THE
YEARBOOK OF ENGLISH STUDIES
VOLUME 21

1991

VOL. 21   1991

THE YEARBOOK

OF

ENGLISH STUDIES

*Politics
Patronage and Literature
in England
1558–1658
Special Number*

Editor

ANDREW GURR

Assistant Editor

PHILLIPA HARDMAN

Reviews Editor

LIONEL KELLY

Modern Humanities Research Association

The Yearbook of English Studies

is published by

THE MODERN HUMANITIES RESEARCH ASSOCIATION

and may be ordered from

The Honorary Treasurer, MHRA

King's College, Strand, London WC2R 2LS, England

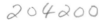
ISSN 0306-2473

ISBN 0 947623 38 8

Printed in Great Britain by

W. S. MANEY AND SON LTD   LEEDS LS9 7DL   ENGLAND

Contents

Contents

viii   *Contents*

EDITORIAL NOTE

The special number for 1992 will be concerned with medieval narrative. The number for 1993 will be concerned with the early plays of Shakespeare. For 1994 the special subject will be Ethnicity and Representation in American Literature. Articles for the 1993 and 1994 issues and books for review submitted to *YES* and *MLR* should be sent to the Editor, Department of English, University of Reading, P.O. Box 218, Reading, Berks. RG6 2AA, U.K.

ANDREW GURR
PHILLIPA HARDMAN

PREFACE

Recent years have seen many new critical accounts of texts, often familiar texts, as participations in cultural and political discourse. In no period has this been more so than in the Renaissance. The present collection of twenty essays on 'Politics, Patronage, and Literature in England, 1558–1658' brings together the work of British and American scholars and demonstrates a range of methodologies, representing historicisms newer and older as they bear upon those themes. The essays derive from papers given at an international conference held at Reading in July 1989, an occasion larger than this selection can suggest, where many literary scholars and historians pooled their interests.

The division of materials into three sections, headed 'Patronage and Audiences', 'Political Readings' and 'Revision and Review', fails to express overlapping matters between the sections but is designed nevertheless as a rough thematic organization. In the first, patronage is considered both in narrow terms, through the study of particular writers or their patrons, and also more broadly, to indicate a social system and its impact on authorship. (This section includes, too, five essays about the conditions of writing for the public stage, part of an interest in the drama maintained in the other sections.) That the import of most of these essays is also political hardly needs saying. In the second section the term politics is likewise applied broadly, both to documents of immediate political function, like *Eikōn Basilikē*, and to those in which political function can be identified as more implicit. The separate existence of a third section, containing corrective readings of two texts to which political interpretation has been extensively applied and a political reading of New Historicism itself, merely indicates that these last three essays have a cautionary or reconstructive function, not that some of the authors of earlier essays in the volume do not also locate their methodologies against existing models.

All in all, this is a collection with a number of interlocking themes, and it touches a variety of sixteenth-century and seventeenth-century writing, poetry and prose, dramatic and non-dramatic, more and less familiar, in a span of a hundred years from the accession of Elizabeth.

Cedric C. Brown

PART ONE
PATRONAGE AND AUDIENCES

Patronage, Poetry, and Print

ARTHUR F. MAROTTI
Wayne State University, Detroit

In the modern institution of literature, itself a product of democratizing tendencies that have been operating over the course of the last 500 years, the social and economic relations of authors, publishers, and readers tend to be hidden or disguised. In the pre-Modern and early-Modern periods, in which literature was more obviously implicated in immediate social relations and had not yet been separated from other forms of discourse into the supposedly autonomous realm of the aesthetic, the relationships of writers, publishers, patrons, and readers were habitually the subject of explicit negotiation. After all, everyone acknowledged that literary communication was socially positioned and socially mediated: styles and genres were arranged in hierarchies homologous with those of rank, class, and prestige. The socio-literary dynamics of manuscript culture carried over into the Gutenburg era in many ways, even as print culture began to transform the intellectual, political, and social order by which it was shaped.

Responding to the heightened awareness of the culture-specific character of literary texts, recent scholarship in the Renaissance period has empha-sized the importance of patronage to literary production and reception. Given the socioeconomic dependency of most writers, especially those who deliberately arranged to have their work printed, patronage was a social and financial necessity, despite the widespread complaints about the decline of such support.[1] Dedicatory letters and poems indicate that writers and

---

[1] This subject has been extensively discussed in the scholarly treatments of the topic of patronage, and the phenomenon is part of what Lawrence Stone has argued is a slow decline of kinship and clientage as the main social organizing principles (*The Family, Sex, and Marriage in England 1500–1800* (New York, 1977)), pp. 125–35. I am indebted to the discussions of patronage in the following: Richard Firth Green, *Poets and Princepleasers: Literature and the English Court in the Late Middle Ages* (Toronto, 1980); Patricia Thomson, 'The Literature of Patronage, 1580–1630', *Essays in Criticism*, 2 (1952), 267–84 and 'The Patronage of Letters under Elizabeth and James I', *English*, 7 (1949), 278–82; John Buxton, *Sir Philip Sidney and the English Renaissance*, second edition (London, 1964, reprinted 1966); the chapters on patronage in H. S. Bennett, *English Books & Readers 1475 to 1557* (Cambridge, 1952), *English Books & Readers 1558 to 1603* (Cambridge, 1965), and *English Books & Readers 1603 to 1640* (Cambridge, 1970); Edwin Haviland Miller, *The Professional Writer in Elizabethan England: A Study of Nondramatic Literature* (Cambridge, Massachusetts, 1959), pp. 94–136; Jan van Dorsten, 'Literary Patronage in Elizabethan England: The Early Phase', in *Patronage in the Renaissance*, edited by Guy Fitch Lytle and Stephen Orgel (Princeton, 1981), pp. 191–206; Michael Brennan, *Literary Patronage in the English Renaissance: The Pembroke Family* (London, 1988).

publishers sought patronage as a way of legitimating and endorsing printed texts, rewarding them for producing such work, and lending prestige to the whole enterprise. Willingly or not, members of royalty and the aristocracy found themselves portrayed in print as the authorizers, protectors, even owners of a wide variety of religious, historical, scientific, polemical, and literary texts, though, it should be noted at the outset, in many cases their connexion with the authors or publishers was slight or non-existent and their names mainly functioned as (misleading) signs of celebrity-endorsement. Through the praise and idealization that supposedly enhanced the patron's current and future esteem and reputation, writers presented themselves not simply as dependents, but also as parties to an (albeit unequal) gift-exchange, empowered by the immediate and continuing efficacy of the print medium whose material features memorialized author and patron simultaneously.

Within the literature of print culture, however, another set of social relations was emerging in which the patron was ultimately eclipsed by the increasing sociocultural authority of authors as well as by the economic and interpretative importance of the reader, the 'patron' of the work as buyer and consumer in the modern sense of the term 'patronage'.[2] One can detect in the juxtaposition of dedicatory letters and epistles to readers an interesting friction developing between the old and new-style patrons, or at the least a complexity in the relationship of author, stationer, patron, and reader that was exploited by both writers and publishers to their own advantage. At issue were the ownership of texts, the control of interpretation, the authority for public literary utterance, the socioeconomic well-being of writers and publishers; that is, the roles of all those who participated in the circuit of literary production and reception.

In focusing on some sixteenth and early-seventeenth-century editions of lyric poetry, I shall pay especial attention to the ways both authors and publishers balanced their dependence on the patrons to whom works were dedicated against their need to appeal to the readers or bookstall 'patrons' who purchased them. I highlight the issues of authorial authority, the evolving roles of publishers and readers, and the status of lyric poetry within the literary institution developing within print culture.

The first Renaissance English poet to have his verse published both in short pamphlet and in collected form was John Skelton. The editions of his works that survive present him as 'Skelton Laureate' or 'Skelton Poet

---

[2] See Karl Holzknecht, *Literary Patronage in the Middle Ages* (1923; reprinted New York, 1966), for the suggestion that a printer like Wynkyn de Worde broke with an older system of patronage and 'courted his new patron, the general public' (p. 115, quoted in Russell Rutter, 'William Caxton and Literary Patronage', *SP*, 84 (1987), 442). Richard Helgerson, 'Milton Reads the King's Book: Print, Performance, and the Making of a Bourgeois Idol', *Criticism*, 29 (1987), 6, remarks: 'Intended to represent the power of the authorial self, print ends by empowering the consumers of that representation. Print makes readers kings.'

Laureat' or 'Skelton Poeta',[3] highlighting his academic credentials and his status as a writer of occasional courtly verse rather than serving as a serious assertion of cultural authority within the print medium: something that might be claimed for the sixteenth-century editions of Chaucer's collected works, for example, Thynne's 1532 volume.[4] The publications contain neither dedications nor epistles to readers by either the author or the publisher: they present themselves simply as a record of what was available in the system of manuscript transmission, the sloppy appearance of the woodcuts and black-letter print suiting the ephemeral character of such pamphlets.

Pre-Elizabethan lyric poets such as Wyatt, Surrey, and the other courtly amateurs did not write for publication or allow their occasional verse to be printed. Wyatt's *Penitential Psalms* (1550) was published posthumously by the stationers Thomas Raynald and John Harrington with a dedication to William Parr, Marquis of Northampton and Earl of Essex.[5] But the first major publication of English Renaissance lyric poetry was Tottel's *Miscellany* (1557), a book that not only inaugurated a fashion for such collections[6] but also self-consciously translated manuscript-circulated verse into the medium of print with a sense of some of the differences between the media.

From the time of Caxton, of course, printers and booksellers enhanced their own position in the circuit of literary transmission, relating to patrons as well as to authors and book-purchasers in self-conscious ways as they developed strategies for marketing publications to an expanding clientèle.[7] In presenting his ambitious poetical anthology to the public, particularly to that portion of it with whom he might have come in contact as the printer holding the patent for publishing common law texts, Richard Tottel depicted himself simultaneously as a connoisseur, a patriot, and an educator, as someone doing a public service for his clientèle rather than as a mercantile exploiter of texts belonging to a social and intellectual élite. His prefatory address, 'The Printer to the Reader', is a clever subterfuge that both flatters his customers and aggrandizes himself:

[3] See, for example, *Skelton Laureate agaynste a comely Coystrowne* (London, n.d.); *A ryght delectable traytise upon a goodly Garlande or chapelet of laurell by mayster Skelton Poete laureat* (London, 1523) at the end of which is a woodcut headed 'Skelton Poeta'.

[4] See the chapter on 'The Renaissance Chaucer: From Manuscript to Print' in Alice S. Miskimin, *The Renaissance Chaucer* (New Haven, 1975), pp. 226–61.

[5] The text of this dedicatory epistle is printed in *Collected Poems of Sir Thomas Wyatt*, edited by Kenneth Muir and Patricia Thomson (Liverpool, 1969), pp. xviii–xix. After highlighting his status as a client to Northampton, Harington explains that he decided, with advice from his friends, to print Wyatt's *Penitential Psalms* so that 'the noble fame of so worthy a knighte, as was thee Auctor hereof, Syr Thomas Wyat, shuld not perish but remayne as well for hys synguler learning, as valiant dedes in mercyal feates' (p. xix). On Northampton, see Ruth Hughey, *John Harington of Stepney: Tudor Gentleman* (Columbus, Ohio, 1971), pp. 37–38.

[6] The earlier collections whose fragments survive as *The Court of Venus* had nothing like the impact of Tottel's book. For a discussion of these Henrician anthologies, see *The Court of Venus*, edited by Russell Fraser (Durham, North Carolina, 1955).

[7] See, for example, Rutter, pp. 440–70. Rutter offers an important corrective to the notion that Caxton relied strongly on patronage, emphasizing rather this printer's techniques of advertising and selling his wares to a book-buying public.

It resteth nowe (gentle reder) that thou thinke it not evill doon, to publish, to the honor of the Englishe tong, and for profit of the studious of Englishe eloquence, those workes which the ungentle horders up of such treasure have heretofore envied thee. And for this point (good reder) thine own profit and pleasure, in these presently, and in moe hereafter, shal answere for my defence. If parhappes some mislike the statelinesse of stile removed from the rude skill of common eares: I aske help of the learned to defend their learned frendes, the authors of this work: And I exhort the unlearned, by reding to learne to be more skilfull, and to purge that swinish grossenesse, that maketh the swete majerome not to smell to their delight.[8]

After praising the verse accomplishments of English authors like Surrey and Wyatt whose writing proves the worth of the undervalued vernacular,[9] Tottel defends his role in the publishing enterprise. He locates the reader midway between the nobility of Surrey and the commonness of the rude multitude, portraying his own printing of the anthology as an act of sharing what was hoarded (courtly coterie literature) to the end of satisfying and edifying an educated audience interested in vicarious contact with courtly eloquence and life. There is an implied argument in this passage: just as the English tongue is equal to the Latin and Italian languages in literary expressiveness, so too are the good gentlemen readers of the volume (and the stationer who serves them) equal, in some sense, to the courtly élite whose writings have been liberated into print. As G. K. Hunter has observed, such printed Tudor poetry provides 'a cultured social world which the reader can join for the price of the book'.[10] In serving his own economic interests, the publisher exploits the hierarchical social structure that the more democratic environment of print helps to undermine. Suppressing the workmanlike activity of editing the poems and of designing titles to replace their lost social contexts with more generalized fictional environments, Tottel functioned as a class mediator taking advantage of print technology's ability to open the closed communications of an élite to a wider audience.

In his prefatory material to *The Paradise of Dainty Devices*,[11] which became the most popular of the Elizabethan poetical miscellanies (largely, as Winifred Maynard has argued,[12] because it presented lyrics that could be sung to well-known tunes), Henry Disle positioned himself as publisher between the broad readership to whom he appealed and the social and intellectual élite that included the patron to whom he dedicated the volume. There is a revealing difference between the title pages of the first (1576) and second (1578) editions: the former emphasizes the quality of the contents

---

[8] *Tottel's Miscellany (1557–1587)*, edited by Hyder Edward Rollins, 2 vols (1928; reprinted Cambridge, Massachusetts, 1966), I, 2.

[9] Elizabeth Pomeroy, *The Elizabethan Miscellanies: Their Development and Conventions* (Berkeley, Los Angeles, 1973), pp. 50–51, compares Tottel's preface and its praise of the vernacular with Lorenzo de Medici's prefatory letter to the *Raccolta Aragonese* (the prototypical Renaissance lyric anthology) and to DuBellay's *Déffense et Illustration de la langue Francoyse*.

[10] 'Drab and Golden Lyrics of the Renaissance', in *Forms of Lyric: Selected Papers from the English Institute* (New York, 1970), p. 8.

[11] Text cited from *The Paradise of Dainty Devices (1576–1606)*, edited by Hyder Edward Rollins (Cambridge, Massachusetts, 1927).

[12] *Elizabethan Lyric Poetry and its Music* (Oxford, 1986), p. 23.

and the status of the contributors: *The Paradise of daynty devises, aptly furnished, with sundry pithie and learned inventions: devised and written for the most part, by M. Edwards, sometimes of her Maiesties Chappel: the rest by sundry learned Gentlemen, both of honor, and woorshippe, viz. S. Bernarde, Jasper Heywood, E. O., F. K., L. Vaux, M. Bewe, D. S., R. Hill, M. Yloop, with others*, but the second emphasizes the benefits to be got by the readership: *The Paradise of dainty deuises. Conteyning sundry pithy preceptes, learned Counsels, and excellent inuentions, right pleasant and profitable for all estates. Deuised and written for the most part, by M. Edwardes, sometimes of her Maiesties Chappel: the rest, by sundry learned Gentlemen, both of honor, and worship, whose names hereafter folowe*. Although the names of the contributors are listed on the verso of the title-page, the impression created is somewhat different in this second edition: 'profitable for all estates' specifies the publication as, among other things, a self-improvement book, morally didactic and utilitarian. By contrast, the dedicatory letter to Lord Compton emphasizes the social status of the poets and the 'delight' (p. 4) to be derived from reading the volume. Though the profit and delight of literature are supposed to apply to all, they often broke down by class lines.

Printed miscellanies are, in many ways, continuous with the practice of transmitting and compiling verse in manuscript: Tottel's collection, for example, resembles the contemporary anthology compiled by John Harington of Stepney;[13] *The Paradise of Dainty Devices* is based on the manuscript collection assembled by Richard Edwards.[14] The first private individual to publish a collection of his own short poems in the Elizabethan period was Barnabe Googe, whose *Eglogs, Epytaphes, and Sonettes* appeared in 1563, six years after Tottel's volume. A kinsman of William Cecil (later Lord Burghley), whose social and political patronge he enjoyed, Googe was a Cambridge-educated devout Protestant whose first published work, a partial translation of Palengenius's *Zodiacke of Life* (1561) was addressed to Cecil, who helped him find service on an embassy to Spain in that year.[15] The publication of his *Eglogs, Epytaphes, and Sonettes* is excused by him with the convenient, and much used, subterfuge that protected gentlemen authors from the 'stigma of print',[16] the claim that the printer was really the initiator of the project, the poet himself when he went abroad having left copies of his poems behind with a friend, 'L. Blundeston', who explains in a commendatory epistle to the reader of the volume:

I trust to fynde the thankfull now in takying this Present from me, which not onely to shewe my good wyll ... by preservynge the worthy fame, and Memorye of my deare frende M. Googe in his absence I have presumed more bouldely to hazard the prynting heareof, though this maye suffyce to excuse well my enterpryse, but also to

---

[13] See *The Arundel-Harington Manuscript of Tudor Poetry*, edited by Ruth Hughey, 2 vols (Columbus, Ohio, 1960), I, 66.
[14] Rollins, *Paradise*, p. xiii.
[15] See William E. Sheidley, *Barnabe Googe* (Boston, 1981), p. 21.
[16] See the classic essay on this topic in J. W. Saunders, 'The Stigma of Print: A Note on the Social Bases of Tudor Poetry', *Essays in Criticism*, I (1951), 139–64.

styrre up thy Pleasure and further thy proffit by readying these his workes, whiche
here I have Publyshed openly unto thee. And so (beyng unstored my selffe) I seake
to satesfie thy learned or willyng desyre with other mens travaeiles. . . . Accept my
goodwyll and way not the valew . . . and so shalt thou encourage others to make the
partaker of the life or farre greater Jewels who yet doubtyng thy unthankefull receyte
nigardly keape them to their own use & privat commoditie. Whear as beynge
assured of the contrarye by thy frendly report of other mens travayles, they could
parhappes be easely entreated to more frely to lend them abroad to thy greater
avayle and furtherraunce.[17]

The middleman in the publishing enterprise, a gentleman to whom manuscript poetry could be loaned by an author, here expresses the same attitude
as Tottel's in claiming that such private treasures should be shared with the
reading public: thus the printed text is a social benefaction rather than an
individual writer's self-advertisement.

The presentation of the collection, however, has the marks of a deliberate
authorial strategy, beginning with a commendatory poem by Googe's cousin
Alexander Neville, a woodcut of his own coat of arms, and a dedicatory
epistle to William Lovelace, 'Reader of Grayes Inne' (p. 9), a man who
shared the culturally rich environment of the Inns of Court, where so many
young poets and translators wrote in the Elizabethan period. Neville's poem
advises Googe to seek wise readers as 'Patrons' (p. 4):

> Go forward styll to advaunce thy fame
>   Lyfes Race halfe ryghtly ron
> Farre easyer tis for to obtain,
>   The Type of true Renowne.
> Like Labours have ben recompenst
>   with an immortall Crowne.
> By this doth famouse *Chaucer* lyve,
>   by this a thousande moore
> Of later peares. By this alone
>   the old renowmed Stoore
> Of Auncient Poets lyve.

(p. 6)

In mentioning Chaucer and classical poets, Neville cites examples of writers
already memorialized through print in the Renaissance. By leaving the
social bounds of manuscript-circulated coterie literature, Googe's poems
could enter an environment in which they and their author, in the face of
contemporary prejudices, could lay claim to a respectable status.

The dedicatory epistle to Lovelace, however, betrays Googe's anxieties
and discomfort in publishing his verse:

Howe lothe I have ben, beyng of long tyme earnestlye requyred, to suffer these
tryfles of mine to come to light: It is not unknowen to a greate nombre of my famyliar
acquaintaunce. Who both daylye and hourely moved me therunto, and lytell of long
tyme prevayled therin. For I both consydered and wayed with my selfe, the grosenes
of my Style: which thus commytted to the gasynge shewe of every eye shuld forth

[17] Text cited in Barnabe Googe, *Eglogs, Epytaphes, and Sonettes* (1563), a facsimile reproduction with an
introduction by Frank B. Fieler (Gainesville, Florida, 1968), pp. 16–18.

with disclose the manifest foly of the Writer, and also I feared and mistrusted the disdaynfull myndes of a nombre both scornefull and carpynge Correctours, whose Heades are ever busyed in tauntyng Judgementes. Least they shuld otherwyse interprete my doyngs than in deade I meant them. These two so great mischiefes utterly diswaded me from the folowynge of my frendes perswasions, and wylled me rather to condem them to continuall darkenes, wherby no Inconvenience could happen: than to endaunger my selfe in gyvynge them to lyght, to the disdaynfull doome of any offended mynde. Notwithstandynge all the dylygence that I could use in the Suppression therof could not suffise for I my selfe beyng at that tyme oute of the Realme, lytell fearynge any such thynge to happen. A verye frende of myne, bearynge as it semed better wyll to my doynges than respectyng the hazarde of my name, commytted them all togyther unpolyshed to the handes of the Prynter. In whose handes durynge his absence from the Cytie, tyll his returne of late they remayned. At whiche tyme, he declared the matter wholly unto me: shewynge me, that beynge so farre past, & Paper provyded for the Impression therof: It could not withoute great hynderaunce of the poore Printer be nowe revoked.... And calling to mynde to whom I myght chieflye commyt the fruytes of my smiling muse: sodaynly was cast before my eyes the perfect vewe of your frendly mynd (gentle Maister Lovelace) Unto whom for the nombred heapes of sundrye frendshyps, accou[n]tynge my selfe as bound, I have thought best to gyve them, (not doubtyng) but that they shalbe as well taken as I do presently meane them. Desyrynge you herein, as all suche as shall reade them especiallye to beare with the unpleasaunt forme of my to hastely fynyshed Dreame, the greater part wherof with lytle advyse I lately endcd, bycause the beginnyng of it, as a senseles head separated from the body was gyven with the rest to be prynted. And thus desyrynge but for recompence the frendly receyvyng of my slender Gyfte, I ende.

(pp. 9–13).

As patron, Googe chose a friend who, as was the case with coterie literary transmission, could serve as an ideal reader,[18] a model of behaviour for the readers and strangers who might buy the published book. Given the disclaimers, and given also the continuing favour of his kinsman and patron Cecil, Googe ran little danger in publishing his 'tryfles'.

When he published his *Epitaphes, Epigrams, Songs and Sonets* (1567),[19] George Turbervile obviously followed the example of Tottel and Googe in presenting socially occasional amorous and non-amorous verse to a book-buying public.[20] Announcing a structure of love-narrative that the final

[18] This portrayal of the patron as ideal reader makes him a figure of mediation between manuscript-circulated verse and printed literature. Other poets repeat Googe's strategy, setting the ideal patron-reader against the carping critics who might condemn the poet's works. Thomas Churchyard, for example, in *The First Part of Churchyardes Chippes* (London, 1575) combines a dedication to Sir Christopher Hatton in which he discusses the proper way of reading his verse with a defensive poem 'To the dispensers of other mens workes that shoes nothing of their own'. In cases such as this the neutral reader is meant to imitate the reading behaviour ascribed to the well-meaning patron.
[19] I cite the text from *Epitaphes, Epigrams, Songs and Sonets (1567) and Epitaphes and Sonnettes (1576) by George Turbervile*, facsimile reproductions with an introduction by Richard J. Panofsky (Delmar, New York, 1977).
[20] One of the features Turbervile borrowed from Tottel is the method of entitling or introducing poems. For example, the generalized 'Lover' is named in the amorous lyrics, producing such titles as 'The Lover extolleth the singular beautie of his Ladie', 'The Lover declareth howe first he was taken and enamoured by the sight of his Ladie', 'The Lover against one that compared hys Mistresse with his Ladie', etc. Panofsky remarks that the 'brief posies' Turbervile appends to poems and the other marks of coterie circulation 'give the reader a sense of participation in the polite recreations of young literary gentlemen' (p. xi).

contents of the collection does not realize (the first printed English lyric
anthology to attempt this arrangement),[21] Turbervile self-consciously presents his work simultaneously as courtly coterie poetry, patronage literature,
and a miscellany for a general readership. He originally dedicated the book
to the Countess of Warwick,[22] expressing gratitude for her acceptance of a
collection shown to her previously, an act that encouraged him to expand it
further in print, even as he denigrates his verse as 'rashe compiled toys'
(sig. *4^v).[23] The same apologetic attitude toward his verse reappears in the
epistle 'To the Reader', where he characterizes his pamphlet as 'a fewe
Sonets, the unripe seedes of my barraine braine, to pleasure and recreate thy
wearye mind and troubled hed withal' (sig. *5^r). He negotiates the respective claims of patroness and readers, telling his general audience 'for thy
solace alone (the bounden dutie which I owed the noble *Cowntesse* reserved) I
undertoke this slender toyle' (sigs. *5^r–5^v) before turning to the more
important issue of the reader's judgement and censure: 'As I deeme thou
canst not, so do I hope thou wilt not mislike it at all. But if there be any thing
herein that maye offend thee, refuse it, reade and peruse the reast with
pacience. Let not the misliking of one member procure thee rashlye to
condemne the whole. I stand to thy judgement, I expect thy aequitie. Reade
the good, and reject the evill: yea rather condemne it to perpetuall silence. . . .
But assuredlye there is nothing in thys whole slender Volume that was ment
amisse of me the Writer, howsoever the Letter goe in thy judgement that arte
the Reader' (sigs. *5^v–6^r). With this appeal for toleration, he then deals with
the amorous subject matter of most of the collection, disingenuously claiming a high moral purpose even as he obviously appeals to the interests of a
young audience: 'Whatsoever I have penned, I write not to this purpose, that
any youthlie head shoulde follow or pursue such fraile affections, or taste of
amorous bait: but by meere fiction of these Fantasies, I woulde warne (if I
myghte) all tender age to flee that fonde and filthie affection of poysoned &
unlawful love. Let this be a Glasse & Myrror for them to gaze upon. . . . And
as I am not the first that in this sort hath written & imployde his time: so
shall I not be the last, that without desarte (perhaps) shalbe misdeemed for

[21] See Panofsky, p. viii. John Erskine Hankins, *The Life and Works of George Turbervile*, University of
Kansas Publications, Humanistic Studies, No. 25 (Lawrence, Kansas, 1940), p. 82, had earlier remarked
'Turbervile is a pioneer in English poetry. He is the first writer to publish a definite and complete
sequence of poems in honor of a mistress, such as that of Petrarch in honor of Laura'.
[22] Most of the works dedicated to Anne Russell Dudley, Countess of Warwick, were from the late 1580s
and 1590s; Turbervile's book is the earliest one dedicated to her, according to the information provided
by Franklin Williams, Jr, *Index of Dedications and Commendatory Verse in English Books Before 1641* (London,
1962), p. 57.
[23] Hankins, p. 35, states 'A number of poems in the volume seem to have been addressed to [Lady
Warwick] before her marriage in November 1565; so we may assign that year as a tentative date for the
earlier collection. Whether these first poems were actually printed, however, or were merely shown to
Lady Warwick in manuscript, we cannot know; there are no indications of an edition of the *Epitaphes* prior
to 1567, except those just mentioned'. If Hankins's hunch is right, the original complimentary poetry to
the youthful Lady Warwick might have been transcribed in a formal presentation copy, a kind of wedding
gift from the poet who was a family client. This, then, could have formed the basis for the expanded
printed collection that, retrospectively, grounded its authorization in the dedicatee's original acceptance
of the verse in manuscript.

attempting the same' (sigs. *6ʳ–6ᵛ). Formulating the presentation of amorous poetry like a typical 'Elizabethan prodigal',[24] Turbervile is conscious of the educational and social denigration of amorous literature, of the readership's tendency to blur the boundary between fiction and actual experience, and, more to the point, of the market for just such ephemeral lyrics.[25] Though he characterizes himself as the 'vassel' (sig. *4ʳ) of his patroness, he appeals to the reader as a 'Friend' (sig. *7ʳ). To those who will not respond to his book with good will he writes a satiric poem, 'To the rayling Route of *Sycophants*', performing an act of exclusion before 'The Table' advertising the contents of the collection that begins (again with an appeal for the protection of his patroness) with an encomiastic poem to the Countess of Warwick that, along with the 'Argument' to the work, portrays her as the fictional mistress in the poetic amorous sequence that follows.[26] Like Samuel Daniel, whose dedication of his sonnet sequence *Delia* also portrays the patroness as the addressee of complimentary love poems,[27] Turbervile defines his amorous verse in a double fashion, first as amorous poetry of compliment and second as literarily self-conscious acts of amorous lyricism in a tradition of such writing derived from Petrarch and from the classical poets of whom Turbervile was so fond.[28] Conscious of the precariousness of his public stance as a publishing poet, Turbervile carefully positions himself in relation to his patroness and to readers both well-disposed and ill, returning at the end of the collection in 'The Authours Epiloge to his Booke' to the importance of the patroness's acceptance of his rough verse.

The two main books in which George Gascoigne printed his lyrics, *A Hundreth Sundrie Flowres* (1573) and *The Posies* (1575), represent sharply differing ways of presenting literary texts to potential patrons and to a general readership. In *A Hundreth Sundrie Flowres*, rather than coming to terms directly with the need to define his role as a publishing author,

---

[24] See Richard Helgerson, *The Elizabethan Prodigals* (Berkeley, Los Angeles, 1976), p. 6.

[25] As someone who, like Gascoigne and the early Ralegh, wrote in the cultural environment of the Inns of Court, Turbervile knew the kind of demand there might be for just such a collection as the one he produced, just as he knew the fashion and market for the translations he produced. Hankins cites Anthony à Wood's biographical account of Turbervile, which places him successively at Winchester College, New College Oxford, and the Inns of Court (p. 5): in the two academic environments, he would have learned to compose certain forms of verse as a part of his classical training; in the latter, he would have been in a social environment that, in the latter half of the sixteenth century generated much poetry and drama.

[26] Hankins, p. 83, remarks 'In Turbervile's *Epitaphes, Epigrams, Songs and Sonets* ... we have a definite poetic sequence in honor of a single mistress ... the Countess of Warwick, who is to be figured forth under the name of Pandora, or Pyndara, while he himself will be represented as Tymetes ... Turbervile includes among his poems a number of epigrams, epitaphs, and verses upon other subjects, but he keeps his sequence always in mind and constantly returns to his main theme. As she is the first subject of his book, so is she the last, and at the end he is able to say to her: "You *Alpha* were when I this Booke begoone ... To be *Omega* now you will not shoonne." To our poet, therefore, must go the honor of introducing the poetic sequence into English'.

[27] Similarly, Thomas Watson in his *Diana* (London, 1592) treats Lady Rich as the beloved praised in his complimentary sonnets.

[28] Turbervile translated Ovid and was influenced by Horace and the poetry of *The Greek Anthology*. See Hankins, pp. 73–75.

Gascoigne hides behind several layers of disguise, turning the editorial
paraphernalia and format of the book into a comical means of hiding and
revealing his own identity. Although his name appears in the titles of poems
included in the volume's table of contents, the work does not openly
proclaim to be the collected works of George Gascoigne. Within the fiction of
its manuscript transmission from 'G.T.' to 'H.W.' to a printer 'A.B.'[29] (the
last differing from the stationer named on the title page, Richard Smith) the
book pretends to be at once an anthology of 'pleasant Pamphlets'[30] and a
collection of manuscript-circulated literature written by various authors
made available to the public without anyone except the publisher taking
responsibility for the act: in 'The Printer to the Reader', a text written
(probably by Gascoigne) in the same ironic tone as H.W.'s later address to
the reader, the publisher complains that, despite G.T.'s and H.W.'s opposition to publication, they are 'of one assent compact to have it imprinted'
(p. 47), leaving him to cope with any public censure of its contents. The most
obvious traces of the printer's actual editorial activities are to be found in the
awkward fit between first and second sections of the work, the former
(running through page 164 of the original edition) including Gascoigne's
two dramatic translations, *Supposes* and *Jocasta*, and the latter (original
pp. 201–445) comprising 'A Discourse of the Adventures passed by Master
F.J.', a collection of occasional lyrics, and the narrative poem 'Dan Bartholomew of Bathe'. Since Gascoigne apparently left England in haste before he
was able to see the publication of his works through the press, the printer was
free to follow his commercial judgement that dramatic texts should be
included in the book because they were much more marketable than lyric
poetry,[31] despite the awkwardness of beginning the second part of the
volume with an address to the reader by 'H.W.' that looks as if it belongs at
the beginning of the volume of 'divers discourses & verses, invented uppon
sundrie occasions, by sundrie gentlemen' (p. 49).

Despite the signals to the contrary, Gascoigne obviously presents his
collected works as more than ephemera. Between praise of ancient poets as
morally instructive in their 'most feyned fables and imaginations' (p. 50) and

[29] In *England's Helicon 1600, 1614*, edited by Hyder Edward Rollins, 2 vols (Cambridge, Massachusetts,
1935), II, 67, the editor notes that 'Frequently "A.B." is used [in Renaissance English publications] as
moderns employ "John Doe"'.
[30] *George Gascoigne's 'A Hundreth Sundrie Flowres'*, edited, with an Introduction and Notes by C. T. Prouty,
University of Missouri Studies 17.2 (1942; reprinted Columbia, Missouri, 1970), p. 47. Further citations
in the text are from this edition. In her edition of Breton, Jean Robertson points out that both Breton and
Gascoigne use the term 'pamphlet' to mean poem, but that Gascoigne seems to make a distinction
between the two in G.T.'s prefatory letter to 'F.J.': 'Marie in deede I may not compare Pamphlets unto
Poems, neither yet may justly advant for our native countrimen, that they have in their verses hitherto
(translations excepted) delivered unto us any such notable volume, as have bene by Poets of antiquitie'
(quoted in Nicholas Breton, *Poems not hitherto reprinted*, edited with biography, canon, and notes by Jean
Robertson (Liverpool, 1967), p. 200. This is the text I cite for Breton's works. Perhaps the term
'pamphlet' (which also designates short, ephemeral publications) is used metonymically to designate the
poetical contents of a manuscript or printed quire or booklet. Clearly, Gascoigne's G.T. distinguishes
casual, occasional literature of the sort that circulated in manuscript from important printed texts
presented with literary self-consciousness.
[31] This point is made by Prouty, *Hundreth Sundrie Flowres*, p. 18.

the citation of the example of Chaucer, whose career is presented as a model for imitation, Gascoigne has 'G.T.' remark in his prefatory letter to the collection: 'Marie in deede I may not compare Pamphlets unto Poems, neither yet may justly advant for our native countrimen, that they have in their verses hitherto (translations excepted) delivered unto us any such notable volume, as have bene by Poets of antiquitie, left unto the posteritie' (p. 50). Despite the many statements denigrating the collection as trivial, immature, and occasional, Gascoigne clearly wishes the publication to constitute a significant cultural achievement, to join the editions of classical authors and of the first canonized English author, Chaucer, as what the printer finally states at the end of the book is a 'good rounde vollume, the which some woulde judge worthy the Imprinting' (p. 220). While trying to use the socioliterary dynamics of manuscript-circulated verse as a protection of his gentility and a defence against some of the consequences of the book's salacious and scandalous content, Gascoigne none the less participates in and attempts to shape the institution of printed literature, the context in which texts take on a monumental character and authors assert a degree of sociocultural authority.

Once the transparent subterfuge of disclaiming responsibility for printing the work had failed, the edition was banned,[32] and its author accused of moral turpitude, Gascoigne responded in the second edition, *The Posies of George Gascoigne Esquire*, by highlighting his authorship on the title page and by prefacing the reorganized collection with three apologetic letters addressed to the ecclesiastical licenser-censors, to young gentlemen, and to the general reader. He also included twenty English and Latin commendatory poems representing the endorsement of his peers (a sign of the literary institution's capacity for self-authorization). Among these, the one attributed to 'The Printer' installs the poet and his works in a tradition that includes both two Medieval English authors, Chaucer and Gower, and sixteenth-century courtly amateurs whose work had appeared in Tottel: Surrey, Wyatt, and Viscount Rochford. The classification system Gascoigne adopted ('Flowers', 'Hearbes', and 'Weeds') suited the medium in which the collection was being presented, allowing for fuller lists of contents (in each section) than had been provided in *A Hundreth Sundrie Flowres*. Exploiting each feature of the publication format as an author controlling the presentation of his revised and corrected collected works (which now include the completed version of the previously incomplete 'Dan Bartholomew of Bathe'), Gascoigne assumed the responsibility of authorship proper to a writer deliberately participating in print culture. He refrained, however, from dedicating the volume to a particular individual and thus from specifically associating the publication with the context of patronage.

---

[32] See Charles T. Prouty, *George Gascoigne: Elizabethan Courtier, Soldier, and Poet* (New York, 1942), p. 79.

Although Gascoigne chose no explicit dedicatee for either *A Hundreth Sundrie Flowres* or *The Posies*,[33] one finds within the collections several poems written in a patronage context, most notably two to Lord Grey of Wilton ('Gascoignes wodmanship' and the verse letter 'Gascoignes voyage into *Hollande*') in the second of which he refers to himself as 'your Lordshippes bound [client] for ever' (l. 286), complimentary verses to Lady Sands and Dorothy Zouche, the deceased Lady Grey of Wilton, and 'Gascoignes device of a maske for the right honorable Viscount Montacute [Montague]'. In the most famous of these, 'Gascoignes wodmanship written to L. Grey of wilton', the author outlines his career, expresses his ambitions, and invites continuing patronage support from an aristocrat well-disposed to assist an articulate gentleman-soldier. It is only in one of the apologetic prefaces to *The Posies* that Gascoigne makes the connexion between this sort of specific act of seeking patronage and the general appeal for patronage he claims was implicit in the very act of publishing his writing. Gascoigne explains that part of his intent in making his writings available to a larger audience through print was to prove his intelligent literacy, his fitness for non-military preferment or political patronage: 'I was desirous that there might remaine in publike recorde, some pledge or token of those giftes wherwith it hath pleased the Almightie to endue me: To the ende that thereby the vertuous might bee incouraged to employ my penne in some exercise which might tende both to my preferment, and to the profite of my Countrye'.[34] Anticipating the obvious objection that a more edifying work might have been better suited to this end, he states that he printed those writings he had available because they could demonstrate the kinds of rhetorical skills he wished to advertise: 'I thought good to notifie unto the worlde before my returne [from military service], that I coulde as well persuade with Penne, as pearce with launce or weapon: So that yet some noble minde might be incouraged both to exercise me in time of peace, and to emploie mee in time of service in warre' (p. 6). In the epistle to Lord Grey of Wilton prefacing the section of *The Posies* containing the military poem 'Dulce bellum inexpertis', Gascoigne narrows his appeal to someone he characterizes as 'an universall

---

[33] In 1575, probably after the publication of *The Posies*, Gascoigne became a client of the Earl of Leicester, through whom he was able to gain employment and a measure of prosperity: see Eleanor Rosenberg, *Leicester, Patron of Letters* (New York, 1955), pp. 166–72 and Prouty, *George Gascoigne*, pp. 87–88. For an excellent discussion of the relation of Gascoigne's writings to his search for patronage and preferment, see Richard C. McCoy, 'Gascoigne's "*Poemata castrata*": The Wages of Courtly Success', *Criticism*, 27 (1975), 29–55. Since the humanist educational programme and its methods of rhetorical training were designed to produce intelligent and versatile men capable of useful service in aristocratic households, the government, and the Church, Gascoigne had some basis for the claim that a demonstration of his writing skills was a way of proving his fitness for preferment, but, of course, occasional and ephemeral poetry, an erotic novella, and an incomplete romantic narrative were hardly the best signs of his seriousness and maturity. As Helgerson, *Elizabethan Prodigals*, pp. 44–57, has pointed out, Gascoigne needed to adopt the role of the reformed prodigal and finally reject such literary trifles, allowing himself only to appear in print as the author of pious and didactic works.

[34] George Gascoigne, *The Posies*, edited by John W. Cunliffe (Cambridge, 1907), p. 5. This is the edition I cite.

patrone of all Souldiours' (p. 140) as he identifies him as one of the persons he hoped to impress and amuse with his earlier book.

Without specific aristocratic patronage, of course, Gascoigne was especially vulnerable to the charges he anticipated in publishing *A Hundreth Sundrie Flowres* and he was forced to answer in the prefaces to *The Posies*. Given the prejudice against amorous prose and poetry in a period whose humanist educational programme trained young men to produce a more narrowly didactic and pious kind of writing, Gascoigne worried about the contents of his collected works, building into the printer's preface and the other editorial interpolations a defence of his subject matter and intentions, even as he teased the reader's imagination with allusions to the erotic content of the volume. Aware of the possible censure of 'the graver sort of greyheard judgers' (p. 47), 'the printer' of *A Hundreth Sundrie Flowres* assures the reader that he has 'wel perused the worke' and can 'find nothing therein amisse' (p. 47), in effect co-opting the role of the ecclesiastical licenser. At the same time, no doubt to arouse the curiosity of book-buyers, he slyly mentions the 'two or three wanton places passed over in the amorous enterprise' and posits a well-meaning 'discrete reader' able, as 'the industrious Bee can gather hony out of the most stinking weede' to 'take a happie example by the most lascivious histories' (p. 47). Emphasizing the 'good moral lesson' to be derived from reading the tragedy of *Jocasta*, calling attention to the 'divers godly himnes and Psalmes' also contained in the volume, the printer concludes that the 'worke is so universall . . . as any mans mind may therwith be satisfied' (pp. 47–48), but highlights the amorous material of the main part of the collection.

The subversion of anti-amorous moralism and the dispersal of literary responsibility for the publication of the whole work are inextricably linked. Recipients of the writing along the line of its transmission: G.T., H.W., the printer, and the reader are, in effect, the ones who must reconcile interest, curiosity, and pleasure on the one hand, with morality and social conventions on the other. Thus, within the frame of 'A Discourse of the Adventures passed by Master F.J.', G.T. establishes a context for both literary and moral judgement and makes *ad hoc* observations as he sustains the narrative line of the work; H.W. assumes that a 'learned Reader' (p. 49) can, as he has done, 'sit and smile at the fond devices of such as have enchayned them selves in the golden fetters of fantasie' and use the work for his 'owne particular commoditie' in a morally responsible way. Gascoigne makes proper reception of his writing, not its contents, the issue, but the strategy had obviously failed when some readers were offended by the salacious material and/or interpreted the story of F.J. as a *roman à clef*.

When Gascoigne assumed full authorial responsibility for publishing the second, revised edition of his work as *The Posies of George Gascoigne*, he addressed first the ecclesiastical licenser-censors, defending his earlier book and the revision: 'It is verie neare two yeares past, since (I beeing in

Hollande in service with the vertuous Prince of Orange) the most parte of these Posies were imprinted, and now at my returne, I find that some of them have not onely bene offensive for sundrie wanton speeches and lascivious phrases, but further I heare that the same have beene doubtfully construed, and (therefore) scandalous' (p. 3.). Because so much of the verse in *A Hundreth Sundrie Flowres* is so obviously rooted in the poet's social experiences, the blurring of the boundaries between the real and the fictional that was normal in manuscript-circulated occasional verse left Gascoigne in the printed edition vulnerable to the charge of 'scandalizing of some worthie personages' (p. 7). Now, in assuming authorial responsibility for his printed works, he could actively define them as literary artifacts rather than real-life communications, thus protecting himself somewhat against the accusation of slandering or exposing actual persons.

Despite the fact that Gascoigne stands forth in *The Posies* as the author responsible for the whole collection of works, and defends the more frivolous amorous compositions as the follies of youth that he has rejected in his maturity, in at least one respect he distances himself from full authorship when he tells the general readership (in the third prefatory epistle) that, of the love poems, 'the most part of them were written for other men' (p. 16). Assuming the identity of the client writer willing to produce verse and prose at the request of patrons or friends, a role later performed by an author such as Thomas Nashe, he explains that 'if ever I wrote lyne for my selfe in causes of love, I have written tenne for other men in layes of lust. . . . though my folly bee greater than my fortune, yet overgreat were mine unconstancie, if (in mine owne behalfe) I shoulde compyle so many sundrie Songs or Sonets. . . . For in wanton delightes I helped all men, though in sad earnest I never furthered my selfe any kinde of way' (pp. 16–17). In this sort of situation, the patrons or commissioners of such verse supposedly bore much of the moral responsibility for the poet-client's productions.

By means of the prefatory epistles in *The Posies*, Gascoigne assumes authorial authority over his writings, defending their fictionality (and literariness) and their didactic value as well as challenging his reader-interpreters both to indulge his youthful excesses and not to perceive what he has done as either immoral or scandalous. The fact that this work was called in by the authorities[35] demonstrates the failure of his strategy to protect himself. Without legitimating precedents, without the intervention of powerful patrons, Gascoigne could not safely translate what looked like the thinly fictionalized private erotic escapades and recreations of a social élite into the public environment of print, nor could he win respect for presenting as his collected works pieces whose genres and subject matter were held in such low esteem. Twenty years later things would have been different; his

[35] Prouty, *George Gascoigne*, p. 79, notes that the Queen Majesty's Commissioners or the Court of High Commission seized *The Posies* in 1576. McCoy, pp. 43–44, observes that two other amorous works were also banned at the same time, *Restoratives to Love* and the ballad-miscellany *A Handful of Pleasant Delights*.

only choice in the mid-1570s was to prove his seriousness as a man of affairs by abandoning secular lyricism and romantic fiction and composing public, religious, and didactic works.[36]

Nicholas Breton, whose first published work, *A Smale handfull of fragrant Flowers* (1575), is dedicated to Lady Sheffield,[37] was willing, despite the suppression of Gascoigne's *The Posies* in 1576, to publish his youthful lyrics in 1577. Perhaps to emphasize the harmlessness of his recreational collection, he (and, perhaps, the printer) entitled it: *The workes of a young wyt, trust vp with a Fardell of pretie fancies, profitable to young Poetes, prejudiciall to no man, and pleasant to every man to passe away idle tyme withall. Whereunto is joyned an odde kynde of wooing, with a Banquet of Comfettes, to make an ende withall. Done by N.B. Gentleman.* Though he relentlessly pursued aristocratic patronage in later publications, Breton emphasizes his gentility in this pamphlet, prefacing it only with 'The Letter Dedicatorie, to the Reader', anticipating differing tastes and judgements in his audience, from whom he invites good will, promising 'perhaps I wyl agaynst the next Terme, provide you some other newe ware for your olde golde' (p. 4). A young gentleman writing for his peers (probably Inns of Court 'termers') relates an 'as you like it' attitude to the economic transaction of book-marketing in which they are both participants. In the poetical 'Primordium' to the small collection, he distances himself from the 'first fruites of [his] brayne' (l. 82), his 'rimes wilde Otes' (l. 84), but his constant reference to his 'Muse' marks his efforts as deliberate attempts to develop an identity as a poet which the apologetic remarks are not meant to obscure.

Breton introduces each of the poems in the volume with the kind of discursive and narrative titles found in Gascoigne, not only marking the occasional character of the pieces and revealing the patronage context in which some were composed, but also providing a metapoetic commentary on his own literary development. For example, he not only wrote at least one poem 'in behalfe of a Gentleman, who travailying into Kent, fell there in love' (p. 120), but also composed at least three pieces when 'a noble man, my right good Lord . . . commaunded me to wryte him some Verses' (p. 28). The poems in the collection are carefully related to the social and literary vicissitudes of an educated young gentleman, conscious of the class hierarchy in which he functions and of the peer group with which he is communicating in print.[38]

The fashion of composing and publishing sonnet sequences or collections of songs and sonnets came to England late in the Renaissance and it took no less an author than Sidney to inaugurate it, albeit posthumously. In the early

---

[36] See Helgerson, *Elizabethan Prodigals*, pp. 50–57.

[37] In this 1575 pamphlet Breton self-consciously presents himself as a young scholar declaring literary ambitions, addressing a pious poem to a patroness as a New Year's gift, a sixteen-page octavo pamphlet.

[38] The discursive introductions to the poems highlight not only the social circumstances of their production but also the poet's own development, the history of which can be visible in the print medium both within a single publication and in a series of printed texts such as Breton had begun.

1580s, however, Thomas Watson published a sonnet collection with all the defensive preliminary gestures an author might use to present such work to a potentially unreceptive public. His anonymous '*EKATOMPATHIA OR PASSIONATE Centurie of Loue* (1582) opens with an elaborate dedication to the Earl of Oxford in which that patron is depicted both as one who caused the poems to be printed and the means for winning it approval. Watson explains that, because the world knew Oxford had read and approved of his verse, 'many have oftentimes and earnestly called upon mee, to put it to the press, that for their mony they might but see, what your Lordship with some likeing had alreadie perused'.[39] Using Oxford's blessing as a celebrity endorsement, Watson also asks him to protect the poems from malicious readers. When Watson addresses 'the frendly Reader' directly, he allows him the freedom to encourage or discourage his composing and publishing further works: 'This toye being liked, the next may proove better; being discouraged, wil cut of the likelihood of my travaile to come' (sig. A4ᵛ). A commendatory letter to Watson from John Lyly, the author of the popular *Euphues* (1578), himself another Oxford writer-client, praises the love poetry to follow, alluding to his own practice of writing amorous lyrics. Finally, there follow six commendatory poems (five in English, one in Latin) praising the work and its author. Despite all this, Watson did not really entice others to write and publish love sonnets.

One of the most significant phenomena relating the publication of poetry to patronage is, of course, the 1579 edition of Spenser's *The Shepheardes Calendar*, dedicated to Sir Philip Sidney. At once the announcement of a significant poetic career, a coyly parodic imitation of the printing house conventions for presentation of classical literature, and a gifting-giving gesture on the part of a client who was also a friend of the dedicatee, this landmark text treated the medium of print with a sociocultural seriousness lacking in most previous poetical pamphlets. Spenser's authorial self-fashioning has, of late, been discussed intelligently by Richard Helgerson, David Miller, and others,[40] and in this context I only wish to provide a reminder of the chronological locus of this publication, after the early miscellanies, the editions of Googe, Turbervile, Gascoigne, and Breton, and before the prestigious publications of the 1590s, many of which were composed during the 1580s. As an author, Spenser also tried to reconcile patronage and publication, social respectability and the print medium, although his love lyrics only appeared after the more prestigious public verse

---

[39] Text cited from UMI/STC Microfilm Reel #400, sig. A3ᵛ. Oxford is also the dedicatee of John Soowthern's sonnet collection, *Pandora* (London, 1584; text cited from UMI/STC Microfilm Reel #354), a book whose audience is identified in the 'Sonnet to the Reader' as 'you that are lyke us amorous' (sig. Aiiᵛ), the group of young gentleman-amorists that would have included the Earl himself.

[40] See Helgerson, *Self-Crowned Laureates*, pp. 55–100; David L. Miller, 'Authorship, Anonymity, and *The Shepheardes Calendar*', *MLQ*, 40 (1979), 219–31 and 'Spenser's Vocation, Spenser's Career', *ELH*, 50 (1983), 197–231; Paul Alpers, 'Pastoral and the Domain of Lyric in Spenser's *Shepheardes Calendar*', *Representations*, 12 (Fall, 1985), 83–100; Jane Tylus, 'Spenser, Virgil, and the Politics of Poetic Labor', *ELH*, 55 (1988), 53–77.

of *The Faerie Queene* had established his identity as a serious national poet.[41] It was, however, the dedicatee of *The Shepheardes Calendar*, Sir Philip Sidney, whose activities both as patron and author had more of an impact on the status of printed literature and the sociocultural authority of the publishing writer.[42]

Once he had become for his contemporaries a Protestant martyr, culture hero, and, after the publication of his various writings in the 1590s, the pre-eminent author of the English Renaissance, Sir Philip Sidney, who had been honoured as a literary patron in life, posthumously exercised some of the sociocultural functions ascribed to living patrons, authorizing the literary texts of writers who invoked his name or followed his example.[43] For instance, as I have argued elsewhere, Sidney's *Astrophil and Stella* in large measure socially legitimated the publication of amorous sonnet sequences in the 1590s.[44] Most immediately it provided the pretext for Samuel Daniel, some of whose poems were printed among the miscellaneous lyrics appended to the first unauthorized edition of Sidney's sonnet collection, to publish *Delia* (1592) and to dedicate it to Sidney's sister, the Countess of Pembroke, whom he sought as a patroness. In characterizing both himself and Sidney as the victims of 'the indiscretion of a greedie Printer' who published 'uncorrected' versions of their lyrics and in explaining that he was, therefore, 'forced to publish' a textually fuller and more authentic version of his collection than Newman had, he simultaneously tried to benefit from the 'fame' and immortality of 'Astrophel'/Sidney. The 'countenance of ... protection' sought from Mary Sidney/Herbert, was both the traditional patronage of a 'happie and judiciall Patroness of the Muses',[45] but also, in effect, the permission for Daniel to associate his work with that of the deceased poet-hero. Thus the function of patron was split between siblings in an interesting way, the brother authorizing the publication of such verse and the sister serving as dedicatee and protector. The Countess is also portrayed as an ideal reader: Daniel expresses his antagonism to the larger audience

---

[41] William Ponsonby's preface to *Amoretti and Epithalamion* (1595) points out that Spenser's 'name sufficiently warranting the worthinesse of the work', he makes bold to publish it in the poet's absence (text cited in *Spenser's Minor Poems*, edited by Ernest De Selincourt (Oxford, 1910), p. 370).

[42] Van Dorsten, p. 200, remarks 'No matter how hard one tries to look for alternatives the new poetry had only one patron: Sidney. Against all odds and almost single-handedly, he provided the ambience and the inspiration that was to initiate one of the greatest periods in European literary history'.

[43] In praising the *Arcadia* Gabriel Harvey refers to Sidney with a chain of epithets, the last of which points to his status as an authorizer of printed literature: 'the Secretary of Eloquence, the breath of the Muses, the hoony-bee of the dayntiest flowers of Witt and Arte, the Pith of moral & intellectual Vertues, the arme of Bellona in the field, the toung of Suada in the chamber, the spirite of Practise in esse, and the Paragon of Excellency in Print' (*Pierce's Supererogation* (1593) in *Elizabethan Critical Essays*, edited with an Introduction by G. Gregory Smith, 2 vols (1904; reprinted Oxford, 1959), II, 264–65).

[44] See my essay, '"Love is not love": Elizabethan Sonnet Sequences and the Social Order', *ELH*, 49 (1982), 396–428.

[45] Samuel Daniel, *Poems and A Defence of Ryme*, edited by Arthur Colby Sprague (1930; reprinted Chicago, 1965), p. 9.

reached through print and, omitting any epistle to readers, presents the book as a gift to one person, who, in effect, became the owner of the text.[46]

In very different circumstances than those of Daniel, Giles Fletcher published his sonnet collection, *Licia*, in 1593 along with 'The Rising to the Crown of Richard the third. Written by him selfe',[47] a poem in the tradition of *The Mirror for Magistrates*. As a former academician with a doctorate in civil law, a government servant with expertise in ambassadorial trade negotiation, and the official Remembrancer of the City of London, Fletcher was a serious man of affairs who could characterize his composition of lyrics both as a gentleman's leisure activity and as a scholar's treatment of the subject of love in a philosophically serious manner.[48] In his pedantic dedicatory epistle to Lady Mollineux, Fletcher defends his writing of love poems by pointing out that 'in other countryes, as *Italie*, and *France*, men of learning and great partes ... have written Poems and Sonnets of Love; but even amongst us, men of best nobilitie, and chiefest familes, to be the greatest Schollers and most renowmed in this kind'. It is not surprising, in this context, that he should mention the name of 'that worthie *Sidney*' (p. 75) in a passage dealing with the affinity of scholarship with gentility: Sidney serves Fletcher's purpose as an example of how social status, learning, patriotism, and amorous writing might be combined.

Like Daniel, Fletcher emphasizes his patroness over his reader, but, while Daniel avoids addressing the reader directly, Fletcher expresses indifference to the reader's judgement in the dedicatory epistle and both insults and patronizes him in a prefatory statement 'To the Reader'. Having depicted Lady Mollineux as the prime mover of his love poetry (that is, an authorizer of its publication), Fletcher tells her: 'For the Reader, if he looke for my letters to crave his favour, he is farre deceived: for if he mislike anie thing, I am sorie he tooke the paines to reade, but if he doe, let him dispraise, I much care not' (p. 76). Since Fletcher assumes that 'our great men ... want leasure to reade, and if they had, yet for the most part, the worse speake worse' (p. 76), he seems to be socially disparaging anyone who buys his book. Hence the comment: 'let the Printer looke he grow not a begger by such bargaynes' (p. 76). Similarly, in the epistle to the reader, he makes the distinction between the few gentlemen of the Inns of Court and the universities who are 'onelie ... fittest to write of Love' and those 'of meane reach ... unfitte to knowe what love meanes', that is, between those who can (neoplatonically) conceive of love as 'a Goddesse ... not respecting the

---

[46] The format of this publication (one sonnet per page with an ornamental border at the bottom of each page) suggests that the printed text was imitating some of the features of a scribally-produced presentation copy of a poetry collection. Mary Lamb, 'The Countess of Pembroke's Patronage', *ELR*, 12 (1982), 177–78, suggests that Daniel might have 'dedicated his *Delia* (1592) to the Countess to gain a position at Wilton'. In the course of her discussion of the Countess of Pembroke, Lamb argues that the extent of her patronage has been greatly exaggerated.

[47] See *The English Works of Giles Fletcher, the Elder*, edited by Lloyd E. Berry (Madison, Wisconsin, 1964). This is the text I cite.

[48] See Berry's account of Fletcher's life, pp. 3–49.

contentment of him that loves but the vertues of the beloved' in contrast to those of 'a vulgare head, a base minde, an ordinarie conceit' who know only 'the love wherewith *Venus* sonne hath injuriouslie made spoile of thousandes' (p. 79). He leaves the reader in an uncomfortable position both intellectually and socially, teasing him by turning interpretive freedom into a kind of helpless dependency: 'If thou muse what my LICIA is, take her to be some *Diana*, at the least chaste, or some *Minerva*, no *Venus*, fairer farre; it may be shee is Learnings image, or some heavenlie woonder, which the precisest may not mislike: perhaps under that name I have shadowed *Discipline*. It may be, I meane that kinde courtiesie which I found at the Patronesse of these Poems; if may bee some Colledge; it may bee my conceit, and portend nothing; whatsoever it be, if thou like it, take it, and thanke the worthie Ladie MOLLINEUX, for whose sake thou hast it' (pp. 79–80). Having asserted his intellectual authority and used his association with his patroness to reinforce his claims to gentility, Fletcher seems unusually hostile to his readership because he fears the vulgarizing potential of print, a danger against which the example of Sidney offered only partial protection, especially since the author of *Licia* could make no pretence that his love lyrics were the products of an unsteady youth. Unwilling to submit himself to reader-censure, Fletcher finally suggests that he can cut himself loose from patronage as well and assert the kind of authorial autonomy that the Sidney model encouraged: after expressing his gratitude to Lady Mollineux and her family, he tells the readers: 'If thou mislike it [*Licia*], yet she or they, or both, or divine LICIA shall patronize it, or if none, I will and can doe it myselfe' (p. 80). In a sense, this idea of the author as his own patron is one that is implicit in the image of Sidney as it develops through the 1590s and beyond. Though thoroughly dependent in his career as a government servant on individual and corporate patronage, Fletcher could at least momentarily imagine an independence that the evolving institution of literature in print culture made it possible to conceive.

Two poetical miscellanies published in the last years of Elizabeth's reign, *The Phoenix Nest* and *A Poetical Rhapsody*, explicitly invoked the memory of Sidney and benefited from the increased social prestige with which he invested printed lyric poetry.

As Hyder Rollins observed, *The Phoenix Nest* (1593), which is the first Elizabethan miscellany edited by a gentleman, is the first such anthology since Tottel to lay emphasis on gentility and to highlight the sonnet as a lyric form,[49] neither feature of which is surprising, given its date and the example of Sidney. After prefacing the prose defence of the deceased Earl of Leicester, which begins the collection, with an address to the reader disclaiming any motive to flatter, the editor opens the poetical anthology with three elegies on Sidney, thus, in effect, presenting the collection under his auspices, making

[49] *The Phoenix Nest, 1593*, edited by Hyder Edward Rollins (1931; reprinted Cambridge, Massachusetts, 1969), pp. xvi, xxxviii.

available to gentlemen-readers the kind of coterie verse whose publication Sidney's sonnets legitimated. 'R.S. of the Inner Temple Gentleman', the editor of the volume, presents the book to the world of polite society without dedicating it to a patron and without a subservient address to readers. The commercial attraction lay in the Sidney aura and the snob appeal of the title page of this attractively printed quarto: *The Phoenix Nest. Built vp with the most rare and refined workes of Noble men, woorthy Knights, gallant Gentlemen, Masters of Arts, and brave Schollers. Full of varietie, excellent invention, and singular delight. Never before this time published.* Largely because the printing of Sidney's sonnets lent a dignity to printed lyric collections, this miscellany could appeal unashamedly to an upscale clientèle.

Francis Davison's dedication of his ambitious miscellany, *A Poetical Rhapsody* (1602),[50] to William Herbert, Earl of Pembroke is explicitly an act of using this patron as a way of establishing contact with the literarily and culturally central name of Sir Philip Sidney, the Earl's uncle. Using the sonnet form for the dedication, Davison praises Pembroke for his 'high and noble minde', 'outward shape', 'Vertue, Valour, Learning', and 'future Hope', before getting to the genealogy of patronage and poetry of which he was part:

> Thou worthy Sonne, unto a peerelesse MOTHER,
> Thou Nephew to great SYDNEY of renowne,
> Thou that deserv'st thy CORONET to crowne
> With Lawrell Crowne, a Crowne excelling t'other;
> I consecrate these Rimes to thy great NAME,
> Which if thou like, they seek no other fame.
>
> (I, 3)

The Earl, evidently, had by this time written some of his own verse, the association with which Davison seeks in order to dignify particularly his own and his brother's lyrics included in the miscellany. Pembroke was thus one poet-patron in a family several of whose members functioned in both roles.

Davison's long epistle 'To the Reader' cloaks the anthology in the Sidney legend and example, using it to authorize not only the printing of his own and his brother's poems but also the act of publishing a collection of occasional lyrics. In defending the writing of verse as an activity worthy of a serious man of affairs, Davison anticipates some of the old prejudices against lyric poetry: 'If liking other kindes, thou mislike the Lyricall, because the chiefest subject is Love; I reply, that Love being virtuously intended, & worthily placed, is the Whetstone of witt, and Spurre to all generous actions: and that many excellent spirits with great fame of witt, and no staine of judgement, have written excellently in this kind, and specially the ever-praise worthy *Sidney* ...' (I, 5). Though obviously using the precedent of Sidney to his own advantage, however, he blames the printer for explicitly exploiting the Sidney name, in effect, ceding to his agency the final editing of

---

[50] Text cited from *A Poetical Rhapsody, 1602–1621*, edited by Hyder Edward Rollins, 2 vols (Cambridge, Massachusetts, 1931).

the miscellany: 'If any except against the mixing (both at the beginning and ende of this booke) of diverse thinges written by great and learned Personages, with our meane and worthles Scriblings, I utterly disclaime it, as being done by the Printer, either to grace the forefront with Sir *Ph. Sidneys*, and others names, or to make the booke grow to a competent volume' (I, 5).

Despite his dismissal of his and his brother's poems as the indulgences of their youth, I believe that Davison wished to associate his work with that of the Sidney–Dyer–Greville circle and with the myth of the martyred shepherd-knight. The collection proper opens with 'Two Pastoralls, made by *Sir Philip Sidney*, never yet published', poems explicitly naming Dyer and Greville as poetic participants and, after an anonymous third poem, continues with the first publication of a pastoral poem by the Countess of Pembroke, before turning to the pastoral verse of the Davisons and others.[51]

Although many writers continued to appeal to Sidney's sister, the Countess of Pembroke, to his nephew, William Herbert, the Third Earl of Pembroke, and to other members of the Sidney–Herbert families for patronage, producing dozens of dedications and complimentary poems, Sidney himself, installed in a developing national literature he helped shape and elevate, became a sign of the growing strength of the literary institution as a self-authorizing entity, less dependent than previously on traditional social and political authority for its existence. The publication of the 1598 folio collection of his works, and the subsequent editions that continued to appear into the next century, both memorialized this author and helped establish the sociocultural authority of printed literature, especially of collected editions in this prestigious format. Certainly the sixteenth-century folio editions of Chaucer contributed to this process, but the Sidney model was more significant: the realization of the possibility of canonizing contemporary or recently deceased writers; folio editions of such authors as Spenser (1611, 1617), Jonson (1616, 1640–41), Shakespeare (1623, 1632), Daniel (1601), Drayton (1619), Beaumont and Fletcher (1647) were, in a real sense, made possible by the printing of Sidney's *œuvres* as was the authorially-planned, but posthumous, publication of his friend Fulke Greville's works.[52]

A writer like Ben Jonson clearly benefited from what Sidney had accomplished. Had not Sidney achieved the sociocultural status he did, Jonson would not have been able to assert so strongly the intellectual and cultural authority he desired for authorship. When he addressed patrons, Jonson was able to pretend to be doing so from a position of strength, often offering moral and intellectual instruction as well as the requisite expressions of humble gratitude and devotion.

---

[51] Although Rollins (*Poetical Rhapsody*, II, 72–74) basically accepts the statement that the printer gave final shape to the anthology, I suspect that the coyly modest Davison at least shared in the responsibility for the inclusion of other poets' works and for the association of the publication with the Sidney name.
[52] *Certain Learned and Elegant Workes of the Right Honorable Fulke Lord Brooke, written in his Youth, and familiar Exercise with Sir Philip Sidney* (London, 1633).

The case of Jonson's first collection of poems provides a good example. Before they appeared in his 1616 folio *Workes*, Jonson evidently intended to publish his *Epigrammes* separately, as the 15 May 1612 entry in the Stationers' Register suggests.[53] The prefatory and introductory material to the collection we find in the Folio were obviously designed for a small volume of epigrams, the kind of work that, in the light of the 1599 Bishops' order against such publications and the mixed reception of Jonson's satiric drama, left the poet especially vulnerable both to the condemnation of his social and political superiors and to the hostility of malicious or offended readers. In the dedication to William Herbert, Earl of Pembroke and in the initial poems to the reader, the book, and the bookseller, Jonson's characteristically hypersensitive attitude toward potential criticism led him virtually to insult the patron, the reader, and the bookseller, the other major parties in the circuit of literary production and reception. Wishing to assert a degree of personal and literary authority and independence in circumstances of obvious social and economic dependency, Jonson inevitably portrays a power struggle taking place with these other agents.

In the epistle to Pembroke, to whom he dedicated the 1611 quarto of *Catiline*,[54] Jonson depicts his own role in a way that ultimately reverses the power relationship between patron and client. Instead of making the usual request for aristocratic protection of his work, something that was especially necessary given the potential retaliation by those who might have felt satirized in the poems, Jonson reformulates the patron's function as the moral responsibility to uphold the conditions of 'truth, and libertie' in which he, like any serious writer, should be allowed to function,[55] a role he tells Pembroke he can perform 'while you are constant to your owne goodnesse'.[56] In his insightful discussion of Jonson's strategies of asserting his authority through the presentation of his texts in print, Timothy Murray notes the ways Jonson 'undercuts his apparent declaration of subservience to his lord' and denies to Pembroke the right to judge the truth-value of his writing.[57] In a strategy he uses constantly in his encomiastic poetry, Jonson instructs his social superior in his duty and challenges him to live up to the ideal image presented in the rhetoric of praise. Moreover, in making the conventional promise to eternize his patron, Jonson casts doubt on the

---

[53] This fact is mentioned in Hoyt Hudson's bibliographical note to *Epigrams, The Forest, Underwoods by Ben Jonson* (New York, 1936), p. [iii].

[54] Helgerson, *Self-Crowned Laureates*, pp. 167–68, notes that this is one of the first play quartos to be dedicated to a particular patron, a sign that Jonson turned away from the popular audience that had poorly received his drama to an intellectually and socially élite readership that would better value what he wrote.

[55] In *The Advancement of Learning* Bacon expresses a hostility to 'the modern dedication of books and writings, as to patrons ... for that books (such as are worthy of the name of books) ought to have no patrons but truth and reason' (Book I, A.3. ix, quoted in Brennan, p. 143).

[56] *The Complete Poetry of Ben Jonson*, edited with an introduction, notes, and variants by William B. Hunter, Jr (1963; reprinted New York, 1968), p. 3. This is the text I cite for Jonson's poetry.

[57] *Theatrical Legitimation: Allegories of Genius in Seventeenth-Century England and France* (Oxford, 1987), pp. 79–80.

worthiness of all those he praises, among whom Pembroke is the first: 'I
returne you the honor of leading forth so many good, and great names (as my
verses mention on the better part) to their remembrance with posteritie.
Amongst whom, if I have praysed, unfortunately, any one, that doth not
deserve; or, if all answere not, in all numbers, the pictures I have made of
them: I hope it will be forgiven me, that they are no ill pieces, though they be
not like the persons' (p. 3). The would-be morally superior poet thus
patronizes patrons.[58]

In the brief epigram addressed to his reader, Jonson is both defensive and
condescending: 'PRay thee, take care, that tak'st my booke in hand, | To
read it well: that is, to understand.' The second epigram, 'To my Booke'
assumes, however, that most readers will be ill-disposed to what he has
written and will misinterpret it. Given his usual attitude toward the general
public, it is not surprising that Jonson objects to the stationer's desire to
reach a broad readership. Contemptuously addressing the bookseller in the
third epigram as 'THou that mak'st gaine thy end' (l. 1), he expresses a
belligerently anti-commercial attitude, objecting to the normal ways of
advertising books, instructing the stationer *not* to

> ... have my title-leafe on posts, or walls,
> Or in cleft-sticks, advanced to make calls
> For termers, or some clarke-like serving-man,
> Who scarse can spell th'hard names.
>
> (l. 7)

Scorning those who might be inclined to lay out the relatively small sums
necessary to purchase a poetical pamphlet, he singles out two of the major
segments of the book-buying public, fashionable 'termers' (both gentlemen
and lawyers in town during sessions of the law courts) who had a taste for
contemporary amorous and satiric literature and the middle-class readers
who wished to improve themselves by imitating the language and behaviour
of their social superiors. In desiring that only the wise seek out his work
(presumably aware of it by word-of-mouth), he imagines, in effect, a
best-non-seller, a publication whose remaindered copies might serve as
grocers' wrapping paper. But, of course, this epigram refers not to the folio
edition of Jonson's *Workes* of which the *Epigrammes* is only a part, a major
joint commercial venture for both publisher and author, but rather to the
slighter poetical pamphlet registered for publication four years earlier, a text
whose fate would probably have been similar to that of other ephemeral
productions, as the many lost copies of dramatic and poetical quartos
suggest.

In the interest of protecting his own moral and literary authority, Jonson
attacks everyone else, everyone, that is, except the king, who is praised both

---

[58] Don Wayne, 'Poetry and Power in Ben Jonson's *Epigrammes*: The Naming of "Facts" or the Figuring of
Social Relations?', *Renaissance and Modern Studies*, 23 (1979), 87, argues that Jonson makes 'a subtle
suggestion that the poems, not the persons, are what serve to codify the standards of the good society'.

as poet *and* patron in the next epigram, the person to whom Jonson's Muse 'should . . . flie' (l. 9). Embedded in the 1616 *Workes*, published while Jonson enjoyed royal favour, the potentially dangerous and ephemeral book of epigrams benefited both from the king's patronage and from the inclusion in a folio, the most prestigious publication format. As Helgerson has demonstrated, then, Jonson's laureate strategy both included and subsumed the kinds of patronage relationships that paradoxically socially elevated poets *and* made it difficult for them to assume independent sociocultural authority.[59]

In 1602, as part of a strategy of currying the favour of the expected heir to the English throne, Sir John Harington sent a copy of his epigrams with a dedication to King James. Unwilling to commit them to print, he exploited them as social currency in the system of manuscript transmission, treating James as his potential patron. When the stationer John Budge brought out the posthumous editions of 1615 and 1618, he took the opportunity of dedicating them respectively to the Earl of Pembroke and to the Duke of Buckingham.[60] In the epistle to the latter Budge wrote:

This *posthume* book is furnished with worth, but it wanteth a Patron. A worthier then your selfe the Booke could not find, nor your Lordship a more patheticall Poet to Patronize. If in Poetry, Heraldry were admitted, he would be found in happinesse of wit neere allied to the great *Sydney*: yet but neere; for the *Apix* of the *Coelum Empyrium* is not more inaccessible then is the height of *Sydneys* Poesy, which by imagination we may approch, by imitation never attaine to. To great men our very syllables should be short, and therefore I make my Conclusion a Petition; That your Lordshippes acceptation may shew how much you favor the noble Name, and nature of the Poet, and Booke. Which I deigned by your Lordshippe I shall think my paines in collecting, and disposing of these Epigrams well placed, and ever rest

Your Lordships most bounden
servant, I. B.[61]

In invoking the example of Sidney, Budge manages to shift his focus from the single text he presents to Buckingham to the whole institution of printed literature, so that it looks as though, in asking for patronage for 'the noble Name, and nature of the Poet, and Booke' he is not just asking for support for an edition of Harington's *Epigrams* but for the newly emerging identities of author and text in print culture. It is no surprise, then, that he should foreground his own important editorial functions in the literary institution of which he is part.

---

[59] *Self-Crowned Laureates*, pp. 101–84.
[60] Brennan, p. 140, points out that Pembroke's influence over the operation of their industry was acknowledged by stationers, suggesting not only that Budge's dedication of Harington's *Epigrams* (1615) was one sign of this fact but also that 'there is an interesting line of descent among some of the stationers associated with the Herberts during James's reign. Both Blount and Shawe had been apprenticed to the publisher of most of Sidney's works, William Ponsonby. Blount continued Ponsonby's practice of publishing high-class literary texts, including volumes by Joshua Sylvester, John Florio, and Samuel Daniel, who all sought the favour of William Herbert'.
[61] Text cited from John Harington, *Epigrams* (1618), facsimile edition (Menston, Yorkshire, 1970), sigs. A3ʳ–A3ᵛ.

By the early part of the seventeenth century, the competition for patronage support for printed texts, the restricted resources of the aristocracy,[62] and the economics of the publishing industry had, in effect, changed the functions of patrons defined in and inherited from manuscript culture. Certainly publishers were more apt to use patrons' names for the purpose of promoting sales of books to a general readership than as signs of an actual clientage in the old sense. Writers could normally hope for little in the way of immediate financial reward in return for dedications, though, depending on their pre-existing status of clientage to particular patrons and patronesses, there were some real social and political benefits to hope for from the patronage system. Multiple dedications,[63] the production of presentation copies with differing preliminary matter tailored to different patrons, the displacement of part of the authorizing function on to commendatory poems,[64] all signal the breakdown of the old system of artistic clientage. In the new vocabulary of printed editions of poetry, the patron-function can, in effect, be transferred to those who buy books, as in Barnabe Barnes's *Parthenophil and Parthenophe* (1593)[65] where the printer refers to the 'friendly patronages' of the 'Learned Gentlemen Readers' (sig. A2ʳ).[66] In the case of published lyric poetry, patrons served multiple purposes: not only were they actual or wished-for dispensers of money, social or political support and

[62] The complaints of authors about the stinginess of patrons or the unavailability of patronage are common. See, for example, Richard Barnfield's *The Complaint of Poetrie for the Death of Liberalitie* (London, 1598), which bemoans his loss of patronage and the substitution of '*Good wordes*' (sig. A3ᵗ) for financial reward. Thomas Nashe continually complained about the difficulty of obtaining patronage, John Marston dedicated *Antonio and Mellida* to 'Nobody' (example cited in Brennan, p. 209) and George Wither dedicated his satiric *Abuses Stript and Whipt* (1613) to himself. In 1600, the printer Thomas Thorpe, in dedicating his first publication, Marlowe's translation of the first book of Lucan, to his stationer-friend Edward Blount, joked about the poor patronage support available for authors and publishers: 'One speciall vertue in our Patrons of these daies I have promist my selfe you shall fit excellently, which is to give nothing' (quoted in Leona Rostenberg, 'Plays, Verse & Masques: Thomas Thorpe, Publisher of "Shake-Speares Sonnets"', in *Literary, Political, Scientific, Religious & Legal Publishing, Printing & Bookselling in England, 1551–1700: Twelve Studies* (New York, 1965), p. 52). For a general discussion of the decline of patronage and the consequent complaints of authors, see the two articles by Patricia Thomson cited above and Miller, *The Professional Writer*, pp. 129–35.
[63] On multiple dedications, see Miller, *The Professional Writer*, pp. 120–21. When he published *The Scourge of Folly* (1611), John Davies of Herford, for example, included a long list of patronage poetry in two sections labelled 'To worthy persons', pp. 183–229, 246–64.
[64] See Franklin B. Williams, Jr, 'Commendatory Verses: The Rise of the Art of Puffing', *Studies in Bibliography*, 19 (1966), 1–14. Ben Jonson, for example, wrote some 35 commendatory poems for other men's works, obviously thinking of peer-endorsement as one of the features of the literary institution. Williams points out that commendatory verse began as a feature of serious humanist publications and later moved to more ephemeral productions: 'Lighter literature, such as English verse and fiction, began to be provided with dedications about 1570, and puffing followed in sequence. In the Jacobean years the vogue extended to frivolous publications' (p. 5). Williams also notes that 'habitual writers of commendatory verses were . . . mainly literary professionals. With the curious exceptions of Sidney and Shakespeare, all the chief poets (including Spenser and Milton) wrote puffs' (p. 6).
[65] I cite the original London text reproduced on UMI/STC Microfilm Reel #982.
[66] The dedicatory poems to the Earls of Northumberland, Essex, Southampton, the Countess of Pembroke, Lady Straunge, and Lady Bridgett Manners appear at the end of the volume, right before the first and only appearance of the author's name. Although they are ways of advertising his social and political connexions and of appealing for favour, they seem in the format of the book to be somewhat beside the point. See the discussion of these poems in Barnabe Barnes, *Parthenophil and Parthenophe: A Critical Edition*, edited with an introduction by Victor A. Doyno (Carbondale, Illinois, 1971), pp. xxvi–xxx.

favour, offices and employment but also, as ideal readers and celebrity-endorsers, they were symbolic or mediatory figures, facilitating the transition from manuscript culture to print culture. They were part of a process in which socially-restricted occasional verse was incorporated into the newly emerging modern institution of literature, an environment in which they were reduced to a minor feature of the publishing format and the subservient author began to enjoy prestige as a member of a new literary and aesthetic élite. For example, even though John Donne and George Herbert did not themselves print their lyric poetry, they posthumously came to assume the general sociocultural authority, fame, and influence that the 1633 publication of their poems helped to solidify for them. The author-centred editions of their works, appearing initially without dedications to patrons,[67] demonstrate that poets could be well-protected, well-respected, and well-installed in a literary institution made visible through the medium of print.

---

[67] In 'The Printers to the Reader', prefaced to Herbert's *The Temple* (Cambridge, 1633), human patronage is specifically ruled out as inappropriate for such a text: 'the dedication of this work having been made by the Author to the *Divine Majestie* onely, how should we now presume to interest any mortall man in the patronage of it?' (sig. *2ʳ).

Apprentice Literature and the 'Crisis' of the 1590s

MARK THORNTON BURNETT

The Queen's University of Belfast

In his influential study of patronage, Werner L. Gundersheimer, following earlier definitions, defines patronage as 'the action of a patron in supporting, encouraging, or countenancing a person, institution [or] work of art'.[1] I would like to try, in this essay, to push further Gundersheimer's notion of patronage to include a more wide-ranging conception of the patron and the patronized. In so doing, I am following the lead of David M. Bergeron who argues in a recent article that one should not ignore paying audiences as major patrons of the drama. Audiences, Bergeron suggests, liberated dramatists and actors from dependence upon a single patron and determined to a large extent how plays evolved, were fashioned and presented.[2]

The patrons upon whom I choose to concentrate are the apprentices of late sixteenth-century London. Apprentices, living with a master who acted *in loco parentis*, bound to work hard, to conduct themselves soberly and to serve for terms of up to seven years, were the consumers of a range of cultural materials — jest-books, ballads, didactic tracts, satirical pamphlets and plays   which shaped their behaviour, social attitudes, and economic expectations.

Evidence for my claim that a large body of literature was addressed to apprentices might be found in their high standards of literacy: apprentices were given pride of place in the dedications and epistles of many writers. Thomas Heywood, in his *The Four Prentices of London* (*c.* 1594), is quite categorical that his dramatic endeavours are intended for 'the honest and hie-spirited Prentises | The Readers'.[3] Richard Norwood wrote self-critically in his journal in 1639 at the age of thirty-nine of his youth in London as a fishmonger's apprentice: 'I had a great delight in reading in vain and corrupt books as *Palmerin de Oliva*, *The Seven Champions*, and others like'.[4] Many companies insisted on literacy as a prerequisite. From the 1520s to the 1540s, seventy-two per cent of the apprentices in the Ironmongers' Company were

---

[1] Werner L. Gundersheimer, 'Patronage in the Renaissance', in *Patronage in the Renaissance*, edited by Guy Fitch Lytle and Stephen Orgel (Princeton, 1981), pp. 3–23 (p. 3).
[2] David M. Bergeron, 'Patronage of Dramatists: The Case of Thomas Heywood', *English Literary Renaissance*, 18 (1988), 294–304 (pp. 294–95).
[3] Thomas Heywood, *The Four Prentices of London*, edited by Mary Ann Weber Gasior (New York and London, 1980), p. 2. All further references appear in the text.
[4] *The Journal of Richard Norwood*, edited by Wesley Frank Craven and Walter B. Hayward (New York, 1945), p. 17.

able to write out a long oath, and the Barber-Surgeons in 1556 were disallowed from taking on any apprentice who could not understand Latin or read and write.[5] David Cressy has found in London and Middlesex in the Tudor and Stuart periods that only eighteen per cent of apprentices were unable to sign their names.[6]

Apprentices could not only read the works in which they were portrayed; they also went to the theatre to watch plays in which they were alternately admonished and extolled. Contemporary pamphlets and plays contain numerous references to apprentices responding enthusiastically to a familiar repertory, gorging themselves on custard and cream or even precipitating violence.[7] These literary allusions are given support by cases in the courts and correspondence: the Common Council issued an order to the Iron-mongers' Company in 1582 instructing them to prevent their apprentices from attending plays and interludes.[8] A group of apprentices came to the notice of the authorities for staging at a London theatre in 1613 a play in which contemporary political dignitaries were represented and subjected to ridicule.[9] Apprentices who belonged to the more prestigious companies may well have been able to afford the theatre prices and to have joined other playgoers on a regular basis. Those apprenticed to smaller companies lower down the scale, one assumes, stole money to meet the admission charges or slipped into the theatres without paying, to continue to experience the staging by dramatists of their immediate, prosaic frustrations and ultimate, lofty aspirations.

In the late Elizabethan and early Jacobean periods, a considerable volume of pamphlets and plays, mainly stressing the civic virtues of hard work and obedience, swelled the market: these works frequently selected the apprentice for particular attention. The issues that these texts address, which I distinguish in the first section of my paper, can be situated, I suggest, in the social and economic problems which menaced the city in the final years of the sixteenth century, manifest in a series of uprisings in London which terrified the metropolitan authorities. With a future stake in the running of their companies, apprentices were sensitive to fluctuations in business and trade. Although these works were ostensibly produced to inculcate obedience, the impression they yield is of ideological uncertainty.

[5] Steve Rappaport, 'Social Structure and Mobility in Sixteenth-Century London: Part I', *London Journal*, 9 (1983), 107–35 (p. 116); Sidney Young, *The Annals of the Barber-Surgeons of London* (London, 1890), p. 309.

[6] David Cressy, *Literacy and the Social Order: Reading and Writing in Tudor and Stuart England* (Cambridge, 1980), p. 129.

[7] *The actors' remonstrance, or complaint* (London, 1643), p. 4; Henry Chettle, *Kind-harts dreame* (London, 1593?), sigs. E4[r-v]; Edmund Gayton, *Pleasant notes upon Don Quixot* (London, 1654), p. 271; Stephen Gosson, *The ephemerides of Phialo, deuided into three bookes* (London, 1579), fol. 88[v]; Thomas Jordan, *The walks of Islington and Hogsdon* (London, 1657), sig. A3[v]. Cf. Andrew Gurr, *Playgoing in Shakespeare's London* (Cambridge, 1987), pp. 5, 6, 227.

[8] Corporation of London Records Office [hereafter C.L.R.O.], Journals 21, fol. 196[r]. Cf. C.L.R.O., Remembrancia I, fol. 325[v].

[9] Sir Henry Wotton, *Letters of Sir Henry Wotton to Sir Edmund Bacon* (London, 1661), pp. 155–56.

At one and the same time encouraged and constrained by their consumers, writers exhorted as they condemned, praised as they voiced anxious disparagement. While expressing worry about the consequences of civil unrest in what has been termed the 'crisis' of the 1590s, authors also rallied apprentices to defend causes of national importance.

At one point the apprentice is the object of unqualified praise. Publications of the moral exemplum genre depicted godly and sanctimonious apprentices, models of dutiful service. Casting an eye back towards his youth, Sir William Sevenoak, a former mayor of London, remembers in a work of 1592:

> To please the honest care my master tooke,
> I did refuse no toyle nor drudging payne,
> My handes no labor ever yet forsooke
> Whereby I might encrease my masters gayne:
> Thus *Sevenoake* livd (for so they cald my name,)
> Till Heaven did place mee in a better frame.[10]

The plodding rhyme-scheme registers Sevenoak's selfless devotion to diligence, his willingness to apply himself to any kind of work, however base, and his refusal to be swayed by other influences. Reflected in the purposeful syntax and unadorned vocabulary is the paradigm of the master and servant working together harmoniously, patiently accumulating profits and good deeds in the present world to ensure their future salvation. Writers employed such god-fearing apprentices to point out the importance of social stability and contentment. For instance Piers, the titular hero of a pamphlet of 1595, after having helped in putting down a rebellion and served a squire and a usurer, has the opportunity to live at court but decides not to take it up: 'for my plaine condition I found them too curious: therefore hetherward I bent my course, intending to live Menalcas man if he accept it, or keepe my owne Heard, when I can get it'.[11] A scene of pastoral calm is presented in the place of the unfamiliarity of the court: Piers's 'course' lies in happily accepting the manacles of serving Menalcas, in amassing sheep rather than money and in anticipating a position that will not affect his essential modesty and humility. In their behaviour, these apprentices thus affirm the inviolability of the *political* structure to which they belong — they espouse the values of the community and the commonwealth; they are ideal members of a strictly hierarchical society.[12]

Popular authors often implied that serving an apprenticeship would lead to material rewards and public honours. Dick Whittington, the quasi-legendary apprentice who rose to be Lord Mayor of London, was celebrated

---

[10] Richard Johnson, *The nine worthies of London* (London, 1592), sigs. C4^{r-v}.
[11] Henry Chettle, *Piers Plainness: Seven Years' Prenticeship*, in *The Descent of Euphues: Three Elizabethan Romance Stories*, edited by James Winny (Cambridge, 1957), p. 174.
[12] For a pertinent expression of this idea, see Bodleian Library, Rawlinson MS poet. 185, fol. 6^v, a 1589–90 ballad in which a father gives advice to his son, newly apprenticed.

in ballads from the sixteenth century onwards; the following extract in which he tells his story is from a 1613 version of an earlier set of verses:

> Brave *London* 'Prentices, come listen to my Song,
> 'Tis for your glory all, and to you doth belong;
> And you, poor Country Lads, though born of low degree,
> See by God's providence what you in time may bee.[13]

The ballad transforms the humdrum existence of the apprentice into exciting prospects of success and prestige. In exhortatory language, it holds out possibilities of ascending into the upper echelons of a company or local government by appealing to servants of all social categories. Courage and duty are equated; they are qualities that will allow the apprentice to promote himself and are part of a divine design in which origins are of no hindrance to the pursuit of civic achievement.

If one set of writers during this period found the apprentice to be of the utmost scrupulousness and integrity, another group voiced a point of view that was altogether more disapproving and hostile. On the one hand, the conduct of apprentices guaranteed the preservation of the social fabric; on the other, it could threaten to throw the established order into chaos and have damaging consequences. For the apprentice who failed to submit himself 'under the yoake', as a contemporary put it, there was little doubt of what troubles lay in store.[14] The results of his neglect were carefully enumerated; a pamphleteer, possibly Samuel Rowlands, wrote in 1602:

There are a certaine band of Raggamuffin Prentises about the towne, that will abusc anie upon the smallest occasion that is, and such men (whom they never came to the credit in all their lives to make cleane their shooes) these dare never meete a man in the face to avouch their rogarie, but forsooth they must have the help of some other their complices. Of this base sort you shall commonly find them at Playhouses on holy dayes, and there they will be playing their parts, or at some rout, as the pulling downe of Baudie houses, or at some good exploit or other, so that if you need helpe, or you thinke your selfe not able to make your part good with anie that you owe a grudge to, no more but repaire to one of these, and for a canne of Ale they will do as much as another for a crowne: & these make no more conscience to beat or lame one, whom they never before saw nor knew, then the knights of the poasts when they are feed out of *Poules* to sweare falsly.[15]

A tone of weary cynicism and sly intimacy characterizes this delineation of apprentices from a low estate. These apprentices indulge rather than abstain, owe allegiance to their own code of behaviour in their rejection of their masters and of other constituted forms of authority. Financial rewards are reaped by the indiscriminate support of local grievances, not by thrift and industry. A group of urban hoodlums, they are part of a complicity as opposed to a company: they embrace no ideals, only a worldliness and a contemptuous disrespect for law, order, and government. In the same mould

---

[13] *The Roxburghe Ballads*, edited by William Chappell and J. Woodfall Ebsworth, 9 vols (London, 1871–97), VII, 582.
[14] B. P., *The prentises practise in godlinesse, and his true freedome* (London, 1608), sig. H3ᵛ.
[15] [Samuel Rowlands], *Greenes ghost haunting conie-catchers* (London, 1602), sig. E3ʳ.

are some lines from a verse satire by Thomas Rogers of 1602–04. The hypocritical Robert Dudley, the Earl of Leicester, will stop at nothing to gain preferment; he recalls:

> The Prentises did likewise take my part,
> As I in private quarrels often tryde,
> Soe that I had the very head and hart,
> The *Court* and *Citty* leaning one my side,
> With flattery some, others with guifts I plide,
>   And some with threats, stearne looks, and angry words,
>   I woone to my defence with clubbs and swords.[16]

By subtly inveigling himself into the good graces of courtier and citizen alike, Leicester seeks to attain royal favour. Once again the apprentices are represented as playing roles: in these verses, having been bribed, they provoke brawls to advance an aspirant's political ambitions. Needing little excuse to take the law into their own hands, they do not hesitate to agitate, excited by the promise of eventual compensation and acknowledgement.

A striking feature of the texts of this limited period, therefore, is the unevenness of the ideas expressed. The apprentice is portrayed as virtuous and restrained even as he joins an unruly throng to rampage in the city streets. But the articulation of contradictory viewpoints does not present irresolvable difficulties: it is rare, for instance, to come across unfavourable opinions prior to the seventeenth century. Most often, the impassioned and easily inflamed apprentice is treated either humorously or exhilaratingly: individual or collective action is vindicated as it protects society from subversive influences. An isolated example of a hot-headed apprentice who is comically drawn is in a jest-book of 1595; a London printer asks his apprentice to fetch him some French mustard, telling him ironically that it is only to be found in France. Gullible and unperceptive, the servant rushes to Billingsgate, boards a ship bound for France and returns home after a year's absence, triumphantly bearing the hard-won condiment:

The said Prentise entring by and by into his maisters Printing-house, and finding a Dutch-man there working at the Presse, straight stept unto him, and snatching the balles out of his hands, gave him a good cuffe on the eare, & sayd: Why how now (Butter-boxe?) Cannot a man so soon turne his back to fetch his maister a messe of Mustard, but you to step straight into his place?[17]

The butt of the joke is at first sight the apprentice who has no conception of the passing of time and thinks his master is able for an unlimited period to do without his services. Stepping out in search of seasoning to sauce his master's food, he returns to find a 'saucy' Dutchman who has ousted his position in the printing-house. But the jest operates on another level, too; in one sense, the apprentice escapes ridicule in that he refuses to be corrupted by his exotic French experience and realizes that he must eventually resume employment.

---

[16] Thomas Rogers, *Leicester's Ghost*, edited by Franklin B. Williams, Jr (London, 1972), p. 18.
[17] Anthony Copley, *Wits fittes and fancies* (London, 1595), p. 129.

The food imagery is suggestive: the apprentice fears his responsibilities are being consumed by the greedy and slippery Dutchman ('Butter-boxe'). As he fills his master's mustard-pot, so he is worried by the possibility that his own place might be filled by a foreign worker.

Unrest and antagonism, then, are legitimized as they defend the political equilibrium. Wrongdoers are routed and traitors brought to justice: apprentices are incited to rise in late Elizabethan literature variously to quash noble feuding and to rescue the unfortunate victims of pickpockets and thieves.[18] In 2 *Henry VI* (1590–91), Peter Thump, an armourer's apprentice, is comforted by his fellows as he prepares to fight his master who has accused him of uttering treasonable words against the state:

1 PREN. Here, Peter, I drink to thee; and be not afeared.
2 PREN. Be merry, Peter, and fear not thy master: fight for credit of the prentices.
PETER.   I thank you all: drink, and pray for me, I pray you; for I think I have taken my last draught in this world. Here, Robin, and if I die, I give thee my apron; and, Will, thou shalt have my hammer: and here, Tom, take all the money that I have. Lord bless me, I pray God, for I am never able to deal with my master, he hath learnt so much fence already.[19]

Despite the fact that Peter dispatches his master in the duel, his action is not condemned: it is given the royal seal of approval. For in death, Horner, his master, reveals that it was he who had entertained treasonable thoughts: 'I confess, I confess treason' (II. iii. 91). The fellowship that Peter shares with the other apprentices elevates him above the separateness and deviancy of political conspiracy. In his concern for his companions, the apprentice is distinguished from his master who thinks only of his own interests and of justifying his accusations. Peter's armour withstands the onslaughts of his enemies, and he successfully affirms the apprentices' 'credit' and fraternal spirit.

Heywood's *1 Edward IV*, in existence in an early version in 1594 but not printed until 1599, contains scenes in which apprentices band together to repel not their employers but the invading army of the rebel, Falconbridge, from the city gates. A chorus of voices chants the principles of the capital; the second apprentice cries: 'And, *London* prentices, be rul'd by me; | Die ere ye lose fair *Londons* liberty', and he denounces the rebels as those 'desperate, idle, swaggering mates, | That haunt the suburbes in the time of peace'.[20] This celebration of civic sentiments culminates in the speech of the first apprentice:

> The Chronicles of *England* can report
> What memorable actions we have done,

[18] Robert Greene, *A Dispvtation betweene a Hee Conny-catcher and a Shee Conny-catcher* (1592), in *The Life and Complete Works in Prose and Verse*, edited by Alexander B. Grosart, 15 vols (London, 1881–86), x, 236.
[19] William Shakespeare, *2 Henry VI*, edited by Andrew S. Cairncross (London, 1962), II. iii. 67–76. All further references appear in the text.
[20] Thomas Heywood, *The Dramatic Works*, edited by R. H. Shepherd, 6 vols (London, 1874), I, 17–18. All further references appear in the text.

> To which this daies achievement shall be knit,
> To make the volume larger than it is. (p. 18)

What is at stake is not so much the city as an ideal of freedom which it represents and which the apprentices are charged to guard and maintain: to this end they gather their forces. Sensitive to their reputation, they are anxious to side against the rabble and trouble-makers associated with the margins of the metropolis. It is, too, to ensure that their pledge of support will be recorded that they oppose Falconbridge, writing themselves into London's posterity.

Issues of class are also underlined in representations of the uprisings of apprentices: discontent is precipitated by gentlemen and gallants as well as by traitors, rebels, and foreigners. A disagreement erupts between Acutus and Graccus, two prosecutors of vice, and some dandies in *Every Woman in Her Humour* (1599–1603), possibly by Lewis Machin, and the hostess of the tavern appeals to the apprentices to separate the fighting parties.[21] On a later occasion in the play, in a parodic reading of an indenture, she drills the apprentices in qualities which they are urged to emulate: 'you must bee|eyed like a Serjeant, an eare like a Belfounder, your con-|science a Schoolemaister, a knee like a Courtier' (IV. i. 14–16). The apprentices in Dekker and Middleton's *1 The Honest Whore* (1604) have certainly taken such instructions to heart. Crambo and Poh, two insulting gallants, enrage George, the journeyman, who rouses the apprentices to rise to correct the hierarchical balance: 'Sfoot clubs, clubs, prentices, downe with em, ah you roagues,|strike a Cittizen in's shop'.[22] The gallants are believed to have transgressed strict lines of social demarcation: the height of abuse, George thinks, is that a tradesman should be beaten in the very place where his business is conducted. His call to the apprentices thus dispels anxieties and resolves the tensions that the conflict has created. Scourges of crime and injustice, the apprentices uphold traditional rights and champion the privileges of civic institutions.

Even greater and more extravagant exploits of apprentices were penned by some writers. A vein of romance and adventure runs through many of these texts: not content with attacking local forms of aberration, apprentices steal abroad to fight traditional enemies and to express their nationalistic inclinations. Contemporary ballads and pamphlets testify to the renown won by apprentices on the battlefield and applaud their heroic deeds.[23] In Heywood's *The Four Prentices of London* (c. 1594), the sound of a drum lures the

---

[21] [Lewis Machin], *Every Woman in Her Humour*, edited by Archie Mervin Tyson (New York and London, 1980), I. i. 302–08. All further references appear in the text.

[22] Thomas Dekker, *The Dramatic Works*, edited by Fredson Bowers, 4 vols (Cambridge, 1953–61), II, IV. iii. 91–92.

[23] Johnson, *The nine*, sigs. D1r, D4r, F3r–F4r; *A Collection of Songs and Ballads Relative to the London Prentices and Trades*, edited by Charles Mackay, Percy Society, 1 (1841), pp. 22–28; William Vallans, *The honourable prentice: or, this taylor is a man* (London, 1615), passim; Hans Werner Willkomm, *Über Richard Johnson's 'Seven Champions of Christendom' (1596)* (Berlin, 1911), p. 15.

apprentices to leave their trades and join the Holy Wars in Jerusalem; *en route*, they liberate not London but Boulogne and other beseiged cities from the Spanish forces. During the course of their campaign, moreover, they indulge in self-congratulation, amatory dalliance, and invective against demagogic tyrants, foreigners, and 'proud *Italians*' (l. 1012).[24] Of a similar character is a pamphlet of 1595 which celebrates Captain James Lancaster and his sea adventures against the Spanish and crystallizes many of the themes we have been identifying; the apprentices are specifically addressed:

> And gallant Brutes which yet are bound,
>   your masters to obay:
> When time shall make you free againe,
>   think then what I now say.
> Learne by this man of woorth to guyde,
>   your selves in everie place:
> By land or sea to gaine renowne,
>   and enemies to disgrace,
> your Countrey then your honor shall,
>   for Prince doe service good:
> and men that see your woorthynes,
>   for you will spend their blood.[25]

The possibility of gaining the freedom of the company is presented as an incentive which stimulates the apprentice to apply himself to his work. Serving an apprenticeship becomes a means whereby he is enabled to shrug off his rawness and inexperience ('Brutes'), assuming instead adult responsibilities ('men'). Only by cultivating patience and determination will he avoid shame ('disgrace'), establish his reputation ('honor') and enjoy dignities and material glory. Finally, an economic dimension is stressed; the lines urge the apprentices to save themselves and to channel their energies into constructing a sound basis for their later achievements.

To try to account for the equal stress placed on contradictory ideas — authors, deriding and exalting the apprentice, instruct him in the same moment to labour and to seek out fame — I move now to a historical reading of these texts, paying particular attention to apprentices' political activism. First, it was not uncommon for apprentices to enlist or to be impressed to fight in foreign wars (in the Low Countries, for example), and the rousing stories in which they appeared might have held a specific interest for some sixteenth and seventeenth-century readers and playgoers.[26] However, it seems more likely that figurations of apprentices' disturbances owed much to rebellions in London throughout the sixteenth century in which they actively participated. On May Day in 1517, 2,000 apprentices demonstrated

---

[24] In its concern with tyranny and megalomania, Heywood's play bears many similarities to Marlowe: see Mark Thornton Burnett, 'Marlovian Imitation and Interpretation in Heywood's *The Four Prentices of London*', *Cahiers Elisabéthains*, 32 (October 1987), 75–78.

[25] Henry Roberts, *Lancaster his allarums* (London, 1595), sig. A4ᵛ.

[26] C.L.R.O., Repertory 24, fol. 98ʳ; Guildhall Library, MS 5570/1, fol. 260ʳ; Public Record Office [hereafter P.R.O.], Req. 2/213/36; *An Analytical Index to the Ballad-Entries (1557–1709) in the Registers of the Company of Stationers of London*, edited by Hyder E. Rollins (Chapel Hill, 1924), p. 29.

anti-alien feelings, sacked the houses of French and Flemish merchants, assaulted the Spanish ambassador, and broke open the gaols. Twelve apprentices were executed after the troubles had subsided.[27] In 1549 there was an unsuccessful attempt to persuade the apprentices to join the Norfolk rebels.[28] A history of apprentice disorder and group activity was available for writers to draw upon; scenes of apprentices taking up their clubs to round on wrongdoers and reform inequalities, then, may have seemed to contemporaries rather more than fanciful speculation and extravagance.

Literary expressions of resentment against gentlemen and courtiers take on a highly-charged resonance when we reflect upon outbursts of class antagonism in which apprentices came into conflict with their social superiors. A proclamation was issued in 1576, for instance, protesting against the violence offered by apprentices towards the pages and lackeys of noblemen.[29] A similar incident caused concern in 1581 when some apprentices in Smithfield assaulted the servants of Sir Thomas Stanhope.[30] In 1584 the apprentices made 'mutines and assemblies' after one of their fellows, sleeping on the grass outside the Curtain, had been kicked in the belly and called a rogue and scum by a passing gentleman.[31] The frustrations culminated in 1590: vagrants and apprentices assembled, attacked the gentlemen of Lincoln's Inn and broke into their chambers.[32] Though the insurrection was put down, it was still necessary to introduce in 1591 stringent measures against unlawful gatherings to prevent further outbreaks of violence.[33]

The key to an understanding of apprentice xenophobia in contemporary pamphlets and plays, I would suggest, can be found in demonstrations against aliens that were a recurrent feature of the period. War and rapid population growth exacerbated already well-established grievances; Dutch and French refugees, in particular, were charged with causing unemployment, a decline in trade, and a rise in prices. Hostilities surfaced in a libel of 1567 and a plot of 1586 hatched by the plasterers' apprentices against the foreign artisans.[34] Again in 1593 a litter of apprentice libels menacing the strangers swept the capital.[35]

Famine and distress were additional problems at this time, particularly in the mid 1590s, and the apprentices took it upon themselves to attempt to

[27] Sebastian Giustinian, *Four Years at the Court of Henry VIII*, translated by Rawdon Brown, 2 vols (London, 1854), II, 70–71.
[28] C.L.R.O., Repertory 12, 1, fol. 122^r.
[29] C.L.R.O., Journals 20, 2, fol. 276^v.
[30] Ian Archer, 'Governors and Governed in Sixteenth-Century London, c. 1560–1603: Studies in the Achievement of Stability' (unpublished D.Phil. dissertation, Oxford University, 1988), p. 11; C.L.R.O., Remembrancia I, fol. 98^r; P.R.O., PC 2/13/452; *An Analytical*, edited by Rollins, pp. 179–80.
[31] British Library (hereafter B.L.), Lansdowne MS 41, fol. 31^r.
[32] C.L.R.O., Journals 22, fols 417^v, 421^r; *Tudor Royal Proclamations*, edited by Paul L. Hughes and James F. Larkin, 3 vols (New Haven and London, 1964–69), III, 60; Roger B. Manning, *Village Revolts: Social Protest and Popular Disturbances in England, 1509–1640* (Oxford, 1988), p. 203.
[33] B.L., Lansdowne MS 66, fols 241^r–42^r.
[34] Archer, 'Governors and Governed', p. 13; B.L., Lansdowne MS 49, fol. 22^r; C.L.R.O., Journals 22, fol. 54^r.
[35] P.R.O., PC 2/20/331.

implement their own solutions to the economic crisis. At Billingsgate in June 1595, in two separate incidents they stole butter and fish in order to sell them at reduced prices.[36] In October 1595 riotous apprentices in Cheapside took off with a cart-load of starch, the property of the Queen's patentee of an unpopular monopoly.[37] Even in 1596 libels which probably complained about the conditions of dearth were still circulating in the city.[38] The existence of unrest suggests a number of further parallels with writings about apprentices: the conviction that aliens were draining sources of employment and stagnating trade was negotiated by authors who promised inviolable opportunities for social betterment. Shortages and dearth were confronted in texts which reassured apprentices with tales of the riches and advantages they might gain if only in youth they remained moderate, disciplined, and abstemious.

Certainly the sense of fraternity and cameraderie among apprentices that pervades Elizabethan literature can be linked to tumults in which they acted in concert to declare their solidarity and to support their members. When a feltmaker's apprentice was imprisoned in the Marshalsea for debt in 1592, his fellows met at a play to plan his rescue. In the attempt, innocent bystanders in Southwark were jostled and hurt, leading to a strengthening of the watch soon afterwards.[39] On 6 June 1595, a silkweaver who faced punishment for having criticized the Lord Mayor was rescued by a crowd of apprentices.[40] An attempt later in the month to imprison in the Counter some servants who had fallen foul of the magistrates gave rise to further apprentice rescue efforts.[41] The discontent came to a climax at the end of the month: encouraged by vagrant soldiers and in revenge for the way in which their fellows had been treated after the butter and fish dispute, on 27 June 1,800 apprentices pulled down the pillories in Cheapside and Leadenhall, and set up gallows against the door of the Lord Mayor, Sir John Spenser.[42] A gathering of apprentices outside the Tower on 29 June, the stated intention of which was to rob the wealthy inhabitants and to take the sword of authority from the governors, resulted in the enforcement of a state of martial law, a search for the culprits, proclamations, a spate of libels, the arrest of the leaders, and on 24 July their execution.[43]

[36] B.L., Harleian MS 2143, fol. 57ᵛ; C.L.R.O., Remembrancia ii, fol. 20ʳ.
[37] Manning, *Village Revolts*, p. 206; P.R.O., PC 2/21/8.
[38] Archer, 'Governors and Governed', p. 17.
[39] B.L., Lansdowne MS 71, fol. 28ʳ; C.L.R.O., Remembrancia i, fol. 341ʳ; P.R.O., PC 2/19/414, SP 12/243/45.
[40] Hatfield House (hereafter H.H.), Cecil Papers, xxxii, fol. 106ʳ.
[41] H.H., Cecil Papers, xxxii, fol. 106ʳ; John Stow, *A Survey of the Cities of London and Westminster*, edited by John Strype, 2 vols (London, 1720), ii, Book v, 303.
[42] C.L.R.O., Journals 24, fol. 22ᵛ; H.H., Cecil Papers, xxxii, fol. 107ʳ; P.R.O., SP 12/252/94 iii; John Stow, *The abridgement or summarie of the English chronicle* (London, 1607), p. 499.
[43] Archer, 'Governors and Governed', p. 9; John Bellamy, *The Tudor Law of Treason: An Introduction* (London, 1979), p. 78; B.L., Lansdowne MS 78, fols 159ʳ, 161ʳ; C.L.R.O., Journals 24, fol. 25ᵛ; *Tudor*, edited by Hughes and Larkin, iii, p. 143; Manning, *Village Revolts*, pp. 209–10; *Select Statutes*, edited by G. W. Prothero, fourth edition (Oxford, 1913), pp. 443–44; Stow, *The abridgement*, pp. 500–01; Stow, *A Survey*, edited by Strype, i, Book i, 65–66; *A students lamentation that hath sometime been in London an apprentice, for the rebellious tumults lately in the citie hapning* (London, 1595), sigs A2ʳ, B4ᵛ.

That the flames of discord continued to flicker after this date would help to shed light on the comments of later writers who fearfully recollected past apprentice troubles or contemplated future dissensions. The Oxfordshire rebels in 1596 planned to join with the apprentices when they marched on London, and more libels were distributed.[44] There were libels circulating in 1597 which claimed that the mayor was 'engaged in a *pacte de famine*', and a further apprentice libel vowing revenge against magisterial injustice was reported in 1598.[45] As late as 1601, a scrivener's apprentice suspected of writing libels was brought before the London Bridewell governors.[46]

We are now in a position to make some more detailed observations about the material conditions which made possible the imaginative shaping of apprentice literature. In one respect, the reasons for authors commending apprentices were economic. At least half of all apprentices in this period of rising poverty failed to serve for seven years; the response of didactic writers was to seek to persuade them that the successful completion of their training was a moral necessity.[47] There may also have been anxieties about the 'liberty' that London enjoyed as a trading capital being eroded: Heywood's apprentices are presented for our approbation as they deliver Syon and Jerusalem from the domination of a foreign power, restoring to them their cultural and religious importance. The contradictions appropriated by this literature are less easy to explain. It needs pointing out, first, that the material authors drew upon for their ideas was potentially dangerous and subversive. Plays in which apprentices performed valiantly could be read as incitements to riot; two of the uprisings, we shall recall, started in or near theatres. One should not be surprised in the circumstances that *The Book of Sir Thomas More*, originally composed in 1592–93, was suppressed by the Master of the Revels, went through endless revisions, and was never staged in a playhouse.[48] Themes of adventure, therefore, served to direct aggression into realms of heroic fantasy: pamphleteers, with one eye on the censors and the other on apprentices who clamoured for new publications, played down economic questions while they resituated contemporary grievances in an exotic environment.

The existence of a literate, theatre-going apprentice population in England in the sixteenth and seventeenth centuries was an essential ingredient in the production of texts which dealt with specifically youth-related preoccupations and interests. Inevitably writers claimed that their work (which had to meet the requirements of apprentices and other consumers)

[44] P.R.O., SP 12/261/10 I-II, B.L., Lansdowne MS 81, fols 72ʳ, 86ʳ.
[45] Archer, "Governors and Governed', p. 17; *Trevelyan Papers, Part II*, edited by J. Payne Collier, Camden Society, 1st ser., 84 (1863), p. 101.
[46] Bethlem Royal Hospital, Bridewell Court Book 1 February 1598–7 November 1604, fol. 228ᵛ.
[47] Ilana Krausman Ben-Amos, 'Service and the coming of age of young men in seventeenth-century England', *Continuity and Change*, 3 (1988), 41–64 (p. 55).
[48] The original date of composition has been suggested by Scott McMillin, *The Elizabethan Theatre and 'The Book of Sir Thomas More'* (Ithaca, 1987), p. 72. For the dates of revision, see Giorgio Melchiori, '*The Booke of Sir Thomas Moore*: A Chronology of Revision', *Shakespeare Quarterly*, 37 (1986), 291–308.

was morally motivated — it was justified to contemplate the deviant as this underlined the established and the normative.

But the apparent meanings of these texts are often ruptured and thrown into doubt. The purging of apprentice frustrations entailed questions about patriarchal power, the concern with domestic order pointed towards more deeply-rooted problems of insecurity, and the representation of servants commanding military forces was a reminder of the more onerous structures of discipline to which the apprentice was obliged to submit. Ultimately, therefore, apprentice literature emphasizes grievances rather than managing their successful resolution and containment.

A number of additional reasons can be proposed to elucidate these inconsistencies. There was an inheritance from earlier literary models, and apprentices occupied a transitional stage in the 'life-cycle' (adolescents who were not yet adults, they were adults who were forced to yield to dictates intended for children). Particularly where political writing with an apprentice element was concerned, the task of playwrights and popular writers was complicated by the conflicting reactions of the authorities to expressions of disorder and by changing alignments among the apprentices themselves.

As the seventeenth century progressed, apprentices, self-styled patrons of the theatre and the literary marketplace and self-elected arbiters of public justice, continued to involve themselves in political movements and authors' pens remained busy: an ever-present danger was that the ghosts of the 1590s would rise again, never having been completely exorcized. In these later texts, contradictions still surfaced, and they were not resolved until apprenticeships came to be irregularly enforced and the powers of the guilds had declined. The writers of the 1590s who attempted to understand the patronizing, politicized system of apprenticeship looked forward to its inescapable collapse and predicted its final demise.

Note:

I would like to thank the following for permission to refer to manuscripts in their possession: the Bethlem Royal Hospital, the Bodleian Library, the British Library, the Corporation of London Records Office and the Marquess of Salisbury.

Patronage, Protestantism, and Stage Propaganda in Early Elizabethan England

PAUL WHITFIELD WHITE

Baylor University, Waco, Texas

The most perplexing problem facing any investigation of the Elizabethan stage during the first two decades of the Queen's reign concerns the evidence. The kinds of source materials that are available during the latter part of the reign are nowhere to be found. We have no equivalent of Henslowe's diary, no extensive records surviving from the Revels Office, no sizeable body of works by a single prominent dramatist, and little hard evidence concerning the repertories of companies and the specific venues where they performed, especially in London. What we do know is that playing was enormously popular even during these years. I have counted some eighty different troupes operating between 1558 and 1576.[1] They range from obscure groups of itinerant town players recorded for only one performance to the major noblemen's troupes of Leicester, Warwick, and Norfolk, touring regularly from year to year in the provinces. What also emerges from the evidence is that in addition to romances, farces, and classical works, a surprisingly large proportion of state-sponsored drama consists of religious interludes, advancing in quite polemical fashion the predominant religious ideology of the Elizabethan governing class. This religious ideology of course was Protestant. It is characterized not only by sworn allegiance to the Queen as Supreme Governor of the Church, but by a distinctly Calvinistic world-view, emphasizing personal religious experience, the primacy of Scripture, God's sovereignty and man's depravity, and showing a pronounced aversion to Roman Catholicism: most notably its political doctrine of papal supremacy, its theological tenets of free will and transubstantiation, as well as its elaborate prescriptions for worship.

In this paper I challenge the persisting opinion that these Protestant religious interludes either were not performed at all (in other words, they appeared only in print) or that they ceased to be performed very shortly after the Royal Proclamation of 16 May 1559, which prescribed that no licence is to be given to plays dealing with matters of religion or the governance of the state. My argument is that the Royal Proclamation of 1559 was not seriously

---

[1] In the absence of a much-needed revision of John T. Murray's *English Dramatic Companies 1558–1642*, 2 vols (New York, 1910), my count is based chiefly on Murray but is supplemented by lists of companies in recent volumes of Records of Early English Drama and the Malone Society Collections, especially *REED: Devon*, edited by John Wasson (Toronto, 1986); Ian Lancashire, *Dramatic Texts and Records of Britain: A Chronological Topography to 1558*, Studies in Early English Drama, 1 (Toronto, 1984); *Norfolk and Suffolk*, edited by David Galloway and John Wasson, *Malone Society Collections*, Volume IX (Oxford, 1980).

enforced, and that indeed Protestant stage propaganda was practised into the early 1570s, after which the growing secularism and commercialism of theatre in London brought polemical interludes into disrepute and decline. Moreover, such stage propaganda was encouraged, at times organized, by the central administration, and was sponsored and protected by all the traditional organizations responsible for producing drama: the royal court, noble households, civic organizations, academic institutions, and the church.

The most explicit evidence of the Elizabethan governing class engaged in encouraging, and even promoting, Protestant stage propaganda, is found during the opening years of the Queen's reign. The Revels Accounts at Court, State Papers, and various other documents, show that pro-Protestant and virulently anti-papist entertainments were popular from the royal court to the streets, taverns, and hostels of London and other cities. During the Christmas revels of 1559/60, the Queen witnessed a elaborate anti-papal spectacle performed by the Court Interluders 'of crows in the habits of Cardinals, of asses habited as Bishops, and of wolves representing Abbots'.[2] In London itself, foreign ambassadors reported the mass mocked, priests derided, and Catholic heads of state satirized in plays and processions through the streets.[3] The practice spread to other cities, such as Canterbury, Ipswich, and Shrewsbury, where city corporations, churches, and schools staged plays denouncing everything Catholic and reviving the advanced Protestantism of Edward VI's reign.[4]

There was of course nothing new about this close alliance between the Protestant pulpit and the stage, nor about the policy that originated at the highest level of government which encouraged and in some instances organized stage polemic. Since 1533 when plays and games satirizing cardinals occasioned Henry VIII's breach with Rome, plays deriding the papacy and proclaiming the new gospel were performed with considerable frequency at court, on village greens, and in guildhalls and churches all over England, especially during Cromwell's term in office and resuming under the relaxed stage regulations of Edward VI. Many of these plays, like many similar ones under Elizabeth, were penned by preacher-playwrights such as John Bale and Thomas Wylley. As Secretary of State, and subsequently as

---

[2] As reported by the Venetian ambassador Il Schifanoya. See *State Papers and Manuscripts Relating to English Affairs, Existing in the Archives and Collections of Venice, and in Other Libraries of Northern Italy*, Volumes I–VII, edited by Rawdon Brown and G. Cavendish-Bentinck (London, 1864–90), VII (*1558–1580*), 11 (no. 10). Cited hereafter as *State Papers: Venice*.

[3] *State Papers: Venice*, 27 (no. 18). *Calendar of Letters and State Papers Relating to English Affairs, Preserved Principally in the Archives of Simancas*, edited by M. A. S. Hume, 4 vols (London, 1892–99), I, 62. Cited hereafter as *State Papers: Simancas*.

[4] For anti-Catholic plays at Canterbury, see Peter Clark, 'Josias Nicholls and Religious Radicalism, 1553–1639', *The Journal of Ecclesiastical History*, 28 (1977), 134–35; Leslie P. Fairfield, *John Bale: Mythmaker for the English Reformation* (West Lafayette, Indiana, 1979), pp. 145–47. For Ipswich, see discussion of Bale's *King Johan* below. For Shrewsbury, see Alan Somerset, 'Local Drama and Playing Places at Shrewsbury: New Findings from the Borough Records', in *Medieval and Renaissance Drama in England*, edited by J. Leeds Barroll, 6 vols (New York, 1984–90), II, 1–31.

Lord Privy Seal, Cromwell advanced beyond his able predecessors in these posts, Bishops Foxe and Wolsey, in organizing state-sanctioned propaganda for the stage.[5] He and his talented office of publicists recognized that in a nation that remained to a large extent illiterate, especially in those outlying regions where Catholicism was most firmly entrenched, drama communicated ideology effectively and entertainingly to the general public in concrete visual and oral terms. The Catholic church itself had proved this through centuries of popular religious theatre. Now, by putting players on the stage in Catholic vestments and parodying the mass (as, for example, one finds in Bale's plays), the Protestant administration could expose popish priests for what the Reformers perceived them to be in reality, actors performing meaningless and illusory rituals. And since the institutions responsible for producing drama remained firmly intact after the Reformation, the Crown, with its many loyal officials strategically placed throughout the realm, could control and exploit the stage, along with the pulpit and the press, as a means of drawing the people away from residual Catholicism and winning broad support for its Reformation policy. As John Foxe would say later in 1562, 'Players, Printers, Preachers be set up of God as a triple Bulwark against the triple crown of the Pope, to bring him down'.[6]

There is little doubt that Cromwell's legacy extended to at least the early years of Elizabeth's reign when William Cecil lived to be the Henrician minister's most able successor as Secretary of State. Cecil's programme of propaganda may not have been as comprehensive as that of Cromwell during the late 1530s, but the evidence is persuasive that he directed anti-Catholic stage propaganda at Court and in the capital at least during 1559 and probably favoured it in subsequent years. That Cecil was actively involved in patronizing stage polemic in the early years is demonstrated in a letter from the Duke of Feria to King Philip of Spain dated 29 April 1559. After reporting the Queen's disapproval of plays containing religious attacks against Spain, Feria states, 'I knew that a member of her Council had given the arguments to construct these comedies, which is true, for Cecil gave them, as indeed she partly admitted to me'.[7] The Spanish ambassador was a partisan observer of the Elizabethan court, but here his remarks may be taken at face value. As Secretary and a Licenser of the Press to both Somerset and Northumberland under Edward VI, Cecil would have had plenty of experience reading Protestant playscripts, which were submitted to his desk along with books for licensing and censorship.[8] A sharp memory would have had little difficulty recalling the contents of such works when they might

---

[5] See Glynne Wickham, *Early English Stages*, second edition, 3 vols (London, 1959–80), I, 277–78.
[6] *Acts and Monuments*, ed. S. R. Cattley, fourth edition, revised and corrected by J. Pratt, 8 vols (London, 1877), IV, 57.
[7] *State Papers: Simancas*, I, 62.
[8] See John N. King, *Reformation English Literature* (Princeton, 1982), pp. 109–11. King regards Cecil among the leading patrons of Protestant propaganda under Edward VI. See also E. K. Chambers, *The Elizabethan Stage*, 4 vols (Oxford, 1922), III, 160.

prove suitable under new circumstances, such as those celebrating the restoration of a Protestant monarch to the English throne. One of these playscripts may have been *Aesop's Fable*, a dramatized beast fable evidently mocking the mass, written and produced by George Ferrers in conjunction with the Master of the Revels, Thomas Cawarden, and performed by the Court Interluders before Edward VI and the Court during Christmas 1553.[9] Since these same producers and performers are believed to have been responsible for the anti-papal beast fable at Christmas in 1559, noted earlier, it seems likely that the latter was either the same work or an adaptation of the Edwardian spectacle of 1553. Moreover, while the Revels Office and the Court Interluders were under the direction of the Lord Chamberlain, Thomas Howard, for the 1559 production, it was the Privy Council who gave its signed approval and it seems more likely that Cecil himself, rather than Howard, commissioned the piece.

There is further evidence of Cecil's patronage, or at the very least his tacit approval, of Protestant religious drama at Court during the 1560s. In August 1564 the Queen made her celebrated visit to Cambridge, where Cecil was Lord Chancellor, and where Protestant religious drama had flourished since the Henrician Reformation. The university was now the seedbed of radical Protestantism. A few days before the Queen's arrival, Cecil went up to the University to discuss with a committee of administrators what sermons, debates, and plays would be suitable for the Queen's pleasure.[10] One of the plays approved was *Ezekias*, performed by the students of King's College before the Queen in King's College Chapel on the evening of Tuesday, 8 August. *Ezekias* was quite possibly staged on at least one earlier occasion, before Cromwell in 1538 while its author, Nicholas Udall, was Headmaster of Eton, the sister foundation to King's College.[11] The play is clearly iconoclastic in nature, as we know from Abraham Hartwell's description of the royal performance, and sees Elizabeth as a latter day Ezekias responsible for destroying false idols and images for her people and redirecting them towards the true worship of God.[12] The topical significance of the play could no more have been missed than the advice the Queen received two years earlier when she saw *Gorboduc*, co-written by Thomas Norton, the translator of Calvin's *Institutes*. That play, too, must have been approved by Cecil, although the Earl of Leicester may have had more to do with its staging at Court, having served as Constable-Marshall at the Inns of Court

[9] See Lancashire, p. 211; *Documents Relating to the Office of the Revels in the Time of King Edward VI and Queen Mary*, edited by Albert Feuillerat (London, 1914), I, 282; L. B. Campbell, 'The Lost Play of *Æsop's Crow*', *MLN*, 49 (1934), 454–57.

[10] The relevant correspondence is found in *REED: Cambridge*, edited by Alan Nelson, 2 vols (Toronto, 1989), II, 230–35; cited hereafter as *REED: Cambridge*. See also Frederick S. Boas, *The University Drama in the Tudor Age* (Oxford, 1914), p. 90.

[11] See Norman Sanders, Richard Southern, T. W. Craik, and Lois Potter, *The Revels History of Drama in English*, Volume II, *1500–1576* (London, 1980), pp. 137–38; cited hereafter as *Revels*, II.

[12] The text of Hartwell's Latin Elegiacs appears in English translation in *REED: Cambridge*, II, 1138–42. See also the account of the play and the Queen's visit in Boas, Chapter 5.

the previous Christmas when *Gorboduc* was first performed. The play offered
the Queen advice not only on the succession, but also on how to rule a
Christian commonwealth, espousing Calvin's own political notion of a
Christian monarchy strongly guided by and indeed ruling in conjunction
with Parliament.

The Queen, while enduring thinly-veiled allegories counselling her on
affairs of state, had little patience for the cruder forms of religious polemic in
performance, at least after the anti-papal show at Christmas 1559. This was
sharply demonstrated at Hinchinbrook shortly after her visit to Cambridge
in 1564. There, during an evening representation of the Marian bishops
Bonner and Gardiner eating a lamb and a dog bone in mockery of the
Sacrament, she walked out, ordering the torch bearers with her and so
leaving the Cambridge student actors in darkness (Boas, pp. 382–85). The
earliest sign of the Queen's attitude, however, came in the spring of 1559. At
that time under pressure from foreign dignitaries to put an end to the
insulting plays attacking the Papacy and Catholic monarchs, she herself
wrote the Proclamation of 7 April in which it was prescribed that a license is
not to be granted to plays dealing with matters of religion or the governance
of the state.[13] This law, as I have already partly demonstrated, was not
seriously enforced. Indeed, this was the conclusion of Spanish amabassador
himself as late as 1562 who reported in a letter that he was tired of
complaining to the Queen of the continuing output of offensive books, farces,
and songs, despite her promise to put a stop to them (*State Papers: Simancas*, I,
247). As Harold Gardiner has observed, 'the establishment of the law [of
1559] was an easy method by which authority could apparently disown an
activity which it was in reality favouring' (Gardiner, p. 66). Ironically, the
Proclamation of 1559, in its later form of 16 May, may have helped to protect
Protestant drama promoting national religious policy. For the very officials
it required to license and monitor plays for performance, noblemen sponsor-
ing touring troupes, and mayors and justices of the peace in the provincial
towns and municipalities, were, in many instances, progressive Protestants
themselves interested in advancing the cause of religious reform. This was
certainly the case of the local magistracy in such cities as Ipswich, Canterbury, Chelmsford, and Leicester, and it is also true of the patrons of some of
the nation's leading noblemen's troupes, as will be seen below.[14]

Up to this point the primary concern has been with Crown patronage of
Protestant stage propaganda to about 1564, and particularly Cecil's involvement. Yet to be considered is the evidence of its continuing practice
throughout the sixties and into the seventies, especially on the popular level.

[13] The Queen's writing of the 7 April Proclamation is mentioned in Holinshed, *The Chronicle of England, Scotland, and Ireland*, 6 vols (London, 1586–87), III, 1184, cited in Harold C. Gardiner, *Mysteries' End* (New Haven, 1946), p. 66; Chambers, IV, 262–63.
[14] For the network of Protestant officials in these cities, see Peter Clark, *English Provincial Society from the Reformation to the Revolution* (Cranbury, New Jersey, 1977); Diarmaid MacCulloch, *Suffolk and the Tudors* (Oxford, 1986); Paul S. Seaver, *The Puritan Lectureships* (Stanford, 1970).

Most critics have been sceptical that it did extend beyond the very early years. Norman Sanders in *The Revels History of Drama in English* suggests that during the 1560s 'there is a general shift in play content away from religious doctrine and towards problems arising from the economic and social changes of the first twelve years of Elizabeth's reign' (*Revels*, II, 21–22). The evidence, however, does not bear this out. Plays dealing explicitly with theological and ecclesiastical issues were written and evidently staged throughout the sixties and well into the seventies. They include Lewis Wager's *Mary Magdalene*, printed in 1564, a play that draws entire passages on religious doctrine from Calvin's *Institutes*;[15] *The Tide Tarrieth No Man*, printed in 1576 and one of the few plays supporting presbyterian reforms; and *New Custom*, printed in 1573, an interlude dealing with the controversial issue of church vestments, about which more will be said shortly.[16] Furthermore, while it is true that some plays such as *Enough is as Good as a Feast* and *All for Money* deal with social and economic issues, like countless contemporary sermons and other religious works by such Calvinist preachers as Crowley, Pilkington, and Gilby they are more concerned with the spiritual implications of wealth and social conduct than they are with temporary, this-worldly solutions to such problems. Another reason given for the rapid decline of Protestant drama during the early sixties is a changed attitude towards drama *per se* by returning Marian exiles of a Calvinist persuasion (Chambers, I, 242). Yet the same year in which Edmund Grindal made his famous rebuke of popular drama to William Cecil (1564) was also the year when *Mary Magdalene* appeared in print, a Calvinist interlude which in its Prologue offers the first defence of the stage in a play by an English dramatist. As I have discussed elsewhere, there were Calvinists who defended the stage and Calvinists who opposed it in Elizabethan England.[17]

In discussing the continuing patronage and practice of Protestant stage polemic in the sixties and early seventies, we must begin with surviving play texts, for they constitute the most explicit evidence that such patronage and practice existed, despite the fact that they represent only a fraction of what must originally have existed. Of the forty-seven extant plays in English printed, reprinted, or surviving in manuscript from 1558 to 1576, twenty-five deal with religious issues, the majority of them anti-Catholic and Calvinist in

[15] See my article, 'Lewis Wager's *The Life and Repentaunce of Mary Magdalene* and John Calvin', *Notes and Queries* 226 (1981): 508–12.
[16] It is possible, of course, that some plays were printed several years after their composition. However, such plays as *New Custom* and *The Tide Tarrieth No Man* treat matters that were highly topical around the time they were printed. See discussion of *New Custom* below.
[17] 'Calvinist and Puritan Attitudes Towards the Stage in Renaissance England', in *Explorations in Renaissance Culture*, 14 (1988), 41–56.

viewpoint and polemical or homiletic in purpose.[18] These plays were written for the most part by either Protestant clergymen or schoolmasters. But were they performed, and if so, by whom, and under what patronage?

As recently as 1950 it was believed that very few of these moral interludes, especially the religious ones, were performed at all. However, this view, originally advanced by E. K. Chambers (Chambers, I, 245), has now been fully discounted by such stage historians as T. W. Craik, David Bevington, Glynne Wickham, Richard Southern, and Alan Dessen, who have praised their theatricality. As Bevington demonstrates, the doubling practices and other theatrical qualities are so sophisticated in such plays as William Wager's *The Longer Thou Livest* and Thomas Lupton's *All for Money* that it is a serious misjudgement to dismiss them as 'anachronisms of a disappearing tradition, lacking a vital audience and written largely by well-wishing clergymen who were out of touch with the times'.[19] Moreover, the nature of the stage directions in many of them indicates that they are actors' scripts rather than readers' texts, which provides further evidence that they probably enjoyed a period on the stage before they got into print and were offered to playing troupes for acting.

It is not difficult to determine the general auspices of these plays, based on the handling of the themes and especially the casting requirements. The Protestant interludes fall basically into two categories, recognizing however that there was some overlapping as well as some exceptions: plays written for school and university production, and plays intended for professional playing troupes (professional here in the sense that they were performed in return for payment).

Protestant drama in the grammar and choir schools, as in the universities and Inns of Court, was designed not only to carry out pedagogical and recreational functions; it was also introduced and encouraged by the authorities to inculcate strong Protestant beliefs and values among England's future political and religious leaders. This is the central point of a chapter on religious drama for students in *De Regno Christi*, a treatise on social reform dedicated to Edward VI as a New Year's gift in 1551, and written by the Calvinist Martin Bucer, Regius Professor of Divinity at Cambridge around the mid-century, who remained a highly influential and esteemed religious authority throughout the Elizabethan period. Following in the footsteps of Ralph Radcliffe at Hitchen, Nicholas Udall at Eton, and Thomas Wylley at

---

[18] The findings are based on 'A Calendar of Plays (1495–1575)', in *Revels*, II, 38–67. Excluded are classical plays in Latin and Greek and the mystery and civic plays, some of which continued into Elizabeth's reign. The Protestant homiletic and polemical plays include *King Johan, Three Laws, The Longer Thou Livest the More Fool Thou Art, Enough is as Good as a Feast, Aegio, Jack Juggler, King Darius, Misogonus, The Cruel Debtor, Mary Magdalene, Lusty Juventus, The Tide Tarrieth No Man, Like Will to Like, Free Will, The Disobedient Child, New Custom, The Conflict of Conscience, All for Money*. Three of these works, *Aegio, Free Will*, and *The Conflict of Conscience*, seem more suited for reading than for performance.

[19] David Bevington, *From Mankind to Marlowe* (Cambridge, Massachusetts, 1962), pp. 54–56. See also Alan Dessen's discussion of the dramatic vitality of these plays in *Shakespeare and the Late Moral Play* (Lincoln, 1986).

Yoxford, Elizabethan schoolmasters and choirmasters were motivated to write and stage plays for their students not only to propagate their own strong Protestant convictions but also to win favour at Court. The most illustrious among these protestant educators were William Hunnis at the Chapel Royal, the probable author of the Calvinist *Jacob and Esau*, and Thomas Ashton, a protégé of Bucer's and the celebrated master at Shrewsbury Grammar School, where Sidney and Greville attended. Both Ashton and Hunnis followed their teaching tenures with responsibilities of greater political significance at Court.[20]

The majority of extant plays of our period, however, were evidently intended for professional touring troupes playing before popular audiences. Of the fourteen early Elizabethan plays which David Bevington has characterized as 'popular' in this sense (*From Mankind to Marlowe*, p. 66), ten are homiletic interludes espousing Protestant religious values. No doubt some of these plays were staged by small bands of players often licensed and patronized by city corporations and other civic institutions. Civic and ecclesiastical records show that there were many such troupes in early Elizabethan England, either bearing the name of the chief player or the name of the city from which they originated. They were made up of unemployed artisans and perhaps also, as Glynne Wickham speculates, the many talented actors, playwrights, and musicians who became free with the dissolution of the monasteries in the late 1530s and forties (Wickham, II, i, 109). John Bale and Lewis Wager are two examples of former monks using their theatrical talent for the new learning.[21] One such troupe of actors was 'the plaiers Peter moone and his co[m]panie' performing before the Ipswich Corporation in 1561.[22] Since Moone, an artisan by trade, had written Edwardian verse pamphlets promoting the Reformation and attacking the 'olde customes' of the Papacy, it is reasonable to suppose that he wrote plays for the company he managed. However, it would not be surprising if it was this troupe which staged Bale's *King Johan* in Ipswich at the time Moone's company is recorded for performance in the local guildhall, since the Elizabethan version of Bale's play was in Ipswich Corporation's possession at that time, although whether or not it was staged for the Queen's visit to Ipswich that very summer is impossible to say.[23]

[20] Hunnis was selected by the Earl of Leicester to take on the prestigious role of devising entertainments at Kenilworth in 1575. For more on Hunnis and the case for his authorship of *Jacob and Esau*, see *William Hunnis and The Revels of the Chapel Royal* (Louvain, 1910), and N. S. Pasachoff, *Playwrights, Preachers and Politicians* (Salzburg, 1975), pp. 16–56. According to Joan Simon, 'Ashton may well have been placed [at Shrewsbury School] by the privy council; a strong Calvinist, he stood well with the earls of Bedford and Leicester, his relations with Cecil were close and he was employed on delicate political negotiations after leaving the school' (*Education and Society in Tudor England* (Cambridge, 1967), p. 315).

[21] Bale was a Carmelite prior at Maldon and Doncaster before his career as a Protestant propagandist under Cromwell's patronage. As Mark Eccles has recently shown, Lewis Wager was a member of the Fransciscan order based at Oxford during the 1530s. See his *Brief Lives: Tudor and Stuart Authors*, in *Studies in Philology*, 79 (Fall, 1982), 123–24.

[22] See 'Players of Ipswich', in *Malone Society Collections*, Volume II, edited by Vincent Redstone, Part iii (Oxford, 1931), p. 261; and Murray, II, 287.

[23] See Peter Happé, *The Complete Plays of John Bale*, 2 vols (Cambridge, 1985–86), I, 7; J. H. P. Pafford, *King Johan*, Malone Society (Oxford, 1931), Introduction.

Most of the extant interludes of the Tudor period, however, religious and non-religious alike, appear to be of noble auspices and performed by noblemen's troupes. According to her recent investigation of Tudor household revels and playing companies, Suzanne Westfall argues that the surviving interludes of early and mid-Tudor England were written by chaplains and choirmasters associated with noble families and that they for the most part appeal to the domestic, social, and political interests of those noble households. It was, then, at the bidding or with the influence of the noble patron, who retained the troupe's playscripts within his possession, that such interludes subsequently found their way into print.[24] One might add that with the advent of the Reformation and Cromwell's propaganda policy of reaching a broad public audience through all channels of communication, including the stage, noblemen's troupes gave increased emphasis to appealing to both nobles and commoners, and that the many printed Protestant interludes 'offered for acting' indicate an 'effort to place topical plays in the hands of itinerant troupes for performance before popular audiences' (King, p. 274).

There is both internal and external evidence to support the notion that noblemen's troupes appealed to mixed audiences. Let us take for example the extant drama of John Bale, which was performed by players patronized by Thomas Cromwell in the 1530s before being revived during the reigns of Edward and Elizabeth. Bale's extant interludes, like their Elizabethan successors, were suitable either for court performance or for staging in popular venues. For example, *King Johan* deals with issues of central importance to the monarchy and the court, depicting characters of royal and noble stature, along with several high ranking clergymen, who carry out the functions of government; hence the appeal of the play to its court audience when it was performed before Cromwell, Cranmer, and their guests at Canterbury in 1538. At the same time it disseminates Protestant religious policy in colloquial language with concrete illustrations understandable to a popular audience, presumably the kind of audience witnessing the play when it might have been taken on tour in the provinces by the Lord Privy Seal's Men between 1536 and 1540. This appeal to a mixed audience of nobles and commoners is typical of most of Bale's works and is also typical of professional Reformation drama of the early Elizabethan period. Lewis Wager's *Mary Magdalene*, for instance, portrays its heroine as a child of noble upbringing (early on in the play we hear of her childhood in the castle of Magdala); like many other youth plays of the time, Wager's interlude offers a lesson to noble audiences on how to raise a child in a godly way. At the same time the play is a dramatized sermon on the nature of religious conversion from a distinctly Calvinist perspective which applies to any spectator, regardless of his or her social class. External evidence for this

---

[24] *Patrons and Performance: Early Tudor Household Revels* (Oxford, 1990), Chapter 3.

mixed audience is found in an eye-witness account of a Protestant moral
interlude performed by a travelling nobleman's company and seen before a
popular audience in the guildhall at Gloucester about 1570. R. Willis reports
that in the play he saw there as a child, *The Cradle of Security*, a prince
represented the wicked of the world, three lady acquaintances impersonating the vices of pride, covetousness, and luxury drew him away from
hearing godly sermons and good counsel, and two old men signifying the end
of the world and the last judgement revealed his spiritual damnation. As in
these other interludes, the characters of *The Cradle of Security* are drawn from
an aristocratic household, and yet the play has a universal religious message
applicable to spectators of all classes in the Gloucester guildhall.[25]

We have now reached the point where we may consider *which* early
Elizabethan noblemen's companies would have been most likely to have
performed these plays. Although it is very probable that many noblemen's
companies, like the one Willis witnessed at Gloucester, were engaged in
performing similar Protestant interludes, naming specific troupes is mostly
guesswork since little hard evidence exists. All we know about the majority of
noblemen's troupes, fifty of which can be identified between 1558 and 1576,
is the name of their noble patron and some of the venues they performed in.
Next to nothing can be substantiated concerning their repertories. The
extant interludes are of little help in this regard, since (unlike so many prose
works) they do not contain dedications or prayers to patrons, with the
exception of the Queen who is conventionally addressed at the conclusion of
several plays.

The companies most likely to have performed Protestant moral interludes
were those sponsored by a noble patron of strong Protestant sentiment, and
it is interesting to note that three of the leading patrons of touring companies
during the 1560s and early seventies were also at the forefront of Protestant
propaganda during these years: the Duchess of Suffolk, the Earl of Warwick,
and the Earl of Leicester. All three protected and supported advanced
Protestant preachers, pamphleteers, and printers engaged in producing
works treating the same ecclesiastical and theological issues found in the
moral interludes.[26] Is it not reasonable to suppose, therefore, that when the
company of one of these nobles appeared before him or her at the household
revels held at Christmas and Easter that a moral interlude reflecting the
patron's religious interests would be presented, and that subsequently it
would have been included in the troupe's touring repertory for performances
in provincial towns across the realm?

---

[25] R. Willis, *Mount Tabor, or Private Exercises of a Penitent Sinner* (London, 1639), pp. 110–14. For the Willis
text and its dramatic context, see *REED: Cumberland, Westmorland, Gloucester*, edited by Audrey Douglas
and Peter Greenfield (Toronto, 1986), pp. 362–64.
[26] See Patrick Collinson, *The Elizabethan Puritan Movement* (London, 1967), Chapter 3. For the extensive
lists of advanced Protestant works dedicated to these patrons, see Franklin B. Williams, *Index of
Dedications and Commendatory Verses in English Books before 1641* (London, 1962).

This must almost certainly have been the case with the Earl of Leicester's Men. Leicester himself was a keen advocate of drama, directly involved in producing it on several occasions. At the Inns of Court for Christmas 1561, and in the royal court in the summer of 1572, he was put in charge of organizing plays, masques, and other entertainments, and of course his festivities in honour of the Queen at Kenilworth in 1575 formed the most celebrated royal visit of the entire reign.[27] We may also be assured that he was responsible for securing an exclusive licence for his company to perform in London in 1574, an example of his protection and the support which dated back to 1559 when he requested permission from the Earl of Shrewsbury for his players to tour in the north of England. That Leicester was not beyond using the stage to advance his own interests was demonstrated in a performance by the players of Gray's Inn which he arranged at Whitehall before the Queen in March 1565. The play centred on a debate between Juno and Diana on the question of marriage, with Jupiter's verdict in favour of matrimony. According to De Silva, the Spanish ambassador, the Queen turned to him and said 'This is all against me' (Wilson, p. 155). In the light of this, and in the light of his probable role in bringing *Gorboduc* to the royal court in 1562 to lecture the Queen on politics, it is not unreasonable to suppose that Leicester either commissioned or encouraged his professional company to promote his ideological views in their plays, for performance not only before him on festive and diplomatic occasions in his residences at Westminster, Paget Place (later Leicester House) in the city, and Kenilworth, but also while touring the midlands and eastern counties, where the Earl had extensive connexions among local magistrates who approved performances in their guildhalls.

Regrettably, not a single play can be certainly ascribed to Leicester's Men prior to 1573.[28] Between that year and 1584 the Revels accounts record some eight plays on classical and romantic themes for performance before the Queen who by this point found religious polemics tiresome and distasteful, and when Leicester may have been manoeuvering for the prized office of the Lord Chamberlain.[29] These apparently non-controversial plays are not necessarily typical of the troupe's entire repertory for both popular and élite audiences during their previous thirteen or fourteen years of touring, especially since the company did not appear at the royal court for almost a

---

[27] For Leicester's appointment as Constable-Marshall of the Christmas entertainments at the Middle Temple in 1561, see *Revels*, II, 34; and Derek Wilson, *Sweet Robin: A Biography of Robert Dudley, Earl of Leicester 1533–1588* (London, 1981), pp. 131–32. For his sharing the responsibilities with the Earl of Sussex in organizing revels at the royal court in June 1572, see J. Leeds Barroll, Alexander Leggatt, Richard Hosley, and Alvin Kernan, *The Revels History of Drama in English*, Volume III (London, 1975), pp. 10–11.

[28] Bevington, *From Mankind to Marlowe*, p. 60, suggests that Leicester's Men performed 'huff-suff-and-ruff' at court in 1560/61, and that this play is really *Cambises* (which includes three comic characters with those names), but the claim is tenuous at best, as explained by T. W. Craik in *Revels*, II, 112.

[29] See Leeds Barroll's discussion in *Revels*, III, 10–11. The plays, none of which survive, are *Predor and Lucia* (1573), *Mamillia* (1573), *Philomen and Philecia* (1574), *Panecia* (1574), *The Collier* (1576), *A Greek Maid* (1579), *Delight* (1580), and *Talomo* (1583). See Chambers, IV, Appendix A, and II, 88–89.

decade before 1573. It is impossible to say precisely, but Leicester's professional troupe must have performed dozens of plays during the sixties and early seventies. Even if it changed its repertory only every other year, a company working with, say, five plays, would have performed thirty or more works between 1559 and 1573.[30] Although classical and romantic interludes were in all likelihood included, some idea of the type of plays performed by Leicester's company during the early years may be gained by noting the belated moralities of Robert Wilson, a member of Leicester's Men during the 1570s and early eighties who, along with James Burbage, was to enjoy a successful career in the Elizabethan theatre. Wilson's *Three Ladies of London* and its sequel, *A Pleasant and Stately Moral*, reflect the puritan religious values as well as the aggressive foreign policy that Leicester himself was known to defend, and as Bevington has observed, these plays are composed in the spirit and form of many surviving Protestant interludes of the sixties, though displaced by the commercial conditions of the stage during the 1580s.[31]

There is good reason to believe that these early Elizabethan interludes are representative of at least some of the plays performed by Leicester's Men in the sixties, since so many of them champion the same Calvinist reforms promoted in polemical works which the Earl evidently sponsored.[32] Eleanor Rosenberg and Patrick Collinson have both scrupulously documented Leicester's extensive patronage of the more advanced Reformers from the outset of the reign, though to what degree he shared their convictions is not clear.[33] One particular controversy that Leicester found himself directly embroiled in during the two occasions it flaired up concerned ecclesiastical vestments. In 1565 he took the side of the nonconformists, known to their opponents as the Genevans, who refused to wear the surplice during communion or any of the other pseudo-Catholic items of clerical apparel prescribed in the Elizabethan Prayer Book, preferring instead the simple attire of a Calvinist minister. We know this from Archbishop Parker's complaints to Cecil about Leicester's protection of the dissenters and from the dissenters themselves who stated that Leicester was their chief patron.[34] In 1573, however, when the issue arose again in the context of the Admonition crisis, Leicester took a more conciliatory role between the bishops and the puritans. This is evident in his arranging for a letter to the leading

[30] The imaginary 'Lord Cardinalls players' in *The Book of Sir Thomas More* (c. 1590) carried a repertoire of seven moral interludes. Westfall, p. 128, suggests that a Tudor company needed three to seven plays to operate efficiently and profitably.

[31] David Bevington, *Tudor Drama and Politics* (Cambridge, Massachusetts, 1966), pp. 138–40.

[32] The list of religious writings dedicated to Dudley between 1561 and 1566 reads like a catalogue of Calvinist works: Jean Veron, *A most necessary treatise of free will* (1561); Robert Fill, *The Lawes and Statutes of Geneva* (1562), William Fulke, *A Goodly Gallerye . . . of naturall contemplation* (1563); *The Commentaries of Peter Martyr* (1564); Pierre Viret, *Christian Instruction* (1565); John Barthlet, *The pedegrewe of Heretiques.*

[33] Leicester's inconsistent nature is nowhere more clearly demonstrated than in his protection of Sebastian Westcote, the Catholic choirmaster of St Paul's School, despite the protests of Archbishop Grindal and other officials. The matter is discussed in Wilson, p. 156.

[34] Eleanor Rosenberg, *Leicester: Patron of Letters* (New York, 1955), pp. 199–229; Collinson, *The Elizabethan Puritan Movement*, pp. 52–53, 74, 92–93; and Wilson, Chapter 11. See also John Strype, *The Life and Acts of Matthew Parker*, 3 vols (Oxford, 1821), II, 393–95, 423, 529.

reformers on the Continent requesting their opinion on the issue, as well as in a statement he made blaming both sides for the problem (Wilson, p. 203; Rosenberg, pp. 200–01).

One play that seems to mirror Leicester's own sentiments relating to the vestment controversy is *New Custom*, which, as indicated earlier, was printed in 1573 and was of professional auspices. *New Custom* is structured around the juxtaposition of two pairs of clergymen. On the one hand, we see two aged popish priests, False Doctrine and Hypocrisy, decked out in the full splendour of Catholic clerical attire; they are pitted against two dynamic preachers barely in their twenties and fresh from Geneva, named New Custom and Light of the Gospel, who wear Genevan gowns and caps, and carry Bibles. Interestingly enough, while the play strongly frowns on, and even ridicules several items of apparel prescribed by the Act of Uniformity and Archbishop Parker's 'Advertisements' of 1564, the play concludes on a moderate note, with New Custom acknowledging his preference for the simpler dress but admitting that these are matters indifferent, adding that the Queen's ecclesiastical laws ought to be observed. It is probable that *New Custom*, like so many moral interludes which underwent considerable revision, was originally written without the moderate conclusion for the vestarian crisis of 1565/66, but by 1573 when the piece was published, the anonymous author or the company in possession of it, in conjunction with its printer Abraham Veale, adopted a more tolerable position on the matter, perhaps in line with playing company's patron, who was perhaps Leicester.[35]

The fact that *New Custom*, with its counsel of moderation on the vestment issue, was printed the same year that Leicester himself was trying to reconcile the bishops and the puritans over this matter may be only coincidental, but the hypothesis that his company was responsible for the piece is not implausible. The play's eleven parts could easily have been accommodated by the company's six actors, as Madeleine Robinson has recently shown.[36] One might add that a play entitled *Old Custom* is listed in the inventory of documents belonging to Leicester's father, John Dudley, Earl of Warwick and later Duke of Northumberland.[37] This play no doubt was performed by Warwick's company during Edward VI's reign, and it is

[35] For a discussion of the play's inconsistencies and of the possibility that more than one author was involved, see T. W. Craik, *The Tudor Interlude* (London, 1958), p. 82.

[36] In her study, 'Dramaturgy of the Anti-Catholic Morality in the Tudor Hall with Special Attention to the Screen' (unpublished Ph.D dissertation, University of Rhode Island, 1980), Robinson reconstructs a theorized performance of this play in the Tudor manor house, Crompton Hall, in August 1572 by the six players known to be in Leicester's Men at that time. The play, however, could be most economically cast with four actors, as the title page of the printed copy indicates. It is possible that Leicester's company only had four actors when the play was first acted, since the troupe fluctuated in size during its history. In 1572, six actors are identified in their letter addressed to Leicester, in 1574, five actors are named in the famous Patent of that year, and in 1583, there may have been as few as three when Laneham, Wilson, and Johnson left for the newly formed Queen's Men (see Chambers, II, 85–91).

[37] See Albert Feuillerat, 'An Unknown Protestant Morality Play', *Modern Language Review*, 9 (1914), 94–96.

conceivable that the company passed into the patronage of Leicester, and that the old play was revised or rewritten with a new name, *New Custom*. The play's topical appeal would have been considerable to both corporations and audiences in such staunch Protestant centres as Ipswich and Canterbury, where Leicester's Men made the most frequent visits while on tour (Murray, I, 39–42). Moreover, considering that the puritan leaders Wilcox and Field were reportedly 'esteemed as Gods' by the London populace at the height of the Admonition controversy in the early 1570s,[38] the play could not have failed to provoke interest in such London venues as the Bell Inn, the Bull Inn, or the Cross Keys.

New Custom is one of several moral interludes of the last 1560s and early seventies which demonstrates that Protestant stage propaganda continued well into the second decade of the Queen's reign. From 1576, however, when the commercial stage began to alienate many committed Protestants from playing as an instrument of religious reform and when a kind of iconophobia became increasingly evident in Reformist teaching (Stephen Gosson exemplifies both these developments),[39] these moral interludes declined rapidly in number. And while noblemen's companies continued to represent their patrons' interests, the players found themselves increasingly less dependent on them for support and more interested in meeting the demands of paying customers in the newly-built theatres in and around London who were their main source of income. Protestant polemical drama enjoyed a brief revival in the 1580s with the Martin Marprelate controversy, but this seems to have been brought to an abrupt halt by the Ecclesiastical Commission formed in 1589, which prohibited all references to religious and political issues in plays. Never again would doctrinal and ecclesiastical matters be so directly and explicitly treated on the English stage.

[38] A remark made by Bishop Sandys of London to Lord Burghley, 5 August 1573; cited in Collinson, 'John Field and Elizabethan Puritanism', in *Elizabethan Government and Society* (London, 1961), pp. 127–62 (p. 138).
[39] Collinson, *The Religion of Protestants* (Oxford, 1982), pp. 234–36.

The Poets' Royal Exchange: Patronage and Commerce in Early Modern Drama

KATHLEEN E. McLUSKIE

University of Kent at Canterbury

In *The Gull's Hornbook*, his parodic consumers' guide to London life, Thomas Dekker informs his gallant gull:

The theatre is your poets' Royal Exchange upon which their Muses — that are now turned to merchants — meeting, barter away that light commodity of words for a lighter ware than words — plaudits ... Players are their factors who put away the stuff and make the best of it they possibly can ... Your gallant, your courtier and your captain had wont to be the soundest paymasters ... when your groundling and gallery commoner buys his sport by the penny and like a haggler is glad to utter it again by retailing.[1]

Dekker's description suggests that, by the early years of the seventeenth century, the theatre and the market have become one: poets provide the commodity which is dealt in by the players and purchased by the audience: patronage has become a matter of commerce and the only patrons the paying audience.

To a significant extent Dekker was right. Individual aristocrats or groups of patrons such as the livery companies can be found paying the players for private performances or lord mayors' shows but they did so in return for a commodity rather than as part of a continuing bond of service and obligations. The playing companies still claimed the patronage of the great nobles and, after 1603, the royal family itself, but this patronage was more in the nature of sponsorship and protection than sustained financial support. Nevertheless modern analysis of the role of patronage in Renaissance drama continues to be divided. Walter Cohen has argued, for example, that

the theatre's economic, social, political and ideological heterogeneity precludes any simple categorisation. An emphasis on effective control of the stage ... points to the nobility and monarchy. ... Yet the large sums of money, the evident quest for profit, and the array of financial instruments integral to the operation of the public stage seem to indicate the dominance of the capitalist mode of production.

David Bergeron, on the other hand, in his discussion of 'The Case of Thomas Heywood', concludes

systems of patronage, familiar in the Renaissance, remained intact; they had not been set aside by a paying theatregoing audience ... Instead of a radical departure from systems of patronage, the dramatists represent an expansion of those systems

---

[1] Thomas Dekker, *The Gull's Horn-Book: or Fashions to Please All Sorts of Gulls*, edited by E. D. Pendry, *Thomas Dekker: Selected Writings*, Stratford-upon-Avon Library, IV (London, 1967), p. 98. Cited hereafter as Pendry.

so that even with theatres established and flourishing and with occasional support from the court or guilds, dramatists nevertheless seek and secure the patronage of noblemen, the oldest pattern of patronage.[2]

Modern theatre historians disagree in part because confusion about the uncertain relationship between patronage and commerce was a leitmotif of early modern commentaries on the theatre. In 1591 Samuel Cox contrasted the new commercial theatres with earlier times in which theatre perform-ances were part of the celebration of seasonal festivities. Then, the players 'had other trades to live off, and seldom or never played abroad at any other times of the whole year ... without making profession to be players to go abroad for gain'. Even in the towns the aim of playing was simply 'to make the people merry; where it was lawful for all persons to come without exacting any money for their access, having only somewhat gathered of the richer sort by the churchwardens for their apparel and other necessaries'. This nostalgic invocation of a coherent community in which playing held its proper place also lies behind Antony Munday's contrast between the modern situation and former times when 'euerie noble mans house [was] a Commonweale in it selfe'. In Munday's view, the new neglect of service and the parsimony of noble lords had allowed players to exploit their aristocratic connexions for financial gain, 'passing from countrie to countrie, from one Gentlemans house to another, offering their service, which is a kind of beggerie ... For commonlie the goodwil men beare to their lordes, makes them drawe the stringes of their purses to extend their liberalitie to them; where otherwise they would not'.

By 1615 Cocke's satiric description of 'A common player' could separate completely the claim of patronage and commerce, denouncing both their economic and the social situation with: 'so howsoever he pretends to have a royall Master or Mistresse, his wages and dependance prove him to be a servant of the people'.[3]

None of these comments can be accepted as social observation. A balance between patronage and commerce had funded the players from the earliest times.[4] However, the wave of anti-theatrical commentary from the 1580s seems to have been particularly concerned with the shift from patronage to commerce and to have dealt with its seeming acceleration in terms which involved more than a sense of economic change. Its tones of satire and complaint and nostalgia manifest the changes in what Raymond Williams

[2] Walter Cohen, *Drama of a Nation: Public Theatre in Renaissance England and Spain* (Ithaca and London, 1985) p. 180; David Bergeron, 'The Patronage of Dramatists: The Case of Thomas Heywood', *ELR*, 18 (1988) 294–305.

[3] E. K. Chambers, *The Elizabethan Stage*, 4 vols (Oxford, 1923), IV, 237, 210, 256.

[4] See M. C. Bradbrook, *The Rise of the Common Player* (London, 1962) Chapter 2; see also Ian Lancashire, 'Orders for Twelfth Day and Night, circa 1515 in the second Northumberland Household Book', *ELR*, 10 (1980), 7–44, in which he notes the comparatively extensive use of players in the Northumberland household but also the widely dispersed travels and varied sources of funding for the troupes of entertainers who worked under the Northumberland name.

has called 'patterns of cultural incorporation',[5] the process by which players and writers, readers and theatre audiences came to terms with the changes in their situation as producers and consumers of culture.

In 1573 an item in The Merchant Taylors' Court books recommended the cessation of play performances in their hall:

wheras at our common playes and suche lyke exercises which be commonly exposed to be seane for money ev'ry lewed persone thinketh hime selfe (for his penny) worthy of the cheif and moste comodious place withoute respecte of any other either for age or estimacion in the common weale which bringeth the youthe to such an impudent familiarity with their betters that often tymes greite contempte of Masters, parents and majestrates followth therof as experience of late in this our common hall hath sufficiently declared.

The Merchant Taylors' observation offers a slightly different focus on the change from patronage to commerce from the anti-theatrical writers. At this performance 'Masters of this worshipful company and their deare frendes coulde not haue entertaynement and convenyente places as they oughte to have had by no provision notwithstanding the spoyle of this house, the charges of this mystery and their juste Aucthoritie which did reasonably requier the contrary'.[6]

Attending a theatrical performance supported by patronage, whether at a great hall or a guild celebration or at the inns of court, was supposed to be a particular kind of social occasion. It involved some financial responsibility on the part of the patron, 'the spoyle of this house, the charges of this mystery'; but it also demanded attention to hierarchy and appropriate deference, bonds of allegiance and obligation which seemed irreversibly threatened by the prospect of buying a product sold by a playing company where 'every lewd person thinketh himself for his penny worthy of the chief and most commodious place'. It is unlikely that this was the first occasion on which the Merchant Taylors had experienced disorder at one of their shows. However the disorder was now attributed to change in attitude to the performance itself. They felt that plays were no longer seen as part of the regular life of the guild but as a separate activity when the rules of order did not apply.[7] Performances had ceased to have a 'use value' as part of the continuing life of the guild and now had only 'exchange value' as a commodity to be bought and sold.

The shift from use value to exchange value was often confused with a shift from élite to popular culture. The Merchant Taylors' disparaging attribution of the new attitude to 'lewd' and 'tumultuous disordered persons' is

---

[5] Raymond Williams, *Politics and Letters* (London, 1979), p. 142. Williams, discussing medieval church building urges the importance of understanding the precise interconnexions between structures of political power, actual relations of production, and patterns of cultural incorporation.

[6] 16 March, Merchant Taylors' Court Books, i, 699: *A Calendar of Dramatic Records in the Books of the Livery Companies of London, 1485–1640*, edited by Jean Robertson and D. J. Gordon, Malone Society Collections III (Oxford, 1954), p. 140.

[7] It is important to contrast this sense of disorder from such periods of *licensed* misrule as feasts of fools and boy bishops when rules of deference and formal behaviour were simply reversed.

quite different from Samuel Cox's image of poor townspeople making merry alongside 'the richer sort' and is echoed in Dekker's later observation that the theatre 'is so free in entertainment, allowing a stool as well to the farmer's son as to your Templar, that your stinkard has the self same liberty to be there in his tobacco fumes which your sweet courtier hath'.[8]

In the world of idealized community, élite and popular culture could combine freely, for there was no question of confusions in status.[9] In the world of commodity production hierarchy is both harder to impose and the more forcibly insisted upon,[10] for the problem with commodification was not merely that everyone could consume commodities. It was rather that the status which particular commodities conferred was available to all. Plays, together with the commercial trade in books, afforded an opportunity for the unlearned to appear learned, removing the controls on the trade in learning which a closed patronage system would have imposed. When Gullio the gallant in the Parnassus plays recites a speech to his lady, Ingenioso the scholar comments, 'we shall have nothinge but pure Shakspeare and the shreds of poetrie that he hath gathered at the theators' (line 986).[11] It was a gibe that was heard again and again. The type of the empty-headed gallant who buys poetry as he buys clothes was a familiar enough figure to be the ironic dedicatee of *The Gull's Hornbook*, where Dekker advises him about 'haunting theatres ... [to] sit there like a popinjay, only to learn play speeches which afterward may furnish the necessity of his bare knowledge to maintain table talk'.[12] Dekker wittily inverts the supposed relationship between purchaser and commodity: for the gallant, a bought knowledge of plays will act as a kind of patronage to maintain him in social relations.

In *The Gull's Hornbook*, the tone of complaint at changing mores is replaced by something much more double-edged. The same complex and ambivalent attitude is found in many other seventeenth-century comments on patronage and the market. The epilogue to Fletcher's *Valentinian*, for example, presents a cheerful acceptance of market relations: 'We have your money and you have our wares!' The wares in question, however, were a specialist commodity produced by people who felt themselves to be superior both to the merchants of those wares and to their consumers. The process of 'cultural accommodation' for writers, as opposed to players, was therefore the more difficult. Randolph's Ascotus in *The Jealous Lovers* for

---

[8] Dekker, *The Gull's Hornbook*, Pendry, p. 98.

[9] Indeed distinctions between élite and popular culture are confused by the élite sponsorship of popular culture. See David Underdown, *Revel, Riot and Rebellion: Popular Politics and Culture in England 1603–1660* (Oxford, 1985), p. 67.

[10] Compare, for example, the confusion of status and conspicuous consumption in the sartorial controversy of the late sixteenth century. See my *Renaissance Dramatists* (Hemel Hempstead, 1989), pp. 112–15.

[11] *The First Part of the Return from Parnassus*, edited by J. B. Leishman, *The Three Parnassus Plays 1598–1601* (London, 1949).

[12] Pendry, p. 73.

example, derides the player who 'deals in wit by retail',[13] and the young scholars in *The Return from Parnassus* are dismayed that they are driven to seek employment with Burbage and Kemp, in spite of the actors' fame:

> And must the basest trade yeeld us releife?
> Must we be practis'd to those leaden spouts
> That nought downe vent but what they do receive. (l. 1845)

The taint of commerce is expressed even more strongly in the common image of prostitution used to describe commercial relations between consumers and literary production: 'for Plaies in this Citie are like wenches new falne to the trade, onlie desired of your neatest gallants while they are fresh; when they grow stale they must be vented by Termers and Cuntrie Chapmen'.[14] Middleton's dedication is typical of the curiously insulting tone of so many addresses to readers, contrasting so markedly with the sycophancy of the dedications to aristocratic or gentry figures which often accompany them. As Nathan Field put it in his dedication to the Reader of *The Woman is a Weathercock*, 'In troth, you are a stranger to me; why should I write to you? You never writ to me, nor I think will not answer my epistle'.[15] It was as though writers had no language with which to address their new patrons. The terms in which the trade in dramatic art could be discussed still had to be set against images of an older, more personal, patron/client relationship.

This personal relationship, however, was, by the seventeenth century, far from the norm. Many of the dedications to printed books acknowledge the practice of multiple dedications and unsolicited dedications which were an uncertain method of gaining favour. Dekker's apparently unsolicited dedication of *News From Hell* to 'Mr John Sturman Gentleman' discusses the difficulties of attracting patronage but seems at the same time to be mocking the practice itself:

> Theise Paper-monsters are sure to be set uppon, by many terrible encounters ... The strongest shieldes that I know for such fights are good Patrons from whom writers claime such antient priviledges, that how-soever they find entertainment, they make bold to take acquaintance of them (though never so meerely strangers), without blushing: wherein they are like to courtiers, that invite themselves, unbidden, to other mens tables, & that's a most Gentleman-like quality; and yet holde it a disgrace, if they receive not a complementall welcome.[16]

Dekker's sarcastic tone is difficult to interpret. He seems to be asking for patronage but denouncing the necessity for asking with satiric images of impertinent opportunism. The alternative to joining the hustle for patrons

---

[13] Discussed in G. E. Bentley, *The Profession of Dramatist in Shakespeare's Time, 1590–1642* (Princeton, 1971), p. 224.

[14] Middleton's dedication to the Reader of the printed text of *The Family of Love*, in Clara Gebert, *An Anthology of Elizabethan Dedications and Prefaces* (New York, 1966) p. 170. Compare Dekker, who declares that the Nine Muses have been raped by Pamphleteers: 'For this goatish swarm are those that, where for these many thousand years you went for pure maids, have taken away your good names. These are they that deflower your beauty'. (Dedication 'To the Reader' of *The Wonderful Year*, Pendry, p. 29).

[15] Gebert, p. 205.

[16] Gebert, p. 163.

was to accept the economics of commercial culture with a pose of sturdy independence. Nathan Field, for example, rejected payment altogether in his dedication to a *Woman is a Weathercock*: 'I did determine, not to have dedicated my play to any Body, because forty shillings I care not for, and above, few or none will bestow on these matters, especially falling from so fameless a pen as mine is yet.'[17] Marston seemed to adopt a similar posture by dedicating the text of *Antonio and Mellida* to the 'most honourably renowned Nobody, bounteous Maecenas of poetry', but the satiric point about the decline of patronage still lingers.

In the Parnassus plays, the young scholars approach the task of seeking a place in the world with a similarly contradictory attitude. The ideal situation for them is the world of the Universities where 'may you scorne each Midas of this age | Each earthlie peasant and each drossie clown' (ll. 54–58). However the absence of patronage forces them to misuse their learning and submits them to such indignities as chasing dogs from the churchyard when employed as a country sexton (II. 168–70) and (horror of horrors) dependence on the whims of a *woman* when acting as a tutor to her indulged and idle children (II. 170–72). The scholars expected their learned education to give them only learned employment, seeking the specialization of economic change, without the commodification which accompanied it. Moreover patronage which accepts commodification but rewards it adequately is equally seen as a corruption of learning. Mardido the drunkard cynically accepts this relationship, declaring:

woulde anie leaden mydas, anie mossy patron have his asses eares deified, let him but come and give me some pretie sprinkling to maintaine the expences of my throate, and Ile dropp out such an encomium on him that shall immortalise him as long as there is ever a booke binder in England. (ll. 167–72)

For his scholar friends, however, the merely financial necessities took second place to the claims of the dignity of learning and the highest ideals for art. Throughout the plays they act out the contradiction between the fundamental material need for employment and an ideology in which art and money were completely opposed. When Stephen Gosson forsook the stage, he was proud to acknowledge his employment as a country schoolmaster, 'where I continue with a very worshipfull Gentleman, and reade to his sonnes in his own house'.[18] The new generation of literary aspirants imagined that no demands that smacked of employment or commerce could be made of true art.

The Parnassus plays are, in places, comic, and the young scholars' unrealistic view of patronage is sometimes presented ironically. However, this uncompromising view of the true role of patronage was fiercely espoused by Ben Jonson. For Jonson the loathed stage presented the antithesis of true patronage which was, in turn, a measure of the political health of the stable

[17] Gebert, p. 204.
[18] *Plays Confuted in Five Actions*, quoted in Chambers, p. 214.

hierarchy he idealized in so much of his writing. For patronage transcended mere payment. In the dedication to *Poetaster*, for example, he assures Richard Martin that 'a thankful man owes a courtesy ever, the unthankful but when he needs it'[19] suggesting a more permanent relationship between poet and patron than the mere exchange of commodities.

Any connexion between financial rewards and poetry is dismissed in the play's opening scene as mere philistinism, a failure to understand a relationship which involves more than cash. Ovid's father, urging him to read the law rather than poetry, challenges him to 'name me a professed poet that his poetry did ever afford him so much as a competencie' (i. ii. 236). But Ovid's father is portrayed as an unsympathetic philistine who is contemptuous of Homer and sees the rewards of public office in terms which are a travesty of true deserving.

The play's Roman setting distances the discussion of patronage from the pressing commercial realities of Elizabethan London. In this idealized world, patronage not only sustains the true poet but also acts as a means of his legitimation. Horace is artistically vindicated as well as financially rewarded by his connexion with Maecenas. The connexion puts him above the desperate efforts of his calumnious rivals:

> Fellows of practised and most laxative tongues
> Whose empty and eager bellies i' the year
> Compel their brains to many desperate shifts. (l. 89)

Poverty was no excuse for profaning the sacred vocation of poetry which was only accorded to those who knew they were true poets by virtue of having true patrons.

However, the commercial world had thrown up a new kind of patron, represented by Tucca, the swaggering captain whose wealth allows him to act as a travesty of a patron. He bails Crispinus when he is arrested for debt, and recommends him to the players not as a true poet but as a means of improving their fortune: 'If hee pen for thee once, thou shalt not need to travell with thy pumps full of gravell any more, after a blind jade and a hamper, and stalk upon boards and barrel-heads to an old cracked trumpet'. (III. iv. 167–70). He even offers to act as patron for the whole company, striking a bargain with the players which is a parody of their relations with their sponsors: 'if you lack a service you shall play in my name, rascals, but you shall buy your own cloth, and i'll ha' two shares for my countenance'. (III. iv. 355–57).

The edge of Jonson's contempt for false patrons may have been honed by the memory of the start of his career when he wrote for the Admiral's Men and was paid by Henslowe for such piece-work as his part in collaboration with Chettle and Porter on 'a Boocke called hoote anger sone cowld' or 'his

---

[19] *The Works of Ben Jonson*, edited by C. H. Herford and P. & E. Simpson, 11 vols (Oxford, 1925–52), IV.

adicians in geronymo'.[20] Throughout his career he voiced most forcibly the tension between the need to earn his living on the stage and his refusal to compromise the high ideals he had of the poet's vocation.

For Jonson, moreover, the difficult relationship between the artist and his audience further complicated the discussion of patronage. Jonson divided his audience into tiers with the theatre audience at the bottom, readers of his text above them, and at the height of expectation the enlightened, learned aristocrat who had the status and the learning to make him an appropriate patron of the arts. On occasion he resorted to the simple oppositions of anti-populist cliché, complaining, for example, to the reader of the printed text of *Sejanus* that it was not 'possible, in these our Times, and to such Auditors, as commonly Things are presented, to observe the ould state, and splendour of Drammatick Poemes, with preservation of any popular delight'.[21] However he was equally disappointed with the reception of *Cynthia's Revels*, which was performed at court. In the induction to *Bartholomew Fair* he presented the connexion between taste and status in its most sarcastically mechanical form. The values of the market are elided with artistic value in the suggested correlation between judgement and seat prices:

It shall bee lawfull for any man to judge his six pen'orth, his twelve pen'orth, so to his eighteene pence, 2. shillings, halfe a crowne to the value of his place: Provided alwaies his place get not above his wit. And if he pay for halfe a dozen, hee may censure for all them too, so that he will undertake that they shall bee silent. (Induction 87–93)[22]

This *reductio ad absurdum* of commercial relations of artistic production was echoed elsewhere.[23] It encouraged the audience to see themselves in a completely different relationship to the art they consumed in books and at the theatre, creating a clear moral and intellectual distinction between the right to judge and the ability to pay.

Nevertheless some of Jonson's contemporaries regarded his efforts to seek enlightened patronage but then denounce his audience when they did not appreciate his work as little more than affectation and hypocrisy. In *Satiromastix*, for example, Dekker mercilessly mocks the self-delusion of Jonson/Horace's attitude to Sir Walter Terril, who has paid him for the epithalamium which we see him labouring over at the beginning of the scene: 'I no sooner opened his letter, but there appeared to me three glorious Angels, whom I ador'd, as subjects doe their Soueraignes: the honest knight Angles for my acquaintance, with such golden baites.'[24] The mockery is

[20] *Ben Jonson*, XI, 307–08.
[21] *Ben Jonson*, IV, 350.
[22] *Ben Jonson*, VI.
[23] For example in the address 'To the Great Varietie of Readers' of the Shakespeare First Folio: 'the fate of all Bookes depends upon your capacities: and not of your heads alone, but of your purses . . . Judge your sixe-pen'orth, your shillings worth, your five shillings worth at a time . . . But, what ever you do, Buy. Censure will not drive a Trade, or make the Jacke go.' (Gebert, p. 259).
[24] *The Dramatic Works of Thomas Dekker*, edited by Fredson Bowers, 4 vols (Cambridge, 1962), I.

being directed partly at Jonson's indulgent play on words, but the most telling satiric hit is at Jonson's delusion that this purchase of his skills requires a response akin to religious devotion. Jonson's assumption of the mantle of Horace, his desire to act as learned mentor of an enlightened élite, was particularly satirized in the contrast between the classical and the modern poet:

heere's the sweet visage of Horace, looke perboylde face, looke; Horace had a trim long- beard, and a resonable good face for a poet, (as faces go now-a-dayes) Horace did not skrue and wriggle himself into great Men's famyliarity, (impudentlic) as thou doost: nor weare the Badge of Gentleman's company, as thou doost thy Taffetie sleeves tackt too onely with some pointes of profit: No, Horace had not his face puncht full of Oylet holes, like the cover of a warming pan: Horace lov'd Poets well, and gave Coxcombes to none but fooles; but thou lov'st none, neither Wisemen nor fooles, but thy selfe. (v. ii. 252)

Horace is made to acknowledge the connexion between his writing and the rights of those who patronize him: 'When a Knight or Sentleman of urship, does give you his passe-port, to travaile in and out to his Company, and gives you money for Gods sake; I trust in Sesu, you will sweare (tooth and nayle) not to make scalde and wry-mouth Jestes upon his Knighthood.' (v. ii. 317) Moreover he is to accord greater respect to those who perform his work and not 'sit in a Gallery, when your Comedies and Enterludes have entred their Actions, and there make vile and bad faces at everie lyne, to make Sentlemen have an eye to you, and to make Players afraide to take your part' (v. ii. 298). Dekker equally mocked the impertinence of a bumpkin like Sir Vaughn trading Horace's verse for 'the reversion of the Master of the King's Revels, or else be his Lord of Misrule' (iv. i. 189), but the final exposure attacks the poet more than the patron.

The battle that Jonson and Dekker engaged in was partly a matter of personal animosity, but it was fought with the ideological weapons of arguments about the status and function of poetry which to a large extent had displaced laments over the decline of aristocratic patronage. The question was the willingness with which 'Every writer must governe his Penne according to the Capacitie of the Stage he writes to'[25] and how far he had the right or duty 'Of baiting those that pay | Dear for the sight of your declining wit'.[26] In these contradictory uses of the language of the market and the language of patronage we can recognize the vital cultural accommodation to a new economic and social system. The writers engaged in these discussions showed some awareness that theirs was a culture of intellectual underemployment where patronage did not accommodate all those with aspirations as artists, and commercial literary production, even in the theatre, was not sufficiently developed to provide full employment for all those who sought a literary career. However, these writers were preoccupied

---

[25] The Printer to the Reader of *The Two Merry Milkmaids*, in Gebert, p. 246.
[26] Owen Felltham, 'An Answer to the Ode of Come Leave the Loathed Stage', in *Ben Jonson*, XI, 339.

with the *relations* of cultural production[27] and so incorporate the language both of social and market relations. Recurring preoccupations of contemporary social concern, the decline of hospitality, the fear of the populace, and the loss of easily established signs of hierarchy provide the terms of the explanation of perceived changes in poetry and learning. They established distinctions between popular and élite audiences, the individual artist against the 'Crew | Of common *Play-wrights*',[28] the discerning reader and the mass market. They provided, moreover, a way of establishing those distinctions as well as describing them which were generated in response to commercial and ideological as well as artistic pressures. The early modern dramatists, the players and the booksellers found themselves dealing with questions of artistic value outside a system in which value was conferred by social function and became a matter of the intersections of taste and commerce and their complex connexions to status, education, and class. Their observations reveal the perennial entanglement of new forms of cultural production with old ideas about what culture could and should do. In a situation in which modern institutions of higher learning are being forcibly, if belatedly, transferred from a patronage to a commercial mode of production, those questions seem particularly pressing.

[27] See above, note 5.
[28] The distinction being made here is between writers, like Jonson, who were masters of the art of tragedy and mere craftsmen, 'wrights' of plays. See 'Cygnus on Sejanus' in *Ben Jonson*, XI, 314.

Rebel Lords, Popular Playwrights, and Political Culture: Notes on the Jacobean Patronage of the Earl of Southampton

In both Houses, the King had a strong party, especially in the House of Lords. All courtiers, and most of the bishops, steered by his compass, and the Prince's presence, who was a constant member, did cast an awe among many of them, yet there were some gallant spirits that aimed at the public liberty, more than their own interest .... among which the principal were, Henry Earl of Oxford, Henry Earl of Southampton, Robert Earl of Essex, Robert Earl of Warwick, the Lord Say, the Lord Spencer, and divers others that supported the old English honour, and would not let it die .... Southampton, though he were one of the King's Privy Council, yet was he no great courtier. Salisbury kept him at bay, and pinched him so by reason of his relation to old Essex, that he never flourished much in his time; nor was his spirit, after him, so smooth-shod as to go always the court pace, but that now and then he would make a carrier that was not very acceptable to them; for he carried his business closely and slyly, and was rather an adviser than an actor.

(Arthur Wilson, History of Great Britain, 1653, pp. 161–62)

I

Since the Essex circle was also that of Shakespeare's patron, and of Shakespeare himself in the 1590s, it has an interest for cultural historians going beyond the question of who was or was not the fair young man of the Sonnets. For the group around Essex included an unusually high number of people with relatively radical political and philosophical views, though not all of them would have supported his adventurist attempt at a coup. Arrogant and individualistic as Essex may have been, to emphasize *only* the personal loyalties and archaic feudal aspects of his faction ('the last honour revolt'), or to see the conflict *only* in terms of a revolt of the 'outs' against the 'ins' at Court, is to miss its wider importance in the history of patronage, and in focusing and dramatizing the 'crisis of authority' felt with varying intensity from the Reformation onwards. It is the 'post-history' of its members and their ideas that is most illuminating; for the critical anti-absolutist attitudes and intellectual allegiances Essex attracted were continuous to a remarkable extent, often in the same families, over several generations between the

Reformation and the Civil War (as J. N. King, Blair Worden, and David Norbrook have variously demonstrated.)[1]

Blair Worden in his paper on *Sejanus* (unpublished) describes Essex as 'a rebel without a theory'. In the sense of theory as a single coherent ideology or a practical political programme he is certainly right. There was indeed no single theory in the Essex circle — rather various strands of anti-absolutist feeling and interest which found space and encouragement there. The milieu included aristocrats who intensely resented their increased economic dependence on the Court and its 'upstart' favourites and the restriction of their military power, but also City Puritan ministers and ambitious army officers; rising diplomats, historians, and Oxford classical scholars; and a remarkable number of writers, playwrights, and poets, involved either as patrons or clients.[2]

The commitment to an active anti-Spanish foreign and military policy in Europe and the New World, and to protection of non-separatist Puritanism at home against increasing persecution by the State church, Essex partly took over from Sidney and from his own stepfather Leicester, together with much of the faction itself, the Dudley family, for whatever reasons, having been protectors of radical Protestants since Reformation times. Along with the bequest of Sidney's best sword, Essex inherited connexions with the Huguenot aristocracy and theories of justified resistance to royal tyranny in religion, expounded by Sidney's friends Mornay and Languet. A new emphasis on scientific history and secular realism in politics came with the rediscovery and English translation of Tacitus, in which Essex himself was especially interested, and which had strong republican connotations. While Puritan preachers and divines looked to Essex as their general against the Popish Antichrist as well as defender of their rights within the established church, his Catholic supporters (many of them fellow-soldiers knighted by him or semi-feudal adherents from the Welsh borders) believed he could ensure greater toleration for loyal Catholics in the succeeding reign, besides careers for military talent; and tolerationist writers dedicated works to him. The very variety of anti-absolutist ideas and oppositional views of history within the Essex circle, openly discussed as they could never have been at Court, may indeed have contributed to Shakespeare's astonishingly multi-vocal drama.

---

[1] John N. King, *English Reformation Literature* (Princeton, 1982); Blair Worden, 'Classical Republicanism in the Puritan Revolution', in *History and Imagination*, edited by Hugh Lloyd-Jones and others (London, 1981); David Norbrook, *Poetry and Politics in the English Renaissance* (London, 1984).

[2] These writers, translators, playwrights, historians, and political thinkers included Shakespeare and his patron the Earl of Southampton; Essex's secretaries Henry Wotton and Henry Cuffe; writers like Spenser, Chapman, Jonson, Daniel, Sir John Hayward, Sir Henry Saville, Sir Henry Neville, George Peele, Gervase Markham; Puritan divines such as George Gifford, Stephen Egerton, and Anthony Wootton; and among literary patrons Fulke Greville, Robert Sidney, and Essex himself. See also the valuable study of Essex's supporters by Mervyn James, 'At a cross-roads of the political culture: the Essex revolt, 1601' in his *Society, Politics and Culture* (Cambridge, 1986).

Essex seems to have imagined himself uniting all the varied and contradictory currents of ideological and practical hostility to the government into a single movement, bound by his own charisma, and this proved a gross overestimation and self-delusion. He expected and gambled on active popular and City support for his revolt, but did not get it, and went to execution as a traitor. His friends had plenty of time to ponder on what went wrong, especially those who were lucky to escape beheading and remained imprisoned in the Tower till Elizabeth's death.

Soon after James's accession, however, the verdict of treason began to be openly questioned, and Essex became retrospectively — and still more in popular culture – a Protestant or even a Puritan patriot-martyr (witness the evidence of Lucy Hutchinson from one end of the political spectrum and the Earl of Newcastle from the other, or Thomas Scot's pamphlet *Robert Earl of Essex His Ghost* in 1624). The ideological and practical alliance which had failed to cohere in the 1590s did so up to a point in the 1620s, with Essex's son the third Earl and Essex's close friend the Earl of Southampton among its most prominent figures, but this time alongside a powerful City interest, many members of Parliament and country gentry, Puritan preachers, professional soldiers, and much of the London working population. Instead of a minority coup by force of arms, dissidence was now expressed within Parliament, the City, and the popular culture.

Economic and political developments during James's reign helped to bring about this alteration, but 'mentalities' were also affected by cultural and ideological influences, including the Puritan preachers and the commercial theatres and London shows, the nearest thing to our modern mass media. The drama did not merely reflect, but helped over a period to articulate and reinforce something like a political public opinion — or rather opinions — despite the variable but ever-present censorship.

To study this process for the Essexians as a group would be a formidable undertaking. I shall attempt only a few tentative ideas on the later patronage of the third Earl of Southampton, next to Essex the main leader of the revolt: and since even that is too large a subject for a single paper, especially on the connexions he may have had with citizen and popular culture.

II

It is at least thought-provoking that Southampton, the only man named by Shakespeare as a personal patron, should later have earned a reputation, both among friends and enemies, as the outstanding 'popular' nobleman of Jacobean times, popular both in the modern and the equivocal Jacobean sense of the word. This seems also to have been how he saw his own role as politician and patron, when he wrote to his friend Sir Dudley Carleton on his belated elevation to the Privy Council in the critical year of 1619:

I had much rather have continued a spectator than become an actor. But I will make the same request to you that I have made to others, not to expect too much of me.

You know well how things stand with us, and how little one vulgar councillor is able to effect. (De Lisle MSS v, p. 221, 233: cited Rowse, *Shakespeare's Southampton* p. 227).

Before considering his patronage in detail we need to recall briefly some of the main facts about the Earl's public life after the Essex revolt.[3]

Immediately on James's accession in 1603 he released Southampton and other Essexians from the Tower and restored him to his honours and titles. The Earl also received important financial grants, notably the farm of sweet wines which Essex had formerly held: James regarded Essex as his committed ally, and was prepared to reward his friends. Southampton, however, was never trusted by Robert Cecil, the powerful Secretary, and failed to get either major office or the high military command he hoped for. After Cecil's death, when Southampton was one of the leaders (with the Earls of Pembroke and Sheffield) of the anti-Howard faction at Court, a reputation for radicalism and even republicanism still kept him marginalized.

Early in James's reign Southampton became a close ally both in business and politics of Sir Edwin Sandys, recognized as the principal leader of opposition and anti-absolutist trends in the Commons from the Parliament of 1604 to the mid-1620s. Southampton was a principal investor in the Virginia Company (among his other business interests), where he was not a mere sleeping partner but played an active role. When Sandys was pushed out of the Treasurership of the Company by James's intervention, Southampton was elected in his stead and continued his policies until the Company's charter was revoked in 1624.

Throughout his life Southampton remained committed to the old Essexian anti-Spanish foreign policy and support for Protestant forces in Europe. On the invasion of the Palatinate in 1618 he pressed strongly for English military aid. He planned to head a force of volunteers and contribute to financing it, but was not allowed to do so, and when a small force raised by voluntary subscription did finally go, Southampton as a Privy Councillor was refused permission to join it: for King James was still pursuing the vain aim of a Spanish alliance and a Spanish marriage for Prince Charles to restore peace in Europe. Southampton continued, in direct contact with the King and Queen of Bohemia, to work for English intervention, openly opposing the policy of the King and Buckingham. In 1621 he was arrested and interrogated, along with MPs Sir Edwin Sandys and John Selden, for organizing 'mischievous opposition' in both Houses of Parliament, and remained under house-arrest for a time. It was apparently the threat to deprive him of the Court grants which formed a large part of his income which induced him temporarily to withdraw from active Parliamentary

---

[3] For this summary I have relied largely on the excellent concise account by G. P. Akrigg, who had access to such Southampton papers as still exist, in *Shakespeare and the Earl of Southampton* (London, 1968) and primary sources cited there. A. L. Rowse, *Shakespeare's Southampton, Patron of Virginia* (London, 1965), though dismissed as of little value by Akrigg, likewise provided some useful references to primary material. Other debts have, I hope, been acknowledged in the text.

opposition; but in 1623 he refused to take the oath demanded of Privy Councillors to support the match.

Finally when the Crown's policy changed in 1623–24, and Buckingham and Prince Charles agreed on the need for some form of military intervention, Southampton was at last appointed to lead a force of 6,000 volunteers to reinforce the English troops already fighting with the Dutch against the Spaniards, an expedition on which he and his eldest son died of fever.

In his discussion of *Sejanus*, Blair Worden suggests that Jonson saw only two alternatives for noble political opponents under a despotic state: futile rebellion, or stoical acceptance and quietism, with the aim of securing minor concessions. Southampton seems consciously to have attempted a third way: to be 'popular', to build support among people outside the Court, and even outside the 'political nation'. His career as patron gives many indications of this fairly consistent, if intermittent, political course.

Southampton was one of the foremost Jacobean aristocrats turning increasingly to business investment — both in industry, in modernizing their estates and in overseas trade and colonization. The landed gentry indeed led the way in such investment in a way which did not happen in any other European country.[4] No craftsman and few individual merchants could have laid hands on the kind of money the earls of Pembroke, Southampton, Salisbury, and De La Warr were able to invest in founding the Virginia Company. For Essexian peers excluded from the highest office at Court by Cecil's distrust, this also offered an alternative opportunity to salvage and extend their wealth and power with a degree of independence,[5] and brought them into contact and sometimes active partnership with City merchants and the new entrepreneurial groups and their ways of thinking.

Southampton himself modernized and rack-rented his estates, pressurizing copyholders into becoming lease-holders by increased fines. He also started a new ironworks at Titchfield and financed the first tinplate mill in England; developed his London property in Holborn and Bloomsbury; sponsored the voyage that led to the foundation of the Virginia Company, of which he was a leading member; belonged to the East India and New England Companies, and backed Hudson's exploration of the North-West passage. As Lawrence Stone says,[6] it would be impossible to draw up a list of merchants or country gentry with such a wide range of interests. Both mining and overseas ventures were high-risk undertakings, well-suited to aristocrats used (as Southampton had been) to losing £1,000 a night gambling.

[4] See T. K. Rabb, *Industry and Empire* (London, 1967).

[5] Similarly Lord Willoughby De Eresby retired to his Lincolnshire estates seeking to recover from his father's debts and build up his fortune by estate improvement, fen drainage, and 'noble traffic', 'he having learned at Venice and Florence that merchandise is consistent with nobility'. Fulke Greville, dismissed from his naval office by Cecil's influence, became a harsh 'improving' landlord on his Warwickshire estates. Edmund Lord Sheffield, later Earl of Mulgrave, another Essexian peer and associate of Southampton, made a fortune out of alum-mining on his lands in Yorkshire.

[6] *The Crisis of the Aristocracy*, abridged edition (Oxford, 1967).

Southampton's own reputation for republicanism went back to his association with Essex's secretary Henry Cuffe, a Puritan Oxford don and one of
the translators of Tacitus, who read Aristotle's political theory with Southampton and Rutland in Paris and was alleged at Essex's trial to have
influenced Southampton with republican opinions. Since Cuffe was not an
aristocrat and did not have the powerful protectors who saved Southampton, he was made a scapegoat and barbarously executed, making a strongly
Puritan speech from the scaffold. Some years later (1607) a philosophical
tract by him, *The Difference of the Ages of Man's Life*, was published and
dedicated to Lord Willoughby De Eresby (another Essex knight) by an
anonymous editor R. M. who claimed to be a servant both of Willoughby
and of the Puritan Lord Montagu of Boughton, whose daughter Willoughby
had just married. The book was several times reprinted, and it is possible
that its religious and political reference was clearer to contemporaries than it
is now.

This reputation was later reinforced by Southampton's association and
friendship, first in the Virginia Company and then in Parliamentary opposition, with Sir Edwin Sandys, who really was a radical thinker as well as a
practical politician, from the time of the 1604 Parliament a consistent
opponent of royal absolutism and determined to limit the prerogative and
assert the rights of the subject in accordance with ideas of natural law. Far
from being the stereotype of intolerant dogmatic Protestantism, Sandys in
his book *Europae Speculum* argued for an alliance against Papal domination by
all the rest of Christendom, including the anti-Papal Catholic republic of
Venice as well as the Dutch republicans. This attitude may well have been
congenial to Southampton, who had converted from his family's Catholicism to Protestantism (probably at some time in the 1590s, though Sandys
claimed the credit for his conversion), but continued personally to protect
individual Catholic loyalists. In the Virginia Company Sandys introduced
the secret ballot for officers, and extended democratic rights to all shareholders, while the general public were allowed to attend the quarterly Court
debates in the gallery. He was accused by his enemies of being ill-affected to
monarchy and of wishing to set up a Brownist republic in Virginia, and did
indeed negotiate with the Leiden exiles about the possibility of their
emigration there. His political intransigence is the most likely reason for
James's intervention in the affairs of the Virginia Company, when he
nominated his own candidates to govern it, declaring 'choose the devil if you
will, but not Sir Edwin Sandys.'[7]

[7] The Company under his leadership was accused of establishing excessive 'popular liberties' and a
'democratic state' in Virginia, to the disgust of those settlers who wished to see strict divisions of rank
established there, and even the introduction of sumptuary laws. See the account of Capt. Bargrave,
HMC 8th Report Part 2, MS of Duke of Manchester, No. 368 p. 45, 16 May 1623.

III

Southampton had been well known in the 1590s as a literary patron, and his release from prison in 1603 was celebrated by several poets: Samuel Daniel, John Davies, possibly Shakespeare among them. Daniel in particular in his *Panegyric Congratulatory to King James* (1603) devoted a long section (fifty-six lines) to praise of Southampton for his heroic constancy and courage under duress, implying that he had been unjustly punished and had nothing on his conscience of which to repent.

> He that endures for what his conscience knows
> Not to be ill, doth from a patience high
> Look only on the cause whereto he owes
> His sufferings, not on his misery.
> The more he endures, the more his glory grows,
> Which never grows from imbecility.
> Only the best composed and worthiest hearts
> God sets to act the hard'st and constant'st parts.

His sufferings, says the poet, have shown the man's true worth, strengthened his reputation and added to his wisdom and discretion. The praise is perhaps extravagant, but it seems true enough that Southampton held to many of his former convictions, although much sobered and matured by his experience in the way he pursued them. If Shakespeare's Sonnet 107 does also celebrate the occasion (as a number of scholars have concluded) it does so in a less pointed and more guarded political way, rejoicing at the patron's unforeseen good fortune and hoping it may last forever.

There were limits, however, to the congratulations allowable. Robert Pricket, who had served as a soldier under Essex, dedicated to Southampton, the Earl of Devonshire, and Lord Knollys a poem *Honour's Fame in Triumph Riding* (1604), honouring Essex as a military hero and denying that he had intended treason, though he had inadvertently been guilty of it:

> Doubtless I think he had no Traitor's heart,
> Gainst Queen and State he did not treason plot.
> No more did they that then did take his part:
> He only strove 'gainst them that loved him not.
> But yet the Law their act did treason make.
> Such hostile arms no subject up must take.
>
> > Thus when he thought an evil to shun
> > A greater evil by him was done.

The show trial was no doubt necessary to preserve order, but the death sentence was not: 'His trial could example give: | Why did not Mercy let him live?' While it expressed what was certainly a popular feeling, Pricket's poem was called in and the publisher interrogated, whether because of a supposed attack on the Earl of Northampton as one of Essex's detractors, or because any kind of public apologia for the rebels was still unacceptable to the authorities (as Daniel was soon to find with *Philotas*). While King James privately spoke of Essex as his 'martyr', the dedication did not protect the tract and may indeed have attracted some suspicion to the dedicatees.[8]

Although Southampton continued to patronize arts and letters (he contributed for example to the foundation of the Bodleian Library), and Chapman, Daniel and the musician Ferrabosco among others dedicated works to him, he did not rival the number and variety of literary artistic dedications of some richer favourites and 'great Maecenases' of the age, such as the third Earl of Pembroke, the Earl of Nottingham, the Earl of Northampton or later the Duke of Buckingham. The list of works addressed to him in Jacobean times is more selective and closely related to his known practical, political, and philosophical interests. His financial position had been greatly eased by James granting him the farm of sweet wines, which Essex had formerly held (and the withdrawal of which by Elizabeth had been one precipitating cause of the revolt). But he still had restraining debts; nor did he command the full favour in the highest quarters at Court that would enable him to secure important jobs for his clients. Thus, for example, Sir Henry Neville, a highly-qualified fellow-Essexian with Puritan and republican interests, though strongly backed by Southampton, failed to get the Secretaryship of State in 1614, King James declaring that he would not have a Secretary imposed on him by Parliament. The Earl's influence made itself felt, however, through links with popular writers and playwrights like Heywood and Wither, popular preachers like William Crashaw, popular education and do-it-yourself writers like Gervase Markham, all contributing to long-term changes in mentalities. The importance of much of this work has been overlooked or underestimated because of what Edward Thompson calls the 'enormous condescension' of later generations of critics towards the ideas, beliefs, expression, and culture of ordinary people in the past where they fail to coincide with our own.

Although Southampton had been keenly interested in the drama in the 1590s — when at a loose end in London he is said to have gone to plays every day — it was no longer possible for a nobleman to maintain his own company to play in the public theatres, as Leicester's Men or Pembroke's Men had done. From the beginning of James's reign the patronage of the chief London theatre companies was taken over by the royal family. Despite their increasing economic independence, the companies still needed aristocratic patrons to secure court performances and stand by them in their collisions with the censor, the Privy Council, or the civic authorities. But the patronage was now exercised through their positions at Court, or more informally as friends or acquaintances of the actors or playwrights.

---

[8] See Akrigg, pp. 139, 142. Another curious tract dedicated to Southampton in 1603, Thomas Powell's *A Welsh Bait to Spare Provender*, which comments obscurely and somewhat flippantly on the Queen's passing and the changes to be expected in the new reign, was issued without a licence and the publisher, Valentine Simms, was fined.

Former Essexians were not appointed to key positions in James's own entourage (since the all-powerful Cecil remained suspicious) but found places in the separate household and mini-court of Queen Anne of Denmark, as well as that of Henry Prince of Wales. Robert Sidney, brother to Sir Philip and to Mary Countess of Pembroke, became Lord Chamberlain to Queen Anne. He was Essexian in sympathy and outlook, even though, like Fulke Greville, on the day of the revolt he had opposed it and helped to besiege Essex House. His friend Southampton was appointed her Master of the Game. Both must have had direct connexions with the two companies licensed to play as her servants, the Children of the Queen's Revels at the indoor, fashionable Blackfriars and Queen Anne's Men (formerly Worcester's Men) at the outdoor, popular amphitheatres, the Red Bull and Curtain. Lucy Countess of Bedford, wife of a peer imprisoned for his part in the Essex rising, was also close to the Queen and a leader in her Court entertainments. Other Essexians, notably Sir Thomas Chaloner, were associated with Prince Henry's household, which had links with the Prince's Men at the Fortune.

Political as well as personal sympathies probably led to the placing of Samuel Daniel, who had been in the household of Lady Pembroke and a protege of Fulke Greville, in a special post as licenser to the Children of the Queen's Revels. While he was licenser the Children put on his play *Philotas* (1605), for which he was interrogated by the Privy Council on the grounds that under the cover of an ancient story it referred too closely and sympathetically to the Essex affair.[9]

It can hardly be accidental that the Children also staged bold and provocative satires on James's court, notably John Day's *Isle of Gulls*, Jonson's *Eastward Ho!*, and Chapman's *Monsieur d'Olive*, an open lampoon on the Earl of Nottingham's showy peace embassy to Spain, as well as Chapman's heavily-censored *Duke of Biron* plays (with their frankly-stated analogies with the Essex revolt), and a lost play satirizing James's ill-fated venture in Scottish silver-mines. Foreign ambassadors were particularly shocked that the Queen could be amused by impudent ridicule of her husband and his favourites. In the various collisions with the government which ensued Daniel lost his special post as licenser, the Queen for a time withdrew her patronage, some of the players went to jail, and James at one point closed *all* the theatres.

Meanwhile the plays put on by Queen Anne's Men in the *popular* theatre were helping to focus opinion in favour of the kind of militant Protestant, nationalist, expansionist outlook with which Essex had been identified in the 1590s as a popular hero for London people. Less directly topical and controversial than the Children's plays, they may have had a more lasting political effect. We do not know how far Southampton's or Robert Sidney's patronage influenced the repertory of Queen Anne's Men; indeed it is

---

[9] Later the posthumous edition of Daniel's *Whole Works* (1623) included a dedication of *Philotas* to Southampton. The original edition (1607) was prefaced by a dedicatory epistle to Prince Henry.

possible that some of the influence went the other way round. However, it is suggestive that their principal playwright, Thomas Heywood, famous for his expression of citizen values, later declared himself to have been formerly Southampton's servant, almost certainly referring to the period when Heywood was a groom of the Chamber to the Queen. It is in his *Elegy for King James* (1625)[10] that Heywood alludes to this connexion:

> Oh give me leave a little to resound
> His memory, as most in duty bound
> Because his servant once.

Scholars have been puzzled by this reference and rather discounted it, on the grounds that Southampton never had a troop of actors; but there is not really much mystery about it. We do not know whether Heywood already had connexions with the Earl in the 1590s, when he was writing plays like the populist *Edward IV*. From 1603, however, when Heywood's company became Queen Anne's Men, he as main dramatist and a shareholder must have had links with Sidney and Southampton, since they held leading positions in her household. From 1604 Heywood with some of his fellow-actors became a groom of the Chamber to the Queen. He marched both in her coronation procession and in her funeral procession in 1619, and signed the patents for the company to act in her name at their usual theatres, the Curtain and the Red Bull. Sidney as the Queen's Chamberlain had the main responsibility for arranging her entertainments, but we know that South-ampton too took a direct interest in bringing commercial companies to play before her. Heywood would not be stretching a point to describe himself as 'Southampton's servant once'.

The *Elegy* is itself a curious poem, which confirms this reading. As well as King James, whom the writer says he did not know personally and who was never his patron, other nobles recently dead are lamented, each in two to four rather perfunctory lines. Praise of Southampton, however, takes up sixty-five lines, a considerable proportion of the whole piece, and a further twenty-eight lines are devoted to the grief of Queen Elizabeth and King Frederick of Bohemia and their children (far more than is said about King Charles). The poet thus uses the occasion to reach a wide audience, and by implication appeal to them to support a policy of active intervention for recovering the Palatinate. The whole thing rather neatly illustrates what Annabel Patterson calls the 'hermeneutics of censorship', written as it is in a kind of code. For example, even if the censor suspects irony in Heywood's description of James as appearing to do nothing and have no policy, but probably less inactive than he seemed, any disrespectful intention can be disclaimed.

---

[10] Thomas Heywood, *A Funeral Elegy Upon the Much Lamentable Death of King James* (London, 1625). Dedicated to the Rt Hon. Edward, Earl of Worcester, PC, 'the unchanged patron of all my weak and unperfect labours'.

Southampton is frankly celebrated here as a lifelong hero of the Protestant cause. His honour is indeed said to derive from this rather than from his lineage: 'The noble deeds in our forefathers shown | May well be termed our grandsires', not our own.' The Earl, however, strove from the first to 'gain a name by art and arms.' His life is briefly but knowledgeably traced, not concealing the ups and downs of favour:

> Cambridge thy pupillage: thy youth the court ...
> Of thy brave valour Ireland witness can,
> Writing thee soldier, even as soon as man ...

He is praised especially as Essex's comrade in arms:

> Let me look back again to Ireland, where
> Methinks I see thee a brave chevalier,
> Commanding others: and so far extend
> Thy worth, as only to be deemed the friend
> Of noble Essex; such thy friendship was,
> Deserving to be charactered in brass,
> And ever read: shrilled with a stentor's breath,
> 'Twixt you it lived, and parted not in death.

Indeed the most concrete praise given to James is that he had the wit to release Southampton from prison and restore him (mostly) to favour:

> Thy patience in thy troubles thousands sing,
> Thy innocence, the goodness of the King,
> Crown'd at's inauguration, whose free grace
> Suited thy merits both with gifts and place:
> And thou whose wisdom seemed obscured but late
> Thought worthy to be councillor of state
> And honoured with the Garter: we find then
> Kings through the breast see more than other men.

This is both well-informed and tactfully partisan. Together with the extended reference to Queen Anne and her brother Christian IV of Denmark (whose invasion of Germany in 1625 was subsidized by England) it seems to confirm that Heywood's links with Southampton through Queen Anne's Men were closer than a mere formality.

Southampton must have appreciated the potential importance of drama in securing popular political support: some Essexians had indeed commissioned Shakespeare's company to stage a performance of *Richard II* on the eve of the revolt. The Earl may well have taken some personal interest in Heywood and the Red Bull repertory from this point of view. But whether this is so or not, their plays bear on what were becoming main interests for him and for many former Essexians: hostility to the Papacy and to Spain (despite the peace concluded in 1604); fortunes to be made by trade with the New World and the Indies; heroic seafights and defence of merchant ships against pirates. The values they dramatize are citizen values, but accord with those of sections of the aristocracy and the rich City venturers meeting a little later in the Virginia Company, of which Southampton, Sidney, and Pembroke were founder members.

Plays like Heywood's *Fair Maid of the West*, *Travels of Three English Brothers*, and *Fortune by Land and Sea* provide not only fantasy, excitement, and escape, but a moral and imaginative climate encouraging young people without land or prospects at home to join overseas exploration and trading ventures, or even face the appalling risks of emigrating to Virginia, in the hope of making their fortune. In one adventure play after another, low-born or trade-fallen heroes from the 'middling sort' — even some on the run from the law — get the chance to make good by overseas trade, privateering, or fighting the pirates.

The Fair Maid of the West, probably an early Queen Anne's play, reprinted as late as 1631, is a fine example, opening with Spencer, gallant lover of the heroine, barmaid Bess Bridges, about to set out from Plymouth with Essex and his followers on the Islands Voyage, not of course merely for prize-money but for glory. As the hero says:

> No, 'tis for honour: and the brave society
> Of all these shining gallants that attend
> The great Lord General drew me hither first,
> No hope of gain or spoil.

The stage directions provide for Essex and the Mayor of Plymouth to appear in walk-on dumb-show parts. Later we are told that Essex has given bags of money to pay off any debts his followers may have run up in the pubs: 'if the captains would follow the noble mind of the general, there would not be one score owing in Plymouth.' This image of the godly nobleman-leader, embodiment of citizen as well as aristocratic virtues, helps to make chaste Bess's later Amazonian exploits, privateering against the Spaniards, rescuing her lover and fighting the pirates, not only exciting but respectable.[11]

Southampton himself at one point in 1617 petitioned James (unsuccessfully) to be allowed personally to lead an expedition on the merchants' behalf against the Barbary pirates, who were becoming an increasing menace to trade. It was apparently Gondomar's influence that led James to veto this scheme. In *Fortune by Land and Sea* (Heywood and Rowley, 1609) young Forrest, son of a decayed gentry family, runs away to sea to escape arrest. He has avenged his brother in a duel, killing the local bully, and because the dead man's family is rich and his family is poor he has no hope of justice. He defeats some notorious pirates (real named villains called Purser and Clinton, who had been commemorated in a broadside tract and ballad of 1583); frees the virtuous merchant they have taken prisoner; seizes their booty, and carries them in irons to London, where they are hanged and he is knighted by the old Queen. The moral is exemplary, and Forrest's triumph

---

[11] Some scholars think this scene dates the play before 1600. But it was certainly performed many times after that date, and survives in the printed text of 1631. Essex, clearly, was still a hero to citizen audiences.

over snobbish enemies at home has its own kind of class awareness. The seafight too is no routine clashing of swords and cutlasses, but a spectacular affair explained with much technical detail about modern warfare, gunnery, and navigation, of a kind we do not find in *Tamburlaine*.

Plays like these, or *The Four Prentices of London*, or *The Travels of Three English Brothers*, or *A Christian Turned Turk*, are close to the chap-book literature which was so widely read by the newly literate, and on which Bunyan later drew for *Pilgrim's Progress*. Not all popular culture is 'carnivalesque' in form. The apprentice's dream of rivalling the knights of old by courage and endurance may be liberating rather than absurd.

Central likewise to the repertories of the popular theatres were a group of plays about English Reformation history, first staged by Queen Anne's Men and Prince Henry's Men about 1604–1608. Most of the playwrights concerned — Heywood, Dekker, Webster, Munday — also worked then or later for the City of London on patriotic street-pageants and shows.

These plays were in tune with the strong traditional anti-Papist, anti-clerical, and nationalist feelings of the popular London audience. Based mainly on Foxe's *Acts and Monuments* (the *Book of Martyrs*) rather than purely on Holinshed's and Hall's chronicles, they helped to reinforce the Foxeian ideal of post-Reformation England as a united Protestant nation, with a destiny to defeat the Antichrist of the Counter-Reformation Papacy through international action, and to bring about the final cosmic victory of true religion and the reign of peace. They may thus have encouraged the drive for overseas expansion, colonization, and conversion of the natives, the imperial myth begun in Elizabethan times. They were not, indeed, the first 'Foxeian' plays. Some were already popular around 1600, notably *Sir John Oldcastle* and *The Life and Death of Thomas Lord Cromwell*, significantly at a time when the Protestant succession was uncertain, and when Archbishop Whitgift's persecution of Puritans in the Church of England (likened by Burghley to the proceedings of the Spanish Inquisition) was well under way. At that time, however, the players could not have presented Elizabeth or her formidable father Henry VIII on stage. After 1603 this became possible: the plays caught a mood of the time and were frequently revived and reprinted up to the 1630s.[12] Middleton's *Hengist King of Kent* and Thomas Drue's *Duchess of Suffolk* (1624) are later examples in the same tradition.

The context may have made the early Jacobean Reformation plays less orthodox in their effect than they may now seem on the page. At the time when they were first staged Whitgift's successor Archbishop Bancroft, with James's approval, was 'harrying the Puritans' out of the Church of England, depriving nonconforming ministers of their livings for refusing to wear vestments or to perform ceremonies they regarded as Popish. Resentment was increased because many of the deprived parsons were highly qualified as

---

[12] We know of eight quarto editions of Heywood's *If You Know Not Me You Know Nobody*, and four of Samuel Rowley's *When You See Me You Know Me*.

preachers (nine of the fourteen deprived in London, among them Essex's former chaplain Anthony Wootton, held University degrees), while 'dumb dogs' (non-preaching ministers) and pluralists were untouched.

In 1604–05 a number of highly respectable mainstream Puritan gentry and MPs who presented petitions to the King in favour of the deprived ministers in their own counties were warned that their combination 'in a cause to which the King had showed his mislike' was little less than treason. When they refused to sign a submission, their leaders, among them Lord Montagu of Boughton and Sir Francis Hastings, were deprived of their local offices as Lord Lieutenants and JPs. As Conrad Russell wryly comments: 'The Government had already begun to tell some of its most hardworking local agents that they were potential traitors. Ultimately the prophecy proved self-fulfilling.' (*The Crisis of Parliaments*, 1971, p. 210). These were influential people, and the attack looked like an assault on the status and power of the gentry which must have shocked those great patrons with whom they were connected. Sir Francis Hastings was a longstanding and highly-respected Puritan MP, who had urged Essex to take on his step-father Leicester's patronage of the Puritans; he was a candidate for Speaker of the Commons and had been on Sandys's Parliamentary committee that drafted the Apology in 1604. Lord Montagu, who was deprived of his Lord Lieutenancy in Northamptonshire, was a cousin of Lord Harington of Exton, who was a patron of mainstream Puritan divines and guardian of James's daughter Princess Elizabeth. Harington's daughter Lucy, Countess of Bedford, wife of a peer imprisoned for his part in the Essex affair, was already Queen Anne's intimate friend and a famous literary patroness. His son Sir John Harington was Prince Henry's closest personal friend.

In their context, these plays bore on the 'crisis of authority', the conflict of loyalty to different religions and the right of the monarch to overrule and dictate to individual consciences. The question whether England was to be Protestant or Catholic — an urgent issue around the time of the Essex revolt when the first Foxeian plays were staged — was sharply raised again by the Gunpowder Plot. Moreover there was a fear among Protestants that peace with Spain might now lead to the erosion of the reformed religion by Popish ceremonies, that they would be cut off from their fellow-Protestants in Europe and forbidden to practise Puritan forms of religion based on preaching and discussion.

The Foxeian plays, though fully orthodox in their expression of obedience to the monarch as head of State and Church, nevertheless transmit images and attitudes which could reinforce militant Protestant, even resistant feeling in the spectators against tyranny in religion. Like Foxe's book itself they have a radical subtext.[13] Although sometimes referred to as 'Elect

---

[13] It is significant that the *Book of Martyrs*, which under Elizabeth had been deemed orthodox enough to be placed by royal order in all churches, under Laud was banned from reprinting.

Nation plays', most of them are neither visionary nor apocalyptic,[14] but concern the conflict of right and wrong (equated with Protestantism and the Papacy) in terms of human behaviour.

These plays began the nostalgic 'harking back to Elizabeth' (Anne Barton's phrase) which in that censored culture so often took the place of overt criticism of James's or Charles's regime. But they can also be seen, like Foxe's book itself, as 'harking back to Grindal' or even to Wycliffe, to the Marian exiles and the radical origins of the English Reformation as men like William Crashaw perceived them. Like the *Book of Martyrs*, the plays incorporated some of the old anti-clerical ideas which (as Anne Hudson has so decisively shown)[15] had been kept alive by persecuted Lollard groups right up to the Reformation itself and the martyrdoms under Henry VIII and Queen Mary[16] — ideas some of which would have been punishable as heresy under Elizabeth, even though she found it expedient for a time to make use of Foxe's work.

Dramatically, these plays could reinforce not only the Protestant cause in general, but some attitudes associated with mainstream Puritanism. They present a new type of hero and heroine, an independent, literate, Bible-reading individual, standing up for conscience and personal interpretation of the Scriptures against bullying bishops or erring monarchs. They speak of the poor as representing Christ (a favourite Lollard theme) and the working people rather than the aristocracy as the firmest supporters of 'true religion'. And the anti-Papal context permits plenty of disrespectful 'carnivalesque' jokes at the expense of anyone in vestments. The popular drama here shows that tendency to outrun the attitudes of its noble patrons which we see again in Middleton's *Game at Chess* (1624).

How far these plays represent an intention by the patrons to influence public opinion we do not know. However, their general line would not have been displeasing to people like Southampton and Robert Sidney, interested in an anti-Spanish political stand both for commercial and strategic reasons. Their impact would have been partly religious, but no less political.

The campaign against royal impositions and monopolies was headed by Southampton's friend and business associate Sir Edwin Sandys, who repeatedly clashed with Government spokesmen in both the 1604 and the 1614 Parliament on the matter, earning James's lasting dislike. As Sandys presented it, the issue was not only an immediate grievance of the 'middling sort' and the consumers, but a question of political power. If the King could raise enough revenue for his needs by introducing impositions and monopolies at will, there would be no need for him to call Parliament or consult with

[14] Dekker's allegorical *Whore of Babylon*, staged by the Prince's Men in 1606 and presenting Elizabeth as the Fairy Queen, is the exception here.
[15] Anne Hudson, *The Premature Reformation* (Oxford, 1988).
[16] This is especially true of Samuel Rowley, whose *When You See Me You Know Me* is particularly disrespectful to Henry VIII and emphasizes the dependence of true religion on the poor. In 1602 he was also the author of some of the anti-Papal clowning episodes in *Dr Faustus*, which appear in the 1616 text and which may have made some use of Foxe.

gentry or city interests at all; it 'struck at the foundation of all our interests' and 'maketh us all bondmen'. 'We have no propriety in our goods as long as the King's prerogative is unlimited, to impose as much upon us as he pleaseth.' The power of the King, he argued, was at first introduced by popular consent, and the authority of the current king was therefore subject to the limitations imposed on his ancestors.[17]

This was the general context of Dekker's searing radical satire in the fable-play, *If It Be Not Good the Devil is In It* (1612), which not only pillories greedy monopolists (a familiar target in the City drama of Jonson, Middleton, and others) but what is much rarer, centres its attack on the monarch responsible. A young King, misled by devils disguised as court favourites, privileges and encourages predatory courtiers and greedy City usurers and merchants to farm the taxes, sell state offices, and prey on the people. The play was rejected by Dekker's usual company, the Prince's Men at the Fortune (perhaps because it was too radically anti-court), and he expressed his gratitude to Queen Anne's Men for taking it on at the Red Bull. The known commitment of the Sandys–Southampton circle to the anti-monopolist case may well have made the players confident of support if they did get into trouble with the censor or the Privy Council, but they seem not to have done so.

When Jonson borrowed Dekker's central idea for a devil-play several years later in *The Devil Is An Ass* (Blackfriars, 1616) he too pilloried the City monopolists and their dupes, but responsibility of the Crown for their extortions is never so much as mentioned. In fact, it is the seemingly 'naive' citizen play that highlights the sufferings of the poor and the corruption of central authority.

IV

William Crashaw, a close associate and follower of the Sandys and Southampton group in the Virginia Company and one of its main preachers and propagandists, was not only a noted anti-Papist scholar, book-collector and controversialist but something of a religious radical, who placed himself consciously in the Wycliffe tradition and got into trouble with the bishops because of his outspoken views.[18] When he had to sell part of his great library, some 2,000 volumes were bought by Southampton to be donated to the new library at St John's College, Cambridge, where he and Crashaw had been contemporaries and where there was a strong Puritan tradition. As Sir Robert Cotton's library was used to supply references for political opposition, so Crashaw's could be for militant Protestantism.[19]

---

[17] See Johann P. Sommerville, *Politics and Ideology in England, 1603–1640* (London, 1986), pp. 66, 79, 154–55.
[18] See P. J. Wallis, *William Crashaw the Sheffield Puritan* (n.p., 1963). This includes a descriptive bibliography of Crashaw's works.
[19] While the library awaited completion these books remained at Southampton House. After Southampton's death his widow sent them on to St John's.

Like many Puritan collectors, Crashaw was particularly interested in Lollard manuscripts and books because they were thought to anticipate reformed thinking, a connexion fostered by Foxe's Book of Martyrs, which traced the origins of Protestantism back to Wycliffe. Crashaw himself translated and intended to publish a famous Lollard dialogue between a knight and a cleric (in which the knight gets the better of the argument), as part of his campaign to expose the falsification of Church doctrines by the Pope and the Jesuits. But although the manuscript he carefully prepared for publication, with a dedication to King James, is still extant, it was apparently never issued,[20] and it seems likely that this was the 'erroneous book' for which, to his 'grief and rage' Crashaw was interrogated by the bishops in 1609 — though the attack was mainly because of his Puritan preaching and writing.

Crashaw made considerable use of his Wycliffite reading in his later polemics, taking over not only the anticlerical, anti-sacramental arguments of Lollard books but some of their popular stylistic devices. The tract he dedicated to Southampton in 1613, entitled 'Consilium Quorundum Episcoporum; the Recommendations of Certain Bishops assembled at Bologna' is a sly burlesque of a conciliar report, used to attack the Catholic Church — the kind of spoof dialogue which was to serve the Protestant cause so effectively a little later in Thomas Scot's *Vox Populi*, the main source for Middleton's *Game at Chess*.

In a polemic in dialogue form of 1623 apparently directed against the Jesuit Dr John Fisher,[21] who had succeeded in converting Buckingham's mother and various court ladies to Rome, Crashaw took up the Jesuit challenge 'Where was your church before Luther?' by arguing that the true Protestant church had originated with Wycliffe in England, long before Luther, and had continued in the underground sects, the Hussites and Waldenses in Europe, the Lollards in England, and others persecuted as heretics, until the Henrician Reformation itself.[22]

As a preacher for the Virginia Company Crashaw denounced those investors who put profit before building a godly colony. 'Tell them of getting 20 in the 100, and how they bite at it, oh now it stirs them! But tell them of planting a Church, of converting 10,000 souls to God, they are senseless as stones.'[23] He argued strongly (in contrast to some other leaders and preachers

[20] The original copy of about 1400, interleaved with a translation by Crashaw and a dedication to King James I, is still extant among the Cosin MSS in the Durham University Library, Cosin MSS V..iii.6 (Wallis, pp. 33–34).

[21] This dialogue, signed WC, is bound up in the Cambridge University Library copy with another tract by H. Rogers. *An Answer to Mr Fisher the Jesuit, his Five Propositions Concerning Luther*, 1623.

[22] The relevance of the debate with Fisher, conducted in the presence of King James, the Countess of Buckingham, and the Duke himself, to the satire in *A Game at Chess* is obvious. The discussion took place in May 1622, but was not published until 1624: 'An Answer to Mr. Fisher's Relation of a Third Conference between a certain B (as he styles him) and himself... given by R. B., Chaplain to the Bishop that was Employed in the Conference'. London, 1624. R. B. was in fact William Laud.

[23] Sermon preached at Temple Church, 1610, before Earl De La Warr and intending colonists on their departure for Virginia. See H. C. Porter, *The Inconstant Savage: England and the North American Indian* (London, 1979), pp. 364–65, 369.

to the company like Robert Gray) that the colonists had no legal or moral right or commandment from God to use force to expropriate and convert the Indians. Nothing must be taken from them 'by power nor pillage'; indeed the tools and skills brought by the English should 'make them much richer, even for matters of this life, than now they are'. They are our brothers: 'The same God made them as well as us, of as good matter as he made us; gave them as perfect and good souls and bodies as us; and the same Messiah and Saviour is sent to them as to us.' If this is starry-eyed, it is at least relatively humane compared with other current attitudes. The Sandys–Southampton faction in the company may not have been exactly the 'sanctified' venturers Crashaw dreamed of (sending out emigrants in coffin-ships and personal corruption were among the charges later levelled against Sandys by the opposing Smythe group, backed by King James).[24] It does seem however that they favoured a softer line towards the Indians (as Raleigh did), less draconian laws, and a greater concern for the long-term rather than the short-term interests of the colony. The controversy over the way to treat the Indians will certainly have been known to Shakespeare when he was writing *The Tempest*.[25]

Crashaw's strong hostility to the Spanish alliance was lastingly expressed when a new gallery was put in to his Whitechapel church to accommodate the ever-increasing audience, with an inscription 'in thankfulness for the safe return of our hopeful and gracious Prince Charles from the dangers of his Spanish journey.' It is the publicity given to the political struggles (at a time when preachers had so recently been forbidden to discuss the marriage) that is striking — a blow at the deference mentality itself.

V

Southampton's involvement in industry, overseas investment, and colonization gave him contacts and a common interest with London merchants and capitalist entrepreneurs in spreading technical and scientific knowledge and providing a modern education for ordinary people. One of the earliest dedications to him (in 1588) is a speech by the mathematician Thomas Hood, introducing his popular City lectures, given in English for the benefit of post-Armada sailors, soldiers, and master-gunners who have practical experience but no Latin.[26] Mathematics and astronomy, he says, are crucial also for navigators, surveyors, cartographers, mine operators, and civil engineers building waterworks 'whose skill being told us we would scarcely

[24] See the account given in Menna Prestwich, *Cranfield* (Oxford, 1966) and the conflicting estimate in H. C. Porter, *The Inconstant Savage*. Some of the allegations against Sandys by the opposing faction in the company appear somewhat dubious (see Bargrave's conversation with Sir Nathaniel Rich, noted above).
[25] The connexions between Southampton and Shakespeare after 1603 are conjectural. In view of the mass of secondary literature, especially on the possible relation of *The Tempest* to the affairs of the Virginia company, I do not attempt to examine the question in this paper.
[26] Thomas Hood, *A Copy of the Speech Made By the Mathematical Lecturer at the House of Mr. Thomas Smith* (London, 1588).

believe were it not lying at our doors.' And such knowledge also furthers religion, for 'there is more required of us concerning heaven than only the view of the outward frame . . . Next to the ordinary means of our instruction, I mean the word, the art of astronomy doth chiefly breed the knowledge of God.'

This was also the kind of thinking behind the foundation, a little later (1596), of Gresham's College, an event celebrated in Heywood's Red Bull play about the great City merchant benefactor Sir Thomas Gresham, Lord Mayor of London (*If You Know Not Me, You Know Nobody*, Part 2, 1605). Here Gresham is seen proudly showing the aristocracy, to whom he is civil but not overly deferential, round his modern educational charities:

> And Lords so please you but to see my schools
> Of the seven learned liberal sciences,
> Which I have founded here near Bishopsgate.
> I will conduct you. I will make it, Lords,
> An university within itself,
> And give it from my revenues maintenance.

In real life, the foundation statutes under Gresham's will required the teaching to be given in English, and in a style based on up-to-date examples to interest ordinary laymen, 'a University within itself' contrasting with the Latinized, élitist and still generally conservative style of Oxford, Cambridge, and the Inns of Court, where modern subjects were little taught. Many of the Gresham's professors (they were supposed to live locally) were directly or indirectly connected with Essexian and Southampton circles. The first professor of Divinity was Anthony Wootton, Essex's Puritan and radical chaplain, who was to be one of the ministers deprived by Bancroft in 1604. Henry Briggs, the professor of mathematics, was a close friend of William Crashaw, and a committed Puritan venturer in the Virginia Company. Matthew Gwinne, first professor of physic, was a former associate of the Sidney group and an acquaintance of Giordano Bruno.[27]

The Virginia Company itself needed to attract as colonists not parasitic gentry looking for an easy life exploiting cheap land and labour, the types represented in the drama by Sir Petronel Flash in *Eastward Ho!*, or perhaps by Antonio and Sebastian in *The Tempest*, but skilled craftsmen and farmers. To reach this highly motivated but unbookish audience required the development of a plain style, of which Hakluyt's *Voyages* and the Company's various reports and propaganda by Crashaw and others set a model.

Gervase Markham, once a member of Southampton's household and a soldier who fought with him in Ireland, had written celebratory poems for the Essex circle in the 1590s, one of them, on the last fight of Sir Richard Grenville, dedicated to Southampton. Later he 'held the plough' for some years as a small farmer, and published a whole series of best-selling

---

[27] For information about Gresham's College, see Christopher Hill, *Intellectual Origins of the English Revolution* (London, 1965), Chapter 2.

do-it-yourself manuals on agriculture, the care of horses and practical soldiering, incidentally far better written in addressing the 'plain honest husbandmen' than either the heroic poems or the blood-and-thunder allegoric melodrama *Herod and Antipater* which he got staged by his friends at the Red Bull in 1620. One of these tracts, entitled *Hunger's Prevention, The Whole Art of Fowling by Sea and Land*, is introduced as 'necessary and profitable for all such as travel by sea and come into uninhabited places, ... and in particular the blessed plantation of Virginia', and dedicated to Sir Edwin Sandys and other venturers in the company. In 1624 Markham was to publish a panegyric on Southampton's final military expedition to the Netherlands.

Emphasis on skills, hard work, and the practical use of learning is also central to the satires, *Abuses Stript and Whipt*, which George Wither dedicated to Southampton and others in 1613, and for which he was imprisoned, probably on the intervention of the Earl of Northampton. Wither includes a verse dedication to Southampton, with others to Pembroke, Sidney, and Lady Mary Wroth — targeting the full Sidney family connexion — and the former Essexian Lord Ridgeway. Within the work itself he praises Southampton's military skill and competence in the satire on *Fear*, where the shamefully unprepared state of English defence forces generally is contrasted with the exemplary training and efficiency given to the Hampshire militia by Southampton as Lord Lieutenant and Captain of the Isle of Wight (a post of some naval importance which he seems indeed to have taken very seriously).

The Scholar's Medley, dedicated to Southampton in 1614 by Richard Braithwait (who describes himself as a friend of Thomas Heywood) is a serious discussion both of how history should be written and of its great value in popular political and social education. Tacitus is the historian strongly preferred by the author, as he had been by Essex. His translators are especially praised for their service (most of them, notably Sir Henry Savile and Henry Cuffe, having been prominent in Essex's circle in the 1590s).

So much is our country benefited by translators, as the neatherd in his hovel may discourse as well of Cornelius Tacitus (if he know his mother's tongue) as our best Latinist. In my opinion no argument better for instruction than that author; and if I should dwell upon one, I had rather insist upon his phrases (though seemingly perplexed) than any other Roman author.

Tacitus is especially recommended as the historian of 'declined States', 'showing the vices of the time, where it was dangerous to be virtuous, and where innocence tasted the sharpest censure; ... where Amici Curiae were Parasiti Curiae, the Court's friends, the Court's popinjays ... the immeritorious in election for greatest honours, and the virtuous depressed because they will not mount by similar means.' The moral for readers of inferior rank is 'rather to live retired, than to purchase eminence in place by servile means.'

The reading of history moreover widens horizons and empowers the middling sort, since 'here may the poor husbandman, at his leisure, receive tidings from foreign courts ... What fitter for the householder to train his children, servants and attendants in (next Divine Writ) than the reading of profitable stories, such as excite to virtue, and stir up their minds to the undertaking of something worthy a resolved spirit' (p. 113). History, says Braithwait, provides encouraging examples of humble workers — farmers, shepherds, gardeners, foresters — who rose to great achievements, like Agricola and Romulus. 'But many have we that we may better imitate than Princes; as their state was eminent, so were their natures depraved.' This is the kind of 'popular Tacitism' which James I especially disliked, and its radical implications are obvious.[28] In dedicating a second edition of the work to Southampton's widow in 1638, Braithwait observed that her late lord 'did highly prize it.'[29]

The old Essex foreign policy, revived by Southampton, Sandys, Sheffield, and their group in 1621, was strongly anti-Spanish and anti-Hapsburg, but it does not follow that all its principal supporters were necessarily committed to a religious–apocalyptic view of England as the elect Protestant nation with a divine mission to annihilate the Popish Antichrist. Some of the clergy certainly saw and presented it in apocalyptic terms. The Puritan lecturer George Gifford had urged Essex to put on white linen and mount his white horse to lead the battle against Antichrist in the manner of Revelations.[30] Pembroke's ally Archbishop Abbot in 1619 believed that Frederick and his armies were about to 'tear the whore (of Babylon) and make her desolate.'[31] But many leaders of the struggle against domination by the Counter-Reformation Papacy and Spain (which it was believed would entail Spanish and Catholic domination in England, as well as loss to Spain of trade with the New World) had always sought alliance with any friendly Catholic forces in Europe. Henri IV did not cease to be a role model for Essex, Southampton, and Prince Henry, or a folk-hero for London people, after his 'politique' conversion to Catholicism. Sir Edwin Sandys, still a leader of anti-Spanish feeling in the Commons, had long stood for an alliance of all anti-Papal powers, including especially the Venetian republic and its leader the patriotic monk Paolo Sarpi, with whom he had written his tolerationist survey of European religion, banned in England by the High Commission.[32] This project was assiduously fostered by the Ambassador to Venice, Sir

---

[28] For the conflict over Tacitus and the radical implications of his work in the early seventeenth century, see Alan T. Bradford, 'Stuart Absolutism and the Utility of Tacitus', *Huntington Library Quarterly*, 46 (1983), pp. 128–38.

[29] In the dedicatory epistle to a later work, *His Catch*, apparently written from prison, Braithwait calls for protection on his godfather Sir Richard Hutton, one of the judges who subsequently held ship-money to be illegal.

[30] *Sermons Upon the Whole Book of the Revelation*. Set forth by George Gifford, preacher of the word at Mauldon in Essex, London 1596. Dedicated to the Right Noble Earl of Essex, his very good Lord.

[31] Cited by S. Adams, 'Foreign Policy and the Parliaments of 1621 and 1624', in *Faction and Parliament*, edited by K. Sharpe (London, 1978).

[32] Translated as *A Relation of the State of Religion*, 1606.

Henry Wotton, formerly Essex's secretary (and mocked by Jonson in *Volpone* as a ridiculous busybody). For Greville in his *Life of Sidney*, and very likely for Southampton, it was the independence and imperialist expansion of England and political resistance to the rival power that came uppermost, a matter of political interests as well as of religious commitment and solidarity with persecuted Protestant brethren overseas.

A section of aristocrats, with their keen sense of honour and their near-monopoly of military command, thus played a crucial if paradoxical role in the effort to bring England into active intervention against the Hapsburgs, and for that matter against extensions of absolute monarchic power. Both in England and the Netherlands they drew on the more cautious men of money, and were pushed forward by more plebeian forces.[33]

When the Government in 1624 finally committed itself to some limited practical assistance to the Dutch against Spain, agreeing that four volunteer regiments (six thousand men) should be raised in England to reinforce the English troops already fighting with the States, the four colonels named were Southampton (as the most experienced military leader of the force), the Earls of Oxford and Essex and Lord Willoughby de Eresby, considered the most likely names to attract volunteers. Significantly they were willing to serve in the relatively humble rank of colonels rather than generals. In 1622 John Knight, a young Oxford scholar, had been imprisoned for a celebrated sermon arguing that 'subjects se defendendo in case of religion might take up arms against their sovereign' — an implicit justification of rebellion against the Spanish match. He had been in the Fleet prison for two years, despite recanting, when Southampton, who had met Knight during his own confinement, secured his release and promptly appointed him chaplain to his regiment. Knight was soon to die of illness contracted in prison, but his release and appointment was symbolic of Southampton's political and religious attitude at the time of his final expedition.[34]

As the expedition was about to leave (characteristically it was delayed by lack of finance) Gervase Markham, who had served under Southampton in the wars, published his panegyric *Honour in his Perfection* (1624), celebrating the consistent record of the four commanders and their families in the Protestant cause since the time of the second Earl of Essex. This was not simply backward-looking nostalgia for the past feudal-chivalric status of the nobility. The tract was evidently written as propaganda to attract money and volunteers. Markham, who had himself worked as a small farmer for many years, was in a position to judge what would appeal to the 'honest, plain-dealing husbandmen' among whom he had lived. He revives the glorious memory of Essex on behalf of his son the third Earl, commends Southampton not only for his courage in the field but as Essex's faithful

[33] See Victor Kiernan, 'Revolution', in *New Cambridge Modern History, Companion Volume*, edited by P. Burke (Cambridge, 1979), pp. 227, 228–30.
[34] See Thomas Cogswell, *The Blessed Revolution* (Cambridge, 1989), pp. 31, 276.

comrade-in-arms, while his praise of Willoughby consists largely of celebrating the heroism and sufferings for religion of his grandmother the Duchess
of Suffolk, famous Marian exile and Puritan patroness under Elizabeth,
about whose life a popular play by Thomas Drue had been running at the
Fortune in the same year.

The credibility of these men as leaders, however, depends on their
competence and acquired military skill rather than mere lineage:

Henry the Great of France called ignorant noblemen golden calves, and all that did
reverence to them were only to perish for idolatry. It was his opinion that noblemen
might be born generous and capable, of virtue, but instruction only makes them
wise.

Having 'infinite oceans' of honour already, these leaders do not seek to make
themselves greater by acquiring more, but to do God's work. 'They clamber
not up to catch the moon but rather to look lower than themselves, that they
might find out heaven.'

Recognizing that Southampton and the expedition have powerful enemies, who 'misinterpret or wish ruin to their proceedings', Markham
resolves as one that lived many years 'where I daily saw this Earl ... that
have seen him undergo all the extremities of war, that have seen him receive
the reward of a soldier ... for the best act of a soldier done upon the enemy'
not to be 'scar'd with shadows' but to speak out on his behalf. Evidently what
Markham calls 'the bastards of the great Whore ... nursed up by the Jesuit'
are believed to be still active against their cause — incidentally a comment
on the view of some modern historians that by the summer of 1624 the
anti-Spanish, anti-Catholic line of A Game of Chess was no longer controversial in England.

VI

Like that of other 'dissident' aristocrats, Southampton's position was
complex and contradictory. While using their wealth to invest in industrial
and commercial enterprises which eventually would provide an independent
source of financial power, they were at the same time operating within the
extravagant Court, and deriving much of their income from the very grants
and pensions they criticized. As 'improving' landlords they fined and
rackrented their copyholders while seeking to build popular support for their
policies.

Within the increasingly solid business alliance of peers, merchants, and a
section of the country gentry, the particular function of peers was not only to
invest money from their rents, but to obtain and keep the necessary
concessions and privileges from the Crown through their Court connexions.
This implied maintaining Court contacts and influence, preferably at the
highest level, the Privy Council, and therefore conflicted with the desire to
lead opposition to the whole foreign and military policy of the Crown.

Principled opposition to monopolies and patents went along with the drive to secure monopoly privileges for themselves, whether to sustain the luxurious lifestyle required at Court or for what they saw as good causes such as the Virginia colony, the repair of defences on the Isle of Wight, or the support of victimized Puritan ministers — there being no other way to operate. Even Southampton, who could barely conceal his hostility to 'boys and base fellows' on the Privy Council, seems to have tried at one point to co-operate with Buckingham, though he could not keep it up. Sandys did so in 1626, and thereby lost his popular influence in his own county of Kent.

These conflicts of interest made alliances unstable and divided families and factions. For individuals they must have meant a frequent sense of self-division and unease. Melancholy and self-doubt in Donne's poetry has been attributed by John Carey to his ambivalence about rejecting his Catholic past. But conflicts between what one believed and what one could say or write (for example about the Spanish alliance), or between what seemed intolerable long-term alternatives (absolute monarchy or mob rule), or between chivalrous ideals and the sordid shifts needed to finance them, seem to have tormented Greville and Southampton as well as Donne. Hence Greville's grim paradox, 'I know the world and believe in God', or Southampton's wry comment on his long-delayed elevation to the Privy Council: 'This preferment I expected not nor wished in my heart ... I had much rather have continued a spectator than become an actor'. Nevertheless the assistance and countenance given by such privileged people to Puritan preachers like William Crashaw, popular educators like the Gresham's professors, radical University lecturers like Dorislaus, satirists like Wither, and dramatists like Heywood, Dekker, later Middleton and Massinger, was probably crucial for historical developments.

Southampton himself seems to have been more a man of action, less a skilful and cautious politician than some others with comparable concerns (Pembroke or Greville), and this makes his convictions and the direction of his influence more obvious. It seems logical that he should finally have commanded a volunteer expedition in 1624 to aid the Dutch republic, and that in the next generation his surviving son and heir fought on the royalist side, while his son-in-law Robert Wallop was a near-regicide and died in prison after the Restoration. From the second Earl of Essex in Shakespeare's time to the third Earl, the Veres, the Fairfaxes, the Sidneys, Brookes, and Nevilles after 1640 a thread of continuity in ideas and patronage can be traced, encouraging but not wholly controlling new trends in popular political culture.

Re-writing Patriarchy and Patronage: Margaret Clifford, Anne Clifford, and Aemilia Lanyer

BARBARA K. LEWALSKI

Harvard University

At this point we know a good deal about how early modern culture constructed women within several discourses: law, medicine, theology, domestic advice. We also know a good deal about the various and complex poetic and dramatic representations of women in the period. But because we have only just begun the recovery and analysis of elusive women's texts from their various archival repositories, we still know very little about how early modern Englishwomen read and wrote themselves and their world. This essay focuses on texts by two noble ladies and a gentlewoman in decline in Jacobean England; and that limitation obviously precludes drawing general conclusions about women of other or even the same ranks in Jacobean society. But I would urge the importance of reading the few women's texts we have found as well as we can, to afford at least some female perspective on issues of gender, ideology, the construction of identity, cultural constraints and resistance, which have become central for scholars in this period.

The trio of women in my title are linked in a network of overlapping relationships. Margaret and Anne Clifford, mother and daughter, engaged in a protracted and notorious legal struggle to contest the will of husband and father George Clifford, third Earl of Cumberland, to maintain Anne's claim to some of his property, titles, and offices, thereby setting themselves against the entire Jacobean patriarchy: male relatives, their husbands, court society, the Archbishop of Canterbury, and King James himself. Margaret Clifford and Aemilia Lanyer may comprise the first English example of female patron and female literary client, and that relationship is at the centre of Lanyer's volume of poems, *Salve Deus Rex Judaeorum*, published in 1611. Anne Clifford and Aemilia Lanyer are linked as rare, and also innovative, female authors: Anne Clifford's diary of 1616 to 1619 is much more personal and introspective than are the few other English secular diaries which survive from that date or before,[1] while Aemilia Lanyer's poems are among

[1] See list of Diaries in *CBEL*, Volume 1, 2259–64; *British Diaries: An Annotated Bibliography of British Diaries Written Between 1442 and 1942*, edited by W. Matthews (Los Angeles, 1959). Also see Paul Delaney, *British Autobiography in the 17th Century* (London, 1969); Sara Heller Mendelson, 'Stuart Women's Diaries and Occasional Memoirs', in *Women in English Society 1500–1800*, edited by Mary Prior (London, 1985), pp. 181–210. The extant domestic diaries were products of a Puritan upbringing, and probably undertaken as exercises in spiritual account-keeping. The *Diary of Lady Margaret Hoby, 1599–1605*, edited

the earliest published by an Englishwoman and include what seems to be the first English country-house poem. Moreover, both texts treat Margaret Clifford as major influence, model, and subject; and both offer a proto-feminist challenge to ideologies and institutions at the centre of Jacobean culture, patriarchy and male patronage.

Received wisdom has it that the Jacobean era was a regressive period for women, as a culture dominated by a powerful queen gave way to a Court ethos shaped by the patriarchal ideology and homosexuality of James I.[2] Anne of Denmark, though an enthusiastic sponsor of and participant in masques, was not otherwise much concerned with literature and learning. Education for Jacobean ladies is said to have declined, especially by comparison with the humanist classical education some Tudor women enjoyed. And beyond question the period saw an outpouring of repressive or overtly mysogynist sermons, tracts, and plays, detailing women's physical and mental defects, spiritual evils, rebelliousness, shrewishness, and natural inferiority in the hierarchy of being.[3]

How is it then, we might ask, that Elizabethan women writers were chiefly occupied with translation, while several Jacobean women wrote and often published original literary works of some scope and merit, among them Lanyer's poems, Clifford's diary and family memoirs, Elizabeth Cary's tragedy *Mariam*, Rachel Speght's elegiac poems and controversial prose; and Lady Mary Wroth's romance *Urania*, her drama *Love's Victorie*, and her sonnet sequence, *Pamphilia to Amphilanthus*? Some enabling factors may include the space opened to other women when Queen Elizabeth's death removed her cultural dominance while leaving in place a powerful female example; the model and sanction for women's literary activities afforded by two influential patroness-poets, Mary (Sidney) Herbert, Countess of Pembroke, and Lucy (Russell), Countess of Bedford; and the evident importance of female communities — mothers and daughters, extended kinship networks, close female friends — as a counterweight to patriarchy. This

---

by Dorothy M. Meads (London, 1930) records her daily prayers and meditations, her constant attention to household management and accounts, her frequent medical and surgical attentions to the sick of the community, but displays little introspection or self-analysis. Grace Sherrington [Mildmay]'s lengthy memoir of her life (*c.* 1570–1617) as child and wife (written in her old age, as a contribution to the education of her daughter and other young people of her class) contains much lively discussion of daily activities and family life; the unpublished manuscript is in the Northampton Public Library, and an account, with excerpts, was published by Rachel Weigall, 'An Elizabethan Gentlewoman: The Journal of Lady Mildmay', *Quarterly Review* 215 (1911), 119–38.

[2] See, for example, Lawrence Stone, *The Family, Sex, and Marriage in England 1500–1800* (London, 1977); Jean Gagen, *The New Woman: Her Emergence in English Drama 1600–1730* (New York, 1954); Roger Thompson, *Women in Stuart England and America* (London, 1974); *The Norton Anthology of Literature by Women*, edited by Sandra Gilbert and Susan Gubar (New York, 1985); Jonathan Goldberg, *James I and the Politics of Literature* (Baltimore, 1983); Antonia Fraser, *The Weaker Vessel: Women's Lot in Seventeenth-Century England* (London, 1984).

[3] See, for example, J. R. Brink, *Female Scholars: A Tradition of Learned Women before 1800* (Montreal, 1980); Felicity Nussbaum, *The Brink of all We Hate: English Satire on Women, 1600–1750* (Lexington, 1984); Linda Woodbridge, *Women and the English Renaissance: Literature and the Nature of Womankind, 1540–1620* (Chicago, 1984); *Re-Writing the Renaissance: The Discourses of Sexual Difference in Early Modern Europe*, edited by Margaret Ferguson, Maureen Quilligan, and Nancy Vickers (Chicago, 1986).

breakthrough to female authorship lends support to recent revisionist studies by Margaret Ezell and others, challenging the supposed rigidity and pervasiveness of patriarchal attitudes and practices in seventeenth-century England.[4] The texts I mean to examine here afford some insight into three women's construction of self and world as they sought to rewrite patriarchy and patronage, supported on the one hand by a sense of female community, and on the other by the firm conviction that God the Divine Patriarch was their ally against the many earthly patriarchs who oppressed them.

First for the Cliffords, mother and daughter, whose stories can be constructed from several kinds of contemporary records:[5] court gossip; dedications; funeral sermons; personal letters (many of them in the Cumbria record office, Kendal); massive tomes of legal records and family papers (called 'The Chronicles') collected by the two women in support of their lawsuits;[6] Anne Clifford's memoirs of her father, her mother, and herself, written about 1653; and especially Anne's Jacobean *Diary* (edited and published for the first and only time in 1923 by Vita Sackville-West).[7]

Anne Clifford's father, George, third Earl of Cumberland, was Queen Elizabeth's official champion in the tilt-yard and a dashing adventurer and privateer on the high seas; her mother was Margaret Russell, youngest daughter of the Second Earl of Bedford, and a noted literary patron whose

---

[4] Margaret Ezell, *The Patriarch's Wife: Literary Evidence and the History of the Family* (Chapel Hill, 1987).

[5] The major modern biographical accounts of Lady Anne are: George C. Williamson, *Lady Anne Clifford, Countess of Dorset, Pembroke & Montgomery, 1590–1676: Her Life, Letters, and Work* (Kendal, 1922), which supplies generous extracts from letters and other documents; Martin Holmes, *Proud Northern Lady: Lady Anne Clifford, 1590–1676* (London, 1976). Other studies include Wallace Notestein, *Four Worthies* (London, 1956), pp. 123–66; and R. T. Spence, 'Lady Anne Clifford, Countess of Dorset, Pembroke, and Montgomery (1590–1676): A Reappraisal', *Northern History*, 15–16 (1979–80), 43–65. For Margaret Clifford the best account remains Chapter 21 in George Williamson's *George, Third Earl of Cumberland (1558–1605): His Life and His Voyages* (Cambridge, 1920). For the documents and letters see: Appendix, Williamson, *Lady Anne Clifford*, pp. 456–520; *Collectanea Cliffordiana*, edited by Arthur Clifford (Paris, 1819); John Chamberlain to Dudley Carleton, Public Record Office, State Papers, Domestic, XVI, 23 (7 November 1605); XLIII, 14 (10 January 1609); XLIV, 6 (3 March 1609); LXXII, 120 (29 April 1613); XC, 122 (15 March 1617); CV, 2 (2 January 1619); CXII, 82 (12 February 1620). Documents or references to Legal proceedings: Clifford MS (Oxford); Hales MS 94 and Hales MS 83 (Lincoln's Inn); PRO SPD XVIII, 1605 (30 May 1608); LXXXIX, 405 (14 November 1616); XC (14 March 1617, 21 March 1620, 10 December 1620, 29 March 1624); CLXII, 212 (10 April 1624); CLXIX (17 June 1630); Cumbria Record Office WD/Hoth/Box 44; WD/Hoth/Box 71/6; WD/Hoth/Boxes 33, 46, 47, 49; WD/Hoth/Additional Records 6, 7, 9, 14, 16, 17, 21; Yorkshire Archaeological Society, Bundle 109.

[6] Margaret Clifford began, and Anne directed the enterprise (notable among family histories for its completeness and accuracy), annotated the volumes, and wrote the memorials of her immediate family and herself. One copy of the three large volumes, called the *Great Books of the Records of Skipton Castle* compiled under Lady Anne's direction is now at Cumbria Record Office WD/Hoth/Great Books. While at Knole Anne Clifford also had the contemporary records and eyewitness accounts of all Clifford's sea voyages collected in a beautiful manuscript entitled *A Brief Relation of the Severall Voyages undertaken and performed by the Right Honourable George, Earle of Cumberland in his owne person and at his owne charge . . . . faithfully collected out of the Relations Observations and Journals of Severall Credible and Worthie Persons Actors and Commanders under the said Noble Earle.* (The original is at the Cumbria Record Office, WD/Hoth/Additional Records #70, and a copy at the Lambeth Palace Library, MS 2688).

[7] An eighteenth-century copy of Anne Clifford's *Lives* of her parents and herself (from the third volume of the *Great Books*) is in the British Library (Harley MS 6177). That MS was printed by J. P. Gilson, *Lives of Lady Anne Clifford and of her Parents* (London, Roxburghe Club, 1916). *The Diary of Lady Anne Clifford*, edited by V. Sackville-West (London, 1923), is based on an eighteenth-century copy (at Knole) of the lost original (Hereafter cited in text and notes by title and page number).

clients included Spenser and Anne's tutor, the poet Samuel Daniel.[8] In his later years George Clifford had notorious affairs with other women and 'parted houses' with his wife, though he repented and was reconciled with Margaret and Anne in 1605, on his deathbed. Anne Clifford, born on 30 January 1590, was her father's only surviving child, so the titles and properties pertaining to the Cumberland earldom legally reverted to his brother Francis.[9] But Anne claimed other castles, estates, titles, and County offices in Yorkshire and Westmoreland which by writ of Edward II were entailed to the heirs general in the direct Clifford line, that is, daughters as well as sons; some of these properties constituted her mother's jointure. Without breaking the entail, George Clifford had willed these estates to his brother also, making a monetary provision for his daughter and giving her the reversion should his brother's male line fail. Anne explained his motives in terms of patriarchal values: 'the love he bore his brother, and the advancement of the heirs male of his house' (*Life of Me*, p. 36). Until her death in 1616 Margaret Clifford masterminded almost continuous legal and domestic struggles to maintain Anne's claims, and Anne continued them until she finally obtained her inheritance in 1643, though only after her uncle and his son died without male heirs.

By her first marriage in 1609 to Richard Sackville, Anne Clifford became Countess of Dorset and had five children by that marriage, three sons who died in infancy and two daughters who survived to adulthood.[10] By her second marriage in 1630 to Philip Herbert she became Countess of Pembroke and Montgomery.[11] However, she did not define herself or her place in society through these marriages, titles, and roles, but referred to herself on every possible occasion and in every possible document as 'sole Daughter and Heir to my illustrious Father'. In 1649 she went North to take possession of her inheritance, defiantly maintaining her authority, her royalism, and her Anglicanism against the Puritan armies occupying her castle at Appleby;[12] and when Pembroke died in 1650 she was ready to enjoy the comparatively privileged status of a wealthy, independent widow. For more than thirty years she ruled her domain as a (usually) benevolent autocrat,

[8] Among Margaret Clifford's clients or would-be clients were: Spenser, Samuel Daniel, Henry Peacham, Thomas Tymme, Henry Constable, Francis Davison. See Franklin B. Williams, Jr, *Index of Dedications and Commendatory Verses in English Before 1641* (London, 1962). Daniel had formerly served as tutor to William Herbert, son to the Earl of Pembroke and Mary Sidney.

[9] Biographical details drawn from: *A Summary of the Records and a True Memorial of the Life of Me the Lady Anne Clifford*, edited by Gilson, pp. 33–34. (Hereafter cited in text and notes by short title, *Life of Me*, and page number); *The Course of Life of this George, 3rd Earl of Cumberland*, edited by Gilson, pp. 5–14; Williamson, *George, Third Earl of Cumberland*; Williamson, *Lady Anne Clifford*, pp. 31–36, 456–57; Holmes, *Proud Northern Lady*, pp. 1–20; Spence, pp. 43–47.

[10] Williamson, pp. 79–83; *Life of Me*, pp. 37–41.

[11] For Philip's character, see Williamson *Lady Anne Clifford*, pp. 160–85; *DNB*, ix, 659–60. No doubt King James's interest was engaged by Herbert's passion for hunting (as well as his good looks).

[12] See the *Memoirs* of her secretary George Sedgwick, reprinted in Joseph Nicolson and Richard Burn, *The History and Antiquities of the Counties of Westmoreland and Cumberland*, 2 vols (London; 1777), I, 294–303. (Sedgwick's original *Memoir* is not extant, except for the segments published herein). Also see her funeral sermon preached by Edward Rainbowe, *A Sermon Preached at the Interrment of Anne, Countess of Pembroke, Dorset, and Montgomery* (London [1676]), pp. 47–49.

combining public and private roles: Lord of the Manor and Lady Bountiful, Sheriff of the County and Grandmother, patriarch and matriarch. She rebuilt her several castles and churches; ordered her estates; established almshouses for poor widows; dispensed patronage and largesse; entertained her numerous grandchildren and great-grandchildren; convened the annual assizes courts, and handpicked the MPs for Appleby and Westmoreland.[13] Early to late she defined her identity through these long-sought roles: 'Baroness Clifford, Westmoreland and Vesey, High Sheriffess of Westmoreland, and Lady of the Honor of Skipton in Craven'. She died in 1676, at the age of 86.

Anne Clifford's memoirs of 1653 represent her as a strong-minded, self-assured woman with a firm sense of personal worth, sitting in confident authorial judgement on all the men who held familial authority over her — father, uncle, husbands — and penning perceptive, fairminded, and judicious evaluations of them. That representation invites the question, how was such an identity constituted within the institution and ideology of patriarchy? Her writings, early to late, suggest some partial answers.

For one thing, she characteristically ranged the various patriarchal authorities against each other, thus opening space for subversion. She was able to maintain great pride in, and a primary identification with, her father by persuading herself that he really intended and expected her ultimately to inherit the property.[14] This strengthened her to resist the authority and claims of uncles, husbands, courtiers, and kings, and to detach herself (she asserts with some pride, and a deft quotation from Sidney's *Arcadia*) from her two husbands' families and concerns:[15]

The marble pillars of Knowle in Kent and Wilton in Wiltshire were to me often times but the gay arbour of anguish. Insomuch that a wise man that knew the insides of my fortune would often say that I lived in both these my lords' great familys as the river of Roan or Rodamus runs through the lake of Geneva, without mingling any part of its streams with that lake; for I gave myself wholly to retiredness, as much as I could, in both those great families, and made good books and virtuous thoughts my companions.[16]

[13] Sedgwick, pp. 300–02; Rainbowe, *Funeral Sermon*, esp. pp. 13, 23–38, 51. Williamson, pp. 226–84, 393–403. Anne's *Day by Day Book* for 1 January to 21 March 1676 (printed verbatim in Williamson, pp. 265–84) is the only extant portion of her diary from the later years.

[14] This is on the basis of the deathbed reconciliation, *Life of Me*, p. 36: 'a little before his death he expressed with much affection to my mother and me a great belief that he had, that his brother's son would dye without issue male, and thereby all his lands would come to be mine; which accordingly befell'.

[15] In retrospect she lumps Dorset and Pembroke together as (for their nobility) among the many blessings Providence bestowed on her, despite the fact that it was her 'misfortune to have contradictions and crosses with them both', *Life of Me*, p. 39.

[16] *Life of Me*, p. 40. Compare *The Countess of Pembroke's Arcadia* (*The Old Arcadia*), edited by Jean Robertson (Oxford, 1973), p. 85. The passage echoes verses sung by Dorus in 'The First Eclogues': 'Come from marble bowers, many times the gay harbour of anguish'.

More important still, at every juncture she finds evidence of God thwarting 'the sinister practices of my Enemies', in defence of her rights.[17] By her reading, the divine patriarch himself frustrated the machinations of the various earthly patriarchs, thereby accomplishing the true desires of her father.

Another major enabling factor was Anne Clifford's emphasis on a matrilineal heritage and kinship network. She consciously took her mother as model, claiming her moral and spiritual heritage from her: 'by the bringing up of my said dear mother, I did, as it were, even suck the milk of goodness, which made my mind strong against the storms of fortune'.[18] Anne's autobiographical writing may have been fostered by Margaret, who herself wrote a brief introspective autobiography in a letter to her chaplain, a poignant and melancholy 'Seven Ages of Women' that breaks off inexplicably after the fifth seventh and represents her life under two tropes: a dance, with backward and forward movements, and a pilgrimage of grief.[19] Anne Clifford was profoundly grateful to her mother for beginning and carrying forward the lawsuits in her behalf, and admired her enormously for her patience in adversity and for her exemplary courage and firmness in opposing the patriarchal power structure: 'so much constancy, wisdom, and resolution did she shew in that business that the like can hardly be paralleled by any woman' (*Life of Margaret Clifford*, p. 26). An exchange of letters between them from 1614 to 1616 reveals Margaret's role as primary strategist and emotional support for Anne, then under great pressure from her husband Dorset (who had many debts and his way to make at court) to accept a cash settlement along the lines of her father's will. Margaret Clifford's long letter of 22 September 1615 is typical:

You writ wisely and I fear too truly for the king and queen, whom you might have had in a more favorable sort, but it was one of your Lord and his friends strategems . . . I have written another [letter] to be delivered to them [the judges] . . . it were best by yourself, if my Lord's [Dorset's] tyranny let it not. Well it seems he hath not tasted of true spiritual comforts that so much forgets that saying of the apostle, he is worse than an infidel that provides not for his wife and family. Then he that has not a heart to defend their rights, wants the true spirit of God. . . . Lay all on me and neither cross him in words but keep your resolutions with silence and what gentle persuasion you can, but alter not from your own wise course . . . . You have written to Masters Crackenthorpe which letter was opened by chance, that whether my Lord would let you or not, if I would have you come [to visit her in the North] you would

---

[17] See her 'Summaries' of the lives of her uncle Francis Clifford (Gilson, p. 14) and her cousin Henry (Gilson, p. 17). To Dorset's brother Edward, who succeeded to the title, she ascribed 'malitious hatred' and constant machinations, which she escaped because her 'destiny was guided by a mercyfull and divine Providence', *Life of Me*, p. 45.

[18] *Life of Me*, p. 36. See also her *Life of Margaret Clifford*, p. 30, citing a 'great divine' who said 'he thought it much more happiness to be descended from so blessed a woman, than to be born heir to a great kingdom'. Anne describes her mother's wide reading (in English translation, since she had no languages), her prudence, and her alchemical knowledge, interests underscored in the great family picture at Appleby, which depicts Margaret holding the Psalms of David, and standing before a shelf holding the Bible, an English translation of Seneca, and (her own) handwritten book of alchemical distillations and medicines.

[19] Reprinted in Williamson, *George, Third Earl of Cumberland*, pp. 285–88.

come against his will. Dear heart be very wary what you say but most wary what you write for they desire to have advantage and to sever my Lord and you, as they let me from my Lord, for you are too near me in resemblance, not of faces but of fortune, which God make better, and me thankful that hath and does overcome in God, which he in mercy grant that you may do in the end.[20]

Reinforcing Anne Clifford's sense of a matrilineal heritage was her belief in her mother's prophetic powers and protective prayers, her delight in tracing uncanny parallels between her mother's life and her own, and her frequent descriptions of her own daughter (named Margaret) as a near-replica of Margaret Clifford.[21] She also found some maternal guidance and protection in a larger female community which included her Russell aunts, the Countesses of Bath and Warwick;[22] Queen Elizabeth, by whom she was 'much beloved' as a child; and Queen Anne, who 'was ever inclyneing to our part, and very gratious and favourable to us' in the controversies over the lands, attributing this to the fact that they danced together in court masques.[23]

Reading and writing were also of primary importance to Anne Clifford's self-definition, and resistance to patriarchy. Her good education she attributes to her mother and her tutor Daniel, while ascribing to her father a single important restriction: '[she] was not admitted to learn any language, because her father would not permit it; but for all other knowledge fit for her sex none was bred up to greater perfection than she'.[24] This evidently meant no Latin, since records indicate that she studied French.[25] Her Jacobean diary and the great family picture she had painted about 1646 provide some record of books read, revealing her special interests in history, literature, and religious classics. During the embattled years 1616 to 1619 she read 'a great part of the History of the Netherlands', Montaigne's *Essays*, the *Fuerie Queene*, Sidney's *Arcadia*, Sandys's *Government of the Turks*, Chaucer, the Old Testament, Augustine's *City of God*, Parson's *Resolutions*, Ovid's *Metamorphoses*, and Josephus.[26] Unfortunately, she does not comment on these books. But we can infer something of what they meant to her from a remarkable letter of 1649 in which she appropriates her literary patrimony as boldly as she did her ancestral lands, echoing Spenser as she claims empowerment through the infusion of Chaucer's spirit:

[20] In the County Record Office, Cumbria (Kendal), WD/Hoth/Box 44. I have regularized the very eccentric orthography.

[21] *Life of Margaret Clifford*, pp. 18–24. See also Williamson, pp. 149, 154, and Anne Clifford's letters of 3 May 1615, and 26 April 1616 to her mother, in the period 16 June 1614 to 26 April 1616, Cumbria County Archives, Kendal, WD/Hoth/Box 44.

[22] They are, she claims, along with her mother 'the three most remarkable ladys for their greatness and goodness of any three sisters in the kingdom', *Life of Margaret Clifford*, p. 24.

[23] *Life of Me*, pp. 36, 38. Of Queen Anne she says 'In my youth I was much in the Courte with her, and in Maskes attended her, though I never served her'.

[24] *Life of Margaret Clifford*, p. 28. In ascribing that prohibition so pointedly to her father, she invites the inference that she herself, her mother (whose education was similarly restricted) and possibly Daniel, did not share the notion that the classical languages were unsuitable for women.

[25] Anne Clifford, *Life of Me*, pp. 35–36. For the account books see T. D. Whitaker, *The History and Antiquities of the Deanery of Craven* (London, 1878), and Williamson, *Lady Anne Clifford*, pp. 58–67.

[26] See Williamson, pp. 498–500; *Diary*, passim.

My love and service to worthy Mr Selden, and tell him if I hade nott exelent Chacor's booke heare to comfortt mee I wer in a pitifull case, having so manny trubles as I have butt when I rede in thatt I scorne and make little of them alle, and a little part of his beauteous sperett infusses ittselfe in mee.[27]

Writing, especially of her Jacobean diary, was evidently crucial to Anne Clifford's construction of herself and her world. By definition the diary is a private genre, yet it seems likely that Anne intended hers ultimately for the Clifford Chronicles, as a record for posterity of her most embattled and momentous years. While lawsuits over women's claims to property or inheritance were common in the era,[28] Anne Clifford's *Diary* offers a rare reading of one such situation by the woman involved, and so offers an intriguing perspective on the engagements of ideology with experience, and on the relation between authoring a text and authoring a self.

The *Diary* begins in the momentous year 1603, with entries which were written up later, but capture the wide-eyed, thirteen-year-old girl's impressions of the flurry of activity and ceremony surrounding Queen Elizabeth's death and James I's coronation: the universal jockeying for position: 'every man expecting mountains and finding molehills'; the court women (herself among them) rushing to meet Queen Anne *en route* from Scotland and killing 'three horses that one day with extremity of heat'; the anxiety caused by her parents' strained domestic relations (*Diary*, pp. 1–12). One remarkable entry reports George Clifford exercising his hereditary right to bear the sword before the King at York, culminating in her own quite astonishing claim to the same privilege: 'because it was an office by inheritance ... it lineally descended to me' (*Diary*, p. 6). The *Diary* resumes in January 1616 and continues through 1619, with the intervening years and the year 1618 lost or deliberately excised; the entries report quotidian affairs but highlight Anne Clifford's legal battles and escalating domestic conflicts with Dorset over her lands.

She reports several scenes of high drama, among them a visit on 17 February 1616 from a phalanx of male kinsmen reinforced by the Archbishop of Canterbury:

Upon the 17th my Lord Archbishop of *Canterbury*, my Lord *William Howard*, my Lord *Rous*, my Coz. *Russell*, my Brother *Sackville* and a great company of men ... were all in the Gallery of *Dorset House* where the Archbishop took me aside and talked with me privately one hour and half and persuaded me both by Divine and human means to set my hand to their arguments. But my answer to his Lordship was that I would do nothing till my Lady and I had conferred together. Much persuasion was used by him and all the company, sometimes terrifying me and sometimes flattering me, but at length it was concluded that I should have leave to go to my Mother [then resident

---

[27] To the Countess Dowager of Kent. British Library ADD MS 15, 232. Compare *Faerie Queene* 4.34.6–7: 'Through infusion sweete | Of thine own spirit, which doth in me survive | I follow here the footing of thy feete'.

[28] See cases cited in T. E., *The Lawes Resolutions of Womens Rights: Or, The Lawes Provision for Woemen* (London, 1632).

on her dower estates in Westmoreland] and send an answer by the 22nd of March next, whether I will agree to this business or not.

Next day was a marvellous day to me through the mercy of God, for it was generally thought that I must either have sealed to the argument or else have parted with my Lord. (*Diary*, pp. 19–20)

Subsequent entries show Margaret Clifford continuing to act as Anne's chief strategist and comrade-in-arms. On 20 March the two women sent from Westmoreland a direct refusal of the judges' award, and when Anne returned to London she left the papers she was supposed to sign with her mother, as a further delaying tactic.[29] Entries over the next two months record mounting emotional turmoil: the 'grevious and heavy parting' with her mother[30] and anxiety over reports of her illness; and her near-desperation as Dorset, alternating between rage and coldness, threatened her with separation, banishment from his residences, and the loss of her daughter Margaret, then two years old. On 9 May he ordered that 'the Child should go live at *Horseley* [with her Sackville aunts], and not come hither any more so as this was a very grievous and sorrowful day to me' (*Diary*, pp. 25–31). On 29 May she reports 'the heavy news of my Mother's death which I held as the greatest and most lamentable cross that could have befallen me' (*Diary*, pp. 29–32).

Anne reports graphically the crisis of January 1617, when the King undertook to settle the matter between Anne and the Clifford heirs. She thankfully takes note of a few (chiefly female) partisans, notably the Queen, who 'promised me she would do all the good in it she could . . . [and] gave me warning not to trust my matters absolutely to the King lest he should deceive me' (*Diary*, pp. 48–49). The entry of 18 January describes a dramatic private meeting with the King:

My Lord *Buckingham* . . . brought us into the King, being in the Drawing Chamber. He put out all that were there and my Lord and I kneeled by his chair sides when he persuaded us both to peace and to put the whole matter wholly into his hands, which my Lord consented to, but I beseech't His Majesty to pardon me for that I would never part from *Westmoreland* while I lived upon any condition whatsoever. Sometimes he used fair means and persuasions and sometimes foul means but I was resolved before so as nothing would move me. . . . All this time I was much bound to

---

[29] *Diary*, pp. 21–23. Dorset responded to the refusal by commanding that the company return to London without Anne; the ladies then drafted a letter, duly notorized, to the effect that she was obeying Dorset rather than her own wishes (lest she be charged with deserting her husband); but after 'much talk' for two nights they determined she should return anyway, to avoid if possible an open separation.

[30] *Diary*, p. 23. Later, she erected a pillar on the spot where the leavetaking took place, in commemoration, Williamson, p. 389. The monument, known locally as 'The Countess' Pillar', was inscribed as follows:

THIS PILLAR WAS ERECTED IN ANNO DOMINI JANUARY, 1654 BY YE RIGHT HONOBLE ANNE, COUNTESS DOWAGER OF PEMBROKE, ETC. DAUGHTER AND SOLE HEIRE OF YE RIGHT HONOBLE GEORGE EARL OF CUMBERLAND, ETC. FOR A MEMORIAL OF HER LAST PARTING IN THIS PLACE WITH HER GOOD AND PIOUS MOTHER, YE RIGHT HONOBLE MARGARET, COUNTESS DOWAGER OF CUMBERLAND, YE 2ND OF APRIL 1616, IN MEMORIAL WHEREOF SHE ALSO LEFT AN ANNUITY OF FOUR POUNDS TO BE DISTRIBUTED TO YE POOR WITHIN THIS PARISH OF BROUGHAM EVERY 2ND DAY OF APRIL FOR EVER, UPON YE STONE TABLE HERE HARD BY. LAUS DEO.

my Lord for he was far kinder to me in all these businesses than I expected, and was very unwilling that the King should do me any public disgrace. (_Diary_, pp. 48–49)

On 20 January, Anne reports an equally dramatic formal session in which she was confronted by an awesome assemblage of power: the King, the Chief Justice, several peers holding court office, lawyers, the Cliffords, and Dorset: 'The King asked us all if we would submit to his judgment in this case. My Uncle _Cumberland_, my Coz. _Clifford_, and my Lord answered that they would, but I would never agree to it without _Westmoreland_ at which the King grew in a great chaff.' Anne read the outcome as a victory, in that she maintained her cause 'led miraculously by God's Providence'; and was saved from public disgrace when Dorset orchestrated her timely departure from the meeting (_Diary_, pp. 50–51). But the king's judgement some weeks later was a resounding defeat: it followed the terms of her father's will, giving the estates to the Cliffords, with reversion to Anne if the male line failed, and £20,000 in installments to Anne — which is to say, to her husband Dorset. However, the final £3,000 depended on her formal acceptance of this agreement, which she flatly refused. So the domestic conflicts continued: she often reports herself 'extremely melancholy and sad', or weeping, or having yet one more 'falling out about the land' with Dorset, who kept her short of cash and even cancelled her jointure in June 1617, restoring it only in 1623, the year before he died at age 35.[31]

John Foxe's female martyrs supply the paradigm for Anne Clifford's self-portrait in her _Diary_ as a loving wife who patiently endures great suffering at the hands of her husband and much of society, but adheres firmly to the right, supported by God 'that always helped me': 'Sometimes I had fair words from him and sometimes foul, but I took all patiently, and did strive to give him as much content and assurance of my love as I could possibly, yet I told him I would never part with _Westmoreland_ upon any condition whatever'. (_Diary_, p. 62). She accepts as facts of life that Dorset's interests and needs are quite different from her own; that his wife and daughter are a small part of his life; that he will have affairs (she takes note of two mistresses and intimates a homosexual relationship with a gentleman-servant);[32] and that his lamentable behaviour to her is authorized by his role as her husband and lord. She also seems to care for him, rejoicing in the occasions when he 'came to lie in my chamber', keeping her tenth anniversary 'as a day of jubilee', and this attachment heightens the emotional cost of resisting his wishes (_Diary_, pp. 58, 62, 88). Remarkably, as she struggles to confront and express these complex feelings, she also determines doggedly to look out for her own interests and those of her daughter. Interestingly

[31] _Diary_, pp. 52–56, 65, 68–72. Jointure properties were made over by the husband to the wife, to guarantee her a fixed income in widowhood.

[32] _Diary_, pp. 70–72, 80, 106. Aubrey notes (_Brief Lives_, p. 100) that Dorset was said to be Venetia Stanley's (later Digby) 'greatest gallant' and to have had 'one, if not more children by her'. Aubrey reports also that he settled on her an annuity of £500.

enough, she does not record a wish to give Dorset a son and heir: rather, as she affectionately records many small milestones and crises in her daughter's life, she seems to see herself responsible to a female line, replicating her own mother's efforts to secure a daughter's inheritance.[33]

On her occasional visits to London and the Court Anne records notable events — the imprisonment of the Somersets, the burning of the banqueting house at Whitehall, the elevation of Buckingham, the death of Queen Anne — but without much comment (*Diary*, pp. 84, 93–102). Chiefly she lived at Knole, the Dorset country house in Kent, occupied with reading, writing, needlework, cards, small exercises of local patronage, visits (including one from John Donne), and general domestic overseeing. At times the disparity between Dorset's situation and her own elicited poignant complaint:

All this time my Lord was in *London* where he had all and infinite great resort coming to him. He went much abroad to Cocking, to Bowling Alleys, to Plays and Horse Races, and commended by all the world. I stayed in the country having many times a sorrowful and heavy heart, and being condemned by most folks because I would not consent to the agreements, so as I may truly say, I am like an owl in the desert.[34]

Anne Clifford's *Diary* presents a self in process, constrained by powerful social forces but struggling toward definition. In it, she claims the importance of her own life, and highlights the factors that empower her: a strong maternal model and some sense of female community; a firm conviction that Divine Providence was engaged on her behalf; a stimulus to self-awareness and imagination through reading; and the act of writing itself, constructing self and world in language. The catalyst seems to have been struggle, leading her to see herself as a kind of female David taking on the Goliath of the patriarchal power structure to claim the rights of a daughter and preserve the interests of a female line. Her later exercise of those rights was due largely to her good luck in outlasting all the men who stood in her way, but the *Diary* records the emergence of a female self able to resist existing social norms and to imagine better ones. We find here not overt rebellion against patriarchy but a subversive re-writing in which Anne Clifford laid stubborn claim to a place of power within it.

Aemilia Lanyer was the self-proclaimed literary client of Margaret Clifford. Her 1611 title page further identifies her as a gentlewoman whose husband has some court connexions, 'Mistris Aemilia Lanyer, Wife to Captaine Alfonso Lanyer, servant to the Kings Majestie'. In the only modern edition of her poems (1978), A. L. Rowse urges the highly tenuous

---

[33] She records, for example, Margaret's fifth birthday, when Dorset 'caused her health to be drank throughout the house', and in the same month she began to sit for her portrait by Vansommer, *Diary*, pp. 104–05. See also pp. 51–54, 66, 72, 82, 110.

[34] *Diary*, p. 48. The Donne visit was from 20 to 27 July 1617, when he preached at Sevenoaks. He was reported to have said of her 'That she knew well how to discourse of all things, from Predestination to Slea-silk', Rainbowe, p. 39.

claim that she is the 'Dark Lady' of Shakespeare's sonnets.[35] The little we know about her is derived chiefly from notes made by the astrologer Simon Forman on her several visits to him. Her father was Baptista Bassano, one of Queen Elizabeth's Italian musicians; she was christened on 27 January 1569; her father died when she was seven, leaving her poorly provided for; and she was mistress for several years to Queen Elizabeth's Lord Chancellor, Lord Hunsdon.[36] Forman claims that she had a reputation for easy virtue, that her 1582 marriage to Alfonso Lanyer, musician to Elizabeth (and later James), was to cover a pregnancy; that her husband squandered her considerable fortune and failed to gain the knighthood he (and she) hoped for from his military expeditions.[37] After his death in 1613 Aemilia engaged in several lawsuits to retain a patent awarded to him; in 1617 she set up a school; and in 1645 she died, at the age of seventy-six.[38]

The title of Lanyer's volume promises, somewhat misleadingly, a collection of religious poetry, a genre thought especially appropriate for women writers: *Salve Deus Rex Judaeorum. Containing, 1. The Passion of Christ. 2. Eves Apologie in defence of Women. 3. The Teares of the Daughters of Jerusalem. 4. The Salutation and Sorrow of the Virgine Marie. With divers other things not unfit to be read.*[39] In fact, the volume contains several kinds of poems, which together offer a protofeminist defence of women and of Lanyer as woman poet. It begins with a series of dedications to royal and noble ladies, in different combinations in the nine extant copies, evidently for different presentation purposes. The most complete versions contain nine dedicatory poems, a prose dedication to the Countess of Cumberland, and a prose epistle 'To the Virtuous Reader'.[40] The

[35] *The Poems of Shakespeare's Dark Lady: Salve Deus Rex Judaeorum by Emilia Lanier*, edited by A. L. Rowse (London, 1978). The edition is based on the Bodleian copy, complete except for the Cookham poem, which is supplied from the British Library copy. Rowse also urges his thesis in *Sex and Society in Shakespeare's Age* (New York, 1974). The links to Shakespeare are very tenuous, even if we grant Rowse's questionable assumption that the sonnets are to be read as straightforward Shakespearian autobiography: the fact that Shakespeare's landlady also visited Forman; that the patron of Shakespeare's company was Lord Hunsdon, father of Lanyer's illegitimate son; and that Lanyer's dark Italian beauty, musical family, literary talent, and questionable moral character, fit the general description of the sonnet 'Dark Lady'.

[36] Rowse, *Sex and Society*, p. 102; *Poems of Shakespeare's Dark Lady*, p. 18.

[37] Forman's notes are from visits to him by Lanyer on 17 May, 3 June, and 16 June 1597, cited in Rowse, *Poems of Shakespeare's Dark Lady*, pp. 11–12, 18. He also recounts efforts to seduce her and implies some sexual contact, but this self-styled Casanova is not a wholly credible witness in such matters.

[38] *Calendar of State Papers Domestic*, 1634–35, pp. 516–17.

[39] The volume was entered in the Stationers' Register on 2 October 1610 by the bookseller, Richard Bonian, and the poems were probably written within a year or so of this date. It was issued twice in 1611, with minor changes in the imprint, and is now very rare. All citations are from the Huntington Library copy of the first issue (STC 15227) with the imprint in four lines, 'AT LONDON | Printed by Valentine Simmes for Richard Bonian and | are to be sold at his Shop in Paules Church- | yard. Anno 1611'.

[40] The British Library copy may be a unique book prepared for the Countess of Cumberland or the Countess of Dorset. It omits the Dedication to Arabella Stuart (probably because she had been taken into custody in March 1611 and sent to the Tower). It also omits the dedications to the Countesses of Kent, Pembroke, and Suffolk, perhaps so as to identify the volume yet more closely with the Countess of Cumberland and her daughter, and to present it only to the obvious Court Patrons: the Queen, the Princess Elizabeth, and the Countess of Bedford who was the Queen's most influential Lady-in-Waiting and the most important Jacobean literary patroness. The Epistle to the Reader is also omitted. The front matter is not reset: but the final sheets are shifted so that the dedications appear in the following order: the Queen, Princess Elizabeth, All Virtuous Ladies, the Countess of Bedford, the Countess of Dorset, the Countess of Cumberland.

title poem is a long meditation on the passion and death of Christ which in fact contains the three other seemingly separate poems listed on the title page, and which is itself enclosed within a frame of 776 lines (more than a third of the whole) comprising elaborate tributes to Margaret Clifford as imitator and spouse of the suffering Christ. The volume concludes with a country house poem, 'The Description of Cooke-ham'; that royal manor was held by Margaret Clifford's brother, William Russell of Thornhaugh, and was evidently occupied by her on occasion during her separation from her husband.[41] Lanyer's volume engages throughout with the ideology and institutions of patriarchy and patronage, re-imagining and re-writing them in feminist terms.

Given the lack of external evidence, what can we conclude about actual patron-client relationships between Lanyer and her several dedicatees? Some deductions are possible from the poems themselves, despite their hyperbole, since Lanyer would fail in her obvious bid for patronage if she were to falsify too outrageously the terms of a relationship. These dedications indicate that in 1611 Lanyer does not enjoy, and is seeking, some entré into Jacobean court circles. The opening poem to Queen Anne recalls nostalgically (and hopefully) the happier Elizabethan times, when 'great *Elizaes* favour blest my youth' (l. 50); that addressing the Countess Dowager of Kent, Susan (Bertie) Wingfield as 'the Mistris of my youth, | The noble guide of my ungovern'd dayes' indicates that she served as a girl in the Countess's household;[42] that to Arabella Stuart claims a long-standing but distant relationship: 'Great learned Ladie, whom I long have knowne, | And yet not knowne so much as I desired'.[43] She does not claim personal acquaintance with Princess Elizabeth, nor with the two major patronesses of the age, the Countesses of Pembroke and Bedford, nor with the Countess of

---

[41] Cookham, a manor belonging to the crown from before the Conquest until 1818, was annexed to Windsor Castle in 1540. It was evidently granted or leased to Lord Russell and occupied by the Countess of Cumberland at some periods during her estrangement from her husband in the years before his death in 1605, and perhaps also during the early period of her widowhood. Anne Clifford's diary records a visit to Cookham in 1603 (p. 15) but there are no entries for the relevant years, 1603 to 1609. We do not know just when or why or for how long Lanyer was at Cookham.

[42] Susan Bertie's first husband was Reynold Grey of Wrest, *de jure* Earl of Kent, who died in 1573. In 1581 she married Sir John Wingfield of Withcall, a member of the Leicester–Sidney faction (knighted by Leicester at Zutphen, one of the twelve honour guard at Sidney's funeral, and a participant in the Cadiz expeditions). Lanyer probably resided with her as a young girl, but certainly before her own marriage in 1592. Lanyer is clearly disingenuous when she disclaims (ll. 43–48) any thought of 'former gaine' or 'future profit' from the Countess. The dedication 'To the Ladie Susan, Countesse Dowager of Kent, and daughter to the Duchesse of Suffolke', associates her with her famous mother whose flight and wanderings with her family during the Marian persecutions were incorporated in Foxe's *Book of Martyrs*. Susan was born in 1554, only a few months before that flight, and Susan herself accompanied her second husband, Sir John Wingfield on his military expeditions, briefly sharing his imprisonment in Breda.

[43] Arabella Stuart, first cousin to James I, was a constant focus for political intrigue during the final years of Elizabeth's reign and the early years of James's, because of her strong title to the throne derived from Margaret, eldest sister of Henry VIII. Forbidden to marry without the King's permission, she did so secretly in July 1610 to William Seymour, grandson of Catherine Grey, an alliance which strengthened her title. When the secret became known, she was taken into custody on 3 March 1611, and after an abortive attempt to escape in June 1611, was lodged in the Tower.

Suffolk, Katherine Howard.[44] On the other hand, the many addresses to and praises of Margaret Clifford throughout the volume identify her as the book's primary patron and audience; they testify to some formal patronage in the past, and to Lanyer's sense of her as the best present hope. However exaggerated, there is clearly some basis for Lanyer's claim that she lived (however briefly) with the Countess and her daughter at Cookham, and that she wrote 'Cooke-ham' at the Countess's behest: 'Those praisefull lines of that delightfull place, | As you commaunded me in that fair night'.[45] Margaret Clifford is also given a unique prose dedication, and proclaimed as the only source and inspiration of the passion poem: 'Great Ladie of my heart . . . . You are the Articke Starre that guides my hand | All what I am, I rest at your command'.[46]

But whatever actual patronage Lanyer may have enjoyed, her dedicatory poems re-write the institution of patronage in female terms, transforming the relationships assumed in the male patronage system into an ideal community. Here the patrons' virtue descends in the female line, from mothers to daughters — Queen Anne and Princess Elizabeth, Margaret and Anne Clifford, Catherine and Susan Bertie, Katherine Howard and her daughters — and redounds upon their female poet-client and celebrant Lanyer. Though Lanyer often excuses her poems as faulty and unlearned by reason of her sex, she finds justification for undertaking what is 'seldome seene, | A Womans writing of divinest things'[47] in the fact that they celebrate divine and female goodness. Since religious poetry is often considered the highest genre,[48] this claim revalues the restriction of women writers to religious subjects, even as her celebration of the several noblewomen for their heroic virtue, extraordinary learning, devotion to the Muses, and high poetic achievement implicitly undermines patriarchal ideology.

The dedication to Queen Anne establishes this community. Its Queen is another Juno, Venus, Pallas, and Cynthia, attracting Muses and Artists to her throne, and its female poet derives her poetics not from classical learning but from 'Mother' Nature, source of all the arts:

---

[44] Later Elizabeth of Bohemia, 'The Winter Queen'. Lanyer honours her primarily as namesake of the great Queen Elizabeth; in 1613 she married Frederick Henry, Elector Palatine. The Countess of Pembroke sister of Sir Philip Sidney and Sir Robert Sidney (of Penshurst), wife of Henry Herbert, third Earl of Pembroke, managed the publication of Sidney's works, wrote some original poetry, and extended hospitality and patronage at her Wilton estate to many writers. Lucy, Countess of Bedford was patron and friend to Donne and Jonson, among many others. Franklin B. Williams, Jr's *Index of Dedications and Commendatory Verses in English Books Before 1641* (London, 1962) lists more dedications and praises to these two noblewomen than to any other persons except members of the royal family. Katherine, Countess of Suffolk was wife to the wealthy and ambitious Lord Admiral and Lord Chamberlain of the Household, Thomas Howard; she alone seems out of place in Lanyer's company of good women, though she and her husband were not yet notorious for the rapacity which led in 1618 to their disgrace and imprisonment for extortion and embezzlement.
[45] 'Cooke-ham', ll. 1–12; 'Salve Deus', stanza 3.
[46] 'Salve Deus', sig. Hv.
[47] 'To the Queenes most excellent Majestie', ll. 3–4.
[48] As, for example, in Sidney's *Defence of Poetry* (London, 1595), sig. C1v–C2; Puttenham, *The Arte of English Poesie* (London, 1589), pp. 22–23.

Not that I Learning to my selfe assume,
Or that I would compare with any man:
    But as they are Scholers, and by Art do write,
    So Nature yeelds my Soule a sad delight.

And since all Arts at first from Nature came,
That goodly Creature, Mother of perfection,
Whom *Joves* almighty hand at first did frame,
Taking both her and hers in his protection:
    Why should not She now grace my barren Muse,
    And in a Woman all defects excuse.

                                    (l. 147)

The other dedications elaborate the would-be patrons' qualities and Lanyer's poetics. She offers her 'first fruits of a womans wit' to Princess Elizabeth, whose 'faire eyes farre better Bookes have seene'; she apostrophizes Arabella Stuart as 'Great learned Ladie ... | so well accompan'ed | With *Pallas*, and the Muses'; she proclaims the Countess of Kent a glass manifesting all virtues to the young Aemilia; and she praises the Countess of Bedford (as Ben Jonson did)[49] for her Knowledge, Virtue and 'clear Judgement'. She urges the Countess of Suffolk to guide her 'noble daughters' in meditating on Lanyer's Passion poem (ll. 49–68), asserting categorically that her poetic vocation and achievement are from God: 'his powre hath given me powre to write, | A subject fit for you to looke upon' (ll. 7, 13–14).

And she appropriates to herself and the Countess of Cumberland the conventional eternizing power of poetry, claiming that her poems 'may remaine in the world many yeares longer than your Honour, or my selfe can live, to be a light unto those that come after'.[50]

Two of the dedications make bolder claims. The longest is a dream-vision narrative describing Lanyer's imagined visit to the Countess of Pembroke, enthroned in Honour's chair with saints, muses, and classical deities singing her Psalm versions and proclaiming her (amazingly enough) 'far before' her brother Sir Philip Sidney 'For virtue, wisedome, learning, dignity' (ll. 147, 151–52). Waking, Lanyer resolves to present her 'unlearned lines' to that better poet, expecting her to value them as 'flowres that spring from virtues ground' and so to recognize Lanyer as her successor in a female poetic line. Her final dedication is a long verse letter praising Anne Clifford as worthy heir to her mother's excellences, virtues, and stewardship of the poor, which, Lanyer intimates, might well be extended to herself. Alluding both to Anne's loss of her lands, and her own loss of contact with Anne, now become Countess of Dorset, Lanyer contrasts male succession through aristocratic titles with a female succession grounded upon virtue and holiness, drawing bold egalitarian conclusions:

---

[49] Cf. Jonson, Epigram 76 which ascribes to her 'a learned, and a manly soule'.
[50] *Salve Deus*, sig. ev.

> What difference was there when the world began,
> Was it not Virtue that distinguisht all?
> All sprang but from one woman and one man,
> Then how doth Gentry come to rise and fall?
> Or who is he that very rightly can
> Distinguish of his birth, or tell at all
>   In what meane state his Ancestors have bin,
>   Before some one of worth did honour win.
>
>   (l. 49)

Lanyer's volume as a whole is conceived as a Book of Good Women,[51] fusing religious devotion with an argument proclaiming the superiority of women to men in moral and spiritual matters and so denying any grounds for their subordination. A prose 'Epistle to the Vertuous Reader' extends the community constructed in the dedications to 'all virtuous Ladies and Gentlewomen of this kingdome' (the potential readership for Lanyer's poems) and makes a vigorous contribution to the centuries-old *querelle des femmes*,[52] in its strident Jacobean embodiment. Denouncing women who speak 'unadvisedly against the rest of their sexe', and 'evil-disposed men who doe like Vipers deface the wombes wherein they were bred', Lanyer marshalls the familiar biblical examples not only to demonstrate women's natural abilities and moral goodness, but also their God-given call to exercise military and political power:

[God] gave power to wise and virtuous women, to bring down their pride and arrogancie. As was cruell *Cesarus* by the discreet counsell of noble *Deborah*, Judge and Prophetesse of Israel: and resolution of *Jael* wife of *Heber* the Kenite: wicked *Haman*, by the divine prayers and prudent proceedings of beautiful *Hester*: blasphemous *Holofernes*, by the invincible courage, rare wisdome, and confident carriage of *Judeth*: & the unjust Judges, by the innocency of chast *Susanna*: with infinite others, which for brevitie sake I will omit. (sig. f 3v)

She then details, with rhetorical force and flair, the singular honours accorded to women by Christ, who chose, 'without the assistance of man ... to be begotten of a woman, borne of a woman, nourished of a woman, obedient to a woman; and that he healed women, pardoned women, comforted women: ... after his resurrection, appeared first to a woman, sent a woman to declare his most glorious resurrection to the rest of his Disciples' (sig. f 3v). In Lanyer's imaginative vision, as in Anne Clifford's, God testifies for women and takes their part.

Lanyer's Passion poem proposes Christ as the standard that validates the various kinds of female goodness her poems treat, and condemns the

---

[51] Lanyer may or may not have known or known about Boccaccio's *De mulieribus claris*, Chaucer's *Legend of Good Women*, or Christine de Pisan's *Livre de la Cité des Dames*, published in 1521 in an English translation by Brian Anslay.

[52] For an account of and bibliography pertaining to this controversy through 1568 see Francis Lee Utley, *The Crooked Rib* (Columbus, 1944); for discussion and listing of later titles see Suzanne W. Hull, *Chaste, Silent & Obedient: English Books for Women 1475–1640* (San Marino, 1982); for an account of the Jacobean controversy and the principal texts, see Woodbridge, *Women and the English Renaissance*.

multiple forms of masculine evil. This poem also undermines some fundamental assumptions of patriarchy, in that it presents Christ's Passion from
the vantage point of good women, past and present. Lanyer as woman poet
recounts and interprets the story. The Countess of Cumberland is the
subject of the extended frame, as chief reader and meditator on the Passion,
as well as exemplary image and imitator of her suffering Saviour. And the
narrative celebrates the good women associated with the Passion, setting
them in striking contrast to the weak and evil men: the cowardly apostles, the
traitor Judas, 'wicked *Caiphas*', 'Proud *Pontius Pilate*', scoffing Herod, the
tormenting soldiers, the jeering crowds.

This theme is sounded first with Pilate's wife, whose plea to save Jesus
leads into Lanyer's remarkable apologia for Eve. She meant no harm in
taking the apple, her guilt was far less than that of the stronger and wiser
Adam, and her gift of the apple to Adam indeed makes her the source of
men's knowledge. Pilate's wife and Eve are taken as representatives of
womankind, while Pilate and Adam represent men:

> Our Mother *Eve*, who tasted of the Tree,
> Giving to *Adam* what shee held most deare,
> Was simply good, and had no powre to see,
> The after-comming harme did not appeare:
> . . . .
> Her weakenesse did the Serpents words obay,
> But you in malice Gods deare Sonne betray.
>
> Whom, if unjustly you condemne to die,
> Her sinne was small, to what you doe commit.
>
> (sig. D-Dv)

Lanyer hereby turns her somewhat dubious exegesis to impressive account,
demonstrating how susceptible the biblical narratives are to very different
interpretations, depending on the interests involved. She concludes with a
forthright declaration of gender equality, denouncing hierarchy and men's
unjust claim to rule:

> Then let us have our Libertie againe,
> And challendge to your selves no Sov'raigntie;
> You came not in the world without our paine,
> Make that a barre against your crueltie;
> Your fault being greater, why should you disdaine
> Our beeing your equals, free from tyranny?
> > If one weake woman simply did offend,
> > This sinne of yours, hath no excuse, nor end.
>
> To which (poore soules) we never gave consent,
> Witnesse thy wife (O *Pilate*) speakes for all.
>
> (sig. D2)

Next, she holds forth the Daughters of Jerusalem as examples of women's
mercy, opposed to men's fierce cruelty. Then comes a long meditation on the
grief-stricken Mother of Jesus as 'Queene of Woman-kind' and sharer in the
Incarnation and Redemption, followed by an account of still other good

women who brought balm to anoint the dead Christ. The long coda associates Margaret Clifford with the Bride of Canticles, as Spouse of Christ and figure for the Church, setting her above all the great women of secular history, and with the greatest saints and martyrs of both sexes, by reason of the love, afflictions, and victories over sin that so closely associate her with Christ.

Lanyer's 'Description of Cooke-ham', in 210 lines of pentameter couplets, may have been written and was certainly published before Jonson's 'To Penshurst', commonly identified as the first English country house poem.[53] Jonson's poem established the terms of a genre that celebrates patriarchy: Robert Sidney's Penshurst is a quasi-Edenic place whose beauty and harmony are centred in and preserved by its Lord, who 'dwells' permanently within it. In sharpest contrast, Lanyer's country-house poem describes a paradise inhabited solely by women: Margaret Clifford who is the centre and sustainer of its beauty and delights, her young virgin daughter Anne, and Aemilia Lanyer, portraying the destruction of this edenic place when its Lady departs (presumably to her widow's dower residences).[54] The controlling topos is the valediction to a place, recalling such classical sources as Virgil's First Eclogue.

An elegiac tone, sustained throughout, is established in the opening lines, as Lanyer bids farewell to the place she associates with her religious conversion and the confirmation of her vocation as poet:

> Farewell (sweet *Cooke-ham*) where I first obtain'd
> Grace from that Grace where perfit Grace remain'd;
> And where the Muses gave their full consent,
> I should have powre the virtuous to content:

In this country-house poem the house itself is barely mentioned: it belongs after all to the Crown, not to the Countess. But the estate is described at length in evocative pastoral imagery, as it responds to Margaret Clifford's presence according to the seasonal round. When she arrives it becomes a *locus amœnus*, putting on all its Spring and Summer loveliness:

> The Walkes put on their summer Liveries,
> And all things else did hold like similies:
> The Trees with leaves, with fruits, with flowers clad,
> Embrac'd each other, seeming to be glad,
> Turning themselves to beauteous Canopies,
> To shade the bright Sunne from your brighter eies:

[53] Jonson's 'To Penshurst' was written sometime before the death of Prince Henry in 1612 (l. 77), but it was first published in the Folio of 1616. Lanyer's poem was written sometime after Anne Clifford's marriage to Richard Sackville on 25 February 1609 (she is referred to as Dorset, the title her husband inherited two days after the marriage) and before the volume was registered with the Stationer on 2 October 1610. If Jonson's poem was written first Lanyer might have seen it in manuscript. Since the Passion poem alludes to the Countess's widowhood, and contains an apology for the author's delay in fulfilling her charge to write about Cookham, it was evidently written after 30 October 1605 and before the Cookham poem.

[54] The valedictory mode of this poem suggests a permanent rather than a seasonal departure, probably related to the Countess's change of residence after she was widowed.

> The cristall Streames with silver spangles graced,
> While by the glorious Sunne they were embraced:
> The little Birds in chirping notes did sing,
> To entertain both You and that sweet Spring.
>
> (l. 21)

Other elements of nature welcome her with an obsequiousness like that of the Penshurst fish and game offering themselves to capture.[55] The hills descend humbly that the Countess may tread on them, the gentle winds enhance her pleasure in the woods by their 'sad murmure'; the rivers deliver up all their fish upon seeing this 'Phoenix'; the birds and animals sport before her. And here, as in the other Eden, the focus of interest is a 'stately Tree', a massive Oak which brings the Countess a view of 'thirteene shires' (if not of all the world) but no temptation, only delights, contentment, and a stimulus to meditate on the creatures and the scriptures.

But this female Eden is already lost. Lanyer complains that Anne Clifford, now Countess of Dorset, is separated from her by 'Unconstant Fortune' (l. 102), and recalls nostalgically her participation in the young Anne's 'sports' at Cookham. The passage obviously exaggerates the intimacy (Lanyer was twenty years older than Anne Clifford and so hardly her playmate) but this timelessness and classlessness is consonant with the Edenic, pastoral ethos imagined for the place. The closing lines fuse pathetic fallacy with seasonal changes in autumn and winter, as (with the ladies' departure) all the beauties of this *locus amœnus* wither in desolation:

> Those pretty Birds that wonted were to sing,
> Now neither sing, nor chirp, nor use their wing;
> But with their tender feet on some bare spray,
> Warble forth sorrow, and their owne dismay.
> . . . .
> Each arbour, banke, each seate, each stately tree,
> Lookes bare and desolate now for want of thee;
> Turning greene tresses into frostie gray,
> While in cold griefe they wither all away.
> The Sunne grew weake, his beames no comfort gave,
> While all greene things did make the earth their grave:
> Each briar, each bramble, when you went away,
> Caught fast your clothes, thinking to make you stay:
> Delightful Eccho wonted to reply
> To our last words, did now for sorrow die:

---

[55] Cf. Jonson, 'To Penshurst', ll. 29–38:

> The painted partridge lies in every field,
>   And for thy mess is willing to be killd.
> And if the high-swoll'n Medway fail thy dish,
>   Thou hast thy ponds that pay thee tribute fish:
> Fat, aged carps, that run into thy net;
>   And pikes, now weary their own kind to eat,
> As loath the second draught or cast to stay,
>   Officiously, at first, themselves betray;
> Bright eels, that emulate them, and leap on land
>   Before the fisher, or into his hand.

> The house cast off each garment that might grace it,
> Putting on Dust and Cobwebs to deface it.
> All desolation then there did appeare,
> When you were going whom they held so deare

(l. 183)

From this ravaged Eden it is a female couple (or rather trio) who depart: the Countess called away by the 'occasions' attendant upon her widowhood; the virgin daughter to her marriage; Lanyer to social decline. Lanyer offers her poem as 'This last farewell to *Cooke-ham*' (l. 205), suggesting that none of them will return to this happy garden state in which women lived without mates, but found contentment and delight in nature, God, and female companionship.

Lanyer's poems provoke many questions we do not yet know enough to answer: What influences and circumstances led her to publish her poetry? How much patronage did she enjoy from Margaret Clifford, or from others? How was her book received? Did she write anything else? And especially, how should we account for the feminist thrust of the volume, which re-writes patriarchy by revising the fundamental Christian myths: Eden, the Passion of Christ, the Communion of Saints, with women at their centre. In 'Cooke-ham' a female Eden suffers its Fall because the structures of a male social order force its female inhabitants to abandon it. In the Passion poem women — from Eve to Herod's wife to Mary to the Countess of Cumberland — are shown to be Christ's truest imitators and apostles. In the dedicatory poems a female lineage of virtue extends from mother to daughter, producing a contemporary community of good women which reaches from Catherine Bertie, Protestant fugitive in Mary Tudor's reign, to the young Anne Clifford. These poems also re-write patronage in female terms, imagining for the poet Lanyer a family of maternal and sisterly patronesses who will honour and reward her celebrations of them and of the female sex.

Of course nothing visibly happened to patriarchy or to male patronage networks as a result of Clifford's or Lanyer's re-writing. But these women's texts themselves display the subversive power of the imagination; they enact resistance and challenge to oppressive institutions, not meek acceptance, and they move beyond dominant gender ideologies to more enabling conceptions. We will be able to read these texts better, as literary works and as cultural documents, when we have progressed further with the excavation and study of texts by early modern women. And we will be able to formulate more precisely our theories of gender, of subjectivity, of cultural containment and subversion in that period when we take such women's texts into account. The re-writings we find may continue to surprise us.

Saving the King's Friend and Redeeming Appearances: Dr Donne Constructs a Scriptural Model for Patronage

M. L. DONNELLY

Kansas State University

In the early spring of 1617, after a long career of suing for favour and seeking the notice of influential people, the experienced courtier John Donne, now a preacher of the Gospel, reflected on the patronage relationship. Given his intense personal experience of frustration and disappointment in seeking advancement, his thoughts on this central institution of his society would hold great interest for us in any case. This occasion holds particular interest, however, for on the twenty-fourth day of March, 1617 [N.S.], Donne's thoughts on patronage took public form in the great outdoor pulpit at Paul's Cross, at the heart of London's life. He was preaching on the King's Day, the anniversary of James's accession, presumably by royal command (although James himself was not present, having departed for Scotland the week before). His audience included, as well as the curious populace, the great — the Lords of the Council and the new Lord Keeper, Francis Bacon, his acquaintance, who was himself a long-suffering seeker of patronage and royal favour. Donne had been in orders a little over two years.[1] His opening of the sacred text reflected deep meditation on the possible spiritual significance of worldly relations, and at the same time hinted at the pressure of personal and perhaps unconscious associations. His remarks on that March day mobilized a cluster of ideas in Biblical analogies and tropes of divinity, collecting echoes of the more or less desperate and eagerly straining letters and verses of his days of secular application and ambition. In this essay I would like to follow some of these connexions and associations from the 1617 sermon back through his earlier, secular writings and forward through later sermons and poems, to shed light on his conception and rationalization of the patronage relationship.

Dr Donne took as his text Proverbs 22.11: 'He that loveth pureness of heart, for the grace of his lips, the King shall be his friend'. As he handles it, Donne makes this text figure in its essentials an idealized relation of patron and suitor, patron and client. The language of grace and calling evoked by the text fits Donne's sense of his worldly situation and prospects, no less than it defines his spiritual condition. Analysing the words of the passage, he

---

[1] Donne was ordained 23 January 1614/15, at the age of forty-two.

meditates at length on the character, seat, acquisition, and retention of purity as a qualification for the recipient of favour, and on false pretenders to purity. He considers love corruptible, subject to satiety, sliding and misdirected, and love incorruptible, ever growing, and rightly placed. He reflects on the gifts and virtues that merit preferment, especially on that service to the State which he makes a precedent condition for favour, and on the exalted significance of the king's title itself, and his friendship.

The general circumstances of Donne's career freight this text with more significance and anxiety than we might at first imagine.[2] From the vantage-point of the first rungs of a ladder of preferment (though not the ladder to secular place and influence that he had initially sought), favoured with the king's grace after years of frustration, Donne seems in this performance to rationalize his place to himself, a place subject to the operations of power in his society. At the same time, in a counter-assertion of conceptual power, he presents to his auditory a moralized model of patronage, one that is, of course, self-affirming. That such a model should borrow a theological armature is, in a sermon, unsurprising. However, examination of other texts, prose and verse letters to friends, poems addressed to patrons or potential patrons, texts written before Donne took orders, and written out of a variety of circumstances and moods, suggest that the attempt is not anomalous, or conditioned simply by its professional context. That is, Donne habitually tried to lay hold of the patterns of worldly success in his culture by casting his reflections on politics and society into theological language: the vocabulary of the miserable sinner redeemed by grace, the syntax of salvation by the inscrutable election of an all-powerful God upon whose will and choice all things turned. A brief review of Donne's own worldly situation and long-frustrated hopes helps us to understand his seizure of theological doctrines of the soul's career as a means of representing worldly advancement or failure. Passages in Donne's life before ordination illuminate the nature of the poet's fears and disappointments, while the texts recording those passages trace the persistence of tropes taken from divinity as a way of translating, representing, or realizing the meaning of that experience.

At the beginning of 1602, the announcement of his clandestine marriage to Ann More lost Donne his secretaryship to Sir Thomas Egerton, Lord Keeper

---

[2] See the remarks of George R. Potter and Evelyn M. Simpson in their *Introductions* to Volume 1 of the *Sermons*: 'His earliest extant sermons have special interest to a student of his career because they reveal the newly made clergyman feeling his way, walking delicately to adapt his discourse to the people and authorities that would judge it and to avoid treading on sensitive toes. They reveal, too, his very natural use of certain ideas he had developed years before his ordination. . . . He was also keenly alive to the all too human mixture of personalities and politics in that church's affairs, and to the necessity of being not only harmless as the dove but also politically wise as the serpent if he was to achieve success in the profession he had adopted' (*The Sermons of John Donne*, 4 vols (Berkeley, Los Angeles, and London, 1953; reprinted 1984), I, 113–14).

of the Great Seal.[3] The loss of that place with its practically assured promise of further advancement at court or in the law meant disaster for a promising career. Having been virtually created from nothing, from the blank prospects of his recusant background, by his diligent and vigorous pursuit of notice, and by Egerton's favour, Donne saw himself at his dismissal dashed into nonentity. From that time until his finally agreeing to enter the ministry of the established church some dozen years later, Donne's energies were consumed in suits and applications, largely fruitless, or in temporary employment which held out either no prospects of advancement, or empty ones. In an unsuccessful appeal to Egerton to be restored to his place, written at the very beginning of his disgrace, Donne's foreboding anticipation of the extent of his ruined state had proved too accurate: 'To seek preferment here with any but your Lordship were a madnes. . . . I have therfore no way before me; but must turn back to your Lordship who knowes that redemption was no less worke than creation'.[4]

Theological conceits like this rueful analogy of the divine work of creation and redemption with the rescue of his worldly hopes come naturally to Donne in situations in which he feels the stakes are high. From his earliest experiences his mind was imbued with the matter of theological doctrine and controversy. His childhood and youth were spent in the fervently Catholic atmosphere of his family's signal adherence to the old faith, he 'being derived from such a stocke and race, as, I beleeve, no family, (which is not of farre larger extent, and greater branches,) hath endured and suffered more in their persons and fortunes, for obeying the Teachers of Romane Doctrine, then it hath done'.[5] His earliest tutors, secured by his mother's care and diligence, were presumably learned Catholics.[6] When as a young man he came to deciding the great question of which church he would embrace, and faced the wrenching prospect of apostasizing from the faith of his fathers, he commenced, according to Walton, a strenuous programme of study to convince his mind of the truth, beginning 'About the nineteenth year of his age . . . seriously to survey, and consider the Body of Divinity, as it was then controverted betwixt the *Reformed* and the *Roman Church*'.[7]

Walton records as one evidence of Donne's diligence in this research that 'about the twentieth year of his age, [he] did shew the then *Dean* of *Gloucester* . . . all the Cardinals works [those of Bellarmine] marked with many weighty observations under his own hand' (Walton, p. 26). Donne's immersion in the study of canon and civil laws during his impecunious years also receives

[3] On the possible advantages accruing to the lost position, see R. C. Bald, *John Donne: A Life* (Oxford, 1970), pp. 93–98. The rise and success of the secretaries who served the Cecils provide further illustration of what Donne could expect; see A. G. R. Smith, 'The Secretariats of the Cecils, circa 1580–1612', *English Historical Review*, 83 (1968), 481–504.

[4] A. J. Kempe, *The Loseley Manuscripts*, 1835, pp. 341–42, cited in Bald, *A Life*, p. 138.

[5] John Donne, *Pseudo-Martyr*, 1610, 'Advertisement to the Reader', cited in R. C. Bald, *Life*, p. 23.

[6] John Carey, *John Donne: Life, Mind and Art* (London, 1981), p. 19; Bald, *Life*, pp. 38–40.

[7] Izaak Walton, *The Lives of John Donne, Sir Henry Wotton, Richard Hooker, George Herbert, and Robert Sanderson* (London, 1927; reprinted 1966), p. 25.

mention from Walton; he testifies to the interest taken in the young man on account of his 'Education and Abilities' by Bishop Thomas Morton, a leading Anglican controversialist and a competent judge of learning, orthodoxy, and skill in disputation.[8] Donne pressed his knowledge of Catholic scholastic thought and the disputed points of divinity into the service of his ambition to attract the attention of the king and those in high places. At Mitcham, having 'destined some days to a constant study of some points of Controversie betwixt the *English* and *Roman Church*; and especially those of *Supremacy* and *Allegiance*' (Walton, p. 38), he employed what he had learned to support the imposition of the Oath of Supremacy (*Pseudo-Martyr*, published in 1610), and to satirize the Jesuits and their activities and claims (*Ignatius his Conclave*, published in 1611). The unpublished and potentially scandalous *Biathanatos* is also a product of his study of civil and canon law, and demonstrates his easy command of the techniques of casuistry and scholastic definition and reasoning.[9] The dyer's hand is subdued to the stuff it works in. Donne's use of the conceptions of religion and the distinctions of 'school divinity' to make sense of experience, far from being the strained product of a desire to shock or a self-conscious affectation, amounts to a habit of mind.[10]

The tone in which he couches comparisons drawn from scholastic divinity and scriptural erudition varies greatly, of course: the same conceit which sounds earnest and profound in one context can sound in another frivolous and even blasphemous. In his letter to Egerton, where the desperation of his plight and the earnestness of his plea no less than the dignity of the recipient would seem to preclude flippancy, the language of religious doctrine articulates in a characteristically hyperbolic way a real, felt likeness. If asked point-blank whether he seriously equated the dashing of his worldly hopes with the damnation of his soul, Donne would undoubtedly have answered that the equation ludicrously over-estimated this world and its values. However, the comparison belies the cool distancing of worldly ambition which conscious doctrinal reflection would entail. It says, in effect, that the greatest misfortune imaginable, the state of lost and fallen souls, is the only conception tremendous enough to convey the wretchedness and desperation of his present worldly condition.

Metaphor taken from the great mysteries of faith affords a particularly weighty closure, wrapping up an argument or clinching an assertion. Comparing Egerton's power to effect Donne's happiness to the divine power of creation and redemption not only represents the intensity of Donne's

---

[8] Walton, pp. 35, 32–35; compare Bald, *A Life*, pp. 202–12.

[9] Bald, *A Life*, p. 200. For further treatment of medieval influences on Donne's thought, see M. P. Ramsay, *Doctrines Medievales chez Donne* (Oxford, 1917), and Louis I. Bredvold, 'The Religious Thought of Donne in Relation to Medieval and Later Traditions', in *Studies in Shakespeare, Milton, and Donne by members of the English Department of the University of Michigan* (Ann Arbor, 1925), pp. 193–232.

[10] Compare Evelyn Simpson, *A Study of the Prose Works of John Donne*, second edition (Oxford, 1948), p. 297.

personal anxiety to his correspondent; the comparison also works to flatter and persuade the person addressed through its attribution of godlike power and its implicit appeal to godlike mercy and beneficence. A similar theological comparison asserting the writer's helplessness and appealing to the mercy of the addressee occurs in a letter to Sir George More. Again, the desperate condition of the sinful soul provides the ground for comparison. Attempting to clear himself of aspersions cast on his character by gossips after his marriage became known, Donne wrote to his irate father-in-law:

as that fault which was layd to me of having deceived some gentlewomen before, and that of loving a corrupt religion, are vanishd and smoakd away (as I assure myself owt of theyr weaknes they are), and that as the devyll in the article of our death takes the advantage of our weaknes and fear, to aggravate our sinns to our conscience, so some uncharitable malice hath presented my debts doble at least.[11]

By this comparison, he at once associates his calumniators with the devil, and himself with a wretch on his deathbed, overcome by debility and terror. The trope nicely combines a vivid realization of Donne's abject dependence on his father-in-law's judgement and a flattering insinuation that Sir George's mercy, like his power, might be God-like.

Repeated use of analogy drawn from religious doctrine, especially when the conceit occurs in a rhetorically pivotal position in different works, gives greater significance to the repeated idea. In contrast to the occasional witty religious reference used once or twice, repeated and stressed conceits and the doctrines they embody must constitute for Donne a particularly satisfying or *convincing* representation of the order of things. The direct comparison of the work of creation to the work of salvation used to close the appeal to Egerton was just such a favourite analogy. So persistently did it occur to Donne and so striking was his use of it that, years after hearing the comparison asserted, Richard Gibson in 1671 writes to Pepys that, reading in *Cabala* (1654) a letter of Somerset's from 1616, he is reminded 'of a Speech of Dr Donn's Deane of St Paules in a Sermon there, vizt, that ye Goodness of God was not soe much seene in our Creation as Redemption, nor soe much that wee are his, as that nothing can take us out of his hands'.[12] Donne's memorable glorification of God's goodness in this comparison is exacted on the one hand by admiration of the immense power and beneficence that created us of nothing and redeemed us from vileness, and on the other by the speaker's

[11] Cited in Bald, p. 7, from Kempe, p. 334.
[12] Quoted in the 1654 edition of *Cabala*, p. 3; Gibson's remark is cited from Bodleian Library, MS Rawl. A174 fol. 372, dated 15 August 1671, and quoted in Bald, p. 412, n. 3. Given Donne's connexion with Somerset's patronage before the latter's fall, it may not be fanciful to suggest Donne as the source for Somerset's conceit, just as Goodyer later used phrases and whole passages from Donne's letters in his own suits and correspondence: see Stanley Johnson's 'Sir Henry Goodere and Donne's Letters', *MLN*, 63 (1948), 38–43, and Bald, *A Life*, pp. 166–68. Indeed, Donne uses a comparison of creation and resurrection in a letter to Somerset, then Viscount Rochester, in the summer of 1613, though in this instance, the ground of comparison is not the goodness of the act, but its difficulty, and resurrection is declared easier than creation *ab nihilo*: see *Letters to Severall Persons of Honour* (1651), facsimile reproduction with introduction by M. Thomas Hester (Delmar, New York, 1977), pp. 290–91.

desperate hunger for assurance that he truly partakes of this grace, that his salvation is no less sure than his creation, and cannot be rescinded or lost.

A glance at the entries in Troy D. Reeves's *Index to Topics*[13] in the Sermons suggests the importance of the topic of Grace for Donne as preacher. Donne's interest long predates his ordination, however. Among the divine analogies illuminating secular poetic contexts ever since Donne's earliest surviving experiments in verse, the idea of Grace is prominent from the beginning.

Characteristically, Donne imagines Grace operating upon nonentity. In relation to Grace, he habitually groups reflections on being saved or redeemed to life from death or nothingness with conceits of imputed merits that cover blackest sin and render the redeemed acceptable to judgement.[14] In both 'The Storme' and 'The Calme', associated with the Island Expedition in August 1597, Donne toys with the concept of nothingness which haunted him throughout his life. Closely related to that concern is the religious application of the idea that a gracious judge can give value to that which in its own nature is valueless or nothing, simply by imputing value that the judge commands.

'The Storme' opens by twisting the conventional conceit that friends are one being into an assertion of nonentity: 'Thou which art I, ('tis nothing to be soe) ...'.[15] Donne proceeds to render self-deprecation the ground of heightened praise of his friend:

> ... a hand, or eye
> By *Hilliard* drawne, is worth an history,
> By a worse painter made; and (without pride)
> When by thy judgment they are dignifi'd,
> My lines are such: 'Tis the preheminence
> Of friendship onely to'impute excellence.
>
> (l. 3)

The friend's acceptance of Donne's friendship is hyperbolically praised by invoking the essentially religious ideas of the sinner's worthlessness and God's graceful imputation of value to the wretched sinner. Climactically in the poem, another creative, redemptive act of grace is called for:

> All things are one, and that one none can be,
> Since all formes, uniforme deformity
> Doth cover, so that wee, except God say
> Another *Fiat*, shall have no more day.
>
> (l. 69)

In 'The Calme', Donne plays with scholastic definitions of animal life in terms of appetite and aversion to prove the non-being of the becalmed mariners (ll. 45–56). Much of the descriptive strategy of both poems turns on

---

[13] Volume 3 of *Index to the Sermons of John Donne* (Salzburg, Austria: Salzburg Studies in English Literature: Elizabethan and Renaissance Studies, no. 95, 1981).
[14] On Donne's obsession with nothingness and the annihilation of personality and of qualities, see John Carey in *John Donne: Life, Mind and Art*, passim, especially Chapter 6, pp. 169–74.
[15] *The Poems of John Donne*, edited by Sir Herbert J. C. Grierson, 2 vols (Oxford, 1912; reprinted 1958), i, 175, line 1; hereafter cited parenthetically by line numbers in text for all quotations from the poetry.

presenting things as deprived of their usual properties or qualities, or as deceiving conventional expectations of identity or function. These conceits climax in the dissolution of both poems into the hyperbolic annihilation of qualities.

In both these poems, Donne exercises his theological fancies at arm's length, as it were, half playfully. He *intends* the compliments to his friend, and half-intends the deprecation of himself, at least as a trial of a role, as a rhetorical stance to play with. And he sees a real, if distant, structural analogy between the mundane relations and experiences he represents, and the divine mysteries and scholastic concepts through which he represents them. Whether or not Donne wrote these verse-letters with a real apprehension of annihilation fresh in mind, the resonance and vividness of much of the imagery gives passages an imaginative presence, a sense of the fuller participation of the complete sensibility, than is conveyed, for example, by a clever image like the comparison to the Three Holy Children in the fiery furnace in lines 27–28 of 'The Calme': 'Who live, that miracle do multiply | Where walkers in hot Ovens, doe not dye.'

In the letter 'To Mr. *Rowland Woodward*', 'Like one who' in her third widdowhood doth professe' (1597?), adverse judgement in the world's eyes again precipitates solemn reflection on God's weightier and final judgement. Woodward appears to have requested copies of Donne's earlier verses, which had been circulating among his familiar friends, and, apparently, beyond. Donne is worried about the reputation for frivolity or worse his elegies and satires may be garnering for him in the minds of those beyond his circle, especially those whose judgement, because of their superior social position or influence, may affect his worldly advancement; he is begging off sending more copies abroad. He wishes influential people to know him by works more in keeping with his education and the profit he has made of it. He sets for himself the sternest standard, blaming himself,

> For though to us it seeme, 'and be light and
>   thinne,
> Yet in those faithfull scales, where God throwes
>   in
> Mens workes, vanity weighs as much as sinne.

Nevertheless, he avers that such sins of omission and vanities need not damn him irretrievably:

> If our Soules have stain'd their first white, yet
>   wee
> May cloth them with faith, and deare honestie,
> Which God imputes, as native puritie.
>
>   (ll. 10–15)

Then, sounding unexceptionably moral and discerning, not to mention theologically orthodox, he declares, 'There is no Vertue, but Religion': 'Manure thy selfe then, to thy selfe be'approv'd, | And with vaine outward things be no more mov'd.' (l. 34) Surely such a poem, violating the protested fallowness of his muse to versify so masterfully the case for the highest ethical carriage and self-control, is a performance, the adoption of a role, written with an eye to circulation like that of the reprehended 'love-song weeds and Satyrique thornes', beyond the eyes of the designated recipient.[16] And yet, despite the calculation, the playing to the galleries, the terms chosen to express the ideas of condemnation and rescue are the religious concepts that have dominated his imagination from the beginning: stain; Fall; loss; Grace; imputed righteousness; assured salvation. The thought of perishing in the world's judgement impels Donne to envisage standing before the Last Judgement, and his self-representation turns to the language of divinity, and turns on grace, imputed purity, and strenuous self-cultivation of virtue, both to 'uplay ... treasure' ('for the great rent day') and to be fruitful of good works (for which surely 'manure thyself' in one of its senses is but a preparation).[17]

Theologically, of course, virtue and merit have nothing to do with the strictest dogmas of imputed righteousness and salvation by grace alone, which Donne's gravitation toward hyperbole keeps evoking. However, the fact that active cultivation of virtue, that is, the subject's doing something himself to procure his salvation, here gets mixed up with grace and imputed righteousness is no accident. True, Donne is fascinated by the idea of God's immense creative and saving power, making the world from absolutely nothing and redeeming a mankind incapable of redemption by any act or virtue of his own:

To enquire further the way and manner by which God makes a few do acceptable works; or, how out of a corrupt lumpe he selects and purifies a few, is but a stumbling block and a tentation: Who askes a charitable man that gives him an almes, where he got it, or why he gave it? will any favorite, whom his Prince only for his appliableness to him, or some half-vertue, or his own glory, burdens with Honours and Fortunes every day, and destines to future Offices and Dignities, dispute or expostulate with his Prince, why he rather chose not another, how he will restore his Coffers; how he will quench his peoples murmurings, by whom this liberality is fed; or his Nobility, with whom he equalls new men; and will not rather repose himself gratefully in the wisdome, greatness and bounty of his Master?[18]

However intellectually satisfying Donne finds that extreme doctrine of unconditional election, emotionally he cannot face its harsh rigour. Not only the emphasis on merits that distinguishes the religion of his childhood, but the need of his own emotional nature to *do* something, to somehow exercise

---

[16] Hester suggests that injunctions to Goodere to burn certain letters suggest that Donne intended his letters as 'public compositions that would circulate among friends as often as not' (*Letters to severall Persons of Honour*, p. xiv), so that the qualities of mind and character displayed in almost any letter, particularly the wittiest, or the most maturely reflective and moral, might be displayed to friends, acquaintances, contacts, and potential patrons.

[17] Given Donne's conversance with legal texts, we must conjecture that he may also intend the word 'manure' to carry a sense, now obsolete but current through the earlier seventeenth century, 'to administer, manage' (*OED*, sv. 'manure', *v.*, 1.).

[18] *Essays in Divinity by John Donne*, edited by Evelyn M. Simpson (Oxford, 1952), p. 87.

some control over his fate, compels him to find a place for striving and for virtue, to represent himself as in some way co-operating with and validating God's election. And of course, compared to the passive role enforced by reliance on unconditional election, the championship of active virtue makes a more favourable self-representation for the eyes of those imagined readers beyond his immediate circle whom he hopes to impress with the self-advertisement of this poem's posture and role.

The impulse to conceive his situation in eschatological terms here is not explicable simply as a mask of hypocrisy, however, any more than the considerable manipulation of the ideas and doctrines in the piece could be said to reflect merely craven fear, either of God's judgement, or the world's. Donne was always sensitive to 'discretion'. Unlike those who would make brusque rudeness a virtue, he conceived a favourable reception among one's fellow men as a crucial element in fulfilling God's demands of service.[19] In his courtship of good opinion, he came to see in the concept of divine Grace a powerful homologue explaining the workings of his social and political world. At the same time, the experienced need for 'appliablencss', for some virtue or grace of manners to *attract* that worldly grace of favour, led him, as he meditated on the reward of the king's friend, to slide from the pure model of God's inscrutable, unconditioned Grace.[20]

In the *divisio* of that first Paul's Cross sermon in 1617, Donne anatomizes the relation between virtue and grace, explicating talents and service as pre-conditions for the granting of favour in an attempt to rationalize the patronage of the great:

But in this Text, as in one of those Tables, in which, by changing the station, and the line, you use to see two pictures, you have a good picture of a good King, and of a good subject; for in one line, you see such a subject, as *Loves pureness of heart*, and hath *grace in his lips*, in the other line, you see the King gracious, yea friendly to such a subject, *He that loveth pureness of heart, for the grace of his lips, the King shall be his friend*. The sum of the words, is, that God will make an honest man acceptable to the King, for some ability, which he shall employ to the publicke. Him that proceeds sincerely in a lawful calling, God will bless and prosper, and he will seal this blessing to him, even with that which is his own seal, his own image, the favor of the King. (I, 183)

In this representation of the text's meaning, the good king figures the patron, the good subject the client or suitor in the patronage relationship.[21] The conceit of the anamorphic image, two pictures involved in one 'table', the

<hr />

[19] See *Sermons* 3, 335–36, and Jeanne M. Shami, 'Donne on Discretion', *ELH*, 47 (1980), 48–66; compare 'Honour is so sublime perfection', lines 37–53.

[20] Compare Carey's claim that, 'To understand this part of his mind correctly ... we must appreciate that veneration for the court and for the grandees who peopled it was so deeply embedded among his imaginative and spiritual impulses that it became an element of his religious belief' (*John Donne: Life, Mind and Art*, p. 113).

[21] 'So also by the name of *King*, both in the Scriptures, and in *Josephus*, and in many more prophane and secular Authors, are often designed such persons as were not truly of the rank and quality of Kings; but persons that lived in plentiful and abundant fortunes, and had all the temporal happinesses of this life, were called Kings. And in this sense, the Kings friendship that is promised here, (*The King shall be his friend*) is *utilis amicitia*, all such friends as may do him good'. *The Sermons of John Donne*, I, 211.

perceived subject depending on the spectator's viewpoint, emphasizes how the predications of king and subject are *relative*: neither can be what it is without the other. This 'reference to one another *by Relation*, as we say in the Schools' is rendered yet more intrinsicate by a further explication of this kind of relation by another conception drawn from divinity, 'The greatest Mystery in Earth, or Heaven, which is *the Trinity*'. Donne concludes: 'As in Divinity, so in Humanity too, *Relations* constitute one another' (1, 184). The use here of the vocabulary and conceptual apparatus of scholasticism to render the inter-illumination of the human by the divine and the divine by the human, is characteristic. By his complication of the symbiotic relationship of servant and king, patron and patronized, Donne telescopes the distance in power between the two, dissolving favour and the grounds of favour, the patron's grace and the client's merit, into one picture, one image which is not to be divided by analysis, but only diversely seen, depending on the point of view.

His treatment of this relation uncovers the defining power of the seemingly less powerful half of the relationship: as the good subject discovers his qualities of goodness in his relation to his king, the good king discovers *his* qualities in relation to his subject. Even more significantly, this reciprocal relationship is presented as governed by God's providence, and fulfilling His will: *God* makes the honest man acceptable to the king; in extending his favour, the king enacts a type of God's Grace. The king's favour is 'the seal' of God's blessing to His virtuous servant. Thus Donne as preacher of the divine Word glorifies the king's favour as an aspect of God's Grace, while at the same time implying the weighty responsibility which rests upon the dispenser of favour as he imitates and enacts the beneficence of the Godhead. 'Neither is this encouragement to this Pureness, and this Grace in our Text, only in the benignity of the King . . . but it is in his duty, it is in his office; for, (as our Translators have expressed it) we see it is not said, The King *will* be; but, The King *shall* be his friend; it is not an arbitrary, but a necessary thing' (*Sermons* 1, 213).

To establish moral virtue as the precedent condition for the patronage relationship is to assert a congruence between virtue and worldly reward that would justify power in its distribution of favour. Reciprocally, Donne empha-sizes in the king's picture extracted from the text by interpretive elaboration that his principal activity, to be friendly and gracious, is specifically qualified as directed toward 'him that hath endeavoured, in some way, to be of use to the Publicke; And, not to him neither, for all the grace of his lips, for all his good parts, except he also *love pureness of heart*' (1, 184). As he *loves* pureness of heart, the king's friend is secured against aspersions that his affections and apparent purity or virtue are simply put on in pursuit of self-interest. He loves purity and goodness for their own sakes and not for whatever gain their attribution to him may procure. Even more forcefully than it justifies power, the asserted congruence of virtue and favour justifies the successful suitor for favour.

The successful suitor, who is successful because he loves virtue, is justified in the first place by that very love. He cannot owe his worldly bliss to base appliances or boot-licking flattery. Loving virtue in his heart, he cannot be a flatterer, or hypocrite, or a counterfeiter of virtue, than which 'there is no foulness so foul, so inexcusable in the eys of God, nor that shall so much aggravate our condemnation' (*Sermons*, 1, 185–86). Moreover, loving incorruptible virtue in his heart, he is justified by the law of contradiction, for he cannot then love the world. To love the world is to set one's heart upon things which are in perpetual flux, like a piece of paper cast upon a stream,

expos'd to the disposition of the tyde, to the rage of the winde, to the wantonness of the Eddy, and to innumerable contingencies, till it wear out to nothing. So, if a man set his heart (we cannot call it a setting) if a man suffer his heart to issue upon any of these fluid and transitory things of this world, he shall have *cor vafrum, & inscrutabile*, He shall not know where to finde his own heart. If *Riches* be this floating paper that his eye is fixed upon, he shall not know upon what course; If *Beauty* be this paper, he shall not know upon what face; If *Honor* and *preferment* be it, he shall not know upon what faction his heart will be transported a month hence. But, if the heart can fix it self upon that which is fixt, the Almighty and immoveable God, if it can content to inquire after it self, and take knowledge where it is, and in what way, it will finde the means of cleansing (*Sermons* 1, 191).

Such justifying love is the gift of the Holy Ghost, a love above even 'the highest degree of other love, . . . the love of woman', for 'All love which is placed upon lower things, admits satiety; but this love of this pureness, always grows, always procceds', filing off the rust in our hearts and purging old habits until 'thou maist see thy face in thy heart, and the world may see thy heart in thy face; indeed, that to both, both heart and face may be all one: Thou shalt be a Looking-glass to thy self, and to others too' (*Sermons* 1, 199).

   Justification of the favoured suitor by placing upon his qualifications the most favourable construction possible continues in the brief middle move-ment of this sermon, analysing the meaning of *Gratia labiorum*. Donne opens with a protestation shaped by his familiarity with the customary practices of *negotium* in high places:

As therefore those words, *A mans gift maketh room for him, and bringeth him before great men*, are not always understood of *Gifts* given in nature of *Bribes* or gratifications for access to great persons, but also of *Gifts* given by God to men, that those *Gifts* and *good parts* make them acceptable to great persons; so is not *Grace of lips* to be restrained, either to a plausible and harmonious speaking, appliable to the humour of the hearer [as flattery is excluded by the premise that the aspirant loves purity of heart] nor to be restrained to the good Offices and Abilities of the *tongue onely* (though they be many); but this Grace of lips is enlarged to all declarations, and expressings, and utterings of an ability to serve the Publick (*Sermons* 1, 206–07).

Donne presses the extended sense of 'lips' as indicating either speaking in general or 'all manner of expressing a mans ability, to do service to that State in which God hath made his station'. So in Proverbs 18.20, '*With the fruit of a mans mouth shall his belly be satisfied, and with the encrease of his lips shall he be filled*; That is, his honest labors in a lawful calling shall enrich him'. Thus,

the *Grace of lips* reaches to all the ways by which a man in civil functions may serve the Publick. And this *Grace of lips*, in some proportion, in some measure, every man is bound in conscience to procure to himself; he is bound to enable himself to be useful and profitable to the Publick, in some course, in some vocation (1, 207).

The gift, the talent, is nothing if it be not employed. The man who keeps himself and his gifts to himself is, as far as the public weal is concerned, no better than a suicide (*Sermons* 1, 209–10). The protestant concept of calling and glorification of the active life emphasized the fact that every man, elect and reprobate alike, ought to be deeply concerned with his 'particular' calling, 'that wherewith God enableth us, and directeth us ... on to some special course and condition of life, wherein to employ our selves, and to exercise the gifts he hath bestowed upon us'.[22] Assurance of calling depends on two things, according to William Perkins: 'Gifts for the calling from God, and Allowance from men'.[23]

John Donne was only too aware how abundantly he was endowed with the former; but both are necessary for assurance and fruit, and during the Pyrford and Mitcham years he fruitlessly pursued allowance from men without significant result. As a clergyman, preaching at Whitehall twenty years after the frustration and sense of uselessness he experienced at Mitcham, Donne himself was no less vehement than Adams, Perkins, Sanderson, and Sibbes in his insistence on the imperative of labour in one's calling:

Be something, or else thou canst do nothing; and till thou have said this, saies our text, that is, done something in a lawful calling, thou canst not sleep *Stephens* sleep, not die in peace. *Sis aliquid*, propose something, determine thy self upon something, be, profess something, that was our first; and then our second consideration is, *hoc age*, do seriously, do scedulously, do sincerely the duties of that calling.[24]

'In a word', he proclaimed in that Paul's Cross sermon, 'he that will be *nothing* in this world, shall be nothing in the next; nor shall he have the *Communion of Saints* there, that will not have the Communion of good men here ...; since he lives the life of a *beast*, he shews that he could be content to die so too, *& accepit animam in vano*, he hath received a soul to no purpose' (*Sermons* 1, 209).

Donne's ambition was boundless and imperative,[25] but he was also, even before he became a clergyman, a religious man. Ambitious as he was, he was yet acutely aware of the mortal danger presented to the soul by worldly ambition and self-love. Susceptible also to 'an Hydroptique immoderate

---

[22] Robert Sanderson, *XXXVI Sermons* (1689), pp. 205–15.
[23] *Works*, I (1612), 760. For other fervent assertions of the centrality of calling and obligation to put God's gifts to use, see the puritan Richard Sibbes, *Bowels Opened* (1639), pp. 17–18. Sanderson and Adams are severe in their hortations: 'where the end of a thing is the use, there the difference cannot be great, whether we abuse it, or but conceal it ... O then up and be doing: Why stand ye all the day Idle? ... in the Church, he that cannot style himself by any other name than a Christian, doth indeed but usurp that too. If thou sayest thou art of the body: I demand then, what is thy office in the Body? ... If thou hast a Gift get a Calling' (Sanderson, *XXXVI Sermons*, p. 46); Thomas Adams thunders, 'To be idle, is to be barren of good; and to be barren of good, is to be pregnant of al evil' (*The Workes* (1629), p. 959).
[24] *Sermons* 8, 176–78; Sermon No. 7, preached at Whitehall, 29 February 1628.
[25] See John Carey, *John Donne: Life, Mind and Art*, particularly Chapters 3 and 4, 'Ambition' and 'The Art of Ambition' for a relentless presentation of Donne's ambition in the least sympathetic light.

desire of humane learning and languages' and a thirst for transcendence, for 'the next life' (*Letters*, pp. 51, 50), that would equally withdraw him from the world, he balanced against those spurs to retirement and contemplation his sense of the imperative of calling, of bearing fruit in this world. What more natural than that he should represent to himself his restless urge to rise in the world, to 'take ... a course, get ... a place', to 'observe his honour, or his grace, | Or the Kings reall ... face contemplate', in terms of his God-imposed duty to use his God-given gifts in such a way as to distribute good more abundantly to his fellow men?

In his years of nonentity, after he had thrown away his prospects through his clandestine marriage, it is the sense of wasted gifts, of rusting in disuse, that returns again and again in his laments to friends. In an often-quoted letter *To Sir H. Goodere*, dated by H. Thomas Hester to September of 1608, he pours out his chafing at his state of idleness, his despair over his lack of a place for his talents:

I would not that death should take me asleep .... I would fain do something; but that I cannot tell what, is no wonder. For to chuse, is to do: but to be no part of any body, is to be nothing. At most, the greatest persons, are but great wens, and excrescences; men of wit and delightfull conversation, but as moales for ornament, except they be so incorporated into the body of the world, that they contribute something to the sustentation of the whole.[26]

The contemplation of the nullity of even the great without occupation breeds corrosive thoughts of his former course, and fall. Trying his thoughts by the most rigorous of standards, divine judgement, he reflects that even his desire to 'try again' may be a trap of damnation, since he must 'fear, that [i.e., that desire to seek a place and scope for his talents] doth not ever [i.e., 'always'] proceed from a good root'. Looking relentlessly into his motives, he sees not only the desire for vocation, but also the egotism which seeks self-gratification and reputation for their own sakes.

I dwell upon these repeated and plangent avowals of his desire to serve, his sense, transcending self-pity, of his nullity, and on his acute casuistry of self-analysis in the midst of his pain, in order to represent as vividly and precisely as possible the state of his mind at the time that he was most assiduously courting potential patronage. Patronage was, certainly, the doorway to a return to what he understood in a purely egotistical way as fullness of life, means, power, and prestige; but it was also 'allowance from men', no less essential to an effectual calling than the talents and gifts that were its ground. For Donne, the patron's favour as an enabling power must have seemed almost what, to a rather different ideological point of view, *money* seemed some 240 years later. In a striking passage from the *Economic and Philosophical Manuscripts of 1844*, Karl Marx spoke of how money, 'being the external, common *medium* and *faculty* for turning an *image* into *reality* and *reality* into a mere *image*', determines that the man who has a *vocation* for

---

[26] *Letters*, pp. 50–51; dated by Hester September 1608 (Introduction, p. xviii).

study, but no money for it, has 'no *effective*, no *true* vocation', while the individual with money for study, whatever his actual capacity for it, has an *effective*, a *true* vocation.[27]

Of course, in Donne's ideology, the medium and faculty for conversion to use, the patron's will and election, is not an *impersonal* agency, and *is* ultimately under divine guidance, as money, for Marx, is not. Donne insists especially upon divine guidance, as he has constructed his model of patronage according to the pattern of the king and his friend, for, to him, 'the King' is just such a superlative as 'God', even in the mouth of the Holy Ghost. 'For, *Reges sunt summi Regis defluxus* (says that Author, who is so antient, that no man can tell when he was, *Trismegistus*) God is the *Sun*, and Kings are *Beams*, and emanations, and influences that flow from him. Such is the manner of the Holy Ghost expressing himself in *Esai*' (*Sermons* 1, 210). Hence Donne could react to the model of the patronage system that he constructed out of the conceptions of divinity, not by rebelling against the medium, favour, defining it as alienating, but by committing himself ever more desperately to laying hold of it, opening himself to its power, even sanctifying it through the analogies he used to understand and describe its operations, all in the fervent hope that, in God's good time and with God's help, grace and favour would eventually be his, and help him to realize his ambitions, and actualize his gifts and virtues in an effectual calling.

---

[27] *Economic and Philosophical Manuscripts of 1844*, in *The Marx–Engels Reader*, edited by Robert C. Tucker (New York, 1972, second edition, 1978), pp. 104–05.

John Milton and the Republican Mode of Literary Production

PETER LINDENBAUM

Indiana University

'It is a shame', lamented Boswell in 1773, acting yet once more as straight man to Dr Johnson, 'that authors are not now better patronized'. To which the unabashed free marketeer of learning responded:

No sir. If learning cannot support a man, if he must sit with his hands across till somebody feeds him, it is as to him a bad thing, and it is better as it is. With patronage, what flattery! what falsehood! While a man is in equilibrio, he throws truth among the multitude, and lets them take it as they please: in patronage, he must say what pleases his patron, and it is an equal chance whether that be truth or falsehood.[1]

Boswell was no doubt merely drawing his friend out, since Johnson had, a moment before, exultantly proclaimed 'We have done with patronage'. Literary critics have tended to disagree over what exactly might have constituted the death knell of the aristocratic patronage system, whose passing Johnson celebrated on several different occasions. A past generation looked most often perhaps to Johnson's own famous 1755 letter to the Earl of Chesterfield, berating that lord for gratuitous commendation after having ignored Johnson seven years earlier when he needed real help, of a monetary kind. Maynard Mack has recently resubmitted an alternative event, Pope's 1714 contract with the publisher Lintot for the subscription and publication of the poet's *Iliad*.[2] As a result of the eight to nine thousand pounds Pope took home from *The Iliad* and *The Odyssey*, he became the first poet to achieve financial independence by means of his poetry alone, without having to rely upon the munificence of some single great figure. I should like to drive the event farther back yet, to Milton's act of publishing *Paradise Lost* on the open market, for what amounted to the meagre sum of ten pounds.

Actually, it is not the publication of *Paradise Lost* alone that might be said to mark the watershed, but the whole shape or progress of Milton's career up to and including the publication of his epic in 1667. For Milton provides us with an example of someone who began his career within the aristocratic patronage system and worked his way free of it. His first major published work was the masque we call *Comus*, the masque itself of course an aristocratic form and written to honour the Earl of Bridgewater's family on the

---

[1] *Boswell's Life of Johnson*, edited by George Birkbeck Hill, revised by L. F. Powell, second edition, 6 vols (Oxford, 1964), V, 59.
[2] *Alexander Pope: A Biography* (New York, 1985), p. 863.

occasion of the Earl's installation, in 1634, as Lord President of Wales. *Comus* is by no means an ordinary celebratory piece; it constitutes, as several critics now have well shown, an effort to educate its aristocratic audience and is, if anything, critical of the cavalier, courtly taste and attitudes that one normally associates with masques.[3] It in no way fawns. But there is ample evidence that the young Milton was enormously pleased not simply with the work itself but also with the aristocratic connexions it implied. He participated in the preparation of the 1637 printing of the masque, restoring some passages from the pre-performance manuscript, adding significant new passages that make its moral point clearer and more substantial; yet he seemed willing to let the work appear anonymously in 1637, as if the property of those for whom it was performed. When he did finally put his name to the masque in print, in the 1645 edition of his *Poems*, he gave *Comus* pride of place, perhaps as the volume's most substantial work, taking it out of chronological order and putting it last among his English poems, after 'Lycidas' of 1637. And he assigned the masque a separate title page in the volume and prefaced it with Henry Lawes's Dedicatory Letter to the Earl of Bridgewater's son, taken from the 1637 edition, and with a letter of commendation to the author from Sir Henry Wotton, provost of Eton College and former ambassador to Venice. In the 1645 volume Milton and his publisher Humphrey Moseley are in part trying to make Milton's name on the coat-tails of others. The title page of the whole volume informs us that 'The SONGS were set in Musick by Mr. HENRY LAWES Gentleman of the KINGS Chappel, and one of his MAJESTIES Private Musick'.

By 1645 Milton had already embarked on his public career as a prose writer, and his twentieth-century biographer, William Riley Parker, has suggested that Milton published the 1645 volume in order to establish a name for himself as something other than a Puritan pamphleteer and a 'divorcer'.[4] But the 1645 volume went virtually unnoticed and it was in prose and public service that Milton's public career remained for the period 1641 to 1660, as he wrote polemical works first on behalf of his religious party, then the government, and then a republic of his own devising. When he did get back to writing and publishing poetry as his main concern, his own religious and political causes were so out of favour that there may well have been no patron willing to be viewed as his supporter. And, of course, to a certain extent Milton did have a patron for *Paradise Lost* after all; please that one reader, God, and no others matter. But the decision to publish *Paradise Lost* on the open market and without benefit of protection or support of some great man represents not simply a religious decision but a political one. In his desire to educate a whole nation through *Paradise Lost*, Milton was

[3] See Cedric C. Brown, *John Milton's Aristocratic Entertainments* (Cambridge, 1985), and John Creaser, '"The present aid of this occasion": The Setting of *Comus*', in *The Court Masque*, edited by David Lindley (Manchester, 1984), pp. 111–34.
[4] *Milton: A Biography*, 2 vols (Oxford, 1968), I, 288; see too the related argument of Thomas N. Corns, 'Milton's Quest for Respectability', *MLR*, 77 (1977), 770–79.

making an essentially republican gesture, one that can be said to be an outgrowth of his own increasing republicanism in the period 1640 to 1660.

To see the full significance of Milton's manner of publishing *Paradise Lost*, we need to consider the various publishing and writing models he had before him, and to do that we can best look back to the Italy Milton visited in 1638–39. For it was there that one could see postulated side by side, and in relatively distinct and pure form, two very different modes of producing literature, what I shall be calling the ducal (or aristocratic) and republican modes respectively. I do not claim that the Italian trip was in any way responsible for Milton's move from the first to the second. Milton's whole Italian trip in fact presents many difficulties and the account Milton provides of it in his *Second Defence of the English People* is fraught with inconsistencies and contradictions. He makes virtually no comment at all on what we have reason to expect ought to have been, for an emergent republican Milton, the culminating point of his whole tour, the stay in Venice. The account, though written in 1654 when Milton was in the midst of his career of public service and leading a life very different from his more private existence of the 1630s, betrays much the same kind of thinking that the 1645 volume of poems does. Milton is eager to tell us about the learned friends he made and to gain his readers' respect by that means. Sir Henry Wotton again makes an appearance and is thanked for that same letter which prefaces *Comus*. And, wishing to portray himself as a Protestant patriot, Milton mentions that sad tidings of civil war in England, which he received when in Naples, forced him to abandon his plans to visit Sicily and Greece, and yet the account he provides reveals that it took him six more months to meander home (and when he got there he did not immediately throw himself into the fray, but rather devoted himself to setting up a school for boys and to two more years of reading). If the trip to Italy does not appear, then, to have been the turning point in Milton's artistic career or his thinking generally that his biographers, following Milton's own lead, like to suggest, the trip does remain of major interest.[5] For, as I have suggested, the Italy Milton saw provides us with fully articulated paradigms of two rather different approaches to literature and the men who create it, paradigms which postulate very different roles for writers in their respective societies.

If Venice did not seem to interest Milton much in 1639, what excited him on his trip, and excited him a great deal, was the welcome he received in Florence and Naples. In Florence, where he remained four months in all, he was evidently taken quickly under the wing of a group of men 'eminent in

---

[5] For the view of the trip as a turning point in Milton's artistic career, see Parker, I, 179–82. In noting the various contradictions in the *Second Defence* account of the journey, I am indebted to a number of papers delivered at the Third International Milton Symposium, held in Vallombrosa and Florence, 12–18 June 1988, most particularly that of Dustin Griffin, 'Milton in Italy: The Making of a Man of Letters?'.

Milton's detailed account of his journey, in *The Second Defence of the English People*, is to be found in the *Complete Prose Works*, edited by Don M. Wolfe and others, 8 vols (1953–82), IV, 614–20. Subsequent references to Milton's prose will be from this edition and marked *CPW*.

rank and learning', members of two different private literary academies, the *Apatisti* and the *Svogliati*, the meetings of both of which Milton attended and from which he emerged with great praise both for his poetic skill and his learning.[6] In Naples he was given the signal honour of particular attention from Giovanni Battista Manso, Marquis of Villa, a nobleman of distinguished rank and former patron to Italy's last great epic poet, Torquato Tasso, and to whom that poet had dedicated his *Dialogue of Friendship*. Manso was a figure of considerable influence, a great patron of the arts and founder and long-time leader of a literary academy, the *Oziosi*, whose meetings were held at his villa. Manso himself seems to have guided Milton around Naples, taken him to the palace of the viceroy, and even visited Milton at his own lodgings. Milton's reception at both these cities, then, plainly appealed to the twenty-nine year old Englishman aspiring to be, and to be recognized as, an up-and-coming poet and scholar. But the account of those two triumphs points to something besides an admiration for John Milton that those two cities had in common, and that is a shared mode of literary production, one very different from that promoted in Venice and that which Milton might be said to have participated in himself in his own later literary career.

The account of the stay in Naples presents us with an arrangement that is familiar enough: it is the traditional patronage system in which the artist strives to gain the attention of a rich patron who in turn provides the material means to enable the artist to continue to ply his artistic or literary trade. The system in Florence implied in the account is a bit more complex, although ultimately the same. Those two literary academies whose meetings Milton attended were both offshoots of the larger, public *Accademia Fiorentina* and that parent academy began its career in the 1540s by being quickly appropriated by Cosimo I, then Duke of Florence and later to be first Grand Duke of Tuscany. Cosimo had provided the members of the academy with a place to meet (initially the Palazzo Medici), with stipends for lectures, and made their elected head a salaried magistrate within his own government, responsible for public instruction and for supervising the book trade within the city. Cosimo secured, as well, the adoption of provisions prohibiting the performance of speeches without permission of his own *auditore*.[7] What such measures did of course was to render the literati of Florence politically harmless, those

---

[6] Milton's attendance at meetings of the *Svogliati* on 17, 24, 31 March 1639 has long been known (it is recorded in the second edition of Volume I of David Masson's *Life of John Milton* (1875)); that he attended meetings of the *Apatisti* too has been assumed but only recently confirmed, by Alessandro Lazzeri's transcription of an eighteenth-century manuscript in Florence's Biblioteca Marucelliana (MS A.36). The manuscript provides a record of the early history of the academy by a later member, Antonio Gori, and on page 53^r, in the midst of a list of members for 1638, appears the name of 'Giovanni Milton inglesi'; see Lazzeri, *Intelletuali e consenso nella Toscana del Seicento: L'Accademia degli Apatisti* (Milano, 1983), p. 74.

[7] For my knowledge of the *Accademia Fiorentina* and the private academies deriving from it, I am indebted to the first chapter of Eric Cochrane's *Tradition and Enlightenment in the Tuscan Academies, 1690–1800* (Chicago, 1961) and his *Florence in the Forgotten Centuries, 1527–1800* (Chicago, 1973); Claudia di Filippo Bareggi, 'In nota alla politica culturale di Cosimo I: L'Accademia Fiorentina', *Quaderni Storici*, 8, no. 23 (1973), 527–73; Armand L. De Gaetano *Giambattista Gelli and the Florentine Academy: The Rebellion Against Latin* (Firenze, 1976), esp. pp. 100–30; Lazzeri (see Note 6 above); the various entries in Michele Maylender's *Storia delle accademie d'Italia*, 5 vols (Bologna, 1926–30).

intellectuals, many of whom had been stirred in the period 1527 to 1530 by Florence's final attempt to banish the Medici and re-establish a republican form of government.

The founders of the *Accademia Fiorentina* in 1540 had included members of the merchant class as well as professional scholars and one of the reasons for gathering was a desire to bridge the cultural gap between artisans and intellectuals. By the time of Milton's trip to Italy such aims seem to have been long since abandoned and the various private academies founded by members of the Florentine Academy existed primarily for the amusement of their upper-class members.[8] A favourite form of entertainment at meetings of the *Apatisti* from 1649 on was a game in which members were called upon to provide learned expositions, studded with quotations from classical and modern sources, of immediate, unthinking, no doubt often meaningless, responses to questions put either to a young member of the academy or to a youth brought in from the street for the occasion.[9] Despite the implications we might draw from that game, the academies were serious enough undertakings, promoting piety, the study and practice of literature, philosophy, philology, in some cases even science. But they were distinctly *not* the place the Medici rulers would go for political advice or for discourses in political theory. The very names of the two academies whose members befriended Milton in Florence — the *Apatisti*, meaning passionless or dispassionate, and the *Svogliati*, will-less or disgusted — express all too conveniently the institutions' detachment from political and social issues of their time. Such names are gestures in self-deprecation, but they point up nicely that these academies, like Manso's *Oziosi* in Naples, were in effect pastoral ventures: as the names suggest, such groups seek detachment from everyday political and social life; they are élitist enclaves, whose members seek separation from more humble sorts, from trade, from *negotium*, in order to devote themselves to art, poetry, the life of the mind. Whether they explicitly state it or not — in the way that Ficino's Platonic Academy, founded for him in 1462 by Cosimo 'Il Vecchio', did state it — such institutions endorse the contemplative life over the active. And much the same stand is implicit in Manso's kind of patronage system. The intellectuals, those *Oziosi*, whom Manso with all the good will in the world led and supported were expected to go about their literary and artistic business at some distance from those holding direct political power. It was expressly written into the statutes of that academy that its members were forbidden to discuss theological questions, Scripture, or issues dealing with public government, which last were to be left to the care of the princes who ruled over them.[10] The reason why Manso did not see even more of Milton than he did, Manso told the Englishman on his

---

[8] Cochrane, *Florence in the Forgotten Centuries*, pp. 204–05; Lazzeri, pp. 8–10.
[9] On the *Sibillone*, see Cochrane, *Tuscan Academies*, p. 4, and Lazzeri, pp. 26–27.
[10] Maylender, IV, 184; for a more detailed study of the procedures and activities of this academy, see Vittor Ivo Comparato, 'Società civile e società letteraria nel primo Seicento: L'Accademia degli Oziosi', *Quaderni Storici*, 8, no. 23 (1973), 359–88.

departure and Milton duly reports in the *Second Defence*, was that Milton had been so outspoken on matters of religion. Manso's attention and patronage were at bottom, then, incompatible with forthright, uncensored statements of controversial religious or political positions.

Venice, too, had its aristocratic patrons and its literary academies, the latter complete with self-deprecatory names. And there is much evidence that Venice's academies did not differ greatly from their counterparts in Florence and Naples. The published work of the leading Venetian literary academy at the time of Milton's visit, the *Accademia degli Incogniti*, suggests that the same kinds of topics were discussed there as in academies in other city-states, questions ranging from the light-hearted or silly (defences of the colour grey, or diatribes against cheese) to those dealing with love (whether absence does in fact make the heart grow fonder) to potentially more serious issues (the dangers of eloquence, or whether that prince is wiser who encourages learning among his subjects or he who seeks to extirpate it). A published collection of biographies of the *Incogniti* reveals that perhaps only a tenth of its members were actually Venetian; the *Incogniti* in their meetings could thus hardly be said to be expressing a particularly Venetian sensibility on behalf of the Venetian populace as a whole.[11] But Venice in the late Renaissance had something besides literary academies and which made for quite a different model of intellectual activity within its bounds: it had the only remaining independent and significant republican form of government among the city-states of Italy. And it had an ideology to match, one which was perceived as a direct extension of that republican form of government. This ideology, a version of that strand of Renaissance humanism that Hans Baron, particularly, has labelled for us as 'civic humanism', favoured the

---

[11] Of the 106 biographies included in *Le Glorie degli Incogniti* (Venezia, 1647), only eleven of the members described (not the total membership) are Venetian. The most authoritative studies of Venetian academies of the late Renaissance are those of Gino Benzoni, 'Aspetti della cultura urbana nella società veneta del '5–'600: Le Accademie', *Archivio Veneto*, 108 (1977), 87–159, and *Gli affanni della cultura: Intellettuali e potere nell'Italia della Controriforma e barocca* (Milano, 1978), pp. 144–200, and of Paolo Ulvioni, 'Accademie e cultura in Italia dalla Controriforma all'Arcadia: Il caso veneziano', *Libri e Documenti* (Archivio Storico Civico e Biblioteca Trivulziana), 5, no. 2 (1979), 21–75. Both Benzoni and Ulvioni paint a relatively bleak picture of intellectual life in the academies covered, noting their increasing homogenization and marginalization as the seventeenth century and the Counter-Reformation wore on, as the academicians talked more and more merely to each other and less to the outside world. In defence of this particular academy, the *Incogniti*, we might note however that, in existence from 1630 to 1660, it came relatively early in the period of Venice's artistic and intellectual decline in the seventeenth and eighteenth centuries and that there is evidence of some unusual intellectual activity among its members, if not always in the performances within the academy's meetings themselves. Several of its members — for instance, Francesco Biondi, Ferrante Pallavicino, and Girolamo Brusoni — seem to have been free-thinking wanderers and Biondi's conversion to Protestantism and employment in the court of England's James I and Pallavicino's execution at the hands of the Inquisition did not prevent them from being considered among the 'glories' of the *Incogniti*. In addition, several of the older members of the Venetian contingent (Cornelio Frangipane, Giovanni Nicolò Doglioni, and Nicolo Crassò) had long and distinguished careers of public service behind them, in Crasso's case as one of those writing in defence of the Venetian state at what was perhaps the high point of its seventeenth-century history, during the Interdict crisis of 1606–07. And if the *Oziosi* in Naples were forbidden to discuss political matters, the founder of the *Accademia degli Incogniti*, Gianfrancesco Loredano, remarked in a discourse of the 1630s on whether it is better for a prince to have ignorant or learned subjects that it is perfectly fitting that political issues be introduced into an academy of fine letters (*Bizarrie Academiche* (Venetia, 1654), p. 106; included as Volume II of Loredano's *Opere*, 5 vols (Venetia, 1653–60)).

active life and promoted the ideal of direct participation in the concerns of government on the part of all citizens in society, among which, naturally enough, would be its intellectuals.[12] Venice thereby endorsed a literary system quite at odds with one that sets intellectuals apart from the rest of society, cloistered in élitist enclaves.

In talking about Venice in the Renaissance, though, we have quickly to acknowledge that we are talking about two different Venices — overlapping entities to be sure, but still different — the actual city with its basically aristocratic mode of governing and what historians call 'the myth of Venice'.[13] The myth in its fullest form claimed that Venice's government had survived unchanged for over a thousand years and had done so primarily because it possessed from its very beginning the ideal combination or balance of the three forms of rule Plato and Polybius had argued was necessary for enduring governmental stability: monarchy, aristocracy, and

[12] See, among many works by Baron, 'Cicero and the Roman Civic Spirit in the Middle Ages and the Early Renaissance', *Bulletin of the John Rylands Library*, 22 (1938), 72–97, and *The Crisis of the Early Italian Renaissance*, revised edition (Princeton, 1966). Eugenio Garin, though concerned more with philosophical than political attitudes, describes much the same phenomenon in his *Italian Humanism: Philosophy and Civic Life in the Renaissance*, translated by Peter Munz (Oxford, 1965 (originally *Der italiensche Humanismus* (Bern, 1947))). I follow William J. Bouwsma (in *Venice and the Defense of Republican Liberty: Renaissance Values in the Age of the Counter Reformation* (Berkeley, 1968)) in viewing Baron's conception of civic humanism as applicable to Venice. Bouwsma's important book has proved almost as controversial as Baron's work before it, having been subject to criticism on the grounds that Bouwsma presents too sharp and perhaps oversimplified a dichotomy between a specifically Renaissance Venice and a Medieval/Counter-Reformation Rome and, secondly, that it may in fact be a mistake to apply Florentine civic humanism to a republic of rather different social and intellectual conditions, a Venice so tightly under the control of a narrowly defined patriciate. For criticism on the first point, see Paul F. Grendler, *The Roman Inquisition and the Venetian Press, 1540–1605* (Princeton, 1977), pp. 26–27n, and James S. Grubb, 'When Myths Lose Power: Four Decades of Venetian Historiography', *Journal of Modern History*, 58 (1986), 43–94 (pp. 56–58); and on both points, see Renzo Pecchioli's review of Bouwsma in *Studi Veneziani*, 13 (1971), 699–708, incorporated into his book *Dal 'mito' di Venezia all' ideologia americana* (Venezia, 1983), pp. 204–32. But Bouwsma's claim that Venetian humanism has a particularly civic thrust to it may not be as startling or controversial as might first appear. Margaret King, in her recent study *Venetian Humanism in an Age of Patrician Dominance* (Princeton, 1986), even while she uses Paul Oskar Kristeller's very different definition of humanism simply as an educational or cultural programme centring around a limited cycle of scholarly disciplines (grammar, rhetoric, history, poetry, and moral philosophy), finds that what was distinctive about fifteenth-century Venetian humanism was the degree to which patricians dominated Venice's humanistic culture. Of the ninety-two 'core' Venetian humanists King examines and bases her study upon, sixty-four were members of the patriciate, and particularly high-ranking ones at that. What this means is that the early humanists of Venice represent and tend to speak for the very group that was responsible for the governance of the city. For a wide-ranging study that traces Baron's civic humanism (and the political attitudes arising from it) from Florence in the fifteenth and early sixteenth centuries to Venice in the later sixteenth century and thence to seventeenth-century England and Revolutionary (and later) America, see J. H. A. Pocock, *The Machiavellian Moment: Florentine Political Thought and the Atlantic Republican Tradition* (Princeton, 1975).

[13] The amount of material on the myth of Venice and its effect on the rest of Europe is now vast. For studies in English alone, see: Zera S. Fink, *The Classical Republicans: An Essay in the Recovery of a Pattern of Thought in Seventeenth-Century England*, second edition (Evanston, 1962), esp. pp. 28–51; Brian Pullan, 'Service to the Venetian State: Aspects of Myth and Reality in the Early Seventeenth Century', *Studi Secenteschi*, 5 (1964), 95–148 (pp. 95–108); William J. Bouwsma, *Venice and the Defense of Republican Liberty* and his 'Venice and the Political Education of Europe', in *Renaissance Venice*, edited by J. R. Hale (London, 1973), pp. 445–66; Felix Gilbert, 'The Venetian Constitution in Florentine Political Thought', in *Florentine Studies: Politics and Society in Renaissance Florence*, edited by Nicolai Rubinstein (Evanston, 1968), pp. 463–500; Eco O. G. Huitsma Mulier, *The Myth of Venice and Dutch Republican Thought in the Seventeenth Century*, translated by Gerard T. Moron (Assen, 1980), pp. 1–54; and Edward Muir, *Civic Ritual in Renaissance Venice* (Princeton, 1981), pp. 13–61. For a recent comprehensive review of the myth itself and the uses modern historians have made of it, see the article of James S. Grubb cited in Note 12 above.

democracy. The doge represented the monarchic element, the Senate the aristocratic, and the Grand Council the democratic. The resulting stability had in turn given rise to a high degree of personal and civil liberty, as was often noted by writers on and travellers to the city. As critics of the myth like Jean Bodin pointed out though, Venice's government was not really so mixed after all. The power of the doge, despite the fact that he was elected for life, was severely limited: he could not act on his own without four of his six elected councillors present, while any four of those councillors could act with him absent; and his actions were subject to review by the Grand Council at his death and his heirs fined if he were found guilty of impropriety. More importantly, the 'many' that the Grand Council, the main electoral body, was purported to represent never at any point in the period from 1500 to 1645 numbered significantly more than one and a half per cent of the total population of Venice: to be a member of the Grand Council and eligible for high elected office, one had to be an adult male descendant of one of the families recorded in the *Libro d'Oro* of 1381. This meant that in 1581, for instance, there were 1,843 members in the Grand Council out of a total population of some 134,890.[14] Venice was in actuality then what we would call today simply a closed aristocracy or an oligarchy, not a mixed polity.

Had there been a legitimately democratic element in the Venetian governmental system, the connexion between the actual Venice and civic humanist dedication to the active life and service to the state (for all citizens) would have been logically firmer and more complete.[15] And it must be admitted as well that the patricians who had complete governmental control of the city-state by no means consistently acted in the high-minded, self-sacrificing, patriotic, and decorous way that their own myth suggested they ought to.[16] In any case and despite this, several generations of writers from

[14] These figures are taken from Fink, *The Classical Republicans*, p. 30, who is indebted for them, by way of John Addington Symonds, to Charles Emile Yriarte, *La Vie d'un patricien de Venise au seizième siècle* (Paris, 1874), p. 96. Yriarte's figures are in basic agreement with more modern studies on Venice's population, for instance, that of James Cushman Davis, *The Decline of the Venetian Nobility As a Ruling Class* (Baltimore, 1962), pp. 62–68.

[15] Defenders of the Venetian political system tended to get around this difficulty either by following the lead of Gasparo Contarini (in *De Magistratibus et Republica Venetorum*, translated by Lewes Lewkenor as *The Commonwealth and Government of Venice* (London, 1599), p. 16) in arguing that the middle classes and lower were mercenary people who work for a living and hence are public servants, not rightly, then, considered citizens; or, alternatively, by talking of the means by which Venetians below the patrician class might participate in the communal life of the city and thereby have reason to feel the government their own, thus instilling in them a sense of loyalty to the state (or at least rendering them quiet). These means included service in governmental offices reserved for professional bureaucrats, participation in the Scuole Grandi (in which long-standing members of the merchant class might serve as officers and work alongside patricians in dedicating themselves to acts of charity parallel to those of the state's procurators), and even popular election of parish priests when vacancies appeared. Contarini touches on this latter approach late in his work (Lewkenor translation, pp. 142–46) and it was developed further by Giovanni Botero in his *Relatione della republica venetiana* (Venice, 1605), fols 42–43, 97–98, and 107–08. It was by such means that the republican civic humanist ideal of active involvement in the affairs of the state might become the ideology not simply of the Venetian patriciate alone but of a fairly large proportion of the Venetian populace. See Brian Pullan, 'Service to the Venetian State', pp. 100–05, and *Rich and Poor in Renaissance Venice* (Oxford, 1971), pp. 99–108.

[16] See Robert Finlay, *Politics in Renaissance Venice* (New Brunswick, New Jersey, 1980), and Donald E. Queller, *The Venetian Patriciate: Reality versus Myth* (Urbana and Chicago, 1986).

and on Venice devoted themselves to promoting a view of the Venetian state as a republican Sparta or Rome and in fact better than those earlier mixed polities because dedicated to peace and civil ends rather than war. And for contemporary Europeans of the mid-seventeenth century, Venice provided a more forceful example of republican dedication to the active life and service to the state than did the Florence where the ideals of civic humanism seem first to have taken root in the Renaissance. This was because Venice's republic continued to live on in the present whereas the period of Florence's vibrant republicanism — in the first half of the fifteenth century and revived briefly from 1494 to 1512 and even more briefly again from 1527 to 1530 — was by now well in the past. And for someone like John Milton in the 1640s and 1650s, Venice's republicanism lived on in a particularly important and relevant way, in the recent examples it provided of scholars and writers like himself who had dedicated themselves to state service.

Foremost among these was Gasparo Contarini, perhaps the single figure most responsible for the dissemination of the myth of Venice throughout Europe, as a result of his having written the *De Magistratibus et Republica Venetorum*, a work which proceeded through some twenty different editions from 1543 to 1650 and in four different languages.[17] By no means a mere governmental propagandist, Contarini was a theologian and a philosopher, a member of the patriciate whose family had provided several doges and who himself served in a number of high governmental positions (ambassador, senator, procurator of St. Mark) before being in effect seized by the church and made a cardinal in 1534. In the next generation Paolo Paruta, though of a lesser noble family, served in a similar series of governmental positions and as official historian of the city. It was his dialogue *Della perfettione della vita politica* of 1579 which gave fullest expression to the Venetian civic humanist preference for and dedication to the active life. Set in the last session of the Council of Trent in 1563, the *Vita politica* pitted Venetian ambassadors and representatives to the Council against prelates who presented Counter-Reformation arguments against commitment to anything in this debased world; they thereby favoured contemplative withdrawal from such a world. What the figures Paruta plainly sympathized with expressed in opposition to such a view was not simply a preference for the active life in this world but an active life dedicated to service to the specifically Venetian state, the mixed or balanced polity of which the then dead Contarini (by the device of remembered conversation from the past) is brought in to praise in the work's final pages.

By far the most important and direct Venetian model for Milton, though, was Paolo Sarpi: Servite friar, philosopher, theologian, historian, religious

<hr />

17 A check of the *National Union Catalogue* and those of the *British Museum* and *Bibliothèque Nationale* reveals: Latin editions in 1543 (Paris), 1544 and 1547 (Basel), 1551, 1557, 1589, and 1592 (all Venice), 1599 (Lübeck), 1626 and 1628 (Leiden), 1636 (Amsterdam); editions of Domenichi's Italian translation in 1544, 1545, 1548, 1551, 1564, 1591, 1630, and 1650 (all Venice); two editions of Charrier's French translation, in 1544 (Paris) and 1557 (Lyon); and Lewkenor's English translation of 1599 (London).

reformer, friend of Galileo, and acquaintance of Sir Henry Wotton, that writer of recommendations for John Milton. Sarpi was a many-sided scholar who in his mid-fifties was appointed official theologian to the Venetian Republic and called upon to defend Venice at the time of one of its greatest crises, during the Papal Interdict of 1606–07. Unlike Contarini and Paruta, Sarpi was not a member of the patriciate, but he plainly lived out the republican civic humanist ideal of service to the state. He is, as well, one Venetian with whose life and work we know Milton to have been very familiar, and increasingly so as Milton himself embarked on his own public career. In his *Of Reformation* (1641), Milton reveals an awareness of Sarpi, albeit a distant one, as 'the great Venetian antagonist of the Pope' (*CPW*, I, 581). Then, evidently in 1643–44, he proceeded to read Sarpi's *History of the Council of Trent* with care and interest, recording some thirteen entries from it in his Commonplace Book under disparate headings ranging from Marriage to Civil War.[18] He then proceeded to make use of this material and other passages as well as in his various proposals for the improvement of conditions in England, in the second edition of *Doctrine and Discipline of Divorce, Areopagitica, Tetrachordon, Eikonoklastes,* and *Likeliest Means to Remove Hirelings,* revealing an awareness of Sarpi's work in both its Italian and English versions. He found no occasion to refer to Sarpi's work in his own flurry of pamphlets arguing for a republic in 1659–60, but it is clear that Venice was on his mind as a possible model — if only in his decision to call his commonwealth's main governing body a Grand Council and to urge that its members sit for life. His true debt to Venice and to independent figures like Sarpi that Venice seemed to foster, though, is not to be seen so much in specific proposals at that time of political desperation as in his phrasing which in itself recalls civic humanist idealism, when for instance in *The Readie and Easie Way* he compares 'the perpetual bowings and cringings of an abject people' under a monarchy to conditions in a free commonwealth (or republic) 'wherin they who are greatest, are perpetual servants and drudges to the public at thir own cost and charges ... yet are not elevated above thir brethren ... [but] walk the streets as other men, [and] may be spoken to freely, familiarly, friendly, without adoration' (*CPW*, VII, 426, 425).

Plainly these Venetian examples do not in themselves account for the increasing political involvement of John Milton. But what I think we can say is that in the course of his public career Milton made the ideals of republican civic humanism his own and secondly, as he did so, he moved from the Neapolitan–Florentine mode of literary production to the Venetian one. It

---

[18] The assumption that Milton read Sarpi's *History* in 1643 and made those entries in his Commonplace Book at that time is based on the fact that the first reference in Milton's prose showing direct awareness of Sarpi's writing comes in a passage added for the second edition of *The Doctrine and Discipline of Divorce* (published probably very early in 1644) and not included in the first edition (published before 1 August 1643); see James Holly Hanford, 'The Chronology of Milton's Private Studies', *PMLA*, 36 (1921), 251–314 (pp. 268–69), and Ruth Mohl's Notes to Milton's Commonplace Book in *CPW*. I, 396 ff. And after *DDD* comes the extensive reliance upon Sarpi in *Areopagitica*, written later in 1644. It is of course possible that Milton started reading Sarpi earlier.

was not a move he made quickly, in the manner of a conversion. Indeed, in many ways Milton can be said to have lived his life in slow motion. Just as he was slow to return to England after having decided to do so in Naples, he was slow to get the 1645 *Poems* into print (publishing in that volume works almost all of which were written before 1637), and he was slow to deliver on his long-standing promise, made implicitly in 'Lycidas' and explicitly in *Reason of Church Government* of 1642, to write something that after times would not willingly let die. And his movement or progress was by no means steady. The 1645 *Poems* probably *was* an attempt to gain respectability, but in the terms I am outlining here, it was a step backward from the type of public, political stance assumed in the anti-prelatical tracts and *Areopagitica* which posit as their ideal subject and audience active, engaged figures who think for themselves and do not seek the protection of established institutions. With its poems in four different languages, its masque and other forms of aristocratic entertainment, its letters of commendation and recommendation, the volume appeals to a coterie audience, insists upon its connexions with the court, and reflects a literary system in which gentlemen-poets do not wish to seem eager to appear in print (it is Humphrey Moseley's claim in the Preface to the volume that he sought out John Milton rather than vice versa).

But if we look at Milton's writing career as a whole, the differences between early and late practices are considerable. One reflection of the change is in the differing presentation of *Comus* within the two editions of Milton's minor poems to appear in his lifetime. In the 1673 edition of *Poems, &c. on Several Occasions*, the privileging of *Comus* has been eliminated. It is still placed after 'Lycidas' but it is no longer last among the English poems, being followed this time by the translations of the Psalms. It no longer has a separate title page and its prefatory material (Lawes's Dedicatory Letter to Viscount Brackley and Wotton's Letter to Milton) has been cut. John Creaser has suggested that the reason for this last change is Milton's dislike of the increasing and increasingly evident royalist politics of the Bridgewater family.[19] This is certainly possible, but it does not explain why Wotton's Letter has disappeared along with that of Lawes and the announcement of who played the masque's various parts. It seems more likely that Milton merely wished to be rid of all the extra paraphernalia that set *Comus* apart in the volume and associated it so strongly with its original setting of aristocratic privilege. The 1673 edition as a whole obviously has much the same flavour and effect as the 1645 *Poems of Mr John Milton* since the later volume reproduces all of the 1645 poems along with some fifteen additions. The Latin part of the volume is particularly close to the 1645 form and continues to include the poems and letters of flamboyant praise from Milton's Italian friends. But the volume as a whole ends with the prose tract *Of Education* and

[19] ' "The present aid of this occasion" ', p. 117.

this, along with the changes in the presentation of *Comus*, reveals a movement, perhaps slight, away from aristocratic privilege and reminders of high-level connexions, in the direction of meritocratic independence, that is, the goal for which one educates young men to begin with; in effect, in a more republican direction.

If we wish, though, to see Milton-as-poet in a fully republican guise and adopting a republican mode of literary production, it is to *Paradise Lost* that we should turn. And to see first of all to what extent Milton had become a follower of Paruta and Sarpi, how attached he had become to the values of civic humanism, we might best look to his whole handling of the active and contemplative lives in his epic.

The old debate between the active and contemplative lives comes up most explicitly in *Paradise Lost* in the council in Hell, in the paired speeches of Moloch and Belial. Both fallen angels present debased versions of the respective stands. Moloch, for instance, favours constant, unthinking action in a suicidal argument that is all too easy for Belial to demolish. Belial, on his part, *sounds* better as he defends the life of the mind and asks, 'who would lose, | Though full of pain, this intellectual being, | Those thoughts that wander through Eternity' (II. 146–48).[20] But as the narrator points out, these are words only 'cloth'd in reason's garb' (II. 226): the lascivious Belial, as his name might well tell us, is not really interested in the life of the mind at all. What is odd and particularly interesting about Milton's handling of the debate is that he is willing to let Moloch's speech go by without comment, whereas he felt impelled to have his narrator place warnings around Belial's speech, evidently so as to put his reader on guard against its false appeal. The appeal to the contemplative life that Belial's speech embodies was, it would appear, perceived by Milton to be particularly and insidiously dangerous.

Milton, in fact, betrays an edginess or uneasiness over the contemplative life and appeals that might be made to it at numerous points in his poem. He grants full contemplation only to the fallen angels in Hell, where a group of lesser devils while away the time until the more active Satan, working on behalf of the whole nation of fallen angels, returns from his scouting expedition. These minor angels 'apart sat on a Hill retir'd' and 'reason'd high | Of Providence, Foreknowledge, Will, and Fate' (II. 557–59), the reward for their intellectual efforts being to find themselves 'in wand'ring mazes lost' (II. 561). They have, in effect, set up an academy of the Italian sort and, given the fact that 'Passion and Apathy' is one of the topics of their discourse, we might (a bit unfairly) call it an infernal branch of the *Apatisti*. And hermits, who might be presumed to practice the contemplative life, are placed among those who sought to reach heaven by vain or too sudden means, a class of beings that seems to have troubled or annoyed Milton to the

[20] Quotations from *Paradise Lost* are from the text of John Milton, *Complete Poems and Major Prose*, edited by Merritt Y. Hughes (New York, 1977).

extent that he departed from his usual adherence to Mortalism in order to give their souls immediate, appropriate punishment after death. The souls of hermits are thus to be found in the Paradise of Fools, along with the builders of the Tower of Babel, Empedocles, Cleombrotus, and embryos, idiots, and friars (III. 444–75). Paolo Paruta passed judgement upon contemplatives in similar terms, likening them to Semele who sought immediate and full apprehension of Jove, only to be struck down by that god for desiring to rise above her proper nature.[21]

But nowhere is Milton's favouring of the active life over the contemplative more remarkable than in his portrayal of Adam and Eve's life in Paradise before the Fall. Paradise is, as we might expect, a place of both action and contemplation in their ideal forms. But there was a theological tradition, and one we can see Milton arguing with, which suggested that Paradise was above all a place particularly suited for the practice of contemplation. It is a tradition reflected in Francis Bacon's statement that though 'it is set down unto us that man was placed in the garden to work therein', that work 'so appointed to him could be no other than work of contemplation'.[22] St John Damascene, to take just one earlier voice from that tradition, thought that 'the one work' man was to perform in Paradise was 'to sing as do the angels ... the praises of the Creator, and to delight in contemplation of Him'.[23] Milton's particular achievement or distinction was to construct the most *un*contemplative Paradise in the whole hexameral tradition. His treatment of Paradise was marked by two relatively original emphases. First, whereas other writers may have insisted that there was some labour to be done in Eden (though of a thoroughly delightful sort),[24] Milton provided Adam and Eve with a particularly exuberant garden that made keeping it in check more difficult than was true of any previous paradisal garden. Much more so than any previous Adam and Eve, Milton's pair had very legitimate work to do.[25] And secondly, Milton took the highly unusual stand of presenting our first parents with the gift of sexual love before the fall.[26] Contemplation tends to be de-emphasized in Milton's Paradise, then, simply because there proves to be so much else for Adam and Eve to do. He has endowed his Paradise with distinctive features which weight the balance on the side of the active life,

---

[21] *Della perfezione della vita politica*, in Paruta's *Opere politche*, edited by C. Monzani, 2 vols (Firenze, 1832), I, 123.

[22] *The Advancement of Learning*, in Bacon's *Works*, edited by James Spedding, Robert Leslie Ellis, and Douglas Denon Heath, 15 vols (Boston, 1860–64), VI, 137–38.

[23] John of Damascus, *De Fide Orthodoxa*, translated by S. D. F. Salmond, in *A Select Library of Nicene and Post-Nicene Fathers of the Christian Church*, edited by Philip Schaff and Henry Wace, Second Series (Grand Rapids, 1955), IX, 29 (Book II, Chapter 11).

[24] See for instance, among many: John Calvin, *Commentaries on the First Book of Moses Called Genesis*, translated by John King, 2 vols (Edinburgh, 1847), I, 125; Gervase Babington, *Certaine Plaine, Briefe, and Comfortable Notes upon Everie Chapter of Genesis* (London, 1592), fol. 10^r; and Thomas Adams, *Meditations upon Some Part of the Creed*, in *Workes* (London, 1629), p. 1130.

[25] See J. M. Evans, *Paradise Lost and the Genesis Tradition* (Oxford, 1968), pp. 242–71.

[26] See my *Changing Landscapes: Anti-Pastoral Sentiment in the English Renaissance* (Athens, Georgia, 1986), pp. 158–77, a reworking of my earlier 'Lovemaking in Milton's Paradise', *Milton Studies*, 6 (1974), 277–306.

and thereby provides a pastoral analogue to the type of stand a civic humanist like Paolo Paruta advocates in his political realm.

Twenty years ago Barbara Lewalski published an article on Adam and Eve's life in Eden, showing how as part of their particularly active prelapsarian existence our first parents undergo an education through trial and error;[27] this education is part of the process whereby Adam and Eve are to be 'improv'd by tract of time' and by steps ascend to God (v. 498, 512). Recently Mary Ann Radzinowicz followed up that study with an article showing how this education continues in the poem after the fall and takes on a particularly political form. Abdiel, Adam, and the reader are expected to correct the false linguistic and political usages and practices of a Satan and a Nimrod and thereby discover for themselves the true bases of freedom, order, and degree. The poem everywhere insists upon freedom of choice, both before and after the fall, and is concerned to promote the discipline and industry that produce an educated meritocracy.[28] While *Paradise Lost* does not, as Radzinowicz observes, endorse any particular political programme or course of action, there is a distinctly republican cast to the whole epic with its insistence upon responsibility for one's own decisions, upon earning one's own freedom and knowledge through a constant process of self-correction. One must be actively engaged at all times in establishing what is politically correct and morally true, just as, in *Areopagitica*, a man may become a heretic in the truth if he accepts that truth merely on the advice of his pastor or the Assembly.

It is in *Paradise Lost*'s thoroughgoing endorsement of constant activity, its portrayal of human life as process, its rejection of stasis as an ideal, that we can see its author's adherence not simply to the tenets of radical Protestantism but to the ideals of civic humanism as well, and to the republicanism closely associated with those ideals. And what is true inside the poem is of course true outside it as well, in the manner of its publication. Milton may ultimately be most interested in finding a 'fit audience . . . though few' for his epic, just as he favoured resting power in the hands of the few in *The Readie and Easie Way* (in an aristocracy of virtue or merit, not blood); but he did not, in publishing his poem on the open market, without patronage, and without introductory commendations, affect to identify that audience in advance. He is letting that fit audience identify itself by its active reading of the poem and is certainly not suggesting that the fit audience is to be found within a certain class of inherited wealth or taste. It can well be argued that *Comus* insists upon the same independence, activity, and personal responsibility that *Paradise Lost* does; but the masque appears in a context that calls up other kinds of associations as well, those of privilege and connexion, a social world

[27] 'Innocence and Experience in Milton's Eden', in *New Essays on Paradise Lost*, edited by Thomas Kranidas (Berkeley, 1969), pp. 86–117.

[28] 'The Politics of *Paradise Lost*', in *Politics of Discourse: The Literature and History of Seventeenth-Century England*, edited by Kevin Sharpe and Steven N. Zwicker (Berkeley, 1987), pp. 204–29.

in which one advances by virtue of the Henry Wottons one knows rather than by one's own active moral virtue.

Humphrey Moseley, the publisher of the 1645 *Poems*, was given in his prefaces to claiming that the works he was issuing were coming naked into the world, even as he pointedly mentioned that various learned 'Academicks' had applauded the poems that follow or indulged in praise of his own high-mindedness for publishing such works for the benefit of his intelligent, clear-sighted, and gentle readers.[29] Although Milton was certainly a known figure after the Restoration, *Paradise Lost* really did come close to entering the world naked in 1667. And this, I would suggest, was as important for later writers seeking independence as the subscription method of publishing which was establishing itself in the course of Milton's lifetime. It is of some significance that it should have been the incipient republican and Puritan prophet, George Wither, who *almost* invented the subscription method of publishing in 1615. In between one work dedicated 'To Himself' (*Abuses Stript and Whipt* (1613)) and another dedicated 'To Anybody' (*Wither's Motto* (1621)), fresh out of Marshalsea Prison and in desperate need of funds, Wither 'put ... out for an adventure amongst [his] acquaintance, upon a certaine consideration' his *Fidelia*, and then at the last minute thought better of the idea, returned all monies, and distributed all copies of the 1615 edition free.[30] But subscription publishing was, initially at least, a commercial venture more than a political one and did not in itself necessarily spell the end of the aristocratic patronage system and lead to political and moral independence for authors, as the fourth edition of *Paradise Lost*, published by subscription by Jacob Tonson in 1688, might well remind us. As was customary in such a mode of publication, the names of the subscribers are provided within the volume itself. For this particular venture, the names are divided according to each letter of the alphabet, but within each letter they are listed in order of aristocratic and social rank, a practice that would presumably make John Milton turn in his grave.

Samuel Johnson both misrepresented and detested Milton's 'acrimonious and surly' republicanism, which he viewed as 'founded in an envious hatred of greatness, and a sullen desire of independence'.[31] But in discussing the originality of Milton's invention at the end of the 'Life of Milton', Johnson had recourse to phrasing that suggests he admired Milton the man and his republican independence more than he let on: 'From his contemporaries he

---

[29] For Moseley's characteristic praise of himself, see his prefatory epistles to Milton's *Poems* (1645), Launcelot Andrewes's *Private Devotions* (1647), and John Suckling's *Last Remains* (1659); and for variations on his publications going forth into the world naked or in unsophisticated manner, see the prefaces to Waller's *Poems* (1645), Cowley's *The Mistress* (1647), and Raleigh's *Judicious and Select Essays* (1650). Moseley's prefaces are conveniently gathered in John Curtis Reed's 'Humphrey Moseley, Publisher', *Oxford Bibliographical Society Proceedings and Papers*, II, Part 2 (1928), 57–142 (pp. 73–103).

[30] The quoted phrase is from the prefatory matter to the 1615 edition of *Fidelia*, sig. A5ʳ; publisher George Norton provides further information in his Preface to the 1617 edition. The prize for having introduced subscription publishing must go instead to John Minsheu for his *Ductor in Linguas* of 1617.

[31] *Lives of the English Poets*, edited by George Birkbeck Hill, 3 vols (Oxford, 1905), I, 157.

neither courted nor received support; there is in his writings nothing by which the pride of other authors might be gratified, or favour gained; no exchange of praise, nor solicitation of support' (p. 194). Johnson is ostensibly talking here about literary rather than monetary indebtedness; but the references to courting, soliciting, and receiving support, gaining favour and exchanging praise, all call up the spectre of the patronage system which Johnson, at some level of his consciousness, saw Milton as helping to lay to rest. There was plainly a great deal more in common between the two writers than Johnson was always willing to acknowledge.

Patronage and the Dramatic Marketplace under Charles I and II

DEBORAH C. PAYNE

The American University, Washington, D.C.

And as an artist, it's terribly confusing to be asked to give something, because then you don't get a measure of what your art is worth. When somebody says, 'I love your work, providing you give it to me' — that's a different thing than saying, 'I love your work and I will pay the going value.' It's a matter of artistic integrity, I think.

J. Seward Johnson on his sculpture, 'The Awakening'.[1]

I   *The Historical and Theoretical Issue*

Customarily, the phrase 'patronage of the arts' means the patronal support of individual artists outside of commercialized marketplace transactions. Less often do we define those terms or outline the cultural practices implied by them. The more flaccid analyses of patronal relations recount bare biographical details: so-and-so functioned as the patron to artist X. More vigorous treatments at least indicate the economic and social obligations common to patronage: direct financial support; the exchange of gifts (such as money for a panegyric); appointment to a post (such as an ecclesiastical advowson); or recommendation to someone who can secure such in exchange for social and political allegiance. Usually, though, literary critics back off from the sort of dispassionate investigation into patronage that social scientists and historians have practised for over a decade.[2] Suggesting that patronal networks limit individual endeavours or that patronal market-places construct literary taste smacks of the overly deterministic, not to mention the sociological. Artistic talent, as we all know, transcends such base considerations; or does it?

Several critical books in the last five years have reread Caroline drama with an eye toward politics and patronage, going so far as to argue the cultural production of literature from Marxist or New Historical positions.[3] But Restoration studies have remained oddly indifferent to such approaches, even when paying lip service to the generalization that the Restoration stage

---

[1] Elizabeth Kastor, 'Waking a Giant Conflict', *The Washington Post*, 1 September 1989, D1–2.

[2] See, for instance, S. N. Eisenstadt and L. Roniger's sociological study, *Patrons, Clients and Friends: Interpersonal Relations and the Structure of Trust in Society* (Cambridge, 1984), or Linda Levy-Peck's critical history, *Northampton: Patronage and Policy at the Court of James I* (London, 1982).

[3] For such rereadings see Martin Butler, *Theatre and Crisis 1632–1642* (Cambridge, 1984); Kevin Sharpe, *Criticism and Compliment: The Politics of Literature in the England of Charles I* (Cambridge, 1987); and R. Malcolm Smuts, *Court Culture and the Origins of a Royalist Tradition in Early Stuart England* (Philadelphia, 1987).

was indeed a 'court theatre'.[4] Thus, an odd contradiction runs through much of the scholarship in the field. By attributing strategic change in the Restoration theatre exclusively to what the sociologist Magali Sarfatti Larson calls the 'ideology of merit' (whereby worthy individuals secure patents, organize companies, and produce plays by equally meritorious dramatists), several critical works obscure how particular historical choices and outcomes in 1660 served well-defined interests.[5] Other studies still loosely invoke the spectre of 'court influence' or patron so-and-so, thereby recirculating historical commonplace without explaining *why* the Restoration theatre developed into the particular social formation it did in 1660.[6] Little wonder, then, that dramatic patronage as a cultural material practice has been overlooked by Restoration scholars: for the most part, the critical literature in the field remains decidedly traditional.[7]

My thesis is predicated upon understanding the essential differences between these respective dramatic marketplaces. Rather than viewing the theatre of 1660 as a 'restoring' of the effete court drama that presumably dominated the 1630s (and therefore uncritically perpetuating G. E. Bentley's reading of the Caroline stage), we should acknowledge the Restoration court's limitation of certain dramatic traditions and theatrical practices. Simply put, reading forward critically from 1630 rather than backwards from 1660 results in a very different Restoration theatre. Prior to the Civil War, patrons of the drama functioned primarily as occasional brokers and protectors to theatres, lending their names and livery to the companies which had once been accused of vagabondage by Puritan-dominated city councils, and backing playwrights and theatre managers before the Privy Council or Revels office during times of censorship or official inquiry. For the Restoration, though, patronage came to constitute the very infrastructure of the theatrical system. To put this historical transformation in more sociological terms, we can say that the theatre goes from being a relatively specific marketplace during the first half of the seventeenth century to a marketplace of generalized exchange by the Restoration. According to the sociologists S. N. Eisenstadt and L. Rongier, these latter

[4] See, for instance, the discussion of the 'social and literary context' in *The Revels History of Drama in English*, Volume v, *1660–1750*, edited by John Loftis, Richard Southern, Marion Jones, and A. H. Scouten (London, 1976), pp. 3–80.

[5] As cited in Stanley Fish's article, 'Authors–Readers: Jonson's Community of the Same', *Representations*, 7 (1984), 26–58 (p. 26).

[6] See, for instance, the brief assertion by Emmett L. Avery and Arthur H. Scouten in *The London Stage, Part 1: 1660–1700* (Carbondale, n.d.) that the 'theatres were restored to an important place in the entertainment of the populace at large and the Court', p. xxx, or, more recently, J. L. Styan's assumption in *Restoration Comedy in Performance* (Cambridge, 1986) of pervasive if unspecified 'court' influence.

[7] This resistance to theory is just beginning to change. Robert Markley's *Two-Edg'd Weapons: Style and Ideology in Etherege, Wycherley, and Congreve* (Oxford, 1988), employs Bakhtin to good purpose in analysing the 'aristocratic' style of the canonical dramatists, and Julie Stone Peters's *Congreve and Print Culture* (Stanford, forthcoming 1990) examines the changing relationship between drama and print technology. A forthcoming collection of essays, *Restor(y)ing the Restoration and Early Eighteenth-Century Theatre*, edited by Deborah C. Payne and J. Douglas Canfield (Carbondale, 1991), rereads the drama of this period through the lens of post-structuralist theory.

marketplaces deliberately limit transactions of 'pure' exchange (in the theatre, this translates into direct payment for varying and competing kinds of entertainment), usually through two strategies: institutionalization of various titles or entitlements, and specifications on social interaction and access to positions.

It can be argued that these limitations colour various aspects of earlier seventeenth-century theatre as well; however, patronage as a system of sporadic brokerage differs markedly from patronage as the construction of an ascriptive-hierarchical marketplace. The assumption of certain aristocratic prerogatives may very well have encouraged the Earl of Suffolk to secure the reversion to the Mastership of the Revels for his client, Sir John Astley, in 1622.[8] It is a similar assumption that emboldened the courtier, Endymion Porter, to intervene with the King on behalf of William Davenant's play, *The Wits*, in 1633/34 over a question of censorship.[9] But these two examples, selected here for their representative nature, are a far cry from the Restoration theatre's institutionalization of various limitations. The issuing of patents exclusively to courtier-dramatists who had proved themselves not only loyal royalists during the Civil War, but also purveyors of particular dramatic forms resulted in a severely curtailed repertory of plays, not to mention a restricted notion of what constituted viable playhouse architecture.[10]

These changes accompanied other ones as well. The loose chain of command, characteristic of the earlier seventeenth-century theatre, running from the court, to the Lord Chamberlain, to the Master of the Revels, and finally to the theatre managers themselves, was quietly centralized through a series of subtle moves. By 1673 the theatre manager for the King's Company just happened also to be the new Master of the Revels. Likewise, the theatre managers for both companies, in addition to controlling the relations of production, owned the means of production as well, making nigh impossible any opportunity for upward mobility amongst the top actors or shareholders of the company except at times of financial crisis or negligence.[11] Streamlining the organizational and regulatory aspects of the theatre companies virtually guaranteed the court's patronal control of theatrical largesse and

[8] For a fuller discussion of this fascinating, but previously overlooked, case study in patronal brokerage, see Richard Dutton's article, 'The Context of Sir John Astley's Sale of the Mastership of the Revels to Sir Henry Herbert', forthcoming in *ELR*. Professor Dutton was kind enough to share this article with me while it was still in manuscript.

[9] *The Dramatic Records of Sir Henry Herbert*, edited by Joseph Quincy Adams (New Haven, 1917), p. 22.

[10] The success of the private theatre model over other competing forms of playhouse architecture is a topic unto itself, and one to which I cannot do justice in this essay. Several recent publications shed some light on this phenomenon, although perhaps not quite from the theorizing perspective one would wish. See John Orrell, *The Theatre of Inigo Jones and John Webb* (Cambridge, 1985); Jocelyn Powell, *Restoration Theatre Production* (London, 1984); Colin Visser, 'The Killigrew Folio: Private Playhouses and the Restoration Stage', *Theatre Survey*, 19 (1978), 119–38.

[11] For a thorough discussion of the organizational problems that beset both companies — especially the King's Company — during the Restoration, see Chapter II on 'Company Organization and Finances' in Judith Milhous's *Thomas Betterton and the Management of Lincoln's Inn Fields 1695–1708* (Carbondale, 1979), pp. 7–25.

eliminated the need for the court masques that had entertained two prior generations of Stuart monarchs.[12] As the Florentine agent, Giovanni Salvetti, observed in his diplomatic correspondence for 24 December 1660, Charles II virtually usurped the public space of professional theatre in the cleverest of public relations ploys: 'Their Majesties the King and Queen . . . meet at the public plays two or three times a week. This, though it was a thing seldom done by his father, does much to win the affections of the people, through letting him be seen so often and so openly'.[13]

II   *Theatrical Choices*

We often overlook what is perhaps the most singular feature of the Restoration stage — that the court, in granting patents after the eighteen-year hiatus of the Interregnum, had an unprecedented opportunity selectively to re-create the stage out of available dramatic and theatrical models. The simple elimination of certain individuals from the potential pool of theatre managers in 1660 ensured the perpetuation of some dramatic traditions and the demise of others. Likewise, the decision to limit sharply the number of theatrical patents and award them exclusively to loyal courtiers ensured that an ascriptive hierarchy dominated the flow of resources within the theatrical marketplace. Prior to the Restoration the situation was quite different. The earlier seventeenth-century theatre had grown piecemeal from the time of the first permanent playhouse structures in London in the 1570s. By the turn of the century London enjoyed a number of rich and varied theatres catering to the tastes of different classes. Sporadic attempts by the court to bring these theatres into line by censoring seditious language or curtailing inflammatory productions were not wholly successful, largely because of the sheer numbers of theatres operating in London, not to mention the decentralized nature of the theatrical hierarchy.[14]

Even the decade before the Civil War, often depicted in traditional histories as offering little dramatic fare outside of 'decadent' court plays, was characterized by variegated artistic activity.[15] The number of playhouses operating by 1632 may have shrunk considerably from their high point at the turn of the century, but they still offered theatregoers the same range of plays, from roaring Elizabethan tragedies to city comedies. Understanding the persistence of these competing and varying traditions up to the closing of

---

[12] Although there are a couple of isolated exceptions to this generalization, most notably, the court production of *Calisto* in 1674/75, as early as 1663 Charles was complaining to his sister of the impossibility of staging a decent masque at court. For a compelling explanation of the Restoration masque's demise see Paul Hammond's article, 'Dryden's *Albion and Albanius*: The apotheosis of Charles II', in *The Court Masque*, edited by David Lindley (Manchester, 1984), pp. 169–83.

[13] John Orrell, 'A New Witness of the Restoration Stage, 1660–1669', *Theatre Research International*, 2 (1976), 16–28 (p. 18).

[14] See, for instance, Philip J. Finkelpearl's article, '"The Comedians' Liberty": Censorship of the Jacobean Stage Reconsidered', *ELR*, 16 (1986), 123–38.

[15] See, for instance, Alfred Harbage's characterization of this decade in *Cavalier Drama*, second edition (New York, 1964).

the theatres in 1642 throws into relief the strategic choices made by the court in 1660 upon reinstituting the stage. As Martin Butler's important study, *Theatre and Crisis 1632–1642*, reveals, the Caroline audience were a heterogeneous mix of Puritan country gentry, London citizens, and aristocrats who supported a theatre of acerbic political commentary, especially in the so-called city comedies of Brome and Shirley (pp. 1–6). Additionally, the genres and playhouses frequented by the plebeian classes continued to flourish until the closure of the theatres in 1642.

What happened to these alternative dramatic traditions? Even the briefest of glances at the origins of the dramatic repertory in the early 1660s tells a revealing tale: of the enormous stock of 'old' plays (pre-Civil War) available for revival, the two patentees vied almost exclusively for the original King's Company repertory, hardly the stuff of popular fare. Indeed, as Robert Hume has queried, what *did* happen to these other plays — the apprentice and guild dramas, the academic tragedies, the patriotic histories, the cheerfully raunchy popular comedies?[16] Clearly, a goodly number were already available in print, if the repositories of countless rare book rooms and libraries in the United States and Great Britain are any indication. As for the companies' rights to those printed plays, that is a more complicated but not necessarily unanswerable question. As Joseph Loewenstein notes, until the late seventeenth century a playtext only acquired abstract property values in the hands of acting companies, who in turn could sell their right in the manuscript to a printer or publisher.[17] Thomas Killigrew, when he assumed control of the newly formed King's Company in 1660, appears to have argued convincingly for the rights to the old King's Company repertory on the basis of a 'continuous' theatrical tradition and a shared name. Killigrew's success in this regard left Davenant with virtually no repertory, not even the right to the plays *he* had written for the King's Company in the 1630s, a dilemma Davenant partially remedied through a counter-petition (Hume, pp. 158–59).

That Killigrew's claim (through company rights) overpowered Davenant's claim (through authorial rights) suggests that the earlier seventeenth-century formulation of property rights in playtexts was still acceptable in the 1660s. Since Davenant and Killigrew were not the only representatives from the pre-Civil War companies still present at the Restoration, presumably other dramatic repertories could be secured through similar claims. For instance, actors and company managers formerly associated with Queeen Henrietta's men, such as Anthony Turner and William Beeston, were still performing in 1659. Monopolization of the theatre companies resulted in the eventual absorption of most of these 'old'

---

[16] 'Securing a Repertory: Plays on the London Stage 1660–5', in *Poetry and Drama, 1570–1700: Essays in Honour of Harold F. Brooks*, edited by Antony Coleman, Antony Hammond and Arthur Johnson (London, 1981), pp. 156–72 (p. 158).
[17] 'The Script in the Marketplace', *Representations*, 12 (1985), 101–14 (p. 102).

personnel (like Turner and Beeston) into the re-established King's Company (Davenant got the younger, less experienced, players by 'raiding' Richard Rhodes's company). Not surprisingly, the dramatic texts originally written for Queen Henrietta's men, by playwrights like Brome, Heywood, and Shirley, were likewise absorbed into the new King's Company repertory along with the personnel. Other plays surfaced at the Restoration via a more circuitous route. For example, the plays Thomas Middleton wrote for Paul's Boys between 1603 and 1606 made their way into the old King's Company repertory (which Middleton later wrote for as well) after the boy's company fell into trouble with the authorities over *The Isle of Gulls* in 1606; from the King's Company the plays emerged into Killigrew's reconstituted troupe some time in the 1660s.[18]

But the plays associated with plebeian theatres, such as the Fortune and Red Bull, were not claimed by anyone.[19] Anonymous plays like *The Two Noble Ladies* or *The Costly Whore* are nowhere to be found in van Lennep's calendar of stage performances, nor are plays by Red Bull dramatists like Thomas May. Even popular Renaissance playwrights whose works were commonly revived on the Restoration stage, like Thomas Dekker and Philip Massinger, had the plays they wrote for the Fortune and Red Bull ignored. *The Whore of Babylon* and *The Roaring Girl*, both plays penned by Dekker for the Fortune playhouse, are neglected, as is Massinger's *The Maid of Honour*, written for the Red Bull. Presumably, the Red Bull repertory was available through extant members of the troupe; that it was overlooked by Davenant and Killigrew suggests a deliberate refusal on their part, especially given the selective choices recounted above.[20]

The degree of dramatic selectivity becomes even more pronounced if we examine the provenance of those plays that constitute what the prompter John Downes calls the 'Principal Old Stock Plays' for Killigrew's company in the early years of the Restoration.[21] Not only were most of the plays from the original King's Company repertory, but an inordinate number were also

---

[18] The performance of John Day's *The Isle of Gulls* not only got the boys' troupe into trouble with James in 1606, but also lost them Queen Anne's patronage. One Robert Keysar, a goldsmith, took over the company, renaming them 'Children of the Blackfriars'; the adult Blackfriars company may have accommodated some of the players as well. See Andrew Gurr, *The Shakespearean Stage 1574–1642*, second edition (Cambridge, 1980), p. 52.

[19] Martin Butler properly warns us against oversimplifying the polarity between élite and popular theatres, noting that within this spectrum 'were all sorts of subtle shadings and fine tunings which have to be observed'. At the same time, he admits that those 'subtle shadings' surface more at intermediate theatres like the Phoenix, Salisbury Court, and the Globe, rather than at the Blackfriars, Red Bull, or Fortune, theatres which do indeed represent extremes in taste. See *Theatre and Crisis 1632–1642*, p. 304.

[20] John Rhodes, one of the contenders for a theatrical patent in 1660, could possibly be a link to the Fortune repertory, although there is some confusion as to whether the bookseller and former wardrobe-keeper at the Blackfriars is synonymous with the manager of the Fortune Theatre. For the former identification, we have only John Downes's not always reliable word; in this instance, he even admits that the information is secondhand ('as I am inform'd'). Parish records suggest that John Rhodes could very well be the same man. See *A Biographical Dictionary of . . . Stage Personnel in London, 1660–1800*, edited by Philip H. Highfill, Jr., Kalman A. Burnim and Edward A. Langhans, 12 vols (Carbondale, 1973–), XII, 318.

[21] *Roscius Anglicanus*, edited by Judith Milhous and Robert D. Hume (London, 1987), pp. 10–24.

stamped by prior royal favour. Out of these fifteen plays, some eight (over half) had been given performances at the court of Charles I, either at the Cockpit in Whitehall, or at the theatre in Hampton Court.[22] Of the twenty-one plays that comprised the secondary list of 'divers others Acted' the same pattern holds true: virtually all of the plays were either owned by the original King's Company outright or eventually acquired by them. But only five plays from this group had received court performances (about twenty-five per cent), perhaps suggesting that royal favour was one of the elements necessary to earn a play its niche in the 'Principal Old Stock Play' category.[23]

By awarding Thomas Killigrew and William Davenant exclusive patents, the court was not only ensuring a theatrical monopoly, it was, in effect, ensuring the perpetuation of the limited dramatic and theatrical traditions the chosen managers represented. Neither manager was a 'man of the theatre' (if by that phrase we mean someone who has worked in many capacities, many venues), as their biographers would have us believe.[24] Rather, their experience of the theatre derived from writing and performing court masques, penning plays for Blackfriars, and, in the instance of Killigrew, scripting a handful of closet dramas for the wandering English court during the Interregnum, hardly a diverse range of activities. Killigrew had no managerial experience prior to the Restoration; Davenant was awarded William Beeston's company of boy players in 1640 only because of the latter's trouble with the authorities. Davenant, part of a theatrical monopoly that would exclude William Beeston (among others) from receiving a patent in 1660, had also benefited twenty years previously from Beeston's disastrous decision to produce Brome's *The Court Beggar* — ironically, a play critical of the Caroline court's awarding of monopolies and patents.[25]

---

[22] I have compiled these lists with the help of G. E. Bentley's *Jacobean and Caroline Stage*, 7 vols (Oxford, 1941–68), especially volumes III and IV.

[23] Nor is this an unreasonable hypothesis on my part. Killigrew, the archetypal politic courtier, secured his upward mobility by using his literary connexions adroitly, at the court of both Charles I and Charles II. As part of Henrietta Maria's circle, he penned the courtly romances she favoured, such as *The Prisoners* (1632–35) and *Claracilla* (1635–36); as loyal servant to the court, he dutifully performed in several masques, most notably *Tempe Restored* (14 February 1632) in which he played 'the Gentleman'. Selecting those scripts for his 'Principal Stock Plays' in 1660 that had pleased Charles II's parents thirty years previously is exactly the sort of literary investment Killigrew had favoured throughout his life. Given the startling number of patents, monopolies, and grants he secured from both courts, in addition to his theatrical monopoly, his investment in favoured genres paid off handsomely. For an unadulterated look at his various schemes, including his distasteful participation in 'begging estates', see the *Calendar of State Papers Domestic* for the years 1637 to 1638; 1660; 1661; 1664 to 1666. Alfred Harbage in his biography of Killigrew suppresses the more lurid incidents and attempts to explain away the better known ones.

[24] For these views, see Chapter 9 in Mary Edmond's *Rare Sir William Davenant* (Manchester, 1987); Arthur H. Nethercot, *Sir William Davenant; Poet Laureate and Playwright Manager* (Chicago, 1938) passim; Alfred Harbage, *Thomas Killigrew, Cavalier Dramatist, 1612–83* (Philadelphia, 1930). All three biographers find themselves at odds with their own evidence, so strongly do they subscribe to the 'ideology of merit'. While believing their subject to be intrinsically worthy of the rewards bestowed upon him, they all work while chronicle careers painstakingly built on court preferment.

[25] Andrew Gurr says that the play which lost Beeston his company of boy players 'was almost certainly Richard Brome's *The Court Beggar*'. See *The Shakespearean Stage 1574–1642*, p. 63. Martin Butler also accepts this attribution as a given; indeed, he even goes so far as to identify several allusions that would have given Whitehall vapours. See *Theatre and Crisis 1632–1642*, pp. 220–27.

In permitting Davenant and Killigrew to manœuvre William Beeston (who, along with John Rhodes and Michael Mohun, had organized independent companies) out of a patent, one can only assume that the memory of the court was long indeed. Moreover, an exclusionary pattern similar to that of the dramatic repertory emerges here. The three 'alternative' theatre managers had first-hand experience of non-élite companies, unlike the two patentees. Michael Mohun trained as a boy actor under Christopher Beeston at the Cockpit (also known as 'The Phoenix' theatre during the 1630s), eventually becoming a key member of Queen Henrietta's men.[26] John Rhodes — if he is indeed the same person, as I am conjecturing here — was either a manager or investor in the Fortune Theatre, one of two notorious 'plebe' houses, in 1637, and perhaps former wardrobe keeper at the Blackfriars. Beeston's first-hand experience of the theatre is the most extensive of the three. William's father, Christopher, was, according to G. E. Bentley, 'probably the most important theatrical figure in London' from 1617 to his death in 1638 (II, 363). Exposure to his father's various companies and to the London theatre world at large figured in his career in several ways. Bentley thinks it likely that, as a child, William acted for his father, experience which later manifested itself in his noteworthy ability in training boy actors.[27] After his father's death in 1638, William took over Beeston's Boys, which he managed until *The Court Beggar* débâcle broke out two years later.

Davenant and Killigrew's lack of practical knowledge about putting together an acting company is quite evident in that first essential year of the Restoration. Neither man actually *organized* a company himself, although the other three contenders for patents were already performing by 1659/60.[28] Clearly, personnel were also available to Davenant and Killigrew. Evidence turned up by John Freehafer indicates that Beeston, for one, put together — albeit without a licence — 'a company of the first rank' in a scant two months after the Restoration.[29] The company of 'old actors' run by Mohun after 1660 was already active in May 1659. And Rhodes's troupe of young actors was performing by February 1660 at the Cockpit in Drury Lane (Freehafer, pp. 7–8). In effect, Davenant and Killigrew — like the so-called 'corporate raiders' of our own time — used a Restoration version of junk bonds to enable their take-over scheme. Exclusionary patents from Charles II himself

---

[26] One of the playhouses 'significantly less exclusive than Blackfriars', according to Martin Butler in *Theatre and Crisis 1632–1642*, p. 304.

[27] Bentley further observes that among contemporary theatre managers and acting coaches, Beeston 'is the first whose ability is mentioned. Thus it is not only as a Restoration manager that he is an important link between the Caroline and Restoration stage, but as the master whose acting technique must have been apparent in the work of several of the most conspicuous Restoration actors'. See *The Jacobean and Caroline Stage*, II, 371.

[28] Davenant was staging 'operas' in London before the Restoration, but these were isolated performances, not the on-going work of a repertory company.

[29] Freehafer's excellent and detailed analysis of the events leading up to the monopolization of the companies supercedes prior accounts in Leslie Hotson and Allardyce Nicoll's theatre histories. See 'The Formation of the London Patent Companies in 1660', *Theatre Notebook*, 20 (1965), 6–30 (p. 13).

prohibited all other companies; moreover, they virtually guaranteed the incorporation of the fledgling theatre companies organized by their three non-élite competitors.[30] Davenant and Killigrew's expertise as courtiers, men who knew how to work the legal system, not to mention the complicated network of access leading to the King's bedchamber, overpowered competing claims of 'professionalism'.[31]

A little-discussed play, *Lady Alimony; or, The Alimony Lady* (London, 1659) suggests that the dramatists and managers remaining in London during the Protectorate who had worked in more popular theatres were well aware of the threat the élite tradition posed to them. Although technically the theatres had been closed since 1642, a number of the citizen playhouses (especially the Red Bull) hosted performances sporadically throughout the period, providing the straggling bands of actors and dramatists who had remained in England with occasional employment. It was during this period that Davenant was released from the Tower in August 1654; he seems to have attended a private show at the Red Bull with Daniel Fleming and Sir George Fletcher in February or March 1655 (Edmond, p. 122). The simple fact of the performance suggests that the Cromwellian regime was not as vehemently anti-theatrical as feared, especially if dramatic fare could be marketed as 'operas' or 'medleys', essentially non-representational modes of performance. Davenant quickly set about staging a number of private musical and pseudo-dramatic entertainments, once again catering to the tastes of an élite audience. By the winter season of 1658/59 he produced two operas at the only fully equipped theatre left in London, the Cockpit in Drury Lane. Even by 1659 Davenant was positioning himself for a complete monopoly of the stage should the restoration of the monarchy come about.[32]

Lady Alimony's comment on Davenant's ambition is extraordinary in several respects. In featuring the first act as an induction scene, it immediately claims alliance with a popular tradition in the Renaissance theatre.

[30] The grant dated 21 August 1660 and stamped under the Privy Signet specifies that 'there shall be noe more Places of Representations nor Companies of Actors of Playes or Operas by Recitative, musick or Representations by danceing and Scenes or any other Entertainments on the Stage in our Citties of London and Westminster or in the Liberties of them, then the two, to be now Erected by vertue of this Authority'. On 5 November 1660 articles of agreement were signed between William Davenant and the members of Richard Rhodes's company which authorized Davenant's legal and financial control. See James Orchard Halliwell-Phillipps, *A Collection of Ancient Documents Respecting the Office of the Master of the Revels* (London, 1870), pp. 20–21 and 27–32.

[31] Although nothing comparable to G. E. Aylmer's superb history of the civil service under Charles I, *The King's Servants* (London, 1961), exists for the Restoration, some of the essays in David Starkey's collection, *The English Court: from the War of the Roses to the Civil War* (London, 1987) give us an indication of the privileged access to the monarch Killigrew would have had as a 'Groom of the Bedchamber'. See especially David Starkey's 'Introduction: Court history in perspective' and Kevin Sharpe's 'The image of virtue: the court and household of Charles I, 1625–1642'.

[32] Nor is this at all a historic impossibility. While quietly staging his 'operas' without the interference, if not with the active approval, of the Cromwellian regime, Davenant would have been aware of the repercussions of the parliamentary upheavals. David Ogg points out that as early as January to April 1659 some members of Richard Cromwell's parliament 'expressed willingness to restore the hereditary peerage to its place in the constitution'. Davenant may very well have been gambling on the return of a monarch who would be sympathetic to the theatre, as well as to his own monopolizing tendencies. See David Ogg, *England in the Reign of Charles II* (1934; reprinted Oxford, 1984), p. 2.

Moreover, the induction includes a playwright-manager, one Timon, who several times longs nostalgically for the 'golden time ... when the Actor could imbellish his Author, and return a Pean to his Pen in every accent', another sentimental evocation of the improvisational nature of the popular theatre (A3v). Shortly after, a hectoring figure, appropriately named 'Haxter', enters with a mandate 'to obstruct [the] Action' of this popular company (several references to 'groundlings' and 'Plebeian incivility' suggest the intended audience).

During the ensuing dialogue it becomes apparent that the 'pragmatical Monopolist' who dispatched poor Haxter is William Davenant. His travels during the Civil War are described in some detail, as are the galloping 'iambicks' of his dramatic verse. Most telling is the direct hit against *The Cruelty of the Spaniards in Peru*, one of the two 'operas' that Davenant produced during the winter season of 1658/59. Timon's response to Davenant's mandate makes the identification apparent: 'present my service to his Naked Savages; Monkeys, Babouns and marmosites', all inhabitants of Davenant's exoticized Peru. He further warns that Davenant should interfere no more 'lest he lose by his out-landish Properties', an allusion to the elaborate staging techniques that Davenant learned — not invented — from working with Inigo Jones on the court masques (B2r). Even from this brief snatch of dialogue, it is clear that the popular dramatists saw the threat posed by the court theatre, especially if the purveyors of that tradition were permitted to usurp everything with the backing of a restored court. At one point Timon wonders: 'Be his monopolizing brains of such extent, as they have power to ingross all Inventions to his Coffer: all our Stage-action to his Exchequer?' The answer, of course, in 1660 proved to be 'yes'.

III   *William Davenant: A Case Study*

Success through the careful nurturing of patron–client relations placed seventeenth-century writers in a peculiarly ambivalent position. While the support of aristocratic patrons serves to authorize the writer's productions, especially given the intertwined hierarchy of aesthetic taste and social class, that very support also calls into question whether genius, inspiration, or artistic excellence plays any part in the creation (or reception) of those self-same literary productions. It is rather like the tired tale of the unknown painter (a film actor will do as well) who is taken up as a *cause célèbre* by art galleries, publicity agents, and society matrons. Years later, awash in money, liquor, and regrets, he pouts that no one 'takes him seriously' — a statement which means that his art is being evaluated in purely economic or social terms, rather than being adequately aestheticized out of vulgar marketplace considerations (and the accusation of 'commercialism' is still the worst insult to befall an artist).

Although it can certainly be demonstrated that class and cultural expectations play as great a role in the production and reception of popular as of élite plays, the artist's success in the former realm is predicated on an assumed detachment from ideology. Professionals — not patrons — determine the selection, production, and payment for plays, thus encouraging the belief that one's genius has spoken convincingly to auditors whose judgement has been formed by experience only. It's not quite the same thing when one's brother-in-law, say, a courtier thick with the Lord Chamberlain, arranges directly for a play. Thus, a central paradox exists at the nexus of patronal/commercial relations. While patronage cannot help but bear witness to the interestedness of kinship or client relations, it still promotes the illusion of a taste rarefied and unsullied by the marketplace. On the other hand, commercialism, while producing the mirage of a largely detached, disinterested, and anonymous audience (who 'get what they pay for'), none the less taints the dramatic artefact with the stench of mere 'lucre'.

This cultural conundrum exists throughout the seventeenth century; indeed, we can see vestigial and transformed versions of it in our own time. An important distinction needs to be made here, though. In a cultural marketplace characterized by specific exchange relationships, the dramatist has the option of targeting his products for different venues (within highly structured parameters, of course). If, like Jonson, he tires of court patronage, he can always retreat to a professional theatre which in turn offers its own hierarchy of taste and reputation. And, not surprisingly, if we stand back and take stock of how the writers within this pre-Civil War marketplace perceived themselves in relation to it, we see them claiming alliance with or opposing factions and camps in a fairly straightforward manner. In a cultural marketplace of generalized exchange, especially one characterized by asymmetrical-hierarchical relations, as was the Restoration theatre, the ability to position oneself in opposition to an artistic foe (and therefore carve out one's cultural identity as a writer) becomes more problematic. Because this later cultural marketplace is constituted commercially, as well as patronally, the writer's sense of validation becomes somewhat confused. Who, or what, authorizes literary endeavours in a generalized exchange marketplace characterized by overt specifications and limitations? How does the writer remain a loyal client to patrons who also prove to be professional rivals? And if patronal interestedness is spurned, where does the professional dramatist retreat to if the popular tradition has been eradicated?

The career of William Davenant, which spans both periods, illustrates not only some of the differences between marketplaces, but also how those differences allowed writers and managers to constitute themselves. Davenant was never what one would consider a 'popular writer'. Early on, élite playhouses, such as the Blackfriars, provided him with box office revenues, while the public sphere of print provided financial remuneration for copyright to his plays. Traditional patronage, though, provided

Davenant with the most lucrative and legitimizing means of employment.[33] Through the court he was awarded direct payment for the extravaganzas he penned, not to mention the lyric poetry and courtly romances that charmed Queen Henrietta Maria. He also performed in several masques, playing the role of the 'Poet' in both *Luminalia* (1638) and *Salmacida Spolia* (1640).[34] Thus, court patronage not only offered him financial remuneration, but also a means of self-reflexive dramatic legitimation: the 'poet' who enabled the court's fantastical royalist fictions. In 1638 the laureateship, the most apparent sign of court favour, followed. From that point on, Davenant never bothered writing for the professional theatre again, even for a playhouse as élite as the Blackfriars.

Largely because of his background — the son of a vintner who succeeded through patronal channels — Davenant's belief in his position as a courtly writer was tenuous indeed.[35] Like many people whose education or social contacts remove them from the social trajectory dictated by birth and economics, Davenant sought to prove himself part of an élite world that was not 'by nature' his own.[36] During Charles I's reign, when Davenant worked exclusively in court and private theatres, he would sporadically attempt to differentiate himself through aesthetic choice (and thereby through class) from the less privileged writers writing for public and citizen theatres. The popular playwrights, in turn, armed with the smug weaponry of popular backing, hurled sallies at the pretences of courtier-writers like Davenant.

[33] As a point of comparison, we might consider Jonson's career. He told Drummond that 'of all his plays he never gained two hundred pounds', whereas from patronage he gained far more, as cited in Richard Helgerson, *Self-Crowned Laureates: Spenser, Jonson, Milton and the Literary System* (Berkeley, 1983), p. 166. Although Davenant never made a similar statement, we can still infer that traditional patronage proved far more lucrative than the box-office proceeds from Blackfriars, a relatively small house. Several of his plays were relative failures, netting him little, whereas the average court payment for masques during the reign of Charles I was £50.

[34] Stephen Orgel and Roy Strong, *Inigo Jones: The Theatre of the Stuart Court*, 2 vols (Berkeley, 1973), II, 87.

[35] Davenant's career is a classic example of advancement through patronage. His first job as a page in the household of the Duchess of Richmond led to employment in the household of Fulke Grevile, Lord Brooke (who was also the patron of Sir Philip Sidney, among other important literary figures). After Lord Brooke's murder by a disinherited servant, Davenant was offered hospitality by Edward Hyde, Lord Clarendon, at the Inns of Court. Both Hyde and Endymion Porter, another friend acquired through Lord Brooke's circle, proved instrumental to Davenant's burgeoning theatrical desires. Hyde, of course, became Lord Chancellor upon the Restoration — a most useful ally for a man with monopolization on his mind. See Edmond, pp. 27–37.

[36] A point impressed upon Davenant after the publication of Books I and II and the uncompleted Book III of *Gondibert* in 1651. In 1653, several of his courtier 'friends' banded together to write 'Certain Verses . . . to be Re-printed with the second Edition of *Gondibert*', an attack on the poem and the poet. Although the quarto and octavo editions of *Gondibert* had featured commendatory verses by Abraham Cowley and Edmund Waller, and advertised the approval of Thomas Hobbes, this élite coterie declared that approval a lie: 'how untruly | All they that read may look'. Moreover, Davenant was assailed for publishing *Gondibert* 'without our consent . . . When we thy best friends to the number of four | Advis'd thee to scribble no more'. The Duke of Buckingham, who would later lampoon the similarly ambitious Dryden (also a laureate with élitist pretensions) in *The Rehearsal*, numbered among Davenant's attackers in these verses. Thus it appears that literary support or consternation divided along class lines. Of his supporters Cowley, the son of a stationer, and Hobbes, an impecunious scholar dependent on tutorial income, shared Davenant's social trajectory; Waller, one of the wealthiest poets in English literature, was stolid gentry but hardly aristocracy. His attackers, clearly piqued that Davenant spurned their advice, remind him of his modest social origins, indifferent education, and resulting lack of taste in verse after verse. See Appendix ii in *Sir William Davenant's Gondibert*, edited by David F. Gladish (Oxford, 1971).

The 1630 quarto of Davenant's ill-fated play, *The Just Italian*, reveals just how deep the mutual antagonism ran. Thomas Carew's commendatory verses blame the debased taste of the audience for preferring the more popular dramas produced by managers such as Christopher Beeston at the Red Bull or the Cockpit theatres to the more élite fare of the King's Company at the Blackfriars (a rivalry which very well could have fuelled Davenant's desire for a monopoly twenty years later). Stung by the town's neglect of his friend's 'strong fancies (raptures of the brayne, | Drest in Poetique flames)', Carew accuses the audience of ignorance and vulgarity:

> These are the men in crowded heapes that throng
> To that adulterate stage, where not a tong
> Of th'untun'd Kennell, can a line repeat
> Of serious sense: but like lips, meet like meat;
> Whilst the true brood of Actors, that alone
> Keepe naturall vnstrayn'd Action in her throne
> Behold their Benches bare, though they rehearse
> The tearser *Beaumonts* or great *Iohnsons* verse
> (as cited in Bentley, I, 224–25)

Andrew Gurr notes that this attack linking Beeston's company at the Cockpit with the citizen fare of the Red Bull found a quick retaliatory reply that same year in the verses appended to Shirley's *Grateful Servant* (p. 201). Some of Shirley's sympanthizers claimed to prefer his 'so smooth, so sweet' verse to the 'mighty rimes, | Audacious metaphors' of Davenant at Blackfriars; likewise, Heywood in Book IV of *The Hierarchy of the Blessed Angels* sarcastically asks of Davenant some five years later, 'How comes it (ere he know it) | A puny shall assume the name of poet'? (Gurr, p. 202). The attacks continued throughout the decade. Martin Butler observes that from 1637 on a number of non-élite dramatists were increasingly challenging the cultural hegemony of private theatres like Blackfriars by banding together and writing commendatory verses for one another in a display of group solidarity. Continuing assaults against Davenant and his patronized circle as 'those who surfeit with their bayes', not only suggest their contempt for dramatists who catered to court tastes (and were rewarded with the 'bayes' of the laureateship accordingly), but who also imposed that rarefied taste upon general audiences (Butler, p. 186).

Paradoxically, although he went to some lengths to fashion himself as a courtier/playwright, Davenant increasingly yearned for the legitimation that professionalism, an ideology of merit that advertises its detachment from 'mere interest', alone can seemingly confer. The barbs from the popular playwrights had found their mark. All that Davenant lacked in order to complete the 'professional' side of his writerly identity was his own company. So keen was Davenant's desire in this regard, that the previous year he secured from Charles I a patent to erect a large theatre in Fleet Street 'in the parishes of Saint Dunstan's in the West, London, or in Saint Bride's, London' (Bentley, II, 421). Either locale would position him securely within the élite domain of private houses, such as the Whitefriars, Salisbury Court, and the Blackfriars, and far from the dread suburban influence of the Red Bull, the Fortune, or the Boar's Head. Some seven months after the 1639 proposal, Davenant withdrew his rights to the patent and promised not to build 'any place in London or Westminster', perhaps yielding to an outcry from other managers. Being awarded Beeston's successful company of boy actors by the court a few months later was not a bad consolation prize.

In the new theatrical marketplace of the Restoration, where the prior distinctions between court, élite, and popular were elided, we see Davenant nervously oscillating between patronized and professional roles, at times enacting both positions at once. While quaffing a cup with professional writers and friends, Davenant could proudly claim that he 'writt with the very spirit that did Shakespeare', thus promoting the fiction of a literary worth based solely on a professional lineage detached from a patronal mode of production. During the Restoration until his death in 1668, Davenant veered between being Shakespeare's putative son, the independent drama-tist, and the court's loyal godchild, the patronized élite poet. For example, shortly after the Restoration, Davenant once again enacted the role of the obeisant servant to the court, even going so far as to praise Charles II openly for *not* rewarding literary merit in writers. In a panegyrical poem, 'To the King's Most Sacred Majesty' (London, 1663), Davenant puts forth the customary justification for poverty (the affliction of poets, as well as the poor), that it actually produces benefits for the indigent 'when Want leads them to God for Remedie' (p. 2). But Davenant goes a step beyond the usual Christian defence to suggest that want keeps poets humble and therefore grateful for patronal reward:

> How happy is Affliction which may come
> Where God allows not Merit any room?
> Kings fit their Gifts to those who them receive,
> And to Affliction so much favour give,
> As may not well to Merit be allow'd,
> Lest those they would encourage should grow proud.
> Kings, wisely jealous, watch how Merit grows,
> That they may know it ere it self it knows.
>
> (p. 3)

Affliction suffered by loyal writers (the *longue durée* of the Civil War's effect on the theatre, or the impoverishment of royalist wanderings abroad) should be rewarded over any question of literary merit. That much is clear. Less apparent, though, is Davenant's astute recognition that merit, as a com-peting ideology, threatens to displace patronage precisely because it empowers writers' sense of independence. Therefore, 'lest those they would encourage should grow proud', kings should scrutinize their literary subjects closely for any overreaching sense of self-promotion or reliance. Affliction, which only kings can ease through patronal gifts, makes for appreciative and obedient poet-playwrights.

Even while urging Charles II not to favour merit over loyalty, Davenant lent credence to the rumour that Shakespeare — everyone's favourite 'man of the theatre' and non-patronized (and therefore disinterested) dramatist *par excellence* — had been his godfather, perhaps even his illegitimate father. John Aubrey, in his brief life of Davenant (which he compiled during the Restoration), records the dramatist's eagerness to establish his proximity to Shakespeare, even at the expense of his mother's reputation, in order to promote his own sense of uninterested professionalism:

Mr. William Shakespeare was wont to goe into Warwickshire once a yeare, and did commonly in his journey lye at this house in Oxon, where he was exceedingly respected . . . Now Sir William would sometimes, when he was pleasant over a glasse of wine with his most intimate friends — e.g. Sam Butler, author of *Hudibras*, etc., say, that it seemed to him that he writt with the very spirit that did Shakespeare, and seem contented enough to be thought his Son. He would tell them the story as above, in which way his mother had very light report, whereby she was called a Whore.[37]

Additionally, in his new position as manager of the Duke's Company after the Restoration, Davenant displayed a self-conscious concern for fashioning himself as a 'professional': someone who introduced innovations into the staging of plays (in this instance, the transference of staging techniques previously reserved for court consumption into the public realm) and who took great care with his actors. It is well known, for instance, that Davenant and his wife personally housed and trained the young actresses who were being newly introduced to the English stage for the first time. He took similar care with other aspects of the company and repertory, from arranging for new plays to the revival of staples from the pre-Civil War period. He may very well have pleaded with Charles II in that panegyrical poem to ignore writers and artists who traded in merit, especially after assessing the relative values of 'patronized' and 'professional' in the Restoration dramatic market-place, but he was not about to relinquish his own burgeoning stock of professional identity — not utterly.

Nowhere do we see more clearly how the transformation to a generalized exchange marketplace (and the accompanying collapse of an enabling distinction between 'patronized' and 'professional') affected Davenant's conception of himself as a dramatist and manager than in the collected *Works* (London, 1673). Published five years after his death and featuring a dedication to the King written by Davenant's widow, Mary, this handsome folio announces itself as a professionalized artefact in the tradition precipitated by Jonson's infamous *Workes*. Interestingly, Davenant did not attempt to publish such a collection prior to the Restoration; the plays written during the 1630s sport the modest quarto and octavo garb that befit the productions of a dramatist who lacks 'professional airs'. One also wonders whether Davenant was willing in the late 1630s to submit such a folio to the public hilarity that greeted his other professional endeavours.

[37] See *Aubrey's Brief Lives*, edited by Oliver Lawson Dick (1949; reprinted Ann Arbor, 1957), p. 85.

11

Because the popular dramatic and theatrical tradition had been virtually eliminated from the Restoration marketplace in the 1660s and early 1670s, the times were more auspicious for such a venture. The title-page specifically informs the reader of Davenant's, the *author's*, careful preparation of the volume: 'Consisting of Those which were formerly Printed, and Those which he design'd for the Press'. The bookseller, Henry Herringman, verifies the information on the title-page: 'I Here present you with A Collection of all those Pieces Sir William Davenant ever design'd for the Press; In his Life-time he often express'd to me his great Desire to see them in One Volume'. Clearly, Davenant wanted to leave for posterity a glimpse of his professionalized self, as the engraved portrait facing the title-page makes apparent: brow graced by literary laurel and shoulder adorned by stately drapery.

Lest the reader recall only the laureatized Davenant, Mary's dedication (which precedes the bookseller's remarks), reminds him/her of Davenant's élite status as a poet patronized by two generations of Stuart monarchs:

I have often heard (and I have some reason to believe) that your Royal Father, of Ever Blessed Memory, was not displeased with his Writings; That your most Excellent Mother did Graciously take him into her Family; That she was often diverted by him, and as often smil'd upon his Endeavors; I am sure he made it the whole Study and Labor of the latter part of his Life, to entertain His Majesty, and your Royal Highness, and I hope he did it Successfully.

Thus the prefatory apparatus to Davenant's *Works* simultaneously internalizes and sustains the complexities of the post-Restoration dramatic marketplace. As the historian of print, Elizabeth Eisenstein, has noted, print technology, precisely because it offered a 'standard' against which variations could be measured, held out to authors the possibility of fashioning a uniquely authorial (and authorized) self.[38] In presenting himself as a 'professional', someone who secured his reputation through merit exclusively, Davenant drew his psychological strength from the residual popular tradition in the pre-Civil War theatre (thus his concern with Shakespeare's lineage) and the emergent bourgeois culture of print. At the same time, Davenant had to survive in a dramatic marketplace where the flow of resources was dominated and limited by a hierarchical élite. In such a marketplace, Davenant could bank on his thirty years of investment in the Stuart monarchy; indeed, because of the unprecedented opportunity to make the theatre anew in 1660, Davenant could become part of that élite in a way never before possible. But for the next generation of theatrical personnel in the 1670s, both the investment and the payoff would prove much more problematic.

---

[38] *The Printing Press as an Agent of Change*, 2 vols (Cambridge, 1979), I, 79–85.

Tasso on Spenser: The Politics of Chivalric Romance

RICHARD HELGERSON

University of California, Santa Barbara

The argument of this paper depends on three dates and their relation to one another. The first is 1580. In that year two small collections of letters between Gabriel Harvey and Edmund Spenser were published in London. These letters contain the earliest surviving reference to Spenser's *Faerie Queene*, which Harvey had been reading in manuscript and did not much like. The second date comes just a year later, 1581. In that year the first five complete editions of Torquato Tasso's *Jerusalem Delivered* appeared in Italy, to be followed in the next eight years by at least six more Italian editions. This enormously popular poem gave literary expression to a debate that had been raging in Italy for some forty years between opponents and defenders of Ariosto's *Orlando Furioso*, a debate over the proper form of heroic poetry. The last date, nine years further on, is 1590, when the first three books of *The Faerie Queene* were published, books which include at least one extensive borrowing from *Jerusalem Delivered* and many briefer echoes. Clearly Spenser had been reading Tasso and had found the Italian's work relevant to the poem he had shown to Harvey some years earlier.[1]

In addressing the relationship between *Jerusalem Delivered* and *The Faerie Queene* I am particularly interested in the way in which Tasso's poem may have served (and can still serve) as an interpretive guide to Spenser's. Whatever *The Faerie Queene* may have meant in 1580 when Harvey first read it, it is likely to have meant something significantly different in 1590 to anyone who had closely studied *Jerusalem Delivered*, as Spenser had. And this would have been the case were the 1590 *Faerie Queene* no more than a printing, as we know it was not, of the 1580 manuscript. In 1580, Harvey charged that Spenser had let 'Hobgoblin run away with the garland from Apollo'.[2] What Tasso forces into

---

[1] For a list of Spenser's borrowings from *Jerusalem Delivered*, see Veselin Kostíc, *Spenser's Sources in Italian Poetry: A Study in Comparative Literature* (Belgrade, 1969).
[2] *The Works of Edmund Spenser: A Variorum Edition*, edited by Edwin Greenlaw and others, 11 vols (Baltimore, 1932–57), x, 472. Subsequent quotations from Spenser come from this edition and are identified by volume and page number with the exception of quotations from *The Faerie Queene*, which are identified by book, canto, and stanza.

view and I think forced into view for Spenser himself was (and still is) the buried political significance of Spenser's Hobgoblinism, the meaning in the immediate context of the newly consolidated early modern state of what the eighteenth century was to recognize, again with Tasso's help, as the 'Gothic' character of Spenser's chivalric romance.

At issue here is less any explicit statement Spenser's poem makes or any thematic 'statement' made by its several episodes (though I will refer later to examples of each) than the meaning of the poem's generic form. In Spenser's generation, the generation born between about 1550 and 1565, a large number of men undertook major textual projects that put England at their centre. One might think, for example, of Sir Edward Coke's *Reports* and *Institutes*, William Camden's *Britannia*, John Speed's *Theater of the Empire of Great Britain*, Michael Drayton's *Poly-Olbion*, Richard Hakluyt's *Principal Navigations of the English Nation*, William Shakespeare's English history plays. *The Faerie Queene* clearly belongs on this list. But in each instance England is represented not only by a certain number of assertions that could be pulled out of context and compared to one another, but also by a particular genre, by a discursive 'kind'. A law report says something about England's legal identity, something about the centrality of precedent, quite apart from anything the individual cases it contains may say. And in doing so, it invests authority in one group rather than another, in judges rather than kings. Each of the genres to which these various works belong performs a similar legitimating act. Each is the implicit advocate of a set of socially grounded interests and of a political ideology associated with those interests. In this *The Faerie Queene* is no exception. Its form had a constituency and a politics, both of which are more easily seen when Spenser's poem is set next to Tasso's. A chivalric romance, like a law report, an atlas, a collection of voyages, or a history play, takes its meaning from an historically located system of differences.[3] For *The Faerie Queene* and its author the most immediately relevant system of differences, both literary and political, was made manifest in *Jerusalem Delivered*.

When eighteenth-century critics called *The Faerie Queene* 'Gothic', they referred to its departures from classical epic design and decorum, to its multiple plotting and its fabulous knight-errantry: precisely those features that sixteenth-century Italian critics had already blamed in *Orlando Furioso*.[4] *Jerusalem Delivered* was designed to answer such objections. It does this, however, not by eliminating Ariostan romance but rather by subordinating it to epic. *Jerusalem Delivered* is founded on a conflict that goes far beyond the

---

[3] For an example of an analysis governed by the terms suggested in this paragraph, see Richard Helgerson, 'The Land Speaks: Cartography, Chorography, and Subversion in Renaissance England', *Representations*, 16 (1986), 50–85.
[4] Eighteenth-century characterizations of *The Faerie Queene* as 'Gothic' can be sampled in *Spenser: The Critical Heritage*, edited by R. M. Cummings (New York, 1971), pp. 206, 224, 229, 232, and 260–61. Bernard Weinberg surveys the debate over Ariosto in *A History of Literary Criticism in the Italian Renaissance*, 2 vols (Chicago, 1961), II, 954–1073.

obvious struggle between Christians and pagans for the possession of Jerusalem. Within the Christian camp itself and within the narrative structure of the poem, the opposed values of epic and romance vie for mastery. Epic finds its prime representative in Goffredo, the divinely chosen ruler of the Christian forces. Romance, as fits its multiplicity of motive and action, has many champions, most prominent among them Tancredi and Rinaldo. Only Goffredo is single-mindedly devoted to the communal cause which brought the crusaders to Jerusalem. The others contribute to that communal cause. Indeed, its success depends on their participation. But each is at some point led astray by other motives and by other desires: by love, honour, or the romantic quest for adventure.

One episode of many will have to serve to illustrate the strongly political terms in which Tasso presents the opposition between his epic and his romance heroes. In Book v Rinaldo slays Gernando, another of the Christian nobles, in a fight over honour and precedence. Despite the plea of Tancredi, who recalls Rinaldo's 'worth and courage' and 'that princely house and race of his', Goffredo resolves to punish the offender. 'If high and low', he answers,

> Of sovereign power alike should feel the stroke,
> Then, Tancred, ill you counsel us, I trow;
> If lords should know no law, as erst you spoke,
> How vile and base our empire were, you know;
> If none but slaves and peasants bear the yoke,
> > Weak is the sceptre, and the power is small,
> > That such provisos brings annexed withal.[5]

'Sovereign power', 'law', 'empire', 'sceptre': these are the dominant terms of Goffredo's discourse of rule. As the commander of the crusading forces besieging Jerusalem, he governs neither a single nation nor a fixed territory. But he is a royal absolutist none the less. His power was 'freely given' him by God, and he refuses to see it diminished. 'Since you are all in like subjection brought, | Both high and low', he tells Tancredi, 'obey and be content' (v. 38). It is precisely such obedience that Rinaldo denies. Indeed, he refuses even to submit to trial.

> Let them in fetters plead their cause, quoth he,
> That are base peasants, born of servile strain;
> I was born free, I live and will die free.

> (v. 42)

For Rinaldo, the free-born nobleman, submission to the law is a sign of servile subjection. The state and its claims must give way before the higher claim of honour and lineage, and that higher claim is indissolubly linked to the behaviour characteristic of romance. Having defied the law, Rinaldo

---

[5] *Godfrey of Bulloigne: A Critical Edition of Edward Fairfax's Translation of Tasso's 'Gerusalemme Liberata'*, edited by Kathleen M. Lea and T. M. Gang (Oxford, 1981), v, 37. Unless otherwise indicated, subsequent quotations from *Jerusalem Delivered* are from this translation and are identified, as is this one, by book and stanza.

rides off in search of 'hard adventures': '*alone* against the pagan would he fight' (v. 52, my italics). If sovereign power is the mark of Goffredo, solitary adventure is that of Rinaldo.

Tasso leaves no doubt concerning the official allegiance of his poem. It supports Goffredo. (The poem was originally called *Il Goffredo* or, in English, *Godfrey of Bulloigne*.) Where Goffredo's inspiration is divine, the moving forces on the other side are demonic. Satan, acting most often through the intermediary of such pagan women as Clorinda, Erminia, and the enchantress Armida, seduces the Christian champions and leads them into romance. Their recovery not only permits the final liberation of Jerusalem but marks a decisive victory of unity over multiplicity, of historic verisimilitude over the marvellous, of antiquity over the middle ages, and, one must add, of the modern absolutist state over its feudal predecessor. 'The old chivalric code is', as one recent critic has remarked, 'denied and overwhelmed in an epic world that reorganizes itself according to a new custom, a world where for the concept of "ventura" (the medieval "aventure") is substituted that of "service," where the role of "knight errant" is suppressed for that of "soldier" to a collective cause'.[6]

That Tasso's epic allegiance is only official, that his poem betrays a 'secret solidarity' with the feudal, romantic ideology that it ostensibly rejects, has been a commonplace of criticism almost since the poem was issued. But if *Jerusalem Delivered* does not make the choice easy, it does make it clear. Here epic stands not only for a supposedly superior literary form but for a whole system of values in which politics has a prominent part. In late sixteenth-century Italy those values were associated with the reinvigorated universalism of the Counter-Reformation church. Elsewhere they would find expression in the absolutist regimes of sixteenth-century Spain and seventeenth-century France. It was in France particularly that critics, though favourably impressed with the unity of Tasso's 'fable', refused to forgive 'the mixture of the Gothic manner in his work'.[7] That mixture and its undoubted imaginative appeal called in question the commitment to absolute authority — aesthetic authority, religious authority, and political authority — on which neoclassicism was founded. Goffredo's obedient assertion of sovereign power had its counterpart in Tasso's acceptance of the classical rules of unity and verisimilitude. Both serve and express what Mervyn James (with particular reference to England) has called 'the dominant theme of sixteenth-century political aspiration': 'the desire and pursuit of the whole'.[8] But the individual aristocratic prowess of Tancredi and Rinaldo, their resistance to royal

[6] Sergio Zatti, 'Cultural Conflict as Military Encounter in the *Jerusalem Delivered*', paper read to the Southern California Renaissance Conference (1983). I have also drawn in my discussion of Tasso on Zatti's book, *L'Uniforme Cristiano e il Multiforme Pagano: Saggio sulla 'Gerusalemme Liberata'* (Milan, 1983). The phrase 'secret solidarity' in the next sentence is borrowed from Zatti.
[7] Richard Hurd, *Letters on Chivalry and Romance* (1762), edited by Hoyt Trowbridge, The Augustan Reprint Society, nos. 101–02 (Los Angeles, 1963), p. 79.
[8] Mervyn James, *Society, Politics and Culture in Early Modern England* (Cambridge, 1986), p. 460.

justice, their solitary feats at arms, their erring loves, belonged rather to the
freer world of Ariostan romance, a world in which the ruler was a marginal
figure and his imperial project of negligible importance. If Tasso's poem was
to satisfy the increasingly repressive and intolerant standards of
seventeenth-century neoclassical judgement, that world of romance had not
merely to be bounded by the epic but wholly replaced by it.

Tasso himself anticipated this need. Tormented by the thought of his own
sinful errancy, he rewrote his poem, transforming the still half-romantic
Liberata into the fiercely correct and generally unread *Conquista*. But long
before making this radically destructive change in his poem, Tasso had
responded to similar doubts with a remarkable post-publication addition.
As early as 1581, the same year as the first complete edition of *Jerusalem
Delivered*, the poem began appearing with a self-protective statement of
authorial intention, 'The Allegory of the Poem'.[9] According to Tasso's
allegorical interpretation civic happiness, represented by the capture of
Jerusalem, is the goal, and Goffredo, who stands for the understanding of the
politic man, is the hero. Solitary enterprise can, from this point of view, only
be condemned. Thus, as Tasso puts it, 'love, which maketh Tancredi and the
other worthies dote and disjoin them from Godfrey, and the disdain which
enticeth Rinaldo from the enterprise do signify the conflict and rebellion
which the concupiscent and ireful powers' (that is, the love and war of the
feudal nobility) 'do make with the reasonable', with the newly rationalized
and absolute power of the state.[10] If the civic enterprise is to succeed these
errant powers must be subjected to their natural master as, to use Tasso's
simile, the hand is subject to the head. Thus, however much the values
associated with the civic life may be qualified in *Jerusalem Delivered* by an
affective preference for romance, Tasso insists that whether one thinks of
politics or of poetics, the public side rather than the private, the side of the
divinely appointed ruler rather than that of the errant knight, must pre-
dominate. In this form and content are at one. The strongly unified epic
must, Tasso clearly feels, be a poem of civic life, a poem in which unity of
purpose and unity of rule are the guarantors of neoclassical conformity.

All this *The Faerie Queene* lacks. Its principal ruler, the Faerie Queene
herself, never appears in the poem and exercises only the loosest and most
intermittent control over its action — or, rather, over its actions, for there are
many. Redcross, Guyon, Scudamore, Artegall, and Calidore are said to have
been assigned their quests by the Faerie Queene, but she does not oversee
their progress in anything like the way Goffredo oversees the taking of

---

[9] Of the twelve pre-1590 editions of the *Gerusalemme Liberata* listed in the British Library catalogue,
seven, including the 1581 Ferrara edition and every edition published after 1581, contain the author's
allegory. Another, Parma 1581 (British Library 1073.g.31.(1.)), clearly had access to it and used it as
the basis for its allegorizations of individual cantos. The allegory is lacking only in the unauthorized and
incomplete edition of 1580 and the Parma (British Library 1489.p.12), Casalmaggiore, and Lione
editions of 1581. It is thus probable that in reading Tasso's poem, Spenser would also have read the
allegory.
[10] *Godfrey of Bulloigne*, p. 90.

Jerusalem. Nor are the quests themselves parts of a unified enterprise, unless
it be on the allegorical level where magnanimity and glory are said to be
central. But in one's experience of the poem such conceptual unity plays
little part, if any. Indeed, what readers of *The Faerie Queene* experience is, in
this regard, not unlike what they would experience in reading Boiardo or
Ariosto: they encounter a large and varied collection of more-or-less
independent adventures that serve no common end. That, in effect, is what is
meant by chivalric romance, what Italian critics of the sixteenth century and
English critics of the eighteenth century meant by the Gothic. As a Gothic
poem *The Faerie Queene*, unlike *Jerusalem Delivered*, allows no place for the
representation of a powerfully centralized and absolutist governmental
order. It acknowledges and celebrates a sovereign lady, but it grants a high
degree of autonomy to individual knights and their separate pursuits, and so
represents power as relatively isolated and dispersed.

In his letter to Raleigh, a letter that is clearly based on Tasso's 'Allegory'
and that presents a reading of *The Faerie Queene* informed by acquaintance
with Tasso's poem, Spenser acknowledges the limited place *The Faerie Queene*
occupies in the epic tradition. Like Tasso, he argues that that tradition has
been divided between the representation of private and public virtues and
remarks that Tasso himself dissevered these qualities, distributing them
between two different characters (or perhaps two different poems), the
'virtues of a private man, coloured in his Rinaldo', those of a political man 'in
his Godfredo'. *The Faerie Queene*, or at least that part of it which he had so far
written, belongs, Spenser says, entirely to Rinaldo's side, to the private side.
Indeed, not only the three books he here presents, but the next nine (only
three of which he actually wrote) will be similarly confined. Together these
twelve books are to portray 'in Arthur, before he was king, the image of a
brave knight, perfected in the twelve private moral virtues ... which, if I find
to be well accepted', he says, 'I may be perhaps encouraged to frame the
other part of politic virtues in his person after that he came to be king
(1. 167–68). Spenser does not refuse the politic in favour of the private, the
king in favour of the 'brave knight', but he does put the politic and the kingly
off to a time that, given the length of the poem, could be expected never to
arrive. A similar split and a similar exclusion mark his representation of
Elizabeth. As 'most royal queen or empress', she is figured by the Faerie
Queene, who, as we have noticed, never enters the poem. Belphoebe, who
does enter it, stands rather for the queen's private person as 'a most virtuous
and beautiful lady'. Again the private side dominates, and the political is
kept waiting for some unreachable narrative prolongation. But that exclusionary deferral is itself an inescapably political act.

Spenser's division of public and private has a long history, going back at
least to Aristotle's separate treatment of politics and ethics. Its history as a
device for describing the Homeric poems and their various successors is
scarcely less long. James Nohrnberg lists some fifteen instances from a

period covering two millennia, from the ancient Greek allegories down through Servius and Macrobius to Landino, Scaliger, and Chapman. Nor is Nohrnberg content to stop with this Western, Græco-Roman line. 'The Indo-European division of the gods, founder-figures, and castes into a kingly or priestly function (Mitra) and a warrior function (Varuna)' also claims relevance. Even this is too narrow a frame for this capacious tradition. 'There seems', writes Nohrnberg, 'to be no reason to restrict this [divided] characterization of heroism to Indo-European culture'.[11] The effect of such wonderfully expansive scholarship is to naturalize and universalize the formal order of Spenser's poem. Freed from all particular location in time or space, the poem resides in triumph with the immortal archetypes. Though Spenser had heard of neither Jung nor Frye, his own evocation of 'all the antique poets historical' aims at a similar elevation. It does something like what E.K. said the antique diction of *The Shepheardes Calender* would do: it brings 'auctority to the verse' (ix. 8). But in Spenser a self-protective motive lurks just beneath the surface, a motive he acknowledges in explaining why he has picked Arthur as his hero. 'I chose the history of King Arthur as most fit for the excellency of his person, being made famous by many men's former works, and also furthest from the danger of envy and suspicion of present time' (i. 167). The present is dangerous and can be approached, if at all, only by the indirection of a pretended universality.

No poetic form, however, is universal. None can escape the particularity of time and ideology, certainly not chivalric romance. The early English humanists' open opposition to chivalry and chivalric romance (think, for example, of Ascham's charge of 'bold bawdry and open manslaughter'), the debate over Ariosto's *Orlando Furioso*, and, most tellingly, the sharp conflict between sympathy and doctrine within *Jerusalem Delivered* all point to the controversial nature of the genre in which Spenser chose to write his major poem. The militant aristocratic autonomy figured by the knight errant was potentially upsetting to reborn classicism, to civic humanism, to bourgeois commercialism, to royal absolutism, and even (as in *Jerusalem Delivered*) to the new military collectivism.[12] Humanist critics and scholars, merchants, ministers of state, and soldiers might thus all find themselves at odds with the chivalric knight. But if chivalry and its representative forms and figures could be highly controversial, they were also powerfully supported by the festive and poetic practices of the Elizabethan court. As Richard Hurd pointed out more than two centuries ago, 'tilts and tournaments were in vogue; the *Arcadia* and *The Faerie Queene* were written' (pp. 116–17).

The Elizabethan vogue for tilts and tournaments is one of the best known and most intensely studied aspects of that 'romantic' age. From the 1570s until the end of Elizabeth's reign the queen's Accession Day was regularly

---

[11] James Nohrnberg, *The Analogy of 'The Faerie Queene'* (Princeton, 1976), pp. 61–63.
[12] Arthur B. Ferguson surveys this opposition to the chivalric revival in *The Chivalric Tradition in Renaissance England* (Washington, D.C., 1986), pp. 83–106.

celebrated with lavish tournaments, and additional tournaments marked other significant court occasions. Indeed, it would not overstrain the evidence to claim that in the last two-and-a-half decades of the sixteenth century the language of chivalry became the primary language of Elizabethan public display, outdistancing even the biblical and classical motifs that had been more prominent earlier. Courtiers became knights, and their queen became a lady of romance.[13] But to recognize the extraordinary importance of the Elizabethan chivalric revival and its part in bringing *The Faerie Queene* into existence is not to dispel the air of potential controversy that, from other sources (including Tasso), we might have supposed to be gathering about Spenser's poem. Elizabethan chivalric display was itself a practice intended to deal with conflict, a way of simultaneously releasing and containing pressures that might otherwise threaten the delicate equilibrium of the Elizabethan state. 'Through its conventions of feudal loyalty and romantic devotion, Elizabethan chivalry confirmed', as Richard McCoy has observed, 'Tudor sovereignty'. But it also gave vent to aristocratic aggression and competition. It thus represented, in McCoy's words, 'a precariously incompatible, sometimes contradictory combination of purposes.... It allowed a kind of compromise between conflicting interests of the crown and her aristocratic courtiers as well as a mediation of factional and personal conflicts among the courtly ranks'.[14]

In a remarkable study of the Earl of Essex McCoy has himself provided an illustration of these conflicting interests and their expression in chivalric display.[15] Celebrated by Spenser as 'Great Englands glory and the Worlds wide wonder', 'Faire branch of Honor, flower of Chevalrie, | That fillest England with thy triumphs fame'.[16] Essex stood, and died, for the martial and aristocratic values that were essential to chivalric romance. In this stance he and Tasso's Rinaldo have much in common. Each is torn between a private code of honour based on a combination of noble lineage and individual military accomplishment and the public duty any subject owes his sovereign. And each has been seen as central to the last of a particular medieval 'kind': Rinaldo the enabling figure of the last Italian chivalric

---

[13] I assume here some acquaintance with the large body of scholarship that has recently been devoted to the Elizabethan chivalric revival. In addition to the work of Ferguson, McCoy, Esler, and James, cited in the notes 12, 14, and 15, see Frances A. Yates, *Astraea: the Imperial Theme in the Sixteenth Century* (London, 1975); Roy Strong, *The Cult of Elizabeth: Elizabethan Portraiture and Pageantry* (London, 1977); Alan Young, *Tudor and Jacobean Tournaments* (London, 1987).

[14] Richard C. McCoy, '"Yet Little Lost or Won": Chivalry in *The Faerie Queene*', paper delivered at Modern Language Association Convention in Houston (1980).

[15] McCoy, '"A dangerous image": The Earl of Essex and Elizabethan Chivalry', *Journal of Medieval and Renaissance Studies*, 13 (1983), 313–29. Similar arguments concerning Essex are made by Arthur Ferguson, *Chivalric Tradition*, pp. 73–74, by Anthony Esler, *The Aspiring Mind of the Elizabethan Younger Generation* (Durham, North Carolina, 1966), pp. 87–99, and by Mervyn James, *Society, Politics and Culture*, pp. 416–65.

[16] *Prothalamion*, ll. 146 and 150–51 (VIII. 261).

romance and Essex the leader of the last English 'honour revolt'.[17] Indeed, for each the end closes in before their individual stories are quite finished. In the final books of *Jerusalem Delivered* Rinaldo is reintegrated into the poem's epic design, becomes once again a dutiful soldier in Goffredo's army. And Essex, who through his trial had maintained a posture of defiant stead-fastness, collapsed before his execution into abject penance, violating 'almost with deliberation . . . all the canons of honour' (James, p. 458). The canons of honour and the canons of romance were rapidly succumbing, as they do succumb in the experience of both Rinaldo and Essex, to a new, more powerfully statist conception of moral obligation, a conception that found support in the unity and verisimilitude of classical literary form. Seen in this way Aristotle's rules (which were really Minturno's and Scaliger's) appear as the literary equivalent of Mervyn James's 'desire and pursuit of the whole'. The 'political culture' of late Tudor England was, in James's words, one 'whose stress [fell] exclusively on the creation and watchful maintenance of wholeness: i.e. on the effective incorporation of the individual into the body of the realm, under its head the queen' (p. 460). Change a word or two and this description would equally fit *Jerusalem Delivered* and the Counter-Reformation literary culture that produced it. In both the political and the literary cultures of sixteenth-century Europe wholeness was emerging as a dominant value.

In its Virgilian intimations, its attempts at unity, and its celebration of Elizabeth, *The Faerie Queene* participates in this cult and these cultures of wholeness. But in its adherence to chivalric romance it remains with the errant Rinaldo and the insubordinate Essex on the Gothic side of the great sixteenth-century cultural divide. Spenser came to know the danger of such errancy and insubordination. In Book v of *The Faerie Queene* an incautious poet, who has spoken ill of Queen Mercilla, is found nailed by his tongue to a post. And since Mercilla's court is the poem's nearest representation of Elizabeth's, the warning is particularly telling. Nor is this the only sign of danger. A sense of peril hangs over the whole of the 1596 instalment. Book iv, the first of the newly published books, begins with an acknowledgement that Spenser's own work has found disfavour in high places:

> The rugged forehead that with grave foresight
> Welds kingdomes causes, and affaires of state,
> My looser rimes (I wote) doth sharply wite,
> For praising love, as I have done of late.

And Book vi, the last of the new books, ends with the Blatant Beast of envy and detraction threatening Spenser's 'homely verse' which, as he again admits, has already been brought 'into a mighty Peres displeasure'.

---

[17] Zatti remarks that '*Jerusalem Delivered* closes historically the season of the chivalric poem' ('Cultural Conflict'). The characterization of the Essex revolt as the last English 'honour revolt' comes from James, p. 416.

That 'mighty peer', the possessor of the 'rugged forehead' of Book IV, is universally identified as William Cecil, Lord Burghley, the lord treasurer of England and the queen's principal counsellor. Educated at Cambridge in a college dominated by Ascham and his humanist friends, Burghley was no partisan of the Elizabethan chivalric revival, nor did he much approve those most prominently identified with it. Essex was, for example, at odds with Burghley and with Burghley's son and political heir, Robert Cecil, throughout his public career. Referring to Burghley and Essex, the French ambassador wrote 'there was always great jealousy between them in everything, one against the other, and a man who was of the lord treasurer's party was sure to be among the enemies of the earl'.[18] In this antagonistic relationship Essex was only taking the place of his political mentor and Spenser's one-time patron, the Earl of Leicester. Spenser himself advertises this Leicester–Essex succession and his own relation to it. Catching sight of Leicester House in the course of his *Prothalamion*, he recalls that it was here

> Where oft I gayned giftes and goodly grace
> Of that great Lord, which therein wont to dwell
> Whose want too well now feeles my freendles case.

(l. 138)

'Yet therein now', he continues, 'doth lodge a noble Peer', the Earl of Essex, whose praises he goes on to sing in words already quoted. From 1579, when he dated a letter to Harvey from Leicester House, to 1596, when he celebrated Essex as 'Great Englands glory', Spenser's strongest associations were with the party that opposed Lord Burghley. No wonder Burghley disapproved of his poetry.

'Spenser [was] the poetic spokesman *par excellence* of militant Protestant chivalry.'[19] This statement by Roy Strong and Jan van Dorsten in their book on Leicester's Netherlands expedition sums up a widely-held view. What I have been arguing is that the Gothic form of *The Faerie Queene* does more than this. In addition to supporting the militant, interventionist policy of the Leicester–Essex faction, Spenser's image of chivalric multiplicity also represents a form of political organization in which the private initiative and private *virtù* (to use a familiar Italian word that includes both *virtue* and *strength*) of individual aristocratic champions plays an exceptionally large part. Whether consciously or unconsciously, Spenser makes his poem the implicit spokesman for a partially refeudalized English polity. The literary authority of Ariosto might at first have naturalized and thus concealed this political orientation, even from Spenser himself. Ariosto's could, after all, be considered simply the accepted way of writing a long heroic poem in the sixteenth century, whatever your politics. But with the publication of *Jerusalem Delivered*, in which the debate over Ariosto found at once literary and political expression, the mask of Ariostan legitimacy would have slipped

[18] Quoted by Conyers Read, *Lord Burghley and Queen Elizabeth* (London, 1960), p. 538.
[19] R. C. Strong and J. A. van Dorsten, *Leicester's Triumph* (Leiden, 1964), p. 3.

badly. Setting Tasso's poem next to Spenser's, anyone could see, as I think Spenser himself saw, how powerful and how powerfully significant his variance from the epic and its statist ideology really was. Faced with this recognition, he may have felt sufficiently uncomfortable to make some effort to unify and to 'Virgilize' *The Faerie Queene*, as many critics think he did sometime between 1580 and 1590. But that effort could not alter the poem's fundamentally multiple and chivalric character. Whatever those qualities had 'said', they went on saying, saying perhaps more forcefully for the very acknowledgement that they were not all that might be said. Like Tasso's, Spenser's is a poem divided against itself. But in it the balance comes down more firmly on the Gothic side.

The chivalric character of *The Faerie Queene* is so pervasive that it is almost invisible to any but the most superficial regard. And because literary critics are taught to eschew superficiality, it does not figure in most recent accounts of the poem.[20] In this the eighteenth-century critics had the advantage. They were not yet much given to our kinds of close reading, or at least they laboured under no institutional constraint requiring them to turn their close readings into published monographs. But they were still deeply involved, as we no longer are, in the Renaissance conflict between classical and medieval forms, and they knew that in terms of that conflict *The Faerie Queene* was a very troubling poem, a poem that in various ways resisted the ordering, unifying, and rationalizing tendencies of the previous two centuries. When John Hughes or Richard Hurd call *The Faerie Queene* 'Gothic' or when Thomas Warton charges, as he did in his *Observations on the Faerie Queene*, that 'Spenser made an unfortunate choice and discovered little judgment in adopting Ariosto for his example, rather than Tasso', they recognize this resistance and reveal that to them it still mattered.[21] This recognition may, as we have noticed, go back as far as Harvey's accusation of Hobgoblinishness, and it continued to be repeated with increasing critical and historical elaboration so long as the dialectic of Greek and Goth remained central to England's self-understanding and self-representation.[22]

But if the mere (and massive) fact of romance design and chivalric action was enough to make a powerful ideological statement, it is nevertheless true that many individual passages of *The Faerie Queene* reveal the ambivalence concerning absolute royal power which underlies the poem's representation of aristocratic autonomy. *The Faerie Queene* is, as many recent critics have insisted, a poem of praise, an important contribution to the cult of

[20] An exception is Michael Leslie's *Spenser's 'Fierce Warres and Faithfull Loves': Martial and Chivalric Symbolism in 'The Faerie Queene'* (Cambridge, 1983). But even Leslie ignores the broader and more pervasive effects of chivalric romance to concentrate on the moral, religious, and historical significance of chivalric symbolism and knightly combat in specific passages.
[21] Hughes in Cummings, pp. 260–61; Hurd, p. 56; Thomas Warton, *Observations on the Fairy Queen of Spenser*, second edition, 2 vols (London, 1762), I, 3.
[22] The dialectic of Greek and Goth is central to my essay 'Barbarous Tongues: The Ideology of Poetic Form in Renaissance England', in *The Historical Renaissance: New Essays on Tudor and Stuart Literature and Culture*, edited by Heather Dubrow and Richard Strier (Chicago, 1988), pp. 273–92.

Elizabeth.[23] But that praise is variously qualified. Not only is the Faerie Queene herself kept out of sight on the poem's furthest periphery, but those figures of royal power that do enter the poem (all dangerously recognizable likenesses of Queen Elizabeth) inspire more apprehension than allegiance.

This is obviously the case of the 'mayden Queene' Lucifera in Book I and her royal look-alike Philotime in Book II.[24] Both represent a demonic perversion of majesty, one that threatens those knights that approach the seat of power with dishonourable subjection. But even the 'gratious' Mercilla, who, like Lucifera and Philotime, is first seen 'Upon a throne of gold full bright and sheene, | Adorned all with gemmes of endlesse price' (V. 9. 27), presides over a court that knows nothing of the chivalric honour Spenser's poem is bent on celebrating. The bright armour of Arthur and Artegall 'did ... much amaze' the clamorous mob of petitioners that filled Mercilla's hall, 'For never saw they there the like array, | Ne ever was the name of warre there spoken' (V. 9. 24). And when, later in the episode, two sons of Belge come seeking aid for their oppressed mother, 'none of all those knights' belonging to Mercilla's court is willing to undertake the enterprise 'for cowheard feare'. So it is the stranger knight Arthur, here figuring Leicester, who

> stepped forth with courage bold and great,
> Admyr'd of all the rest in presence there,
> And humbly gan that mightie Queene entreat,
> To graunt him that adventure for his former feat.
>
> (V. 10. 15)

Mercilla 'gladly' grants his request, but both the initiative and the subsequent action are his doing, not hers. If Lucifera and Philotime represent a perversion of honour, Mercilla's court betrays a passive neglect of it, though to say so in any less veiled way than Spenser does would be to risk the fate of the tongue-nailed poet Bonfont/Malfont.

In Book II Mammon tells Guyon that from his royal daughter Philotime alone 'Honour and dignitie ... derived are' (II. 7. 48). In his proem to Book VI Spenser says something very similar of and to his own 'most dreaded Soveraine': 'from you all goodly vertues well | Into the rest, which round about you ring' (VI. proem. 7). This monarchic claim to a monopoly on honour, dignity, and virtue is precisely what marked the shift from a feudal to an absolutist regime. Spenser's description of Elizabeth as the unique fount of virtue contributes to this shift, but his parodic ascription of similar authority to Philotime questions it. And in the context of Book VI, the Book of Courtesy, even the positive assertion is so qualified that monarchic authority seems to be in competition (sometimes losing competition) with other, more

---

[23] This view has been elaborated in two book-length studies: Thomas H. Cain, *Praise in 'The Faerie Queene'* (Lincoln, 1978) and Robin Headlam Wells, *Spenser's 'Faerie Queene' and the Cult of Elizabeth* (London, 1983).

[24] Michael O'Connell discusses these two figures and their likeness to Queen Elizabeth in *Mirror and Veil: The Historical Dimension of Spenser's 'Faerie Queene'* (Chapel Hill, 1977), pp. 52–54 and 105–07.

private sources of validation. The book begins 'Of Court it seems, men Courtesie doe call', but its narrative finds its prime representatives of courtesy far from court, in the woods and countryside. Indeed, one of the most attractive of those representatives, the old shepherd Melibee, berates the 'roiall court' as a place of vanity, delusion, and idle hopes. And at the allegorical centre of the book, in the scene on Mount Acidale, the poet puts his own love in the privileged place hitherto reserved for the queen.[25] He apologizes for the substitution, but he makes it all the same.

Such displacements are anticipated earlier in the poem when the queen herself, in her 'private' guise as Belphoebe, is removed from the court and made to speak against it.

> Who so in pompe of proud estate (quoth she)
> Does swim, and bathes himselfe in courtly blis,
> Does waste his dayes in darke obscuritee,
> And in oblivion ever buried is.

(II. 3. 40)

And, significantly, it is in this private role that she values 'deedes of armes and prowesse martiall' most highly. 'All vertue merits praise', she says, 'but such the most of all' (II. 3. 37). Where Mercilla presides over a 'cowheard' court (the class slur in Spenser's spelling of *coward* is surely no accident) and where even the Faerie Queene recalls the heroic Artegall before his 'reforming' work is thoroughly complete, Belphoebe herself bears, if not the instruments of war, at least those of the warlike chase. Divided from her royal power, in her private body, the queen appears as a martial figure, a fit exemplar of Spenser's heroic creed. But enthroned in her public body, she misleads, deflects, frustrates, or simply fails to nourish chivalric valour. It is thus appropriate that Spenser should have chosen to represent the deeds of Arthur as 'a brave knight . . . *before* he was king' rather than his achievements *as* king. Kingship in the modern 'politic' and absolutist sense is inimical to knightly, aristocratic virtue.

If *The Faerie Queene* expresses much ambivalence concerning the strongly centralized monarchic order that was to a large degree the very enabling condition of its existence, it entertains no similar doubts concerning the aristocratic myth of natural, inborn superiority. Virtuous ploughmen, salvages, and shepherd lasses regularly turn out to be the foundling offspring of nobles and kings, while base-born upstarts are just as regularly betrayed by their pride, insolence, and cowardice. Unlike those humanists who favoured virtue over lineage and who argued that the state might recognize virtue with the reward of noble title (as Elizabeth did for Sir William Cecil), Spenser

---

[25] I discuss this substitution in *Self-Crowned Laureates: Spenser, Jonson, Milton and the Literary System* (Berkeley, 1983), pp. 92–96. It should be noted that in this passage from Book VI Spenser's resistance to the monarch comes not from the aristocratic position that underlies chivalric romance, but rather from still another position, neither monarchic nor aristocratic, that is Spenser's as poet. Calidore, the chivalric knight, is as unwelcome and disruptive a figure on Mount Acidale as the queen.

refuses to envisage the separation of blood and virtue.[26] 'Shame is to adorne', he charges, with the 'brave badges' of arms and knighthood one 'basely borne' (VI. 6. 36), but

> O what easie thing is to descry
> The gentle bloud, how ever it be wrapt
> In sad misfortunes foule disformity.
>
> (VI. 5. 1)

What then are we to make of his claim that 'the general end ... of all the book is to fashion a gentleman or noble person in virtuous and gentle discipline'? This, it must be insisted, is fashioning of a quite limited sort. Spenser does not mean to make gentlemen of what he calls 'cowheard villains'. That, he supposes, would be impossible.[27] His aim is rather to perfect the well-born in the discipline appropriate to their class.[28] And central to that discipline, as Spenser teaches it, is an aristocratic independence that would make a Leicester or an Essex a dangerous figure in the Tudor–Cecil state, just as a similar romantic and chivalric discipline and a similar insistence on the prerogatives of blood make Rinaldo a disruptive figure in the regime governed by Goffredo. The difference between Spenser and Tasso is that Spenser endorses claims of birth that Tasso admires but ends by reducing to obedience.

That reduction was essential to the making of the modern state and it was powerfully under way in Tudor England. New men and the service of a new monarchy were, as we have noticed, turning the state into the unique fount of honour. Without such changes *The Faerie Queene* would have been quite literally inconceivable. Yet, as much as it is the product of a new monarchic centralism, *The Faerie Queene* resists that centripetal force. It represents an uneasy and unacknowledged compromise between a monarch who gives both poem and nation whatever unity and identity they have and individual aristocratic knights whose adventures are the glory and the safety of the nation. Private virtue, '*ethice*' in the term of Spenser's letter to Raleigh, is made the sole instrument of public action. Instead of a princely Goffredo at the head of a highly organized and complexly equipped army, solitary knights embody England's Protestant destiny in *The Faerie Queene*, destroy the enervating Bowre of Blis, overcome the enemies of Belge and Irenae, capture the Blatant Beast. In a letter to Sir Philip Sidney, Sidney's political guide, the Burgandian humanist Hubert Languet, warned his pupil against independent action on behalf of the Belgian states.

---

[26] It would perhaps be more accurate at this point to substitute '*The Faerie Queene*' for 'Spenser'. On the value of lineage and heroic endeavour, the poet was less certain than his poem. In *The Teares of the Muses*, he mocks those 'mightie Peeres' who 'onely boast of Armes and Auncestrie' (VIII, 65). Such mockery has no place in *The Faerie Queene*.

[27] This impossibility is illustrated by the efforts of the baseborn Braggadocchio to learn horsemanship, 'a science | Proper to gentle blood' (II. 4. 1). Compare young Tristram, whose knightly behaviour shows him to be 'borne of noble blood' (VI. 2. 24) despite his rude upbringing.

[28] Frank Whigham exposes the contradictions implicit in such a project in *Ambition and Privilege: The Social Tropes of Elizabethan Courtesy Theory* (Berkeley, 1984).

It is not your business, nor any private person's, to pass judgment on a question of this kind; it belongs to the magistrate, I mean by magistrate the prince, who, whenever a question of the sort is to be determined, calls to his council those whom he believes to be just men and wise. You and your fellows, I mean men of noble birth, consider that nothing brings you more honour than wholesale slaughter; and you are generally guilty of the greatest injustice, for if you kill a man against whom you have no lawful cause of war, you are killing an innocent person.[29]

In their principal quests Spenser's knights are not guilty of such injustice. Their actions are licensed by the magistrate. But they do enjoy an autonomy that such Elizabethan generals as Leicester and Essex excrcised only with peril and reproach. Though tempered by statist ideology, the chivalric form of *The Faerie Queene* strengthens the association that Languet (like many humanists before him) blames, the association of aristocratic honour with 'wholesale slaughter', an association that, as Languet realizes, menaces the monarch's authority as the sole dispenser of justice.

In standing against neoclassical order and verisimilitude, Spenser's Gothic image of England stands against the rationalizing tendencies of the modern state, tendencies that determined the form of *Jerusalem Delivered*. This oppositional stance is the constant preoccupation of his various proems. In each Spenser sets what he calls 'antiquity', a time that belongs rather to the idealizing historical imagination than to any particular period but whose most prominent features are romantic and chivalric, against the present, with the unfailing proviso that his dread sovereign mistress be understood as exempt from all blame. Indeed, antiquity and the queen are repeatedly presented as the twin sources of his poem. But clearly there is a tension between them, a struggle in Spenser's effort to fit 'antique praises unto present persons' (III. proem. 3). That tension and that struggle were not, however, his alone. They belonged equally to the militant Protestant faction with which, through most of his career, he was associated: to Leicester, to Sidney, to Essex, and to the many lesser figures who supported them. Bridled by a parsimonious queen and a cautious minister, the members of this faction found themselves, like Tasso's Tancredi and Rinaldo, repeatedly torn between private honour and public duty. By enforcing the claims of duty, both civic humanism and Aristotelian neoclassicism worked to restrict and ultimately deny the aristocratic cult of honour. Spenser's chivalric romance pulls the other way. It enlarges the sphere of honour and identifies private virtue with public obligation. *The Faerie Queene* represents a nation of indistinct boundaries and uncertain political organization, at once British and Faerie, but it leaves no doubt concerning the value of lineage and heroic endeavour. For all its claims to some larger truth, claims that generations of critics have expanded and elaborated, Spenser's poem thus served a quite particular, even partisan, ideology, a Gothic ideology of renascent aristocratic power.

[29] *The Correspondence of Sir Philip Sidney and Hubert Languet*, edited by Steuart A. Pears (London, 1845), p. 154.

The Farce of History: Miracle, Combat, and Rebellion in *2 Henry VI*[1]

RONALD KNOWLES

University of Reading

It has long been a critical commonplace that the low-life scenes of the two parts of *Henry IV* have a dramatic complexity which shows a distinct maturity in Shakespeare's early dramatic art. Perhaps A. P. Rossiter's is the best known point of view. Rejecting the simple view of Falstaff as a morality figure he found greater 'complexities ... which often result from the use of comic parallelism of phrase or incident. That is, of parody, critically used, or of travesty-by-parallel'. This resulted, he said, from a bi-focal view of persons and history, and the ironic mode of drama generated an 'essential ambivalence'.[2] It will be argued here that this celebrated mode of the *Henry IV* plays is anticipated, more than is usually recognized, in the experimentation of *2 Henry VI*, in the miracle, combat, and rebellion scenes.

Such anticipation of the technique of the *Henry IV* plays has been hinted at before, but not fully realized. Rossiter himself (p. 58) noted in passing 'the grotesque, Hieronymus-Bosch-like sarcastically-comic scenes of Cade's rebellion', in which Shakespeare 'achieved something remarkable'. Also, in one of the major studies of all the English Histories since Rossiter's time, Moody E. Prior gave voice to a gradually revised general view in his consideration that 'the three parts of *Henry VI* are the rich ore out of which the later plays are refined'.[3] The present essay will show by means of cultural and historical placement that the technique is already essentially in place, and that it already represents a dynamic reconsideration of the main historical materials out of which the play is made.

The most important case is that of the Cade rebellion. It is, however, foreshadowed by the miracle of St Albans and by the trial by combat between Horner and Peter. In the long first scene of the second act of *2 Henry VI*, the miracle episode is flanked by the hawking and the arrest of the Duchess of Gloucester. It has not been difficult to assign dramatic function to the scene itself. Hereward T. Price, for example, sees in it a dramatic 'touchstone' for the chief characters: 'We see Henry's simple faith based on an unquestioning mind, Gloucester's scepticism and quiet penetration, the

[1] At the outset of this study Sydney Anglo provided several valuable antiquarian references, while Andrew Gurr kept me abreast of current criticism. I am indebted to Cedric Brown for suggestions during composition.

[2] *Angels with Horns* (London, 1961), pp. 46, 51.

[3] *The Drama of Power* (Evanston, Illinois, 1973), p. 9.

Queen's cruel laughter at the horrible punishments afflicted'. To Price 'Shakespeare steps outside his plot in order to show the deeper undercurrents in the society he is depicting'.[4] If, however, we also bear in mind Rossiter's 'comic parallelism of phrase or incident' the 'miracle' can be seen to have a level of ironic integration within the main action of the *Henry VI* plays.

In order to gain, Saunder Simpcox and his wife claim that his sight is restored by the divine miracle of St Alban. Gloucester exposes the deceit by getting Simpcox to identify some colours. The parallel can hardly be accidental with the linked sequence of events in *1 Henry VI*, IV. i, where the king is blind to the consequences of choosing the colour red, and most characters act out the pretence of what is later called 'Deceit bred by Necessity' (*3 Henry VI*, III. iii. 68).[5] In the Paris coronation scene of *1 Henry VI* we can see a potentially tragic imbalance between loyalty and allegiance, betrayal and faction, as the action unfolds. Talbot's heroism is offset by Falstaff's cowardice and Burgundy's defection, and Gloucester's authority is overwhelmed by the factionalism of the Yorkist Vernon and the Lancastrian Basset, backed by their noble patrons. Yet King Henry foolishly chooses the colour red:

> I see no reason if I wear this rose,
> That anyone should therefore be suspicious
> I more incline to Somerset than York.
>
> (l. 152)

The business of colours is entirely Shakespeare's invention, with no hints in the sources.

This scene, showing Henry's political blindness, comes after the Temple Garden scene, also Shakespeare's invention, in which it is asserted by both sides that even the blind or near-blind can 'see' the truth of argument and thus choose the white or red rose. For Richard Plantagenet 'truth' is so 'naked ... That any purblind eye may find it out' (II. iv. 21), while for Somerset truth is 'so evident, | That it will glimmer through a blind man's eye' (II. iv. 24–25). The central symbolic action of the scene then follows in the choice of red and white roses.

To a certain extent a metaphorical reading of the miracle scene of *2 Henry VI* is encouraged by the way Shakespeare opens and closes it: the characters themselves allegorize the hawking at the beginning, and then, towards the end, use the 'miracle' to get at each other:

> CARDINAL   Duke Humphrey has done a miracle today.
> SUFFOLK   True; made the lame to leap and fly away.

[4] 'Mirror Scenes in Shakespeare', in *Joseph Quincy Adams Memorial Studies*, edited by James G. McManaway (Washington, 1948), p. 104.

[5] References are to the Arden editions by Andrew S. Cairncross: *1 Henry VI* (London, 1962); *2 Henry VI* (London, 1957); *3 Henry VI* (London, 1964).

GLOUCESTER   But you have done more miracles than I;
You made in my day, my lord, whole towns to fly.

(l. 153)

This technique of deriving ironical metaphors from actual circumstances occurs later also when the accused Gloucester, about to be led off as a prisoner, warns the king 'Ah! then King Henry throws away his crutch | Before his legs be firm to bear his body' (III. i. 190). Seeing the 'Honour, Truth and Loyalty' (III. i. 203) of Gloucester, the king is nevertheless blinded by his tears and sees only 'with dimm'd eyes' (III. i. 218). Shakespeare added Simpcox's lameness to the historical sources, and presumably a crutch was carried on stage, since he is said to be 'not able to stand' (II. i. 146). Simpcox's wife's parting words are 'Alas! sir, we did it for pure need' (II. i. 150), the plangency of which is somewhat modulated by the comic flight of Simpcox and the ironic echo of his earlier answer to the Queen's question as to whether he came 'here by chance, | Or of devotion, to this holy shrine?'. 'God knows', he says, 'of pure devotion' (II. i. 87–89). His 'pure devotion' is somewhat impure, his blindness and lameness are fake, and the miracle bogus. In contrast, the unremitting, single-minded purity of Henry's devotion has rendered him politically blind and lame, as Gloucester's image makes plain, and only a miracle can save him amidst 'Deceit bred by Necessity'. No miracle is forthcoming.

Shakespeare was under no necessity to use the St Albans material for his story. In choosing to do so he gave the scene ironic point in the literal and metaphorical significance of devotion, colours, and blindness in *1* and *2 Henry IV*. Something similar is seen in his inclusion of the combat scene of Horner and Peter. Here Shakespeare also employed the mode of travesty, but with greater comedy and more concentration and force.

The trial by combat in Act II scene iii has of course attracted some attention. Many years ago Clifford Leech saw something like ironic point, considering that 'the formal combat between the armourer and his man is a parody of chivalric encounter: in a way remarkably sophisticated for this early drama, it implies a critical attitude towards the warring nobles whose quarrels are grotesquely mirrored in this fight between two simple men, one terrified, one drunk'.[6] More recently Ralph Berry has discussed the trial as a unifying image for the whole play: the play's 'essential form', he says, 'is that of the Trial. The processes of a Trial — charges, investigation, arraignment, defence, verdict, sentence, and execution — compose the pattern that orders *2 Henry VI*'.[7] Of the combat won by the apprentice, and celebrated by the king for the revelation of 'God in justice' (l. 106), Berry concludes 'I put it that the play does not invite us to share the view of Divine Providence advanced by Peter and King Henry' (p. 6). That might be easily granted.

[6] *Shakespeare: The Chronicles*, Writers and their Work, 146 (London, 1962), p. 17.
[7] *Shakespearian Structures* (London, 1981), p. 2.

However, I believe that a sharper perspective can be gained by focusing on details such as double ale and the weapons used, and identifying their specific social contexts, for the incident needs interpreting both with regard to historicity and to current social attitude. The chronicles themselves provided very little detail of the circumstances of the combat, but, to judge from his manner of introducing the action — 'the appellant and defendant ... to enter the lists' (ll. 49–50) — it is evident that Shakespeare knew that the combat was under the auspices of the courts of chivalry. Recognition of this helps us to gauge more precisely the burlesque nature of the scene.

Incurring the criticism of Parliament, which feared encroachment on the courts of common law, Richard II had fostered the power and scope of the civil court of chivalry to the extent that the articles of deposition against him included specific details of this abuse. It eventually became possible for any treason appeal to come before this court, although there were conditions which had to be fulfilled. In cases of treason trial by combat was used when there were no witnesses and no evidence, so that one man's word simply stood against another's, provided that both parties were of good repute and not felons.[8] The practice reached its height under Henry VI. Thus Cater and Davy, the originals of Shakespeare's Horner and Peter, appeared in historical fact in the chivalric setting of the lists at Smithfield.

They may seem an odd pair to have done so, but there were other cases concerning parties of less than knightly standing. A few years earlier, in 1441, for example, two thieves fought in combat 'at Totehill' according to Stow,[9] on what appeal he does not say, and in 1426 'a gentleman, Henry Knokkis' defended himself against an appeal of treason made by 'a certain plebian tailor' beneath the walls of Edinburgh castle.[10] Even more strangely, an elderly friar was ordered under Henry IV to fight a woman, who had accused him of treason, with one arm tied behind his back. (The charge was then withdrawn.) The *Brut* chronicle, also, records a fight to the death between a 'Welsh clerk' and a knight.[11]

By the Tudor period, such combat was considered against the law of arms. Spenser makes this clear by showing Calidore at first dismayed to see Tristram, who is 'no knight', slay a knight, 'which armes inpugneth plaine'.[12] In Shakespeare's day, in a work which the playwright may have consulted for the combat scene of *Richard II*, Sir William Segar spelled out 'What sorts of men ought not bee admitted to triall of Armes'.[13] Generally, 'the triall of Armes apperteineth onelie to Gentlemen, and that Gentilitie is a

---

[8] Anthony Tuck, *Richard II and the English Nobility* (London, 1973), pp. 124, 198; J. G. Bellamy, *The Law of Treason in England in the Later Middle Ages* (Cambridge, 1970), p. 143. G. D. Squibb, *The High Court of Chivalry* (Oxford, 1959), is the authoritative study.
[9] *The Annales* (London, 1615), p. 381.
[10] G. Neilson, *Trial by Combat* (Glasgow, 1890), p. 275.
[11] Bellamy, pp. 145–46.
[12] *The Faerie Queene*, VI. ii. 7. I am indebted to Anthea Hume for this reference.
[13] *The Book of Honor and Arms* (1590) and *Honor Military and Civil* (1602), Scholars Facsimiles and Reprints (New York, 1975), p. 30. See the introduction by Diane Bornstein for discussion of *Richard II*.

degree honorable, it were not fit that anie persons of meaner condition, should thereunto be admitted' (pp. 30–31). In this judgement, amongst the ineligible, beside 'Theeves, Beggers, Bawdes, Victuallers, persons excommunicate, Usurers, persons banished the Armie', is ranked 'everie other man exercising an occupation or trade, unfit and unworthie a Gentleman or Soldier'. To sum up, then, Richard II had promoted a situation in which history itself would furnish burlesques of chivalric practice, whilst Tudor aristocratic exclusivity had heightened awareness of decorum. Thus when Horner and Peter appeared on stage in the 1590s, one drunk, the other terrified, and both carrying less than knightly weapons, the resulting burlesque confirmed the comic tenor of Peter's petition:

PETER   Against my master, Thomas Horner, for saying that the Duke of York was rightful heir to the crown.
QUEEN   What say'st thou? Did the Duke of York say he was rightful heir to the Crown?
PETER   That my master was? No, forsooth: my master said that he was, and that the king was an usurer.

(I. iii. 25–30)

Yet that exaggeration of the comic will prove to have its serious point.

Details of the combat deserve investigation. It is removed from the traditional Smithfield venue to a 'Hall of Justice'. *Gregory's Chronicle* mentions that Cater (like Davy, it is assumed) was in 'harnys' (harness) that is, a suit of armour.[14] Shakespeare mentions a curious weapon, a 'staff with a sand-bag fastened to it', but no armour. The treason-duel of chivalry, usually on horseback, was never fought without a sword and spear. Shakespeare's weapon, in fact, is closer to the weapon of the duel-of-law, the baton.[15] Sir Samuel Rush Meyrick, the Victorian antiquarian, was somewhat baffled by the weapons of Horner and Peter: 'Shakespeare arms his combatants with batons and sand-bags at the end of them, yet this is the only authority I have met with for the use of this latter appendage'. He then proceeded to speculate that 'probably such were the weapons of the lower class of people, and were therefore considered by him as appropriate to the parties'.[16] He quotes Samuel Butler's *Hudibras* in support — 'Engaged with money-bags, as bold | As men with sand-bags did of old' — and suggests a comparison with the fool's baton and bladder. As early as Warburton's edition of the play, in fact, Butler had been used as a gloss, as H. C. Hart recounts in his edition of 1909, where, however, he shows no certainty as to what the weapon actually was.[17] The weapons are in fact combat flails, as distinct from the metal military flail or the agricultural wooden variety.

[14] *The Historical Collections of A Citizen of London in the Fifteenth Century*, Camden Society New Series XVII, edited by James Gardner (London, 1876), p. 187. John Nichol's *Illustrations of the Manners and Expenses of Antient Times in England* (1797), AMS Press Facsimile (1973), pp. 217, 220, prints the writ for the combat and the costs for disposal and execution.
[15] See Neilson, pp. 188–89, for a detailed comparison.
[16] *A Critical Inquiry into Antient Armour*, 3 vols (London, 1842), II, 125.
[17] *The Second Part of King Henry the Sixth* (London, 1909), p. 66.

Reference to them seems to be rare, but an excellent illustration survives in one of the most detailed examples of a Renaissance festival book, *The Triumph of Maximilian* (1526), with woodcuts by Hans Burgkmair and others. Plate 33 shows 'Five men with (leather) flails' preceding similar numbers of men with quarterstaves, lances, halberds, battleaxes, and various swords and shields, all collectively representing *gefecht*, explained by the editor as 'combats on foot, considered beneath the notice of nobility or royalty until they were fostered by Maximilian, who took part in them himself'.[18]

The Triumph of Maximilian Plate 33.

By choosing flails with sand-filled leather bags Shakespeare placed a weapon associated with the lower orders in the high-born milieu of chivalric combat, bringing on his combatants without the expected arms and armour. He also made other significant alterations to the chronicle material. As has always been recognized, Shakespeare links the armourer's treason with

[18] *The Triumph of Maximilian I, with a translation of descriptive text, introduction and notes by Stanley Applebaum* (New York, 1964), p. 7.

York, although it was not so linked in the chronicles. In the sources the armourer is the innocent party and his servant the guilty. Holinshed, for example, following Fabyan, found Davy a 'false servant' and Cater 'without guilt', while Grafton, following Hall, saw Davy as 'a coward and a wretche'.[19] That wretchedness could follow from the cowardice, or it might be that Davy is called wretch for falsely accusing his master — presumably the latter, since the chroniclers see ultimate justice in his execution at Tyburn.

In assessing these alterations, we should not miss the question of drink. All sources except Gregory record the drunkenness of the Armourer, but Shakespeare makes a significant change in the liquors consumed. Grafton, following Hall again, records 'Malmsey and Aqua vite'; Holinshed 'wine and strong drinke'; Fabyan 'wyne and good ale', whilst Shakespeare has 'sack', 'charneco' and 'good double beer' (ll. 60–64). The last item is the telling detail. By the sixteenth century there had developed an association between festive wassail, that is to say, extra-strong ale ('double beer' or 'double ale'), and riot and sedition. In John Bale's *King John* (1584), for example, Sedition enters, crying

> No noise among ye? where is the merry cheer
> That was wont to be, with quaffing of double beer?
> The world is not yet as some men would it have.[20]

Charles Hobday has noted the subversive meanings of 'merry' as egalitarian freedom in the sixteenth century generally and in Shakespeare in particular, quoting the declaration of one of Cade's followers that 'it was never merry world in England since Gentlemen came up' (IV. ii. 9).[21] Again, in *The Life and Death of Jack Straw* (1593) Tom Miller, the comic rebel-clown, says of the notorious John Ball 'You ... | Find him in a pulpit but twice in the year, | And I'll find him forty times in the ale-house tasting strong beer', and in a ludicrous self-indictment he promotes himself as 'a customer to help away ... strong ale'.[22] From this we can understand the import of Cade's 'reformation' when he 'will make it a felony to drink small beer' (IV. ii. 64–65). Double beer only for the rebels! In other words, the Armourer's 'treason' is further damned by association with drunken insurrectionaries.

Hall introduced the notion of Horner's height and strength: 'he beying a tall and a hardye personage'. Shakespeare changes this subtly to Horner's superior technique: Peter knows that 'I am never able to deal with my master, he hath learnt so much fence already' (ll. 75–76). Advantage is all on the side of the master, except for his over-confidence encouraged by drink. It

---

[19] Raphael Holinshed, *Chronicle* (1577), 6 vols (London, 1807–08), III, 210; Robert Fabyan, *The New Chronicles of England and France* (1516), edited by H. Ellis (London, 1811), p. 168; *Grafton's Chronicle*, 2 vols (1569; London, 1809), I, 628; *Hall's Chronicle* (1542; London, 1809), pp. 207–08.
[20] *Elizabethan History Plays*, edited by William A. Armstrong (London, 1965), p. 80.
[21] 'Clouted Shoon and Leather Aprons: Shakespeare and the Egalitarian Tradition', *Renaissance and Modern Studies*, 23 (1979), 68.
[22] W. Carew Hazlitt, *A Select Collection of Old English Plays*, 15 vols (London, 1874), V, 381, 483.

could therefore seem that when the Armourer is struck and confesses treason before dying, Peter has 'prevail'd in right' (II. iv. 95–96); right seems to have defeated might, so that the combat could be seen as divinely ordered. As Segar puts it:

all Nations ... have (among many other trials) permitted that such questions as could not be civilie prooved by confession, witnesse, or other circumstances, should receive judgement by fight and combat, supposing that GOD (who onelie knoweth the secret thoughts of all men) would give victorie to him that justlie adventured his life, for truth, Honor, and Justice. (sig. A^{2v-r})

Hence the king's pious response to what has taken place: 'And God in justice hath reveal'd to us | The truth and innocence of this poor fellow' (II. iv. 98–99). The king may see it simply; the audience is more likely to see an irony: it sees the 'right' result produced by oddly circumstantial means, by Horner's incapacity through drink. If this is Providence, it is of a kind difficult to credit, except in the simple mind of this king.

The effects produced in this episode show the kinds of complexity so often celebrated in the *Henry IV* plays. In reshaping this historical material, Shakespeare created comic matter in a burlesquing of the chivalric code, in such a way as to create an ironic inversion of the main lines of action in the play, perhaps of the action of all three *Henry VI* plays. The combat scene lies in the middle of these plays, in which an overall pattern can be discerned of a falling into a world of brute force, in the demise of chivalry in Talbot's death, in the ineffectuality of Christian piety in Henry VI, and the rise of Machiavellian *virtù* in Richard of Gloucester. Everywhere Might seems to be overcoming Right, both in the small instance:

PLANTAGENET   Now Somerset, where is your argument?
SOMERSET   Here in my scabbard, meditating that
                          Shall dye your white rose in a bloody red
                                                              (*1 Henry VI*, II. iv. 59–62)

and in the large confrontation:

WARWICK   Do right unto this princely Duke of York,
                     Or I will fill the house with armed men ...
                     He stamps with his foot, and the soldiers show themselves
                                                              (*3 Henry VI*, I. i. 172–73)

Momentarily the comic outcome of the combat scene seems to militate against this general tendency, and to affirm that Right might conquer Might. But such is the travesty of the combat as combat that we seem to have instead an ironic pointing up of the issues, a reminder of what ideally might be rather than an affirmation of Right. To have turned the chronicles around in such a way seems to have been to invoke and then to call in question any sense of divine ordinance in human affairs, and to direct us further towards the conduct of weak men.

The most developed instance of this technique is, however, in the rebellion of Jack Cade in Act IV, for which the comic scenes of the St Albans miracle and the treason combat seem a kind of preparation. Jack Cade is arguably the most complex figure of the *Henry VI* plays. The complexity of his case derives from three compounded categories, the historiographical, the cultural, and the artistic. Shakespeare follows his contemporaries' propagandistic conflation of Cade's 1450 rebellion with that of Jack Straw and Wat Tyler of 1381. From a cultural point of view Cade's presentation has an affinity with the topsy-turveydom of the Lord of Misrule and the World Upside Down, while in artistic terms it is related to the Vice and the clown. Yet, ultimately, Cade is an inverted image of authority, both its distorted representative and its grotesque critic.

The historical Jack Cade was rather different from the rebels of 1381. Though Brents Stirling points out Cade's execution of Say and Cromer and the freeing of prisoners, he concludes that 'most of the violence and outrage in Shakespeare's version of the Cade uprising came from the chronicle story of the earlier Peasants Revolt', from which was taken the anti-literacy of the rebels, the wish to kill all lawyers, the destruction of the Savoy and the Inns of Court, the destruction of state documents, and the ascription to Cade of Wat Tyler's belief that 'all the laws of England should come forth of his mouth'.[23] Cade, on the contrary, was impressively personable and articulate, in the words of Holinshed 'a young man of goodly stature and right pregnant wit', 'sober in talk, wise in reasoning, arrogant in heart, and stiff in opinion' (p. 220). Hall considered that Cade, far from being illiterate, was 'not only suborned by techers, but also enforced by pryvye scholemasters' (p. 220). Initially Cade's forces were in fact relatively disciplined, and on behalf of his supporters he presented the fully documented 'Complaints of the Commons of Kent'.

The earlier, mid-Tudor depiction of Cade in *The Mirror for Magistrates* (1559) is moral and theological. He is heard insisting on the principle of non-resistance to divinely appointed rulers and the individual's responsibility to 'follow reason' and 'subdue their wylles' and 'lust', rather than allow the vagaries of Fortune to rule over them. In the prose discussion following Cade's speech his insurrection is seen as an example of God using rebels to chastise irresponsible rulers and overmighty subjects.[24]

By the 1590s Cade's rebellion was generally seen more in political than theological terms. Brents Stirling has shown how a conflation of the rebellions of 1381 and 1450 was further linked by conservative propagandists to English nonconformity and to the German Peasant War, by way of the Anabaptists and John of Leiden. John of Leiden was decried for the lowness of his trade, tailoring, and Jack Cade was turned by Shakespeare, without any indication in the sources, into a 'clothier' and a 'shearman' (IV. ii. 4, 127), that is, one who sheared the nap in the finishing stages of cloth

---

[23] *The Populace in Shakespeare* (New York, 1949), pp. 22–23.
[24] William Baldwin, *The Mirror for Magistrates*, edited by Lily B. Campbell (Cambridge, 1938), pp. 170–80.

production. Both declared themselves kings, both were opposed to learning, both proclaimed that all would be held in common and that money was to be banned. Given these parallels, it is unlikely that Shakespeare's presentation of Cade as a clothier could be made without some of the audience seeing such parallels implied in a richly compounded stage figure. Shakespeare pointedly concentrates on the anti-literacy of the 1381 rebels and adds a theme of his own, the critique of dress. In doing so he focuses on the authoritarian gradation of society manifested by the sumptuary laws and benefit of clergy.

We hear from Medvedev and Bakhtin that 'ideological reality', that is, the 'philosophical views, beliefs or even shifting ideological moods', are 'realized in words, actions, *clothing*, manners, and organizations of people and things' [my italics].[25] Consider, for example, the sack of the Savoy, John of Gaunt's house, in 1381: the rebels 'seized one of his most precious vestments, which we call a 'jakke', and placed it as a lance to be used for their arrows. And since they were unable to damage it sufficiently with their arrows, they took it down and tore it apart with their axes and swords'.[26] It has been suggested, somewhat fancifully, by Thomas Pettit that this represents 'an effigy for ritual slaying, *sparagmos*, the tearing apart of the sacrificial victims in many ancient renewal ceremonies'. More soberly Pettit draws a parallel with the rough treatment of the festival dummy figure of Jack o'Lent. However, if we note Sir Samuel Rush Meyrick's observations (p. 68) on the 'Jakke' — it was a strengthened tunic used as armour yet lined with silk — we can see the symbolic provocation of such a thing. The Latin of Walsingham's chronicle, *vestimentum preciosissimus ipsius*, indicates that such a garment was uniquely noble, combining the martial and the gentle. This the rebels singled out amidst the general havoc. John Ball spoke for them: the nobles, he said, 'are clothed in velvet and soft leather furred with ermine, while we wear coarse cloth'.[27] In fact, Shakespeare did not need to be prompted by a specific incident, for such occurrences derived from the system of visual class distinction being legally enforced in his own day.

Although they seem often to have been more honoured in the breach than the observance, sumptuary laws persisted with various amendments in statutes and proclamations from the reign of Edward III until their final repeal by James I in 1604, even appearing in hortatory form as an Elizabethan homily.[28] They attempted to impose the quality, colour, kind, cost, and length of material worn by everybody, from monarch to serf, in order to

---

[25] P. N. Medvedev and M. M. Bakhtin, *The Formal Method in Literary Scholarship* (Johns Hopkins, 1978), p. 7, cited by Michael D. Bristol, *Carnival and Theatre* (New York and London, 1985), p. 20.
[26] Thomas Pettit, '"Here comes I, Jack Straw": English Folk Drama and Social Revolt', *Folklore*, 95, no. 1 (1984), 12.
[27] *A Radical Reader*, edited by Christopher Hampton (London, 1984), p. 51.
[28] See, particularly, 1 Henry VIII c 14, 6 Henry VIII c 1, 24 Henry VIII c 13, *The Statues of the Realm* (London, 1817), III, pp. 8, 122, 432; 1 and 2 Philip and Mary c 2, ibid, IV, 239; Paul L. Hughes and James F. Larkin, *The Tudor Proclamations*, 3 vols (New Haven and London, 1969), particularly II, nos 464, 542, 601, 646, and III, no. 697; 'An Homily Against Excess of Apparel', in *Certain Sermons or Homilies* (Oxford, 1894), pp. 274–83.

distinguish their degree.[29] Summarizing the period 1400–1600, Harte found that 'the sixteenth-century Acts contained a vision of society that was more complex and hierarchical' than in some earlier periods (p. 136). Elizabeth punctiliously followed the strictures of the statute of 1533, which had reversed the relative liberality of former law. The 1533 statute contained 'exceptionally minute provisions limiting the use of silk and silk-wrought materials, according to the rank or income of wearer, between those kinds that could be used in different garments of external wear' (Hooper, p. 435). All materials, in varying combinations, were graded according to social standing. At the top end, 'none . . . except earls and all superior degrees, and viscounts and barons in their doublets and sleeveless coats . . . shall wear . . . cloth of gold, silver, or tinsel; satin, silk, or cloth mixed with gold or silver, nor any sables'. At the lower end, 'no servingman in husbandry or journeyman in handicrafts taking wages shall wear in his doublet any other thing than fustian, canvas, leather, or wool cloth'.[30]

Prompted by Elizabeth in 1559, the Privy Council inaugurated a system of surveillance by suggesting to the city corporation 'that two watches should be appointed for every parish, armed with a schedule of all persons assessed to the late subsidy . . . in order to see that the prohibition against silk trimmings was being obeyed' (Hooper, p. 437). The dividing line between gentleman and plebeian was that between him whose annual income, after all taxes, was five pounds and him whose income was 'forty shillings'. The sartorial manifestation of this in the gentleman was 'silk in his doublet or jackets', whereas the man below gentry rank could not wear silk at all, not even as decoration on 'any shirt, or shirtband, under or upper cap, bonnet, or hat'.[31] Class consciousness would have been most acute at this dividing line, and at least a century of discrimination, which all of the audience would have recognized, informs Jack Cade's contemptuous remark, 'As for these silken-coated slaves, I pass not' (IV. ii. 122).

Bevis's play on words at the opening of the Cade scenes — 'I tell thee, Jack Cade the clothier means to dress the commonwealth, and turn it, and set a new nap upon it . . . for 'tis threadbare' (IV. ii. 4–6)[32] — alludes to Cade's particular occupation, but in this topsyturvy world he would indeed act the king and he has his own sumptuary proclamation: 'I will apparel them all in one livery' (IV. ii. 71). According to Stubbes in the *Anatomy of Abuses* (1583),

[29] See E. Baldwin, *Sumptuarie Legislation and Personal Regulation in England* (Baltimore, 1926); Wilfrid Hooper, 'The Tudor Sumptuarie Laws', *English Historical Review*, 30 (1915), 433–49; N. B. Harte, 'State Control of Dress and Social Change in Pre-Industrial England', in *Trade, Government and Economy in Pre-Industrial England*, edited by D. C. Coleman and A. H. John (London, 1976), pp. 132–65. I am indebted to Anne Curry for these references.
[30] *The Tudor Proclamations*, no. 542, p. 280.
[31] *The Tudor Proclamations*, no. 697 (1588), pp. 5–6.
[32] For a topical interpretation of this in terms of a 1590s industrial dispute between capitalist free marketeers and the guilds, between those who wished to export unfinished cloth and those in London's finishing crafts, see Richard Wilson '"A Mingled Yarn": Shakespeare and the Cloth Workers', *Literature and History*, 12 (1986), 171–72. In the Utopian context of IV. ii. 62–72 Bristol (p. 89) sees topical economical reference to inflationary prices.

the Lord of Misrule invests 'everie one of these his men . . . with his liveries, of green, yellow or some light wanton colour',[33] and it has been conjectured that 'Jack Cade may have used the Whitsun festivities of 1450 to forward or cover his enterprise'.[34] Cade's 'livery' as part of his visionary utterances recalls 'the simple gray cloth in which all Utopians dress'.[35] On the other hand, Pettit records of the 1381 revolt that 'according to the presentiments of the York jurors, the leaders of the disturbances there "gave caps and other liveries of one colour to various members of their confederacy"' (p. 10). (Ironically, for all the messianic fervour of the German Peasant Revolt, 'one of the demands of the insurgents was that they should be allowed to wear red clothes like their betters'.)[36] Cade's 'livery', like his 'regality' and the Lord of Misrule burlesque, apes that of the great households with their liveried retainers,[37] like those overlooked in earlier sumptuary laws and granted special dispensation by Elizabeth in 1588: 'the servants of noblemen and gentlemen may wear such livery coats as their masters shall allow them, with their badges or other ornaments of any velvet or silk to be laid or added to their said livery coats.'[38]

At one point Shakespeare may have had a sumptuary proclamation in mind. The word 'sumptuous', found only four times in his plays and only in the histories, is used in Lord Say's protest of probity, innocence, and moderation: 'Is my apparel sumptuous to behold?' (IV. vii. 95). This may be an ironic echo of the proclamation in which Elizabeth authorized temporary detention to prove the correctness of dress and degree, 'because there are many persons that percase shall be found in outward appearance more sumptuous in their apparel than by common intendment'.[39]

However that may be, it is certain that Cade plays sharply with words when first confronting Lord Say: 'Ah, thou say, thou serge, nay, thou buckram lord!' (l. 25). Punning on the name, Cade sees Say's reduced circumstances in terms of a coarsening, from 'say' (silk) to 'serge' (wool) to 'buckram' (a rough linen). Materials correspond to their reversed positions, but beyond the cruelty of the wit there may be a finer dramatic point. Cade's first line had been, 'Well, he shall be beheaded for it ten times' (l. 22). As this sentence sinks in, he seems to be prompted by the change visible in Lord Say's face to add the 'buckram Lord!' In the sixteenth century 'buckram'

[33] Cited by Pettit, p. 10.
[34] H. M. Lyle, *The Rebellion of Jack Cade*, Historical Association Pamphlet G16 (London, 1950), p. 9; cited Pettit, p. 4.
[35] *Utopia, Yale Edition of the Complete Works of St Thomas More*, Volume IV, *Utopia*, edited by J. H. Hexter (New Haven, Connecticut, 1965), Introduction, p. xli; cited Bristol, p. 91.
[36] James Laver, *A Concise History of Costume* (London, 1972), p. 86.
[37] As a corrective to the one-sided view of peasant revolt in Norman Cohn's influential study *The Pursuit of the Millennium* (London, 1957), see F. Gaus, 'Social Utopias in the Middle Ages', *Past and Present*, 38 (1967), pp. 16–17, and Rosamond Faith, 'The "Great Rumour" of 1377 and Peasant Ideology', in R. H. Hilton and T. H. Aston, *The English Rising of 1381* (Cambridge, 1984), p. 73. Both studies indicate how certain conservative beliefs could have radical political implications.
[38] *The Tudor Proclamations*, no. 697 (1588), p. 7.
[39] Ibid., no. 646 (1580), p. 457. The phrase 'sumptuous apparel' occurs three times in the homily 'Against Excess of Apparel'.

had, beyond the literal meaning of the 'kind of coarse linen or cloth stiffened with gum or paste' (*OED*, 2), a figurative meaning of 'stiff', 'starched', 'stuck-up'; or 'that has false appearance of stress' (*OED*, 4b). Not wishing to provoke the rebels, perhaps, Lord Say had appeared modestly dressed before them, without the distinction of his degree. Here 'buckram' may also capture Cade's perception of Say's sudden realization of vulnerability, a superiority of bearing stiffening in shock before the judgement of Cade. And the latter does not let class-based invective drop, as is seen in the following charge of printing books and prompting literacy, and in his rounding on the modest lord, 'Thou dost ride in a foot-cloth, dost thou not?' (ll. 44–45), pointing to the undeniable luxury of trappings which give his remarks justification: 'Marry, thou ought'st not to let thy horse wear a cloak, when honester men than thou go in their hose and doublets' (v. vii. 47–49).

Symbolic of the 'honester men' are the 'leather apron' (IV. ii. 12) and 'clouted shoon' (IV. ii. 178). Drawing on the work of Keith Thomas and including the example from this play — 'Spare none but such as go in clouted shoon' — Charles Hobday notes of the clouted shoe, the peasant's hobnailed boot, that ' "clubs and clouted shoon" was a proverbial phrase for a peasant revolt which crops up in Norfolk in 1537, and again in 1549 in connection with Kett's rebellion, and in Leicester in a recusant prophecy of 1586'.[40] Class contempt is echoed in Bevis's 'The nobility think scorn to go in leather aprons' (IV. ii. 12). Unlike aristocratic dress, peasant wear changed relatively little during the Middle Ages. The one common innovation, particularly for smiths and tanners, was the leather apron. This remained an emblem of the lower orders right into this century,[41] a sign of difference as clear as that of spoken language.

From symbolism of clothing we may move to the crucial question of literacy. 'We are all branded on the tongue', said Dr Johnson, but in the earlier period the crucial difference was between those who were branded on the thumb and those who were executed instead, according to their inability to read. At the heart of Cade's assault on literacy is his accusation addressed to Lord Say: 'Thou hast appointed justices of peace, to call poor men before them about matters they were not able to answer. Moreover, thou hast put them in prison; and because they could not read, thou hast hang'd them' (IV. vii. 39–43). As in the matter of treason combat, history itself furnished grotesque materials, seeming travesties, in the matter of the law of benefit of clergy. In the Middle Ages benefit of clergy was the privilege, available to ordained clerks, monks, and nuns accused of felony, of being tried and punished by an ecclesiastical court. As a consequence of the statute of *Pro Clero* (1350), which extended the privilege to secular clerks who helped the

---

[40] 'Clouted Shoon and Leather Aprons', p. 69.
[41] C. Willett Cunnington and Phillis Cunnington, *A Handbook of Medieval Costume* (London, 1973), pp. 178–79. Phillis Cunnington and Catherine Lucas, *Occupational Costume in England from the Eleventh Century to 1914* (London, 1967), passim.

clergy in church services, it was later extended to all who could demonstrate the ability to read in Latin their 'neck verse', Psalm 51.1. By the sixteenth century royal courts had taken control, as benefit of clergy had become an involved law which could exempt those found guilty of certain felonies from the severity of the heavily used death penalty.[42] But what of those unable to read, who confronted the death penalty? Consider the case of one John Trotter, who claimed benefit of clergy when accused of murder during the reign of Edward III. Though illiterate he seemed able to 'read' the Psalter. He could still 'read' the verse even when a suspicious judge turned the book upside down. It transpired that a kind-hearted gaoler had allowed two boys to coach him. He was found guilty as a laymen, but if the boys had succeeded in teaching him to read more convincingly, his claim to clergy would have been upheld, though the gaoler would have been punished.[43] Such was the travesty of law in history.

Cade's charge to Lord Say applies a logic of inversion and reversal. Instead of being sentenced to death in effect for not being able to speak Latin, Lord Say is condemned for his words on Kent, '*bona terra, mala gens*'. 'Away with him! Away with him! He speaks Latin' (ll. 54–55). Because of Cade's logic, in reciprocating authoritarian self-justification in kind, it is impossible to reject his judgement without recognizing the preposterousness of such law in the actual world: this manifest injustice in the play serves to reveal the injustice of all justice based on class.

By adding the Clerk of Chartham episode to the historical confrontation with Lord Say, Shakespeare furthered Cade's comprehensive rejection of authority and law made manifest in writing. The precedents for anti-literacy in the 1381 revolt had nothing as systematic as the allusions in Act IV, which include materials, 'parchment', 'wax . . . seal', 'pen and ink-horn'; production, 'paper-mill', 'printing'; education, 'grammar-school', 'noun', 'verb'; and law, 'justices of the peace', 'clerk', 'courthand', 'obligations', 'letters'.

However, as in the previous episodes discussed, it is impossible to rest securely in the sense of simple affirmation of value. As if to surrender subversion to inconsistency, to surrender the social critic to anarchic clown, Shakespeare also shows Cade as feudal monarch manqué: 'there shall not a maid be married, but she shall pay to me her maidenhead, ere they have it. Men shall hold me in capite' (ll. 5–8). Rather than 'reformation' here, Jack will insist on his proprietory right, his *droit du seigneur*.

In these scenes of the play everything is qualified and compromised by the comic mode of the presentation of Cade, particularly when we consider that if the play was acted by Lord Strange's men it is highly likely that the part went to the principal comedian, Will Kemp. It is considered that the Pembroke company, referred to on the bad quarto title-pages of *2* and *3 Henry*

---

[42] W. S. Holdsworth, *A History of English Law*, 17 vols (London, 1903), III, 294–302.
[43] Leona C. Gabel, *Benefit of Clergy in England in the Later Middle Ages*, Smith College Studies in History, 14, nos 1–4 (October 1928–July 1929, Northampton, Massachusetts), p. 73.

VI, grew out of Lord Strange's Men, for whom all three parts of *Henry VI* were written.[44] Two of Strange's men, Holland and Sinklo (or Sincler) are named respectively in *2* and *3 Henry VI*.[45]

The leading comic performer in Strange's company was Kemp. It would therefore appear likely that Shakespeare knew that he could act Jack Cade. Considering Kemp's later Shakespearian roles as Peter in *Romeo and Juliet* and as Dogberry in *Much Ado About Nothing*, Michael Hattaway feels that 'it is safe to conjecture that such players were type-cast and that playwrights wrote parts with their particular skills in mind'.[46]

Internal allusions indicate this to have been the case with Kemp and Cade. In Act III, scene i the Duke of York in soliloquy recounts his suborning of Cade and recalls his fighting prowess in Ireland: 'And fought so long, till that his thighs with darts | Were almost like a sharp-quill'd porpentine' (l. 362). He then elaborates with a further simile: 'And, in the end being rescu'd, I have seen | Him caper upright like a wild Morisco, | Shaking the bloody darts as he his bells. (l. 364) In that allusion to the Morris dance C. L. Barber saw an apt image: 'Such an upstarting, indomitable gesture is perfect for a leader of a rising which is presented as a sort of saturnalia'.[47]

The claim for saturnalia may be overstated, but there is a point here, for how appropriate it would be if the actor playing Cade was the most celebrated Morris dancer of his day, an obvious draw for a popular and impatient audience. (If so, this was in fact to be his first extensive acting role.)[48] The character York refers to Cade, but the actor of York may be ushering the famous dancer on to the stage.

Again, just before his demise, Cade remonstrates with his sword: 'Steel, if thou turn the edge, or cut not out the burly-bon'd clown in chines of beef ere thou sleep in thy sheaf' (IV. x. 55–57). David Wiles has shown that 'in Shakespeare ... the word "clown" is never found outside stage directions unless used *of* or (for ironic effect) *by* the character who is designated as *the* clown of the play'.[49] Kemp's famously athletic capers meant that he was well-built, thus, ironically, he is 'the burly-boned clown' about to be chined by Iden. What is more, if Sinklo, a notoriously thin actor,[50] was cast as Iden, his invitation to compare physiques — 'Set limb to limb, and thou art far the lesser' (l. 45) — has a farcical point reminiscent of the burlesque of the earlier Cade scenes.

There are some comparable cases. As we have seen, Tom Miller the clown appeared with the rebels in *The Life and Death of Jack Straw* (1593), and in the

[44] Hanspeter Born, 'The Date of *2, 3 Henry VI*', *Shakespeare Quarterly*, 25 (1974), 323–34.
[45] Ibid., p. 333. See Part Three, ed. Cairncross, p. 66.
[46] *Elizabethan Popular Theatre* (London, 1982), p. 90.
[47] *Shakespeare's Festive Comedy* (Princeton, New Jersey, 1959), p. 29.
[48] See one of Tarlton's *Jest Book* anecdotes: 'It chanced that in the midst of a Play, after long expectation for *Tarlton*, being much desired of the people, at length he came forth.' Quoted by A. J. Gurr, *Playgoing in Shakespeare's London* (Cambridge, 1987), pp. 125–26.
[49] *Shakespeare's Clown* (Cambridge, 1987), pp. 68–69.
[50] E. W. Talbert, *Elizabethan Drama and Shakespeare's Early Plays* (1963; reprinted New York, 1973), p. 13.

play *Sir Thomas More* (1593), to which Shakespeare contributed, Will Kemp acted the clown amidst the rebels, as Wiles shows (pp. 80–81). Such figures could also symbolize the collective nature of an insurrectionary mob, 'the unruly sort of clowns', as Sidney has it, reminding us that the rustic buffoon provided the early model for the stage clown.[51] Shakespeare's portrayal of Cade incorporated both cultural and theatrical traditions.

Enid Welsford points out the process whereby the court fool and the public fool 'came to be reunited in the person of "the Lord of Misrule", "the Abbot of Unreason", "the Prince of Fools" who is none other than the traditional mock-king and clown, who has adopted the appearance and behaviour of the court-jester'.[52] Furthermore, Morris dancing was associated with the Lord of Misrule and his train. With the decline of folk custom and ceremony the spirit of misrule survived in 'the "immoderate and inordinate jove" of the Elizabethan clown, jig dancer, and "jeaster", who was accustomed, as Thomas Lodge wrote "to coin bitter jests, or to show antique motions, or to sing baudie sonnets and ballads", and who indulged in "all the feats of misrule in the countrie"'.[53] The 'jig', the celebrated specialism of Kemp, as C. R. Baskerville has shown, included 'legal parody', 'satire on the ills of society', and allusion to the Utopian Land of Cockaygne — all features of the Cade's scenes. In the theatrical tradition the clown as comic actor aped his betters yet scoffed at ranks or classes, made mock prophecies, indulged in chop logic not without some pointed wisdom, yet scorned learning.[54] Again, all are palpably there in the Cade scenes but in a compounded form incomparably more dynamic than theatrical predecessors, especially when it is recalled that Kemp is not performing as a clown accompanying Cade, but is both impersonating Cade acting clownishly, and derisively evaluating such action as from without, for Kemp as clown ridicules Cade the historical personage. If this surmise about Kemp acting Cade is right, Shakespeare's major innovation in the early history of the clown was to have him act a historical figure of some moment in the chronicles. The dialectic between the ideology of propagandist history and the conventions of art as modified by carnival inversion give the Cade scenes their uniquely ambivalent power.

There are other signs of strange conflations and inversions. At the beginning of Act IV, scene ii, a carefully placed qualification triggers a particular expectation. 'Come get thee a sword', says Bevis, 'though made of lath'. Editors point out that this was the weapon carried by the Vice in the old morality plays. (Feste's song in *Twelfth Night*, IV. ii. 127–30, puts it

---

[51] Cited by Christopher Hill, 'The Many Headed Monster in Late Tudor and Early Stuart Political Thinking', in *From the Renaissance to the Counter-Reformation*, edited by Charles H. Cater (London, 1966), p. 298. See Wiles, pp. 61–72, for an extended discussion of the word 'clown'.
[52] *The Fool* (London, 1968), pp. 197–98.
[53] Robert Weimann, *Shakespeare and the Popular Tradition in the Theatre* (Baltimore and London, 1978), pp. 23–24.
[54] Talbert, Chapter 2, 'Aspects of the Comic', pp. 7–60, especially pp. 56–60 on the Cade scenes.

plainly enough: 'like to the old Vice . . . Who, with dagger of lath, in his rage and his wrath, | 'Cries "Ah, ha!" to the devil.') But no sooner has the audience been invited to measure the historical Cade against a Vice figure such as Sedition, than it finds Bevis and Holland invoking the World Upside Down. Deriving from classical *adunata* (or *impossibilia*) and the medieval *drolerie*, the pictorial tradition of the World Upside Down found on sixteenth-century broadsheets depicted a range of social and natural inversion. The social aspect concerns us here — such images as the peasant rides, the king walks; the servant arrests his master; 'the peasant judges the judge and teaches or refuses the advice of the learned' and 'the thief (or poor man) takes the judge or policeman to jail'.[55] Following Holland's observation on the nobility's scorn for leather aprons, Bevis adds: 'Nay, more; the king's Council are no good workmen' (IV. ii. 13–14). On which Holland muses: 'True; and yet it is said, "Labour in thy vocation"': Which is as much to say as, "Let the magistrates be labouring men"; and therefore should we be magistrates' (IV. ii. 15–17). Holland specifically travesties 'An Homily Against Idleness', restricting the meaning of 'labour' to what the homily distinguishes as 'handy labour', while elaborating on 'divers sorts of labours, some of the mind, and some of the body' including the 'vocation' of 'governing the commonweal publicly', and so on.[56] The world is turned upside down first by turning language upside down: the King's magistrates are considered poor 'workmen' who should therefore carry out manual labour in a revised vocation, thereby taking the place of the regular workmen, like Bevis and Holland, who would assume their office. The judges will be judged, and the judged will become judges, as we see in the following scenes with the Clerk of Chartham and Lord Say.

A larger dimension of burlesque can be seen in the way that Shakespeare carefully made Cade not merely claim the throne but also echo York himself. More than any other critic, David Riggs assembles a persuasive catalogue, saying that Cade imitates his patron York's 'claims to royal ancestry (IV. ii. 37–50), his intention to purge Henry's court of "false caterpillars" (IV. iv. 36; see also IV. ii. 61–67, IV. vii. 28–30), his detestation of all things French (IV. ii. 159–65), his admiring recollection of Henry V (IV. ii. 149–52), his distaste for "bookish rule" (IV. ii. 81–104), his insistence on martial eminence as requisite for aristocratic station (IV. ii. 76), and his easy association of martial bravery and material prosperity (IV. ii. 61–72)'.[57] Furthermore, as has always been recognized, Cade parodies aristocratic genealogy (IV. ii. 37–47), reflecting on a major concern through the *Henry VI* plays in general, and referring to York's claims in particular.[58] It has also

[55] David Kunzle, 'World Upside Down: The Iconography of a European Broadsheet', in *The Reversible World: Symbolic Inversion in Art and Society*, edited by Barbara Babcock (Ithaca and London, 1978), p. 51.
[56] *Certain Sermons or Homilies* (Oxford, 1894), p. 460.
[57] *Shakespeare's Heroical Histories* (Cambridge, Massachusetts, 1971), p. 124.
[58] For example, see Prior, pp. 112–13.

been claimed, more provocatively, that 'Cade's ramshackle army is the antimasque to York's rebellion'.[59]

To all this may be added a further suggestion that Shakespeare created 'travesty-by-parallel' with history itself, by having Cade burlesque the royal entry of the king. The real King Henry VI, returning to London from his coronation in Paris, first assembled his entourage on Blackheath before the entry, during which, as Fabyan records (p. 605), the conduits of Cheapside ran with wine, a festive tradition. In the play Cade and the rebels assemble on Blackheath, then, after his violent entry and his declaring himself 'Lord of this city', he gives orders that 'the pissing-conduit run nothing but claret wine the first year of my reign' (IV. v. 1–4), 'King' Jack even has his royal rhetoric, not echoing King Henry, but echoed by King Henry. His followers deserting him, 'Was ever feather so lightly blown to and fro as the multitude' (IV. viii. 54), asks Cade; his subjects deserting him, 'Look, as I blow this feather from my face ... such is the lightness of you common men' (3 Henry VI, III. i. 83, 88), observes Henry, the failed King echoing the mock king.

Shakespeare repeats this technique in the action, with execution by decapitation. The chronicles express uniform horror at the execution of Lord Say and Sir James Cromer, Cade having their heads hoist aloft 'and at every corner have them kiss' (IV. vii. 130). In fact the historical Cade's action, repeated by Shakespeare, duplicated at least one earlier atrocity. In 1381 Suffolk rebels bore the heads of Lord Chief Justice, Sir John Cavendish, and the prior of Edmondsberie, 'making them sometimes as it were to kisse'.[60] Cade's protracted, cruelly delayed sentence and execution of Lord Say stresses a barbarity which in more summary execution elsewhere in the plays, though less apparent, is no less real. The depiction of Cade here is not simply the expression of anti-egalitarianism, the anarchic many-headed monster run wild, rather the recognition that such rebellions become a grotesque mimicry of the barbarism of feudal hierarchy. In 3 Henry VI Shakespeare has Warwick order that York's head be replaced by Clifford's on York gate (I. iv. 180; II. vi. 85), a duplication reflecting the Cade scene and which is not in the sources.

The miracle, combat, and rebellion scenes each comment on the main action by developing a comedy that is never free from irony. Even moments of high comedy are darkened by the larger context, creating a particular dialectic between kinds of relief, between relief as release and relief as projection, as in the plastic arts, making distinct by contrast of plane, colour, or line. Here that making distinct by contrast is done in terms of image, allusion, and action. The audience's affective response is checked by this intellectual recognition and compromised by a cumulative irony which, in turn, encourages through anticipation the relief of laughter. Where at one moment we respond to inversion, distortion, and burlesque, at another we

[59] Robert Ornstein, A Kingdom for a Stage (Cambridge, Massachusetts, 1972), p. 51.
[60] Holinshed, II, 744.

find they have become a version, reflection, and duplication. The serio-comic dialectic moves from the stage and becomes not a movement from plot to subplot, but a dialectic between art and life, the play and history.

The ideological certainties of chronicle history have gone. History is dynamically reconstituted by the relativistic freedom of art. We confront not the farce of subplot but the possible farce of history in which self-interest, dishonour, and barbarism invert, distort, and burlesque fealty, honour, and love, while protesting their integrity. But this sense of travesty is critical, not dogmatic, and we are made both participants in, and spectators of, the historical process, by the transformation of foreshortened dramatic time. This is the essentially critical function that these scenes promote, from the tentative beginning at St Albans to the confident staging of Jack Cade, in which Shakespeare drew most fully on the resources of history, culture, and art.

The Politics of Stuart Medievalism

JOHN D. COX

Hope College, Holland, Michigan

When Ruskin coined the term 'Mediaevalism', he did so as a way of contrasting what he saw as a distinctive visual style with two other historical styles, 'Classicalism' and 'Modernism'. Ruskin's terms have since been broadened to include much more than visual style, but his aesthetic preoccupation still clings to 'medievalism'.[1] As a consequence, comparatively little has been said about the *political* implications of turning to the Middle Ages as a model of style or behaviour. On the face of it, those implications would seem to be conservative and authoritarian. Divine right monarchy, theocracy, social and cosmic hierarchy, theological descriptions of authority, all are political ideas that originated in the Middle Ages or achieved dominance then, and all belong to the decidedly conservative end of the political spectrum. One immediately thinks, for example, of how medievalism flourished in the reactionary political atmosphere of nineteenth-century England, when a theological definition of authoritarian order from the past appealed to those with power and privilege as they confronted the threat of political revolution and rapid social change.

But while a nostalgic perception of the medieval authority undoubtedly characterizes the nineteenth century, that understanding did not arise then for the first time. Every river has a source, and what might well be thought of as the river of nineteenth-century medievalism is no exception. Just as the conception of the 'middle ages' itself had to arise some time after what we think of as the Middle Ages, so medievalism as a nostalgically conceived repository of political conservatism had to arise at some point after the thing itself had passed, or at least was perceived to have passed. What I want to suggest here is that the key ingredients of what would eventually emerge as nineteenth-century medievalism can be found in the seventeenth century and specifically in the rise of Stuart absolutism under James I.

To be sure, in laying down the foundations of centralized power, the Tudors had consciously preserved and in some cases revived certain symbols and rituals of power that had arisen much earlier and were essentially neo-medieval, for they had been rendered obsolete in practice by Tudor policy itself. Court rituals such as the tournament or the disguising, for

---

[1] See, for example, the journal *Studies in Medievalism*, which takes 'medievalism' in almost precisely the same way Ruskin defined it. See *Ruskin's Works*, 11 vols (Chicago and New York, 1871, VI: 105. For an account of the Victorian medievalism Ruskin represents, see Alice P. Kenney and Leslie J. Workman, 'Ruins, Romance, and Reality: Medievalism in Anglo-American Imagination and Tast, 1750–1840', *Winterthur Portfolio*, 10 (1975), 131–63).

example, were products of deliberate archaism, and they have sociological counterparts in Spenser's literary medievalism, in royal portraiture, and in the highly ornamental armour of the late sixteenth century. Neither the skills of the tournament nor outrageously expensive armour made any practical military sense in the age of gunpowder, and the passionate pursuit of obsolescence under Elizabeth in fact has an explanation in the dynamics of centralized power. As Lawrence Stone has pointed out, the Tudor monarchs systematically reduced the real power of their competitors by substituting education for military domination as the primary sign of social privilege.[2] This substitution created a new social élite whose first loyalty was to the crown, but the old standards of privilege did not simply disappear: they were transformed from real means of violent coercion into symbolic forms that were politically innocuous. The more idealized these forms were, the more effective they became as impressive symbols, hence the wealth expended on court pageantry and the ornamentation lavished on impractical armour. The new élite had to master these symbolic forms in order to compete effectively with the old nobility. Sir Philip Sidney's ambition expressed itself, for example, both in his surpassing military horsemanship and his eloquence in verse: the old and new signs, respectively, of social privilege. Sidney thus begins his *Apology for Poetry* with a seemingly offhand allusion to Italian horsemanship, thereby signalling the easy grace and authoritative control that he admires both in riding and in writing.[3]

Under James I, the cultivation of what might be called artistocratic military medievalism at first continued apace, despite the king's personal distaste for the martial arts. Indeed, Prince Henry may well have sought to distinguish himself from his overbearing father by making himself a foremost practitioner of archaic military skills in the Elizabethan manner.[4] In doing so, he was probably laying the groundwork for a foreign policy that would also have been distinct from his father's: a militantly Protestant policy that assumed a combative stance over against Spain, in contrast to James's pursuit of peace.[5] Henry's deliberate revival of Elizabethan court chivalry thus perpetuated the politics of Tudor medievalism, and Henry therefore represents important continuity between the Tudors and Stuarts where medievalism is concerned.

But Henry did not survive his father's ninth year on the English throne, and at about the time of the crown prince's unexpected death in 1612, Stuart medievalism takes an important new turn. This turn has to do with the strategic royal affirmation of popular culture, for this affirmation is not only

[2] *The Crisis of the Aristocracy, 1558–1641* (Oxford, 1965), pp. 242–50.
[3] *An Apology for Poetry*, in *Elizabethan Critical Essays*, edited by G. G. Smith, 2 vols (London, 1904), I, 150–51.
[4] See Roy Strong, *Henry, Prince of Wales and England's Lost Renaissance* (London, 1986) and Jerry W. Williamson, *The Myth of the Conqueror. Prince Henry Stuart: A Study of Seventeenth-Century Personation* (New York, 1978).
[5] Williamson, pp. 75–107.

a Stuart innovation and an explicit means of solidifying power; it is also the direct progenitor of nineteenth-century medievalism. Let us first consider what popular culture is in this period, and then turn to James's response to it and the contrast between his response and Elizabethan attitudes. Popular forms of Elizabethan pastime were not distinguished from courtly forms merely on the basis of taste. Bear-baiting, play-acting, football, morris-dancing, wake ales, and Maying were not only less erudite and refined than triumphs, disguisings, tournaments, and guild shows; the popular forms were regarded as subverting political stability as well as good taste. This does not mean that individual aristocrats did not affirm such activities. Elizabeth herself had a taste for bear-baiting; she and James both patronized the office of the Master of the Royal Game of Bears, Bulls, and Mastiff Dogs, an office that was purchased by Philip Henslowe and Richard Alleyn for £450 in 1604.[6] The Royal entertainment at Kenilworth in 1575, which is unusually well documented, included numerous folk elements, some of them reappearing in Jacobean masques decades later.[7] But Elizabeth's personal taste did not, in this case, create policy, for by far the dominant attitude during her reign was that popular pastimes were a serious threat to public and national order. This attitude seems to have been shaped about equally by ruling-class fear of popular riot and by widespread anti-Catholicism. Muriel Bradbrook has amassed evidence that Elizabethan public gatherings indeed tended to be riotous, and denunciation of popular pastimes can be heard from every quarter.[8] Apprentices were forbidden to engage in sports and pastimes even as late as the Restoration. A 1595 Shoemakers' ordinance forbade apprentices and journeymen to make or play with footballs without the consent of the guild masters.[9] In May 1575, no less an establishment figure than the Bishop of Winchester, Thomas Cooper, gave order for the suppression of 'church ales, May games, morris dances, and other vain pastimes'.[10] Cooper was later lampooned by the Puritan satirist, 'Martin Marprelate', so he can hardly have been perceived as a Puritan sympathizer; rather, he spoke for an anti-Catholic majority opinion. In short, Elizabethan opposition to popular culture was by no means confined to Puritans or to radical reformers in the English church. Rather, opposition was largely defined by a strong sense of social superiority and by the widely perceived threat of Catholicism throughout Elizabeth's reign.

---

[6] *Henslowe's Diary*, edited by W. W. Greg, 2 vols (London, 1908), II, 35–41. On popular culture in general in this period, see David Underdown, *Revel Riot and Rebellion: Popular Politics and Culture in England, 1603–1660* (Oxford: Clarendon Press, 1985) especially pp. 44–72.
[7] A folk figure called Captain Cox appeared at Kenilworth, for example, and reappeared in Jonson's *Masque of Owls* (1626), edited by C. H. Herford and Percy and Evelyn Simpson, *Ben Jonson*, 11 vols (Oxford, 1925–52), VII, 781–86. For commentary, see Percy & Simpson, X, 700–03 and Muriel C. Bradbrook, *The Rise of the Common Player* (London, 1964), p. 151.
[8] Bradbrook, pp. 96–118.
[9] O. Jocelyn Dunlop and R. D. Denman, *English Apprenticeship and Child Labour* (New York, 1912), pp. 189–90.
[10] Quoted in Bradbrook, p. 142.

During the reign of Elizabeth's successor, however, the situation changed. Even before he took the English throne, James published a book of advice to his infant son, in which he advocated royal affirmation of popular pastimes for strategic political reasons, not merely because he personally approved of them. To be sure, James was like everyone else who possessed a degree of privilege or power in his assumption that the lower classes were unstable, dangerous, and threatening: 'But unto one fault is all the common people of this kingdom subject, as well burgh as land, which is, to judge and speak rashly of their Prince, setting the commonweal upon four props, as we call it, ever wearying of the present estate and desirous of novelties.' But James advocates something besides suppression to deal with this threat. Severity, he urges, should be tempered and mixed with mildness in order to induce 'just praise of your so well moderated regiment. For I know no better mean than so to rule as may justly stop their mouths from all such idle and unreverent speeches and so to prop the weal of your people with provident care for their good government that justly Momus himself may have no ground to grudge at'.[11] In other words, the inherent threat represented by commoners is to be prevented in part by encouraging limited expression of popular mirth and thus winning the support of the populace rather than merely alienating them:

In respect whereof, and therewith also the more to allure them to a common amity among themselves, certain days in the year would be appointed for delighting the people with public spectacles of all honest games and exercise of arms, as also for convening of neighbors, for entertaining friendship and heartliness by honest feasting and merriness. For I cannot see what greater superstition can be in making plays and lawful games in May and good cheer at Christmas than in eating fish in Lent and upon Fridays. (*Basilikon Doron*, p. 27)

Eventually, in 1618, James decided to put his policy into effect in England, and he did so specifically to counter the rising threat of Puritan resistance to the crown. In that year he published *The King's Majesty's Declaration to His Subjects Concerning Lawful Sports To Be Used*, more commonly called *The Book of Sports*.[12] As Leah Marcus has recently argued, this royal edict was conceived as a political double play.[13] Not only was *The Book of Sports* supposed to restrain the potentially subversive energy of popular pastimes; it was supposed to disallow a major structural plank in the platform of the Puritan opposition, by repudiating *their* opposition to holidays and festivals.

Marcus has extensively documented the literary impact of *The Book of Sports*, and her argument need not be repeated here. What needs to be emphasized instead is that James's policy can be distinguished from Elizabethan practice and that the Jacobean distinction effectively created an

---

[11] *Basilikon Doron*, in *The Political Works of James I*, edited by C. H. McIlwain (Cambridge, Massachusetts, 1918), p. 27.
[12] In *Minor Prose Works of James VI and I*, edited by James Craigie, Scottish Text Society (Edinburgh, 1982).
[13] *The Politics of Mirth* (Chicago, 1986), pp. 1–23.

attitude that would resurface in nineteenth-century medievalism. By isolating Puritan opposition to popular pastime, James drew the sting of anti-Catholic antagonism to holiday mirth under the Tudors. An apparent alliance therefore seemed to form between crown, church, and festive-minded commoners, and this alliance would be the basis of the 'cavalier' party in the seventeenth century, as it would be the basis of medievalism two centuries later. Consider, for example, Macaulay's assertion, in his *History of England*, that 'nothing ... so strongly distinguished the Church of England from other Churches as the relation in which she stood to the monarchy. The King was her head'.[14] The alliance of church and crown is something Macaulay regards as important and unique, and he eloquently scorns the Puritans who resorted to biblical precedent in opposition to this alliance:

The prophet who hewed in pieces a captive king, the rebel general who gave the blood of a queen to the dogs, the matron who, in defiance of plighted faith, and of the laws of Eastern hospitality, drove the nail into the brain of the fugitive ally who had just fed at her board, and who was sleeping under the shadow of her tent, were proposed [by the Puritans] as models to Christians suffering under the tyranny of princes and prelates.[15]

Summarizing the points that Puritans opposed, Macaulay revealingly lists cavalier affectations indiscriminately with popular pastimes — a characteristically *Stuart* combination of qualities:

It was a sin to hang garlands on a Maypole, to drink a friend's health, to fly a hawk, to hunt a stag, to play at chess, to wear lovelocks, to put starch into a ruff, to touch the virginals, to read the Fairy Queen. ... The fine arts were all but proscribed. The solemn peal of the organ was superstitious. The light music of Ben Jonson's masques was dissolute. Half the fine paintings in England were idolatrous, the other half indecent [16]

Spenser's *The Faerie Queene*, Ben Jonson's masques, and the fine paintings of England are, of course, exclusively aristocratic products, and they would not be in Macaulay's list along with hanging garlands on a Maypole if he derived his conception of the nostalgic ideal he is describing from the Tudor period. His sources, in fact, are Dryden and the royalist pamphleteers of the Restoration, who revived and adapted the Stuart politics of James I.[17]

If Macaulay had wished, he could have found earlier examples of the model he nostalgically admires, but he could not have found them before

---

[14] Thomas Babington Macaulay, *The History of England*, edited by T. F. Henderson, 5 vols (London, 1931), I, 47.
[15] Macaulay, I, 70.
[16] Macaulay, I, 70–71.
[17] For an excellent description of how Restoration royal apologists revived the early Stuart ideology of kingship, see Nicholas Jose, *Ideas of the Restoration in English Literature, 1660–71* (Cambridge, Massachusetts, 1984), pp. 17–30.

the accession of King James.[18] Typically late Elizabethan seems Richard
Carew's *Survey of Cornwall* (1602) in which a friend offers to defend sports,
only to be refuted by the author: 'the best curing was to cut it clean away.'[19]
The earliest printed defence of popular pastime is Henry Chettle's *Kind
Hart's Dream* (1592), but Chettle undertakes to defend only play-acting, and
he does so in the face of Robert Greene's moralistic attack on playwrights in
Greene's Groatsworth of Wit. Sidney defends plays too, of course, in the *Apology
for Poetry* (printed in 1595), but his aim is also very far from defending
popular sports per se; indeed, he censures the vernacular drama precisely
because it does not conform closely enough to neo-classical expectation, and
that expectation had definite aristocratic implications, as we shall see.

In fact, the earliest published general defence of popular pastimes is
Jacobean: Humphrey King's *An Halfe-penny Worth of Wit, in a Penny Worth of
Paper* (London, 1613) appeared five years before *The Book of Sports* itself. The
early appearance of this work suggests that James's strategy was eliciting
support well before his policy was officially promulgated. King writes in a
popular style, consciously reviving the early sixteenth-century manner of
John Skelton, in order to evoke nostalgia for 'the merry time' he describes:

> Let us talke of *Robin Hoode*,
> And little *Iohn* in merry Shirewood,
> Of Poet Skelton with his pen,
> And many other merry men,
> Of May-game Lords, and Sommer Queenes,
> With Milke-maides, dancing o're the Greenes,
> Of merry *Tarlton* in our time,
> Whose conceite was very fine,
> Whom Death hath wounded with his Dart,
> That lov'd a May-pole with his heart. (sig. E)

Though King decries papal superiority in the church and treats courtly
excess with moralistic disapproval (sig. C2v–D), he reserves his harshest
criticism for the 'Sectaries' who curse the state, rail at the clergy, and preach
against Maypoles and Whitson ales (sig. D2v–E). His defence of the monarchy and the established church, his resistance to Puritans, and his
nostalgic view of popular pastimes represent a quintessentially Jacobean
attitude that anticipates precisely the attitude championed by Macaulay.

Evidence for the distinction I am making between the politics of Tudor
and Stuart medievalism can be found in drama of this period as well. We
have already noticed Sidney's distinction between classical and Italian

---

[18] This claim pertains to published sources only. A manuscript poem by Puttenham offers a qualified
defence of games and 'country sport' in the 1570s, but this poem was not published until W. R. Morfill
edited it in *Ballads from Manuscripts, Part II. Ballads Relating Chiefly to the Reign of Queen Elizabeth* (Hertford,
1873), pp. 72–91. Puttenham may well have refrained from publishing his sentiments because the climate
of opinion was so contrary to them. For whatever reason, I have been unable to find any other defence of
popular pastime (aside from drama) before 1613. I am grateful to David Norbrook for the reference to
Puttenham.

[19] Richard Carew of Antony, *The Survey of Cornwall*, edited by F. E. Halliday (London: Andrew Melrose,
1953), p. 142.

drama on one hand and English drama (as Sidney knew it) on the other: the latter is deficient, Sidney thinks, because it lacks neo-classical decorum. Sidney's distinction anticipates the distinctiveness of Jacobean medi-evalism. For Sidney's stylistic reservations about vernacular drama are social reservations too: he subscribes to the classical separation of styles that reserves noble subject matter for the high style and relegates common subjects to the low style. This separation extends to genre as well: tragedy is for high subjects in the high style; comedy, for common subjects in the low style. Hence his rejection of

these gross absurdities, how all their plays [i.e., the English plays Sidney knew of] be neither right tragedies nor right comedies, mingling kings and clowns, not because the matter so carrieth it but thrust in clowns by head and shoulders to play a part in majestical matters with neither decency nor decorum. So as neither the admiration and commiseration nor the right sportfulness is by their mongrel tragi-comedy obtained. (1, 199)

'Sportfulness' is the term Sidney identifies with comedy, because both comedy and sports have common (lower-class) connotations. Even where comedy is concerned, he prefers plays that produce 'delight' rather than 'laughter', because 'laughter almost ever cometh of things most dispropor-tioned to ourselves and nature', whereas 'delight hath a joy in it, either permanent or present' (1, 199). 'Ourselves' is meant to be taken universally in this sentence, but given Sidney's social sense of decorum in genre, 'ourselves' comes perilously close to meaning 'us aristocrats'.

Sidney's recognition of stylistic and social decorum is the same recog-nition that governed Jonson's sense of genre, including his sense of the court masque, a form he frequently used to defend the Jacobean policy regarding popular pastimes. Indeed, Jonson was keenly impressed by Sidney's *Apology*, and he sought to put its precepts into practice whenever he could. Kings never appear in his comedies, for example, and clowns have no place in his tragedies. Even the masque maintains this decorum, for commoners are invariably banished with the antimasque, which exists largely to demon-strate royal virtues by default. Since professional actors were used in the antimasque, it is a striking example of what Stephen Greenblatt has called 'the circulation of social energy'.[20] For in the Jonsonian division between masque and antimasque, Jacobean policy found a receptive complement in dramatic form, and form reinforced social reality: popular sports (repre-sented in this case by the commercial theatre) were simultaneously affirmed and decorously kept in their place by the very structure of the masque itself.

As a way of illustrating how the special decorum of the Jonsonian masque embodies Jacobean policy in a specific case, let us consider two dramatic works that can be dated within a dozen years of each other, one late Elizabethan and the other early Jacobean. The two works in question are Shakespeare's romantic comedy, *Twelfth Night*, with a date of about 1600,

[20] *Shakespearean Negotiations* (Berkeley and Los Angeles, 1988), pp. 1–20.

and Jonson's masque, *Love Restored*, produced in 1612. One of many points in common between these two works is their association with the popular festival, Twelfth Night, alluded to in Shakespeare's title and celebrated as the occasion on which Jonson's masque was performed. Indeed, this play and masque have so many points in common that one might at first be inclined to cite Shakespeare's *Twelfth Night* as an Elizabethan example of what I am proposing as a distinctively Jacobean medievalism. In Shakespeare's play, for example, we witness a marked opposition between a character actually called 'puritan' several times (that is, Malvolio) and a fun-loving fellow commoner whose name, 'Feste', reflects his love of festivity. These two serve a noble lady, Olivia, who initially disapproves of Feste and favours Malvolio. Yet after the latter's hypocrisy is made clear to Olivia, she eschews him in favour of his mirthful competitor, who has spent his time throughout the play in singing catches, drinking to all hours of the night, and generally acting in the carefree but irresponsible way that commoners were supposed to act. In short, if one reads *Twelfth Night* selectively, one can make of it a virtual allegory of the Jacobean policy that was first officially formulated almost two decades later. The madcap festival alluded to in the title has no direct bearing on the play, except that the play finally vindicates popular festivity, and Twelfth Night is a major popular festival.

Where Jonson's *Love Restored* is concerned, Jeffrey Fischer and Leah Marcus have left little doubt that this particular masque is a brilliant early defence of the policy James would later put into effect in the *Book of Sports*.[21] In this case, though the title does not allude to Twelfth Night, the staging of *Love Restored* on Twelfth Night is a clue to its meaning, which involves a defence of popular pastime. This masque, Marcus observes, is 'about the inability to make a masque' (p. 29). The first character to appear is Masquerado, who attributes his impotence in staging a masque to Cupid's hoarseness and lack of court favour. Understood allegorically, this opening statement indicates that a masque is impossible because masques celebrate the harmony promoted by love, and love presently has no voice or effect at court. The truth of Masquerado's observation is borne out when a character enters who appears to be Cupid but is actually Plutus — not love but the love of money. His true nature is revealed when he begins talking like Malvolio, rejecting Masquerado and 'the merry madnesse of one hower' (l. 35) that masques provide. The paradoxical dilemma of the antimasque is finally resolved only when love is restored with the appearance of the true Cupid, who banishes Plutus and acknowledges that his own energy derives from

> The Majestie, that here doth move,
> [And s]hall triumph, more secur'd by love,
> Then all his earth.
>
> (l. 247)

---

[21] Jeffrey Fischer, '*Love Restored: A Defense of Masquing*', *Renaissance Drama*, n.s.8 (1977), 231–44; Marcus, pp. 24–38.

The 'Majestie' Cupid refers to, of course, is King James, whose presence at the masque Cupid acknowledges in these lines. As always in Jonson's masques, the solution to the problem embodied in the antimasque is the epiphany of royal power. In this masque, the king is the source of true court harmony because he is conceived neo-platonically as the source of the love that makes harmony possible.

Love Restored explicitly vindicates popular pastime by including another character in the antimasque, who is essential in preparing the way for the true Cupid. This character is Robin Goodfellow, a product of native English folklore, who was already familiar to the popular stage because of his appearance as Puck in Midsummer Night's Dream. Robin's function in Love Restored is to bring three things to the masque that Masquerado himself cannot bring, namely, the energy of popular pastime, the recognition of Plutus's imposture, and an understanding of what true love is at court. The fact that the simple rural Robin can recognize true majesty when Plutus cannot is a powerful vindication of popular devotion to the monarchy and a rejection of festivity when it takes the form of mere lavish expense — the love of money. In Love Restored popular pastimes are not dangerous to the crown, as the Tudor conception would have held, because the channelling of their energy in devotion to the crown is appropriate and fruitful. This is why Robin's rhetoric becomes more elevated as he draws nearer to his revelatory purpose in the masque: in effect, his own nature is elevated (or made socially acceptable) as it fulfills its true purpose of devotion.

Despite their superficial similarities, Twelfth Night and Love Restored embody very different political conceptions of popular pastime. While Jonson defends festivity as long as it is tied to royal power, Shakespeare grants it an autonomy that makes it potentially threatening and subversive. Take Feste's relation to the ruling class, for example. While no actual monarch attended Twelfth Night, Shakespeare does put rulers on stage in that play, thus violating the decorum prized by Sidney and Jonson. Moreover, the ruling class he stages is foolish, fallible, and capable of change — even of improvement — thus violating the static image of royal perfection that Jonson would later create in the masque. Both Orsino and Olivia are 'sick of self love', the disease that Olivia finally recognizes in Malvolio, and while they are curable, in contrast to Malvolio, their cure is wrought at least in part by Feste, a mirth-loving subordinate. Indeed, at one point Feste actually instructs Olivia that she is a fool, making her laugh in self-recognition and thus progress toward her own cure (1.5.54–69). Feste's subordination to Olivia is highly ambiguous, and he certainly remains irreducibly himself throughout Twelfth Night; he is not elevated or morally transformed, as Robin is elevated in Love Restored. Feste is on the margins of the courtly pale from beginning to end, and the strength of his energy is signalled in his literally being given the last word, the haunting and enigmatic lyric 'When that I was and a little tiny boy'. Contrastingly, the taming of Robin in Love

Restored is unequivocal: he is banished with the antimasque, decorously compelled (with all the other characters who were played by professional actors) to defer to the dignity of the courtiers who danced the masque proper.

It is easy to overstate Feste's subversiveness, of course, and I call attention to it only because it contrasts so strikingly with the relatively emasculated energy of Robin in *Love Restored*. A similar contrast can be seen in Puck of *Midsummer Night's Dream*. In comparison to his folklore model, Puck is tame indeed, but like Feste he is outside the orbit of royal control — indeed of human control — for Puck and Oberon have the last word in their play, as Feste does in *Twelfth Night*. *Midsummer Night's Dream* ends with the fairies blessing the royal marriage bed, though the high-minded duke has denied that fairies even exist. Fairies and human beings in this play do not have a symmetrical impact on one another; the weight of influence runs heavily in favour of the fairies. If Shakespeare is defending popular mirth, he conducts his defence very differently from the way Jonson conducts his. Rather than insisting on the subordination of popular pastime to royal control, Shakespeare grants holiday mirth an energetic and potentially threatening autonomy. If festivity serves royal purposes, it does so almost inadvertently and in a larger scheme of things, in which royalty itself plays a diminished role.

What Leah Marcus has called 'the politics of mirth' is thus very different for Shakespeare from what it is for Jonson, and I would urge that this difference is related to broader differences between the Elizabethan and Jacobean regimes — differences that tell us something about the politics of medievalism. To be sure, even in his Jacobean plays Shakespeare eschews the decorum that Jonson consistently observes, but the reasons for his doing so cannot be detailed here.[22] It is enough to note for now that the decorum prevailing in all Jonson's masques is a decorum that makes profound obeisance to royal power. The politics of Jonson's style anticipates the politics of neo-classical style itself, with its insistence on harmony, balance, symmetry, and hierarchy — an insistence anticipated in Sidney's *Apology*. The adaptability of this style to the class structure of English society accounts for its irresistible appeal from the sixteenth to the eighteenth centuries. Moreover, the Romantic revolution only superficially challenged that appeal. Whatever nineteenth-century medievalism may owe to Romanticism, it owes much more to a social conception in which all people know their place and are glad to remain in it. The nostalgic appeal of such a conception goes a long way to explaining medievalism both in the seventeenth century and the nineteenth.

---

[22] For an explanation of Shakespeare's violation of Jacobean decorum, see John D. Cox, *Shakespeare and the Dramaturgy of Power* (Princeton, 1989), pp. 194–221.

Cowley's Verse Satire, 1642–43, and the Beginnings of Party Politics

THOMAS OSBORNE CALHOUN

University of Delaware

Political parties which are recognized and named by the 1680s were not much in evidence prior to the civil wars. Although conditions for party formation had been developing since the Reformation, the vertical model of king/subject held the cultural imagination and so defined political reality. By 1640, however, other models could be conceived: for instance, Oliver St John could speak of a ruling parliament as a 'great body politic' comprehending 'all from king to beggar',[1] and verse satire of the 1640s, as we shall see, provides some evidence that political activity could be perceived as a function of party organization. I will argue that satire of Horatian kind, in particular Cowley's second satire, helped to make the new political vision possible. The genre both reflects and alters its subject, and the form which it imposes brings an otherwise vague political structure into clearer focus.

The phenomenon of party politics has been broadly described by a number of social and literary historians. Lawrence Stone, for example, puts the origins of political parties in the 1570s and 1580s, when 'a vacuum of religious zeal was created by the non-preaching, non-proselytizing, absentee clergy of the church established by Elizabeth' which 'was filled by two groups of dedicated and determined men who differed utterly in their religious loyalties and beliefs'. The first was made up of seminary priests, who built a post-Reformation Catholic minority. The other was a group of Puritan ministers and preachers, either Marian exiles returned or younger men whose muses were Protestant martyrs. Stone cites J. E. Neale's judgement that the Puritan lobby in the Elizabethan House of Commons was the first political party in English history, and adds that 'the congregations clustering around the Puritan lecturers in the urban churches of the 1620s and 1630s were the models for ideological party organization'.[2] Mark Kishlansky, who studies political party formation through parliamentary selection, locates evidence for political organization in shifts from 'unified choice' candidates to contests. Kishlansky cites David Underdown's broad formula that 'between the Elizabethan era ... and the crisis of the Popish

---

[1] St. John's speech on Strafford (Thomason E 208[7]), as cited by William Palmer, 'Oliver St. John and the Legal Language of Revolution in England: 1640–1642', *The Historian*, 51, no. 2 (February 1989), p. 282.
[2] Lawrence Stone, *The Causes of the English Revolution* (London, 1972), pp. 82 and 103 (citing Neale's *The Elizabethan House of Commons*).

Plot something of decisive importance happened which changed the character of [parliamentary] elections', and then he narrows the frame, saying that
'beginning with the selections to the Short and Long Parliaments ... the
underlying nature of the process of parliamentary selections began to
change'.[3] This, then, is the time when evidence allows us to reconstruct and
perceive a change. Some contemporaries, as well, had by now begun
thinking about government and society in new ways. By 1642, for instance,
Thomas Hobbes's *De Cive* was completed, published, and he had begun
work on *Leviathan*.

When we turn to literary evidence of 1640–43, we find that by 1642
pre-war politics had become the predominant subject for poets, and that
satire, the medium for modulating and expressing anger, had become the
expected genre. Indeed, much of the study of poetry in these years calls for
distinctions between one kind of satire and another. As far as Abraham
Cowley is concerned, we find that he was amongst those who considered that
religious categories serving to define organized groups since the Reformation
were anachronistic, and that beneath the familiar labels 'Puritan' and
'Papist', which he examines, there lay a different political reality. We also
find that the kind of satire he chose to write helped to determine his
perception of the political subject.

Kinds of satire are most readily distinguished by form. Lyric or ballad
satire is written in song forms. The *Rump Songs* are of this type, and during
the early 1640s many poets — including John Denham and John Cleveland
— turned to 'invective song'. Prose satires also abound, such as Richard
Overton's *The araignment of Mr. Persecution ... By reverend youngue Martin
Mar-Priest ... Printed by Martin Clawe-Clergie for Bartholomew Bang-Priest*,[4] and
this example is not the only one which reveals Martin Marprelate (senior)
and his seven pamphlets (1588–89) as the historical model for prose satirists.
This form verges on dramatic satire when the text is spoken by a persona or
written as dialogue. For convenient example, one incorporating a medley of
prose, dialogue, and song, and organized in religious categories, there is the
anonymous 1641 *Dialogue Betwixt Rattle-head and Round-head ... with the
Argument against Bishops*.[5]

[3] Mark A. Kishlansky, *Parliamentary Selection: Social and Political Choice in Early Modern England* (Cambridge, 1986), pp. 15–18; D. E. Underdown, 'Party Management and the Recruiter Elections, 1645–
1648', *English Historical Review*, 83 (1968), 235.
[4] Wing STC 0620. The second edition of this prose satire, as stated in the imprint, was published in
'Europe' in 1645. The text is a precursor of Bunyan's *Pilgrim's Progress*. Richard Overton was also in the
business of writing and publishing verse satires. His *Lambeth Faire, Wherein you have all the Bishops Trinkets set
to Sale* was published anonymously in 1641, but a second edition with marginal annotations, printed by
R. O. and G. D. in 1642, announces Overton as author. The *Articles of High Treason Exhibited against
Cheap-side Crosse, with the last Will and Testament of the said Crosse*, a medley of verse, dialogue, and prose, was
written by R. Overton and printed for R. Overton in 1642. These satires are topically similar to Cowley's,
but their political outlook is in direct contrast.
[5] Thomason E 134 (19), printed in London for 'T. G.' This satire may be the first instalment of a
pamphlet series that includes *The Resolution of the Round-Heads* (Thomason E 132[39]) and *The Answer to the
Rattle-Heads Concerning their fictionate Resolution of the Round-Heads ... their former scurrilous and illiterate
Pamphlet* (Thomason E 132[30]). All of these end with an invective song.

This *Dialogue* features Roger Rattle-head, a discontented Papist, and the equally distraught Alexander Round-head. As their dialogue begins, they are ideologically opposed along traditional lines. At the end, for no reason other than their shared hatred of the hierarchy of bishops, they are in utter agreement, so much so that they join together in an 'invective song':

> *Bishops hold your wonted prattle,*
> *Rather now provide for battle*
> *An enemy ha's vow'd to rattle*
> > *Your tippets from your Crown.*
> > Round-heads Round . . .
> *We give you warning ere we come,*
> *We mean such Birds as you to plumme* . . . (A4v)

A third character, 'Neut.', who represents the writer's point of view, enters the dialogue expecting to moderate an argument between opposing religious parties. Mid-way through, however, he is forced to exclaim: 'hold, hold my Masters, I came to be partners with you in your Religions, but now I fear you'l turn Cat ith' pan and be both one; and so betwixt two stooles, my arse fall in ground' (A3v).

This satire has virtually no intellectual content. It just records a perception that the expected religious categories do not define the anti-hierarchy movement, and concludes with an unveiled threat. The idea that Puritans are siding-up with Papists is not at all new. In 1640 John Corbet had disguised himself with the pseudonym Lysimachus Nicanor, a Jesuit, to write the *Epistle Congratulatorie* . . . *of the Societie of Jesu, to the Covenanters of Scotland* and to show links between Papists and Scots presbyters. The label 'Papist', now virtually a euphemism for 'dangerous and unpatriotic', was tacked on to any number of factions, especially the Arminian bishops, in order to discredit them.

Michael McKeon writes that 'at the beginning of the seventeenth century, the dominant categories for describing political conflict were by and large religious categories', but that 'by the end of the century this was obviously no longer the case'. Popular movements begun for the ostensible purpose of church reform, 'reforming the Reformation', turned to other political and economic causes. John Milton's prose works, chronologically scanned, show his shifting from anti-prelatical tracts to those addressing human rights, and 'some of Milton's contemporaries learned to regard sectarian terminology as essentially political in nature, and therefore to see its customary ascendancy as a mystification of more fundamental motives'.[6] McKeon views this as a dimension of Restoration culture. Abraham Cowley, however, Milton's contemporary and political adversary, saw the point as clearly as anyone and broadcast it in his influential verse satires of 1642 and 1643.

---

[6] Michael McKeon, 'Politics of Discourses and the Rise of the Aesthetic in Seventeenth-Century England', in *Politics of Discourse*, edited by Kevin Sharpe and Steven N. Zwicker (California, 1987), p. 37.

Verse satire, or Roman satire, is of another order from the prose pamphlet satires and invective song. Because of its genre-orientation it represents considered, modulated anger, not just arses falling between two stools. Its formal characteristics, pentameter lines rhyming in couplets, obviously make it a more controlled form than prose. Its longer line gives a more weighty bearing than popular song forms. Roman exemplars, Horace, Persius, and Juvenal, provide the models for differing degrees of constraint and hence different perceptions. Julius C. Scaliger is first among renaissance theorists to distinguish between two kinds of Roman verse satire (*Poetices Libri Septem* [1581], III, 98), and Joseph Hall echoes the distinction in the way he subtitles his *Virgidemiarum* (1597): Books 1–3 are subtitled 'tooth-lesse Satyrs', while Books 4–6 are *'byting Satyres'*. We can substitute 'the way Horace wrote' and 'the way Juvenal wrote' to express these terms according to their Roman exemplars.

The distinction between toothless and biting satire arises again in 1641, in the Milton/Hall debates. Milton enters the exchange between Bishop Hall and 'Smectymnuus' with his unsigned *Animadversions upon the Remonstrants Defence Against Smectymnuus* (1641). His intent is to associate the Remonstrant Arminian, Hall, with the Papists. In the course of this exercise in scurrilous labelling, he recalls the *Virgidemiarum* subtitle: 'You love toothlesse Satyrs; let me informe you, a toothlesse Satyr is as improper as a toothed sleekstone, and as bullish'.[7] By 'bullish" Milton means ridiculous, a contradiction of terms, and he intends the allusion to papal bulls.

A retort to Milton's attack on Hall was published in 1642: *A Modest Confutation of a Slanderous and Scurrilous Libell ...* (Thomason E 134/1).[8] 'Why', the Modest Confuter asks, 'in the name of Philology, is a toothlesse Satyr improper? why Bullish?' (p. 9). According to Horace, a true satirist does not write to 'bite' or injure. He spares the person but strikes at the vice — more or less as Hall did in his *Characters*. Toothless satires, or *'Satyrae incolumes*, are ... in opposition to *Satyrae mordaces*, biting or toothed Satyrs, such as for their loose insolencies were by Law forbidden to the Ancients' (p. 10). Milton's reply, in *An Apology Against a Pamphlet call'd A Modest Confutation* (1642), takes the philological argument to its logical conclusion. 'Toothless satire' is bullish contradiction, Milton proclaims, for it takes 'away the essence of that which it calls itself. For if it bite neither the persons nor the vices, how is it a Satyr, and if it bite either, how is it toothlesse, so that toothlesse Satyrs are as much as if he had said toothlesse teeth'.[9] While Hall's confuter argues for 'legal' and generic constraint, Milton urges that

---

[7] *The Complete Prose Works of John Milton*, general editor, Don M. Wolfe, 8 vols (New Haven and London, 1953), I, 670. This tract is edited by Rudolph Kirk.

[8] Milton thought this rejoinder to have been written either by Bishop Hall or, possibly, by Robert, his eldest son, or another close acquaintance. It is not by Joseph Hall, but whoever wrote it clearly knows Hall's satires and wants to defend them.

[9] *The Complete Works of John Milton*, I, 916. This tract is edited by Frederick L. Taft.

satire 'ought to ... strike high, and adventure dangerously at the most eminent vices among the greatest persons'.

While we might hear Horace *redivivus* arguing with Juvenal in all of this, we ought to consider that it is going on with about as much disingenuousness as is possible. Hall is defending his privileged status, one for which he laboured by defending the ecclesiastical establishment with voluminous argument and example, and the younger Milton adventures dangerously to tear him down. Both of them do battle on a field where the power of the word is the unquestioned mutual assumption. It is this field that Abraham Cowley came to survey, then to dominate, in 1642–43. He too believed that satires, as much as sermons, could reflect as well as alter the course of the nation's inner conflict.

Cowley's first verse satire is of the mordant kind, though its Juvenalian heritage has been thoroughly screened through John Donne. Its title, on the authority of manuscripts, is *The Puritans Lecture*; it first appeared in print under the title *A Satyre against Separatists* in two editions of 1642.[10] The poem cannot have been completed by 23 April 1642, when Hotham refused the king entry into Hull — a topical allusion in lines 131–34. There are other references in the satire to events of 1641 and 1642 but none to the civil war. Lines 89–90, describing the lecturer, 'His stretcht-out voyce sedition spreds a farre, | Nor does he only teach but act a warre', imply that war is still only being rehearsed. So *The Puritans Lecture* was probably completed before August 1642. Cowley was at Cambridge at the time.

This satire takes the form of an epistolary account of a journey, following Donne's Satire 2. The narrator and the unnamed 'Sir' to whom the letter is addressed implicitly share a point of view which is reasonable, learned, conservative, and patriotic. As in the prologue to *The Guardian*,[11] Cowley speaks from the prospect of reason and privilege, Cambridge, about another place, London, where the irrational body politic has been seen in action. The focal character of the satire is the Puritan lecturer, whom Cowley associates with the 'many headed beast *Smectimnius*' and with the muse of both, William Prynne.

Cowley's early plays show that he had a good ear for idiomatic speech, and this satire offers a vivid portrait of the lecturer at work, speaking in a nasal drone, emphasizing the unexpected word or phrase, drawing out hums and haws as though the sounds had meaning. When the lecturer cries out that

[10] The satire was reprinted in 1648, 1660, 1675, and 1678. It has recently been edited by Thomas O. Calhoun and Laurence Heyworth for *The Collected Works of Abraham Cowley*, Volume 1 (Associated University Presses, 1989). The manuscript copies (British Library MS Egerton 2725, Princeton University MS Taylor/Restoration 3, and Yale University MS Osborn f.b. 108) are assessed and the title *The Puritans Lecture* is explained in this edition.

[11] Cowley's satirical drama was presented before Prince Charles, at Cambridge, March 1642. Copies of its prologue and *The Puritans Lecture* circulated together. Cf. British Library MS Egerton 2725.

people's feelings have been numbed, that the passions of 'the *Wauld O Lawd*'
are only lukewarm, some women in the congregation go teary-eyed and start
to sob.

As the lecture moves interminably on, the lecturer's ostensible subject,
'Israels sinnes', is gradually forgotten and his real concerns emerge. The
hierarchy of bishops is targeted, then hierarchy in general. 'Down, down
ev'n to the ground must all things goe' (l. 93). His anger begins to surface,
and 'Not a kinde sillable from him can God get | Till to the Parliament he
comes at last; | Just at that blessed word his furie's past: | And here he
thankes God in a loving tone, | But *Laurd*, and then he mounts, *All's not yet
done*' (ll. 98–102).

> Next he cuffs out set Prayer, even the Lords,
> It binds the spirit he sayes as 'twere with cords,
> *Yea with whipcords, beloved*; Next must authority goe,
> Authoritie's a kind of binder too.
> First then he intends to breath himselfe upon
> Church Government: have at the King anon.
> The thing's don straight, in poore six minutes space
> *Titus*, and *Timothy* have lost their place;
> Nay with th'Apostles too it eene went hard,
> All their authority two thumps more had mard;
> *Paul* and St. *Peter* might be sure o'the doome
> Knew but this frantick foole they'd bin at Rome.
>   Now to the State he comes, talkes an alarm,
> And ath' malignant party flings his arme,
> Defies the King, and thinkes his Pulpit full
> As safe a place for't, as the Knight does *Hull*.
> What though no Magazeen laid in there be
> Scarce all the Guns can make more noice then he.
> Plots, plots he cries, ther's jelousies, and feares,
> The politick Saints shake their notorious eares.
>   (*The Puritans Lecture*, l. 117)

Among the 'politick Saints' listening to the lecture are groups for whom the
occasion serves as a magnet. These groups, including organizations of urban
employers and employees, male and female, are all presumably concerned
with religion, the welfare of their souls. However, as the satire portrays them,
they are more concerned with gaining status and power. They are loosely
affiliated, but their political party lacks a name. In lines 57–59, for example,
a 'Shee-zealot' rages into view, shouting that bishops are the limbs of
Antichrist and identifying herself as a member of the 'what d'you call it
party'. The 'Prentizes' who formerly showed their strength by abusing
citizens on the streets and beating up whores on holidays now band together
to root out Popery, so they say. In fact, it is 'their brave intent | Wisely
t'advise the King, and Parliament: | The worke in hand they'le disaprove or
back ...' (l. 157). The apprentices are demanding a voice in government. A
group of women enter with a long petition that they are preparing to present

Parliament,[12] opposing pluralities, popish idolatries like signing the cross, surplices, organ music, and (we find out at last) the customary exclusion of women from preaching. The women seek the pulpit-status of the lecturer.

These are the voices heard at the lecture. Cowley listens to them, mimics, and mocks. He cannot bring himself to sympathize with their motives, but he has listened carefully enough to hear, beneath the slogans and rallying cries, what those motives are. The Puritan's lecture is an occasion for political organization. Those who were previously disenfranchised, 'the Kingdomes dirt and sinke', are the ones who come not so much to listen as to speak up and sign on. Cowley satirizes them all, as a Cambridge student seeing through Roman eyes. *O tempora o mores*, he says.

Juvenalian, mordant satire is one-sided. It has a fixed point of view, with which the reader is expected to align. The political vision that this kind of satire supports is similarly one-sided. It is a one-party system, and those who act outside it are the satirist's targets. They are ignorant and irrational. Horatian satire is more balanced, if not entirely two-sided. Cowley's second verse satire, or two-thirds of it (lines 1–207 of 302), is of this kind.

Cowley wrote *The Puritan and the Papist* at Cambridge. He had probably completed most of it by 23 March 1643, when his M.A. and ejection from Trinity College were, almost simultaneously, granted and near the time he left Cambridge for Oxford. By March 1643, the skirmishes or battles at Powick Bridge, Edgehill, and Brentford, all mentioned in the satire, had taken place. An authorized edition of the satire was printed in Oxford, later in 1643.

This satire begins with a conceit, extended for 200 lines, developing the 'Puritan-Papist' theme which Corbet, the creator of Rattle-head and Round-head, and other satirists and polemicists had recently repopularized.

> So two rude *waves*, by stormes together throwne,
> Roare at each other, fight, and then grow *one*.
> *Religion* is a *Circle*; men contend,
> And runne the round in dispute without end.
> Now in a *Circle* who goe contrary,
> Must at the last *meet* of necessity.
> The *Roman* to advance the *Catholicke cause*
> Allows a *Lie*, and calls it *Pia Fraus*.
> The *Puritan* approves and does the same,
> Dislikes nought in it but the *Latin name*.
> He flowes with these devises, and dares *ly*
> In very *deed*, in *truth*, and *verity*.

[12] See Samuel Rawson Gardiner, *History of England from the Accession of James I to the Outbreak of the Civil War*, 10 vols (London and New York, 1883–84), x, 163 on the women's 'long petition' concerning popery and idolatry. The petition was presented on 4 February 1641/42, one day before the House of Lords passed the Bishops Exclusion Bill. *A True Copie of the Petition of the Gentlewomen, and Tradesmens wives, in and about the City of London,* along with an answer to the women reportedly given by John Pym at the door of Parliament, was printed by R. O. [Richard Overton] and G. D. in 1641/42. The degree to which women's rights are claimed in this document may be assessed by its concluding statement: 'We doe it not out of any selfe conceit, or pride of heart, as seeking to equall our selves with Men . . . But to discharge that duty we owe to God . . . and the cause of the Church' (sig. A4).

> He whines, and sighes out *Lies*, with so much ruth,
> As if he griev'd, 'cause he could ne're speake truth.
> *Lies* have possest the *Presse* so, as their due,
> 'Twill scarcely, 'I feare, henceforth print *Bibles* true.
> *Lies* for their next strong Fort ha'th' *Pulpit* chose,
> There throng out at the *Preachers mouth*, and *nose*.
>
> (*The Puritan and the Papist*, l. 1)

Part of this is witty, if not scurrilous counter-labelling. Cowley is confronting John Pym's charges, advanced in Parliament, that popish factions in court were dividing the king from his people. In reply, he portrays Pym and the Puritan Parliament, with their pulpit and lying lecturer installed, as the true subversives.

The form of the satire, however, deriving from the opening conceit, is one of balancing antitheses, which rhyme if they do not reconcile opposites.[13] Ruth Nevo praises the satire: 'The stopped couplet ... admirably serves the purpose of the double-criticism ... This level of [satiric] style, rationally based, seriously intended, and salted with neat couplet wit, will not be attained again until the Restoration.'[14] There are places in the satire where Nevo's point is particularly well taken. Lines 57–62 serve as an example.

> They keepe the *Bible* from *Lay-men*, but ye
> Avoid this, for ye have no *Laytie*.
> They in a forraigne, and unknowne *tongue* pray,
> You in an unknowne *sence* your prayers say:
> So that this difference 'twixt ye does ensue,
> *Fooles* understand not *them*, nor *Wise-men you*.

Here the form and sense of the lines combine perfectly, the two sides balanced in the couplets, though the weight of the critique bears clearly on the Puritans.

None the less, we should be wary of making *The Puritan and the Papist* into something neater than it is. While he jests somewhat at practices of Roman Catholics, Cowley ridicules the Puritans, and if we consider an extended

---

[13] Cowley's formal approach in *The Puritan and the Papist* is, broadly considered, Horatian. His mediating muse, however, is John Marston whose 'Satire 4', printed with *The Metamorphosis of Pygmalion's Image, and Certain Satires* (London, 1598), contains the genesis of Cowley's opening conceit and some of the argument. Marston writes:

> So have I seen the fuming waves to fret,
> And in the end naught but white foam beget ...
> So have I heard a heretic maintain
> The church unholy, where Jehovah's name
> Is now adored, because he surely knows
> Sometimes it was defiled with Popish shows;
> The bells profane, and not to be endured,
> Because to Popish rites they were inured.
> Pure madness! ...

These lines are 17–18 and 63–69 from 'Satire 4', as printed in *The Works of John Marston*, edited by A. H. Bullen, 3 vols (Boston and New York, 1887), III, 280 and 282. Marston's main target in this satire, somewhat ironically from our perspective, is both the raillery and the 'toothless gumming' of the young Joseph Hall.

[14] Ruth Nevo, *The Dial of Virtue* (Princeton, 1963), p. 62.

sequence of couplets we will find that the topical and rhetorical structure is more irregular than Nevo likes to think. The opening lines of the poem, cited above, offer a typical example, with the Papist side presented in two lines, 7–8, and then ten lines given to the Puritans. Cowley shows his bias, but he is by no means a Papist, and the reader is not able readily to know what the sides really are.

Cowley uses the antitheses to expand his view of contemporary events and returns to the comparison when he needs a fresh charge. As he extends his observations, a third party enters the picture. The Cavaliers appear at lines 39, 53–54, 77–78, and by line 207 the witty exercise and religious masquerade is ended. After the couplet '*Three Kingdomes* thus ye strive to make your owne; | And, like the *Pope*, usurpe a *Triple Crowne*' it is clear that religious contrariety is no longer the issue. 'Such is your *Faith*, such your *Religion*', Cowley concludes. 'Let's view your manners now.'

In the last third of the satire, old labels and the religious groups they have been attached to give way to a new perception. One can still talk in terms of king and subject, but no present episode, political or military, can be described in those terms. Instead, there is opposition, more or less balanced in strength, between two organized, political groups: the Puritan Parliament with the lecturer on his parliamentary pulpit, swaying Pym from any centrist position; and the Cavaliers, drawn to Oxford by Falkland and so, at this time, allied with king and court.

Cowley refers to the opposing parties as 'You' and 'We', clearly indicating his Cavalier allegiance and no longer expecting the readers he addresses in the second person to align with him. Still, the synthesizing argument goes on. The Cavaliers and the 'popular party' are portrayed to some degree as brothers in parliamentary crime. Here are some of the points, in paraphrase: Ship Moncy was unjustly taken, you say; but with more injustice you've taken away the ships. You called the ecclesiastical court of High Commission a tyranny and forced its disbanding, only to found your own 'High Committee'. You accused the court of bribery, only to mimic the same corruption. The king protected delinquents, preventing their appearance to answer charges of Parliament; then delinquents protected Parliament, when the king was prevented from arresting the 'five members'.

If the political motive of this display is the same as it had been in the first part of the poem — to satirize with an appeal to common reason; to jest division back to one-party unity — that motive is not, in the end, well served. The breach is too wide, and the immediate future is predicted along lines of open hostility. Former factions, if they were that, are now separate organizations. But the kind of satire Cowley writes, following the Horatian model, serves extremely well to delineate the two-party subject. The form requires that the poet look at his subject in a way uncalled for by Juvenalian or mordant satire. The form requires that he see more than he had in *The Puritans Lecture*, whether he likes it or not.

Cowley's two-party political satire was widely distributed over the course of forty years. Henry Hall, the Oxford publisher and printer, issued *The Puritan and the Papist* as a quarto dated 1643. A second quarto, without title-page or date, was probably printed in the same year. The satire appears under the title *Sampsons Foxes* in a third quarto, pen-dated 22 June 1644 in the Thomason copy. Next, Cowley's poem was dismembered to create two shorter satirical characters — 'The Sub-Committee' and 'The Zealous Sectary' — appearing in *The Character of a Moderate Intelligencer*, dated 29 April 1647 in the Thomason copy. Ten mid-to-late seventeenth-century manuscript copies of *The Puritan and the Papist* survive. These are independent of the printed texts, and all but one of the manuscript copies are more or less complete. This is a remarkable statistic for a poem of over 300 lines.

Finally, *The Puritan and the Papist* was printed under Cowley's name in *Wit and Loyalty Reviv'd* (1682). Shaftesbury's party, spurred by Titus Oates's 'Popish Plot' (1678), had brought the nation to the brink of another civil war. Many believed that '1641 was come again'.[15] By this time, Cowley's readers may have understood 'Whig' for 'Puritan' and 'Tory' for 'Cavalier'.

---

[15] The opinion is cited by G. M. Trevelyan in *A Shortened History of England* (Harmondsworth, Middlesex, 1959), p. 341.

Books as Memorials:
The Politics of Consolation

WARREN CHERNAIK
Queen Mary and Westfield College, London

My starting point is the curious fact that our knowledge of the poetry written during the 1630s, in the reign of Charles I, comes largely from a series of books published in the 1640s and 1650s after that reign had ended, as conscious memorials and acts of homage to the dead. Defeat can have two contrasting effects, to expunge or to drench in falsifying retrospective sentiment: Auden, in lines which gain additional irony from the author's unsuccessful attempts to disown them, claims that 'History to the defeated | May say Alas but can never help or pardon'.[1] My own thoroughly non-revisionist view is that history can say a great deal more than this, depending on what questions we ask it. The works discussed in this essay all actively seek to give a pattern to history, and in doing so both defy time and serve its sovereign power, in conscious acts of imaginative intervention. The curious belatedness of these twice-born poems enacts a process by which the 'flying minute', rapidly slipping out of sight, is transmuted into a made object, a testament.[2]

One striking instance of the phenomenon I am describing is the publication in 1648 of Herrick's *Hesperides*, in times the author characterizes as 'untuneable', destructive of the spontaneous pleasure from which art springs: 'Wither'd my hand, and palsie-struck my tongue'.[3] The volume begins and ends with a series of highly self-conscious references to his 'Book', the literal object which a reader may hold in his or her hand. The Latin epigrammatist Martial, a principal source and inspiration for Herrick here as in other respects, regularly treats literary production in material terms, emphasizing not the act of composition but of dissemination.[4] But what in Martial is almost an act of witty disavowal (in one epigram he asks his book — using the diminutive 'libellus' — to slow down or come to a conclusion because the copyist is becoming fatigued, in another he describes the reader

---

[1] 'Spain 1937', in *The English Auden*, edited by Edward Mendelson (London, 1977), p. 212.
[2] 'His Poetrie his Pillar', line 5, in *The Poetical Works of Robert Herrick*, edited by L. C. Martin (Oxford, 1956), p. 85; subsequent references are to *P.W.*
[3] 'To his Friend, on the untuneable Times', line 10, *P.W.*, p. 84. One of the few critics to discuss the structure of *Hesperides* is Ann Coiro, in 'Herrick's *Hesperides*: the Name and the Frame', *ELH*, 52 (1985), 311–36.
[4] The best and fullest account of Herrick's indebtedness to Martial is Gordon Braden, *The Classics and English Renaissance Poetry* (New Haven and London, 1978), pp. 180–94, which treats the address to his Book among other motifs; see also the illuminating discussion of Herrick's classical imitation in Graham Parry, *Seventeenth-Century Poetry: The Social Context* (London, 1985), pp. 154–87.

as yawning and becoming irritated) takes on in Herrick a characteristic elegiac tone:

> Goe thou forth my booke, though late;
> Yet be timely fortunate.
> It may chance good-luck may send
> Thee a kinsman, or a friend,
> That may harbour thee, when I,
> With my fates neglected lye.
> If thou know'st not where to dwell,
> See, the fier's by: *Farewell*.[5]

Herrick's lines are precisely poised between the hope of gaining immortality through art and the ironic recognition that such survival is largely a matter of luck, that neither men or books are likely to escape the fires that consume all things. A similar sudden darkening of tone, expressed in a characteristically laconic way, occurs in 'To live Merrily, and to trust to Good Verses', which pays convivial tribute to the Roman poetic tradition both in its conscious literary echoes and in its dramatis personae. Art is celebrated here in terms of domestic intimacy, with poet and reader meeting as friends, joining in a series of toasts to the Latin poets whose memory they honour:

> Now, to *Tibullus*, next,
> > This flood I drink to thee:
> But stay; I see a Text,
> > That this presents to me.
>
> Behold, *Tibullus* lies
> > Here burnt, whose smal return
> Of ashes, scarce suffice
> > To fill a little Urne.[6]

The first eight and the last eight poems of *Hesperides* all concern themselves with 'his Booke', *Hesperides* as 'first-borne child' from which its parent must part: 'I brake my bonds of Love, and bad thee goe, | Regardlesse whether well thou sped'st, or no' (p. 6). However the author may direct and counsel his prospective readers, with instructions 'When he would have his verses reade', warnings 'To the soure Reader', or an 'Argument' summarizing its contents, he recognizes that he has no control over its reception, or indeed any guarantee that it will find a reader. In the closing poems, life and art are seen as coterminous, drawing to an end simultaneously: in the lines 'To his Booke' that I quoted before, coming near the end of the sequence, the book is literally 'late', the product of old age and harbinger of approaching death (which the next three poems explicitly treat).

Hesperides is unusual in that it is designed by the author as his own funeral monument, an old man's book: Herrick was fifty-seven when it was published, and it was his only book. The volume is carefully shaped out of a large

---

[5] 'To his Booke', *P.W.*, p. 334; Martial, *Epigrams*, iv. lxxxix; vi. lx, translated by W. Ker (London, Loeb Classical Library, 1961); Braden, pp. 181–85.

[6] Lines 37–44, *P.W.*, p. 81. As Graham Parry points out in his helpful commentary (pp. 158–60), the last stanza quoted echoes Ovid's elegy to Tibullus (*Amores* iii. 9. 39–40).

number of individual pieces written over a period of twenty years or so, mostly epigrams *upon* or epistles *to* specific occasional subjects and recipients, arranged to serve as a *summa*, the record of a life. The closest analogy in seventeenth-century verse is Herbert's *The Temple*, the work of another master craftsman, except that Herbert's book is private, an overheard dialogue of man and his heavenly master, where Herrick's book is in its essence social, treating the reader as 'a kinsman, or a friend'.

None of the other authors I am discussing took the same direct responsibility for supervising the production of a volume of poems. In each of the other volumes, the roles of creator and preserver, recorder, or memorialist of the individual occasion and collector, transcriber, assembler of dispersed fragments into a whole, are separated. But the similarities of Herrick's book and a number of others published during the interregnum are striking.

A few titles and dates may help to make my point. A single publisher, Humphrey Moseley, issued the following volumes during the Civil War period: *Poems, &c., written by Mr. Edmund Waller* (1645: the &c. consists of three speeches to Parliament); *Poems of Mr. John Milton* (1645); *Fragmenta Aurea. A Collection of All the Incomparable Peeces, written by Sir John Suckling. And published by a Friend to perpetuate his memory* (1646); *Poems, with a Maske, by Thomas Carew Esq* (third edition, 1651); and *Comedies, Tragi-Comedies, with other Poems, by Mr. William Cartwright* (1651). These volumes are only a fragment of Moseley's large output as a specialist literary publisher during the interregnum years, which also includes such comparable collections as *Poems &c. By James Shirley* (1646); *Steps to the Temple. Sacred Poems, With other Delights of the Muses. By Richard Crashaw* (1646); *Clarastella; Together with Poems occasional, Elegies, Epigrams, Satyrs. By Robert Heath, Esquire* (1650); and *Olor Iscanus. A Collection of some select Poems, and Translations, Formerly written by Mr. Henry Vaughan Silurist. Published by a Friend* (1651).[7] Many of these collections of poems contain a self-advertising preface by Moseley, commenting on the '*Care & Pains*' he took in collecting and therefore preserving from oblivion

---

[7] On Moseley's career, see the full and useful account by John Curtis Reed, 'Humphrey Moseley, Publisher', *Oxford Bibliographical Society Proceedings and Papers*, 2 (1927–30), 57–142, which includes a list of works published by Moseley and texts of the prefaces and epistles dedicatory prefixed to these volumes. A recent account of Moseley's career as a publisher, emphasizing his royalist allegiances, is in Lois Potter, *Secret Rites and Secret Writing: Royalist Literature, 1641–1660* (Cambridge, 1989), pp. 19–22; see also Thomas N. Corns, 'Ideology in the *Poemata* (1645)', *Milton Studies*, 19 (1984), p. 196. A number of the volumes published by Moseley have been reprinted in recent years by Scolar Press, and the Scolar reprint of Waller's 1645 *Poems* includes a copy of a catalogue circulated by Moseley, listing 340 books. It is striking what a small proportion of Moseley's publications consist of sermons and tracts, the mainstay of most contemporary publishers. According to Reed, between 1644 and 1659 his entries in the Stationer's Register 'record the publication of the best literature of the period .... The quality of the books is remarkably high' (p. 64). As well as the volumes of poetry mentioned, he published many plays and a large number of translations from the French, German, and Italian: the catalogue begins with 'Various Histories, with curious Discourses in humane Learning'.

the scattered leaves of the author in question.[8] Images of resurrection or of funerary monuments are frequent in Moseley's rather garrulous prefaces, as they are in the many commendatory poems, commissioned by the publisher, with which the collections begin, and these commendatory poems regularly make reference to the tributes of friendship, as do the title-pages of the Suckling and Vaughan volumes. Such motifs are especially frequent in those collections where the author is either dead or silenced by what Herrick calls 'the bad season', the untuneable times.

But since we lost our *Author*, let us save what we can of him; his *Poems* we see come first to hand, as in a great Shipwrack the lightest Treasure swims uppermost.[9]

That quotation comes from Moseley's preface to Cartwright's poems, which together with his sumptuous edition of the *Comedies and Tragedies* of Beaumont and Fletcher (1647), contains the largest number of commendatory poems (Moseley seems in each case to have approached every poet passing through London that year) and the fullest and most explicit treatment of the theme of poetry as consolation, the only stay against a '*Tragicall Age*' of civil war.

The *Care & Pains* was . . . more than you'd easily imagine, unless you knew into how many hands the Originalls were dispersed. They are all happily met in this Book, having escaped these *Publike Troubles*, free and unmangled.[10]

Moseley's political sympathies are clear enough from his prefaces: he supported the established church and episcopacy, he spoke of Charles I with reverence, he had little use for rebels or conventicles. But it is interesting how even in those volumes published in the early stages of the Civil War, with relatively little explicit political content, and consisting largely of poems written during an age of peace, Moseley manages to turn the physical book into a statement of allegiance. The oddest case is that of Milton, who is virtually kidnapped by Moseley and transformed against his will into a royalist. The title-pages of the Waller, Milton, and Carew volumes are substantially identical, all calling attention to the musical settings of the lyric poems contained in the book: 'The Songs were set in Musick by Mr Henry Lawes Gentleman of the Kings Chappell, and one of his Majesties Private

---

[8] *Comedies and Tragedies. Written by Francis Beaumont and John Fletcher* (London, 1647), Sig. A3v. Such prefaces appear in seven of the volumes listed above. The exceptions are the Carew volume, issued in 1640 and again in 1642 by another publisher, Thomas Walkley, from whom Moseley bought the rights, and the Shirley volume, which contains a preface and postscript signed by the author. A commendatory poem in the Cartwright volume by Joseph Leigh addressed 'To the Stationer (Mr Moseley) on his Printing Mr Cartwright's Poems' provides an exhaustive list of the wits of the age ('brave *Suckling*', 'melting *Carew*; learned *Crashaw*', 'hopeful *Stanley*') 'Whose high Achievements Thou hast brought to light, | Setting forth Wits who best knew how to write' and urges Moseley to 'Gather up' yet more volumes of named poets as yet uncollected. (*Comedies, Tragedies, With other Poems*, Sig. *1–1v).

[9] 'To the Reader' (not paginated), Cartwright (1651); 'The bad season makes the Poet sad', *P.W.*, p. 214.

[10] Beaumont and Fletcher (1647), Sig. A3v–A4.

Musick'.[11] The Milton, Carew, and Shirley volumes all follow the same format, beginning with poems 'Compos'd at several times' (that is the wording of the Milton title-page; an alternative formula is 'Poems upon several occasions', the running title in the Waller volume), arranged in roughly chronological order, and ending with a masque. Milton scholars have generally assumed that the poet himself is responsible for the design of the volume: Louis Martz, in his influential essay 'The Rising Poet', emphasizes the 'integrity' of the authorial conception: 'Milton's original arrangement creates the growing awareness of a guiding, central purpose that in turn gives the volume an impressive and peculiar sense of wholeness . . . . It is clear, from many indications, that Milton has designed his book with great care to create this impression.'[12] But the striking similarities between this volume and others published by Moseley at approximately the same time suggest a role for the publisher at least as significant as that of the author in creating what Martz calls 'a tribute to a youthful era now past'.[13] None of the other volumes can be called authorized in any sense, with details of printing supervised by the author. In each case, the unsettled times, and a concern for the 'honour and esteem of our English tongue' (the phrase comes from the Milton volume, but equivalent statements can be found in many of the others) have caused the publisher to take the initiative.

Like the present condition of the Author himself, they are expos'd to the wide world, to travel, and try their fortunes: And I believe there is no gentle soul that pretends any thing to knowledge and the choycest sort of invention but will give them entertainment and welcome.[14]

Now there are certain obvious differences among these poets: Suckling, like Carew, was dead, Waller 'expos'd to the wide world' in exile, Milton active as a writer of prose pamphlets on the other side. Though the causes of Waller's exile are not explicitly stated in Moseley's preface, the volume itself

---

[11] This is the wording of Milton (1645); Waller (1645) reads 'All The Lyric Poems in this Booke were set' and Carew (1651) 'his late Majesties'. A similar phrase is used in the Suckling volume, though not in this case on the main title-page. The Lawes settings and the association of title-page and frontispiece with 'the recent courtly style', but not the similarity of the title-pages of the Waller and Carew volumes, are discussed in Louis Martz's important essay 'The Rising Poet, 1645', in *The Lyric and Dramatic Milton*, edited by Joseph H. Summers (New York, 1965), pp. 6–7.
[12] Martz, pp. 4–5. Thomas N. Corns, in 'Milton's Quest for Respectability', *Modern Language Review*, 77 (1982), 777–79, sees the publication of the 1645 *Poems* as one of several attempts by Milton in the mid 1640s 'to dissociate himself from the archetypal sectary', asserting his 'high culture', 'his social status and aspirations', 'his establishment connexions' throughout the volume. More recent accounts have emphasized the radical Protestant elements in the 1645 *Poems* as well as the gestures toward 'the Caroline courtly tradition': see Parry, pp. 188–92; and Michael Wilding, *Dragons Teeth: Literature in the English Revolution* (Oxford, 1987), pp. 7–20.
[13] Martz, p. 5. Corns, though he sees the publication of the *Poems* in terms of a coherent Miltonic polemical strategy of self-presentation, concedes that the author and publisher may have 'worked closely' together in designing the volume: 'Nor are we certain what part the publisher, Humphrey Moseley, played in initiating the publication and determining the format of the volume, though Milton must have been closely involved in its preparation' (p. 778). Wilding is the one critic who suggests a need to distinguish 'between Milton's activities and those of his publisher' . . . Milton may not have known of Moseley's intention, may not have agreed with it, may have gone along with it as many an author has gone along with a publisher's promotional strategy that he or she was not in agreement with' (pp. 8–9).
[14] 'An advertisement to the Reader', Waller (1645), Sig. A4v.

situates the author squarely in the royalist camp. Its first four poems are addressed to the King, all utilizing the conventions of panegyric for concrete political ends, and the poems that follow, addressed in the language of elegant compliment to the Queen, the powerful Countess of Carlisle, and various members of the Sidney family, all breathe the air of the court. Waller's political position at a time closer to the date of publication is spelled out in detail in a selection of parliamentary speeches, 1640–43, which concludes the volume.[15] The Suckling volume, *Fragmenta Aurea*, is even more mixed in genre, since only about a quarter of it contains Suckling's occasional poems and lyrics. The second part of the volume contains 'Letters to diverse Eminent Personages: Written on several occasions', a mixture of personal letters of gallantry and friendship, the record of a courtier's life, and pamphlets on political and philosophical subjects which use the conventions of epistolary address: 'To Mr Henry German, in the beginning of Parliament, 1640', 'An Account of Religion by Reason. A Discourse upon Occasion presented to the Earl of *Dorset*'. The final portion of the volume includes three plays acted at the private theatres, the last of which, *Brennoralt* (1640), is explicitly topical, aimed like some of Waller's panegyrics to persuade, urging certain policies against others.[16] In these two volumes, and several of the others published by Moseley, the royalist sympathies of the author are made explicit. Yet even here the appeal to potential readers in the introductory material assembled by Moseley is not partisan, fighting over the battles of the Civil War. Instead, the poems of each author, as written and then as collected, are seen as precious relics rescued from 'that *Oblivion*, which our *Best Labours* must *come* to at last' (the passage is quoted from the preface to Vaughan's *Olor Iscanus* (1651), which also uses Herrick's image of the funeral pyre), and as testaments of friendship.[17]

The prefaces to the Suckling and Milton volumes employ a common strategy, as they seek to establish a community of 'knowing Gentlemen' in which the readers can be enrolled, making these poems extensions of the poet's conversation. Thus, for Suckling,

It had been a prejudice to Posterity they should have slept longer, and an injury to his own ashes. They that convers'd with him alive, and truly (under which notion I comprehend only knowing Gentlemen) ... will honour these posthume Idaea's of their friend: And if any have liv'd in so much darknesse, as not to have known so

---

[15] The speeches, which are bound together with all but one of the 1645 editions of Waller's *Poems*, have separate pagination and were printed separately. The title-page mentions that Waller was 'lately a Member of the Honourable House of Commons'. For a contrast between the Waller and Milton volumes, laying stress on Waller's royalist allegiances, see Raymond B. Waddington, 'Milton among the Carolines', in *The Age of Milton*, edited by C. A. Patrides and Raymond B. Waddington (Manchester, 1980), pp. 340–45.

[16] There is a highly interesting discussion of *Brennoralt* in its political context, providing specific advice (disregarded) to the King similar to that in his letters published in *Fragmenta Aurea* and reflecting 'anxieties and dissent existing in tension within the court', in Martin Butler, *Theatre and Crisis 1632–1642* (Cambridge, 1984), pp. 76–83.

[17] Henry Vaughan, *Olor Iscanus* (London, 1651), Sig. A6–A6v. For further discussion of *Olor Iscanus*, see Parry, pp. 97–100.

great an Ornament of our Age, by looking upon these Remaines with Civility and Understanding, they may timely yet repent, and be forgiven.[18]

It may well be that the inclusion of letters by Henry Wotton and Henry Lawes, situating Milton within a cultured community of friends — Lawes, the original Thyrsis of Milton's masques, writes of *Comus* in a letter included in the volume that 'the often copying of it hath tir'd my Pen to give my severall friends satisfaction' — is Moseley's attempt to defuse Milton's reputation as puritan polemicist, suggesting that the commonwealth of art and learning transcends politics.[19] Though a publisher's puff is not strictly comparable with the ethical proof of a constructed authorial persona in a tract, in certain respects the language with which Moseley commends Milton is strikingly Miltonic in its tone towards its readers and its assumptions about literary tradition. This may suggest a degree of collaboration between author and publisher, or a shared ideal of 'Civility and Understanding' which can broadly be categorized as humanist.

It is the love I have to our own Language that hath made me diligent to collect, and set forth such *Peeces* both in Prose and Vers, as may renew the wonted honour and esteem of our English tongue . . . These are not without the highest Commendations and Applause of the Learnedst *Academicks*, both domestick and forrein . . . I know not thy palat how it relishes such dainties, nor how harmonious thy soul is; perhaps more trivial Airs may please thee better . . . . That incouragement I have already received from the most ingenious men in their clear courteous entertainment of Mr. *Wallers* late choice Peeces, hath once more made me adventure into the World, presenting it with these ever-green, and not to be blasted Laurels.[20]

What all the passages in prose and verse I have been citing have in common is an element of direct address or apostrophe, in one way or another combining praise with lament. Like Milton's *Areopagitica* (1644), they treat books as living things, and the publication or circulation of a book as a resurrection from the dead:

For Books are not absolutely dead things, but doe contain a potencie of life in them to be as active as that soule was whose progeny they are; nay they do preserve as in a violl the purest efficacie and extraction of that living intellect that bred them. I know

---

[18] Sir John Suckling, *Fragmenta Aurea* (London, 1646), Sig. A3–A3v.

[19] The 1637 edition of *A Maske Presented at Ludlow Castle* contains the letter by Lawes but not the letter by Wotton. Martz emphasizes the 'strong Royalist associations' of the prefatory material printed with *Comus* (p. 7), and Corns the patronage of 'establishment figures' (p. 778). But the appeal of this prefatory material, as a whole, is less limited. Cedric Brown in *John Milton's Aristocratic Entertainments* (Cambridge, 1985), argues the case for a 'reformist programme' in *Comus* and suggests that Lawes rather than Milton bore primary responsibility for the revisions in the text of the masque as it was performed in 1634 (pp. 153, 171–78). David Norbrook similarly sees *Comus* as an 'attempt to rethink masque conventions in the light of an apocalyptic Protestant ideology', in 'The Reformation of the masque', *The Court Masque*, edited by David Lindley (Manchester, 1984), p. 106.

[20] Milton (1645), Sig. a3–a4. Compare *The Reason of Church Government* (1642): 'There ought no regard be sooner had, then to God's glory, by the honour and instruction of my country . . . . For which cause . . . I apply'd my selfe to that resolution . . . to fix all the industry and art I could unite to the adorning of my native tongue . . . . Neither doe I think it shame to covenant with any knowing reader, that for some few yeers yet I may go on trust with him toward the payment of what I am now indebted, as being a work not to be rays'd from the heat of youth, or the vapours of wine, like that which flows at wast from the pen of some vulgar Amorist or the trencher fury of a rhyming parasite', (*Complete Prose Works*, edited by Don M. Wolfe and others, 8 vols (New Haven and London, 1953–82), I, 810–11, 820).

they are as lively, and as vigorously productive, as those fabulous Dragons teeth; and being sown up and down, may chance to spring up armed men . . . . As good almost kill a Man as kill a good Book; who kills a Man kills a reasonable creature, Gods Image; but hee who destroyes a good Booke, kills reason it selfe, kills the Image of God, as it were in the eye. Many a man lives a burden to the Earth; but a good Booke is the precious life-blood of a master spirit, imbalm'd and treasur'd up on purpose to a life beyond life.[21]

The edition of Richard Lovelace's *Lucasta: Epodes, Odes, Sonnets, Songs etc.* published in 1649 (not, for a change, by Moseley) bristles with references to the author's military status. In twenty pages of commendatory poems, nearly all call the author 'Colonel Richard Lovelace', and several of the authors identify themselves by their own rank in the defeated army. Lovelace is praised for uniting action and contemplation, as an ideal knight motivated by the 'desire of Glory' in arts and arms, wearing both the '*Delphick* wreath and *Civic* Coronet'.[22] Several of these poems assume the stance of Milton's Moloch, pretending, with a degree of bravado, that victory is just around the corner. But two of the poems are elegiac in tone, presenting 'the shrill noise of drums' as incompatible with and destructive of the cultivation of the arts. The poems by Marvell and the otherwise obscure John Pinchbacke, like Marvell's 'Upon Appleton House' (which, addressed as it is to the retired general of the parliamentary army, can hardly be called royalist), present a world in which 'all the graces from the Land are sent, | And the nine Muses suffer banishment' — or, in Marvell's commendatory poem, 'These vertues now are banish't out of Towne, | Our Civill Wars have lost the Civicke crown'. The spirit of poetry, as Marvell and Pinchbacke characterize it, is generosity — a 'more gentle' quality in both senses of the word — in which the muses' servants are united in the bonds of friendship:

> Our times are much degenerate from those
> Which your sweet Muse, which your fair Fortune chose,
> And as complexions alter with the Climes,
> Our wits have drawne th'infection of our times.
> That candid Age no other way could tell
> To be ingenious, but by speaking well.
> Who best could prayse, had then the greatest prayse.[23]

The problem which both poets address, like Lovelace himself in 'To Lucasta. From Prison', contemplating the wreck of his hopes in 'a universall mist | Of Error', is how to preserve the values of the past in a 'time distracted', a loathed and hostile present. Pinchbacke, rather than associate Lovelace with the departed time of peace, distinguishes him from his fellow

[21] *Complete Prose Works*, II, 492–93.
[22] Joseph Hall, 'To Colonel Richard Lovelace, on the publishing of his ingenious Poems', in Richard Lovelace, *Lucasta* (London, 1649), Sig. a8. The commendatory poems and elegies addressed to Lovelace in *Lucasta* (1649) and *Lucasta. Posthume Poems* (1659) are printed in *The Poems of Richard Lovelace*, edited by C. H. Wilkinson (Oxford, 1930). For this particular poem, see *Poems*, pp. 9–10.
[23] Lovelace, *Poems*, pp. 5, 8; 'Upon Appleton House', line 338, in *The Poems and Letters of Andrew Marvell*, edited by H. M. Margoliouth and Pierre Legouis, third edition (Oxford, 1971).

poets Carew and Waller as, like Marvell's 'Unfortunate Lover', 'forced to live in Storms and Warrs':

> Well might that charmer his faire *Caelia* crowne
> And that more polish't *Tyterus* renowne
> His *Sacarissa*, when in groves and bowres
> They could repose their limbs on beds of flowrs:
> When wit had prayse, and merit had reward
> And every noble spirit did accord
> To love the Muses, and their Priests to raise.[24]

The aim of poetry in dark times is to console. Pinchbacke identifies this consolation as specifically aimed at the losing side 'in the past wars':

> To divert our sorrowes by thy straines,
> Making us quite forget our seven years paines.[25]

Herrick, in one poem, 'The Bad Season Makes the Poet Sad', explicitly associates a personal sense of loss with the defeat of royalism, and the destruction of the old order is seen as a disease infecting the land:

> Dull to my selfe, and almost dead to these
> My many fresh and fragrant Mistresses:
> Lost to all Musick now; since every thing
> Puts on the semblance here of sorrowing.
> Sick is the Land to'th'heart; and doth endure
> More dangerous faintings by her desp'rate cure.
> But if that golden Age wo'd come again,
> And *Charles* here rule, as he did before did Reign ...[26]

But only rarely does Herrick rely on nostalgia or the hope of a magical transformation in which awkward fact is whisked away; more often in his poems, life and death are described as a continuous process, cyclical, with no fixed boundaries: 'Thus times do shift, each thing his turne do's hold; | *New things succeed, as former things grow old*' (*P.W.*, p. 285).

When Milton in 1655 writes a 'bad season' poem, it has none of the direct political relevance of the poems just considered. Neither he nor the friend he was addressing, a Cromwellian puritan, had any regrets about the end of the monarchy. But in most other significant respects, it resembles these poems and their classical models: in the association of inner and outer weather, the suggestion that the processes of time are inevitable and beyond our control, and the praise of friendship and its attendant ceremonies as the best of all consolations in dark times.

---

[24] Lovelace, *Poems*, pp. 5, 51; 'The unfortunate Lover', line 60. Leah. S. Marcus, in *The Politics of Mirth: Jonson, Herrick, Milton, Marvell, and the Defense of Old Holiday Pastimes* (Chicago, 1986), p. 217, makes the shrewd point that Marvell, who knew perfectly well that 'most of Lovelace's poetry had been written during wartime', deliberately misdated Lovelace's poems to emphasize the poet's 'adherence to bygone ideals'.

[25] *Poems*, p. 5. Together with this reference to Jacob's seven years of labour, Pinchbacke also compares Lovelace to Orpheus, who 'made the damned to forget their smart' (ibid.).

[26] *P.W.*, p. 214. Herrick's royalism is emphasized in a number of recent studies: see, for example, Marcus, pp. 140–68; and Peter Stallybrass, '"Wee feaste in our Defense": Patrician Carnival in Early Modern England and Robert Herrick's "Hesperides"', *English Literary Renaissance*, 16 (1986), 234–52.

> *Lawrence* of vertuous Father vertuous Son,
>   Now that the Fields are dank, and ways are mire,
>   Where shall we sometimes meet, and by the fire
>   Help wast a sullen day; what may be won
> From the hard Season gaining: time will run
>   On smoother, till *Favonius* re-inspire
>   The frozen earth; and cloath in fresh attire
>   The Lillie and Rose, that neither sow'd nor spun.
> What neat repast shall feast us, light and choice,
>   Of Attick taste, with Wine, whence we may rise
>   To hear the Lute well toucht, or artfull voice
> Warble immortal Notes and *Tuskan* Ayre?
>   He who of those delights can judge, an spare
>   To interpose them oft, is not unwise.[27]

We do not expect to find Milton writing in praise of wine, food, and idleness; the refined hedonism of these lines is more like what we customarily associate with the Cavaliers, the world of 'Tourneyes, Masques, Theaters' which Carew so eloquently evokes in defiance of the rival claims of war's 'shrill accents' in his letter to Aurelian Townshend.[28] Milton's principal literary model is Horace's Epode XIII (Horrida tempestas caelum contraxit), which also serves, together with Anacreon XXXIV, as inspiration for Lovelace's 'The Grasse-hopper'. The 'o'reflowing glasse' as defence against the bitter winds of winter is not the exclusive property of one party, and neither are the more lasting consolations, celebrated by these poems, of art and friendship. Though the sustained, grave music of the lines, the inter-weaving of Biblical and classical allusions, the judicious tone — is there any other drinking song which includes the words 'judge', 'spare', and 'not unwise' in its closing lines? — are all characteristically Miltonic, yet the parallels with Lovelace's poem, written a few years earlier, are striking:

> Thou best of *Men* and *Friends*! we will create
>   A Genuine Summer in each others breast;
> And spite of this cold Time and frosen Fate
>   Thaw us a warme seat to our rest.
>
> Thus richer then untempted Kings are we,
>   That asking nothing, nothing need:
> Though Lord of all what Seas imbrace; yet he
>   That wants himselfe, is poore indeed.
>
>   (*Poems*, pp. 39–40)

'The Grasse-hopper', like Milton's sonnet and many of the poems we have been discussing, is addressed to a named friend who is presumed to share in the values expressed: friendship, it is implied, is not a matter of mere contiguity, but ethical choice. The 'cold Time and frosen Fate' of Lovelace's poem reflect and allude to the particular circumstances of royalist defeat, but

---

[27] Sonnet xx, in *The Poetical Works of John Milton*, edited by Helen Darbishire, 2 vols (Oxford, 1952–55).
[28] 'In answer of an Elegiacall letter upon the King of *Sweden* from *Aurelian Townsend*, inviting me to write on that subject', lines 2, 95, in *The Poems of Thomas Carew*, edited by Rhodes Dunlap (Oxford, 1949).

Lovelace like Milton in his sonnet uses the occasion to set forth a coherent moral position which, the poet suggests, transcends these circumstances. As an ethical statement shaped by an artist, Lovelace's testament of friendship enduring through dark times, like Milton's, has a resonance far beyond its initial occasion.

What was the King's Book for?: The Evolution of *Eikon Basilike*

ROBERT WILCHER

University of Birmingham

On the very day on which Charles I played out his most 'memorable scene'[1] in front of the Banqueting House, copies of the book that was to disseminate the myth of 'the Martyr of the People'[2] throughout Europe were in existence.[3] That book, *Eikon Basilike*, has been called 'the most widely read, widely discussed work of royalist propaganda to issue from the English Civil War'.[4] Much of the discussion, however, has concentrated on the question of its authorship and more recently on its effectiveness as a performance which deliberately conceals its status as a printed text and serves to complement the theatrical triumph on the scaffold.[5] It is the purpose of this paper to interpret some of the stylistic features of the text itself in the context of what is known about its composition and printing in order to construct a hypothesis about the evolving nature and function of 'the king's book'.

Charles himself, who was so adept at promoting his own image through the arts of masquing and painting,[6] had apparently first hinted at the role which was to be so potent in the ideology of Interregnum royalism. On 2 December 1642, he had written to his cousin, the Marquis of Hamilton, explaining his attitude towards an uncertain future:

---

[1] The phrase is from Andrew Marvell's lines on the execution in 'An Horatian Ode upon Cromwell's Return from Ireland': '*He* nothing common did or mean | Upon that memorable scene.'

[2] So Charles I styled himself on the day of his death. See *King Charles His Speech Made upon the Scaffold at Whitehall-Gate Immediately before his Execution* (London, 1649), p. 6.

[3] In a letter written from Clapham in Bedfordshire on 5 February 1649, Dr Hammond, a former chaplain of the king, stated that he had received the 'fruits' of his master's 'retirements' on 1 February, only two days after the execution. (See Francis F. Madan, *A New Bibliography of the Eikon Basilike*, Oxford Bibliographical Society Publications, new series III (1949), p. 165.)

[4] *Eikon Basilike: The Portraiture of His Sacred Majesty in His Solitudes and Sufferings*, edited by Philip A. Knachel (Ithaca, New York, 1966), p. xi. All further quotations will be from this edition, and page references will be incorporated into the text.

[5] Two books by Revd Christopher Wordsworth, *"Who Wrote Eikon Basilike?": Considered and Answered in Two Letters* (London, 1824) and *Documentary Supplement to "Who Wrote Eikon Basilike?"* (London, 1825), contain the fullest discussion of the authorship issue and reprint all the evidence then available. Francis F. Madan has assembled all that is currently known about the authorship and printing of *Eikon Basilike* in the appendices to his *New Bibliography*, cited in Note 3 above. The iconographical aspects of the work are discussed by Richard Helgerson, 'Milton Reads the King's Book: Print, Performance, and the Making of a Bourgeois Idol', *Criticism*, 29 (1987), 1–25 and by Graham Parry, *The Seventeenth Century: The Intellectual and Cultural Context of English Literature 1603–1700* (London, 1989), pp. 38–41.

[6] See Stephen Orgel, *The Illusion of Power: Political Theater in the English Renaissance* (Berkeley, Los Angeles, and London, 1975), pp. 77–87; Richard Ollard, *The Image of the King: Charles I and Charles II* (London, 1979); Graham Parry, *The Golden Age Restor'd: the Culture of the Stuart Court, 1603–42* (Manchester, 1981); R. Malcolm Smuts, *Court Culture and the Origins of a Royalist Tradition in Early Stuart England* (Philadelphia, 1987).

yet I cannot but tell you, I have set up my rest upon the Justice of my Cause, being resolved, that no extremity or misfortune shall make me yield; for I will be either *a Glorious King, or a Patient Martyr*, and as yet not being the first, nor at this present apprehending the other, I think it now no unfit time, to express this my Resolution unto you.[7]

As the decade wore on, it became ever more appropriate to cast the king in the character of the 'suffering servant', ready if need be to make the ultimate sacrifice in the cause of his church and his nation.

The inception of the work itself goes back almost a year. It was at Theobalds, not long after his final departure from London in January 1642, that Charles had first voiced the idea of defending himself with his pen against the libels of his enemies. Some of his most intimate companions, including Edward Symmons, a loyal Anglican clergyman, questioned the advisability of opening the old wound of Strafford's death, but Charles went ahead with his project and 'the continuation of His Divine Meditations, which He had gone along with to the Successe of that day', was among royal papers which were captured at the Battle of Naseby in June 1645. This manuscript was eventually 'recovered above all expectance, and return'd to His Majesties Hand'.[8] There is evidence that the king used the time passed in close confinement at Holmby, between 16 February and 4 June 1647, to resume work on a vindication of his actions since the calling of the Long Parliament, and it is assumed that it was during his subsequent sojourn at Hampton Court in the custody of the Army, between 24 August and 11 November 1647, that he recovered the papers lost at Naseby.[9] The compiler of the authoritative modern bibliography of *Eikon Basilike* is confident that the accumulated evidence 'leaves no further room for doubt as to the existence by that time of substantial writings of the King, composed at different times, and comparable in subject-matter, though not identical in form, with the published *Eikon*'.[10] Of particular importance is the testimony of Sir John Brattle, which was first published by Richard Hollingworth in 1692:

In the year 47 King Charles, having drawn up the most considerable part of this book, and having writ it in some loose papers, at different times, desired Bishop Juxon to get some friend of his (whom he could commend to him as a trusty person) to look it over, and to put it into an exact method; the Bishop pitch'd upon Sir John's Father, whom he had been acquainted withal for many years, who undertaking the task, was assisted by this his son, who declares, he sate up with his Father some nights, to assist him methodizing these papers, all writ with the King's own hand:

---

[7] Gilbert Burnet, *The Memoires of the Lives and Actions of James and William Dukes of Hamilton and Castleherald* (London, 1677), p. 203.

[8] This evidence is from *The Princely Pellican* (pp. 4–7 and 21–22), an anonymous reply to early doubts about the authorship of 'the king's book' which appeared towards the end of May 1649. Madan attributes it to John Ashburnham, a former Groom of the Bedchamber.

[9] Both Major Huntington and Dr Dillingham, Master of Emmanuel College, Cambridge, claimed to have seen part of the manuscript at Holmby (Madan, p. 128, n. 12). See Madan, p. 128, for the return of the lost papers.

[10] Madan, p. 128.

thanks be to God, Sir John is yet alive, and is ready to give the same account to any man that asks him.[11]

At about the same time that the Brattles were 'methodizing' the king's manuscript, Edward Symmons was preparing to print his own vindication of Charles I in a work which played a highly significant part in the evolution of *Eikon Basilike*.[12] Several years before, Symmons had put together a defence of his royal master against 'those Aspersions cast upon Him by certaine persons, in a scandalous Libel, Entituled, *The Kings Cabinet Opened*'.[13] The offending pamphlet had made public the damaging correspondence between Charles and his queen which had fallen into the hands of Parliament at Naseby in 1645. Circumstances had more than once prevented Symmons from publishing his work, but in 1647 (as he informs his readers in a prefatory epistle dated 25 October), 'some friends' persuaded him to 'put it to the Presse', and he speculates that 'perhaps God had a speciall Providence in this also, peoples hearts were not then so capable to receive a *Vindication* of their Soveraign from a fellow-Subject, as now they are even forced to be, by that illustrious eminency of his *graces* which hath beamed forth in his dark condition' (pp. A2^{r-v}). Having argued the case for Charles at painstaking length in the first twenty-five sections of *A Vindication of King Charles: Or, A Loyal Subjects Duty*, Symmons abandons the traditional methods of point-by-point refutation of his opponents for a daring experiment in iconography. He recognizes that the battle for the allegiance of those 'Christian friends' to whom the book is addressed is to be fought not only with reasoned arguments, but also with images. Up to now, he has been engaged in the task of dismantling a version of the king's character and conduct deliberately created by his enemies to mislead the English people:

they hoped to portray him forth, according to the *Image* of him in their owne minds, by wresting his expressions to the highest pitch of misconstruction, and charging upon him their own conditions; but through Gods help, those *filthy Garments* they arrayed him with, are taken off, and sent home to their proper owners. (p. 241)

Symmons will, in fact, contest the false image of the king *mis*-constructed in their own image by his denigrators, with a *re*-constructed image more in harmony with recent history as perceived by a 'loyal subject':

wherefore I will present him once againe, as habited in another *mantle*, more truly his, then that other was, though put upon him (for the most part) by the same men; in opposition of that Act of theirs, which I have undone, I will set him forth in Christs *Robes*, as cloathed with *sorrowes*; and shew what a perfect similitude there hath been and is, between our *Saviour* and our *Soveraign* in the foure last years of both their sufferings. (p. 241)

---

[11] Quoted by Madan, p. 128.
[12] Charles E. Doble first suggested the importance of Symmons's role in the conception of 'the king's book'. See 'Notes and Queries on the *Eikon Basilike* II', *The Academy*, No. 577 (26 May 1883), 367–68.
[13] Edward Symmons, *A Vindication of King Charles: Or, A Loyal Subjects Duty* (1648). The quoted words are from the title page.

There follows a series of parallels between the period of Christ's public ministry and the experiences of Charles I between 1642 and 1646. And, warns Symmons, the series may not yet be complete:

In a word, as Christ was belyed, slandered, betrayed, bought and sold for money, reviled, mocked, scorned at, spit on, *numbred among transgressors*, and judged to be such a one from his great misery, and from the successe his enemies had against him, and at last put to death; even so hath the King been used in all respects, by his rebellious people, who have alreadie acted all the parts which the Jewes acted upon the *Son of God*, the last of all only excepted, which may also be expected in the end from them, when oportunity is afforded. (p. 246)

Symmons was here erecting a model for much of the most effective royalist propaganda that was to appear in the wake of the regicide; and by assigning the roles of the Pharisees who persecuted Christ and the Jews who clamoured for his crucifixion to the members of the Long Parliament and Charles's rebellious subjects, he was deliberately stealing the rhetorical clothes of his antagonists, whose preachers had made such capital out of analogies between their own struggle against episcopacy and tyranny and the Old Testament captivities of the tribes of Israel. The English nation were the new Israelites, indeed, as Protestant propaganda never tired of proclaiming, but the evidence of four years of civil war suggested to Symmons that the Chosen People would pursue the biblical parallel to its bitter end and hound the king they had spurned to an ignominious death:

Well, when he is dead, as I think no wise man expects otherwise, but that they will murder him openly, or secretly shorten his dayes, if they can get him, and God doe not in a miraculous manner againe deliver him; for as nothing but Christs Crucifixion would please the Jewes of old, so nothing but the Kings extinction will satisfie the malice of some in this Age: but I say, when he is dead, we shall in this one thing imitate *Pilate*, and publish to all the world his accusation and cause of his death, This shall be his Title: *Carolus Gratiosus, Rex Anglia*: CHARLES *the Gratious, King of England, was put to death by the Pharisaicall Puritans of his Kingdome, only because he was their King, and in many respects so like unto Iesus Christ the Worlds Saviour.* (p. 250)

There is no way of knowing how far Charles had himself begun to develop the analogy between his own situation and that of Christ in the 'loose papers' that were put 'into an exact method' while he was at Hampton Court, but the later chapters of the *Eikon Basilike* exploit it quite extensively, and it looks as if the printed version of the 'king's book' owed a considerable debt to Symmons's *Vindication*.[14]

It was, in fact, through his association with Symmons, who had been his contemporary at Cambridge in the 1620s and the incumbent of a neighbouring living in Essex at the outbreak of the Civil War, that John Gauden, who later claimed that the 'book and figure was wholy and only my invention,

---

[14] Doble examined the similarities between the two texts and concluded that the evidence pointed to a 'direct obligation to Symmons's work on the part of the writer of the *Eikon*', p. 368.

making and designe', first came into contact with the king's writings.[15] A servant later testified that Gauden had made a copy of a manuscript lent to him by Symmons, which must have been the 'methodized' version of the royal papers prepared by the Brattles in the autumn of 1647.[16] It is conceivable that Symmons, who had recently prepared his own defence of the king for the press, saw the potential for a more spectacular propaganda coup in a vindication under Charles's own name and recruited his former acquaintance to carry the project through.[17] However he became involved, Gauden had completed his redaction of the work by the beginning of June 1648.[18] His plan was to publish it under the title 'Suspiria Regalia', but he was advised by Lord Capel to seek the king's approval before proceeding. The start of the negotiations between Charles and Parliament at Newport provided the necessary opportunity and the manuscript was entrusted to the Marquis of Hertford.[19] The king evidently gave his blessing to the enterprise, since he is said to have 'sometimes corrected and heightened' Gauden's 'sheets', and in October was making preparations for the work to be published by Richard Royston, who later affirmed 'that his late Ma^ty of blessed memory King Charles the first did sent to him about Mich[ael]mas before his Martirdome to provide a Presse for hee had a Booke of his owne for him to Print'.[20] The king having been removed from Newport by the Army on 1 December, and the process of bringing him to trial having been set in motion, Gauden, according to his wife's testimony, 'did Resolve to print it

---

[15] Gauden made his claim in a letter to the Earl of Clarendon dated 21 January 1661, the text of which is given in Wordsworth's *Documentary Supplement*, pp. 15–17. Gauden matriculated sizar from St John's College at Michaelmas 1619, and took his B.A. in 1622–23 and his M.A. in 1626; Symmons matriculated sizar from Peterhouse at Easter 1621, and took his B.A. in 1624–25 and his M.A. in 1628. Gauden became Dean of Bocking, Essex, in 1642; Symmons was Rector of Raine, Essex, 1630–43. (See the entries in volumes I and IV of *Alumni Cantabrigienses*, compiled by John Venn and J. A. Venn (Cambridge, 1922 and 1927).)

[16] This evidence came to light in a letter of Mr Le Pla, minister of Finchingfield in Essex, dated 27 November 1696, which was first printed in the second edition of Thomas Wagstaffe's *A Vindication of King Charles the Martyr* (London, 1697). It is quoted by Madan on page 129:

> William Allen . . . was servant to Dr Gauden for several years, and at last married one of his family . . . I fell into a discourse with him about Dr Gauden and the King's Book. He said most people thought his Master to be the author of it, or to have had the chief hand in it, or to that purpose. I told him I could never believe it, for some reasons I then gave him. Whereupon he smiled, and told me, He believed he could say more to that business than any man besides him; for that Dr Gauden told him he had borrowed the Book, and was obliged to return it by such a time; that (besides what other time he might imploy in it) he sate up one whole night to transcribe it; that he (William Allen) sate up in the Chamber with him, to wait upon him, to make his Fires, and snuff his candles.

[17] Gauden's later claim that the book was entirely his own invention and design could not have been refuted by appeal to Symmons, who died on 19 March 1649 at Gravesend as he was on his way to Holland with a manuscript of *Eikon Basilike*.

[18] Mrs Gauden, in an account of the composition and printing of *Eikon Basilike* probably written in 1662 soon after Gauden's death, states that 'when my Husband had writ it: he shewed it to my Lord Capell' (Wordsworth, *Documentary Supplement*, p. 43). As Madan points out on page 130, this must have been before Capel was besieged in Colchester from the middle of June 1648.

[19] Mrs Gauden's narrative is again the source of this information. (See Wordsworth, *Documentary Supplement*, p. 43.)

[20] The information that the king himself approved and corrected Gauden's manuscript also comes from Mrs Gauden by way of a bishop who knew her well in later life (Symon Patrick, 'A Brief Account of My Life', in *The Works of Symon Patrick, D.D., Sometime Bishop of Ely*, edited by Alexander Taylor, 9 vols (Oxford, 1858), IX, 566). Royston's statement is reprinted by Madan, p. 153.

with all the sped that might be ... only hee then added the Esay upon denying his Ma: the attendance of his Chaplins, and the Meditation upon Death.'[21] She adds that 'the instrument wch my Hus: imployed to git it printed was one Mr. Simons a Devine' — a fact corroborated by Royston himself, who also records that it was on Christmas Eve that the manuscript was delivered into his hands.[22] Printing went ahead forthwith and the proof sheets were with Symmons by 14 January.[23] It was while the book was actually in the printing-shop that Gauden's title of *Suspiria Regalia, or, The Royal Plea* was changed to *Eikon Basilike*.[24]

As one might expect, the complexity of the process by which 'the king's book' achieved a final form left its mark on the text itself. Although no reference is made to an editor, the intervention of some third party between the 'private reflections' of 'His Sacred Majestie' and their appearance in the public medium of print is implied in the third-person titles at the head of each chapter. There is also a curious inconsistency in the use of tenses, which may betray the variety of hands and the lack of temporal continuity in its composition. The title-page proclaimed the work to be a portrait of the late king 'in His Solitudes and Sufferings'. Such a formula might be taken to suggest that its contents were intended to be read as the fruits of his long captivity, as a prisoner successively of the Scots at Newcastle, of the English Parliament at Holmby, and of the Army at Newmarket, Hampton Court, the Isle of Wight, Hurst Castle, and Windsor. In conformity with this, most of the chapters that dwell upon specific events adopt a retrospective stance and supply a commentary which draws upon the wisdom of hindsight. In Chapter 3, for example, a past tense narration of how he went 'to the House of Commons to demand justice upon the five members' in January 1642 prompts a sad reverie by the later Charles on the subsequent disasters that he had done his best to check with this timely intrusion upon the proceedings of the rebellious parliament: 'I endeavoured to have prevented, if God had seen fit, those future commotions which I foresaw would in all likelihood follow some men's activity, if not restrained, and so now hath done, to the undoing of many thousands; the more is the pity' (p. 13).

Other chapters, however, are couched in a present tense which creates the impression of an immediate and unresolved situation. For example, the account in Chapter 22 of the king's flight from Oxford to join the Scottish army in the spring of 1646 presents him as ignorant of the sequel: 'I must now resolve the riddle of their loyalty and give them opportunity to let the world see they mean not what they do but what they say' (pp. 134–35). The drama continues to unfold in the present tense in the next chapter, which

---

[21] Wordsworth, *Documentary Supplement*, p. 44.
[22] See Madan, p. 153.
[23] See Madan, p. 164.
[24] Evidence for a change of title while the book was in the printing-shop comes from one of the men who set up the first edition, who also states that it was suggested by Jeremy Taylor. (See the account of *Dr Hollingworth's Defence of K. Charles the First's Holy and Divine Book* (1692) in Madan, pp. 141–42.)

takes place some eight months later, after he has been handed over to the English and incarcerated at Holmby:

Yet may I justify those Scots to all the world in this, that they have not deceived me, for I never trusted to them further than to men. If I am sold by them, I am only sorry they should do it and that my price should be so much above my Saviour's. . . . The solitude and captivity to which I am now reduced gives me leisure enough to study the world's vanity and inconstancy. (p. 137)

As one would expect, if the bulk of the papers 'methodized' by the Brattles and used by Gauden as material for the text of *Suspiria Regalia* were penned by Charles during 1647 while he was being held at Holmby, most of the chapters dealing with earlier events consist of past tense narrative and present tense commentary. When the period of 'Solitudes and Sufferings' is approached, it is natural for the present tense to take over, as it does consistently in Chapters 22–28 — a sequence which begins with the king seeking refuge with the Scots and ends with Gauden's fabrication of 'Meditations upon Death, After the Votes of Non-Addresses, and His Majesty's Closer Imprisonment in Carisbrook Castle'. The title of this late addition serves primarily to assign Charles's spiritual preparation for martyrdom to the year 1648, since the move to the Isle of Wight in November 1647 and the circumstances of the vote in the following January make no substantial contribution to the content of the chapter. Other chapters — such as 16, 'Upon the Ordinance against the Common Prayer-Book' (mainly a reasoned Anglican defence of set forms of worship), and 20, 'Upon the Reformation of the Times' — are more in the nature of general essays on topics that were of concern throughout the decade.

This leaves a handful of sections that stylistically disrupt the steady development from the philosophically distanced past to the more poignant immediacy of the writer's imprisonment and isolation. Chapters 7, 10, and 11 are concerned with a number of things which happened in the months preceding the outbreak of civil war in 1642: Henrietta-Maria's departure for the Low Countries in February;[25] Parliament's wresting of control of the armed forces from the king by the Militia Ordinance in March; the Nineteen Propositions of June. In each of these meditations, retrospective narrative gives way to the more dramatic impact of the present tense. In the first, political circumstances have compelled the queen to seek refuge overseas. Charles's gloss on the 'scandal of that necessity which drives her away' reads like the work of a man engaged in the process of coming to terms with the shock of what is happening to him, rather than the contemplation of an old sorrow by one looking back over five years of disappointment and defeat:

that she should be compelled by my own subjects and those pretending to be Protestants to withdraw for her safety, this being the first example of any Protestant subjects that have taken up arms against their king, a Protestant. For I look upon

[25] In his note to Chapter 7 on page 29, Knachel assumes that the king is referring to Henrietta-Maria's final flight from England on 14 July 1644. Her earlier visit to Holland in 1642 to raise men and munitions fits more appropriately into the chronological sequence of the first eleven chapters.

this now done in England as another act of the same tragedy which was lately begun in Scotland; the brands of that fire, being ill-quenched, have kindled the like flames here. (p. 30)

The writer of Chapter 10 takes the stance of a beleaguered monarch anxious to prove himself innocent of hostile intent towards his people. Opening with the assertion, 'How untruly I am charged with the first raising of an army and beginning this civil war,' he goes on to protest that his very 'unprepared-ness' for any kind of military action 'testifies for me that I am set on the defensive part, having so little hopes or power to offend others that I have none to defend myself' (p. 46). In Chapter 11, the man who meditates on the Nineteen Propositions, put to him by Parliament in June 1642, seems to forgo or not have access to the historical perspective provided by his later 'solitudes':

Although there be many things they demand, yet if these be all, I am glad to see at what price they set my own safety and my people's peace, which I cannot think I buy at too dear a rate, save only the parting with my conscience and honour. If nothing else will satisfy, I must choose rather to be as miserable and inglorious as my enemies can make or wish me. . . . Here are many things required of me, but I see nothing offered to me by the way of grateful exchange of honour or any requital for those favours I have or can yet grant them. (pp. 52–53)

Sandwiched between the retrospective treatment of the king's repulse from Hull in Chapter 8 and the dramatic present of the protestations of Chapter 10 is an account of the outbreak of hostilities, which mobilizes the resources of both these temporal perspectives. It opens with the king struggling in the toils of historical circumstance:

I find that I am at the same point and posture I was when they forced me to leave Whitehall. What tumults could not do, an army must, which is but tumults lifted and enrolled to a better order but as bad an end. My recess hath given them confidence that I may be conquered. (p. 38)

Out of the midst of the confusion of 1642 — and the date of the utterance is pointedly inscribed in the text — he speaks in tones of hurt and baffled innocence:

Are the hazards and miseries of civil war in the bowels of my most flourishing kingdom the fruits I must now reap after seventeen years living and reigning among them with such a measure of justice, peace, plenty, and religion as all nations about either admired or envied? (p. 39)

For several more pages, an analysis of the immediate past — the activities of the London mobs, the Root and Branch Bill, the removal of the right of bishops to sit in the House of Lords — is presented from the perspective of the summer of 1642. Then there is a marked transition to the historical vantage-point of the captive king of a later period, who writes from the bitter experience of more than three years of fighting and seeks to absolve himself from all responsibility for starting it:

This is the true state of those constructions pretended to be in point of justice and authority of Parliament, when, I call God to witness, I knew none of such consequence as was worth speaking of a war, being only such as justice, reason, and religion had made in my own and other men's consciences. (p. 42)

Looking back now, from 1647, he has a clearer view of the consistent policy of those who were determined to find a pretext for taking up arms against him: 'That this is the true state and first drift and design in raising an army against me is by the sequel so evident that all other pretences vanish' (p. 43). He concludes with an expression of gratitude that, 'in the midst of all the unfortunate successes of this war on my side', he has been able to take comfort from the certainty of his own innocence, which was never 'any whit prejudiced or darkened' (p. 44).

Two explanations suggest themselves for these shifting time perspectives, one emphasizing the rhetorical strategy, the other the historical origins of *Eikon Basilike*. The first would argue that Gauden cleverly used the medium of the present tense to heighten the dramatic appeal of his subject at crucial moments in the story; the other would ponder how far Gauden was reflecting the variation of tenses in his source manuscript — that collection of 'loose papers', composed 'at different times', which had been organized 'into an exact method' while the king was at Hampton Court. The Brattles may have done little more than arrange the documents into roughly chronological order. Gauden's contribution may have consisted of devising the format of a series of meditations,[26] which would have entailed a certain amount of rewriting, adding some of the more general essays (such as that on the Book of Common Prayer), and completing the 'Portraiture' with Chapters 24 and 28, which highlighted the pathos of the 'solitude they have confined me unto' (p. 141) and brought the narrative more or less up to date.

It may well be that Charles, who was seen working on a manuscript at Holmby, had there composed the majority of the 'loose papers' dealing with the period 1640 to 1645 — the material written largely from the perspective of 1647 which became Chapters 1–21. The immediacy of the account of the decision to leave Oxford and seek refuge in the north in Chapter 22 suggests that Charles's resumption of sustained work on the project mooted at Theobalds in 1642 dated from his sojourn in Newcastle, before he was transferred to Holmby. The present-tense reflections on his betrayal by the Scots in Chapter 23 locate themselves clearly during the Holmby period itself. Chapter 24, on 'the Army's Surprisal of the King at Holmby', and the letter to the Prince of Wales, which ends 'Farewell till we meet, if not on earth, yet in heaven' (p. 171), are presumably the latest additions not certainly attributable to Gauden's own invention.

Such a reconstruction of the work's composition leaves open the possibility that drafts of the anomalous present-tense meditations (Chapters 7, 10, and 11, and the first part of 9) antedated by some years the period of

---

[26] The author of *The Princely Pellican*, however, claims that the king himself was induced 'to end every *Meditation* with a *Psalme*' (p. 12) by his frequent reflections upon the troubles of King David.

confinement at Newcastle and Holmby which gave Charles the leisure to undertake a retrospective assessment of his career since 1640. Perhaps, if they were among the captured writings that were returned to him at Hampton Court, they were not available when the Brattles 'methodized' the king's 'loose papers', and were only later incorporated into the text by Gauden, who for some reason omitted to harmonize their temporal stance with that of the surrounding material.

There remains the question of the book's purpose. When he first discussed the idea of drawing up a vindication of his actions in 1642, and even when he set about putting his papers in order in 1647, Charles himself can hardly have anticipated that publication would coincide with the final bloody act in his long-drawn-out contest with Parliament. Similarly, Gauden's redaction in the early months of 1648 must have been intended as a contribution to a battle for political power that had not yet been irrevocably lost. Even as late as October, when Charles had approved and corrected Gauden's manuscript and alerted his publisher, the work must have been regarded as a means of strengthening his hand in the negotiations with the parliamentary commissioners at Newport by exciting popular sympathy for a captive and persecuted monarch. His unexpected removal to Hurst Castle on 1 December and the subsequent movement of events confirmed the resolve of Gauden (or should it be Symmons, if he was the moving spirit in the whole enterprise?) 'to print it with all the speed that might be'; and Symmons deposited the augmented manuscript with Royston on the same day that the House of Commons appointed a committee to make arrangements for the trial. Was this a last ditch attempt to rally public opinion to the king's defence, or does the addition of the 'Meditations upon Death' earlier in December indicate that those closest to the king had bowed to the inevitable and were already planning a propaganda coup that would transform the execution into a martyrdom? References to the danger of violent death in earlier chapters had been in the context of military action, as in the comment that 'the hazards of war are equal, nor doth the cannon know any respect of persons' (p. 39). Death on the scaffold seems to have replaced death on the battlefield in the scenario imagined by Gauden in Chapter 28 with its spectators and triumphing adversaries, and the imminent end is now presented as more or less unavoidable:

That I must die as a man is certain. That I may die a king by the hands of my own subjects, a violent, sudden, and barbarous death, in the strength of my years, in the midst of my kingdoms, my friends and loving subjects being helpless spectators, my enemies insolent revilers and triumphers over me, living, dying, and dead, is so probable in human reason that God hath taught me not to hope otherwise as to man's cruelty. However, I despair not of God's infinite mercy. (pp. 173–74)

It may be that the last-minute change of title from *Suspiria Regalia, or, The Royal Plea* to *Eikon Basilike* marks the final acknowledgement by those responsible for producing 'the king's book' that it was too late for any 'plea' to influence the result of the trial. In those last weeks of January, it must have become clear that 'The Portraiture of His Sacred Majesty' would enter the public consciousness as a martyred monarch's bequest to a grieving nation rather than the political vindication of a king who would have been prepared to lay down his life for his country's peace.

'A rationall of old Rites':
Sir Thomas Browne's *Urn Buriall* and
the Conflict over Ceremony

ACHSAH GUIBBORY

University of Illinois at Urbana-Champaign

Sir Thomas Browne's *Urn Buriall*, for all its claims of universality, is distinctly a product of its time, addressing issues that were hotly contested during the period of the English Civil War. Browne's famous treatise on funeral rites is an interesting test case for the relations between literature and politics during the seventeenth century, in part because its subject may not strike us as being overtly political. Browne is political though not quite polemical; he engages with politically controversial issues, yet is detached in his paradoxical, sceptical approach.

Religious controversy was inseparable from politics during this period. During the 1640s Parliament repeatedly legislated matters of religion. They passed various ordinances for the reformation of religion, abolishing episcopacy as the form of church-government, and calling for all 'monuments' of 'Idolatry' in churches (such as altars, tapers, and crosses) to be removed and destroyed.[1] Particularly relevant for my reading of Browne, on 4 January 1645 Parliament banned the use of the Book of Common Prayer 'in any Church, Chappel, or place of public Worship';

The Lords and Commons assembled in Parliament . . . resolving, according to their Covenant, to reform Religion according to the Word of God, and the Example of the best Reformed Churches . . . do judge it necessary that the said Book of Common Prayer be Abolished . . . [and that the many statutes for uniformity of prayer, service, and administration of sacraments from Edward VI on] be and stand from henceforth repealed, void and of none effect.[2]

Seven months later, Parliament extended the ban on the use of the Prayer Book to private worship, enumerating punishments for violating the ordinance: £5 fine for the first offence, £10 for the second, and a year in prison for the third. All prayer books remaining in parish churches and chapels were to be carried to committees of respective counties where they were to be disposed of 'as the Parliament shall direct'.[3]

---

[1] See, e.g., ordinances of 12 June 1643 (in John Rushworth, *Historical Collections*, vol. 5 (London, 1721), 337), 26 Aug 1643, 9 May 1644, and 27 May 1648 (in *Acts and Ordinances of the Interregnum, 1642–1660*, edited by C. H. Firth and R. S. Rait, 2 vols (London, 1911), I, 265–66, 425–26, 1143).

[2] Rushworth, v, 785.

[3] See the 23 August 1645 *Ordinance of the Lords and Commons Assembled in Parliament For the more effectual putting in execution the Directory For public worship* (London, 1646), pp. 5–8.

In banning the Book of Common Prayer, Parliament outlawed the performance of its various ceremonies, including the rites enjoined under 'The Order for the buriall of the dead'. After the ordinance of 4 January, it was illegal to bury a person according to the rites of the Church of England. As a replacement for the Prayer Book, Parliament decreed instead that the *Directory for Public Worship of God*, created by the Westminster Assembly, be used (Rushworth, v, 785). Rejecting the Church of England's liturgy and 'the many unprofitable and burdensome Ceremonies contained in it', the *Directory* gave legal force to the long-standing Puritan objection to the use of religious ritual. The *Directory* expressly stated that

When any person departeth this life, let the dead body, upon the day of Buriall, be decently attended from the house to the place appointed for publique Buriall, and there immediately interred, without any Ceremony.

And because the customes of kneeling down, and praying by, or towards the dead Corps, and other such usages, in the place where it lies, before it be carried to Buriall, are Superstitious: and for that, praying, reading, and singing both in going to, and at the Grave, have been grosly abused, are no way beneficiall to the dead, and have proved many wayes hurtfull to the living, therefore let all such things be laid aside.[4]

One wishes to know what exactly were the burial practices in England after Parliament made the *Directory* legally binding. It has been suggested that it may not have been widely used, despite the Parliamentary order, and Claire Gittings, in her excellent study of death and burial in early modern England, notes that at least a few burials were performed in church with the old rites. But the evidence about funeral practices in these years is sparse and inconclusive. If (as Browne comments) we are hopelessly ignorant about the particulars of our future state after death, we also know frustratingly little about funeral practices during the Civil War and Interregnum. For as Gittings remarks, 'the breakdown of the system of ecclesiastical records during the Interregnum inevitably hampers attempts to discover what actually was the practice of the time'.[5]

---

[4] *A Directory for the Public Worship of God* (London, 1645), pp. 73–74. Cf. 'The order for the buriall of the dead' in the 1638 *Book of Common Prayer*. For an important statement of the Puritan position, see the 1572 'Admonition to the Parliament', which objected to having 'a prescript kinde of service to burie the dead: And that which is the duety of every christian, they tie alone to the minister, whereby prayer for the dead is maintained' (reprinted in *Puritan Manifestoes: A Study of the Origin of the Puritan Revolt*, edited by W. H. Frere and C. E. Douglas (London, 1907), p. 28). In 1634, John Canne vigorously repeated these objections, echoing the *Admonition* and the Scottish *First Book of Discipline* (1560) as he insisted that he and the other 'Nonconformists' want the corpse to be buried 'without all kind of ceremony heretofore used' (*A Necessitie of Separation from the Church of England* (Amsterdam, 1643)), p. 102. I am grateful to Dennis Kay for alerting me to Henry Machyn's diary, which describes in some detail an unceremonious Protestant funeral he witnessed in 1559 (*The Diary of Henry Machyn ... from A.D. 1550 to A.D. 1563*, edited by John Gough Nichols (New York and London, 1848), p. 193). See Kay's important discussion of the diary entry and of changes in funerals precipitated by the Reformation in *Melodious Tears: The English Funeral Elegy from Spenser to Milton* (Oxford, 1989), Introduction.

[5] Claire Gittings (*Death, Burial and the Individual in Early Modern England* (London, 1984)) has questioned 'just how effective the Puritan insistence on simple burial was even during the Civil War and the Interregnum itself' (p. 54), but her data (given in Tables 5 and 6 in her 'Statistical Appendix') actually show a sharp drop in the number of burials in church and funeral doles after 1640. There is also a radical decrease during these years in the number of surviving probate accounts, which are her source of

Written between May 1656 and 1 May 1658, Sir Thomas Browne's *Urn Buriall* was published in 1658, two years before the liturgy and rites of the Church of England would be restored. As a text examining burial practices in different historical times, countries, and cultures, it seems at times curiously modern in its archaeological, anthropological approach. But in his concern with burial rites, Browne takes as his subject what was the site of contemporary religio-political conflict — humanly ordained ceremony, of which burial rites are a particularly important example.

The fact that *Urn Buriall* is an antiquarian piece has led modern readers to feel that it is a work appropriate to Browne's singular fancy, but quite remote from the heated political concerns that absorbed Browne's contemporaries. But it is worth noting that seventeenth-century antiquarian studies did not always remain disinterested; they often had applications for the contemporary politics of religion.[6] Browne himself suggests the connexion between distant past and immediate present when he tells his friend Thomas Le Gros in the dedication that these urns have 'voices' that 'speak' to the present.[7] They have something to tell which is not just a timeless truth about human mortality and the universal desire for immortality, but particularly timely during the period of the Civil War and Interregnum, when the liturgy and ceremonies of the Church of England had been prohibited by Parliamentary law. For, as I will show, Browne's examination of burial practices is in part a defence of burial rites and, indeed, of ceremony more largely. Browne begins with a focus on the recently discovered urns and on specific burial customs, emphasizing their ritualistic nature and significance; but just as he moves from the particular Norfolk urns to the ways humans have ceremoniously treated the dead body, so his concerns broaden from specific rites of burial to large conclusions about the role of religious ceremony.

Though the causes of the English Civil War are complex, conflict over religious worship certainly contributed to its outbreak.[8] The reign of Charles I witnessed increasingly intense controversy over the role of ceremony in religion. Under the influence of Laud, there was an increased emphasis in the Church of England on ceremony, formality, and uniformity in religious worship, an emphasis that sorted well with Charles I's own taste

---

information about funerals, and this makes it especially hard to generalize about what actually happened. That a few traditional church burials were held does not necessarily mean that the *Directory*'s prescription for burials without religious ceremony was not widely followed, since the church burials are referred to by contemporaries as noteworthy, hence probably as exceptions to the usual practice. We simply do not have enough information to be able to draw firm conclusions.

[6] See John Selden's *Historie of Tithes* (London, 1618).

[7] *Urn Buriall*, in *The Works of Sir Thomas Browne*, edited by Geoffrey Keynes, 4 vols (Chicago, 1964), I, 131.

[8] See Nicholas Tyacke, *Anti-Calvinists: The Rise of English Arminianism c. 1590–1640* (Oxford, 1987), and John Morrill, 'The Religious Context of the English Civil War', *Transactions of the Royal Historical Society*, 5th series, 34 (1984), 155–78 and J. Sears McGee, *The Godly Man in Stuart England* (New Haven, 1976). On religious differences, see also Peter Lake, 'Calvinism and the English Church 1570–1635', *Past and Present*, no. 114 (Feb. 1987), 32–76.

for ceremony and order within his court.[9] Laud ordered the observance of all ceremonies in the Prayer Book and in the Canons of 1604, and insisted on the appropriateness of such things as the priest's wearing the surplice, making the sign of the cross after baptism, kneeling at receiving the sacrament, and bowing at the name of Jesus. This emphasis on orderly ceremony and bodily gestures provoked much resistance among those who felt such ceremonious worship was opening the way to the return of Roman Catholic idolatry.

Much was written on both sides of the issue of ceremonial worship. For all the differences among writers on each side, distinct and incompatible ideologies characterize the 'Anglican' defences of ceremony and the 'Puritan' attacks on ceremonial worship.[10] Anglican defenders of ceremony emphasized its symbolical function. According to John Burgess, who had earlier been a non-conforming minister but in 1631 published a justification of ceremonies by Charles I's 'special command', ceremonies — the 'outward' part of worship — are 'expressions of internal', spiritual devotion.[11] Though 'sensible' or corporeal, they have 'Mysticall signification'.[12]

Ceremonies were also valued for their 'memorative' function, their ability to work on the memory through sensible means. In an effort to distinguish the ceremonies of the Church of England from the 'superstitious' use of them by the Church of Rome, apologists emphasized the function of ceremonies as 'memoratives' or 'memorialls'. Since our knowledge, even in religious things, comes through the bodily senses, we need 'sensible objects' to understand and be reminded of spiritual truths.[13]

The attention to the body, as well as the belief in the symbolic and memorial functions of material ceremonies, was particularly evident in Laud's concern with 'the outward face of Religion'. In dedicating his *Conference with Fisher* to Charles I, Laud explained that though 'the Inward

[9] Kevin Sharpe, 'The Image of virtue: the court and household of Charles I, 1625–1642', in David Starkey and others, *The English Court: from the Wars of the Roses to the Civil War* (London, 1987), pp. 226–60. See also R. Malcolm Smuts, *Court Culture and the Origins of a Royalist Tradition in Early Stuart England* (Philadelphia, 1987), Chapter 8 ('Religion').

[10] McGee has argued for the usefulness and necessity of distinguishing between 'Anglicans' and 'Puritans', despite difficulties with these terms. I am using the terms much as he does, with a sense that there are differences and variety within each group: 'Puritans are those whose highest priority was the dissemination of "godly preaching" throughout England. It was their vision that England could then move towards complete "reformation" in their sense, meaning the establishment of a "piety and moral order" which was distinctive.... Anglicans were those more or less content with the episcopal organization and liturgy of the Church of England ... [and this includes] even those who became critical of Laud [but still] made their highest priority the maintenance of a domestic peace within which they could work for a distinctively anglican "piety and moral order"' (*The Godly Man*, pp. 9–10). See also John F. H. New, *Anglican and Puritan: The Basis of their Opposition, 1588–1640* (Stanford, 1964). On conflict over ceremony, see McGee, *The Godly Man*, Chapter 3.

[11] John Burgess, *An Answer Rejoyned to that Much Applauded Pamphlet ... A Reply to Dr. Morton's Generall Defence of three Nocent Ceremonies* (London, 1631), pp. 185, 158.

[12] Thomas Morton, *A Defence of the Innocencie of the Three Ceremonies of the Church of England* (London, 1618), pp. 85, 88. Morton, a Calvinist, was no Arminian and was not part of Laud's group. His treatise encouraging conformity was written in James's reign. But his defence of ceremony is important for the controversy as it developed under Charles I. Morton's *Defence* was attacked by William Ames, who Burgess in turn refuted, elaborating upon Morton's position. Thus Morton's earlier treatise became worked into the Laudian defence of ceremony.

[13] Morton, p. 58; Burgess, p. 278.

Worship of the Heart' is essential, the external, bodily worship of God in the church is 'the *Great Witnesse* to the World, that Our heart stands right in that Service of God'. So long as 'we live in the Body', we need 'External helps'.[14]

Laud's insistence on conformity, on 'the beauty of holiness', and on rites and gestures involving the body triggered resistance among Protestants wanting a 'purer' worship. Though Laud's attention to the body was based on his belief in the interrelation between spirit and sense, critics of ceremony saw all this attention to bodily rites as 'carnal' idolatry and pride. Peter Smart, who had been punished for preaching a sermon in 1628 against the ceremonial 'innovations' of John Cosin, Bishop of Durham, brought charges against him, in which he mocked Cosin's bodily gestures in worship: the 'poore people of Durham', Smart charged, have been 'miserably misled' by [your] upstartings, downe-squattings, east-turnings, crossings and kissings of altar-clothes, and the elements of bread and wine; with your frequent and profound duckings and prostrations before your most sumptuous Altar'.[15] Prynne and Burton attacked the carnality of the prelates and their ceremonies in similarly colourful language. Instituted by man not God, ceremonies, they argued, are merely 'humane inventions' and hence idolatrous.[16]

The 'Puritan' attack on ceremony as 'carnal idolatry' reached its culmination in the 1640s in the iconoclastic desecration of churches and cathedrals, the parliamentary ordinances for 'the utter demolishing, removing and taking away of all Monuments of Superstition or Idolatry', and the ordinance abolishing the Book of Common Prayer, with all its ceremonies and rites.[17] The same day that Parliament passed the ordinance against the Prayer Book, they passed the bill of attainder against Laud, charging him with 'high treason' for trying to bring back popery. Five days later Laud was executed. Even after his death Laud defied the Puritan dislike of ceremony, for, as the seventeenth-century historian Rushworth notes, he was buried according to the 'rites' that had just been prohibited.[18]

[14] William Laud, *A Relation of the Conference Betweene William Lawd ... and Mr. Fisher the Jesuite ...* (London, 1639), Dedicatory Epistle to King Charles. See also Sears McGee, 'William Laud and the Outward Face of Religion', in *Leaders of the Reformation*, edited by Richard L. DeMolen (London and Toronto, 1984). Peter Lake, 'Lancelot Andrewes, John Buckeridge, and Avant-Garde Conformity at the Court of James I' (forthcoming in *The Mental World of the Jacobean Court*, edited by Linda Levy Peck), convincingly argues that the antecedent for the 'style of piety' associated with Laud and the Arminians in the 1620s and 1630s is to be found in Richard Hooker in the 1590s and, after him, in Lancelot Andrewes and John Buckeridge in the reign of James I.
[15] 'Articles, or instructions for Articles, to be exhibited by his Majestie's Heigh Commissioners, against Mr. John Cosin, Mr. Francis Burgoine, Mr. Marmaduke Blaxton, Doctor Hunt, Doctor Lindsell, Mr. William James, all learned clerks of the Cathedrall Church of Durham', in *The Correspondence of John Cosin*, Publications of the Surtees Society, vol. 52 (London, 1869), p. 165. On the 'carnal' ceremonies, see also Henry Burton, *A Replie to a Relation of the Conference Betweene William Laude and Mr. Fisher the Jesuite* (n.p., 1640); John Bastwick, *The Answer of John Bastwick ... to the exceptions made against his Letany ...* (London, 1637), and William Prynne's numerous polemical treatises.
[16] Morton argued that God left men the 'liberty' to 'invent' ceremonies (pp. 56, 71); in 1631, Burgess's emphasis, however, is on the church's authority to impose them (see, e.g., pp. 228–38).
[17] *Acts and Ordinances*, I, 265–66, 425–26, 1143. See also John Phillips, *The Reformation of Images: Destruction of Art in England, 1535–1660* (Berkeley, 1973).
[18] Rushworth, v, 785.

Browne's *Urn Buriall* gains significance when read within the context of this conflict over ceremony. This highly complex work speaks to the issue of ceremony and uses the urns recently discovered in Norfolk as an occasion to explore the various ways in which humans have treated death and the place of ceremony in human experience. Implicitly, *Urn Buriall* defends the legitimacy of burial rites, and of ceremony more largely. It shares and confirms the arguments of those who had defended ceremony in the Church of England. But *Urn Buriall* is a paradoxical, problematic work, for another voice in Browne's text speaks of the vanity and absurdity of these rites. The contradictions make *Urn Buriall* a fascinating text, incorporating conflicting discourses about ceremony.

Browne's sceptical, paradoxical bent of mind ensures that *Urn Buriall* cannot simply be read as a Laudian defence of ceremony. Nevertheless, his work shares much of the ideology that energizes the apologists for religious ceremony. Browne approaches his inquiry into the variety of human burial practices with the assumption that these practices are *significant*; they have meaning. Browne's discussion of burial customs in the first three chapters discovers the 'reason' or logic underlying these customs: 'Some being of the opinion of *Thales*, that water was the original of all things, thought it most equall to submit unto the principle of putrefaction, and conclude in a moist relentment. Others conceived it most natural to end in fire, as due unto the master principle in composition, according to the doctrine of *Heraclitus*' (p. 137). In each of these cases, the practice symbolizes an attempt to return to the origin of things in the hope of renewed life. The fact that there is some 'reason' behind burial rites is what enables them to function symbolically. The idea of significant ceremonies links Browne's discourse with defences of religious ceremony.

Browne's attempt to give a 'rationall of old Rites' is based on his belief that 'all customes were founded upon some bottome of Reason' (p. 137) — exactly the argument made by the apologists for religious ceremony. Peter Heylyn, for example, Laud's chaplain and biographer, argued that customs such as the consecration of temples and altars were natural and founded on reason. Speaking of the patriarchs and early Jews, he observed that 'Nature ... informed them that proper and peculiar places were to be set apart to Gods publick worship'.[19] In contrast to the Puritan opposition between Scripture and custom or tradition (identified with error) is the 'Anglican' argument that, besides divinely ordained ceremonies, there are rituals and customs that have their 'foundation in nature' and reason and thus can be properly observed.[20] A similar sense of custom appears in Bishop Cosin's notes on the Book of Common Prayer — significantly for my purposes in his discussion of the Office for the Buriall of the Dead, where he defends the

[19] Peter Heylin, *Antidotum Lincolniense* (London, 1637), p. 69; on nature and reason's place in the development of ceremony, see John Pocklington, *Altare Christianum* (London, 1637), pp. 4–5, 154.
[20] See T. R., *De Templis* (London, 1638), p. 101.

customary funeral banquet after the burial by saying it is 'a custom taken from the Jews, as they took it from natural reason'.[21]

Much of Cosin's commentary indirectly responds to the Puritan rejection of ceremony. He criticizes 'that unchristian fancy of the puritans, that would have no minister to bury their dead, but the corpse to be brought to the grave and there put in by the clerk, or some other honest neighbour, and so back again without any more ado'.[22] For Cosin, ceremony is necessary, and his belief that 'custom' is reasonable is closely tied to his strong feeling for historical continuity. Cosin stresses the connexion between Jewish and Christian customs, and argues for the antiquity of current practices such as singing psalms at funerals or praying for the dead.[23] In Cosin's discussion of burial rites, as in other Laudian defences of ceremonial worship, there is a deep sense of historical continuity, a sense that ceremony is a natural, universal human instinct.

In the defences of ceremony there are glimmerings of an anthropological interest in human behaviour which comes to fuller light in Browne's work. The author of *De Templis: A Treatise of Temples* looks for a common denominator in the practices of various cultures. He observes that wherever temples were built they always looked towards the east; they were consecrated as holy places through rituals that are 'founded in nature' and hence universal. Offering a kind of anthropological survey of various religions, the author concludes that 'All nations, from the beginning of the World, have beene naturally inclined, to build and adorne Temples, as if it were impossible for a humane life, to be lead here upon earth, without them'.[24]

The anthropological interest we see in *De Templis* is even stronger in Browne. As he surveys the customs for dealing with the dead body, he mentions Christian and Jewish burial practices alongside those of other cultures — Greeks, Chaldeans, Persians, Indians, Egyptians, Scythians, Romans. Whereas Puritans insisted on clear separations between Christian and pagan, between the godly and ungodly, Browne's first three and a half chapters show continuity underlying the diversity of human experience. All cultures have taken special care for the body at death. Ulysses desired a 'noble Tomb after death', and even 'the rigid Jews were wont to garnish the Sepulchres of the righteous' (p. 147). Though we might expect Christians to care less about the body, with their faith that all is 'reparable by a resurrection', Browne points out that they too have displayed 'careful consideration of the body' at burial (p. 157).

What emerges from Browne's survey of burial customs is a sense that, for all their diversity and particularity, there is a single symbolic significance underlying these rites. All the customs represent attempts to continue

[21] John Cosin, *Notes and Collections on the Book of Common Prayer*, in *The Works of ... John Cosin* (Oxford, 1855), v, 171.
[22] Cosin, *Works*, v, 168; this is in the 1619 notes.
[23] Cosin, *Works*, v, 165, 170.
[24] *De Templis*, pp. 139–40.

connexions with the living and renew bodily life after death. The pagan custom of burying things which 'delighted, or ... were dear' to the dead person (p. 144), the burial of the tears of friends in a vial, the inclusion of evergreen bay leaves in the tomb of St Humbert, the pictures of the holy candlestick in an old Jewish burial cell, or the pictures of cypress, Lazarus, or Jonas in the cells of ancient Christians and martyrs, all these represent symbolically hopes for another life.

When in Chapter IV Browne turns to Christian practices, we might expect him to distinguish them from pagan, but instead he insists on the similarity, as he shows that even pagan customs symbolically represented the hope for immortality:

Christian invention hath chiefly driven at Rites, which speak hopes of another life, and hints of a Resurrection. And if the ancient Gentiles held not the immortality of their better part, and some subsistence after death; in severall rites, customes, actions and expressions, they contradicted their own opinions: wherein *Democritus* went high, even to the thought of a resurrection, as scoffingly recorded by *Pliny*. ... who would expect from *Lucretius* a sentence of *Ecclesiastes*? Before *Plato* could speak, the soul had wings in Homer. ... *Lucian* spoke much truth in jest, when he said, that part of *Hercules* which proceeded from Alchmena perished, that from *Jupiter* remained immortall. Thus *Socrates* was content that his friends should bury his body, so they would not think they buried *Socrates*, and regarding only his immortall part, was indifferent to be burnt or buried. (p. 158)

If the desire for immortality is universal, so is the function of funeral rites to represent this human desire. All funeral customs, everywhere, no matter how seemingly bizarre, signify 'the natural expectation and desire' for some further state to come, 'unto which this seemes progressionall, and otherwise made in vaine' (p. 163).[25]

Browne remarks that from ancient times Christians have used ceremonies to 'gloss' the deformity of death, to 'take off brutall terminations', and to symbolize their faith in resurrection (p. 157). This comment links Christian practices with analogous pagan ones. But it also defines a norm against which the parliamentary prohibition against burial rites demands to be evaluated. Browne's reference to the 'civil rites' of Christians (p. 157) may be calculated to imply that, in deference to Parliament's prohibition of religious ceremonies, he is only concerned with secular rites (the *Directory* allowed 'civill respects' at burial).[26] Yet the term 'civil' also meant 'well-ordered', 'not barbarous', 'civilized', 'refined', and 'humane' (*OED*, 7–9, 11), all appropriate meanings. In this sense, Christian rites, which 'handsomely gloss' (or give a fair appearance to) the 'brutal' deformity of death, are a mark of civility.

[25] Browne's insight seems confirmed by the work of twentieth-century archaeologists and anthropologists. The earliest human ritual behaviour (*c*. 500,000 B.C.) was occasioned and motivated by death; by *c*. 50,000–60,000 B.C., human beings were engaging in elaborate funeral rites which indicate a belief in a postmortem existence (see David E. Stannard, *The Puritan Way of Death: A Study in Religion, Culture, and Social Change* (Oxford and New York, 1977), Introduction).

[26] *Directory*, p. 74.

It is a distinctive mark of human beings to have ceremonies, although Browne observes that some animals perform burials or have 'exequies'. If even animals have burial rites, to have no rites at all would place humans beneath the animals. The discovered urns remind us of the universality of burial ceremonies, this 'universal truth' making it evident that the Puritan abolition of burial rites radically disrupts and violates human practices that go all the way back to the earliest recorded antiquity.[27]

It is significant that Browne does not directly describe the burial rites of the Church of England in his survey of burial customs. This may be a rhetorical strategy, a way of dealing with the parliamentary prohibition against the ceremonies. The indirection, the specific references to so many customs except the Anglican ones, is 'safe', yet paradoxically draws attention to those absent rites. There is, I think, a further significance to the felt 'absence' of the burial rites of the Church of England. As Browne attempts to date and identify these urns in Chapter 2, references to ancient customs of Romans, Britons, or Danes which ceased to be practised suggest that burial customs are mortal — they eventually 'expire' (p. 146). Perhaps this is what is happening to the burial customs of the Church of England. The strong apocalypticism of the final chapter suggests the impending extinction of all human civilization. From his Royalist perspective, the destruction of English culture, seen as the disruption of the long history of man as a ceremonial creature, may well mark the end of time.[28]

However, if he does not describe the burial rites of the Church of England, he indirectly inscribes them in his text. As in the rites themselves, he interweaves mortality with the promise of resurrection. He gradually shifts his emphasis from the universality of death to the availability of another life only for those who believe in Christ, and concludes by anticipating the end of the world. Much as the Church of England's rite ends with the idea that 'whoever believeth' in Jesus Christ shall live, so Browne towards the end of *Urn Buriall* sadly insists that only Christians will have their hopes for an afterlife fulfilled. Moreover, the fifth and final chapter eloquently echoes the passages from 1 Corinthians 15 on the resurrection that actually form the central part of the burial service.[29] Inscribing the prohibited service in his own text, Browne preserves remnants of his own culture for whatever posterity there may be. Ironically, however, this final chapter serves as a funeral oration for burial rites themselves, as it defines a present in which so

[27] In his important book on *The Puritan Way of Death* in New England, Stannard has argued that, in contrast to their counterparts in England, New England Puritans during the mid-seventeenth century developed a heightened concern with funeral ritual: 'in virtually every aspect ... the New England Puritans ritualized death as only the most non-Puritan of pre-Restoration Englishmen would have dared do' (p. 117). Stannard explains this special development in American Puritanism as linked to the growth of an 'introspective tribalism' (see Chapter 5, 'Death and Burial', pp. 96–134).
[28] Jonathan F. S. Post, *Sir Thomas Browne* (Boston, 1987), gives a politically more optimistic interpretation in his interesting suggestion that *Urn Buriall*'s message is finally one of 'preservation and continuity', of 'survival' by 'living underground' during a time of Puritan ascendancy (pp. 131–34).
[29] See 'The order for the buriall of the dead' in the 1638 Book of Common Prayer.

little time is left until the end of the world that it seems absurd to expect those rites to fulfil a memorative function. No need for 'Monuments' when there will be no generations left to remember us:

We whose generations are ordained in this setting part of time, are providentially taken off from such imaginations. And being necessitated to eye the remaining particle of futurity, are naturally constituted unto thoughts of the next world, and cannot excusably decline the consideration of that duration, which maketh Pyranmids pillars of snow, and all that's past a moment'. (p. 166)[30]

Behind the universalism of this 'metaphysical' statement is Browne's keen sense of the particulars of the political moment.

Urn Buriall is a paradoxical, sceptical, ironical, perhaps deeply divided work. If Browne's text is a defence of ceremony there are also voices in the text that point out the futility and vanity of funeral customs, voices that become most persistent in the fifth chapter. Browne's discourse on burial customs is contaminated by the Puritan attack on ceremony which raised questions that apparently struck a responsive chord in Browne's sceptical, ever inquiring mind. The text of *Urn Buriall* voices conflicting religious ideologies competing for dominance in the seventeenth century.

Although Browne's examination of burial customs shows that the invention of ceremony is an essential impulse of human nature, there is also a persistent sense of the ultimate absurdity and futility of these rites, with all their attention to the body. There is often an ironic edge, for example, in his description of substances buried in the grave that were found 'fresh', or the bay leaves in St Humbert's tomb that were 'found green . . . after an hundred and fifty yeares' (p. 149). Though from one perspective, burial rites are marks of civility, decency, and humanity, from another, all the decorations of tombs and urns, all the ceremonies, seem ways of 'glossing' or covering over the brutal 'deformity' of death. If Browne appreciates the art of these 'glosses', he is also impelled to expose the brutal reality of death and decay that art strives to conceal. By Chapter 5 the urns have become 'Emblemes of mortall vanities', since they symbolize the many diverse attempts of human beings to create for themselves an earthly, material immortality: 'to subsist in bones, and be but Pyramidally extant, is a fallacy in duration' (p. 165). All the efforts of antiquity to preserve names, to build monuments or pyramids, to gain an earthly immortality are 'vanity, feeding the winde, and folly' (p. 168). 'In vain do individuals hope for Immortality, or any patent from oblivion, in preservations below the Moon' (p. 168). Although burial rites and customs represent with elegance the human desire for immortality, they

---

[30] Browne continued to show an interest in monuments. In *Reportorium, or Some Account of the Tombs and Monuments in the Cathedrall Church of Norwich* (1680), he tried to retrieve and record information about the 'noble and considerable persons' who had been buried in the cathedral, as a way of counteracting the iconoclastic destruction of 'about a hundred brasse Inscriptions torne and taken away from grave stones and tombs' during the period of 'the late civill warres' (*Works*, III, 123). His concern to preserve names late in his life, his sense of the importance of monuments, should make us wary of accepting as Browne's 'final' position on the matter statements in *Urn Buriall* about the vanity of monuments that seek to preserve individual identity.

are ineffectual in their attempts to ensure a continuation of life, and they are 'carnal' in their concern with the body rather than the soul. The Puritan distrust of ceremony as a mark of pride and carnality finds an echo in Browne's mockery in Chapter 5 of ceremonies concerned with the body:

There is nothing strictly immortall, but immortality. Whatever hath no beginning may be confident of no end . . . . the sufficiency of Christian Immortality frustrates all earthly glory, and the quality of either state after death makes a folly of posthumous memory. God who only can destroy our souls, and hath assured our resurrection, either of our bodies or names hath directly promised no duration. . . . But man is a Noble Animal, splendid in ashes, and pompous in the grave, solemnizing Nativities and Deaths with equall lustre, nor omitting Ceremonies of bravery, in the infamy of his nature. (p. 169)

The irony is heavy here, and the association of ceremony with infamy as well as splendour seems much closer to the Puritans than to Laud.[31] Seen from this perspective, there is a folly even in Christian concern with the body in death. Indeed, Browne's remark that God has not directly promised the resurrection of our bodies or names is startling, especially after he has just detailed all the concern among Christians, Jews, and pagans with the position in which the body is buried.[32] It effectively comments on the emphasis on bodily resurrection not only in the various pagan customs he has described but also in the Prayer Book's rite itself, which invokes (with some changes) Job's words (19. 25–27): 'I know that my Redeemer liveth, and that I shall rise out of the earth in the last day, and shall be covered again with my skinne, and shall see God in my fleshe yea, and I my self shall behold him, not with other, but with these same eyes.' Browne's insistence that we have no way of understanding what our resurrected state will be (possibly only the unindividuated soul will rise) suggests that perhaps even Christian rites such as those in the Common Prayer Book place too much emphasis on the body, on an immortality modelled on earthly life. His scepticism about whether our individual personalities will be preserved at the resurrection critically reflects on the 'increased personalization' evident in the development of funeral art forms from the thirteenth to the seventeenth centuries. As the historian Philippe Aries has shown, monumental tombs, funeral inscriptions, and wall plaques from this period all indicate a new and increasing 'desire to render the burial place individual' and to preserve identity.[33]

[31] Post notes that Browne's rejection of monuments in the final chapter seems consonant with a Puritan dislike of icons (p. 132).
[32] Cf. Canne's attack on the 'superstitious' practice in the Church of England of 'laying the dead in the grave, viz East and West, that he may rise with his face to the East' (pp. 102–03). Gittings distinguishes the traditional Anglican attention to the dead body, seen as the temple of the spirit, from the extreme Puritan 'insistence on the simple disposal of the corpse, which they viewed with such disgust' (pp. 46–47).
[33] Philippe Aries, *Western Attitudes toward Death: From the Middle Ages to the Present*, trans. Patricia M. Ranum (Baltimore and London, 1974), pp. 47–50.

Certainly, Browne's ironic perspective on all the attention to the body evident in human burial customs marks his distance from Laud,[34] with his extraordinary emphasis on the body. Laud insisted on the necessity of physical ceremonies as 'external', material 'helps' to men while they 'live in the body', and even suggested in a speech to the Star Chamber (1636) that 'a greater Reverence (no doubt) is due to the Body, then to the Word of our Lord'.[35] Browne shows the human dependence on and attachment to the body, but he finally insists on the limits of the body ('Circles and right lines limit and close all bodies, and the mortall right-lined circle must conclude and shut up all' (p. 166)), and on the limits of bodily ceremonies.

We thus see in *Urn Buriall* radically contradictory perspectives which do not admit of any firm or easy resolution. There is a kind of indeterminacy in this text but it is historically and culturally specific. It both defends ceremony as natural, necessary, and universal, and exposes ceremony as vain, carnal, and ineffective. The balance shifts from the first chapters, with their recognition of the reason behind customs, to the final two chapters, with their insistence on the irrationality of customs; from a Laudian emphasis on continuity and universality in human experience, to a Puritan sense of firm divisions between Christian and pagan, between the few who will be saved and those multitudes 'without hope'. Yet it is not a matter of a simple progression.[36] If the anti-ceremonial implications of the final chapter drastically compromise the defence of ceremony which animates so much of the work, so also the rather grim, inflexible conclusions of that last chapter seem inadequate to the generosity of spirit and flexibility which characterize Browne's approach to human experience throughout most of the text. Moreover, if the Christian God only promises resurrection of the soul, not the body, then (Browne's protests to the contrary) Christianity itself fails to match the human desire for continued bodily life.

Finally, we see in Browne, for all his love of ceremony, the secularization of ceremony that, as Keith Thomas has argued, was a major consequence of the Protestant Reformation.[37] Rejecting the older belief that ceremony has a

[34] Browne's relation to Laud has been the concern of two recent essays on *Religio Medici*. Michael Wilding sees Browne as anti-sectarian, a polemically conservative, even reactionary supporter of law and order (*'Religio Medici* in the English Revolution', in *Dragons Teeth: Literature in the English Revolution* (Oxford, 1987), Chapter 4). While Wilding's argument is provocative, he oversimplifies Browne's 'position'. A more balanced assessment is provided by Jonathan F. S. Post, 'Browne's Revisions of *Religio Medici*', *SEL*, 25 (1985), 145–63. Post sees a complex, basically moderate position and places Browne at a distance from Laud's extremism. On Browne's 'Anglicanism' in *Religio Medici* in the context of religious controversy, see also Raymond B. Waddington, 'The Two Tables in *Religio Medici*' in *Approaches to Sir Thomas Browne: The Ann Arbor Tercentenary Lectures and Essays*, edited by C. A. Patrides (Columbia, 1982), pp. 81–99.
[35] William Laud, *The History of the Troubles and Tryal of ... William Laud*, edited by Henry Wharton (London, 1695), p. 224; and *A Speech Delivered in the Starr-Chamber, on Wednesday, the XIVth of Iune, MDCXXXVII. At the Censure of Iohn Bastwick, Henry Burton, and William Prinn ...* (London, 1637), p. 47.
[36] I diverge here from Walter R. Davis, '*Urne Buriall*: A Descent into the Underworld', *SLitI*, 10 (1977), 73–87, and Leonard Nathanson, *The Strategy of Truth* (Chicago, 1967), pp. 191–94, who emphasize progression and see Christian Faith as the culmination of Browne's discourse.
[37] Keith Thomas, *Religion and the Decline of Magic* (New York, 1971), Chapter 3. Gittings also discusses the increasing secularization of post-Reformation funeral rituals (pp. 12, 42, 56–57, 221, 224).

material efficacy, Protestantism redefined legitimate ceremony as a 'commemorative rite' not a magical one. The extreme Puritan rejection of religious ceremony in the period of the English Civil War secularized ceremony much further than Calvin and Luther had envisaged, restricting rites to a civil arena. This cultural process of the secularization of ceremony is evident in Browne's tendency to approve of those customs which have practical effects, for example, pouring oil upon the pyre, which facilitates the burning, or the custom of burying coins or medals, which helps 'posterity' make 'historicall discoveries' (p. 160). Once ceremony is secularized, its role is circumscribed. Although Browne suggests that ceremony is necessary to us (and thus should not be prohibited), and although he is indisputably Anglican in mentality and commitment, he drastically restricts the role and importance of ceremony. Burial rites symbolize and represent the universal desire for immortality, but whether Christian or pagan, they are powerless to effect that desire. Ceremony is a legitimate 'human invention', but it is a human invention none the less, with no supernatural, magical power to effect any transcendence of the physical. As human art, ceremony can only, with more or less elegance, *express* human desire.

'In those days there was no king in Israel':
Milton's Politics and Biblical Narrative

MARY ANN RADZINOWICZ

Cornell University, Ithaca, New York

When Milton set out a programme to reform English culture in *The Reason of Church Government*, one goal was 'the procurement of wise and artfull recitations sweetned with eloquent and gracefull inticements to the love and practice of justice . . . instructing and bettering the Nation at all opportunities' (*Complete Prose*, I, 819–20).[1] Hence he listed in the Trinity Manuscript fifty-three Old Testament stories fit for the project. Twenty-two of the fifty-three biblical plots he listed concern the period of the first eight books of the Old Testament, when 'there was no king in Israel'. They comprise nine tales from Genesis, one from Exodus, four from Numbers, two from Joshua, six from Judges, and one from Ruth. The pastoral from Ruth concludes the premonarchic stage of scriptural history, a stage that apparently had for the young Milton the attraction of a clear alternative. In those days *either* justice spoke to 'the bettering of the nation', *or* its silencing indicated kingship, whether in Israel or England.

The biblical narratives in the Trinity Manuscript are part of a political programme just as much as notebook entries of used and unused ideas.[2] *Pace* William Riley Parker, it is not true that Milton never thought of them again after jotting them down haphazardly from an open Bible. By the time he wrote *The Reason of Church Government*, many had a past in Milton's political prose, all had a future. In polemic he treats Scripture as a series of practical case histories rather than the clear instructions of God and does the best he can to read Scripture accurately. The theological examination of the Bible in *De Doctrina Christiana* between the 1640s and his death freed him to think

---

[1] All references to Milton's prose are given in the text from *The Complete Prose Works of John Milton*, general editor, Don M. Wolfe, 8 vols (New Haven, 1953–82). All references to Milton's poetry are to *The Works of John Milton*, general editor, Frank Allen Patterson, 18 vols (New York, 1938). Also consulted: *An Index to the Columbia Edition of the Works of John Milton*, compiled by Frank Allen Patterson assisted by French Rowe Fogle, 2 vols (New York, 1940).

[2] William Riley Parker writes: 'Milton picked up a Bible, leafed through it, and jotted down ideas as they were suggested to him. Most of these notes he probably never thought of after the moment. . . . He skipped Leviticus as unfruitful', *Milton: A Biography*, 2 vols (Oxford, 1968) I, 191. James Pequigney writes: 'Milton contemplated no tragedies on classical, and Shakespeare wrote none on scriptural themes. Considerations besides religious and patriotic ones probably determined Milton's choices. Italian critics, among them Castelvetro and Tasso, argued the preferability in epic and tragic poems of historically true over entirely feigned fables. Milton would seemingly concur and Shakespeare would not', *A Milton Encyclopedia*, general editor, W. B. Hunter, 8 vols (Lewisburg, Pennsylvania, 1980) VIII, 76. Richard Helgerson writes: 'the very thoroughness of his search, moving book by book through the Bible and century by century through British history, reveals the lack of any specific aim', *Self-Crowned Laureates: Spenser, Jonson, Milton and the Literary System* (Berkeley, California, 1983), p. 248.

about it politically elsewhere.[3] The liberty of prophesying is Milton's paradigm for political liberty. Furthermore, although I will not reargue the point here,[4] his political treatment of premonarchic biblical history itself inscribes a history that one might characterize as an irregular but consistent movement away from identifying England as God's chosen agent of the Millennium towards urging human responsibility for justice everywhere, in England, Canaan, Egypt, or Israel. Here I shall argue first that Milton's chosen premonarchic plots serve not a theoretic but a republican politics, and second that he saw them to be open to political interpretation because of the two distinct strands of narrative history and theological redaction constant in them.

Milton's selections cover several political stages in pre-monarchic Israel: nomadic patriarchy up to and after the Flood, tribal agrarianism on alien soil, Egyptian slavery, exodus under religious leadership, the conquest of Canaan, tribal confederacy, and finally tribal union in a settled land. He read the total sweep of pre-monarchic history in the Hebrew Bible as a demonstration of personal and institutional responses to secure political and religious freedom. His subjection of narrative history to reasoned judgement, pieced together across the fabric of his poetry and prose, constitutes an education in politics. To search premonarchic history with Milton is not to find a God-given blueprint, the one true way of organizing a society. For Milton the politics derived from the Bible is the discovery of human freedom to act to secure human freedom. A poet seeking to emphasize theocracy might privilege prophecy over Biblical history; emphasizing the human management of government, Milton turns to narrative. Hence my title preserves the duplicitous and ironic moral it has in the Bible. The last words of Judges: 'In those days there was no king in Israel: every man did that which was right in his own eyes', signify a dichotomous detestation of primitive disorder, a theological preference for a time when God was king in Israel but a political preference for a time when Israel can claim a native culture unified under an orderly monarchy. Milton, who managed to politicize even versification when he called his an 'ancient liberty recover'd to Heroic Poem from the ... modern bondage of Rimeing',[5] disputed the redactor's double moral, re-examining the Bible to relieve modern bondage. My particular instances are Abraham, Samson, and Joshua.

---

[3] See Maurice Kelley's Introduction to *The Christian Doctrine* in *The Complete Prose Works of John Milton* for an account of the stages of its composition. *C.P.*, VI, 15–28.

[4] Generally useful in tracing the evolution are the following: Christopher Hill, *Milton and the English Revolution* (New York, 1977); Michael Fixler, *Milton and the Kingdoms of God* (London, 1964); Mary Ann Radzinowicz, *Towards Samson Agonistes: The Growth of Milton's Mind* (Princeton, 1978), and 'The Politics of *Paradise Lost*', in *Politics of Discourse: The Literature and History of Seventeenth-Century England*, edited by Kevin Sharpe and Steven N. Zwicker (Berkeley, California, 1987), pp. 204–29; Keith Staveley, *Puritan Legacies: Paradise Lost and the New England Tradition, 1630–1890* (Ithaca, New York, 1987) and the unpublished article, 'The World Was All Before them: Milton and the Rising Glory of America'.

[5] See Staveley, 'The World Was All Before them: Milton and the Rising Glory of America', p. 10.

I have chosen Abraham to represent the patriarchal period, but the antediluvian patriarchs could quite as well be represented by Noah. Milton's prose handling of the Noah narrative is no less nor differently political than that of the Abraham cycle, as one would have predicted from the emphasis in *Paradise Lost* on Noah's detestation of imperialism 'much waste | Subduing Nations', (XI. 791–92) and hence his arguments for 'paths ... full of peace', as well as his indifference to 'custom, and a World | Offended' (XI. 810–11). In Genesis, after the landing on Ararat Jehovah gave to Noah one general law: 'Whoso sheddeth man's blood, by man shall his blood be shed' (Genesis 9.6). Milton called this text in *Eikonoklastes* (*C.P.*, III, 586) 'The first express Law of God giv'n to mankind', 'a Law in general to all the Sons of men', 'a most ancient and universal law'. He said the law showed that the patriarchs in the days when there were no kings in Israel devised their own governments, bound only by that rule of charity. He interpreted '*Noah* and the Patriarkes before the Law' as a political 'patterne of that Christian prudence, and liberty which holy men by right assum'd of old' (*Tetrachordon*, *C.P.*, II, 637–38). Contemporary criticism so little recontextualizes this material politically, however, that its focus in the scene is resolutely on Adam's tears. Likewise, I have chosen Joshua and Samson to represent the stages of military conquest of Canaan and of tribal confederacy, although Milton's Trinity Manuscript list offers alternative choices just as politically useful to him through his œuvre.

From the Abraham cycle in Genesis, Milton listed the topic, 'Abram in Aegypt'. (The title refers to one of the two wife-sister stories in Genesis 12 and 20 involving Abraham. The first features Pharoah in Egypt; the second, Abimelech in Philistia. A repetition of the two stories, featuring Isaac, Rebecca, and Abimelech, occurs in Genesis 26.) Milton quite fully sketched a plan for another plot, 'Abram from Morea, or Isack redeemd'. That sketch adds to the Genesis story (i) Sarah's premonition, 'sorrow and *per*plexity accompanied with frightfull dreams', (ii) an account of her by someone 'passing through the mount in the time that Abram was in the midwork ... hence [her] lamentations, fears, wonders', (iii) a scene showing Abraham's people 'discoursing ... divers ways, bewayling the fate of so noble a man faln from his reputation, either through divin justice, or su*per*stition or coveting to doe some notable act through zeal', and (iv) Abraham's return 'with a great Train of Melchizedec ... conduct[ing him] ... home with joy' (*C.P.*, VIII, 557–58).

Genesis, almost unequivocally, stresses obedience to God: three times a voice calls and Abraham answers obediently, he assures Isaac that God will provide a lamb, the story is twice given the moral: obedience pays. First, the place of sacrifice is renamed Jehovahjireh (the Lord will provide); second, the angel promises 'thy seed shall possess the gate of his enemies'. Under that unequivocal theology, however, is an equivocal human politics. Abraham's building an altar in a land not his is tantamount to planting a

territorial flag. Seventeenth-century maps enshrine the territoriality sig-
nified by altar-building; emblems of altars are regularly drawn on them to
mark boundaries.[6] Similarly, Joshua tells the story of an altar built 'not for
burnt offering, nor for sacrifice: But that it may be a witness between us, and
you, and our generations after us ... that your children may not say to our
children in time to come, Ye have no part in the Lord' (Joshua 22. 26–27).
The building of that altar is not a religious act of piety but a political act of
alliance. Likewise the sacrifice of a son commonly tropes territorial war; and
the promised possession of the gate of the enemy tropes land conquest.

In contrast, Milton openly stresses the equivocality of the story in his
version. In his account Abraham's people variously explain the event, even
as misplaced zeal or superstition; Sarah's love of her son is as sacred as
Abraham's love of his God; neither God nor angel speaks, and likewise
suppressed is the scriptural prologue announcing a Job-like temptation as
well as the epilogue congratulating Abraham. The Genesis version uses
Abraham's increasing isolation to trope an inwardness of meaning and
deflect its latent political force, whereas Milton's version throngs the final
scene with a train of friends. He uses Melchizedec in the Abram sketch to
represent the power of political alliance and not the institution of clergy, as
he is used in the Book of Hebrews. In his polemical prose Milton frequently
draws on Melchizedec's alliance with Abraham to argue against a paid
clergy and the system of tithes. His detestation of both involves his equation
of the liberty of prophesying with individual political liberty; it also hints at a
strong class hostility to hierarchy. The sketch as Milton developed its
ambiguities exemplifies his confident distinction between narrative history
and the editorial moralizing of the textual redactors.

Milton takes a similar interpretive liberty with the Samson story in *Samson
Agonistes*. He brings Dalila on in an extra-biblical scene to argue the claims of
love or personal life; he gives Siloa's Dread no direct role; and he similarly
offers multiple contradictory explanations of the mimesis. The plan for
Abraham suggested 'bewayling the fate of ... a man faln ... either through
divin justice, or su*per*stition or coveting to doe some notable act through
zeal'. While Samson exonerates the Almighty from destining his fall by
inculpating his own pride (374–75), the Chorus allies him with others who
have unsuccessfully attempted to free their nation, left

> to the hostile sword
> Of Heathen and prophane, thir carkasses
> To dogs and fowls a prey, or else captiv'd;
> Or to the unjust tribunals, under change of times,
> And condemnation of the ingrateful multitude.
>
> (l. 692)

Their words are equally apposite to premonarchic Israel and Restoration
England. Dalila places worship of Dagon and the 'holy One of Israel' on the

---

[6] I am grateful to Kenneth Knoespel of Georgia Institute of Technology for confirming this point.

same footing, to imply that Samson was superstitious to think that 'what [he] motion'd was of God' (l. 222). The moral of these mixed readings together with Samson's silence between the pillars is the freedom of each reader to make Scripture hang together for himself; that freedom grounds a political hope, the 'new acquist of true experience'. Milton read both Abraham and Samson as historically usable and transferable figures.

In aiming at a face value reading of scriptural history, Milton was not naïvely unaware of the fictionality of much scriptural history. Modern anthropologists express, of course, doubts about the historicity of the so-called history that had occurred to Milton himself. Thus Edmund Leach writes 'King David and King Solomon are no more likely to be historical than are King Agamemnon and King Menelaus'. He adds 'The distinction between myth and history is not necessarily clear cut. It need not be inconsistent to affirm that an historical record has mythical characteristics and functions'.[7] That is, if myth is not history, history may be made myth. Milton thought along similar lines with a similar balance of belief and doubt, when he wrote 'It is true that the other books, particularly the historical ones, cannot be certainly ascribed to a particular date or author, and also that the chronological accuracy of their narrative often seems suspect. Few or none, however, have called in doubt their doctrinal part' (*C.P.*, VI, 588–89).

The Abraham cycle thematizes the establishment of a durable culture as part of a premonarchic history running from Genesis through Judges. That long narrative and each of its segments is throughout given a dichotomous explanation: on the one hand, Israel's holding of land upon which to ground its culture is permanent, the result of inheritance, purchases, treaties, and freely renewed divine promises; and on the other hand, Israel's landholding is contingent, the reflection of its fluctuating worthiness.[8] Milton's tragic sketches also offer dichotomous explanations, turning on human action, after which, if at all, comes God's accord. His sketch for a Phineas play ends with his repeated moral: 'after all arguments drivn home then the word of the lord may be brought acquitting and approving phineas' (*C.P.*, VIII, 560). Similarly, Milton's assignment of multiple motives and purposes to the Queen in the Herod sketch, the even-handedness of his argument in the Lot sketch 'where is disputed of incredulity of divine judgements and such like matter', his weighing of human motives in the Tamar sketch so that she is 'excus'd in what she attempted', and his humanity in allowing that 'Jeroboam beeing bad himself shod so greive for his son that was good', all

---

[7] Edmund Leach, *Genesis as Myth and Other Essays* (London, 1969), p. 114.
[8] See Joel Rosenberg, *King and Kin: Political Allegory in the Hebrew Bible* (Bloomington, Indiana, 1986) pp. 88–89. From the anthropological point of view, the implications of the first explanation would be exogamous: marriages and cultic exchanges with foreigners could be held to promote the security of Israel. The implications of the second would be endogamous: the racial and sexual purity or exclusivity of the chosen people could be held to be symbolic of their religious answerability to God's instructions.

exemplify liberty of interpretation used to prove the justice of public decisions taken as Israel becomes a settled culture.

The story 'Abram in Aegypt' on Milton's list incorporates an assessment of political expediency in a test of cultural permanency. Twice Abraham's chance of fathering an heir and keeping his people together is about to vanish; hence he represents his wife, 'a fair woman to look upon', first to Pharoah, then to Abimelech as his sister. If she is known to be his wife, he will be killed to make her accessible; to add a sister to one's harem, murder is unnecessary. Each time his deceit is exposed, but he is sent on his way loaded with gifts by the sovereign host. While Edmund Leach accepts Abraham's explanation given not to Pharoah but to Abimelech that Sarah was his half-sister, both children of Terah by separate unspecified mothers, and interprets both wife-sister stories as myths approving Hebrew endogamy as against Egyptian exogamy, Milton relying on Abraham's earlier silence judges him in moral terms a dangerous liar 'whose story [to Abimelech] about Sarah being his sister, though it was intended only to save his own life, was, as he might have learned from his previous experience [with Pharoah] in Egypt, likely to lead men who did not know the truth into sin and unlawful desire' (C.P., vi, 760–61).[9]

In each of the two stories Abraham's politic accommodation secures Israel; the Bible redactor, however, tells each as a narrative of divine help: 'the Lord plagued Pharoah and his house with great plagues because of Sarai'; 'The Lord had fast closed up all the wombs of the house of Abimelech, because of Sarah Abraham's wife' (Genesis 12.17, 20.18). Not at all reluctant to take up biblical narratives involving politically manipulated sexuality, Milton reads each of the stories of Abraham's wife-sister deception historically as well as morally. Setting forth 'the duties of magistrate and people TOWARDS NEIGHBORING STATES [in] peace or war', he uses Abraham's treaty with Abimelech, after Sarah's release, to instance lawful 'treaties with the wicked' 'to strengthen the existing peace, or ... friendship between neighboring states' (C.P., vi, 801).

My title comes not from the patriarchal period, however, represented here by Abraham, but from the period of Judges or tribal confederation. Samson's ambiguous epitaph is written in Judges 16.30: 'The dead which he slew at his death were more than they which he slew in his life.' The next chapter comments 'In those days there was no king in Israel, but every man did that which was right in his own eyes'. Before serving as the last word in Judges and the verdict upon that historical period, the verse also introduces the story of Micah and the story of the Levite's concubine in Gibeah, one Milton listed as 'Comozontes or the Benjaminits ... or the Rioters'. In Scripture a Levite and his father-in-law, lest riotous 'sons of Belial' sodomize

---

[9] Leach, p. 48.

a houseguest, give them the Levite's wife. She is raped, murdered, dismembered, and parts of her corpse sent around to rouse tribal vengeance. The horrifying story makes the repeated comment in Judges seem an unequivocal condemnation: when there were neither kings nor the constant kingship of God to order Israel, the unruly people did damnable things.[10] Milton the radical republican declines that reading, for the reign even of good king David brought its own atrocities (he planned plays on David's pollution of Bathsheba, and Amnon's rape of Tamar). In those days there was a king in Israel, and what the monarch did was not right in Milton's eyes. Furthermore, he interprets the biblical narratives of the period of Judges as of Genesis, so that political decisions in that period occur where political decisions are always made, among men and not in the courts of heaven. To a modern reader Milton is right to represent political decisions, whether made in the days when there were no kings in Israel or in his own day, as human choices and not divine commands. Nevertheless, when Milton makes polemical application of some events in scriptural history to his own times, the modern reader may well misdoubt his conclusion. He politicized the Comozantes story, for example, in *A Defence of the People of England* in 1651 stressing popular consent of 'all Israel' to a war of vengeance:

What teachings of law or religion ever instructed men to consider their own ease and the saving of money or blood or life more important than meeting the enemy? . . . All Israel saw that without much shedding of blood she could not avenge the outrage and murder of the Levite's wife; did they think that for this reason they must hold their peace, avoid civil war however fierce, or allow the death of a single poor woman to go unpunished?

(*C.P.*, IV, 431)

We read naïvely if we seek a simple endorsement of our own views, pacific or otherwise, in his work. But we read blindly if we doubt that biblical history was evidence to him in discovering his own politics or that he took the liberty to interpret scripture as instrumental to political freedom.

I turn now to the political stage of military consolidation in Joshua for my final instances. Referring selectively but about fifty times in his œuvre to Joshua, Milton confines himself to three main actions: Joshua's personal leadership and the two episodes in the conquest of Canaan listed in the Trinity Manuscript as 'Achan' and 'Josuah in Gibeon' (*C.P.*, VIII, 555). His actual use overrides two presumptive uses. It might be presumed that Milton read Joshua as typology; it has been presumed that he derived from it an ideology of holy war. The Book of Hebrews found two types of the faithful in Joshua: 'By faith the walls of Jericho fell down after they had been encircled for seven days. By faith Rahab the harlot did not perish with those who were disobedient, because she had given friendly welcome to the spies'.

[10] For reflections on the story and on Milton's interest in it see Phyllis Trible, *Texts of Terror: Literary-Feminist Readings of Biblical Narratives* (Philadelphia, 1984), p. 84; Louise Simons, '"An Immortality Rather than a Life": Milton and the Concubine of *Judges* 19–21', forthcoming, p. 7; Cedric C. Brown, *John Milton's Aristocratic Entertainments* (Cambridge, 1985), p. 67.

Nowhere in Milton's œuvre do the walls of Jericho fall down; Rahab makes her rare appearances as often in matrimonial as in typological contexts. Only in *Paradise Lost* does he interpret Joshua as the type in whom Moses's unfulfilment shaded into Jesus's fulfilment, leading his people into the promised land (xii. 307–14). Since Milton locates the promised land not in time but beyond it, however, Old Testament heroes of faith by his typology are instructive precedents to modern men, not just foreshadowers of Christ's offer of salvation in the New Testament. To defer 'fulfilment' to a future time is to enable the present and the past to be seen as politically continuous. Hence, outside *Paradise Lost*, Milton is interested in Joshua as leader not type. Regina Schwartz argues that 'the typological language of "fulfilment," of shadows and truth, is alien to Hebraic — and postmodern — understandings of textuality'.[11] I would add that notwithstanding his endorsement of typology as one biblical hermeneutic in *De doctrina Christiana* Chapter 30, Milton's acknowledgement of correlative typology and the deferral of fulfilment to the end of time in effect reinstated the Old Testament as historical precedent for the seventeenth century, not in the form of God's over-ruling human choice but in the form of educative instancing.

The other presumption is that Milton values Joshua for articulating an ideology of holy war. Michael Lieb, in *Poetics of the Holy*, highlights Joshua's role as God's conqueror of the Promised Land.[12] Lieb's reading of Joshua as a conquest account of holy war is indisputable, but to that account Milton's references are virtually non-existent. Lieb cites four verses as definitive of the ideology of holy war; Milton alludes to none of them. A view of war as unholy inspires his first reference to Joshua. Satan, in *In quintum Novembris*, disguised as Saint Francis stands by the Pope's sleeping head and urges him to scotch England's king lest he 'trample with godless feet your holy neck' (l. 111; Columbia *Works*, I, part 1, 244). Joshua said 'unto the captains of the men of war.... Put your feet upon the necks of these kings ... for thus shall the Lord do to all your enemies' (10. 24–25). Milton turned Joshua's solemn ritual into melodramatic provocation.

The three subjects in Milton's actual, not presumptive, interest — Joshua as historical leader and the tragedies of Achan and the five kings of Gibeon — share striking thematic material. In each God either permits or rejects human exceptions to or extensions of his revealed will, as if '[God] made our Laws to bind us, not himself... For with his own Laws he can best dispence' (300–14). In each case, Joshua's emphasis jars with Milton's moral and political sense. Unlike John Donne, who once wrote 'O God, if thou hadst not said it, I would not have believed it', Milton thought '[God] hath taught us to love and to extoll his Lawes, not onely as they are his, but as they are just and good to every wise and sober understanding' (*C.P.*, ii, 297–98).

---

[11] In 'Joseph's Bones and the Resurrection of the Text: Remembering in the Bible', *PMLA* 103 (1988), 114–24.
[12] In *Poetics of the Holy: A Reading of 'Paradise Lost'* (Chapel Hill, 1981).

I take it that means 'O God, if it weren't good and rational to my best understanding, it would not have been you that said it'. Accordingly he handles the Achan and Gibeon stories so as to show that the politics of Exodus promise the people 'no ultimate struggle but a long series of decisions, backslidings and reforms'.[13]

Milton's political reading of Joshua's leadership begins with him as disciple to Moses. In *Areopagitica* Milton notes how Joshua, on the report that Eldad and Medad were prophesying, said to Moses 'My Lord Moses, forbid them', and was answered 'Enviest thou for my sake? Would God that all the Lord's people were prophets, and that the Lord would put his spirit upon them'. Milton twice equates Joshua's 'testy mood of prohibiting' with 'licencing' to rebuke the suppressors. In the *First Defence*, he finds Joshua no precedent for kingship: 'the Reubenites and Gadites promise to obey Joshua: "According as we hearkened unto Moses in all things . . . so but God be with thee as he was with Moses"' states 'a qualification', and implies a contract not a divine appointment of a king (*C.P.*, IV, 346). Milton adds 'some . . . deny that their fathers should have recognized any king but God, though such a king was given to punish them. With those teachers I cast my vote' (*C.P.*, IV, 366). Similarly, he reads God's commission to Joshua, 'go over this Jordan, thou and all this people, unto the land which I do give to them', not as millennial fulfilment but as the initiation of years of human struggle, during which the people repeatedly remember past comfort and would choose a captain to lead them back to Egypt. And he reads Joshua's last words in a political light. He glosses 'And if it seem evil unto you to serve the Lord, choose this day whom ye will serve; whether the gods which your fathers served that were on the other side of the flood, or the gods of the Amorites, in whose land we dwell; but as for me and my house, we will serve the Lord' (24.15) as showing 'Thus magistrates should protect religion, not enforce it' (*C.P.*, VI, 797). Milton's Joshua has limitations; even as he more or less succeeds in his mission, he is subjected to a political education. Milton makes no distinction between Joshua's sobering political history and that of England, seeing that 'pharaonic oppression, deliverance, Sinai and Canaan are still with' his seventeenth-century countrymen.[14]

Milton likewise derives a political moral from the tragic and equivocal story of Achan set into the pattern of current struggles of his own day. In *A Letter to a Friend, concerning the ruptures of the Commonwealth*, dated 20 October 1659, for example, he (like Cromwell before him) warns the leaders of the army against planning secret coups by alluding to Joshua's discovery that the defeat at Ai was due to the transgression of Jehovah's covenant by Achan, who hid part of the Jericho spoils, knowing them anathema to take. In a 'Declaration for a Solemn Fast' by Cromwell on 14 March 1656, Cromwell had asked the people 'to discover that Achan which had so long

---

[13] Michael Walzer, *Exodus and Revolution* (New York, 1985), p. 148.
[14] Walzer, p. 149.

obstructed the settlement of these distracted nations'. In *Healing Questions*, Vane replying implied that Cromwell himself was Achan. Milton in a further application turned the allusion against Lambert's *coup d'état* of 13 October, as motivated by the 'close ambition' of certain officers.[15] In Scripture, after an investigation, Achan confesses; he, all his sons and daughters, and his asses and sheep are stoned, burned, and disgracefully buried under a great heap of stones. Joshua then takes and utterly razes Ai. Having hanged its king on a tree until eventide and buried his body under a heap of stones, Joshua builds an altar to the Lord before which he recites the whole law of Moses. The terrible landscape with its hanging tree and disgracing cairns compromises the altar-building as a religious act to expose its force as a territorial claim.

The mass execution of Achan and his family opens a gap between religious and moral codes, a gap that widens in the subsequent tale of the five kings against Gibeon. The tale is one of a sequence interrogating the allowable limits of human disobedience to God's laws and the justice of his laws and penalties. It follows the destruction of Jericho out of which Rahab and her kindred were saved by a deviation from God's command: 'And ye shall dispossess the inhabitants of the land and dwell therein' (Numbers 33.53). With impunity Joshua's agent abandons the letter of God's command and perhaps its spirit, to favour a benefactress of Israel.[16] The Achan story reports a holocaust during the conquest of Canaan in accord with God's command. It leads to the parallel instance of the annihilation of five kings at Gibeon.

Responding to the moral gap that opens between divine and human justice and mercy in these episodes, Milton defends God's command not as it is God's but as it is consonant with human law. He reads the conquest of Canaan as literal and instructive history, but defends the stoning and burning of Achan's children as just. In *Christian Doctrine*, he writes:

It is not only a constant principle of divine justice but also a very ancient law among all races and religions, that when a man has committed sacrilege ... not only he but also the whole of his posterity becomes an anathema and a sin-offering. This was so ... in the punishment of Achan, Josh. vii. 24, 25. When Jericho was demolished, the children paid for the sins of their fathers, and even the cattle were given up to slaughter along with their masters.... Indeed, sometimes a whole nation is punished for the sin of one citizen, Josh. vii.... This feature of divine justice, the insistence upon propitiatory sacrifices for sin, was well known among other nations, and never thought to be unfair ... Again, a man convicted of high treason, which is only an offence against another man, forfeits not only his own estate and civil rights but also those of all his family, and lawyers have decided upon the same sentence in other cases of a similar kind.

(*C.P.*, vi, 385)

[15] *C.P.*, viii, Introduction to *A Letter to a Friend*.
[16] See Meir Sternberg, *The Poetics of Biblical Narrative: Ideological Literature and the Drama of Reading* (Bloomington, Indiana, 1987), p. 498.

Although God permitted Rahab and her family to be made exceptions to general destruction for 'with his own laws he can best dispence', in *Christian Doctrine* Milton uses the Achan affair to show that divine anathema is reasonable to men.

What conclusions are to be drawn from Milton's selectivity and emphasis in interpreting Joshua and premonarchic history? First, he adopts a face-value historical reading that consistently finds human beings answerable for human actions. Secondly, very much aware of his own historical moment, he bends the face-value reading of the biblical history towards the history he himself wishes to live through. He uses historical evidence as a polemicist, as in invoking Achan against military profiteering. An ideological resort to history, far from unique to Milton, gives early biblical history another pattern than the theocentric. Milton knows that by the revolution of time he lives in an era entirely different from Joshua's, and yet in asserting the normative value in episodes from Joshua, he treats history as composed of segments of usable truth capable of application throughout time. If those truths are not learned, human beings are doomed in some sense to repeat that history. Thirdly, scripture shows him that, if not a nation, a chosen individual may be 'Improv'd by tract of time' (*PL*, v, 498). For Milton, Joshua makes a paideutic journey from smallness of mind and envy to serenity in death, freely collaborating in Israel's epic. Joshua sums up his heroic life: 'I have given you a land for which you did not labour, and cities which ye built not and ye dwell in them; of the vineyards and oliveyards which ye planted not do ye eat' (24.13). Milton echoingly sums up the tragedy of Commonwealth England:

For *Britain* . . . as it is a land fruitful enough of men stout and courageous in warr, so is it naturallie not over fertil of men able to govern justlie and prudently in peace . . . For the sunn, which wee want ripens witts as well as fruits; and as wine and oyle are imported to us from abroad, so much ripe understanding and many civil vertues bee imported into our minds from forren writings and examples of best ages.

(*C.P.*, v, 451)

If biblical stories are not usually taken to represent in Milton 'forren writings and examples of the best ages' from which to learn to 'govern justlie and prudently in peace' with 'ripe understanding and many civil vertues', that is owing not to Milton's failure to read scripture politically but owing to our own failure as Miltonists, over-enthusiastic about prophecy or theology, to read its histories at all.

'We are one mans all':
Jonson's *The Gipsies Metamorphosed*

MARTIN BUTLER

University of Leeds

One of the offshoots of the recent trend of revisionism in historical studies of the early Stuart court has been a revaluation of attitudes towards political panegyric, and towards the discomfort which modern readers tend to feel with the form. For a long time, the stock responses of modern commentators to political compliment in verse have fluctuated uneasily between two poles. They have tended to deplore the apparent artistic prostitution involved in panegyric, or they have sought to alleviate discomfort by prioritizing the formal dimensions of the genre, thus off-loading the political into the category of the aesthetic.[1] More recently, some scholars have been coming increasingly to argue that the modern discomfort with panegyric is misplaced: that self-presentation was endemic to the Renaissance profession of letters, that solicitation of a patron was bound up with notions of honour, obligation, and reward, and that factionalism amongst aristocratic patrons meant that patronage avenues often cut across the configurations of ideology and political loyalty.[2] And yet, as David Lindley has shrewdly urged in an important essay called 'Embarrassing Ben: the masques for Frances Howard', this discomfort is unlikely to go away entirely, for it has been fuelled by the unease that was occasionally expressed by court poets themselves.[3] Patronage might have been a desirable alternative to the compromises that had to be made in the literary market-place, but it was not free from painful dilemmas of its own. In order to maintain goodwill, the poet as client would have to make his social and political priorities acceptable to his patron, and thus he might well be involved in marginalizing any doubts he had about that which he was expected to praise. A poet might have

---

[1] For a comparable analysis, see David Norbrook, *Poetry and Politics in the English Renaissance* (London, 1984), pp. 1–6.

[2] See especially Linda Levy Peck, ' "For a King not to be Bountiful were a fault": Perspectives on court patronage in early Stuart England', *Journal of British Studies*, 25 (1986), 31–61; for an example based on Jonson, see R. C. Evans, *Ben Jonson and the Poetics of Patronage* (London, 1989).

[3] D. Lindley, 'Embarrassing Ben: the masques for Frances Howard', *English Literary Renaissance*, 16 (1986), 343–59, reprinted in *Renaissance Historicism*, edited by A. F. Kinney and D. S. Collins (Amherst, Massachusetts, 1987), pp. 248–64.

to accommodate his hesitations about his subject matter within the format of praise, or he might have to suppress them altogether. Either way, the writing of panegyric was likely to involve a complex private negotiation with plenty of scope for embarrassment for the poet and for difficulties of interpretation for the modern reader. Did the poet really mean all that he said?

As the poet who achieved the most spectacular success in translating his talents into rewards at the early Stuart court, Jonson is the figure for whom this problem is most acute. For all that Jonson constituted himself as the leading panegyrist of the Jacobean court, from time to time unmistakable signs of embarrassment about his role come to the surface of his panegyrics. For example, there is the constrained, conditional praise of the posture of godly militancy associated with the youthful Prince Henry in the 1610 *Barriers*; there is the ironical counter-masque, *For the Honour of Wales*, that he was forced to produce after *Pleasure Reconciled to Virtue* failed to please; and, most telling of all because done tacitly, there is the suppression from the folio texts of *Hymenaei* and *A Challenge at Tilt* of the occasions which they had been designed to celebrate, the two marriages of Frances Howard which, in the retrospective view from 1616 had come to seem profoundly embarrassing. Crucially, though, in the 1620s, as international crisis on the continent provoked an answering transformation in the political scene at home, the evidence of Jonson's discomfort with his court role becomes more substantial and more sustained. In a series of poems from this decade, Jonson gave vent to feelings that did not, on the whole, find their way into the masques that he was writing at the same time for James and Charles. 'An Epistle to a Friend to Persuade him to the Wars', 'An Epistle Answering to One that Asked to be Sealed of the Tribe of Ben', 'An Execration upon Vulcan', and 'A Speech According to Horace' all lashed out against the decline of honour, the pusillanimity of the nobility, the vices of the world of fashion, the popular enthusiasm for news, the flattery of great men, and even the empty glories of the court masque itself.[4] Jonson may not have been taking over wholesale the attitudes and satirical voices of the so-called Spenserian poets, whose response to the mood of the times was bitter and disillusioned, but there certainly seems to have been a gap between what he thought suitable for unpublished poems, and what in the masques was proper to be said. If in his earlier plays Jonson explored a stoical perspective on politics that sought to reconcile internal dissent with outward conformity,[5] in the late 1620s that balance seems personally to have become an exceptionally difficult one. David Norbrook has argued a powerful case for seeing Jonson's artistic problems at this time as bound up with his sense of being personally compromised, reluctant to praise the court unreservedly, yet unhappy about any more radical alternative.[6]

---

[4] There is a brief consideration of these poems by Sara Pearl in 'Sounding to present occasions: Jonson's masques of 1620–25' in *The Court Masque*, edited by David Lindley (Manchester, 1984), pp. 60–77.
[5] This formulation is taken from an unpublished lecture on *Sejanus* by Blair Worden.
[6] Norbrook, *Poetry and Politics in the English Renaissance*, pp. 224–26, 245–47.

Inevitably, the text on which these issues come to rest is *The Gipsies Metamorphosed*, the one Jonson masque commissioned specifically by the powerful and charismatic court favourite, Buckingham. In the summer of 1621 Buckingham was seeking to celebrate the acquisition of his new house in Rutland, Burley-on-the-Hill. Bought by a courtier with local roots but who spent most of his time in London, and refurbished at the then staggering cost of £28,000,[7] Burley was indeed built to envious show and violated most of the social and ethical norms enshrined in *To Penshurst*. If ever a commission could have embarrassed Jonson, this was the one, and indeed the text constructs Buckingham in a way that is teasingly problematic. In the masque, Buckingham and six close associates, including his brother John, Endymion Porter, and Viscount Feilding, disguise themselves as gipsies, tell the fortunes of the assembled company, and pick the pockets of a band of gullible yokels who turn up to have their hands read. The gipsies then depart in order to shed their clothes and tawny faces in readiness for their final reappearance as magnificent courtiers, and to cover their absence a ballad is sung about the cannibalistic feast given to the devil at Devil's Arse cavern in Derbyshire by the gipsies' founder Cock Lorel, the culmination of which is the devil's cataclysmic fart which gave the cavern its name. Both the vulgarity of the masque and its casting of Buckingham as the leader of a gang of shiftless and rapacious vagrants have troubled modern interpreters, and in the principal current discussion, by Dale B. J. Randall, the view is advanced that Jonson could not have meant what he said and that his masque was designed not to applaud Buckingham but covertly to discredit him. In Dale Randall's account the masque insinuates a disparaging view of the patron under cover of strategic ironies, and accommodates feelings of disrespect which are intense but otherwise inadmissible.[8]

The difficulties with this view of the masque are many and severe. All the external evidence about the masque's reception is against it, for Jonson was paid £100 by Buckingham in advance of the performance, was granted the reversion of the office of Master of the Revels shortly after, and was rumoured narrowly to have missed being knighted.[9] Plainly, if Jonson did build a subversive subtext into his masque, it did no damage to his career at Whitehall. Equally difficult to circumvent are the circumstances of performance of the masque. Presumably Buckingham had a say in determining the role he was to dance, and presumably there were rehearsals at which Buckingham could have objected to anything which he found untoward, especially as Jonson would have been on hand at Burley.[10] And again, if

---

[7] Roger Lockyer, *Buckingham* (London, 1981), p. 63.

[8] D. B. J. Randall, *Jonson's Gypsies Unmasked* (Durham, North Carolina, 1975).

[9] B. Jonson, *Works*, edited by C. H. Herford, P. Simpson, and E. Simpson, 11 vols (Oxford, 1925–52), I, 97, 237.

[10] I owe the point about rehearsals to Graham Parry. Jonson's presence at Burley (or at Belvoir) is demonstrated by the last-minute addition of the fortune for the Countess of Exeter, which he must have been there to write.

Jonson was seeking to criticize Buckingham by indirection, it is hard to see how or where such a message might be received in the Burley audience, given that this was a domestic celebration amongst family and kin (a problem all the more acute at the Belvoir performance a few days later, where the host was Buckingham's father-in-law, the Earl of Rutland: if Jonson insulted Buckingham, he must have insulted Rutland too).[11] On the other hand, Professor Randall's view does at least underline the fact that this is an unusually transgressive masque, in which polarities that on such occasions were normally kept separate (such as that between silent aristocratic masquer and speaking professional antimasquer) were here uniquely elided, and in which the poet was for once unusually unconcerned about disguising his complicity in the mechanics of courtly myth-making. Even as the masque praises Buckingham that praise is, if not subverted, at least rendered problematic.

In order to address some of these problems, I intend to look at the masque's circumstances of production: first at the context of its performance at Burley in August, and then at Jonson's revisions for the performance at court, probably a month later. The wider public context of the masque (beyond Buckingham's housewarming at Burley) was the parliament of 1621, in the summer recess of which the masque was performed.[12] The parliament had been summoned in response to a recent crisis in European politics, to the circumstances of which I shall return at the end of this paper. James was seeking parliamentary backing for new and changing foreign policy options, but since he still had unresolved diplomacy on foot when parliament met in January, foreign affairs were shelved and the first session was allowed to drift onto domestic grievances, in particular the critical matter of monopolies. Monopolies raised constitutional issues, as they were an aspect of the prerogative powers of the crown, but the skirmish over them in 1621 was given its excitement by the knowledge that it constituted an indirect attack in the direction of the favourite. Buckingham's cousin, Sir Giles Mompesson, and his brothers Sir Edward and Kit Villiers were implicated in two of the most notorious and obnoxious monopolies, respectively those for alehouses, and for gold and silver thread, and the attack on these patents contained an element of serious risk for Buckingham himself. Buckingham saved his skin by throwing in his hand with the cause of reform, in the anticipation that James would prevent the attack from proceeding beyond dispensable officers of state. In the Lords he fell on his knees before the king and pleaded that if any aspersion fell on him he should be censured accordingly; before the two houses, he affirmed his willingness to pursue the guilty, even if they should include his two brothers. Meanwhile, his client

---

[11] There is also the problem that the success and popularity of Jonson's masque is testified to by the large number of manuscripts of all or part of it which have survived.

[12] The most authoritative, though controversial, recent account is by Conrad Russell, *Parliaments and English Politics 1621–1629* (Oxford, 1979). See also R. Zaller, *The Parliament of 1621* (Berkeley, 1971).

Lionel Cranfield deflected the Commons' fire towards the referees for the patents, who had been responsible for certifying their legality, and before the attack could get far in Buckingham's direction another erstwhile client and the leading referee, Sir Francis Bacon, was abandoned to the parliamentary wolves. After Easter James warned Parliament not to pursue monopolies further than was necessary, and although Buckingham was the subject of sensational accusations in the Lords, his friends rallied around him. Subsequent proceedings in this session did him no further damage, and the letter-writer John Chamberlain commented 'thus we see that great men weakly opposed, thereby become the stronger, and it is no small comfort to him and his (as he professes) that he is found parlement proofe'.[13]

It has to be remembered that there had been no parliament since Buckingham's arrival in favour, and that this session therefore constituted the first real test of his ability to survive. Buckingham had faced this test and had emerged triumphant, and in August 1621 he had some reason to feel self-confident. Jonson was being asked to celebrate a favourite who had just demonstrated that his power was not merely temporary and who had been vindicated from his critics' aspersions by a profession of integrity and by the support of the king. *The Gipsies Metamorphosed* addresses these circumstances by presenting a fable in which the favourite's integrity is playfully questioned but, under the friendly eye of the king, is found to be above suspicion and intact.

In the speech of welcome which met James at Burley Buckingham was figured as the king's creature, so overwhelmed by his sense of obligation and gratitude as to be reduced to a silent statue. 'The Master is your creature; as [is] the place', said the porter at the king's entrance (B16),[14] and the ensuing masque dwelt on the power of the clientage relationship between Buckingham and his royal master to legitimize and transform Buckingham's ambition. In the opening section of the masque the favourite and his associates are introduced as if they were mercenary opportunists. They present themselves as amusing entertainers, but they have light fingers and no regard for law. After they have danced their entry, the Patrico (their presenter) points out to them the richness of the audience now assembled before them, and suggests they might make use of this chance to steal away with some rare jewel, or even with a great lady or two; the gipsies should set aside their usual trivial tricks and really benefit from an unprecedented opportunity for profit (B120–207). The third gipsy (Endymion Porter) responds by agreeing and urges the Captain (Buckingham) to do so in obedience to the gipsies' Magna Carta, which is 'To judge no viands

---

[13] J. Chamberlain, *Letters*, edited by N. E. McClure, 2 vols (Philadelphia, 1939), II, 374.
[14] All quotations are from the authoritative edition by W. W. Greg, *Jonson's Masque of Gypsies in the Burley, Belvoir and Windsor Versions* (London, 1952). A line number prefixed with a 'B' indicates a quotation from the Burley text, a 'W' a quotation from the Windsor text. I have silently standardized Greg's italic passages to roman (as this is merely a convention to distinguish between parts of the Burley version with differing textual authority).

wholsome that are bought' (B222). In this spirit Buckingham advances to
the king, but as he reads James's hand and affects surprise at discovering
from his mount of Jupiter that he is a monarch, the character of his address
changes. From trickster soliciting an unwary victim, he modulates into a
servant dutifully acknowledging his master, in effect anticipating that later
physical metamorphosis by dropping his gipsy cant in favour of a language
of obligation and loyal praise. Instead of this part of the masque affirming
Buckingham's mercenary character, the suggestions of opportunism are
whited out in an act of submission from a dutiful client to a royal patron, and
in the wake of this symbolic acknowledgement the ironies that continue to
attach themselves to Buckingham are licensed within the bond of trust
between king and favourite. Dale Randall points out that in the fortune-
telling sequence that follows there are many references to theft (of men's
hearts) and to the fact that the Villiers women are wedded to gipsies, but the
prevailing atmosphere is less satiric than playful and amorous. With the
patron-client relationship sanctified, the encounters between lesser
members of the clan can be witty rather than disturbing.

So there is reason to read this opening sequence as not so much subverting
Buckingham as questioning his motives in order that they may be royally
vindicated. Dale Randall's point, though, is that however entertaining the
gipsies are the role is boobytrapped against the performer, and that the
association of Buckingham with gipsydom is enough to create a current of
doubt about him which is not accommodated by the act of submission as
loyal servant to the king. And yet if Jonson's development of the role raises
this possibility, he chooses not to exploit it. Rather, the aspects of gipsy life
on which Jonson seizes work to ends precisely opposed to those that
Professor Randall argues. As the public relations man says in Caryl
Churchill's *Serious Money*, there is ugly greedy, and there is sexy greedy. In
Jonson's masque, it seems to me, it is incontestably the case that Buckingham and friends are sexy greedy. They may be tainted with vagrancy, but
they are neither brutal nor sordid; their gipsydom is sanitized so that they
have all the gipsy graces but few of the drawbacks.[15] The men are jolly and
vigorous, as the Patrico says,

> They are of the sorts
> That love the true sports
> Of King Ptolomaeus,
> Our great coryphaeus . . .
>
>   (B144)

and the women are Cleopatras who will readily be seduced by the fun
(indeed, the masque opens with the comical story of Justice Jug's daughter

---

[15] A useful standard of comparison is George Wither's remark in *Wither's Motto* (London, 1621) that he
would not applaud a great man just for having beautiful looks: 'If beautiful he be, what honor's that? | As
fayre as he, is many a Beggars brat' (sig. B2v). Wither plainly expects his reader to regard beggary as
inherently nasty and the comparison as insulting.

who ran away with the gipsies). Besides, though the gipsies are outlaws, their transgressions do not disrupt considerations of order. In his song at their first appearance the Jackman insistently reassures the audience that the gipsies are not wildly anarchic and that there is no need for the men to draw their swords:

> Draw but then your gloves we pray you,
> And sit still, we will not fray you,
> For though we be here at Burly,
> We'd be loath to make a hurly.
>
> (B116)

Plainly, these are not exactly figures to turn the world upside down; if these gipsies take liberties, they will restrict them to what will be acceptable to their audience. Furthermore, in the conduct of their performance the decorums of the event remain intact. Buckingham may transgress masquing norms by taking a speaking role, but the fortune-telling exactly observes the niceties of social and political protocol. The fortunes of king and prince are told first, then the members of the family are addressed in descending order of seniority. Only then are the ludicrously banal yokels introduced, at the furthest possible remove from the stately exchanges appropriate to the king and prince. This impression of astute control beneath the apparent disorder is confirmed by the respectful treatment of Buckingham himself. It is he who tells the king's fortune and leads the dances, but he takes part neither in telling the subsequent fortunes, nor in the pickpocketing. The event may seem to disrupt decorum, but Jonson's formal organization preserves the favourite's privilege and dutifully acknowledges his precedence. Nor, in running over the family fortunes, does Jonson admit any mention of the brothers Edward and Kit, who had narrowly escaped censure over the patent for gold and silver thread. If this masque is supposed to be disparaging Buckingham's family, these two names are conspicuous by their absence.

It seems to me that if the playful, teasing tone of this masque resembles anything else in the literature of the time, it is most like the letters that passed between Buckingham and King James. Buckingham, who was not above signing himself off with the words 'I kiss your warty hands', conducted a correspondence with James remarkable for the archness with which he cast himself in the role of loveable rogue, overtly conscious of his hold over the king and of the extravagance of the king's rewards. While his customary signing of himself as James's 'humble slave and servant and dog, Steenie' is amusing enough, there is a sharper edge to the ingratiating familiarity with which he addressed James as his 'Dear dad and gossip' which probably derives from the fact that in the morality drama the term 'dad' could be a mode of address from the figure of the Vice to the Devil on whom he was dependant.[16] Rather like the masque, Buckingham's letters drew James into

[16] For an example, see Shakespeare's *Twelfth Night*, iv.ii.131.

a game of coy roles which paraded the extravagantly intimate nature of their relationship and made dangerous fun out of it. Buckingham plainly had his own private uses for abasement and knew its value as a tool of power: playing at being a dog was one way of reinforcing the absoluteness of his command over the king's trust. Nor was *The Gipsies Metamorphosed* the only occasion on which Buckingham performed publicly in a seemingly demeaning part. In the 1620s there appears to have been something of a vogue for court theatricals in which aristocratic performers were cast in vulgar and comical roles, some of which were also speaking parts: for example, in a show at Salisbury in 1620 several courtiers (including three people involved in *The Gipsies Metamorphosed*) masqueraded in roles such as a cobbler, a bearward, a baboon-carrier and a puritan.[17] Of course to masquerade as gipsies could seem to be rather too near the knuckle for a favourite who headed a clan of upstart nobility achieving a stranglehold over patronage and favours, but (as Tom Cogswell points out)[18] it was customary for courtiers on progress humorously to speak of themselves as gipsies. In presenting the Villiers family to the peripatetic King James as dashing and courtly gipsies, Jonson was doing little more on the surface than actualizing a common courtly figure of speech.[19]

It still might be argued, of course, that the second half of the masque makes doubts more overt which the first half has entertained in order to dispel. If the first action shows thieves turning into bantering entertainers, the second half shows entertainers who really do steal things from the local yokels, and caps it with a scurrilous parody of Buckingham's entertainment in the ballad of Cock Lorel's feast. Certainly the pickpocketing has potential for doing serious damage to Buckingham, and it draws on that rich vein of popular complaint that satirized courtiers as thieves, rascals, or beggars.[20] Possibly it functions as reinforcing an attitude of ambivalence towards Buckingham; possibly it is a warning to Buckingham about the way he is perceived in England at large. More striking, to my mind, is the tendency of the laughter in this episode to cut less against the gipsies than against the

[17] See *Calendar of State Papers*, Venetian series [hereafter CSPV], 1619–21, p. 390 and note. On this particular courtly vogue, see my essay 'Jonson's *News from the New World*, the "running masque" and the season of 1619–20' (forthcoming). It is known that Buckingham was, unorthodoxly, an *antimasquer* in the Queen's masque of January 1627 (the text of which has not survived).
[18] In a personal communication.
[19] The other interesting point about gipsies, of course, is that when they arrived in Europe they presented themselves as peripatetic nobility exiled from Egypt on religious grounds, and astonishingly, they were entertained at some European courts on this basis. Just about the last European court to treat them as bona fide nobility was the Scottish court, in the mid-sixteenth century. For the history and customs to which Jonson alludes, see S. Rid, *The Art of Juggling* (London, 1612); A. V. Judges, *The Elizabethan Underworld* (London, 1930); H. T. Crofton, *English Gypsies Under the Tudors* (Manchester, 1880); D. Macritchie, *Scottish Gypsies Under the Stewarts* (Edinburgh, 1894); W. Simson, *A History of the Gypsies* (London, 1865); A. L. Beier, *Masterless Men: The Vagrancy Problem in England 1560–1640* (London, 1985); G. M. Spraggs, *Rogues and Vagabonds in English Literature 1552–1642* (unpublished PhD dissertation, Cambridge, 1980). I am very grateful to Gill Spraggs for first arousing my interest in Jonson's masque and sharing her speculations about it.
[20] On this subject, see Spraggs, *Rogues and Vagabonds in English Literature*; and my own *Theatre and Crisis 1632–1642* (Cambridge, 1984), pp. 215–16, 220–27, 258–59.

yokels. If the tradition of satire on court beggars is being invoked, it is being appropriated in such a way as to defuse its potential for reflecting on Buckingham, who is at one with his audience in this episode in finding the yokels ridiculous. Unlike the gipsies who are glamorous and magical, the yokels are clodhoppers who can barely scrape together ninepence between them, who scarcely have the intellectual wherewithal to work out which are the gipsies and which the audience, and whose fortunes all involve some kind of graceless homely insult. The robberies are ludicrously insignificant, for all the items stolen are overvalued by their owners: they include worthless sentimental keepsakes such as an enchanted nutmeg, a vulgar ballad, even a puritan tract (which the gipsies joke they are only too pleased to hand back (B763)). The yokels blame themselves, rather than the gipsies, for not looking after their things better (B712–14), and they praise the gipsies for being so clever: 'here be those can lose a purse in honour of the Gypsies. . . . Much good doe 'hem with all my heart, I doe reverence 'hem for't' (B668–73). Most crucial of all, the gipsies do not actually run off with their booty but return it whence it was stolen, leaving the yokels overcome with admiration for them: 'Excellent y'faith, a most restoratiue Gypsie . . . Ile neve'r trust my judgement in a Gypsie againe. A Gypsie of quality believe it' (B774–81). Possibly there is criticism here; perhaps the only way Jonson could safely depict Buckingham as a thief was by showing him giving his pickings back. But it is difficult not to feel that the thrust of the episode as a whole works towards defusing rather than reinforcing anxieties about the Marquis, especially since the treatment of the yokels dovetails so conveniently with the wider insistence on Buckingham's role as local host and the hospitality of his entertainment. The Patrico's comments on the pickpocketing episode are that it demonstrates not only how Buckingham transcends complaints about thievery but also displays his largesse and sense of local responsibilities:

> We scorne to take from yee,
> We'had rather spend on yee;
> If any man wrong yee,
> The thiefe's among yee . . .
> For he we call Chiefe,
> (Ile tell't you in briefe)
> Is so farre from a thiefe,
> As he gives you reliefe,
> With his bread, beere, and biefe . . .
>   (B770, 908)

The effect of Buckingham's presence on this particular local community is not to divide it, but to unite it in tipsy festive solidarity and traditional attitudes of deference.

So too for the ballad of Cock Lorel. There clearly is a symbolic interchange going on here, between Cock Lorel's palace under the hill and Buckingham's palace on top of another hill, between the lower bodily functions associated with one and the message about power enshrined in the other, but it is an interchange that appears to reinforce rather than subvert James's authority. In the ballad Cock Lorel treats the devil to a bizarre human banquet that translates James's real-life banquet into a grotesque cannibalism, but eating people is not wrong at the Devil's Arse cavern since the figures on whom the devil dines are all middle-class types the symbolic digesting of whom is likelier to have amused the king than angered him. The list of culinary victims begins with a show of evenhandedness, for the hors-d'œuvres are a puritan and a promoter (that is, an informer), one of whom was offensive to James, the other to his subjects. But as the song proceeds it becomes clear that the devil's menu breaks down into two broad categories. In the first group there are low-life citizen characters: a usurer, a cuckold, a harlot, a captain, and so forth, and in particular figures who represent the service industries that supplied the city world of fashion: tailors, sempsters, feather-men, tire-women, and perfumers. In the second group, the cooking in-gredients are taken from the ladder of legal and civic authority: a lawyer, a justice of the peace, his clerk, a constable and jailor, two aldermen, an alderman's deputy, a churchwarden, and the mayor of a town. This may be an anatomy of civic life, but it is adapted to the outlook of a king who was hostile to the growth of the London world of fashion and anxious about collisions of interest between metropolitan power and royal authority. The ballad may appear to disrupt the body of state with a subversive eruption of grotesque physical processes, but it reaffirms the authority of the King's body by presenting figures who have come into conflict with his power as being ingested, digested, and turned to mere bad gas. It is, so to speak, a loyal fart that the devil vents, and the point was made explicit in stanzas added later in which the devil's stink was said not only to have given the cavern its name but to be the origin of another royal hate, tobacco (W940–51). No wonder the king liked it, and the ballad circulated widely in manuscript.[21]

At the end of the masque the Buckinghamites are reintroduced trans-formed into magnificent courtiers, and as the masque dissolves into praise of the king the earlier doubts about the character of Buckingham's favour are whited out in the dazzle of royal glory. Says the Patrico:

> I can (and I will) . . .
> [Bring] the Gypsies were here,
> Like Lords to appeare,

[21] Alternative versions of some stanzas (printed by Herford and Simpson, x, pp. 633–34) make the connexion clearer, as they include a holy sister, a 'silent teacher' (= a silenced minister?) and a traitor on the devil's menu. The roots of the Cock Lorel ballad lie in popular satire, particularly in the visual and verbal propaganda that was inspired by Lollard and Lutheran attacks on monks and friars, which often showed the devil eating or excreting fat churchmen. See R. W. Scribner, *Popular Culture and Popular Movements in Reformation Germany* (London, 1987), pp. 277–99, and Chaucer, *The Summoner's Prologue*. This sort of imagery was current in the seventeenth century, for it turns up again in anti-clerical propaganda of the Civil War.

With such their attenders,
As you thought offenders,
Who now become new men
Youle know 'hem for true men . . .

(B896, my italics)

By this stage of the masque Jonson can afford openly to allude through the mouth of the Patrico to Buckingham's evasion of parliamentary censure and posture of future good behaviour; the closing panegyric ties expressions of devotion to the king to compliments to the favourite and celebrates the renewed bond between them. For all the teasing problematization of Buckingham earlier in the masque, then, the reservations that it appears to admit are accommodated and, if not dispelled, then contained within the reassuring context of Buckingham's promise of reform, his duty to the king, and his hospitality at his local seat. In the interests of a triumphant conclusion Jonson chooses to suppress his knowledge that Buckingham was both a new owner of Burley and an absentee, but given that the revel was staged on Buckingham's home territory it is hard to see what else he could have done. As the Patrico concludes, 'Both good-men and tall, | We are one mans all' (B921).

However, when the masque was repeated at court in September its circumstances were somewhat different, and Jonson took account of these differences by making substantial alterations to his text in the intervening month. At Windsor Buckingham was dancing not before an audience of family and friends but before the court grandees who had held the London fort while James was on progress in August, and though the masque still works for Buckingham that work is more in the nature of an act of negotiation than of ready vindication and display. Moreover, while Jonson's alterations still do not make the masque appear to disparage Buckingham, in the revised version the praise of the favourite has become significantly more conditional. Here, if anywhere, there are suggestions of a wobble in Jonson's attitude towards his patron.

Basically, Jonson's alterations shift the masque from a Buckingham event to a James event. Compliments to the family disappear, the Cock Lorel ballad is extended and a new song is added invoking a blessing on the king's five senses. Inevitably, all allusions to Buckingham's hospitality are cut, and the vindication of the gipsies can no longer be achieved, as it was at Burley, by positioning Buckingham as a channel of deference between king and locality. Instead, the gipsies truly could have been perceived as interlopers at the Windsor feast, and they are forced to earn their exoneration much more strenuously. A newly-written prologue sounds a note of uncertainty at the start by apologizing that the masque is being repeated again:

Wee may striue to please
So longe, some will say, till we growe a disease:
But you Sir, that twice
Haue gracd vs alreadie, incourage to thrice;

> Wherein if our bouldnes your patience inuade,
> Forgiue vs the fault that your fauour hath made.
>
> (W15)

The new prologue distinctly takes notice of worries that under Buckingham's influence James was devoting too much time to revel, and its address is defensive and apologetic, though it seeks to turn the accusations away from Buckingham by asserting that such 'faults' are not of his doing but a matter of royal grace and 'fauour'. None the less these doubts are not stilled, for they resurface uneasily in the badinage that introduces the fortunes, in which the Patrico is now made to say that the gipsies have their eyes on the Georges and Garters worn by the courtiers, as well as on the privy purse and the great seal,

> That when our trickes are done
> Wee might seale our owne pardon.
> All this we may doe
> And a greate deale more too.
>
> (W196)

The foregrounding of anxiety about the rapaciousness of the Villiers clan was made much more resonant and serious at Windsor, and it was answered by verses added to the king's fortune in which Buckingham was made to acknowledge his sense of gratitude and obligation to the monarch:

> May still the matter wayte your hand,
> That it not feele or stay or stand,
>   But all desart still ouerchardge:
> And may your goodnes euer finde
> In mee, whome you haue made, a minde
>   As thanckfull as your owne is large.
>
> (W313)

Perhaps Jonson was using the revised fortune to impose a promise of good behaviour on the favourite; more probably, Buckingham himself wished to use the opportunity to make a reassuring display of submission. Whichever way we interpret it, however, it is clear that the nature of the event has shifted. Buckingham no longer approaches James as an easily familiar friend, but as one competitor among many in the courtly environment seeking to demonstrate his worthiness of reward. Moreover, in the presence of his competitors, the extravagance of the rewards which he has engrossed is apologized for not in terms of Buckingham's sense of individual merit but in terms of the arbitrariness of the royal grace to which all are subject and which alone is responsible for placing its favours wheresoever it will. The justification for Buckingham's success, it is implied, lies not with the favourite's pursuit of reward but with the king who at his own pleasure makes men or mars them.

The other major change at Windsor was to the lesser fortunes which were now spoken not to members of Buckingham's family but to the great aristocrats and officers of state in attendance. Consequently the nature of the transactions taking place at this point in the masque was entirely altered, and the effect was to put Jonson's light-hearted fable under considerable strain. Some of the figures who are addressed here were already firm friends of Buckingham. The new Lord Keeper, John Williams, for example, was a client of the Marquis and had been among those advising Buckingham earlier in the year to throw in his hand with the reform of monopolies; his reward was to be moved up into the office left vacant by the fall of Bacon.[22] Similarly, the Earl of Arundel, who is given a particularly warm and full fortune by Jonson, had acted as a close ally of the Marquis in the Parliament, speaking up in Buckingham's defence when he was insulted in the Lords; he too had been promoted in the summer, to Earl Marshal.[23] Other recipients of Buckingham's good wishes, however, were men of whom he was less sure and whom it was politically tactful to solicit with expressions of friendship. Particularly, the Duke of Richmond and Lennox, the Marquis of Hamilton, and the Earl of Pembroke were powerful and established noblemen (two of them relatives of the King) who looked on Buckingham with different degrees of distrust and who were resentful of the favours engrossed by a parvenu. Hamilton was easiest to deal with, for he was about to marry a Villiers connexion, and could be complimented besides for his recent success in carrying through royal policy in Scotland, having been instrumental in imposing the unpopular Five Articles of Perth on the 1621 Scottish Parliament.[24] His fortune is gay and confident. Pembroke, on the other hand, was Buckingham's most influential rival at court and functioned sporadically as his leading opponent from within Whitehall; the fortune he is given is altogether more wary and polite. Moreover, these three aristocrats (and some of the other courtiers addressed, such as Lord Treasurer Mandeville) were opposed to the prevailing pursuit of marital alliance with Spain on grounds of ideology or principle, and were prepared to work to different ends from Buckingham's over foreign policy. These were men towards whom it would behove Buckingham to build poetic bridges of trust.

The effect of this on Jonson's masque is to make the central portion of the text intensely problematic. From having been a playful and intimate family game, the lesser fortunes become the masque's business centre in which Buckingham negotiates a public and symbolic version of that goodwill which it would have been his aim to preserve informally at court. It is difficult not to feel a considerable discomfort about these central exchanges: their tone is markedly more constrained than the lively banter of the Burley version, and the underlying seriousness of Buckingham's bridge-building towards his

[22] Lockyer, *Buckingham*, p. 95.
[23] R. Zaller, *The Parliament of 1621*, pp. 121–22. See also K. Sharpe, 'The Earl of Arundel, his circle, and opposition to the Duke of Buckingham', in *Faction and Parliament* (Oxford, 1978), pp. 209–44.
[24] M. Lee, Jr, *Government by Pen: Scotland under James VI and I* (Urbana, 1980), Chapter 5. On the Protestant grandees, see Tom Cogswell, *The Blessed Revolution: English Politics and the Coming of War 1621–1624* (Cambridge, 1989), pp. 100–05.

fellow courtiers sits uneasily with the fanciful masquerade in which it is embedded. Further, in order to achieve an appearance of rapprochement between favourite and peers, Jonson was forced to elide the competition and mistrust that undoubtedly characterized their relationships, and to manipulate Buckingham into a posture of humility that runs counter to the promotion of him elsewhere in the text. Each of the lesser fortunes very pointedly addresses the various lords in terms not of their private circumstances or identity but of their role in the royal household, as chamberlain, treasurer, steward, and so forth. This enables Jonson to situate Buckingham in the role not of favourite condescendingly addressing competitors or inferiors, but of servant to the king complimenting his fellow-servants on the diligence of their labours. Thus the possibility of horizontal competition is rewritten in terms of the vertical relationship of service to the same royal master. Even so, Buckingham's self-effacing pretence that he is just one good servant among many still resonates uncomfortably with the masque's celebration of his special relationship with James. If Jonson's solution was less than wholly successful in its new context, these were structural problems that arose from the contradictory imperatives of an occasion on which Buckingham needed to capitalize on his success without discountenancing other powerful men competing in the same arena. Subsequent additions to the encounter with the yokels, in which the clowns express their feelings of pleasure in the gipsies and their willingness to join their order, sought to buttress Buckingham's image in the absence of the countervailing allusions to his hospitality: in delighting both king and clown, Buckingham is made to look like a figure whose charisma cements the solidarity of society at large.[25]

It is clear, then, that *The Gipsies Metamorphosed* performs different work in its two versions, that its entertaining of doubts about Buckingham serves a wider end of accommodating or transcending such doubts, and that the pursuit of this agenda was trickier at Windsor than it was on Buckingham's home territory. But what of Jonson's own particular perspective on the negotiation between grandees in which he was a temporary pawn, that potential for 'embarrassment' which I have offered as the conceptual framework for this paper? We do not have Jonson's private views on the events of 1621, though they are unlikely to have been simple, for he was a friend and admirer of the man who took Buckingham's fall for him in Parliament, Sir Francis Bacon, as well as of John Selden, who was one of four men involved in the attack on monopolies who were slung into prison over the summer in a pettish display of courtly vindictiveness. If Jonson did feel embarrassed about the case he was being asked to negotiate, that embarrassment was likely to have been at its height in the writing of the fortune for the new Lord Keeper, given that only in January of the same year he had been

---

[25] On the function of the Windsor fortunes, it is worth noting Simon Adams's observation that before 1623 Buckingham had few reliable allies on the Privy Council. See his 'Foreign Policy and the Parliaments of 1621 and 1624' in Sharpe, *Faction and Parliament*, p. 154.

enthusiastically hymning 'the wisdom of my king' in having such a man as Bacon in the same office (*Underwoods*, 51.20). Though the Lord Keeper's fortune talks about the integrity of his performance in office, it is significantly cast in the future tense, and the couplet 'You doe not appeare | A Iudge of a yeare' (W400) is, to say the least, an understatement: Williams was a cleric with little legal experience, and to fit him for this post he was having to undertake urgent remedial law lessons.[26] So too Jonson steeled himself sufficently to write a conventional poem of praise for the fortune of Lord Treasurer Mandeville, singling out the pureness of Mandeville's palm and his expectations that he would soon set the exchequer out of debt, but he could scarcely not have been aware that Mandeville had been as deeply implicated in the offensive monopolies as Bacon and had escaped the parliamentary attack only by the skin of his teeth, nor that he had no real financial expertise but had bought the office along with his title for £20,000 and had only held it since December. If Jonson was not embarrassed by these things, he could hardly have escaped a retrospective embarrassment when a few days later Mandeville was kicked upstairs in order to be replaced by a Buckinghamite who was a real financial wizard, Lionel Cranfield.[27] The tangled circumstances surrounding these two fortunes suggest how difficult it was to write panegyric at this time without becoming compromised in one direction or another.

And yet if Jonson was rendered seriously uncomfortable by these circumstances or by the commission, he does not allow his discomfort to impinge beyond the margins of the masque. Certainly the teasing representation of Buckingham leaves plenty of space for private reservations about the favourite, but, as I have been arguing, that space is mapped in such a way that apparent ironies have a tendency to double back into praise. Buckingham appears at one and the same time as self-confident courtier and as the courtier's demonized mirror, but though that radical perception is allowed subliminally to trouble the masque, Buckingham's mastery of his complex role is on the whole a source of theatrical power rather than of subversion. Of course it may well be that in the summer of 1621, when the court's control over unauthorized political expression was becoming increasingly assertive, Jonson had no choice but to knuckle under. James had issued a proclamation in December 1620 against 'excess of lavish and licentious speech in matters of state', and followed it up in July 1621 with an even severer proclamation against political discourse from 'all manner of persons, of what estate or degree soever', threatening serious reprisals and urging subjects to inform on offenders. The Venetian ambassador commented in August that as a consequence 'the progress has continued in

[26] S. R. Gardiner, *History of England 1603–1642*, 10 vols (London, 1883–84), IV, 136.
[27] Gardiner, *History of England*, IV, 23–24, 227, 46; Russell, *Parliaments and English Politics*, pp. 101, 104, 110–11, 125 n.

profound silence'.[28] Drayton was one poet to be found complaining at this time that matters of state must remain 'misteries', and Wither similarly wrote that these 'guilty' days are so 'captious' that 'such as of their future peace haue care, | Vnto the *Times* a little seruile are'.[29] Jonson was demonstrably aware of the difficulties of political expression in 1620 and 1621, for in his 'Epistle to a Friend, to Persuade him to the Wars' he complained about the swarming of spies and informers and observed sardonically that 'even our sports are dangers' (*Underwoods*, 15.38). Plainly, the space for dissent at this time was exceptionally marginal and fraught with danger.

On the other hand, it is possible to argue that on grounds of ideology there was in fact a concordance between Jonson's attitudes and those of Buckingham, and that on this basis Jonson's praise of Buckingham may have been less compromised than has been supposed. The aspect of *The Gipsies Metamorphosed* that I have saved till last is that the masque takes up a position on matters of foreign policy, and it is here that there are interesting similarities of ideological outlook between Jonson and Buckingham. To explicate these it is necessary to return to the circumstances that lay behind the calling of the 1621 Parliament. The sequence of events from the assumption of the Bohemian crown by James's son-in-law, Prince Frederick of the Rhine, to the eventual forfeiture of the Palatinate has been too often told to warrant rehearsal here.[30] Suffice it to say that in 1621 James was faced with the dilemma of saving the Palatinate without jeopardizing his long-term diplomatic aim of a marital alliance with Spain to balance the marriage of his daughter to the Protestant Frederick. Plainly, the loss of the Palatinate would be a disastrous blow to England's international prestige, and some protection had to be given even to errant royal children, but James was unhappy about seeming to condone what appeared to him to be a rebellion of Bohemian subjects against their legitimate monarch, and he wished too to prevent what he saw as a local quarrel between German princes from escalating into a full-scale European conflagration along religious divisions. Deeply antipathetic to chiliastic enthusiasm for a godly war which, with some reason, he anticipated would be unnecessary, impractical, and suicidal, he preferred to hope (unjustifiably as it turned out) that he could rely on Spanish help in restraining the retribution of the Austrian Habsburgs. By soliciting Spanish assistance, James sought to continue pursuing his aim of marriage while making the Spanish match conditional on the safeguarding of the Palatinate. On the other hand, in order to

---

[28] *Stuart Royal Proclamations*, Volume I, edited by J. F. Larkin and P. L. Hughes, 2 vols (Oxford, 1973), p. 520; CSPV 1621–1623, p. 117.
[29] M. Drayton, *Works*, edited by J. W. Hebel, 5 vols (Oxford, 1931–41), III, 206; Wither, *Wither's Motto*, sig. A6ʳ.
[30] The classic narrative from the English point of view is by S. R. Gardiner, *History of England*, Volumes III and IV. This now has to be modified by Cogswell, *The Blessed Revolution*, and Adams, 'Foreign policy and the parliaments of 1621 and 1624'.

convince Spain that he meant business, James needed to look ready and able to protect the Palatinate from Habsburg armies. It was substantially to this end that a war-hungry Parliament was called, but because James wished in the long term to continue a policy of Spanish alliance there was a large element of sabre-rattling involved, and despite the seeming shift in royal policy criticism of the marriage was still not tolerated. James's response to the anti-Spanish sermons and pamphlets which the summoning of Parliament produced was the 1620 proclamation forbidding discussion of affairs of state.

The Gipsies Metamorphosed addressed itself to foreign policy in the fortunes of the king and prince, and in the Burley version Jonson was scrupulously observant of the king's intentions. Despite the crisis in James's diplomacy, in which his policy aims had all but collapsed, Jonson gave Buckingham lines praising James for the 'command | You have upon the fate of things' (B289), and despite the parliamentary enthusiasm for war James was praised for trying to 'ballance business' and make 'All Christian differences cease' (B295–96). Addressed as 'prince of your peace' (B260), a monarch with no aggressive territorial ambitions, he was still, in an obvious allusion to the fate of Frederick and Elizabeth, a father who has 'care of your barnes' (B267), though in praising James for choosing to be 'just' Jonson could well have been riposting to those who regarded the royal punctiliousness about whether Frederick's actions were legal or not as a distraction from the need for firm and urgent backing:[31]

> For this, of all the world you shall
> Be stiled James the just, and all
>   Their states dispose, their sons, and daughters,
> And for your fortune, you alone,
> Among them all, shall work your owne
>   By peace, and not by humane slaughters.
>
>   (B300)

James was being praised as a figure who had a leading role to play in Europe, but it would be a role that eschewed the military option. Indeed, by casually referring to James as 'top of all your neighbour kings' (B293), Buckingham was made implicitly to sanction James's disregard for the option of leaguing with the Dutch republic, whose twelve-year truce with Spain had expired in April. The threat of English intervention in Flanders might have tied Spain's hands, but Jonson's phrase represents European politics as entirely a matter of goodwill between monarchies.

Prince Charles's fortune, which follows, was little more than a panegyric of the proposed marriage with the Infanta. Jonson alludes to the proposals that had been floated in January that in the present climate a better match for the prince might be with France ('See what states are here at strife | Who

---

[31] Gardiner, *History of England*, III, 331–32.

shall tender you a wife' (B318)),[32] but the fortune goes on roundly to endorse the Spanish option. However, as Tom Cogswell has recently been arguing, the perspective of Charles and Buckingham on the Spanish match may not have been quite the kingly one.[33] Buckingham and Charles were respectful of James's diplomacy and hoped for a diplomatic resolution to the crisis and one that would safeguard friendship with Spain, but there is some evidence to suggest that they were concerned for the loss of honour involved in the English failure to defend the Palatinate, and anxious about putting the reality of Spanish promises to the test. Tom Cogswell argues that the 1623 trip to Madrid looks less quirky and unprecedented when seen as an attempt to bring matters to a clear-cut head by a prince who had already shown concern about the safety of his sister, as well as an ambition to cut a figure in Europe. In this context it is striking that some of the additions made to the Windsor version of the masque have the effect of complicating and toughening its foreign policy line, though still remaining deferential towards the king.

In his additions to the prince's fortune Jonson reiterates and underlines the commitment to the Spanish match, for he imagines not only Prince Charles married but the production of a little grandson to play between the king's knees. The success of the Spanish alliance is thus predicted even more confidently, for it promises assurance of succession to the English throne: succession, needless to say, that takes precedence over any child of the hot-headed Frederick. But Jonson also adds three stanzas cautiously anticipating the time when Charles himself will take over from his father, and in the process he associates him with what sounds very much like a more energetic posture on Europe. Charles will not only relieve the old age of his father by taking over some of his labours, he will 'by being longe the ayde | Of the empire, make afraide | Ill neighbours' (W355), a suggestion which can only be interpreted by reference to the current concern about protecting the Palatinate. Further, in anticipating the fame which Charles will eventually achieve as king, Jonson avers that 'your name in peace or warres | Nought shall bound vntill the starres | Vp take you' (W364), a formulation of expectations about Prince Charles ('in peace *or* wars') which suggests that Jonson envisages for him a style of kingship more interventionist than that of his father, and one which would not automatically eschew military options.[34] These additions strikingly alter the balance of priorities enshrined in the two royal fortunes and, as if to reaffirm the shift of outlook introduced into the revised version of the masque, Jonson includes amongst the lesser fortunes a panegyric to the Earl of Buccleuch, a Scottish nobleman who

---

[32] Gardiner, *History of England*, III, 388–90.
[33] Cogswell, *The Blessed Revolution*, pp. 58–69 and *passim*.
[34] Jonson echoes this formulation again in the *Ode to Himself* written after the failure of *The New Inn* in 1629.

personally commanded British forces on the continent, praising his honourable military bearing and his brave intentions of returning to the fray.[35] The compliment to Buccleuch is all the more distinctive given that he is the only recipient of a fortune who was not a member of the royal household or privy council.

There has been a tendency to think of Jonson as essentially a panegyrist of the Jacobean peace, and indeed he seems to have been deeply in sympathy with James's eirenic and non-confessional line on Europe, and equally strongly averse to the 'pocket statesmen' and those whose support for intervention in Europe on religious grounds carried the potential for the inflaming of social tensions at home. But in the critical conditions of the 1620s, as the Palatinate was inexorably overrun and James's diplomacy came to look compromised and ineffectual, Jonson may well have started to ask himself which statesmen were those who to his mind best guaranteed peace with honour. Certainly he could have had little sympathy with those noblemen, such as the Earls of Southampton and Pembroke, who would willingly have countenanced warfare on principles of godliness. On the other hand, James's pursuit of friendship with Spain at whatever cost had produced little beyond empty promises of aid and seemed unlikely to be able to procure the Palatinate's return. In such circumstances it may well be that Jonson could have come to entertain expectations that Charles and Buckingham might promote an acceptable middle way that avoided the disadvantages of either of the alternatives. A measured but effective overseas strategy, led in a properly circumscribed way by Buckingham and Charles, would have fulfilled Jonson's criteria for honourable warfare. Unlike the popular and bellicose enthusiasm for war, its objectives would have been carefully limited and legitimate; rather than a godly, confessional conflict it would have been a campaign for honour that was headed by men of social and political trustworthiness; its sponsors would have respected and upheld royal authority, and would have been inclined to discourage rather than to exploit popular participation in politics. If these were the criteria that governed Jonson's thinking, there is reason to suppose that he may have been led to look in the direction of Buckingham, and through him to Charles, as men in a position to legitimize military enterprise that respected the ideological priorities of monarchy. In this perspective, Jonson's praise of peace in the masque can be reconciled with his seemingly contradictory praise of individual courage in a worthy cause which resounds obsessively through his more private writings in the 1620s. Peace with honour marks out

---

[35] W. Fraser, *The Scotts of Buccleuch*, 2 vols (Edinburgh, 1878), I, 242–72. Buccleuch was certainly fighting on the continent in the years 1627 to 1633, though there is no documentary evidence to put him there earlier. However, Jonson's verses seem to imply strongly that he was even at that moment en route to Germany. It should be added that although James sponsored no military campaigns of his own, he was prepared to allow the occasional troop of volunteers to go abroad, so long as they were generalled by aristocrats he could trust.

a political space which there was some reason to hope Buckingham might be induced to occupy.[36]

So despite the problematizing of Buckingham which Jonson has made the central issue in *The Gipsies Metamorphosed*, I find myself on the whole forced towards the conclusion that, in the early 1620s at least, Jonson felt less uncomfortable with the favourite than some writers would have us believe, and that given the disturbingly polarized politics of the time he was prepared to suppress whatever doubts he might have had about him; indeed, that his relationship with Buckingham was more sustained and significant than this single direct commission seems to suggest. For, after all, since 1617 Jonson had been writing masques which, though they were focused politically on the king, still functioned as vehicles for displaying Buckingham's histrionic qualifications, and sometimes celebrated occasions at court which were days of honour for Buckingham too (for example, *A Vision of Delight* was performed on the day in 1617 when Buckingham was invested with his earldom). He asked Buckingham personally to intervene in 1619 when Selden ran into trouble at Whitehall over his *History of Tithes*.[37] He was himself listed among the members of the proposed Academy of Honour which Buckingham was pushing Parliament to establish in 1621.[38] And it may not be entirely irrelevant that the one time in this period when he is to be found complaining that he was being excluded from the production of court celebrations, in 'An Epistle Answering to One that Asked to be Sealed of the Tribe of Ben', it was in the summer of 1623 when Buckingham was out of the country at Madrid. Buckingham's patronage record was more impressive in the visual arts than it was in the field of letters, but if Jonson was prepared to take direct support from the favourite he would have been in company with Donne, Bacon, Carew, and Herrick, as well as with lesser men such as Richard Corbett, Endymion Porter, Edmund Bolton, Sir John Beaumont, and Sir John Maynard. With the favourite increasingly monopolizing patronage and honours, it is far from inconceivable that Jonson could have felt that it was going to be necessary for him to make himself acceptable in this quarter, though to adopt a less mercenary analysis, it is likely that Jonson felt ideologically more at home with Buckingham than he did with many other potential patrons.

It is worthwhile paying attention to the implications of the rewards which Buckingham was pushing in Jonson's direction in 1621. The Academy of Honour, which was discussed in Parliament but got no further, would have placed Jonson amongst a panel of élite men of letters and courtiers whose function would have been to censor translations of secular works published in foreign languages, and 'to give to the vulgar people indexes expurgatory and expunctory upon all books of secular learning published in English,

---

[36] For full documentation, see my essay 'Jonson and war' (forthcoming).
[37] Herford and Simpson, xi, 384–85.
[38] E. M. Portal, 'The Academ Roial of King James I', *Proceedings of the British Academy*, 1915–16, 189–208.

never otherwise to be public again'. In addition to this control over non-theological opinion, the proposed Academy would have the duty of compiling an authorized version of British history, 'and thereby to correct the errors and repress the ignorance and insolencies of Italian Polidores, Hollandish Meterans, rhapsodical Gallo-Belgias and the like': in other words, a history devoid of those popular patriotic and religious enthusiasms which were ever challenging the royal position on Europe.[39] When the Academy failed to materialize the reward that was found for Jonson was the reversion of the office of Master of the Revels, a post that promised him not only financial security, but a permanent place within the upper levels of the royal household and effective censorship over the entire English theatre. While modern scholarship has amply documented Jonson's material success in his career at court, I do not think that it has been generally appreciated how powerful and extensive was the control over the intellectual life of his contemporaries that at one time he seemed likely to be given. When in *The Gipsies Metamorphosed* Jonson figured the relationship between James and Buckingham in terms of an idealized patron–client bond, he may well have successfully insinuated his own claims for consideration in the chain of clientage; but it may also be the case that Charles and Buckingham recognized in Jonson a man whose ideological priorities rendered him sympathetic to their own values at the beginning of a decade that promised to be socially and politically problematic.

[39] Portal, 'The Academ Roial of King James I', p. 196.

Political Interpretations of Middleton's
A Game at Chess (1624)

T. H. HOWARD-HILL

University of South Carolina

Few readers today would wholeheartedly endorse Swinburne's characterization of Middleton's play as 'one of the most complete and exquisite works
of artistic ingenuity and dexterity that ever excited or offended, enraptured
or scandalised an audience of friends or enemies — the only work of English
poetry which may properly be called Aristophanic'.[1] Yet it is worthwhile
recalling Swinburne's words for they locate *A Game at Chess* in an interpretative context unique in the history of early English drama. Most plays
written for public theatres have failed to survive their brief lives on stage. Of
the proportion that publication preserved for later generations, very few are
accompanied by records of their reception. Thomas Middleton's *A Game at
Chess* alone, surviving in two authorial (or partially-holograph) manuscripts, four other scribal transcripts, and three contemporary editions, is
accompanied by a long eye-witness account of a performance, fourteen other
reports of performances and the events surrounding them, and ten other
documents that show official responses to the play's performances.[2] This
large extent of contemporary witness to the play's unexampled run of nine
performances obliges literary scholars to undertake a double task. They
must of course relate the play to the circumstances in which it was written
and performed in terms of its own structure and language. But exceptionally,
they must also account for the very fact of its existence, in terms of its
documented reception. The sheer extent of the documentation surrounding
the play, besides its own topicality, has tended increasingly in recent times to
alter perception of the play's compositional matrix. Whereas earlier it was
possible to regard the play simply as belonging within the canon of the
playwright, or as an exceptional theatrical event, the tendency in recent
years is to consider *A Game at Chess* primarily as if it were a *political* event.

In this century *A Game* has been situated with considerable precision
within the context of events following the return to London of Prince Charles
and Buckingham from Madrid on 5 October 1623. Quite early in the modern
history of its interpretation the play was characterized as propaganda for the
prevailing English attitudes which, at the time of *A Game*'s performances
between 5 and 14 August 1624, were almost uniformly anti-Spanish and

---

[1] *Thomas Middleton*, edited by Havelock Ellis (London, 1887), p. xxiii.
[2] These documents are described, and most of them are printed, in my forthcoming Revels Plays edition
of *A Game*. New transcripts are given there in original spelling.

anti-Catholic.[3] Following recognition of the profoundly nationalistic and sectarian values of Middleton's play, it was a small step to the assumption that such a play would not have been written — and certainly could not have been performed — without strong political sponsorship. Consequently much of the modern (and presumably best-informed) literature about *A Game* concerns itself to identify the contemporary personages under whose sponsorship the play might have been written. Literary critics cannot be indifferent to the outcome of what is apparently an exclusively historical concern, because identification of a sponsor, inevitably reinforcing estimation of the play's status as political propaganda, focuses attention on the playwright's purposes (and therefore, the quality of his achievement) in a peculiarly limiting way. The question of sponsorship, therefore, is the central topic of this paper.

Contemporary Englishmen immediately recognized *A Game at Chess* as a play of political content and significance, and, indeed, a risky enterprise for all concerned. John Woolley doubtless reflected a common understanding when he wrote to his master William Trumbull at Brussels that 'assuredly had so much ben donne the last yeare, thei had everyman ben hanged for it'.[4] As it turned out, no one was hanged for it, an irrefutable confirmation that the political climate of 1624 was significantly altered from that of 1623. George Lowe presciently reported to Sir Arthur Ingram on the third day of performances that 'it is thought that it will be called in and the parties punished'.[5] And John Holles, Lord Haughton, attracted to visit the playhouse for the first time in some ten years, suggested that 'surely thes gamsters must have a good retrayte, else dared thei not to charge thus princes actions, ministers', nay their intents'.[6] Woolley, writing again to Trumbull on 20 August, could suggest the nature of the 'retreat': the Master of the Revels had licensed the play 'it is thought not without leave from the higher powers I meane the P. and D., if not from the K. for they were all loth to have it forbidden, and by report laught hartely at it'.[7]

Further, contemporary commentators — only one of whom had actually seen the play on the stage — were quick to penetrate the veil which Middleton's adoption of the metaphorical device of the chess-game apparently threw over the identities of contemporary persons. In this they were followed by the nineteenth and early-twentieth-century literary historians. The identities of the play's two most blatantly impersonated characters were

---

[3] The usual dates (*cf.* G. E. Bentley's 'Annals', *JCS*, VII, p. 54) are 6–17 August. See Howard-Hill, 'The Unique Eye-Witness Report of Middleton's *A Game at Chess*', forthcoming in *R.E.S.*: Holles's account facilitates the re-dating which B. M. Wagner ('New Allusions to *A Game at Chess*', *P.M.L.A.*, 44 (1929), 827–36) had preferred in 1929 (p. 833).

[4] Berkshire C.R.O., Reading. Trumbull alphabetical correspondence 48/134.

[5] H.M.C. *Report on Manuscripts in Various Collections*, VIII (1913), 27.

[6] Holles Letter Book, Nottingham U.L., NeC 15405, 11 August 1624.

[7] Berkshire C.R.O., Reading. Trumbull alphabetical correspondence, 48/136. Notice that prior approval is assumed from the reported reaction to the event itself. Woolley would later report a rumour 'that the Players are gone to the Courte to Act the game at chess before the King' (28 August, 48/137), but there is no other evidence for this.

transparent: the Black Knight was Don Diego Sarmiento de Acuña, Conde de Gondomar (1567–1626), Spain's hated resident ambassador in England from August 1613 to July 1622, and the Fat Bishop was Marc Antonio de Dominis, Archbishop of Spalato (1566–1624). Nobody got _them_ wrong. The relationships amongst the pieces in chess made identification of the White King, Knight, and Duke as James, Charles, and Buckingham respectively a simple matter, and the Black King was evidently Philip IV of Spain. Nevertheless, the contemporary commentators were strangely various in their identification of the other pieces, and later annotators pursued topicality so deep into the ranks of the minor pieces that inevitably they could not agree. Woolley correctly identified the Black Duke as Philip's _valido_, Don Gaspar de Guzman, Conde-Duque de Olivares (1587–1645) but Thomas Salisbury, less up to date with Spanish politics and overlooking the play's reference to 'a sun-burnt, tansy-faced beloved, | An olive-coloured Ganymede' (v. iii. 211–12) took him to depict the Duke of Lerma.[8] Woolley incorrectly took the Black Queen to represent the Infanta Maria, attributing her a prominence in the play that the text does not support. The eye-witness Holles was no more accurate. He named the Black Bishop simply as 'the Spanish bishop' when the text identified him more than once (i. i. 44–45, 296) as the Father-General of the Jesuits. Salisbury's identification of the Black Bishop as the Pope was less excusable as he seemed to have had access to a text of the play.[9] Later commentators were no more accurate. A. W. Ward took the White Queen to be Anne of Denmark who had died in 1619; he was followed by Wagner. Fleay and Bald were more plausible in identifying her with the Church of England.[10] For Fleay the White Bishop was John Williams, Archbishop of York (1582–1650), but Bullen was undoubtedly correct to see him as the Calvinistic George Abbott, Archbishop of Canterbury (1562–1633). The roles the chess pieces acted in the play enabled their identification with the corresponding functions in English or Spanish society, but they had no strong individual colouring in the play. On the other hand some at least of the minor pieces were strongly characterized but not in a way that made their association with contemporary persons completely plausible. The leading characters of the main plot, the Black Bishop's Pawn and his accomplice the Black Queen's Pawn, were taken by Bullen and Pastor to represent Father Henry Floyd (1563–1641) or Fray Diego de Lafuente 'padre Maestro' (Sherman), and Mrs Mary Ward (Fleay) or Donna Luisa Carvajal (Pastor) respectively.[11] But my favourite is Fleay's identification of the male White Bishop's Pawn as 'Carandeleto's

---

[8] B.L. Additional MS 29,492, fols 33v–35.
[9] 'the Bishop stood for Roomes corrupted chayre', B.L. Add. MS 29,492, fol. 34r.
[10] F. G. Fleay, _A Biographical Chronicle of the English Drama, 1559–1642_ (London, 1891); _Thomas Middleton: 'A Game at Chess'_, edited by R. C. Bald (Cambridge, 1929), p. 11.
[11] _The Works of Thomas Middleton_, edited by A. H. Bullen, 8 vols (London, 1896), vii, 4; A. Pastor, 'Un Embajador de Espana en la Escena Inglesa', _Homenaje ofrecido a Menedez Pidal_ (Madrid, 1925), pp. 241–61; J. Sherman, 'The Pawn's Allegory in Middleton's _A Game at Chess_', R.E.S., 29 (1978), 147–59.

mistress'. Clearly, their inconsistency aside, most of the identifications are far removed from historical (topical) or theatrical plausibility. They illustrate a prevalent tendency amongst readers of *A Game at Chess* to take it as a puzzle that will yield its secrets if only the right key can be found.

One last example of the decoding of the minor chess pieces in terms of topical relevance provides a useful case study. The White King's Pawn makes a sensation in the play when his white doublet is thrown off and he is revealed to be Black underneath. From the first lines of the White King's speech of reproof at III. i. 263–76 Bald identified him as Lionel Cranfield, Earl of Middlesex (1575–1645) whom Buckingham had brought down early in 1624. All others who put a name to the White King's Pawn (Bullen, Pastor, Morris) except Ward (who named the Earl of Somerset) reasonably saw him as a sketch of Sir Toby Matthew (1557–1655) who had become a Jesuit priest in 1614 and was despatched to Madrid to advise Charles and Buckingham in 1623.[12] But the only reporter who saw the play took him to be Bristol and no one else of the contemporary commentators mentioned Middlesex in connexion with *A Game at Chess* at all. Comparison of the early version of *A Game* preserved in the Archdall-Folger manuscript and the full version that most people read reveals that Middleton altered the role of the White King's Pawn, which had been strongly coloured by its model, Sir Toby Matthew, to represent the disgraced Lord Treasurer by the most economical of means. He retained all the lines appropriate to the concealed Catholic sympathizer and ally of Spain and simply added two passages (I. i. 317–21, III. i. 265–67) to denote Middlesex. Consequently, it is not surprising that no one identified this synthetic character correctly before 1929. If the play was conceived as an anatomy of the political situation in the middle of 1624, and particularly if it was expressly written as propaganda, it seems in this particular grossly to have missed its mark. One might think that if the play were commissioned with an auxiliary aim to enlarge Middlesex's disgrace, it would have been somewhat more pointedly written.

Many plays, particularly of the Jacobean period, exist with speeches on which contemporary or modern critics could justifiably place political constructions. Usually, however, any observations that might have been taken to have contemporary relevance were shrouded by being set in peculiar circumstances or foreign settings, thus enabling all concerned to disavow their English application should the need arise. But Middleton's play, the depiction of Error's dream of a game of chess, barely attempted to conceal that it was a commentary on the prevailing political situation. That it would do so and that it would be read so was inevitable from the moment Middleton chose chess as his enabling metaphor. It was a disguise meant to reveal rather than to conceal. The transparent identity of the Black Knight

---

[12] The process whereby the early version of the White King's Pawn's role was changed to enable his identification as Cranfield is discussed in my 'More on "William Prynne and the Allegory of Middleton's *Game at Chess*"', *N&Q* forthcoming.

as Gondomar, with repeated references to his notorious fistula, provided the key and the rest was obvious. The Palatinate was a 'lost piece' said Sir Benjamin Rudyerd in the Commons debate in James's fourth and last Parliament.[13] Middleton, following Thomas Scott, proclaimed the affair as merely one move in a complex game in pursuit of world domination, the 'universal monarchy' of Spain. The chess pieces were monarchs, noblemen, and statesmen. The public theatres had long been enjoined to refrain from the performance of plays 'wherein either matters of religion or of the governance of the estate of the commonwealth shall be handled or treated, being no meet matters to be written or treated upon, but by men of authority, learning and wisdom, not to be handled before any audience but of grave and discreet persons' (Proclamation, 16 May 1559).[14] The sanction James recalled to memory to warrant the prohibition of performances of *A Game* was 'a commaundment and restraint given against the representinge of anie moderne Christian kings' in plays, an injunction unknown to Chambers's and Bentley's theatrical histories but doubtless effective, even if it were just an extension of the restraint just quoted. Holles was right to note that 'suche a daynty [was] not every day to be found', and to conclude that the play was 'more wittily penned, then wysely staged'. Inevitably, such an extraordinary theatrical event requires extraordinary circumstances to explain it.

How the play ever reached the stage has exercised many modern minds to explain, but James himself was mostly concerned to know why 'the first notice thereof should bee brought to him, by a forraine Ambassador, while soe manie Ministers of his owne are thereaboutes and cannot but have heard of it'.[15] This remonstrance reminds us of a point often neglected in recent literary criticism — that the king was not the exclusive authority in the state and that there were many great men who had a responsibility as well as an interest to ensure that *A Game* was not left to play unchecked.[16] Nevertheless, it was, until Spain's ambassador, Don Carlos Coloma, reported the event to James on 7 August, asking that the 'authors and actors be punished in a public and exemplary fashion'.[17] If there was a conspiracy to mount *A Game at Chess*, then it would seem to have been remarkably widespread. Even the remnants of the pro-Spanish faction which Buckingham had deserted early in 1624 raised no outcry against a play that Holles characterized as 'a foule injury to Spayn, no great honor to England'.

So far as I can discover, the suggestion that Middleton had political auspices for the writing of *A Game* was first made by Louis B. Wright in 1928.[18] He thought that it was 'probable ... that *A Game at Chess* was

---

[13] Quoted from C. Russell, *Parliaments and English Politics, 1621–1629* (Oxford, 1979), p. 171.
[14] Modernized from E. K. Chambers, *The Elizabethan Stage*, 4 vols (Oxford, 1923), IV, 263.
[15] *State Papers (Dom.)*, James I, vol. 171, no. 39.
[16] The same observation is relevant to the theory that the production of *A Game* was delayed until James had left London for his Midlands progress.
[17] *State Papers (Spain)*, P.R.O. SP94/31, fol. 132.
[18] '"A Game at Chess"', *TLS*, 16 February 1928, p. 112.

conscious political propaganda for the policy of intervention in the Palatinate in behalf of Elizabeth and Frederick, a policy strongly favoured at this time by Prince Charles and Buckingham'. He suggested that Middleton would hardly have written a play that he could forsee would displease James 'without some assurance of reward'; he had 'authority from some source high in power, most likely Buckingham'. After requiring some explanation for the fact that 'the cautious, timorous Herbert should have licensed without reservation an obviously political play' and noting that the 'actors and playwright escaped with slight, if any, punishment', Wright concluded that the 'most probable explanation of Middleton's and Herbert's boldness is that the ruling favourite, Buckingham, and the Heir Apparent, Charles, sponsored or, at least actively approved a play which had for one of its chief theses a propaganda for the reclamation of the Palatinate'.[19] Wright, therefore, was adopting E. C. Morris's notion that the play mainly allegorized the matter of James's daughter and son-in-law and the Rhine Palatinate.[20] R. C. Bald, who was about to publish his influential edition of the play, quickly pointed out that 'no one seems to have found any allusion to the Palatinate' at the time.[21] Therefore, if Charles and the Duke were using the play for a specific political purpose, their plan seems to have misfired.

Bald went on to draw two potent red herrings across the trail. He mentioned as evidence against Buckingham's patronage a passage in one of Chamberlain's letters to Carleton that 'seems actually to suggest that Buckingham, taking offence at the references to himself in the play, was responsible for its suppression'. He quotes Chamberlain: 'the worst is in placeing him [Gondomar], they played sombody els, for which they are forbidden to play that or any other play'.[22] But, writing on 21 August, days after the authorities had moved against the players, Chamberlain was in a position to know that the initial and specific reason for the suppression of the play was that it represented 'his Majestie, the Kinge of Spaine', that is, a

---

[19] Wright conspicuously does not allow the King's Men a significant role in the production of the play. If performances were to expose them to punishment, they would require assurances from men in authority. If then they had such assurances, why were they nevertheless brought to answer before the Council. 'Conspiracy' theories must account for the players' as well as the author's participation. Also, Middleton's 'assurance of reward' would be the sale of a highly profitable play to the King's Men; sponsorship was not necessary to make the venture remunerative to him. The characterization of Herbert as cautious and timorous (which does not seem to be correct) can only be justified by his conduct *after* the *Game* affair; he had been in his office for a very short time, having been knighted as Master of the Revels on 7 August 1623, and, as Adams (J. Q. Adams, *The Dramatic Records of Sir Henry Herbert, Master of the Revels, 1623–1673* (New Haven, 1918)) shows, apparently escaped controversy in the execution of his office before August 1624. The terms 'sponsored' and 'actively approved' suggests that they did not encourage the writing of the play but led the playwright and/or players to believe that its performance would not have serious consequences for them. It is not clear that Wright intends *prior* approval or not.
[20] 'The allegory in Middleton's *A Game at Chess*', *Englische Studien*, 38 (1907), 39–52.
[21] *TLS*, 17 May 1928, p. 379. This remains true even though many more documents have come to light since the publication of Bald's edition in 1929.
[22] *State Papers (Dom.)*, James I, vol. 171, no. 66; SP14/171.

'moderne Christian king'.[23] (No contemporary documents give any indication that either Buckingham or Charles had anything to do with the suppression of *A Game*). Further, Bald comments, 'the references in the play to . . . Buckingham are not always complimentary . . . Middleton, it is clear, was no partisan of Buckingham'. The matter of Middleton's attitude to the favourite is beside the point. In the play the White Duke (as well as the White King) is treated with almost slavish deference.[24] The White Duke's self-accusations of gluttony, fatness, and lechery in order to lure the Black House into self-discovery needed to have some foundation in fact for the sake of plausibility. Even so, there is no reason to believe either that the spectators did not enjoy the few references to Buckingham's 'flesh-frailties' or that they revealed Middleton's animus towards him. Such accusations set within the fiction of a device within the presentation of a dream hardly have the weight to exclude Buckingham as a potential patron, as Heinemann (pp. 158–59) does.[25]

John Dover Wilson, in a review of Bald's edition in which error and fantasy struggle for dominion, adopted Wright's suggestion that Sir Henry Herbert would not 'have issued the licence unless he had first covered himself completely by securing the approval of the Court' (p. 110). Wilson was so enthusiastic that he found that 'the most natural explanation' for the two months delay between Herbert's licence on 12 June and the first performance in August was that the time was 'partly taken up with private performances of the play at the instigation of the war party at Court'.[26] These events have left no trace in the documents that survive. Then in 1957 W. Power concluded that only 'the Prince, and he alone, could have given Middleton an assurance that a licence would be issued' (p. 533).[27]

However, lurking in the background all the while, strangely neglected by the seekers of political sponsors for Middleton's play, was Herbert's immediate superior and kinsman, the Protestant Lord Chamberlain, William Herbert, third Earl of Pembroke. Margot Heinemann found 'the evidence pointing to him as an important figure behind the play . . . varied and telling, if not conclusive' (p. 166). She noted that it was Pembroke who had apparently interceded with James on behalf of the King's Men.[28] Her most

---

[23] *State Papers (Dom.)*, James I, vol. 171, no. 39; SP14/171. Margot Heinemann (*Puritanism and Theatre; Thomas Middleton and Opposition Drama under the Early Stuarts* (Cambridge, 1980)) claims that the 'someone else' was James himself (p. 160, n. 19) but the official documents show clearly that representation of the King was not a cause for the play's suppression.

[24] Indeed all the White pieces who might be subject to contemporary identification — except the renegade White King's Pawn and the Fat Bishop of course — were portrayed with the utmost decorum and respect. None of the official documents complains of the depiction of White House pieces.

[25] J. R. Moore ('The Contemporary Significance of Middleton's *A Game at Chesse*', *P.M.L.A.*, 50 (1935), 761–68), claiming that Herbert 'would hardly have passed [the play] without the approval of some of his superiors' (p. 767), takes Buckingham as the most likely courtier to have 'furthered the production of the play' (p. 768).

[26] *The Library*, 4th ser., 11 (1930), 105–06.

[27] 'Thomas Middleton vs. King James I', *Notes & Queries*, 202 (1957), 526–34.

[28] B. L. Egerton MS 2623, fol. 28. Pembroke did not, we should note, intervene on the playwright's behalf: the Council was directed to continue their efforts 'to fynd out the originall roote of this offence, whether it sprang from the Poet, Players, or both'.

valuable point was that 'Pembroke, as Lord Chamberlain, was the senior official responsible for the control of the drama' as well as 'the personal patron of the King's Company, which staged it' (p. 166). At last a crucial element in the chain from sponsor to playwright to performance was accounted for. However, Thomas Cogswell gave Pembroke and Heinemann short shrift in 1984.[29] Asking 'what factions at court were behind this remarkable foray into popular politics' (p. 275) — or rather, barely disguising the assertion with the interrogative voice — he finds the answer within a few lines: 'the production of a public entertainment which reviled the monarch and diplomats of an ostensibly friendly state must have had the encouragement and protection of a powerful court faction'; 'it was the same broad-based "patriot" coalition that had been so successful in the 1624 Parliament' (p. 281), orchestrated by Buckingham under Charles's aegis, with Pembroke's co-operation.[30] When we notice how a proposition for examination and discussion in the 1920s and 1930s has become an assumption in the 1980s, it should not be surprising to find that Jerzy Limon asserts that four plays and a mask written for performance in 1624 were 'a part . . . of a campaign of political propaganda, carried out on an unprecedented scale and initiated in the last months of 1623'.[31] Elsewhere, 'it was not a spontaneous reaction of the dramatists of the period against the mishandling of England's foreign policies by the court, but a consciously contrived campaign, initiated and sponsored by a group of politicians whose goal it was to use all means available to win the support of both nobility and commons' (p. 2). However, Limon is unable to 'prove who in particular "stood behind" a given performance, or publication' (p. 2) and when he comes to discuss *A Game at Chess* he remarks simply that he finds it 'plausible that [Buckingham and Prince Charles] sponsored the production' (p. 98). I am citing Limon's valuable and interesting book here simply to illustrate the tendency of modern scholarship on the auspices of *A Game*. Once possibly protected or even influenced by this or that great man of state, the play now is the product of a conspiracy on a grand scale, so great that we cannot begin to say who was responsible for it.

At this point I should say who the sponsor of *A Game* was. However, certain impediments exist. First, there is not an iota of documentary evidence to establish that anyone other than the playwright, the censor, and the players had any connexion with the play before it was performed. That fact, I know, to some will be conclusive evidence of a conspiracy: there must have been a sponsor for this political play because he covered his tracks so

[29] 'Thomas Middleton and the Court, 1624: *A Game at Chess* in Context', *Huntington Library Quarterly*, 42 (1984), 273–88.
[30] Cogswell puts the play very convincingly into its historical context but makes no effort to distinguish amongst Buckingham's version of the Spanish marriage negotiations, Middleton's concerns, and the popular view of Anglo-Spanish relations to which pamphlets like Thomas Scott's *Vox Populi*, pt. 2 (see his p. 278), testified.
[31] *Dangerous Matter; English Drama and Politics in 1623/24* (Cambridge, 1986), pp. 7–8.

well. However, the second point is that, the play having been viewed by multitudes of Londoners of all social classes, it is reasonable to expect that performances of *A Game* would have been recognized as a smart political move by a faction of the court. In fact, none of the contemporary commentators, most of whom were reporting common gossip about the play, perceived it as a political device for the advantage of any court party at all. Even the Spanish ambassador, who should have been prompted to drive a wedge between the monarch and his favourite (as indeed he had earlier attempted to do) made no such allegations. If there was a political conspiracy to mount performances of the blatantly anti-Spanish play, then it was exceptionally successful: nobody at the time identified it, nobody reported it, and nobody accused anyone of seeking to profit by it. Looking more or less disinterestedly at the lack of evidence and the sponsorship theories that have been propounded, it is hard not to regard them simply as a form of the *post hoc, propter hoc* fallacy; that is, if someone benefits from an event, he must have intended or participated in the event. There is no doubt, and Cogswell has shown in admirable detail, that the ideology of *A Game* was that of the anti-Spanish party; the play's rationalization of the romantic expedition to Madrid was Buckingham's as he had related it to the Select Committee of Parliament in February 1624. But it was also the pamphleteer Thomas Scott's view of the journey; indeed, everyone in England (except perhaps poor Bristol) in the first half of 1624 knew very well that the only reason why Buckingham had exposed the body and soul of the heir apparent to Spanish Catholic injury was to discover their nefarious purpose for world domination. (Although why that desperate expedient was required after the affair of the Rhenish Palatinate is questionable). Charles, Buckingham, and the anti-Spanish, anti-Catholic Pembroke might indeed have conceived some benefit from the play's performances (and certainly they had no strong interest in punishing the perpetrators after the event), but the plausibility of their interest cannot be erected into the fact of prior active sponsorship without documentary support.

Nevertheless, two other considerations can be examined. One general point is the suitability of plays as vehicles for political propaganda, the other is the suitability of the particular play, *A Game at Chess*, for the particular purposes any of its suggested patrons may have contemplated.

On the first question a play written not too many years before 1624 affords the best evidence. Fletcher and Massinger's *Sir John van Olden Barnavelt* dramatized the downfall of the Dutch patriot executed on 13 May 1619. News of Oldenbarnevelt's death reached England quite quickly and the first account of his execution was registered in the Stationers' Company register on 17 May.[32] Someone quickly saw the dramatic possibilities of a *de casibus* tragedy based on Oldenbarnevelt's life. The collaborators wrote the play

---

[32] T. H. Howard-Hill, 'Buc and the Censorship of *Sir John van Olden Barnavelt* in 1619', *R.E.S.*, 39 (1988), 39–63, gives a full account of the background to and composition of this play.

quickly, drawing on readily available published materials just as Middleton was to do later for *A Game* — the last datable reference in *Barnavelt* notes the demotion of Barnavelt's son on 14 July — and the play was ready for performance on 20 August, when it was stayed by the Bishop of London. The sole surviving manuscript gives evidence of considerable attention by the then Master of the Revels, Sir George Buc. Nevertheless, even though the play was collaborative (which should have hastened the composition), and even though the King's Men must have wished to be timely in the representation of the fate of the play's protagonist, it still took three months to reach the stage. Cogswell commented approvingly on the theatre's advantage for purposes of propaganda, in being able to reach a large public within a short span of time.[33] What he did not consider was that drama is particularly unsuitable — since it is a collaborative venture of a playwright and a company of actors — as a means of responding in a timely fashion to particular political necessities.

Furthermore, the public theatre was not so highly esteemed that the use of plays as specific political tools in factional disputes would have commended itself to men of worth. If Cogswell is right Buckingham would have been using *A Game at Chess* to gloss over his role in the Spanish marriage negotiations, not to inflame the common people who were already strongly opposed to Spain. None of the contemporary references to the play, however, shows much perception of sophistication: they talk mainly of the unprecedented impersonations of Gondomar and De Dominis. The play was 'a vulgar pasquin' (Holles), 'a very satiric thing' (Salvetti), a work 'of no great merit' which 'drew great crowds from curiosity at the subject' (Valaresso). Its treatment by modern historians also helps to put the event in perspective. *A Game at Chess* is not mentioned in such important works as Minna Prestwich's definitive biography (*Cranfield: Politics and Profits under the Early Stuarts* (Oxford, 1966)) of Lionel Cranfield, the Earl of Middlesex (the White King's Pawn), D. H. Willson's *King James VI & I* (London, 1956), B. Coward's *The Stuart Age* (London, 1980), Roger Lockyer's fascinating *Buckingham* (London, 1981), or J. H. Elliott's *The Count-Duke of Olivares* (New Haven, 1986): Coloma had directed his report of the scandal to Olivares, but if the matter had been of concern to the Spanish court, the modern historian did not account it worthy of mention. 'The wonder lasted but nine dayes', as Chamberlain remarked,[34] creating a barely perceptible ripple in the chronicles of time. Sir Francis Bacon who was no stranger to the philosophy of Macchiavelli observed that 'in modern states play-acting is esteemed but as a toy' (*De Augmentis*) and therefore, I contend, not commendable as a political instrument. Nevertheless, when he continues with the reservation, 'except when it is too satirical and biting', he describes the case of *A Game* exactly.

---

[33] Cogswell, pp. 283–84.
[34] *State Papers (Dom.)*, *James I*, vol. 171, no. 66; SP14/171.

But let us suppose for one moment that Buckingham, or Charles, or Pembroke, or any or all of them in combination, directly or through clients or well-wishers, decided to employ drama to gain public acceptance of their views. What kind of play was written to the commission? Comparison of the early Archdall-Folger manuscript with the revised form of the play represented by Middleton's holographic Trinity College manuscript allows us to form a pretty clear idea of the play. I shall report conclusions briefly.[35] It seems that composition of the play was at least well advanced in May 1624 for Middleton drew upon two pamphlets (Thomas Scott's *The Second Part of Vox Populi* and John Gee's *The Foot out of the Snare*) licensed and published in that month. The two short passages intended to change the White King's Pawn from Sir Toby Matthew to Middlesex could very well have been added in May or June because Middlesex was convicted on 12 May. In any event, it looks as if the version of the play that Herbert licensed on 12 June was essentially that represented by the Archdall manuscript; it lacks about 310 verses of the full version. Assuming that Middleton was commissioned to write a political play, this is what the sponsor got. The most extensive part was that of the Black Knight, Gondomar, drawn mainly from Scott's *Vox Populi* pamphlets. He is shown to deceive the White House successfully until he finally over-reaches himself in the last scene. Informed political commentators suggested that the play would be 'prohibited once the King has notice of it, because they cannot tear Count Gondomar so much by revealing his fashion of dealing, without depicting him against their will as a man of worth, consequently reflecting weakness on those that gave him credence, and that daily dealt with him' (Salvetti); Valarcsso, the Venetian ambassador, judged that 'The Spaniards are touched from their tricks being discovered, but the king's reputation is affected much more deeply by representing the ease with which he was deceived'.[36]

The roles of the White Knight and Duke, on the other hand, were not large: they appear in only five of the play's fifteen scenes, mainly in IV. iv, v, v. i, iii which represent the visit to Madrid and the discovery of the Black House. (However, marriage was not the motive for the visit, by either party). The main White House character was the White Queen's Pawn, second only to the Black Knight in extent of lines, and prominent in nine scenes. The Pawn's plot, in which the Black Bishop's Pawn and Black Queen's Pawn — both Jesuits — attack a figure representing the pristine virtues of Anglicanism, is primarily a moral allegory. It has even less political significance than the comparable allegory of *The Faerie Queene*, Book 1 because no contemporary reporter even noticed the main plot of the play. It was Middleton's own invention, apparently owing nothing to printed sources, and comprises the fundamental structural as well as ethical basis of the play.

---

[35] The introduction to the Revels Plays edition discusses the composition, licensing, and revision of *A Game* in some detail.

[36] B.L. MS Addit. 27,962, vol. C, fol. 189; *State Papers (Ven.), 1623–1625*, no. 557, p. 425, SP99/25.

The early version has other deficiencies from a political standpoint. A pressing thorn in Buckingham's flesh in the middle part of 1624 was Bristol who was vainly trying for an opportunity to defend himself in the Lords against Buckingham's charges of treason in relation to the marriage negotiations. Middlesex was no longer a political force in June but Bristol was: he survived to charge Buckingham with treason, in May 1626. Politically, it would be strange that Bristol had no role in *A Game*, particularly in that the White King's Pawn's part was revised to acknowledge Middlesex's downfall rather than to contribute to Bristol's. Further, the Pawn's plot shows the White Queen's Pawn apparently entrapped by a false contract of marriage, good propaganda against the aborted Spanish marriage perhaps but, one might think, an unwelcome reminder of the negotiations for another Catholic marriage then going on in France. I can see no reason why the great men suggested as sponsors of the play would have thoroughly approved of the early version of *A Game* hypothetically written to their commission.

Then the play was revised. With political sponsorship it would be reasonable to expect that the weaknesses I have noted would be reformed, and that the political content of the play would be reinforced. Setting aside the quite small additions to the White King's Pawn's part already mentioned, the revision consisted predominantly of the addition of another character, the apostate Archbishop of Spalato as the Fat Bishop. He had returned to Rome in January 1622 and even as the play was being performed was languishing in an Inquisition cell. De Dominis had no significance for English politics in the middle of 1624 and his addition weakens the political force of the play. Middleton had made a point of associating Gondomar (Black Knight) and the Father-General of the Jesuits (Black Bishop) in various plots (II. i. 162–225, II. ii. 44–99, 215, 242–43, III. i. 153–54 and IV. ii), in order to show the conjunction of the secular and religious instruments of Spanish ambition. However, he added the Fat Bishop — who was a self-aggrandizing buffoon with mostly a comic function in the play — at the expense of the Black Bishop, conferring many of the second's speeches on him, together with the allegorically significant attempt upon the White Queen. This substantial revision attenuates rather than reinforces the political impact of the play and seems to have been owed to no more serious desire than the players' need for a fat part for their clown that would enhance the play's comic value.

In conclusion, the play itself and the manner of its composition gives no support to those who would see in it an instrument of state policy. It would, I contend, be foolish to make a play the fulcrum on which issues of state balanced. The players were merely 'the abstract and brief chronicles of the time' (*Hamlet*, II. ii. 524, Riverside edition), not agents in the game of statecraft. *A Game at Chess* was allowed and performed because it suited the temper of the age in a brief halcyon period of national unity. To make more of it is to diminish its value as witness and drama.

New Historicism for Old: New Conservatism for Old?: The Politics of Patronage in the Renaissance

M. D. JARDINE

King Alfred's College, Winchester

Meaning, we have learnt from Saussure, resides in difference, and the new historicists will not thank me for threatening in my title to render them meaningless.[1] It is, on the contrary, the increasing significance of new historicism in English studies, particularly in the Renaissance, that obliges us to look closely at and, perhaps, to adapt Terry Eagleton's metaphor, to act as customs officers to keep out dangerous influences. For those like myself who firmly believe in the need to relate texts to historical context and hence read them politically, it might appear somewhat ungrateful to enquire critically into a movement (if that is what it is) that has made it fashionable to do just that. However, history can be used progressively or conservatively, as the British Prime Minister is fully aware, and we must be clear exactly what we are presenting to our students or using in our research. The object of this paper is to examine the politics of new historicism, principally by relating it to old historicism and to competing views of the Renaissance patronage system.

Old historicism has been the object of much recent hostility (E. M. W. Tillyard is referred to more often now than when his work was current), not least from new historicists seeking to distance themselves. It is charged with representing a conflict-free society, nostalgically, from the perspective of a troubled present, revealing less about Shakespeare's age than his own, with its need, during the Second World War, to emphasize the importance of order and social cohesion, which he found in Shakespeare to be 'so taken for granted, so much part of the collective mind of the people, that it is hardly mentioned'.[2] This conception of order 'must have been common to all Elizabethans' (p. 17). Even those shortly to form opposing groups in the

---

[1] What 'new historicism' means is itself the subject of controversy. H. Aram Veeser, in the introduction to a recent collection of essays on the subject, distinguishes between 'oppositional' and 'Right New Historicists'; see *The New Historicism* (New York and London, 1989), p. x. For a good brief account of the divergence of opinion within new historicism see in the same volume Vincent Pecora, 'The Limits of Local Knowledge', pp. 243–76, especially p. 244.

[2] E. M. W. Tillyard, *The Elizabethan World Picture* (London, 1943), p. 17. It is interesting to compare Stephen Greenblatt's argument in *Shakespearean Negotiations: The Circulation of Social Energies in Renaissance England* (Oxford, 1988), that allusion to subversive activity, in this case atheism, does not mean that there was any such thing in reality, 'rather [it] registers the operation of a religious authority ... that confirms its power by disclosing the threat of atheism' (p. 22).

English Revolution were bound together by what we would call this dominant ideology: 'The Puritans and the courtiers .... had in common a mass of basic agreements about the world, which they never disputed' (p. 12). Whereas some historians have identified this period as one of transition producing tensions which culminated in revolution, the old historicists found a cultural homogeneity and a static, unitary, or monologic social formation, symbolized by the notorious Great Chain of Being, a model of strength in unity and harmony celebrated in the great art of the time. There is an uncomplicated fit between the reality of an orderly society, its ideology of order, and its aesthetic production. The values enshrined in this 'world picture' are permanent and universal, any lapses being no more than regrettable blips in the smooth current of history. It is a powerful expression of the historical myth of consensual homogeneity, the British way of moderation and order which we claim to have exported around the globe and to which Matthew Arnold and, later, T. S. Eliot, gave wider currency as a means of fending off working-class revolt.[3]

John Buxton's *Sir Philip Sidney and the English Renaissance*, recently appearing in a third, revised edition (London, 1987), is a later manifestation of this version of British history which usefully serves as an example of old historicism applied to the study of patronage. Buxton's positive representation of Renaissance English patronage as the source of national unity and artistic achievement has been extremely influential and still colours much writing on the subject.[4] Like Buxton the new historicists also see patronage as occupying the central place in the cultural politics of the period. Because its presence in society is diffuse and difficult to delimit, both historicisms can make claims for its totalizing capacity which are hard to dispute. There are strong links to be made between Renaissance patronage and contemporary politics, as patronage promotes hegemony based on personality cult centred on the great patronus, and it serves as an alternative to social systems based on principles of communality and public ownership. It typically operates in a covert way, unlike coercive power-wielding; its power and influence are based on an ideology of service and interdependency designed to maintain the status quo by agreement rather than force. Patronage study leads to a focus on circular relations of mutuality rather than conflict of interests between groups bidding for power. As Paul Millet puts it, 'Patronage is one of the methods by which the rich seek to control the poor',[5] but it is, in theory at least, held in place by willing subjection.

Buxton's objective in publishing his account of Sidney's influence as a patron of letters was to reverse what he saw as a process of cultural and social

[3] For a detailed discussion see Chris Baldick, *The Social Mission of English Studies* (Oxford, 1983).

[4] For recent work on patronage see *Patronage in the Renaissance*, edited by Guy Lytle and Stephen Orgel (Princeton, 1981); Arthur Marotti, '"Love is not Love": Elizabethan Sonnet Sequences and the Social Order', *ELH*, 49 (1982), 396–428; Don Wayne, *Penshurst: The Semiotics of Place and the Poetics of History* (Madison, 1984); Robert C. Evans, *Ben Jonson and the Poetics of Patronage* (Lewisburg, 1988).

[5] *Patronage in Ancient Society*, edited by Andrew Wallace-Hadrill (London, 1989), p. 16.

decline rooted in Romanticism, offspring of the French Revolution, which had led poets into the illusion that poetry is 'self-expression' (p. vi) and that they were able to 'write for mankind' (p. vii), absurdities apparently absent from a patronage system. As a poet himself he longed for the spirit of the war years when poets were 'making articulate a shared experience' (p. viii), a sense of common purpose which had been lost. There is nothing quite like a war for generating camaraderie, but Buxton saw the way forward after the war in a revival of patronage, replacing social division with an ideology of service: the way the Elizabethans had 'met a challenge not unlike ours' (p. viii). Buxton's study assumes the absolute determining power of the patronizing class and the absence of contestation. Sidney is depicted as having almost single-handedly 'brought about' the golden age of English poetry by his patronage. There are no flaws in the system (he dismisses Jonson's report that Spenser bitterly refused £8 from the Earl of Essex as he lay starving), which uses example, encouragement, and mutual respect as its only lubricants. Needless to say the literature produced by such a system celebrates the established order of things. As for the drama of the time, the main focus of new historicism, Tillyard, though admitting that 'At first sight [it] is anything but orderly' (p. 17), claims that one can detect Shakespeare's conformity because speeches supporting orderliness 'seem to be utterly his own' (p. 116).

Such untheorized dependence on instinct to gauge an author's politics is totally alien to the new historicist sophisticates. However, in the conclusions they reach concerning the relationship between literature and the status quo there seems little difference. At first sight this might seem absurd, as one of the defining characteristics of new historicism has been its interest in subversive or transgressive elements in texts, in contrast to and partly in reaction against old historicism. To understand new historicism one has to understand the intricate process whereby it starts with conflict and subversion and ends up with an Elizabethan world picture as controlled and contained as Tillyard's. The way that old historicism dealt with contestation was to write it out of history by careful selection of material. The new historicists' grounding in deconstruction allows or even encourages the disclosure of oppositional voices, but on the understanding that such voices are always already contained.[6] In his critique of metaphysics, Jacques Derrida's demonstration (at the time viewed as politically progressive) that what was excluded from the norm, that is, the 'other', was a necessary part of it, has been rendered politically regressive by the simple but effective move of

---

[6] This is the nub of the issue. For an excellent analysis and critique of the development of ideas through Derrida and Paul De Man which arrives at the position that 'all gestures of deviation must remain surreptitiously conformist', see David Simpson, 'Literary Criticism and the Return to "History"', *CritI* 14 (1988), 721–47. For an interesting attempt to defend Foucault and new historicism from the charge of 'overtotalization' and 'political quietism', see Mark Maslan, 'Foucault and Pragmatism', *Raritan* 7 (1988), 94–114. In place of the argument that capitalism produces an under-class and then contains it, Terry Lovell develops a marxist argument that it produces such a class and fears it: see *Consuming Fiction* (London, 1987).

making politics and culture a unitary totality beyond which there can be no uncontained position of contestation. Following Derrida's argument for 'the interiority of exteriority' (*Of Grammatology*, p. 314), the excluded have been included with a vengeance, apparently not only powerless but unable to contest their position in any way that is not already contained in advance.[7]

Both old and new historicisms posit a society of moulded selves, which for the former represents an idyllic prospect of harmony and accord, for the latter a nightmare vision of Foucauldian carceration. Just as the old world picture was a product of its time in war-torn Britain, so the new variety is born of political defeatism in contemporary politics, with reactionary governments apparently impregnably entrenched on both sides of the Atlantic, with the means to ensure perpetual power. Looking back in history the new historicists seem to be saying 'Look, it was always thus'. Hence the Renaissance emerges as a unitary totality, described suitably vaguely as 'power', which both enables and controls everything, like some transcendental credit-card system. This structured domination is located in the patronage system, and a question that must be asked of new historicism is whether the patronage system was so all-pervasive as to have had the power to shape millions into conforming uniformity. The historical moment of such pervasive power can more persuasively be seen as that of the modern corporate state, which has at its disposal a daunting technology of social control. When Greenblatt represents Shakespeare as 'the principal maker of what we might see as the prototype of the mass media',[8] he supports his case for cultural complicity of patronized authors in the subjectification of the subject only at the expense of historical accuracy. Patronage literature certainly played its part in generating the cult of royalty which the establishment felt to be essential in the face of internal and external (Catholic) threats, but to argue that there is no position outside of that maintained by government propaganda is to repeat the old historicist fallacy. The modern media's role in maintaining the status quo is well documented, but Shakespeare's is not, as David Morse has recently argued in a book that takes old historicism as its target:

Tillyard's account of the 'doctrine of rebellion' has the familiar univocal flavour: he simply asserts that rebellion is universally condemned and deplored. Tillyard bases his case once more on the Homilies and assumes that the arguments against rebellion commanded as total an assent as ever Big Brother received in Orwell's *Nineteen Eighty-Four*. Yet there were many arguments on the other side. There was a long and popular tradition of revolt against unjust kings and the fact that this was in no way part of establishment thinking does not make it any the less real.[9]

[7] Feminist critics have found reactionary implications in new historicism in the comfort it offers to a patriarchal status quo. See Carol T. Neely, 'Constructing the Subject: Feminist Practice and New Renaissance Discourses', *ELR* 18 (1988), 5–18; Jane Marcus, 'The Asylums of Antaeus: Women, War, and Madness — Is there a Feminist Fetishism?', in *The New Historicism*, pp. 132–51; Judith L. Newton, 'History as Usual? Feminism and the New Historicism', in *The New Historicism*, pp. 152–67.

[8] Stephen Greenblatt, *Renaissance Self-Fashioning: From More to Shakespeare* (Chicago, 1980), pp. 223–24.

[9] David Morse, *England's Time of Crisis: From Shakespeare to Milton: A Cultural History* (London, 1989), pp. 21–22.

The patronage ideal, as celebrated by Buxton and others, was of a willing, idyllic sharing of values and culture, of mutual benefit in the interest of art. The new historicist version represents this as a power circuit, with art reduced to a 'cash for propaganda' level: 'The poet's gift — both his talent and his offering — is the power to create symbolic forms, to create illusions which sanctify political power; his expectation is a reciprocal, material benefit'.[10] What links the historicisms is the assumption of complicity and totality. The power depicted by new historicists is not something that is up for grabs; nothing like, say, the struggle between capital and labour for the power that comes with control of the means of production. It is diffuse and pervasive, consisting of what Clifford Geertz, a major influence on new historicism, calls an 'ordered system of cultural symbols [which] ... provides a "symbolic outlet" for emotional disturbances generated by a social disequilibrium'.[11] Symbols in all forms of representation (all texts, including notions of the 'real' are collapsed together here) are an enabling device to help us get by. Thus, to use an example from Geertz, when labour attacks capital this is no more than a role-playing stance against a 'symbolic enemy', a ritualized game-playing, not a 'real' power struggle. Or when anti-trade union legislation is condemned by the unions as a 'slave-labour act' this is not a label (i.e., literally true) but a 'trope'. Geertz calls this 'the expressive conception of politics', which he defines as, 'the conviction that the principal instrumentalities of rules lie less in the techniques of administration than in the arts of the theatre' (p. 331). (Compare Greenblatt's 'Theatricality ... is one of power's essential modes'; or Goldberg's 'political reality, ordinary events, and staged ones are all matters of representation'.)[12] The function of such 'theatre' is, of course, the maintenance of order. Representation does not 'reflect', as it would for old historicists, it orders. This lies behind such new historicist insights as Greenblatt's 'Prospero's magic is the romance equivalent of martial law'.[13] My problem is in accepting that there is nothing outside either Prospero's representational skills or those used by, say, South African media manipulators.[14]

The result of what Joseph Loewenstein has described as an inscribing of English theatre 'within a dialectic of tense dependence on the interests of the

---

[10] Louis Montrose, '"Eliza, Queene of shepheardes", and the Pastoral of Power', *ELR*, 10 (1980), 153–82 (p. 168).

[11] Clifford Geertz, *The Interpretation of Cultures* (London, 1973), p. 196.

[12] Quoted by Thomas Cartelli, in 'Ideology and Subversion in the Shakespearean Set Speech', *ELH*, 53 (1986), 1–25 (p. 8). In this essay Cartelli expresses the fear that some new historicists might 'overestimate [Shakespeare's] political radicalism', in reaction against old historicism. He prefers 'the middle ground'.

[13] *Shakespearean Negotiations*, 156.

[14] See Martin Orkin, 'Cruelty, *King Lear*, and the South African Land Act of 1913', in *Shakespeare Survey*, 40 (Cambridge, 1988), 135–44, for a politicized historical reading which avoids the 'producing subversion for containment' line of new historicism. Further evidence of recent opposition to the new historicist theory of containment from American critics who wish to approach texts by way of historical context comes from Karin Coddon's '"Unreal Mockery": Unreason and the Problem of Spectacle in *Macbeth*', *ELH*, 56 (1989), 485–502.

new monarchy',[15] in a patronage/propaganda circuit, is a reading of texts which cancels out oppositional voices. Thus, for Stephen Orgel it cannot be admitted that Caliban (the colonized native) falls outside Prospero's (Elizabeth's) cultural patronage. Even the restless native must be incorporated in a virginal embrace (the Queen, Virginia, Miranda) in which lay 'not only civilization but the promise of infinite bounty within a hegemonic order'.[16] Prospero, of course, moves his drama 'toward reconciliation' (p. 64), made possible by Orgel's refusal of an external position for Caliban: 'However abhorrent the attempt on Miranda's chastity may be to Prospero, the essential, enabling idea behind it can only have come from him.' (p. 55) Caliban was always already within the hegemonic order: 'Ralegh's designs on the virgin land … were as much Caliban's as Prospero's' (p. 66). In a typical new historicist vertiginous leap from the single item to the total bill, Orgel assures us that these ideas 'inform Elizabethan and Jacobean political behaviour generally' (p. 66), a statement of which Tillyard would have been proud. Elizabeth moves from being, in Geertz's description, 'the center of the center' (adding 'it was allegory that lent her magic, and allegory repeated that sustained it')[17] to occupy the margins also, her power sustained by theatrical illusion, so that in Elizabethan England as at every other time and place, 'Every people gets the politics it imagines' (p. 204).

This method of cultural semiotics which new historicism borrows from Geertz predetermines that all cultural practice will have a function familiar from old historicism (and new criticism), that of resolving conflict in celebratory harmony and aestheticizing power, a danger of which new historicists themselves are becoming aware, as Don Wayne observes: 'We run the risk of aestheticizing power in a new formalism that traces relationships among documents of various kinds. Such intertextual relations in a given historical moment will then operate in our criticism in the way that generic categories, narrative functions, and stylistic devices did formerly.'[18] The link between 'relations of power' and 'textual relations' is clear, and reflects new historicists' determination to avoid essentialism; the difficulty for them is that they flee from that only to embrace a totalization of power that is in itself essentialist. The structuralist focus on relations also brings with it structuralist problems with history, particularly diachrony, and agency. 'History' is supposedly brought in by way of what Greenblatt labels 'shadow stories', the 'non-literary' parallel texts which he and his followers juxtapose with the canonized texts of the period. The crucial manoeuvre for

[15] Joseph Loewenstein, 'Plays Agonistic and Competitive: The Textual Approach to Elsinore', *RenD*, 19 (1988), 63–96 (p. 82).
[16] Stephen Orgel, 'Shakespeare and the Cannibals, in *Cannibals, Witches and Divorce: Estranging the Renaissance*, edited by Marjorie Garber (Baltimore, 1987), pp. 40–66 (p. 66).
[17] Clifford Geertz, 'Centers, Kings, and Charisma: Reflections on the Symbolic of Power', in *Local Knowledge: Further Essays in Interpreting Anthropology* (New York, 1983), p. 129.
[18] Don Wayne, 'Power, politics and the Shakespearean text: recent criticism in England and the United States', in *Shakespeare Reproduced: the Text in History and Ideology*, edited by Jane Howard and Marion O'Connor (London and New York, 1987), pp. 47–67 (p. 61).

the new historicists is from 'shadow' text to literary text, as on this fragile thread hangs suspended their massive generalizations about this (and all other) periods. As Carolyn Porter points out in a close analysis of a Greenblatt article: 'The question arises: what kind of relationship, precisely, is being posited between Harriot's *Report* and that Elizabethan culture so as to underwrite the transposition of the power/subversion model from the one to the other? Notably, this question never arises for Greenblatt.'[19] The new historicists' most eye-catching results have been the product of dazzling intertextual cross-reference, but in offering readings based on the relations between canonized texts and marginal 'shadow' texts they expose themselves to Joseph Loewenstein's charge of distorting history by an 'attenuated selection of things', in their preference for one powerfully symbolic text over the steady accumulation of less spectacular material.

We locate creative activity — both the fashioning of art-objects and of selves — in an attenuated political nexus; where art or psychology is articulated in relation to power, power has not been much examined outside the institutional grid of monarchy, aristocratic family, court, or church. Power and politics can institutionalize themselves otherwise. To study literary activity as if patronage or parenting were nearly the exclusive structures of constraint and nurture, or as if their only supplements were Church and textual canon, will be to miss much that shaped authorship.[20]

Their choice of bizarre and dramatic texts lends support to their contention that all that is accessible to us is an aesthetic or cultural realm; that differences between text and context, literary and non-literary should be collapsed.[21] The question of influence of one text/author on another does not arise, as it is the *sharing* of ideas which carries significance, a procedure which is much less open to query than source-hunting. Old historicists also took 'shadow' texts, but theirs were in support of the Tudor myth of cosmic and social order. New historicism has deliberately fastened on the transgressive texts ignored by Tillyard only to arrive at the same myth of Tudor absolutism, and the same focus on canonized texts, the patronage culture, and the ruling élite. Jonathan Goldberg's account of the genesis of his *James I and the Politics of English Literature* is representative:

I was interested in mapping strategies of representation *shared by* [my emphasis] Jacobean authors and their monarch. The emphasis now is on the *re-* in representation, the haunting spectacle of duplication that unmoors texts and events from a

---

[19] 'Are We Being Historical Yet?', *SAQ*, 87 (1988), 743–87 (p. 759).
[20] Joseph Loewenstein, 'For a History of Literary Property: John Wolfe's Reformation', *ELR*, 18 (1988), 389–412 (p. 394n).
[21] In perhaps the most perceptive critique of new historicism available Lee Patterson contemplates the price that it has had to pay for its absorption of the historical into the textual: 'To adopt an interpretative method that assumes that history is not merely known through but constituted by language is to act as if there are no acts other than speech acts. But while we can all agree that language cannot be prised off the world ... this does not allow us to abandon the category of the historically real entirely. History is impelled by consequential and determinative acts of material production.' See *Negotiating the Past: The Historical Understanding of Medieval Literature* (Madison, 1987), p. 62.

positivistic view of history or literature. What is *real* is the *re-*, perhaps itself a recovery of the nothing into which texts slide.[22]

It is not that literature is about politics, that it has a political content, rather it shares the same social function as politics —the perpetuation of power. As there is nothing to reveal in the text in the way of its politics, Goldberg's 'unmooring' replaces unmasking as the requisite critical activity. To read against the grain is what those with a political axe to grind do for a living (Don Wayne refers to such activity as 'mere ideological reflexes').[23] Texts do not disclose history; they form part of the relations of power which *is* history. To read a text as allegorical (i.e., referring to 'real' persons or events) is as misguided a 'mooring' as that practised by the sailors who mistake a whale for dry land in *Paradise Lost*. By cutting the cord to the world of material practice in order to prevent the text leaking into history new historicism has bereft itself of any claims to be making a progressive contribution to contemporary criticism or contemporary politics.

If texts cannot be read against the grain to lay bare their ideological workings, neither it seems can there be *intentionally* subversive authors/texts. According to Laura Stevenson, 'Elizabethan authors . . . had only one set of values at their disposal — aristocratic values. To them, the idea that two social groups might conflict with each other on ideological grounds was unthinkable.'[24] At one stroke most of the dramatic content of Renaissance English plays, it seems to me, is erased, much as Tillyard managed to do. This over-arching 'set of values' is presented in new historicism as being co-extensive with the patronage system. Because 'conflict on ideological grounds was unthinkable', one would look in vain for opposition to the system itself, although authorial complaint about departure from the patronage ideal is an acknowledged possibility, and it is here that new historicists admit the existence of critical perspectives. One can point to the many attacks on the failure of patronage,[25] particularly by authors, or to the representation of the patronage system as viciously corrupt, in plays like *Sejanus* or *Timon of Athens*, the answer will come back that here we see art and artists contributing to the gradual process of reform and adaptation by which the hegemonic order assures its preservation. Hence the replacement of patronage by market forces is not a major social upheaval but the evolution of patronage (paying customers being the new patrons) towards democracy. To respond to the new historicist revision of history one can, of course, only argue from texts, and it is now more important than ever that

[22] Quoted by Jacques Lezra in 'Pirating reading: The Appearance of History in *Measure for Measure*', *ELH*, 56 (1989), 255–92 (p. 286n).

[23] Don Wayne, *Penshurst: The Semiotics of Place and the Poetics of History* (Madison, 1984), p. 173.

[24] Laura Stevenson, *Praise and Paradox: Merchants and Craftsmen in Elizabethan Popular Literature* (Cambridge, 1984), p. 8.

[25] See, for example, John Danby, *Poets on Fortune's Hill* (London, 1952), and Muriel Bradbrook, 'No Room at the Top: Spenser's Pursuit of Fame', in *Elizabethan Poetry*, edited by J. R. Brown and B. Harris (London, 1960), pp. 91–110.

critics on the left to argue strenuously for the presence of competing sets of values and practices, before human struggle to overthrow systems which kept them from power is removed from our record of the past.

Although the strategy of containment admits criticism, the new historicist version of patronage and the service ideal is inevitably close to the way in which its proponents at the time wished it to be seen, as the more the system is presented as corrupt and inefficient the less persuasive are the claims for automatic containment from within a unified culture. There are strains and tensions, but Laurence Stone's case for the English Revolution resulting from 'half a century of ineptitude ... in the handling of the patronage system',[26] could not be admitted. Their ignoring of the fact that patronage would be ideologically abhorrent for certain religious and social groupings who found themselves on the same side in the Revolution — note, for example the Puritan demands for the election of ministers by the congregation, and the fact that after the collapse of the monarchy authors like John Milton wrote for the public not a private sponsor — leaves them without an explanation for this historical event. As Lee Patterson laconically observes, 'It is sometimes difficult to remember, in reading New Historicist accounts, that the English Renaissance reached its culmination in 1642 with a revolution.'[27] What is certainly true is that the patronage/service ideal was a powerful symbolic fiction (in the Geertzian sense) which was vital at the time, and has been since, in helping to generate the myth of the golden age of England. The civilizing embrace of the Elizabethan patrons produced, in old historicist eyes, 'an extraordinary cultural and spiritual unity'.[28] Michael Foss, an old historicist, laments the loss of such unity with the rise of professionalism, as does Buxton; in place of productive interdependence 'the arts began to suffer the booms and depressions of the business cycle'. (p. 186)

Because they cannot admit the sort of conflict that would manifest itself in revolution, the new historicists find themselves sharing a bed with the old, despite having contempt for its lack of theoretical rigour. Thus, in Don Wayne's new historicist counterpart to Buxton's study of patronage, *Penshurst: The Semiotics of Place and the Poetics of History*, we find the same civilizing embrace being celebrated and nostalgia for aristocratic cultural tradition manifested. He finds contradictions where for Buxton there were none, but he is attracted to the poem because of the way in which they are reconciled in an ironic structure: 'It is a great poem because of a certain complexity of structure and of feeling ... [It] simultaneously asserts an ideology and places it in question.' (p. 20) This aesthetic ordering lifts Jonson's ode out of its immediate context and provides us with the timeless liberal humanist message of gradualism and political consensus: '[it] can be said to liberate a potential for future social praxis along bourgeois egalitarian lines.' (p. 154)

---

[26] Laurence Stone, *The Crisis of the Aristocracy 1558–1641* (Oxford, 1965), p. 141.
[27] *Negotiating the Past*, p. 64n.
[28] Michael Foss, *The Age of Patronage* (London, 1971), p. 186.

Jonson is not only 'fed' by patronage, it 'consecrated his genius', and like Buxton Wayne is drawn towards the idealized image of mutuality: 'A visit to Penshurst will confirm, even today, the legitimacy of certain utopian elements in Jonson's text: the atmosphere is still bucolic.' (p. 133) In seeking to avoid 'naively reflectionist' approaches Wayne thus obliterates the historically specific price that had to be paid for this bucolic atmosphere to be created. Neither Jonson's poem nor Wayne's reading of it satisfactorily resolves the contradictions between the celebrated service ideal ('the image of responsible, benevolent, yet authoritative management', (p. 135) and the conditions of servility which it concealed. For this reader new historicists appear to share with the old a fascination for certain privileged literature born of a marriage between genius and aristocratic taste and wealth. As Buxton puts it: 'The Elizabethan poet was not given some cash and told to express himself: he was invited to Wilton and asked to express his opinion about the suitability of the hexameter in English.' (p. 25)

Although Louis Montrose, in his comments on Renaissance patronage, characteristically urges that 'literary criticism must note the social truth [i.e., 'unattractive scrambling'] behind dazzling court entertainment', he argues that this awareness of the unacceptable face of patronage is 'sublimated' in 'courtly cultural forms', and he, too, follows the old historicists in seeing a falling off with 'the dubious and anxious freedom from patronage conferred on writing by the printing press'.[29] Montrose is the most sensitive of the new historicist commentators on patronage, but he shares the general historicist tendency to view the patronage relationship as one of straightforward mutual benefit of the back-scratching variety; it is a short step from here to the denial of the possibility of opposition. Hence for Montrose pastoral must be viewed as 'an authorized mode of discontent — rather than a critique made in the terms of a consciously articulated oppositional culture'.[30] As Philippa Berry has pointed out in her recent study of Queen Elizabeth, Montrose's entrapment within the new historicist circle of containment disallows admission of the truly radical impact of there being a female monarch, and, hence, a female at the centre of the patronage network. Quoting his 'Elizabeth's rule was not intended to undermine the male hegemony of her culture ... Indeed, the emphasis upon her *difference* from other women may have helped to reinforce it', Berry argues that 'Although reformulated in the terms of the new historicism, this recuperation of Elizabeth's gender simply mirrors that effected by the traditionalist scholarship of Francis Yates ... Elizabeth's presence on the English throne for forty-four years certainly did not end the patriarchal structure [but] ... it *was* a radical event.'[31]

[29] Louis Montrose, 'Celebration and Insinuation: Sir Philip Sidney and the Motives of Elizabethan Courtship', *RenD*, 8 (1977), 3–35 (p. 6).
[30] Louis Montrose, 'Of Gentlemen and Shepherds: The Politics of Elizabethan Pastoral Form', *ELH*, 50 (1983), 415–60 (p. 427).
[31] Philippa Berry, *Of Chastity and Power: Elizabethan Literature and the Unmarried Queen* (London and New York, 1989), p. 61.

The new historicist conservatism has been particularly damaging in its criticism of Renaissance drama, where the effect has been to incorporate the theatre within the hegemonic order as absolutely as did old historicism. It is significant that Margot Heinemann's emphasis on the commercial nature of the theatre and its development away from court-centred patronage, placed in a strikingly different historical context of growing conflict between social groups, results in conclusions which are completely at variance with the new historicist position.[32] Where she finds evidence of conflict arising from a complex and changing relationship between theatre and state the new historicists produce plays which can only be 'authorized modes of discontent'. Leonard Tennenhouse is representative of this trend: 'stagecraft collaborates with statecraft ... [the monarch's body] authorized other symbolic forms of power, so that they in turn might authorize that body.'[33]

In presenting Shakespeare as a vehicle for nationalism, Tennenhouse joins the long line of critics from Arnold onwards who have sought to put the Bard to such use, culminating in the current deployment of his holograph image on credit cards. When Thomas Cartelli writes of Shakespeare's 'negative capability of fading into the woodwork of his culture'[34] it is difficult to distinguish his position from old historicist Patrick Crutwell's view of the homogenization wrought by Elizabethan patronage: 'These blending groups — Church, aristocracy, gentry, scholars, poets, dramatists: an extraordinary cultural and spiritual unity.'[35] What is involved here is a struggle between two explanations of outstanding cultural achievement: the historicists explain it in terms of national unity and a cultural homogeneity now unfortunately lost, while materialist critics see it as the product of conflict and diversity during a period of transition. One group is and the other is not willing to see something good coming out of social conflict; great art is the natural product of historicism's mutual accord between artist and patronizing class.

Frank Whigham, in a similar demonstration of collusion between art and the establishment, concludes that courtesy literature contains 'a repertoire of actions invoked by, and meant to order, the surge of social mobility that occurred at the boundaries between ruling and subject classes'.[36] To pursue the point, Greenblatt tells us in his recent *Shakespearean Negotiations* that allusion to subversive activity, in this case atheism, does not mean that there was any such thing in reality, 'rather [it] registers the operation of a religious

[32] See Margot Heinemann, *Puritanism and Theatre: Thomas Middleton and Opposition Drama under the Early Stuarts* (Cambridge, 1980).

[33] Leonard Tennenhouse, *Power on Display: The Politics of Shakespeare's Genres* (New York and London, 1986), pp. 15–16.

[34] Thomas Cartelli, 'Ideology and Subversion in the Shakespearean Set Speech', *ELH*, 52 (1986), 1–25 (p. 25n).

[35] Patrick Crutwell, *The Shakespearean Moment* (London, 1954), p. 131.

[36] Frank Whigham, *Ambition and Privilege: The Social Tropes of Elizabethan Courtesy Theory* (San Marino, 1984).

authority ... that confirms its power by disclosing the threat of atheism'.[37] This monolithic power 'not only produces its own subversion but is actively built upon it'. (p. 30) We know that Elizabeth had a sophisticated spy network, but Greenblatt's conclusion, borrowed from Kafka, that 'There is subversion, no end of subversion, only not for us' (p. 39), seems more appropriate as a motto for the CIA. In place of Tillyard's Great Chain of Being Greenblatt offers 'opposed and interlocking forces that held Tudor society together' (p. 47) — tension rather than harmony to be sure, but the result is just the same. In place of a received and agreed 'world picture' we have a massive and mass-consumed con-trick, connived at by artists and the state, based on theatrical representation, by means of which the patron class, with the monarch at its head, holds all in place: 'Royal power is manifested to its subjects as in a theater, and the subjects are at once absorbed by the instructive, delightful, or terrible spectacles and forbidden intervention or deep intimacy.' (p. 65) Oppositional theatre is an impossibility: 'Theatricality ... is not set over against power but is one of power's essential modes' (p. 46). The point is hammered home with exemplary clarity: 'The subversive voices are produced by and within the affirmations of power; they are powerfully registered but they do not undermine that order.' (p. 52) Does Greenblatt mean that the audience did not rush out into the streets, as from an Agitprop event, to mount a violent challenge to the system? Does the 'order' at the end of a Shakespeare play effectively obliterate all that has gone before? It is hardly surprising that we find Greenblatt agreeing with Norman Holland's crudely reductive reading of 2 Henry IV: 'The right people of the play merge into the larger order; the wrong people resist or misuse that order.' (p. 52)

The Foucauldian power-circuit is complete; an invisible hand has turned on the generator and the machine ticks over nicely without human agency; here in Britain we would have no trouble privatizing such an efficient system, one devoid of labour problems that can harness and monopolize all available power and that is beyond public scrutiny or control. It is clear why patronage is so central for the historicists, because it can be presented as the perfect closed circuit of negotiation or exchange, a circulation between patron/client/text to imply origin without the problems of determination inherent in a base-superstructure model. The formulation Greenblatt prefers is a 'complex circulation between the social dimension of an aesthetic strategy and the aesthetic dimension of a social strategy' (p. 147). Censorship, like open repression, is revealingly left out of the exchange, as it breaks this cosy circle and breaches the fiction of efficiency whereby power, Antaeus-like, needs, desires, and stimulates subversion. In Greenblatt's

---

[37] Stephen Greenblatt, *Shakespearean Negotiations*, p. 22. Given the deep gloom which hovers over this further study of the subjectified subject it is hardly surprising to find Greenblatt craving for a critical practice sealed off from history: 'There are days when I long to return to the close-grained formalism of my youth.' (p. 2)

narrative of history censorship becomes a nonsense. Why on earth bite the hand that feeds you? As Annabel Patterson observes,

New Historicist approaches to the topic of control elide rather than explain the conditions in which Shakespeare's theatre was required to operate. The impersonality of the Foucauldian and Althusserian models cannot account for specific cases of intervention and nonintervention by the authorities; nor for the famous instances of textual censorship.[38]

She appeals for a 'rehistoricizing' which would be personal, local, material, and human, and take account of specifics.

James Holstun makes a similar case in his 'Ehud's dagger: Patronage, Tyrannicide, and "Killing No Murder"',[39] although his targets include right-wing revisionist historians. The outrageous dagger strapped to the thigh of the would-be tyrannicide, like the IRA bomb that nearly killed Margaret Thatcher, represent a point of reference so far removed from the assumed wishes of the establishment that it arguably cannot be what Montrose calls 'an authorized mode of discontent'. New historicists would challenge this argument by claiming that the more extreme the acts of subversion the more secure the powerholders. This is why it is necessary to shift the argument away from individual acts/texts to movements, such as republicanism or socialism, towards which these acts/texts might be seen to contribute. Revisionism and new historicism are flourishing at a time when we are told that oppositional movements are waning (while, paradoxically, insecurity is waxing). But history cannot be left to be re-written by this double design to render invisible the real struggles of women and men to overthrow systems which denied them access to power.

How close the relationship is between revisionist historians and new historicists is plain from a recent article by Kevin Sharpe in which he applauds new historicism and refers approvingly to Clifford Geertz, from whom we are to learn that 'the exercise of power is itself a cultural practice, integral to and dependent upon the mores and expectations, rituals and symbols of any social group; that power, especially in pre-modern societies that lacked armies, professional bureaucracies, and the techniques necessary for the foundation of authority on force, depended upon perception.[40] It is, revealingly, a short step from the homogenizing Geertzian power-circuit to a version of history which totally erases the English Revolution:

Given cultural differences and a political divide into civil war it was all too easy for historians to make the simple conclusion that the Civil War was a clash of cultures. . . . Political and literary historians even seized on such simplistic antitheses [such as 'Milton and the Cavalier poets'] to *explain* the origins of the Civil War

---

[38] Annabel Patterson, '"The Very Age and Body of the Time His Form and Pressure": Rehistoricizing Shakespeare's Theater', *NLH*, 20 (1988), 91–104 (p. 94).
[39] This was delivered at the conference on patronage at Reading University in July 1989 and is awaiting publication. I am grateful to Dr Holstun for access to the full version of his excellent paper.
[40] Kevin Sharpe, 'Review Article: Culture, Politics, and the English Civil War', *HLQ*, 51 (1988), 95–135 (p. 95).

in two rival cultures — ignorant of or unconcerned by, the shared values and assumptions, the many individuals who belie a thesis of polarity. (p. 96)

One wonders why and how these individuals were able to emerge from their shared world picture to slaughter each other on the battlefields; and is it really 'simplistic' to 'polarize' Milton and the Royalist Cavalier poets? Milton seems keen to establish such a polarity in most of his writings, as were Royalists to differentiate their beliefs from his: not much sign of sharing here. American new historicists should note that in denying social conflict based on conflicting beliefs, they join forces not only with the new breed of revisionist historians but the British Prime Minister herself, who, during the bi-centenary celebrations in France, deplored the excesses of the French Revolution and praised the British people for avoiding revolution and progressing by way of consensus.

It is entirely consistent that her government prefers patronage to a planned economy, and individual acts of charity to a welfare system, but patronage should not be left to the revisionists since there are ways in which it can be of use to materialist historians. Though marred by its selective focus the Buxton model of patronage, in which the patron stimulates and even determines the client's art-work, is at odds with the new historicist model which suppresses agency and prefers to depersonalize the system. The products of patronage are often occasional and historically specific; of all texts they are the most likely to bear the trace of the material circumstances of their production and are therefore resistant to the aesthetics of intertextuality. Furthermore, the fact that there were various forms of patronage, such as that provided by guilds, challenges the new historicist model of power as an exclusively centrifugal force with the monarch at the hub, a model which pays no attention to either 'the growth of bourgeois literature or the explosion of London's power as a commercial centre'.[41] Margot Heinemann's work on opposition drama, and Michael Bristol's on carnival must also cast doubt on any unitary model of patronage.[42]

Since it views the theatre as, in Tennenhouse's words, 'a forum for staging symbolic shows of state power',[43] new historicism is forced to discount the possible impact on the shaping of material of having the paying public as a vital source of income. Admittedly there is no consensus, but new historicists could not admit Werner Gundersheimer's argument that

The political and social orderings in European societies in the Renaissance are mirrored in their structures of patronage. Could Shakespeare's awareness of this point have led him to prefer the support of the London crowds to that of a single *patronus*? If so, we may view his career as less a product of than as departure from and

[41] Joseph Loewenstein, 'John Wolfe', p. 6.
[42] See Margot Heinemann, *Puritanism and Theatre*, and Michael Bristol, *Carnival and Theatre: Plebeian Culture and the Structure of Authority in Renaissance England* (New York and London, 1985), and his 'Carnival and the Institutions of Theater in Elizabethan England', *ELH*, 50 (1983), 637–54.
[43] *Power on Display*, p. 39.

perhaps a challenge to, the traditional relationships that define patronage in the Renaissance.[44]

This is anathema to David Bergeron:

The case of Thomas Heywood in the 1630s makes clear that systems of patronage, familiar in the Renaissance, remained intact; they had not been set aside by a paying theatregoing audience.... I do not think that Shakespeare's dramatic career represents any kind of challenge to the system of Renaissance patronage.[45]

Characteristically Bergeron sets the 'natural process' of gradual change against the claims of 'challenge' to the patronage system. The circulation of power does not, it seems, extend to the sharing of power by London citizens in determining the nature of their popular theatre, just as there is a tendency in new historicism to ignore that literature which was produced by the professional writers whose dependency on a patronus was either sporadic or non-existent. Given what Robert Weimann describes as the 'homogenization of discursive space that post-structuralist theory assumes' then 'the appropriation of cultural power and communicative action by unsanctioned social groups'[46] becomes an impossibility. In pursuit of such homogeneity new historicism appears to suppress middle-class and popular culture; this alternative culture is incorporated and rendered invisible: 'Many in Shakespeare's audience ... though outside the immediate parameters of the empowered community ... were part of the same nation whose welfare was inextricably linked to that of the aristocracy.[47] In their beginning and ending with aristocratic patronage we can observe the route by which the new historicists re-write history to agree with the right-wing revisionist historians.

Alan Sinfield has argued that Renaissance patronage was not a monolithic system but a precarious means of holding on to power by regulating the distribution of favours,[48] an anti-meritocratic method that was bound to cause great discontent. Authors at this time, and particularly playwrights with alternative sources of income from the press or paying customers, were likely to have had a tense and complex relationship with the patronizing class, suggesting the possibility, in Sinfield's terms, of a 'structural position from which state ideology might be perceived critically'. The uncertain status of author and literary text placed literary activity in a peculiarly sensitive position, which can explain such apparent contradictions as radical theatre under royal patronage. The theatre companies were enmeshed in the

---

[44] Werner Gundersheimer, 'Patronage in the Renaissance: An Exploratory Approach', in Lytle and Orgel, *Patronage in the Renaissance*, pp. 3–26.
[45] David Bergeron, 'Patronage of Dramatists: The Case of Thomas Heywood', *ELR*, 18 (1988), 294–304 (p. 304).
[46] Robert Weimann, 'Shakespeare (De)Canonized: Conflicting Uses of "Authority" and "Representation"', *NLH*, 20 (1988), 65–81 (p. 79).
[47] Leonard Tennenhouse, *Power on Display*, pp. 39–40.
[48] 'Power and Ideology', p. 271.

transition from the service ideal to the market economy, as Michael Bristol points out:

The social position of the players and of their work was based on two contradictory presuppositions — that they were engaged in a business or industry and that they were engaged in 'service' to their aristocratic patrons ... the players are at one and the same time at the bottom of the social scale and yet somehow affiliated with its highest and most privileged spheres.[49]

Under such circumstances it is surely possible to doubt new historicist claims that state 'theatre' and public theatre were co-extensive, and that the patronage system was monolithic. It seems more likely that the system was breaking down under the impact of a developing market economy, in which the theatre in particular was embroiled.

As with patronage, so with the service ideal. Behind the success of service as a key element in the social stability of the Elizabethan period was the Christian doctrine of obedience, of the family to the father and servant to master. In these relations duties came before rights in what was viewed as a natural obligation, naturalness being the vital component in the effectiveness of the service ideal, indeed the supposed voluntary nature of the relationship still partly colours the contemporary significance of the term. Such idyllic mutuality is immediately threatened by the introduction of payment into the contract; the buying and selling of labour has none of the emotional appeal of the feudal ideal of service. For this reason we find Japanese industrialists seeking to establish in modern factories the lineage loyalties and kinship networks which characterized the medieval 'familia regis'. It is not payment but ideology that ensures good service. To sell one's labour to the highest bidder is a crude relationship, and one which offers potential power to the seller, hence the need for the retention of the mystifying ideology of service (the only expanding area of the British economy). But this could not be the same service that underpinned the Renaissance patronage system. Capital needs labour to separate mind from body, whereas feudal service integrated the two. Francis Barker has argued that it was with the arrival of the disembodied Cartesian subject that the body became supplementary and hence ready for exploitation by capital: 'Disinherited and separated, the body is traduced as a rootless thing of madness and scandal; and then finally, in its object aspect, it is pressed into service.'[50] The object of 'service' under capitalism would now, however, be absent, invisibly replacing the patron at Penshurst or the monarch at court. I would argue that it is in the Renaissance period in England that the strains resulting from this transition between divergent concepts of service are most apparent. Disguised by use of the same term these are not shared values and ideas, as historicism would have it, but are antagonistic.

---

[49] 'Carnival and Theatre', p. 648.
[50] Francis Barker, *The Tremulous Private Body: Essays on Subjection* (London and New York, 1984), p. 67.

Monarchs did, as the new historicists observe, use theatrical display to perpetuate the service ideal, and it was certainly a vital, calculated element of their strategy for maintaining power. Greenblatt quotes Bishop Goodman's account of one of Elizabeth's 'staged' exits from Council: 'This wrought such an impression upon us, for shows and pageants are ever best seen by torchlight, that all the way long we did nothing but talk of what an admirable queen she was, and how we would venture our lives to do her service.'[51] But to move from noting such methods of ideological control to arguing that *all* forms of representation, including the public stage, are necessarily also symbolic shows of state power is to overlook the fragile nature of the service ideal and the patronage system in a society that was changing rapidly. As David Norbrook puts it in a recent powerful critique of new historicism: 'What precipitated the crisis of the English Revolution was arguably the recognition of Charles I and Laud that it was almost too late to keep Britain within their ideal model of an elegant, theatrical, Renaissance absolutism.'[52] The allegiance of all authors all of the time to a system that was under strain and on which they were not absolutely dependent cannot be assumed. Because the new historicists, like the old, have left themselves with no way of mapping or accounting for change, they are trapped in essentialism and totalization.

Perhaps reluctantly in some cases, they inevitably share revisionist historian Jonathan Clark's judgement of the period, that 'the so-called forces of reaction were in fact always dominant . . . any changes . . . were short-term adjustments only'.[53] Does this include the adjustment to Charles I's head, one wonders? This alliance threatens to become the new orthodoxy. There are clear warning signals when the editor of *Renaissance Drama* actually invites contributions which 'explore the ways in which chaos is ritualized to contain and/or encourage social, political, and religious disorder'.[54] Ritualized chaos leaves conflict safely in the aesthetic realm; in such a way does 'real' human struggle get written out of history. This development is particularly unwelcome in Britain at a time when revisionists are devising a history syllabus for the new national curriculum. Will all schoolchildren learn the smooth evolution of British consensus history (with the odd short-term adjustment) to triumphant democratic monarchy? It is less than fortuitous that the new English syllabus will have the new historicism to hand so that schools can avoid confronting unpleasant 'antitheses' or 'theses of polarity' and learn to celebrate the strength and continuity of the nation's 'shared values and assumptions'.

The crucial question facing literary critics after a dose of new historicism is whether there are ways of reading patronage literature, or any literature, as

[51] *Renaissance Self-Fashioning*, p. 167.
[52] David Norbrook, 'Life and Death of Renaissance Man', *Raritan*, 8 (1989), 89–110 (p. 110).
[53] Quoted by Christopher Norris, 'Postmodernising History: Right-Wing Revisionism and the Uses of Theory', *Southern Review*, 21.2 (1988), 123–40 (p. 135).
[54] Mary Beth Rose, *Renaissance Drama*, 19 (1988), vi.

anything other than a reproduction of the dominant ideology. One way might be to select texts which parade themselves as oppositional and independent of patronage. But this still leaves us with the works of many authors who sought and received the protection and succour of patronage, with its concomitant service obligation. Bringing history to bear on texts in new historicist fashion seems to mean that any oppositional ideas that they present cannot have been, in David Norbrook's phrase, 'advanced for serious consideration'.[55] To respond to this challenge, which has far-reaching implications for readings of Renaissance texts, materialist critics have to be able to rescue a text like *Sejanus*, by an author apparently committed to monarchy, as a play in which republican ideas *are* for 'serious consideration' and not, in new historicist fashion, cancelled out by a process of aesthetic absorption. The case needs to be put that even texts written by a client/author can, as Alan Sinfield puts it, 'produce a critical perspective' and be read as 'sites of contest'.[56] To offer a reading of *Sejanus* that denies that it is a savage attack on a corrupt patronage system and that republicanism is presented positively as an alternative system seems to me a gross distortion of the play, and certainly one that renders it less interesting. It is also to contribute to a revision of history that would produce the absurdity of republicanism suddenly flaring up out of nowhere in 1649.

If this is where the long road from structuralism to deconstruction has got us then it is no surprise to find even committed anti-marxists like Robert Young wishing to pull back from the political consequences of these recent developments: 'What is needed is a new model that can include conflict, in which incompatibility provides more than an aporia, and yet which does not require that such differences are subsumed — and dissolved — into the nostalgic notion of a collective unity.'[57] New historicism can, as we have seen, 'include conflict', but only to dissolve it in just such a way. British critics are becoming more aware of its reactionary impact and, like Young, looking for alternatives. David Norbrook, noting in new historicism the 'odd mechanism by which violent politicization emerges in a kind of bleak estheticization' (p. 93) which 'risks turning the whole of history into a poetical text' (p. 101), links this, as does Joseph Loewenstein, to its attenuated focus, its 'renewed emphasis on patronage, on the role of a small courtly élite in setting the agenda' (p. 102). For him the way forward is to 'take account of areas of agency' which new historicism has neglected: 'intellectual history, Parliamentary politics, and radical religion' (p. 108). Isobel Armstrong argues from the evidence of a live production, directed by Peter Bogdanov, in order to challenge the logic of the politics of containment: 'That the conservative reading can be so palpably upended made one

[55] David Norbrook, *Poetry and Politics in the English Renaissance* (London, 1984), p. 20.
[56] 'Power and Ideology', pp. 271 and 275. Sinfield prefers the 'sites of contest' formula to one claiming subversiveness in texts. He does this in order to resist closure, but it leaves him in a political limbo, disallowing the potential for texts contributing to historical change.
[57] Robert Young, 'The Politics of "The Politics of Literary Theory"', *OLR*, 10 (1988), 131–57 (p. 155).

doubtful about Greenblatt's case.'[58] To combat the idea of a 'resistance' that is 'ultimately self-deceived', Catherine Belsey proposes a history 'of conflicting interests, of heroic refusals, of textual uncertainties. It tells of power, but power which always entails the possibility of resistance.'[59] Christopher Norris, in noting a 'fashionable relativist trend that undermines critical reason', warns that 'we in Britain are living through a period when it is vital to maintain a due sense of the difference between fact and fiction, historical truth and the various kinds of state-sponsored myth that currently pass for truth.'[60] Contrast this with Goldberg's claim that 'political reality, ordinary events and staged ones are all matters of representation',[61] the advertiser's world-view in which what you see 'staged' before you is all that there is.

This is the phenomenon of conservatism which looks to sweep all before it in a post-modernist free-for-all, while the political left, it is rumoured, can do no more than reach for a helping brush. The character Arruntius in *Sejanus* is left alive by the great patron and power-broker, Sejanus, because his oppositional activity only serves to defeat his own cause ('We must keep him to stalke with'). In the brave new historicist world we are all Arruntiuses now, doomed to serve the interests of those whom we like to think we are subverting.[62] New historicists need to bear in mind that this is precisely the frame of mind that all totalitarian governments seek to foster, as it is the most effective corrosive of active resistance. They need also to take note of the fact that their reading of history is shared by the most reactionary of bedfellows. I am conscious of a warning given by Catherine Gallagher: 'New Historicism confronts Marxism now partly as an amplified record of Marxism's own edgiest, uneasiest voices .... To dismiss such challenges as the mere echoes of reactionary defeatism would be a serious mistake.'[63] I take the point, but from the perspective of a Britain in the midst of a government campaign to snuff out the small remains of trade union power and privatize the great national utilities against the wishes of the majority, while the media tell us that actively to oppose is to play into the government's hands, I am afraid that is exactly how it looks to me, except that I would not use the term 'mere'.

---

[58] Isobel Armstrong, 'Thatcher's Shakespeare', *Textual Practice*, 3 (1989), 1–15 (p. 10). She sees the task ahead as being 'to consider how a democratic account of language — a democratic textual practice — can empower the dispossessed'. (p. 13)

[59] Catherine Belsey, 'Towards cultural history — in theory and practice', *Textual Practice*, 3 (1989) 159–72 (p. 172). She seeks to distinguish between new historicists and cultural materialists in this paper, a difference which 'lies in the inscription of struggle'.

[60] Christopher Norris, 'Postmodernising History: Right-Wing Revisionism and the Uses of Theory', p. 128.

[61] Jonathan Goldberg, *James I and the Politics of Literature* (Baltimore and London, 1988), p. 177.

[62] It should come as no surprise that Goldberg sees *Sejanus* as a representation of the 'all-embracing powers' of monarchy, with the play's republican ideas simply appropriated by the emperor, and as for Arruntius 'Even Arruntius is part of the imperial performance, an allowed voice giving Tiberius scope for his acts. Politics makes all the world a stage.' (*James I and the Politics of Literature*, p. 181.)

[63] Catherine Gallagher, 'Marxism and the New Historicism', in *The New Historicism*, pp. 37–48 (p. 47).

Reviews

Middle English Dialectology: Essays on some principles and problems. By ANGUS
McINTOSH, M. L. SAMUELS, and MARGARET LAING. Edited and introduced by
MARGARET LAING. Aberdeen: Aberdeen University Press. 1989.
xiv + 295 pp. £24.90.

This book contains a collection of nineteen papers, all but one of which have been
published earlier. The earliest dates from 1956. Thirteen of the papers are by Angus
McIntosh, four by M. L. Samuels, and two by Margaret Laing. In 1986 Aberdeen
University Press published *A Linguistic Atlas of Late Middle English*. This atlas was the
culmination of a project initiated by Professor McIntosh which had been under way
for many years. The papers in this volume could be said to form part of the
background to the atlas in that they show the development of the theory and
methodology behind it and also how the results obtained can be exploited in Middle
English studies. However, a companion collection of essays devoted to the language
of Chaucer, Gower, and Langland containing work by Professor Samuels and
Jeremy Smith has been published by Aberdeen University Press and this explains
why these authors are represented either not at all or less completely in this volume.
It is also planned to issue a collection of essays by Professor Benskin, and so none of
the work he has published is reprinted in either collection. The original project
focused on late Middle English, and now a second project is concentrating on early
Middle English. It is important to appreciate this background in order to understand the rationale of this collection.

That the atlas was published at all is a tribute to Professor McIntosh's persever-
ance in effecting a change in the attitudes of Middle English scholars to the written
word. Before, and even since, many of these articles appeared, editors were
interested only in establishing the best text of the work they were editing and
historical linguists were principally concerned with tracing the history of the sounds
of English. Consequently neither paid much attention to the many later manuscript
versions of texts which existed because they were dismissed as corrupt. The novelty
of Professor McIntosh's approach was to work with the written characters on the
page and for this purpose it made no difference whether the text was a late, 'corrupt'
copy or not, because it soon became clear that it was possible to construct
inventories for individual scribes. On the basis that some manuscripts could be
localized on external grounds, it emerged that it was possible to build up a grid of
scribal profiles which could be plotted on to the map of England so that texts which
were otherwise impossible to localize could be slotted into that map through the fit
technique. If the text was long enough and contained enough features, these would
limit the place into which it could fit on the map. Sometimes the fit was so accurate
that a text could be localized to within five miles. Naturally, in order to avoid
differences which can arise over time, a restricted time span of a hundred years, 1350
to 1450, was chosen — a period in which manuscripts in English become much more
common. Over the last thirty years the scribal profiles of a large number of
manuscripts have been recorded and it is that work which has formed the basis of the
atlas.

The possible applications of the information thus obtained are manifold and some
of them are expounded in the essays in this book. Because it is now possible to plot
manuscripts on a grid, such problems as the extent of Scandinavian penetration, the

development of a standardized language, and the limits of particular types of vocabulary can be approached in a more rigorous way. The technique also has important implications for the editing of medieval texts. As all manuscripts of a particular work are examined it may become clear whether individual copies contain a mixed dialect, made up of the language of the copyist, or whether the copyist was able to impose his own linguistic conventions on the text. In the latter case the copyist may well leave some relict forms and may indeed take a few pages to get into his stride. Analysis and localization of the different manuscripts allow us to see what the potential inter-relationship of the extant manuscripts is and hence to plot their gradual dissemination both geographically and chronologically. In this connexion Margaret Laing's previously unpublished paper on 'Linguistic profiles and textual criticism: the translation by Richard Misyn of Rolle's *Incendium Amoris* and *Emendatio Vitae*' is important. She is able to show from her analysis of these texts what the relationship among the extant manuscripts is and how the text circulated; it also provides us with fascinating information about the way scribes treated their exemplars in the fifteenth century. Her conclusion that her paper 'illustrates how textually and linguistically based approaches to the study of manuscripts may be combined. Used interactively, the two disciplines may greatly increase our understanding of the relationships between texts, manuscripts and scribes. Together they can provide the means to confirm or refute hypotheses based on the results of either when pursued in isolation' (p. 210) is fully justified. Its importance for the future cannot be overestimated.

The atlas is too expensive for most individuals to purchase for their private libraries. This collection of essays provides the methodology behind the atlas and examples of the way in which its material can be exploited. It will be essential reading for all who are interested in the history of Middle English or in the editing of Middle English texts. It brings important articles from a wide variety of journals together and makes them available at a price that even modern academics can afford.

University of Sheffield   N. F. Blake

The Track of the Repetend: Syntactic and Lexical Repetition in Modern Poetry. By Laury Magnus. New York: AMS Press. 1989. viii + 255 pp. $37.50.

Repetition, Laury Magnus reminds the reader at the start of this study, 'is central to the single most important element of both Platonic and Aristotelian poetics — mimesis' (p. 1), and has been central to much thinking in the history of theory. But modern criticism and theory, she claims, has ignored the fact 'that time is central to the workings and power of repetition' (p. 2). This might lead the reader to suspect that the author will correct this 'omission'; but this is not so. As the subtitle of her study suggests, any kind of theoretical and philosophical concern with repetition cedes place here to questions of syntax and matters of formal — even formalist — concern.

Half the book is a study of the refrain in poetry. Two categories of refrain are outlined: the traditional and the modern. Within the traditional, there are four types: simple, complex, cumulative, and antithetical (these last three all being called types of 'complex' refrain), each of which is explained, discussed, and exemplified. In the modern category there is a fifth type (which is also 'complex'): the disjunctive refrain. These refrains and their formal effects on poetry are exemplified through readings of Yeats, Dylan Thomas, Auden, T. S. Eliot, Whitman, Stevens, and others.

The disjunctive refrain, it is argued, is used by modern poets 'to articulate their sense of the cultural discontinuity of the modern world' (p. 71). This offers the theoretical key to this work. Professor Magnus seems throughout to hold to some theory of mimetic form, in which the formal and syntactic manoeuvres of a refrain will repeat or represent — and thereby reinforce — the supposed content of the poetry. This is theoretically extremely simplistic: could *all* those disjunctive refrains really be more or less about the same thing: 'man's [*sic*] loss of faith in tradition and authority, in religion and politics, in the social institution and the family, even in science and technology' (p. 71)? It is paradoxical, though a common effect of some early structuralisms, that within the extremely rigid and schematic formulations of a typology of repetition as advanced here, the readings of individual texts which are supposed to substantiate the thesis turn out to be extremely arbitrary and lacking in any philosophical rigour.

There is an obvious legacy of some involvement with structuralist methodology here; but the book, theoretically, has simply been incapable of moving beyond the structuralist problematic. Despite the assertion of time's centrality, for instance, there is no analysis of the refrain or of poetry at all here which takes into account the one thing which Professor Magnus says is lacking in other work: the temporality of the experience of reading. Critics, we are told, have failed to see the poem as an event in time. Well, what about, for random examples, Blackmur and Burke (both of whom thought of poetry as an event in time), Riffaterre (especially in his direct engagement with Jakobson over 'Les Chats', referred to here but not commented on as a matter of temporal concern), Stanley Fish (whose most influential work has been concerned precisely with the temporality of reading and what it makes a reader do in the time of reading), not to mention a whole different school of theory with a different attitude to time: marxism. There is here no question of the relation of time to history, and as a result no philosophy of the repetend. There is a useful layout of what might be called a 'rhetoric of repetitions' (pp. 19–21) which recurs from time to time in the study. This, in its rhetorical niceties, would have formed a much better ground for the kind of neo-formalist study proposed here; and it is this passage which serious critics or thinkers concerned with repetition in language will want to use and develop.

Professor Magnus might well have been advised to go on the track of the misprint, with which the text is unfortunately riddled.

UNIVERSITY COLLEGE DUBLIN   THOMAS DOCHERTY

Rethinking Bakhtin: Extensions and Challenges. Edited by GARY SAUL MORSON and CARYL EMERSON. Evanston, Illinois: Northwestern University Press. 1989. viii + 330 pp. $36.95 (paperbound $12.95).

Half of this volume is given to versions of previously published essays and chapters that extend or challenge Bakhtin's ideas: Gary Saul Morson and Linda Hutcheon on parody, Ann Shukman and Caryl Emerson on Bakhtin and Tolstoy, the late Paul de Man on 'Dialogue and Dialogism', and Aaron Fogel on 'Coerced Speech and the Oedipus Dialogue Complex'. These substantial essays all take on some new implications in their new contexts, but I shall concentrate my remarks on the three essays that appear in *Rethinking Bakhtin* for the first time.

Michael André Bernstein contributes a piece entitled 'The Poetics of *Ressentiment*' that stands to 'dialogism' as Huxley's 'Wordsworth in the Tropics' stands to Wordsworthianism: it highlights the dark implications of dialogism that Bakhtin's enthusiastic and cheerful readers typically ignore but it does not engage the complexity of Bakhtin's texts or ideas. Professor Bernstein rethinks Dostoevsky's *Notes from the Underground* more than he rethinks Bakhtin.

In their introduction, which is really two separate essays, Professors Morson and Emerson do rethink both their own earlier thoughts on Bakhtin and the thoughts of other important authorities on his work, especially Bakhtin's biographers Michael Holquist and Katerina Clark. The first part of the introduction, '"Toward a Philosophy of the Act"', challenges the claims of Professors Clark and Holquist that 'Bakhtin's works are ... really a theology in code' and that 'all of Bakhtin's later ideas are already present in the early texts'. The reading Professors Morson and Emerson present of Bakhtin's early fragment 'Toward a Philosophy of the Act' — a text to which until recently only Professors Clark and Holquist have had access — finds ethics rather than theology at its centre, and the reading the editors offer of his intellectual development divides his career into four periods with distinctive concerns and terminologies.

The second part of the introduction, 'The Disputed Texts', reviews the evidence cited by Professors Clark and Holquist for attributing works of Valentin Voloshinov and Pavel Medvedev to Bakhtin; though Professors Emerson and Morson 'long accepted assurances that convincing evidence would be forthcoming', they now find the evidence unconvincing and distinguish sharply between Bakhtin's 'lifelong dislike of Marxism' and the 'sincerely Marxist' works of his colleagues and urge us to consider the 'genuinely dialogic' relations among Bakhtin, Voloshinov, and Medvedev. They do not deny that 'Bakhtin's ideas exercised a profound influence on his friends' books', but they ask 'If Bakhtin influenced Voloshinov and Medvedev, why could they not have influenced him' to develop 'theories of language and literature that were sociological without being Marxist'? I find their case compelling and will try henceforth to distinguish among the authors of what we can still call the 'Bakhtin School'.

The two introductory essays share an emphasis on the importance for Bakhtin of distinctive individual positions in the world. For him, they argue, 'I alone occupy a particular place at a particular time, no one else can be in my place at my time'. Having acquired theoretical knowledge, they go on, 'we must impart a "tone" to it and "sign" it — that is, we must "acknowledge" it'. The 'real dialogue' they would reinstate among Bakhtin and his friends 'is destroyed by the attempt to make a "synthesis" (dialectical or otherwise) that conflates distinct voices'.

What is disconcerting for me is that Professors Morson and Emerson make these claims in a conflated editorial voice that makes no distinction between their own particular places, times, or tones. They *both* sign the essay and speak in a first person plural that would seem to demand explanation in the context of their emphasis on Bakhtin's radical account of individual responsibility and his radical suspicion of the 'forfeiture of singular participation in the name of representation'. A Bakhtinian analysis of joint authorship would seem to be called for here and in the case of Professors Holquist and Clark as well.

Mathew Roberts's new essay 'Poetics Hermeneutics Dialogics: Bakhtin and Paul de Man' would be worth the price of the volume to anyone interested in Bakhtin's place in recent literary theory. Drawing as Professors Morson and Emerson do on Bakhtin's as yet untranslated fragment 'Toward a Philosophy of the Act', Mr Roberts lucidly elaborates the parallels between Bakhtin's and Heidegger's responses to Kant and Dilthey and shows how the differences in their responses affect the differences between Bakhtin and de Man. Mr Roberts gives the best account I have read of both Bakhtin's and de Man's relations to twentieth-century phenomenology, showing how the 'fundamentally different attitudes to the dialogic and hermeneutic epistemologies' produce the 'mutual unintelligibility of their perspectives on meaning'.

Rethinking Bakhtin also contains the first English translations of Bakhtin's 1929 Prefaces to Tolstoy. One wishes that it contained an English translation of 'Toward a Philosophy of the Act'.

UNIVERSITY OF TOLEDO, OHIO   DON H. BIALOSTOSKY

Discontended Discourses: Feminism/Textual Intervention/Psychoanalysis. Edited by
   MARLEEN S. BARR and RICHARD FELDSTEIN. Urbana and Chicago: University
   of Illinois Press. 1989. viii + 250 pp. $29.95 (paperbound $12.50).

Discontented Discourses is a mine of brilliants. The essayists in this anthology bring us
many important insights into a variety of texts, ranging from Woody Allen's films to
Virginia Woolf's novels to Jane Gallop's essays. Bringing together the discourses of
feminism and psychoanalysis, they unearth the disease at the heart of Western
culture: we are afraid of the Other; we try to disarm it, naturalize it, become it.
   In the first section of the book 'Language and Disconnection', the focus is on
language and the need to disconnect language from its 'natural' links. In 'Not One
of the Family: The Repression of the Other Woman', Helena Michie claims that the
language of feminism, with its emphasis on sisters and the pre-Oedipal dyad of
mother and child, leaves no room for the Other. In 'Feminism and Psychoanalysis:
A Family Affair?' Terry Brown speculates about the place of the woman in
masculine discourse. Must she always be Cordelia, uttering 'nothing'? Using her
own relationship to a male mentor (Norman Holland), Dr Brown questions the
woman's connexion to psychoanalytic discourse and urges us to seek a different
position from the unconscious from which to speak. Pamela L. Coughie ('Virginia
Woolf's Double Discourse') is troubled by feminist readings of *Orlando* which
propose (impose?) androgyny as the novel's solution to women's and men's sexual
dilemmas. Dr Coughie believes that not enough attention has been paid to the
novel's duplicitous, self-contradictory language, which helps the hero/heroine
escape the gender constructions imposed by the various cultures (s)he passes
through. In 'The Case of Two Cultures: Psychoanalytic Theories of Science and
Literature', Ruth Salvaggio asks how can we escape engendering discourse (seeing
science as masculine, literature as feminine)? She suggests that the bisexual nature
of psychoanalytic discourse may give us a way to 'reposition ourselves and continually participate in the reconstruction of discourse and identity' (p. 69).
   The essays in the second edition, 'Representation and Distortion', examine the
distorted representations of women in the many different discourses of our culture.
Richard Feldstein ('Displaced Feminine Representation in Woody Allen's
Cinema') suggests that throughout Allen's work, the woman is always marginalized. He believes the danger is that we tend to think of Allen as apolitical or
even sympathetic to women, but he is neither. In fact, he disavows the (m)Other. In
'"Laughing in a Liberating Defiance": *Egalia's Daughters* and Feminist Tendentious
Humor', Marlene S. Barr turns to a feminist utopian novel and to Norman Holland
to understand what makes feminists laugh and why women sometimes find something funny even when men do not. Professor Barr concludes, 'Above all, the
[feminist] reader laughs [when reading *Egalia's Daughters*] because she can use the
text to confirm her feminist identity' (p. 97). Judith Roof, in 'The Match in the
Crocus: Representations of Lesbian Sexuality', looks at the difficulties literary and
psychoanalytic discourses have had representing lesbian sexuality. She begins with
brief readings of works by men, and then turns to novels by women: this procedure
allows her to demonstrate beautifully just how much more successful women are at
representing lesbian sexuality. Like Dr Roof, Victoria Frenkel Harris ('Scribe,
Inscription, Inscribed: Sexuality in the Poetry of Robert Bly and Adrienne Rich')
balances a male discourse against a female discourse and finds the male discourse
less effective. Bly wants to value feminine intuition and subjectivity, but he can only
reverse the usual hierarchy. On the other hand, Rich 'subversively reshapes' our
view of gender and of women's 'marginal status'.
   The third section, 'Theory and Disruption', looks at ways women have disrupted
the text, their own as well as others. Elizabeth A. Hirsh ('Imaginary Images:

"H.D.'', Modernism, and the Psychoanalysis of Seeing') demonstrates how H.D. disrupted her own texts as well as Pound's. Pound wanted to remove the 're' from 'representation', but H.D. refused to accept the Modernist privileging of interpretive metaphor/Images over decorative metaphor/Images. In her tantalizingly brief essay 'Rereading J. S. Mill: Interpretation from the (M)Otherworld', Christine Di Stefano suggests that liberal political theory with its emphasis on the autonomy of the self is based on a masculine subject. Consequently, Mill's feminism only works for women who are like liberal men and adopt 'a masculine posture in the world and toward the (m)other' (p. 168). Looking for the (m)Other in Mill's discourse allows us to disrupt his text.

The last two essays are both the longest and the most difficult. Cheryl Herr's essay 'Fathers, Daughters, Anxiety, and Fiction' brings a real daughter into the story of feminist discourse disrupting patriarchal discourse. Lucia Anna (Joyce's schizophrenic daughter) just as surely disrupts her father's self/text as Hélène Cixous's *Angst* restructures the male discourse of anxiety as ritualistically played out in Dickens, Joyce, or Barthelme. However, though Dr Herr faults earlier critics for overlooking the person Lucia, I am not sure she completely avoids this trap. She relies too completely on men's retellings of Lucia's story (Richard Ellman's biography, Joyce's letters). I wish that she had tried a little harder to read Lucia's own words (retellings).

Ellie Ragland-Sullivan's 'Dora and the Name-of-the-Father: The Structure of Hysteria', also attempts to bring to the forefront the real woman marginalized in a male discourse. She contends that Dora's (Ida Bauer's) story is lost amidst the profusion of discourses generated by her link with Freud. Dr Ragland-Sullivan believes that a Lacanian analysis might yet save her (or, at least, her story), for it would try to release her desire from the prison-house of the destructive family. Despite the essay's many fascinating insights into Dora and Lacan, a very important question has not been answered: Could Lacan have helped Dora? Although Dr Ragland-Sullivan contends that Lacan has helped women to use psychoanalysis as a tool to move outside the 'family novel', I remain unconvinced. How successful has Lacan been with his woman patients, for example, with actual anorexics and bulemics (whom Dr Ragland-Sullivan identifies as our modern-day hysterics)? Where are the 'real' women with real problems in all this theorizing?

As a reader-response critic, I also felt uncomfortable with the title and all it implies. To paraphrase David Bleich, discourses are not discontented, people are. I wish the contributors had at least occasionally been willing to acknowledge this. Perhaps this reluctance to acknowledge that readers have power and that reading is always situated is also the source of my last quibble with this book. I found the introduction very hard to read; I wish the editor had spoken less about the texts and more about why *these* essays were selected for *this* particular book. In other words, I would have liked, both in the introduction and throughout the book, a little more emphasis on context and a little less relentless focusing on text.

GETTYSBURG COLLEGE   TEMMA F. BERG

Teaching Women: Feminism and English Studies. Edited by ANN THOMPSON and HELEN WILCOX. (Cultural Politics) Manchester and New York: Manchester University Press. 1989. x + 211 pp. £27.50 (paperbound £7.95).

Ann Thompson's and Helen Wilcox's preface mentions their hope that *Teaching Women: Feminism and English Studies* 'will be of practical use as well as intellectual interest to everyone involved in' feminist pedagogy. The essays included in the book's five parts ('Access for Women', 'Valuing Women's Experience', 'A Course of

Our Own', 'Women and the Male Canon', and 'Beyond the Boundaries of "English"') certainly accomplish the editors' objective. *Teaching Women* thoughtfully documents efforts to establish feminist pedagogical niches within patriarchal educational enclaves. The contributors view feminist criticism as 'an instrument for personal, institutional and social change' (p. 74); they teach each student to achieve self-respect by valuing her own linguistic style and personal experience.

Teaching Women is about space. Contributors tackle issues regarding what should be done within relatively newly-acquired and hard-won classrooms of their own. They reveal that a feminist classroom is, unfortunately, still a marginal space. Its institutional position is aptly described by feminist (and female) science fiction writer James Tiptree Jr's protagonist who observes that women occupy a chink in the world machine ('The Women Men Don't See'). Feminists' chink in the patriarchal academic world machine is an evolving intellectual space relegated to an inadequate institutional space. As Patsy Stoneman explains, many British feminists work within a single discipline and their 'teaching practices are determined only partly by pedagogic ideas, and largely by the crannies of institutional space which we can infiltrate or commandeer' (p. 96). Or, in Allison Easton's words, 'I don't now feel like Ellador in Ourland, but more like Alice in Wonderland at the Mad Hatter's Tea Party where three creatures (all male) are seated who say it is *their* table and shout "no room, no room"' (p. 158).

To evoke another imaginative work, contributors imply that the feminist teacher enacts the 'Cinderella' plot. She becomes the academy's wicked step sister when undertaking feminist transformations. The 'shoe' of patriarchal academic acceptability simply does not fit her. As Penny Florence explains in her afterword, 'One problem common to all the essays in the book is that feminist courses and essays do not fit into the institutions that host them' (p. 194). While reading these essays about feminist teachers and their students, it struck me that both teaching and feminism receive low priority within many university endeavours. Dr Florence speaks to this issue: 'Rather than teaching, what is rewarded is contributing to a self-defined body of intellectual knowledge. . . . It is not coincidental that it should be a feminist book that brings together teaching practice, course content, institutional relationships, students' experiences and aesthetics' (pp. 194–95).

Teaching Women confronts the rather ludicrous fact that most universities do not value teaching and that most scholarly books silence pedagogical discourse. It creates a space and place for change by describing teaching practices which humanize what Elaine Hobby describes as 'the brutal world of academe' (p. 21). Instead of binding their feet in shoes that do not fit, the contributors stride into classrooms which are laboratories for creating feminist designs.

Teaching Women rightly insists that although feminist space within the academy is marginalized, it is none the less important. According to Patsy Stoneman, 'Institutionally small and constrained, our course might seem an ivory tower; but in terms of people and ideas, even a small course can be an empowering house' (p. 107). Feminist teachers can change the patriarchal academic world. Dr Florence closes the collection with a personal direction to the reader to imagine such change: 'I want you to pause before leaving these pages to allow through into consciousness at least the possibility of a new educational reality' (p. 198).

Teaching Women adroitly documents the beginning stages of feminist efforts to create change within academic institutions. The contributors emphasize that feminist critics 'do continue to exist within the dominant culture, and before we can change it we must learn to (re)read it without succumbing to its assumptions' (p. 112). They (re)read the dominant academic culture by insisting that teachers are learners. Created in a scholarly atmosphere hostile to the notion that teaching is important, *Teaching Women* reaffirms the importance of teaching people. The anthology asserts that women can in fact widen their chink in the male world machine. 'The possibility of a new educational reality' (p. 198) constitutes womankind's first small step toward constructing a brave new feminist world. Within this remade world, university personnel who fail to value teaching — not feminist educators — will be misfits.

I want you to read *Teaching Women: Feminism and English Studies* so that you can contemplate creating learning environments which inspire new social roles and rules.

VIRGINIA POLYTECHNIC INSTITUTE   MARLEEN BARR

The Brain of Robert Frost: A Cognitive Approach to Literature. By NORMAN N. HOLLAND.
    New York and London: Routledge. 1989. viii + 200 pp. £30.00 (paperbound
    £9.95).

First of all, and as Norman Holland quickly tells us in his opening chapter, this book is not really about Robert Frost's brain: 'I want to use Frost as a way to think about any brain, not just Robert Frost's, as it engages literature and language' (p. 1). But even this is not quite true. *The Brain of Robert Frost* is really about a theory of reader response developed already in such earlier works as *The Dynamics of Literary Response* (New York, 1968), *Poems in Persons* (New York, 1973), and *5 Readers Reading* (New Haven, 1975), all of which worked with an essentially psychoanalytic approach. The major thrust of this newer book is to reground that theory on cognitive psychology and recent brain research, and thus to give it more the look of hard science (and the glamour that goes with that), yet without substantially changing its central tenets. The discussion is carried out in Professor Holland's engagingly personal style, and, like the earlier *Poems in Persons*, in the tone of an introduction.

The opening chapter lays out the basic argument: first, neuroscience has now advanced to the point where we can begin to 'connect behaviours that we describe at a psychological level to physical structures in the brain' (p. 6); second, the brain modifies its circuitry according to patterns of use during early childhood, so that 'childhood experience . . . shapes the final architecture of the individual brain' (p. 8), and thus presumably its cognitive style; third, neurological studies of perception have contributed to a 'feedback' model of mental process that has overturned the mechanistic 'stimulus-response' model of early twentieth-century psychology; and finally, the new 'feedback' psychology proposes an account of literary experience quite different from and superior to the 'stimulus-response' model that pervades most modern literary criticism. In other words, texts do not simply act upon readers, or cause effects; readers act upon texts, and their experiences are the results of individual feedback processes and individual cognitive styles. One may ask whether Professor Holland really needs neurology to arrive at these conclusions; he has certainly arrived at them before without it. Further, one may wonder whether his first two premises about the brain adequately warrant his claims: studies of restored cognitive function in brain-damaged children, for example, suggest that remarkably similar abilities and styles can arise from radically different neural arrangements, and that one cannot simply equate a particular mode of personality with a particular neural circuitry. One might also note that, at this date, the neurologists are far from confident about assigning specific anatomical loci to the various feedback processes hypothesized by cognitive psychologists.

The rest of the book more or less serves to amplify the argument of chapter 1, and for much of the time the 'brain' largely drops out of the picture and gives way to 'mind'. This is especially noticeable in Chapters 2 to 4, as we examine, first, the cognitive style of Robert Frost as manifest in his writing (Chapter 2) and in his reading of Edwin Arlington Robinson (Chapter 3), and then the cognitive styles of six professors reading Robinson also (Chapter 4). All this is very much a reprise of Professor Holland's earlier work: Frost and the professors are seen to interpret literature (and the world) according to their particular 'identity themes', and to be increasingly different from each other as the interpretive issues become more open-ended. In Chapters 5 and 6, 'brain' makes a slight reappearance, but quickly gives way to cognitive feedback-theory, which is illustrated with the astonishingly simple example of driving a car on a twisty mountain road in Crete (Chapter 5), and then applied to writing and reading (Chapter 6). In the final Chapters (7–9), the feedback model of reader response confronts and defeats the stimulus-response 'metaphors' underlying most modern criticism (Chapter 7) and the teaching of literature (Chapter 8); the closing chapter more or less sums up the case for feedback. The critique of post-structuralist theory and *Rezeptionästhetik* in these chapters is incisive, and the discussion of implications for teaching is highly useful. Throughout, however, one has the feeling this book is meant for beginners: aside from the wrinkles added by neurology and cognitive psychology, those familiar with Norman Holland's important earlier work won't find much new here.

PENNSYLVANIA STATE UNIVERSITY   JEFFREY WALKER

Towards a Literature of Knowledge. By JEROME J. McGANN. Oxford: Clarendon Press. 1989. xiv + 138 pp. £16.50.

'What is the truth of imagination?' This is the question which motivates Jerome McGann's new book, the substance of which is drawn from his 1988 Clark lectures. In asking that question, Professor McGann seeks an alternative to the powerful Kantian and Romantic traditions which restrict literature's truth-functions to those of formal coherence and self-sufficiency. It is his contention that a 'literature of knowledge' exists to challenge the dominant assumptions of this more familiar Romantic 'literature of power'. 'Knowledge', in this context, entails an orientation toward the social and rhetorical, and to that extent poses serious questions about the kind of 'truth' to which the 'poetics of sincerity' and 'internal colloquy' lays claim. For the writers chosen to represent this alternative tradition — Blake, Byron, Rossetti, Pound — 'truth' is to be understood not as a particular content to be articulated, but as an activity (here the existential and deconstructive seem to merge in Professor McGann's approach): 'poetic truth is not conceptual; it is a process of knowing', a process which, in making of the poem 'a rhetorical situation', opens up the text to the play of *social* contradictions which mark its operation within the 'public sphere'.

For Professor McGann it is indeed contradiction which animates the 'literature of knowledge'. Each of the four writers examined here would in one way or another have subscribed to Adorno's view that 'Truth is the antithesis of existing society', but, as Professor McGann points out, Adorno also acknowledges that 'no art escapes complicity with untruth, the untruth of the world'. So Rossetti, for example, while seeking to establish the 'truth of the imagination' as something which stands apart from a vulgar materialism, creates in practice 'a style designed to function within a marketing and commercial frame of reference'. Knowledge, then, turns out to be a knowledge of limits; and it is, says Professor McGann, 'real, objective knowledge because the poetic field remains, finally, under the dominion of experience and not of consciousness'.

The particular interest of this account lies in Professor McGann's discussion of contradiction as an essentially non-dialectical element of poetic discourse: 'contradiction is not dialectic, it is asymmetry'. This 'asymmetry' allows truth and error to reside together in a poetics which is thoroughly context-based and grounded in the materiality of its medium. It is this materiality (rather oddly termed 'the physique of poetic discourse') which exposes those limits by which poetic truth is defined. Hence the importance of Blake's claim that his work 'giv[es] a body to Falshood that it may be cast off for ever', for, as the gouged erasures of some of his printing plates show, the trace of that 'body' remains, bound in a 'dialogical' relation to the truth which the writer seeks to express.

In a different way, the same set of issues is relevant to Pound's *Cantos*. For all Pound's attempts to control that work and to submit his materials to the discipline of some 'totalitarian' form, the 'objectivist' style which he chose had the effect of continuously submitting authorial truth-claims to those structures of judgement everywhere invited by his techniques of juxtaposition and contiguity. Professor McGann concludes that 'Pound's texts, like Byron's, enter a dialogue with their readers; this is what Pound, like Byron before him, wanted'. The point is well made, but in context it might leave the reader wishing for a more clearly political sense of the nature of such 'communicative exchange'. Certainly, that terminological nod to Habermas opens perspectives on a 'public sphere' which extend far beyond (for example) the relatively closed world of Hobhouse's annotations to Byron's poem. It is to be hoped that Professor McGann will explore them further at some later date.

UNIVERSITY OF SUSSEX   PETER NICHOLLS

Kenneth Burke: Literature and Language as Symbolic Action. By GREIG E. HENDERSON. Athens: University of Georgia Press. 1989. xiv + 216 pp. $27.50.

Kenneth Burke has been a name to reckon with in literary criticism for more than fifty years, but during most of that time he has been a somewhat marginal figure. Unlike most of the New Critics, with whom he had certain connexions, he was a thoroughgoing theorist and comparatively little of his output was devoted to the analysis of literary texts. His interests also ranged far beyond literature in the narrow sense. With the ascendancy of theory in recent years, however, his stock has risen and he has been seen as bridging the gap between native American criticism and continental theory. But contemporary critics still have problems in accommodating his work, though such critics as Fredric Jameson and Frank Lentricchia have written about him recently. Most of Burke's books are inordinately long, deal with a great variety of subjects, and are idiosyncratically structured. This has made his work difficult to use by critics and teachers. As J. Hillis Miller has remarked: 'Though Burke is a great critic, one of his limitations is the difficulty of getting out of his work a practical procedure for teaching, for criticism, for interpreting works. Derrida's procedures are more assimilable to teaching' (*Criticism*, 24 (1982), 107).

Greig E. Henderson's book would serve a useful purpose if it could go some way towards altering this situation. In contrast to William H. Rueckert's earlier study (*Kenneth Burke and the Language of Human Relations* (Berkeley and Los Angeles, 1982)), it aims to be synchronic in approach. A study that created a coherent order out of the diversity and discursiveness of Burke's texts would be highly desirable, especially as Professor Henderson believes that Burke's work 'manages to yoke together formalist and sociological approaches to literature' (p. 3). In a critical climate in which the major conflict is between Derridian or de Manian textualism and new historicist contextualism Burke, Professor Henderson implies, may offer a way of overcoming this split.

Does this book, then, succeed in making Burke's work usable by critics and teachers or in suggesting that Burke successfully reconciles intrinsic and extrinsic criticism? I think the answer must be no or not quite. Professor Henderson admits that he does not believe Burke achieves total consistency but he struggles even to demonstrate a limited amount of coherence. Thus he writes not very confidently: 'Burke seems to be saying that freedom and determinism are compatible within the confines of a dramatistic terminology of motives' (p. 124), and refers to 'the dubious realm of what Burke "really" means' (p. 125). Professor Henderson demonstrates that he is a capable summarizer of the ideas of several thinkers but his accounts of Burke are less clear. This suggests, I think, that Burke's merits are not as a systematic thinker (though the connexions between Burke's dramatistic theory of language and the work of such theorists as J. L. Austin are rightly pointed out), but lie rather in his ability to generate striking ideas which have great resonance. For example, Professor Henderson quotes the following statement from *A Grammar of Motives*: 'we must always be admonished to remember, not that an experiment flatly and simply reveals *reality*, but rather it *reveals only such reality as is capable of being revealed by this particular kind of terminology*' (p. 131). Professor Henderson also gives a useful account of Burke's later 'logological' stage and shows that he has lost none of his power to intrigue.

Though the book may fail to derive from the diversity of Burke's writings a critical procedure that is easily usable or teachable or to suggest convincingly that Burke's work formulates a theory that will reconcile intrinsic and extrinsic critical approaches, it does remind one that Burke is a critic whose work continues to generate insights.

University of Dundee   K. M. Newton

Dimensions of the Sign in Art. By Albert Cook. Hanover and London: For Brown
    University Press by University Press of New England. 1989. xiv + 262 pp.
    £23.25; $42.00.

The publication of a new book by Albert Cook inevitably raises high expectations; these are largely fulfilled. His erudition in these wide-ranging essays is character-istically impressive, moving effortlessly from Longinus to Lyotard, Plato to Panofsky, but it does raise an unresolved methodological problem: that of insuffi-cient discrimination. It may seem ungenerous to complain of an embarrassment of riches, but I believe that the text is clotted with such a wealth of data as to verge on indigestibility. (An analytic index would have helped.) Take the theoretical first chapter, for instance, which attempts in effect a survey of western aesthetics. Typically we are offered just a paragraph on each major thinker, accompanied by glancing footnote asides on aesthetic debates that are taken out of context and often bear only tangentially on the exposition in the text. Professor Cook's considerable learning is beyond question, but the briskness of his summarizing and sampling is ultimately frustrating, giving a misleading impression of superficiality. The same phenomenon characterizes his later digressions on the functions of colour or of the mirror in cultures ranging from New Guinea to Egypt. Such material is fascinating but, one feels, its inclusion is a self-indulgence. Elsewhere chapters on specific artists cite such a plenitude of individual works (only thirteen of which are illustrated), often devoting no more than a sentence to each, that the argument becomes submerged in a catalogue of annotations. The style is also all too often a barrier to comprehension. There are epigrams of suggestive brilliance: 'Magritte's surrealism can be defined as a redefinition of and an advance upon the fusion of a realistic surface and allegorical moments in the painting of the Low Countries generally' (p. 184). But elsewhere the phrasing is sometimes unfortunate or downright opaque: 'These faces leave all the years of portraits behind to a world in collusion to repress the fierceness that their haunted impenetrability unleashes' (p. 96).

These reservations aside, however, no reader could fail to learn considerably from Professor Cook's reflections. He argues that technical problems in art are indivisible for both artist and viewer from a contemplative experience of 'immersion' or 'sublimity'. It is accordingly not surprising that Professor Cook devotes his first essay to Turner. His discussion of the 'sublime' is influenced neither by Post-modernism nor by recent criticism of Romantic literature. Instead the declared focus is on 'Mind, Eye, and Brush', to demonstrate in Turner's canvases the interplay of imagination with reality and with the inherited significance of cultural codes and painterly conventions. The discussion is well-informed but largely a digest of existing critical positions. Skirting epistemological issues, Professor Cook also avoids questions of handling. Yet Turner's late works raise similar problems to late Monet and may arguably — as John House's work on Monet indicates — best be illuminated by detailed attention to the marks of the brush. Curiously, Professor Cook also ignores Turner's apocalyptic concerns, where his treatment of historical and visual deliquescence sometimes parallels that of Shelley (the English Romantic poets are another Venetian context that remains unexamined). The chapter on Goya also offers little that is new; the assertion that Goya throws ethical questions into unprecedented relief being supported by a descriptive commentary on his etchings. By contrast there are stimulating chapters on mirrors in Renaissance art and on colour in painting. In pursuing his unexceptionable argument that paintings are often unified by chromatic variations on a single hue, Professor Cook perhaps foregrounds this communicative element in artificial isolation from other composi-tional devices but his close readings of Titian's paintings display considerable sensitivity. (A minor point: the Vienna *Tarquin and Lucretia* is now not attributed to Titian himself.)

The second half of the book is extremely assured. Professor Cook is at his most authoritative in exploring the interaction of word and image and he offers an outstanding account of the intricate contradictions among sign systems in the work of Duchamp and a fine survey of Klee's fusion of verbal and visual wit in the light of his *Das Bildnerische Denken*. Magritte's paintings are illuminated through his own distinction between resemblance and similarity (*'similitude'*), the discrepancies between 'reality' and its incongruent artistic reflection. There is an interesting essay on Ernst's collage novels, although here the emphasis on verbal/visual interaction is less appropriate. For Ernst's narratives offer an encyclopaedia of melodramatic clichés, from cinema as well as from nineteenth-century popular illustrations. To neglect this complex visual intertextuality is also to overlook the ironic contextual displacements within the texts produced by visual rhymes, whether of gesture, posture, or compositional format.

HOCHSCHULE ST GALLEN   ALAN ROBINSON

Crossing the Shadow-Line: The Literature of Estrangement. By MARTIN BOCK. Columbus: Ohio State University Press. 1989. x + 170 pp. $25.00.

This study extends Conrad's sense of the 'shadow-line' to discuss literature that moves out from celebrating 'the cultural episteme' into a more visionary world dependent on a disorientation of the senses. It traces a tradition from 'The Ancient Mariner' though De Quincey, about whom Mr Bock writes well, to Baudelaire, Poe, and Rimbaud, and Joyce, who is narrowed by the discussion to stress him as a successor to Rimbaud, and Djuna Barnes. Two last chapters go outside this tradition, by looking at Conrad, whose fiction involves different modes of sensual deprivation, and Malcolm Lowry. These last chapters seem separate from the thesis, which otherwise uses some interestingly interlocked figures, but the study otherwise stirs up some very empiricist objections. Does Eliot refer to 'an association of sensibility' (p. 68), for instance? Mr Bock refers repeatedly to 'the cultural episteme', which it is claimed derives form Foucault's *The Order of Things* but it has no Foucauldian resonances, and elsewhere seems identified with 'contemporary Christian civilization' (p. 64), and is also just 'the culture' (p. 76). This simply collapses any possible critique of the historical conditions the Romantics or the Modernists, for instance, were involved in; it makes the dominant culture monolithic and yet at the same time comically easy to subvert if any text describing an individual psychic journeying, not dependent on an empirical sense of reality, can do it. Texts that question the episteme are dubbed 'heretical', because they distinguish themselves from those other canonical texts 'that reflect that Christian mythos of the cultural episteme' (p. 140). Not many texts remain canonical, then.

The study lacks a sense of necessary differentiations. Is it true that 'The Ancient Mariner' begins a process of linguistic disorientation that culminates in *Finnegans Wake* (p. 76), or that it is a Barthesian 'text of bliss' (p. 143) — Barthes's *jouissance*? It is not a wish to deny the Modernism (a term never used here) instinct in romantic writing that prompts denial of this: nor a sense that the treatment of Coleridge requires an instatement of cultural and religious orthodoxy in Wordsworth: yet Wordsworth's sense of radical disconfirmation of self and experience at certain moments of crisis, such as the crossing of the Alps, is much less contained in a consensual way of seeing than Coleridge's. Rather, the treatment of 'The Ancient Mariner', though making useful points, fails to register how the text belongs to a tradition of writing that allows for the existence of the isolate (as the Wandering Jew, for instance). Keats's sense of Coleridge's irritable reaching after fact and reason suggests how his poetry, perhaps unlike Wordsworth's, which does register disorientation, both in those frequent senses of being lost and in what de Man calls Wordsworth's interest in mutilation, does seek to reinscribe itself in traditional orthodoxies. This suggests that Mr Bock's model is far too simple. The sense that the writers he describes 'cross the shadow-line of heretical space' allows for no Foucauldian or Bakhtinian sense that discourses operate within contested spaces, that definitions and redefinitions of the liminal and acceptable are modified within each text, or that the nineteenth century is the site of contests for dominant modes of writing: between fantasy and realism, between romanticism and forms of modernism.

In *Yale French Studies* in 1984, John Frederick Logan suggests that 'the question of intoxication provides a key to understanding the entire nineteenth century' ('The Age of Intoxication', *Yale French Studies*, 50 (1974), 94). Mr Bock is aware of the importance of drugs for cleansing the doors of perception of the bohemian artist, and buried within this book is a more interesting thesis about the artist as addict, enlarging the senses in a way inseparable from a revolution of the word. But arguments are not developed. A treatment of 'estrangement' might have involved reference to Marx; Nietzsche would have been invaluable for the relationships of this breakdown of the rational to the Dionysian, but Freud seems an important omission. De Quincey, author of the word 'unconsciously' in 1823 (so *O.E.D.*) is the confessional writer (but confession implies a desire to return to the world of the dominant and familiar that Mr Bock takes his writers to be refusing) whose explorations lead him towards a psychic exploration that is inseparable from that discourse which, it needs seeing, leads to Freud, and to the learning of the split, non-unitary character of subjectivity. The given texts' radical edges are not felt, or felt rather dully as when Mr Bock says that the most sympathetic readers of *Nightwood* and *Under the Volcano* lie outside the mainstream of society, lesbians and transsexuals for one, alcoholics for the other novel. Strange literalism. He lacks the measure of what the 'cultural episteme' he writes of permits and what it denies.

UNIVERSITY OF HONG KONG   JEREMY TAMBLING

Elegiac Fictions: The Motif of the Unlived Life. By EDWARD ENGELBERG. University Park and London: Pennsylvania State University Press. 1989. xviii + 283 pp. $29.95.

It seems perfectly appropriate that Edward Engelberg's most recent book should recall to mind his first, and best, interpretative endeavour: the 1964 study of 'patterns in W. B. Yeats's aesthetic' which takes for its epigraph the poet's description of Byzantium under Justinian (from *A Vision*), a paean of praise to the artificers who could make 'a vast design . . . seem but a single image'. As in a previous study 'From Consciousness to Conscience, Goethe to Camus', however, Professor Engelberg has elected to diversify his focus, with the result that the 'single image' (in *Elegiac Fictions* the 'motif of the unlived life' foregrounded by its subtitle) is distributed *through* and *across* a 'vast design', rather than perceived at the acme of its expressive potential as (in Yeats's formulation) 'the work of many that seemed the work of one'. Whilst it is evident that *A Vision* is far from being a procedural model for the literary critic seeking to trace the various manifestations of a motif from the opening moves of Romanticism to what Professor Engelberg identifies as the 'endgame' of Modernism, something comparably governed by crystallizations of the *Zeitgeist*, and by the vagaries of chance and choice which are subsequently received as determinants of an epoch, surfaces throughout *Elegiac Fictions*. Fifteen authors — Lermontov, Turgenev, Brontë (Emily), Tolstoy, Kafka, Chekhov, Mann (Thomas), James (Henry), Ibsen, Faulkner, Joyce, Woolf, Flaubert, Hemingway, and Beckett — figure prominently in Professor Engelberg's chapter titles, and the one chapter with no specific exemplars of its theme adds four more (Goethe, Rousseau, Byron, and Pushkin) for good measure. This is about as near to God's plenty over the past two centuries as anyone could be expected (if not actually encouraged) to aspire, and not surprisingly a very long book, well over a hundred and twenty thousand words, has been brought to birth in an attempt to respect the depth and complexity of more than thirty works of more or less classic status, the majority of which receive extended discussion of the kind one might find in an article devoted to any one of them. Each, however, surrenders some individual, not to say idiosyncratic, features in proportion to the emphasis Professor Engelberg exerts on the privileged motif that conditions his response to them.

Elegiac Fictions could only have undertaken to plead its massive (but also limited) brief on the basis of its author's distinguished career as a teacher of Comparative Literature, with each new semester offering tempting and occasionally irresistible opportunities to add another cluster of mosaics to a work already in progress. Yet it is difficult, in spite of what is shown to be a corporate (if very various) concern with 'the unlived life', to feel that any inevitability controls Professor Engelberg's account of it. The urgency and verve which not unnaturally, though often paradoxically, attends a given author's exploration of this issue is largely, if not wholly, dissipated by criticism that gravitates, by very virtue of its range, towards paraphrase and plot summary, enlivened by occasional shifts of perspective reflecting differentials rather than similarities. Whether anyone's tolerance or patience can be expected to survive the volume as a whole, beyond the discussion that has prompted one to turn to it, seems very doubtful, with so much imperturbable academic blandness on display. In his Introduction Professor Engelberg writes: 'A review of literary suicides in the last century and a half would be worth a separate study; so would an analysis of the various kinds of literary renunciation. But Death, Negation, Ennui, "The Super-fluous Man", the void — all have been subjected to detailed attention. The "unlived life" in some way subsumes them all.' It would surely have been more prudent to substitute 'to some extent' in what would actually have served equally well as a concluding paragraph, suitably situated at the furthest possible remove from the reassurance — almost as disturbing as it is amusing — that 'with cosmic despair we shall deal very little, except in Chapter 1'.

UNIVERSITY OF READING   JOHN PILLING

Marx & Modern Fiction. By EDWARD J. AHEARN. New Haven and London: Yale
    University Press. 1989. xvi + 231 pp. £17.95; $26.00.

In his preface Edward J. Ahearn tells us that his study is intended 'to delineate a number of leading concepts and analyses in Marx's writings as a whole and then to show — through detailed interpretations of a range of novels — the richness of these arguments for literary study'. Aware of the charge of reductiveness that is so often brought against Marxist criticism — and against Marx himself — he argues that the 'Method of Political Economy' section of the *Grundrisse* 'combines awareness of the specificity of artistic forms with a theoretical finesse concerning the relation between concept and concrete detail in economic history and social analysis'. However, even if Professor Ahearn is right about Marx's critical acumen, he does not succeed in putting it to profitable use.

After a (very) brief introduction to some key concepts (alienation, mode of production, etc.), the author turns to the seven novels he has selected for discussion. In three long chapters he pairs *Pride and Prejudice* and *Madame Bovary*, *The Golden Bowl* and *Ulysses*, *Le Père Goriot* and *Absalom, Absalom!*, and then devotes a final analysis to *Moby-Dick*, always insisting that 'Marx's depiction of the growth of European capitalism and its impact on the non-European world is the appropriate context in which to read modern Western fiction'.

Professor Ahearn's critical commentary is, on the whole, unobjectionable. Who would want to deny that 'the city-country division becomes the central locus for the expression of Emma's romance-reality problem' or that '*The Golden Bowl* is even more extreme than *Pride and Prejudice* in presenting personal relations in financial terms'? It is, at times, informative, especially with respect to *Pride and Prejudice* and *Madame Bovary* (in both novels the libidinous aspects of status and ownership receive careful consideration), and it establishes interesting parallels between Balzac's Vautrin and Faulkner's Sutpen. But it is also given to restating the obvious — worse, it insists on relating the obvious to Marx's writings at a level that one can only call pedestrian and that raises the question why Marx is brought in in the first place: 'At the end, illustrating Marx's argument about owning and being, Charlotte possesses Verver's millions but is hardly any longer appreciated — the prince calls her stupid.' In fact, to quote one of the wry ironies of Melville's Ishmael, 'if your apothecary by mistake sends you poison in your pills, you die', and offer as commentary that 'here the economic relation is very nearly one of life and death', is to invite spontaneous laughter.

But the main objection to Professor Ahearn's approach must be that it does not escape the reductiveness he seeks to avoid. To read Emma Bovary's 'passion' and 'destiny' in socio-economic terms is to ignore the psychological condition that makes her so susceptible to the trappings of capitalism. To claim that 'global exploration and commerce, spearheaded by whaling, is the true historical subject of *Moby-Dick*' or that another of Ishmael's ironies (his suggestion that the whaling house of Enderby & Sons lags 'not far behind the united royal houses of the Tudors and the

Bourbons, in point of real historical interest') shows an 'emphasis on international economic history [that] recalls Marx's linking of capital cities and the world market' is not only reductive, it is bewildering, as is the final claim that 'virtually everything in these novels is conditioned, if not determined, by the economic'. (This last claim is all the more surprising since at the outset we were told that Marx is not a determinist.)

Professor Ahearn's study has the merit of spelling out the importance of the socio-economic in the passages he has selected for detailed analysis, but it falls far short of what it promises.

UNIVERSITY OF UTRECHT   HANS BERTENS

Mask and Scene: An Introduction to a World View of Theatre. By DIANA DEVLIN. Basingstoke and London: Macmillan. 1989. 221 pp. £25.00 (paperbound £7.95).

Diana Devlin, a teacher and director of theatre and recently administrator of the International Shakespeare Globe Centre dedicated to reconstructing the playhouse near its original site, has given her new book *Mask and Scene* an intriguing title. Both that, and her avowed intention to examine theatre as a multi-cultural phenomenon not limited by historical demarcations or geographical boundaries promise an original perspective. This expectation, however, is only sporadically met, since her contention that theatre has developed in parallel ways in East and West demands consistently rigorous analysis of a comparative nature that Ms Devlin delivers only occasionally, as, for example, in her fascinating brief treatment of the horse as stage prop in world drama.

Even the introductory nature of this volume — the suggestions for research and readings for further study appended at the end clearly point to secondary-school or lower-college level as the intended audience — cannot fully excuse the sketchy handling of most topics. Curiously, in light of what is emphasized in the book's title, there is no discussion of the use of literal masks in modern drama, as in Yeats's plays; and, perhaps even more curious and certainly potentially misleading, is Ms Devlin's statement that 'the creation of the scenic effect [is] an aspect of theatre that could be largely dispensed with', since she argues that 'the essential needs are time, space, actor and audience for the creation of a play'.

Interesting notions abound, but too much of the time these are just mentioned and then dropped: the Globe resembled architecturally the early Chinese theatres; theatre marginalized the masses from 1600–1800; the acting in Noh aims for the effects of Expressionism; naturalism on stage replicates the scientific method; anti-colonialism coincides with the re-emergence of indigenous forms; stage nudity is itself a costume; gender-switching demonstrates acting's appeal as a 'risky' business in which performers gain 'excitement' by 'courting danger and disapproval', and so forth. Twice, Ms Devlin refers admiringly to the importance of the Indian treatise *Natya Sustra, Doctrine of Dramatic Art* without ever hinting at its contents, and the lack of any attempt to handle the notion of comic structure in drama reduces all stage comedy to escapist or satiric — hardly adequate in the case, for instance, of Shakespeare. Finally, a number of her generalizations and conclusions require some bolstering: *Why* has scenic illusionism dominated in the West while a more simple creation of images in the spectators' minds has been a hallmark of theatre in the East? *Why* does social revolution lead to innovation in stage design? *How* in more exact terms can the screen in cinema and television be regarded as analogous substitutes for the masks performers sometimes wear? *What* contemporary examples might support the claim that when truth is pluralistic rather than 'unchanging' and 'permanent' a civilization's drama will be more varied and novel?

Ms Devlin attempts to provide a sense of the richness of the world's dramatic repertoire by synopses of sixteen texts from Sophocles's *Antigone* through Soyinka's *Death and the King's Horseman*, though even these are sometimes not without their problems; she seems unsure of the specific 'crime' (the forged signature) of Nora in *Doll House*, for example, and suggests that 'the mythical pattern of death and rebirth' governs *The Cherry Orchard*, when Chekhov's seasonal imagery would seem to support those who question the regenerative close of that play. Her discussion of the element of 'performance' in theatre through a detailed account of one production (the Royal Shakespeare Company's 1978 mounting of *Macbeth* at the Warehouse) is, however, a complete success, though an accompanying production photograph would have enriched a chapter that is already the book's real pleasure. (The publisher has included three-dozen line illustrations, some beautifully simple, others too fussy for their size.) The author's style is serviceable throughout, although the appropriateness of several chapter subheadings (for instance, 'The invisible function of theatre') is never made clear in the treatment of the subject, and once in a while an awful sentence has escaped the editor's eye: 'In any performance be open to what seems to be being demanded of you, and be willing to give it.'

In short, Ms Devlin's *Mask and Scene* often tantalizes but seldom satisfies. It would be better to send one's introductory students to a little volume like Martin Esslin's more narrowly conceived *An Anatomy of Drama* (London, 1976), or one's more advanced students to his recent *The Field of Drama: How the Signs of Drama Create Meaning on Stage and Screen* (London, 1988) to start them thinking intelligently about the conventions of drama and the nature of the communal theatrical experience throughout history and in their own lives.

PURDUE UNIVERSITY, WEST LAFAYETTE, INDIANA   THOMAS P. ADLER

Rediscovering Hellenism: The Hellenic Inheritance and the English Imagination. Edited by
    G. W. CLARKE. Cambridge, New York, Port Chester, Melbourne, and Sydney:
    Cambridge University Press. 1989. xiv + 264 pp. £30.00; $55.00.

In the 1850s Edward Lear sketched the sites of Greece, provoking Tennyson to song: 'Illyrian woodlands, echoing falls.' Among his watercolours is one of the Temple of Apollo at Bassae, now in the Fitzwilliam Museum, Cambridge. Centre stands the temple, Doric columns flawless, marble honey turning to gold. Behind, indigo-mauve, rise the triple peaks of Ithome while in mid-distance goats browse, the whole framed by the generous branches of an oak. At much the same period Robert Smirke also rendered the temple, its columns listing, its architraves eaten by time, the floor piled up with the debris of centuries. In his essay on 'The Arcadian vision', one of the many delights of this fine book, J. Mordaunt Crook reproduces Smirke's picture, but not Lear's. His point, however, is contrast. For Smirke's painting belongs to a literal Arkadia, Lear's to a fabled Arcady; Smirke's to an historic Hellas, Lear's (and Tennyson's response) to that resistless and far from extinct cult known as Hellenism.

The ten essays here assembled amount to a history of that cult. In 1816 it reached London with the Elgin Marbles. Despite Byron's strictures at the audacity of their pillage, the Marbles were reputable, and they were News. So excited was the painter Fuseli at their arrival that he ran all the way to Park Lane to see them, colliding with a flock of sheep *en route*. Haydon escorted Keats, who reported himself 'a sick eagle looking at the sky'. Later Keats stood entranced before a Grecian urn. His plight is so moving because he knew no Greek. But what had gripped the English?

They were not, of course, the instigators. Early travellers to Greece were for the most part British and French, but the enthusiasts and interpreters were German. It was Johann Winckelmann who gave us Hellenism as a sort of serene Apollonian essence, epitomized in his eyes, as in Lessing's, by the Hellenistic Laocoön. Winckelmann had no more visited Greece than had Goethe or Hölderlin, both of whom perpetuated the craze. Germany produced the brightest scholars none the less; it also synthesized an Hellenic ideal annexed by other nations for reasons of their own. In England, the gist was threefold. Hellenism was first, as Frank M. Turner illustrates, the means by which a native élite debated the issue of democracy in terms that *demos* could not understand. It was secondly, as James Bowen demonstrates, the model through which British public schools recast themselves in the mould of philosopher–guardians presiding over an increasingly intractable world. Thirdly and most famously, it was the method by which Matthew Arnold attempted to keep the nastier aspects of industrialism at bay even if, as Stephen Prickett mercilessly proves, he got his terminology, and his history, woefully confused in the process. Should not the Barbarians have been harrassing the Hellenes, and the Philistines the Hebrews? The closing epic simile of 'The Scholar Gipsy' has a shy Tyrian trader, *ergo* a Philistine, fleeing some loutish Greek hoplites, relaxing only when he beaches on African shores frequented by 'dark Iberians', friendly Phoenicians. A tricky moment for Arnold until Professor Prickett sails to the rescue, tracing the Hellenes of *Culture and Anarchy* to Coleridge's quasi-ecclesiastical Clerisy of clergymen, dons, and schoolmasters: all guardians of a sort. As we twitch our sable gowns, are we even now exempt? Arnold-like and slippered, the wraith of Leavis stalks among us still.

At the root, of course, lies Plato, or rather Benjamin Jowett's version of Plato: a proto-Christian gentleman and Jolly Good Chap. In 1879, in *The Journal of Philology*, Henry Jackson published a series of articles claiming that the dialogues were a mutually inconsistent sequence which could only be understood in strict historical context. Jowett would have none of it: 'The dialogues of Plato are poems.' So the dialogues became Forms peering over us as we toiled grubbily below. It was all too good to last, and a recoil naturally set in. So pervasive was Hellenism in Germany however that Nietzsche, whose Dionysianism may owe something to Bachofen, could only express his reaction in Greek terms. Thenceforward the ideal was less Fifth Century Athens than Thrace, whence the Bacchic hordes swept down to do Nice and Terrible Things. Greece grew pagan, and lurid as Tylor and then Frazer unveiled the mystery cults. In his culminating essay Anthony Stephens can do little more than glance at these later developments, so perhaps Dionysus deserves another book. This one is absorbing, though it has some odd *termini ad quem*. Penelope Wilson gives us Gray's Pindar, but little beyond (what of the nineteenth-century ode?), and Peter Tomory follows 'the fortunes of Sappho' to 1850, nineteen years before a rubbish tip near Crocodopolis in Egypt yielded a mass of her fragments which had been used for mummy wrappings. So it is the sublime and heterosexual Sappho we get, Sappho in the arms of Phaon rather than Andromeda, though there are other Sapphos, Swinburne's for instance.

In the twentieth century, Dionysus Rules Okay though Apollo too has his moments. A schoolmaster once defined an intellectual for me as 'someone who reads Plato at bus stops'. I later traced this to Macaulay, where the Platonist has his feet on the fender. With this book, let us warm ourselves.

ROYAL HOLLOWAY AND BEDFORD NEW COLLEGE, LONDON   ROBERT FRASER

Orthodox Heresy: The Rise of 'Magic' as Religion and its Relation to Literature. By STODDARD MARTIN. Basingstoke and London: Macmillan. 1989. viii + 322 pp. £35.00.

Modern magic is the creation of the late nineteenth century. Worried about religion, daunted by science, our great-grandparents raised a monolith on the plinth of fallen

Christianity. The inscription on the stone bore various names: Theosophy; Sweden-borgianism; Spiritualism; Christian Science. Eclecticism was the order of the day, and, however heady the proliferation, sectarianism was out. Just as late Victorian anthropologists sought a common structure beneath man's cultural and social experience, so the mystics of the period sought an elixir distillable from all religions as truth. Much — but not all — of this has passed away. In the late 1960s, on an equivalent personal mission, I followed some of these decaying certainties across wintry Brighton and Hove. It was a marvellous place to start; a treasure trove of mystical dinosaurs.

In the twentieth century the action moved to America, where the spadework had already been done by sages tired of Europe's religious hegemony: Emerson, Mary Baker Eddy, even William James, people whose contribution Stoddard Martin might have done more to examine. Increasingly as one might expect the focus moved to the West coast, where mid-twentieth-century California proved ripe for the likes of Aleister Crowley and L. Ron Hubbard. Dr Martin is himself an American, and takes these latter-day manifestations more seriously than many of his European colleagues might have done. To guide us round this maze we need someone with just enough empathy to maintain our interest and sufficient scepticism to keep protest at bay. Dr Martin comes with uniquely mixed qualifications: endless curiosity and tolerance combined with an engaging illiteracy concerning the wider context. One of the few men I know to have read right through Madame Blavatsky's *The Secret Doctrine*, he has also painstakingly investigated the cognitive structure of such movements as the Golden Dawn, Anthroposophy and Scientology. If nothing else, his is an historical handbook of the occult.

Nor is his subject trivial. Somewhere along the line somebody had to write a study of late-nineteenth-century revivals of magic, if only as essential background for such figures as W. B. Yeats. But problems there are. To begin with, Dr Martin seems incapable of distinguishing between ancient magic and its modern revivals. The rites of Eleusis, the Isis and Orphic cults are dutifully displayed, but such phenomena, though magical in the Frazerean sense of attempting to orchestrate nature, were never in the modern sense 'occult', drawing as they did on sources of myth and spiritual enlightenment commonly revered. More importantly, as his title betrays, Dr Martin cannot distinguish between magic and religion. He is, furthermore, indifferent to the wider debate out of which Victorian occultism sprang.

Throughout the period of the *fin-de-siècle* and even later, questions of the para-normal occupied a centrality in the intellectual market-place inconceivable to us now. The cults investigated here teach us not to view science and religion too naïvely as opposites. Seen from one angle, occultism represents a training of scientific method on immaterial things. The results have been mixed: as pure science occasionally fascinating, as applied science worrying in the extreme. But, even in one's anxieties, it is a help thus to be informed.

ROYAL HOLLOWAY AND BEDFORD NEW COLLEGE, LONDON ROBERT FRASER

The Old English Physiologus. Edited by ANN SQUIRES. (Durham Medieval Texts, 5)
 Durham: Durham Medieval Texts. 1988. x + 137 pp. £4.00.

Beowulf: An Imitative Translation. By RUTH P. M. LEHMANN. Austin: University of
 Texas. 1988. viii + 119 pp. $14.95 (paperbound $5.95).

The Old English *Physiologus* consists of what are generally printed as three poems, the substantially complete *Panther* and *Whale* and the fragmentary *Partridge*, amount-ing to 175 lines or so in all. In the opinion of the late Stanley Greenfield, 'the allegorical nature of the Old English *Physiologus* is simple and its poetry, for the most part, mediocre'.

In her Preface and Introduction Ann Squires lays emphasis on the homiletic character of the Old English *Physiologus*, and she follows most modern opinion in holding that it constitutes 'a single and complete work . . . in which the significance of each poem is only to be fully understood in the context of the other two' (p. 22).

The Introduction provides in traditional form brief accounts of the manuscript and of matters of date, authorship, language, metre (fairly detailed), and sources (Greek and Latin texts, with translations, are supplied in appendices). The main discussion of artistic qualities is in the section on 'The design of the Old English *Physiologus*' (pp. 22–30).

Dr Squires believes that the Old English *Physiologus* constitutes 'ideal material for an introductory course on Old English'. In the notes, she records many parallels to individual words and phrases, from both verse and prose texts ('to help the beginner gain a feel for the poet's style within the Old English tradition' and 'to support the contention that these poems . . . belong as much to the native prose homiletic tradition as to the poetic' (p. i)). I am not convinced that beginners will be able to draw worthwhile conclusions from these citations.

On the other hand, I think such readers will need more help with immediate problems of translation than is always to be found here. They will stumble over, for example, *geond worl[d] innan* (*Panther* 4b) and (13b) and in neither case will their problems be completely resolved by the information given. The difficulties of *Panther* 8b–11a are not greatly clarified in the course of thirty-eight lines of notes. (Amongst other things, I do not understand the relevance of the reference to 'the dat.+inf. construction' at the end of the note to l. 9a. At the foot of p. 48, as elsewhere, the citation of other scholarly works is substantially correct but irritatingly inaccurate in its details.) The translation (p. 53) of the somewhat intricate passage *Panther* 20b–30a leaves *æghwæs* (24a) unaccounted for.

The note to *sundes* (*Whale* 15b) would have benefited from reference to Roberta Frank's article '"Mere" and "sund": two sea-changes in *Beowulf*', in *Modes of Interpretation in Old English Literature: Essays in Honour of Stanley B. Greenfield*, edited by Phyllis Rugg Brown and others (Toronto, 1986), pp. 153–72, and in the note to *reonigmode* (*Whale* 23a) it would have been appropriate to mention Hans Schabram's article 'Etymologie und Kontextanalyse in der altenglischen Semantik' (*Zeitschrift für vergleichende Sprachforschung* 84 (1970), 233–53; see pp. 249–50). I think Dr Squires, who says that 'the gloom of *reonig* connects with hell and *rest* with the grave . . . so that . . . the implication seems to be of spiritual weariness and darkness which ironically finds pleasure in such a resting place', here as in other places finds subtlety of meaning beyond the limits set by our knowledge of Old English. It is unconvincing to leap, in the note to *Whale* 53b–54a, from the observation that '*weler* occurs rarely in Old English poetry except in the Psalms' to the claim that 'the collocation of *muð* with *ontynan* (and *weler*) in the Psalms, e.g. *PPs* 58.7, 62.4, 80.11, 118.131, would no doubt, for a reader who would know the Psalter by heart, raise ironic echoes for this description of the whale's gaping mouth as well as recalling images of hell as the open maw of a monstrous animal'. (The parallels cited are not particularly close, nor is *PPs* 62.4 even a collocation of the type it is supposed to illustrate.) Such inferences are ones that inexperienced readers will be all too readily encouraged to make by the piling up of parallels which is a feature of these notes. The last suggestion in this note, that the passage 'may also reflect Matthew 7.13', seems to be plucked straight out of the air.

The edition assembles some useful information and makes some enlightening comments. Nevertheless, it is not clear that it manages quite to serve the needs of either novice or scholar.

Ruth P. M. Lehmann's *Beowulf: an Imitative Translation* declares itself to be 'more or less imitative of Germanic alliterative verse' (p. 16). Although not quite the first attempt to produce an alliterative Modern English verse rendering, it strives to remain particularly close to the typical metrical patterns as analysed by Sievers. Whether this helps the modern reader in his or her appreciation of the poem is debatable. It involves some straining of the norms of Modern English usage, and there is an antique ring to many of the terms and phrases used. In this version of *Beowulf*, as in many others, people 'fare forth' brandishing 'falchions' and 'glaives', and actions are 'featly' performed. It will not, I think, bring anyone much closer to an understanding or appreciation of *Beowulf*, though its style may appeal more to some tastes than to others.

St Peter's College, Oxford   T. F. Hoad

Arthurian Literature VIII. Edited by Richard Barber. Woodbridge, Suffolk and Wolfeboro, New Hampshire: D. S. Brewer. 1989. 206 pp. £27.50.

In line with established practice this latest volume of *Arthurian Literature* offers a pleasing diversity in its coverage, although at the same time two of the essays are sufficiently close in subject-matter to offer oblique commentaries on one another. The longest piece is a useful translation by D. D. R. Owen of the early thirteenth-century *Romance of Fergus* by Guillaume Le Clerc. The aim of the translation, 'to provide an acceptably literal rendering' (p. 85) which can be used alongside an edition of the text, inevitably entails a certain stiltedness in expression; but the text is readable, and lively enough to convey a sense of what is lost, thereby encouraging the reader to return to the original French. The brief introduction and commentary serve much the same function, in that both highlight the literary context in which the romance should be read, emphasizing the extent to which Guillaume's poem acts as a parodic counter-point to the romances of Chrétien de Troyes and the Continuators of the *Perceval*, written only a generation before. But whilst here Chrétien's romances are taken to be the paradigm from which Guillaume deliberately deviates, Jan Janssens in his essay suggests that the idealism of the supposed model is, itself, open to doubt.

In an exhaustively thorough reading of *Le Chevalier de la Charrette* Dr Janssens argues that irony permeates the text. Some of the argument is familiar, for example the blasphemous nature of Lancelot's adoration. But the conclusion forcefully points a contrast between the egoistical love of Guenièvre and the altruism of the emotion displayed by the daughter of Bademagu. (The issue of Chrétien's responsibility for the overall design of the poem, even though it was completed by Godefroi de Liegni, is carefully considered.) Dr Janssens argues that Lancelot's acceptance of the love which the *pucele* offers him, 'de type conjugal' (p. 73), means that the romance should be seen as a 'chanson de change' in which a lover abandons his lady for another, rather than as an exemplification of a 'courtly' ideal. He concludes that the denouement rebounds, as a kind of grotesque joke, on Chrétien's patron, Marie de Champagne, since she is implicitly associated with the fictional 'grande dame', Guenièvre.

No such complexities underlie the works of the fifteenth-century writer, John Hardyng. His *Chronicle* survives in two versions, testimony to his pursuit of royal patronage and reward under changing political circumstances. E. D. Kennedy examines his deployment of the stories of Joseph of Arimathia and Galahad, and convincingly elaborates upon the thesis that the impetus behind the original composition was Hardyng's desire to promote the claim of the English crown to Scotland; his case is that Hardyng included the grail material as counter-propaganda to contemporary Scottish attempts to prove the independence and antiquity of the Scottish church. The tantalizing glimpses which Professor Kennedy gives of differences between the two versions of the *Chronicle* emphasize the desirability of an edition of the first of these, although the particular interests aroused by this piece will be satisfied by Felicity Riddy's edition of the Arthurian portions of the texts for the series *Middle English Texts* (Heidelberg, forthcoming).

By way of contrast Elizabeth Archibald's essay is a reconsideration of the sources and nature of the theme of incest in the Arthurian legend. The literary evolution of the theme from slight beginnings in Geoffrey of Monmouth's *Historia* and the early Vulgate texts is charted fully, and there is a lengthy analysis of the ways in which the pattern of incest and parricide in the story of Arthur and Mordred differs from those of other traditions in which similar events can lead to self-discovery, repentance, and even sanctity. Some attention is also given to the literary and historical reasons which may have impelled Arthurian writers to explore incest. But in spite of the detail which accompanies the argument, what in some ways appears to be the most intriguing aspect of the study is left undeveloped: that is, how is this episode from Arthur's history dealt with by individual authors? Malory, for instance, may indeed have deflected 'the anger of the barons entirely onto Merlin' when all the innocents born on the same day as Mordred are massacred in an attempt to thwart the prophecy (p. 20), but does this event leave lingering echoes in the text for the reader; or must we simply regard it as another instance of the incomplete assimilation of diverse and contradictory source materials? Are other writers more successful than Malory in presenting a coherent vision of Arthur's fateful, if unknowing, mistake in sleeping with his half-sister?

Such qualifications apart, the volume as a whole demonstrates the continuing strength of this series, which lies in bringing together informative and stimulating essays and, not least importantly, providing the space for more extended discussion than is practicable in other contexts.

UNIVERSITY OF BRISTOL   CAROL M. MEALE

'Piers Plowman' and the New Anticlericalism. By WENDY SCASE. (Cambridge Studies in Medieval Literature, 4) Cambridge, New York, New Rochelle, Melbourne, and Sydney: Cambridge University Press. 1989. xvi + 249 pp. £30.00; $49.50.

This study freshly investigates features in *Piers Plowman* that satirize or attack the friars. Study of Langland's antifraternalism is not a new subject, but Wendy Scase finds that previous students, by only linking it to its earliest sources in the thirteenth century and in Fitzralph, have failed to take into account developments that occurred after Fitzralph and were contemporary with *Piers Plowman*. Her thesis, then, is that the antifraternalism of William of St Amour and other thirteenth-century figures, inherited and partly transformed by Richard Fitzralph in the middle of the fourteenth century, changed into a general anticlericalism during the 1370s and 1380s. Evidence for this development comes from writings by such polemicists as Hardeby, Conway, Maidstone, Ashwardby, Nicholas Hereford, Woodford, several Benedictines, and Wyclif. In this development *Piers Plowman* has its own place and function. To trace it, Dr Scase discusses a number of relevant passages from the poem in light of, predominantly, Fitzralph's works and contemporary controversies, and further draws on early reader-responses to the poem that have been preserved for us in the margins of various manuscripts.

This thesis is developed by detailed discussion of four major subjects with a variety of subordinate topics. Chapter 2, for example, deals with the priestly power of absolution. By investigating such topics as the question who was a penitent's 'proper priest' (to whom he or she was required to make confession at least once a year), the demand for and theory of restitution, the satirical topos of friars as *penetrantes domos*, and the intellectual preparation and learning of priests, Dr Scase shows that while these topics had been part of antifraternal satire, in the later fourteenth century they were developed into aspects of anticlericalism. For instance, the early friars claimed that their own *clergie* made them better priests than the normal parish clergy. Their opponents attacked them as self-seeking and hypocritical university men and stressed instead the valuable simplicity of a relatively unlearned parish clergy. But in *Piers Plowman* 'neither the treatment of clerical learning, nor that of clerical ignorance, constitutes a defence of priestly powers' (p. 43). Instead, the poem, together with some other polemical works, develops certain implications in these topics that would deny the claim of any priest's spiritual power. Thus, salvation may be seen as independent of clerical learning and efficacy (cf. *Piers Plowman*, B.xv.372–90); or, due to the development of lay literacy, listening to clerical authority might be replaced with private reading of the newly created works of spiritual guidance in the vernacular, to which *Piers Plowman* itself belonged.

This evolution is similarly traced with respect to the subjects of poverty (Chapter 3), possession of worldly goods and their endowment (Chapter 4), and criticism of the religious life and religious orders (Chapter 5). Each of these chapters, again, takes up several subordinate topics, among which I mention as a particularly clear and suggestive example the transformation of earlier satire against *gyrovagi* (false hermits, monks wandering outside their cloister) into an attack against 'lolling' which, in the C-text, embraces both friars and unbeneficed secular clergy.

In tracing such developments, Dr Scase constantly refers back to Fitzralph, analyses relevant polemical works of Langland's time, and keeps her eye firmly on differences between the poem's three (or four) versions as well as Langland's apparent distance from Wyclif. The repeated evocation of such a complex network makes her exposition at times difficult to follow; and it might have been helpful to have a fuller exposition of Fitzralph's theory of civil dominion early in her study, since that patently formed the conceptual source of so many later developments. Further, one wonders how much her focusing on antifraternalism and its claimed transformation into anticlericalism has caused Dr Scase occasionally to lose sight of larger contexts for the discussed topics in canon law and in contemporary nonpartisan preaching. For instance, the example of ancient hermits and friars, or the topos that wealthy prelates enjoy their income while they allow their altars to deteriorate in the rain, surely was used in complaint literature against the greed of the clergy elsewhere without the general anticlerical implications that are postulated here. Similarly, the question of who is a penitent's 'proper priest' and the subject of restitution recur in canon law as well as in late-fourteenth-century pastoral manuals. Dr Scase may well be right that these topics formed part of a 'new anticlericalism'; on the other hand, in many instances I would question if Langland's text requires or even allows her revised reading.

But such questions must remain matter for further scholarly debate. It will be clear from my summary that Dr Scase's study is not concerned with literary criticism, nor does it aim at elucidating *Piers Plowman* as a poem, even though it has some important implications for the critical understanding of particular passages. But as an investigation of anticlericalism in *Piers Plowman* and in contemporary polemics, the book highlights and investigates an important aspect of fourteenth-century thought to which the poem apparently contributed and which explains its appeal to its readership in the fifteenth and sixteenth centuries. As such, this study is an important scholarly contribution to intellectual and church history.

UNIVERSITY OF PENNSYLVANIA   SIEGFRIED WENZEL

A Game of Heuene: Word Play and the Meaning of 'Piers Plowman B'. By MARY CLEMENTE
DAVLIN, O.P. (Piers Plowman Studies VII) Woodbridge, Suffolk, and
Wolfeboro, New Hampshire: D. S. Brewer. 1989. 147 pp. £25.00.

The Bishop of Durham claims that God is not imperialist, never forcing proofs of his
presence upon men by performing miracles or directing experience in any other
obvious way. Mary Davlin takes rather the same view of God, and believes that
Langland does as well. Because his God is immanent within the stuff of experience, she
argues, 'he went out of his way to avoid the clarity of scholastic distinction, choosing
instead word-play, ambiguity, and a slippery double vocabulary' (p. 115). A pun, she
argues, keeps different meanings simultaneously in play, involving the reader in a
game which reflects not only the shifting possibilities for good and evil of experience,
but also the 'secrets' of God. Certain words, like 'truth', 'kynde', and 'love', are
polysemous concepts (p. 34), meaning different things at different times and with the
possibility of meaning them at the same time. Thus, for example, 'Truth' in Passus
XVIII thinks of herself as only one very limited judicial meaning of truth, but comes
through the arguments and events of the Passus to encompass the much deeper and
more loving meanings of the word, and so eventually to reflect the God whose name
she bears. Evil characters, on the other hand, use such words shallowly, limiting their
meaning in what Schmidt calls 'anti-puns', and reflecting only their own hypocrisy.

Passages from B.I, XI, XII, and XVIII are analysed in great detail to show the
simultaneous latent meanings enriching the poem; 'Dowel', for example contains
within it both the verb 'to do' and the verb 'to dwell', so that 'fals folk' who 'wandren
. . . and wasten' (VIII. 196–98) oppose both its stability and its activity (p. 50). The
larger structure of this dream poem, like the experience of the world and of God from
which it is drawn, demonstrates these same active ambiguities and inner meanings,
and the reader must be as receptive as the dreamer himself to the complexity of its
meaning. The whole poem is read as a kind of walnut simile, though more like an
onion than a nut.

Now this approach has definite advantages. It undoubtedly enhances one's
appreciation of the poetry, and is often very illuminating of dark passages, particularly where the darkness is caused by Langland's apparent illogicality rather than
by our lack of knowledge of his culture. But because the author hardly ever ventures
into this wider context to find other contemporary uses of the words she analyses,
her approach is self-enclosed, and sometimes short-circuits into circular arguments
about recurrent words. More evidence that polysemous words like 'truth' and
'suffer' were in fact used 'monosemously' by other writers, would also help to
demonstrate that Langland was indeed using them as puns. As it is, I suspect that
words always had complex resonances, and that Sr Davlin is recovering the richness
of Middle English rather than the deliberate wit of Langland. But as she herself says
when discussing the intentionalist fallacy, this need not really matter so long as our
awareness is heightened. And this is certainly an exciting and enjoyable book to
read, even if the experience is a bit like drinking sparkling wine without much in the
way of ballast to prevent one's becoming drunk.

CAMBRIDGE   ANNA BALDWIN

Piers Plowman: A Glossary of Legal Diction. By JOHN A. ALFORD. (Piers Plowman
Studies, V) Cambridge: D. S. Brewer. 1988. xxxi + 170 pp. £29.50.
Nature and Salvation in 'Piers Plowman'. By HUGH WHITE. (Piers Plowman Studies, VI)
Cambridge: D. S. Brewer. 1988. viii + 128 pp. £25.00.

John A. Alford's splendid *Glossary* is to be welcomed not only for the inherent
fascination and convenience of all good dictionaries and word-lists, but because of

the stimulus it will provide to the study of the diction not only of Langland but of many of his contemporaries. The introduction refers to the inadequacy of general dictionaries for the interpretation of poetry: their reduction of creative extremes to a level norm, their inability to scan more than the immediate context. The specialized topic of the law affords instead an illuminating distortion, casting an oblique light that throws into relief not only, for example, the 'daring literalism' of Langland's usage, but also the pervasive presence of legal terminology in a wide range of late medieval literature (not that the position of the law in the argument of *Piers Plowman* is all that oblique, of course, as Professor Alford argues here and elsewhere). In vocabulary as in other things, it seems, Langland was both innovator and tradition-alist, playing his part, on the one hand, in the importation of Latin and French legal terms into English, while on the other, 'in his choice of vocabulary (if indeed he really had a choice), Langland was simply using the words best suited by tradition to his subject matter'.

Where the definitions coincide, as they usually do, with those of the *OED* and *MED*, they are assembled more conveniently for the student of the poem around the legal themes and associations. But the insistence at many points on more technical legal senses helps the reader to focus more sharply on Langland's poetic activity. Best of all are the cross-references and numerous citations both from *Piers Plowman* and from other literature. We are thereby alerted to the peculiar resonance some words acquire in the development of the poem, as well as to the interest of other writers in related themes and ways of treating them. When the book's general aim to encourage appreciation and study is so effectively served, it is unnecessary to question the inclusion or omission of individual words and citations; one can only regret that there could not be simply more of the same.

Many of Professor Alford's entries, for example, *ingratus*, 'resoun', and 'lawe' itself provide helpful commentary, expansion, and modification of the discussion in Hugh White's book. *Nature and Salvation in 'Piers Plowman'* is itself more an exploration of vocabulary than the thematic study its title might suggest, at its best conscientiously seeking a pattern in Langland's terminology of *kynde wit*, *kynde knowynge*, the *kynde*, and Kynde personified. The account is appropriately restrained, punctuated with perhapses and footnotes to accommodate modification and contradiction from other perspectives. Dr White's concern is consciously not the background of ideas but 'the complexities of the text itself', which he takes to be evidence of 'a poet not securely in control of his material'. Indeed an important concomitant of his argument about nature and salvation is the assumptions it makes, or the conclusions it suggests, about the process of the poem's composition.

Throughout the three texts Dr White traces the development in Langland of an optimistic conception of the *kynde* and its role in man's salvation under the scrutiny of the poet's own 'unillusioned honesty'. In particular *kynde wit* suffers a reverse from its positive role in the foundation of society and as Piers Plowman's guide to Truth, first in the Visio under suspicion of Pelagian heresy, and then disparaged by Ymaginatif, only to be restored in the final Passus in a new form that emphasizes submission to God's will, and reflects the poem's increased concern with God's activity rather than man's. Dr White follows a parallel development in Langland's personification of Kynde as God, from the unproblematic picture of creator and created in B ix, to the Kynde of Passus xx, who brings disease and death and presides over the collapse of Unity. Dealing here with the existence of evil within Kynde's dispensation, Langland is seen reaching an optimistic understanding of a natural order that accommodates man's fallen nature.

The argument, fragmented at first by the division into terms, accumulates conviction as it deals with the God of Nature and with *kynde*ness. Dr White understands Langland's innovative personification of Nature as related to the

Chartrian goddess largely by a kind of ironic contrast that lends piquant overtones to the portrayal of a male figure who promotes death, and whose realm is criticized by Will for Reason's failure to follow man rather than the other way about. The chapter on 'Being Kynde' reaffirms Langland's optimism, expressing an 'essential unity of human and divine' in the central significance of *unkyndenesse* as a sin, on the one hand, and on the other, *redde quod debes* as an expression of *kynde*. What Dr White calls 'the accommodation of the negative within the idea of the natural' he sees as peculiar to Langland, setting him apart from Gower and Chaucer, a more convinced believer in the *felix culpa* than Milton. The end of *Piers Plowman* manages to be optimistic while at the same time forcing the reader to confront 'a realm of moral confusion, beyond the poem' but also enacted in it.

In characterizing such accommodations and reconciliations of opposites, it is difficult for Dr White to avoid an impression of something too neatly 'successful', quite at odds with his own appreciation of the fluidity and opportunism of Langland's use of terms like *kynde*, whose essential ordinariness as well as their breadth of reference resists attempts at an academic stability of meaning. That appreciation is expressed with refreshing scepticism in his discussion of *kynde knowynge*. Although at certain points it may be possible to identify the knowledge referred to with *synderesis* or even *sapientia*, the primary sense of *kynde knowynge* is 'not a single entity, but a manner of knowing various things', the sense of *kynde* in the phrase being 'proper' rather than 'natural', while the object of knowledge remains to be specified. It is possible thus to clear Will of the charge of misusing terms in his search for knowledge.

Despite the fundamental questioning in his approach, and willingness to see change and multiplicity of meaning, Dr White himself at times seems to treat names such as Kynde Wit as entities between which Langland's argument moves, rather than, for instance, to regard Langland's topics as constants for which he seeks new names and changing images. This is a difficult distinction to insist on, especially with Langland, but it might be exemplified by the Pardon Scene. Here Dr White takes Piers's change of direction as a genuine rejection of a way of life, guided by *kynde wit*, with which he has become dissatisfied, where Burrow, for example, sees the real change rather in Langland's attitude to his image of agricultural labour. It is in the treatment of *kynde wit* that Dr White's approach seems least successful by being oddly out of key with the poet's procedures. He interprets Ymaginatif's discourse at the start of B XII as a redefinition of *kynde wit* necessitated by Will's idealization of the unlearned labourer, and indeed it is somewhat provoking to find *kynde wit* ranged here with *clergie* in opposition to a supposedly blessed lack of learning. Ymaginatif is certainly delivering a warning about the insufficiency of unaided *kynde wit* for salvation, and even its danger when misdirected. But rather than redefining *kynde wit* as 'high intelligence and wisdom', his list of the 'great wits', such as Aristotle, is surely intended to demonstrate that even advanced users of the faculty can come to grief. Ymaginatif, like Studie, is warning against intellectual pride, not suggesting that *kynde wit* is an exclusive preserve. In Ymaginatif's discussion of the relative importance of *clergie*, *kynde wit*, and grace, Dr White's interest in the survival or otherwise of *kynde wit* as an entity leads him to stress contrast and distinction where Ymaginatif seems intent rather on showing an almost mysteriously complex interrelation. Similarly at the end of the poem, although there is no explicit rejection of Kynde Wit, Dr White sees the mere absence of the personification as a significant absence, where another reader might notice rather a shift of focus requiring a single figure rather than a pair at the close to represent the pilgrim soul. It is a matter of emphasis, no doubt, made more delicate by the characteristic involvement of form with content in Langland. Any attempt, such as this, to tease out patterns of meaning, is welcome even, or perhaps especially, where it raises further questions.

With all the neatness of some of his solutions, the *Piers Plowman* that emerges is the one Dr White characterizes in his introduction, 'questioning its own solutions and revising what had looked like its conclusions'. His answer to Professor Alford's recently restated question of the poem, 'What is it?' would be less a poem than a record of Langland thinking by means of one. Far from planning mistakes and false starts as ironic instruction for his audience, this Langland can even be found responding to his own creations almost as if they had equal status with himself: 'after Ymaginatif's appraisal Langland is unable to look upon *kynde wit* again as sanguinely as he once had done'. Dr White is often a persuasive guide to such strangely dramatic processes.

UNIVERSITY OF READING   DAVID WILLIAMS

Troilus and Criseyde. By GEOFFREY CHAUCER. Edited by R. A. SHOAF (from the text of A. C. BAUGH). East Lansing: Colleagues Press. 1989. xxxii + 312 pp. £19.50.

Chaucer and Langland: Historical and Textual Approaches. By GEORGE KANE. Berkeley and Los Angeles: University of California Press. 1989. x + 302 pp. $32.50.

This collection of George Kane's essays and lectures from 1965 to 1986 is arranged according to logic rather than date. His classic essay on 'The Autobiographical Fallacy in Chaucer and Langland Studies' leads to four essays on Chaucer, three on Langland, and two arguing the main theme, 'Langland and Chaucer: an Obligatory Conjunction'. There follow four essays in textual and editorial matters, and finally two on critical methods.

Professor Kane offers all these essays as 'period pieces' (p. ix) and has therefore, presumably, decided not to alter, revise, or even supplement. This has an adverse effect only on the final two essays. In spite of detailed quotation there are no notes to essay 15, 'Criticism, Solecism: Does it Matter?' (published in 1976 as 'Some Reflections on Critical Method' from a lecture given in 1967, as the Contents page says); and in essay 16, 'Outstanding Problems of Middle English Scholarship', first published in 1977, it is frustrating, for example, to have Professor Kane give his view of Root's *Troilus* but not of Windeatt's. There is a need for some revision, though much remains valid. Professor Kane's salutary scepticism about the very possibility of trying to determine common authorship of the *Gawain* group remains relevant (p. 234), but one would like to have read his response to sketchy recent attempts to produce quantitative evidence (R. A. Cooper and D. A. Pearsall, 'The *Gawain* Poems: A Statistical Approach to the Question of Common Authorship', *Review of English Studies*, n.s. 39 (1988), 365–85). Given his advocacy of computer analysis of Middle English alliterative poetry, one would also have like to see him respond to conclusions based on such analysis by Hoyt Duggan, which would deny the modulation in which, according to Professor Kane's persuasive account, Langland's poetic excellence is grounded. All in all, scholarship and critical discourse have changed too much for re-publication to satisfy without at least an afterword.

How astringent in tone such an afterword might have been may be gauged from Professor Kane's own sharp handling of Chaucerian textual scholars, both recent (in essay 14) and less recent, such as Manly and Rickert (essay 13), who are magisterially downgraded. There is no room for generosity in Professor Kane's standards: 'we must not tolerate, in ourselves or others, shortcomings such as have invalidated some previous scholarship' (p. 241). He insists on the need for advanced textual, historical, and linguistic skills as a precondition of literary scholarship. His own example runs to prolific expertise in medieval philosophy and theology, and could hardly be more impressive or exemplary. He also insists that criticism should be learned and logical, and his own is both.

The first ten essays give this volume its coherence. They show Professor Kane to have been a pioneer in urging that 'Langland and Chaucer belong together' (p. 124); 'They seem to me to have more in common than Langland has with any of the alliterative poets, or Chaucer with Gower' (p. 282, note 1). He sets out to diminish at every turn the perceived distance between the two. The criticism here is subtle and balanced, full of incidental riches. He explains plausibly how and why Chaucer's reading of Machaut 'would promote eclecticism, a practical and pragmatic treatment' (p. 40), and he anticipates Minnis with illuminating remarks about the Franklin's Tale as a series of choices making sense only in a pagan setting. There is fine commentary generally on 'The Perplexities of William Langland'.

Professor Kane's account of Langland happily concentrates on making readers feel that *Piers Plowman* is, after all, great poetry, only then addressing content and even here assuring us that 'Langland was not writing as a professional theologian but as a highly intelligent and tolerably well-informed poet making poetry for his own comfort out of the thought and feeling of his time' (p. 121). The account of Chaucer's poetry, however, proceeds in the reverse direction, assuming our appreciation of the style and trying to toughen our minds to its substance: not only does Chaucer move 'from court poet to moralist, and in particular to moralist preoccupied with *trouthe*' (p. 48), but also 'in at least some of his poetry, he is more a moral philosopher than a moralist' (p. 67). The interest of narrative for such a poet is as a vehicle for examining moral choice.

Much here seems valuable and corrective. Yet it may be easier to accept Professor Kane's Langland than his Chaucer, in presenting whom, oddly, Professor Kane comes perilously close to some sort of autobiographical fallacy, if not exactly the one he diagnosed: 'Chaucer is no longer able to acquiesce in his own heart in the pretence of courtly love' (p. 22); 'So in the end Chaucer did return to the moral stance' (p. 31). There is also some tendentiously humourless reading: 'adulteries' in the Manciple's, Miller's, Shipman's, and Merchant's Tales 'amount to an augmentation of squalid deceit that silences in the end the laughter generic in the fabliau' (p. 48). Many will fail to agree; and given that Chaucer's interest in such tales occurs late in his career, such a judgement is critical to the entire argument.

Of the several misprints in the volume, the best, suitably for the editor of *Piers Plowman*, transforms 'The Liberating Truth' into 'The Literating Truth'.

Professor Kane's erudite and brilliant essay on 'Chaucer, Love Poetry and Romantic Love' should be mandatory reading for all medievalists. It would be an antidote to the misrepresentation of *fine amour* that occupies under three pages of R. A. Shoaf's brief introduction to *Troilus and Criseyde* — an introduction from which we learn, for instance, that 'Boethius was not a quitter' (p. xxv). This is an edition addressed to undergraduates, and simplification is a keynote, or rather a keyword ('To help readers relate initially to each character, a keyword is provided here for that character', p. xxi). There are problems, the least of which is probably the text. Surprising as it is to see Baugh's edition exhumed (and the justification offered is singularly weak), Baugh's text presumably offered fewer copyright problems than Windeatt or Riverside or even Robinson; and on the logic of this edition any text, other than Root's based on Corpus 61 might do for 'the first-time reader' — though after Windeatt it is mildly irritating to have, for example, Virgil, Ovid, Homer, Lucan, and Statius in v. 1791 'pace' once again rather than 'space'. The Shoaf edition gives a large print version, glosses on the page and a few footnotes in which translations and comments are undifferentiated in format or fount. Readers for whom such aids are necessary are yet assumed to know their way round the terms 'nominative', 'accusative', 'genitive', and 'dative' (p. xix).

The pity is that Colleagues Press has missed a major opportunity. For we really do lack an ideal undergraduate edition of *Troilus and Criseyde*. Ever since Windeatt we have known what it should contain: a reliable text, some apparatus and a full English translation of *Il Filostrato* — dismissed by Professor Shoaf, as in the bad old days, in one sentence. The keyword for this edition, unfortunately, is misconceived.

UNIVERSITY OF SYDNEY   DAVID LAWTON

Chaucer and the Law. By JOSEPH ALLEN HORNSBY. Norman, Oklahoma: Pilgrim Books. 1988. x + 180 pp. $32.95.

Chaucer's Universe. By J. D. NORTH. Oxford: Clarendon Press. 1988. xvi + 577 pp. £60.00.

Was Chaucer an Inns of Court Man? The harder and rarer question is what was an Inn of Court in Chaucer's time. Too often Chaucer is seen through a Renaissance perspective. Both authors, with their fourteenth-century expertise, would agree on this. Thanks to the magisterial work of J. H. Baker and Samuel Thorne (*Readings & Moots at the Inns of Court*, Volume II, Selden Society 105 (London, 1990)) a clearer picture is emerging. Legal training was not London-based until the 1340s; a recently discovered contract of 1323 assures a young man four years' support among the apprentices 'at our lord the king's court of Common Bench, wherever the said Bench should be in England'. Baker concludes that the existence of a school of law is proved by moot exercises in or before the time of Edward I. But we cannot at this early period give to *process* a local habitation and a name. So a well-established legal training in the common law was available to Chaucer in his youth even though it would be anachronistic to identify a particular inn. The hypothesis floated on Renaissance evidence by Edith Rickert (*Manly Anniversary Studies* (Chicago, 1923)) cannot be scuppered as simply as readers of E. W. Ives (*Common Lawyers of Pre-Reformation England* (Cambridge, 1983)) might wish.

Must literary history always 'hop behind' recent historical findings? Joseph Hornsby's 'hunch' that it would be rewarding to study Chaucer and the law proves correct although the well-read author is not himself at the pit-face of primary research in that area. If Dr Hornsby simplifies by relying upon Ives's conclusion that the Inns did not offer a legal education early enough in the fourteenth century for Chaucer, nevertheless his decision to follow T. F. Tout and R. F. Green (*Poets and Princepleasers* (Toronto, 1980)) and to look at Chaucer's administrative experience gives the reader a refreshingly broad perspective. The value of Dr Hornsby's book lies in his decision to examine Chaucer's work for evidence of his knowledge of canon as well as common law. Some of his most interesting writing focuses upon the distinction between sin and guilt: alerting the reader to the importance of 'intention' in ecclesiastical law — the factor which decides the question of damnation.

In looking closely at Chaucer's language Dr Hornsby finds no extraordinary mastery or display of esoteric or technical aspects of either canon or common law; he chooses three broad categories. Most of the poet's allusions to criminal law are general or philosophical. Chaucer shows a mastery of the nuances of the law of agreements that is consistent with a mercantile background. Dr Hornsby is most interesting on 'intention' in the canon law; he exonerates Dorigen in 'The Franklin's Tale' from her thoughtless and unintended bargain but fails to satisfy me as to the motivation of her chivalrous husband, for Arveragus holds her to the *letter* not the *intention* of her agreement. Interesting too is Dr Hornsby's review of recent critical battles over the troth-plighting of Troilus and Criseyde in the light of fourteenth-century cases of breach of promise of marriage. Whereas Chaucer's pagans, Dido and Aeneas, in the *Legend of Good Women* exchange vows recognized as legally viable by Pope Alexander III's decree on clandestine marriages, no English church court would have declared Troilus and Criseyde married on the evidence of formulae in Chaucer's poem. The church would not have recognized in any of their words clear intention of marriage. He goes on to argue that Troilus's and Criseyde's only clear agreement was made as a metaphor of feudal troth. Dr Hornsby shows that Chaucer has altered Boccaccio to emphasize the parallel between Calkas's political treason, its consequent dangers for his daughter, and her final metaphoric treason. Criseyde, breaking her troth, is arguably more treasonous than her father who merely betrayed his feudal superior while she, accepting Prince Troilus's feudal homage, betrays her 'vassal'.

A more accessible form for this useful research might be a reference glossary of legal terms with short factual essays introducing the most difficult concepts.

J. D. North has divided his *Chaucer's Universe* in anticipation of two kinds of reader. In Part I as the genial eagle he explains 'the elements of Chaucerian cosmology' arguing cogently that Chaucer's interest in astrology developed to sophisticated mastery of the latest astronomical theories and tables. These chapters along with the work of Lynn Thorndike (and in much shorter compass) provide an admirable survey of the range of scientific source books available in Chaucer's life-time. Part I may become required reading for most serious students of the poet, yet the Copernican-born deserve a little more elementary guidance in Ptolemy's epicycles and deferents before submitting to the black-belt mathematical calculations (pp. 144–45). The novice is referred to some of the author's earlier works for technical help. Professor North writes for a readership with prior interest and some experience of the subject; they will not be disappointed.

Part II: 'Allegories interpreted' is more controversial, drawing cosmic subtexts from Chaucer's literary works. Those familiar with the pages of tide-tables at the back of Dickens's manuscript of *Great Expectations* must pause in similar awe before the incontrovertible evidence of Chaucer's engagement with serious astronomy; but they may still demur as Professor North finds cosmic allegories governing the structure of each hitherto familiar poem. Beginning with the 'Squire's Tale', six other Canterbury Tales are considered as well as the *Parliament of Fowls*, *Troilus and Criseyde*, and the *Legend of Good Women*. It is impossible in short space to do justice to the intricacy of some of his arguments. Briefly, he sees Chaucer as adapting intractable source material by making current astronomical and astrological observations, using allegories of these stars to infuse contemporary relevance into old stories. The reader may discover that 'a tale told yesterday of Troy might be told tomorrow of London' (p. 401). Thus a remarkable conjunction of Saturn and Jupiter becomes a structural feature of 'The Knight's Tale' and Professor North sees in the layout of Theseus's temples a configuration of the heavens observed by Chaucer on 3 May 1388. Similarly in *Troilus and Criseyde* an observed conjunction of Jupiter and Saturn of 9 June 1385 portends not only the 'smokey rain' of Book III but recalls a similar configuration at the fall of the Troy. It follows ('as the night the day') that the works in their present forms are unlikely to pre-date these cosmological events. In such genial company it seems churlish to disagree; the learning is great, the approach is sound. Yet such confident reliance upon observed reckoning leaves little scope for Chaucer's imagination. When the encoded cosmic allegory is expounded few chapters present an irrefutably simple congruity of tale and 'allegory'; in every case there are troublesome, discordant details which need special pleading. But this apparent weakness stems from Professor North's integrity. He will not hide what does not fit, so great is his faith in the approach, and his hope for the student who will get it perfectly right. In Part II Professor North's least controversial work is on *The Complaint of Mars* where cosmic allegory is evident to most readers. The notes are full of previous battle scars; responsive to criticism, eminently reasonable he has changed his mind about some of the claims but not the scope of his pioneering work: 'Kalenderes enlumyned ben they' (*Review of English Studies,* 20 (1969) pp. 129–54, 257–83, 418–44).

When we have mended our ways, abandoned accessible but inappropriate Renaissance star charts, learned with little Lewis to position our rete, set our computer to the configuration of the heavens in June 1385 we may recover the perspective of Chaucer's ideal readers, those scholars who 'read the heavens as assiduously as they read committee minutes today' (p. 297)! Perhaps many will be content with the humbler possibilities open to Chaucer's auditors past whose ears the *Parliament of Fowls* sped too fast to have served as a calendar and almanac.

Those who are persuaded by the introduction to skip Part I will not only miss the best but will have difficulty in Part II with the Wife of Bath's horoscope (p. 298), and with technical vocabulary such as 'apse line' and 'unequal hours'. In a book so beautifully produced, full of detailed charts and appendices, small errors leap forth: Plutarch for Petrarch (p. 110), Antenor was not 'one of Troilus's brothers' (p. 368); greater expertise would be needed to check the mathematics. But even those fully equipped by Part I and following the detailed calculations for the chapter head-lined *Parliament of Fowls* will be set back by the misprint which delivers these arguments to illuminate *The House of Fame* (p. 358).

Even if on literary grounds one rejects Professor North's precise dating, the cumulative effect of his approach is persuasive. In *Troilus and Criseyde* Chaucer's English heavens mitigate with their planetary aspects, exaltations, and conjunctions the heavy blame placed on Criseyde by the poet's source books. Weighing Professor North's plaything of the planets against Dr Hornsby's guilty heroine we may reserve critical judgement. Yet what impresses in these two books is the vigilance required in reading Chaucer, the constant need to know the full range of technical meanings of his words. For such guardians of Chaucer's richness, many thanks.

CAMBRIDGE UNIVERSITY   MARIE AXTON

The English of Chaucer and his Contemporaries: Essays by M. L. Samuels and J. J. Smith. Edited by J. J. SMITH. Aberdeen: Aberdeen University Press. 1989. vi + 126 pp. £17.50.

For two or three decades the emphasis of Middle English literary research has been upon the manuscripts which preserve the literature. It is therefore appropriate that major advances in linguistic research should also have been concerned with the written medium: with spelling rather than sounds. Both the stimulus for these developments, and their monument, is the *Linguistic Atlas of Later Middle English*, in which Professor Angus McIntosh, Professor M. L. Samuels, and their colleagues have shown how scribal spelling may be used to reconstruct the copying history of a manuscript, in favourable cases to locate its place of origin, and sometimes even to throw light on the career of individual authors and copyists.

In the present volume Jeremy J. Smith draws together those papers arising from the methodology and data of the *Atlas* project which bear principally upon the language of Chaucer, Gower, and Langland. He provides also an Introduction, Bibliography, and indexes of persons and manuscripts, along with some up-dating in the Notes, and cross-referencing to the *Atlas*. Of the eight papers included, five by Professor Samuels, and a collaborative one by Professor Samuels and Dr Smith, have been previously published; two by Dr Smith are new. This requires no apology, however, since the significance to Middle English studies of the intellectual enterprise which gave rise to this collection cannot be over-emphasized: this book should not be overlooked by anyone seriously interested in medieval English studies.

Such a recommendation may be taken to imply that this is a repository of undisputed truths, and consequently rather dull: but this is not so. The papers reproduced are sometimes controversial and even polemic in tone. That on 'Chaucerian Final '-E'' represents a decisive historical victory still worthy of commemoration; but the papers on 'Chaucer's Spelling', and especially that on 'The Scribe of the Hengwrt and Ellesmere Manuscripts of *The Canterbury Tales*', still reek of gunpowder. Professor Samuels's reconstruction of Chaucer's spelling depends upon the assumption that palaeographers have been correct in identifying the scribe of the Ellesmere and Hengwrt manuscripts as an individual, whose own varying spelling practices can then be traced in other manuscripts, and distinguished from Chaucer's own. This assumption was threatened by Professor Vance Ramsey (*Studies in Bibliography*, 1982) in an article which precipitated a debate whose latest shot is Dr Smith's 'The Trinity D-Scribe and his Work on Two Early *Canterbury Tales* Manuscripts'. Here, he contests Professor Ramsey's view that spelling variation indicates that the scribes of Corpus Christi, Oxford 198 and Harley 7334 are likewise distinct. It is convincingly demonstrated that each manuscript is a *mischsprache*, sharing with the other certain layers of dialectally common provenance: one is consistent with the Chaucer original, another with the South-Western origin of the copyist himself. Certain distinctively Gowerian forms probably arose from the demonstrable copying career of this scribe. Thus spelling practice, related to a copyist's history and habits in several manuscripts, is shown to complement palaeographic opinion.

The second new paper, 'Spelling and Tradition in Fifteenth-Century Copies of Gower's *Confessio Amantis*', deals with a number of diverse matters: the status of Gower as an *auctor*, suggested by the emergence of a characteristic orthography in Gower manuscripts; the behaviour of Scribe D in relation to emerging standardization; the role of orthographical studies as an adjunct to current codicological work on the Gower textual tradition. The paper closes with an appendix giving rather abbreviated details of the dialectal characteristics of all known manuscripts of the *Confessio Amantis*.

The remaining, previously published, papers in this highly-recommended collection are: 'The Language of Gower', 'Langland's Dialect', 'Spelling and Dialect in the Late and Post-Middle English Periods'.

UNIVERSITY OF SHEFFIELD   J. D. BURNLEY

Approaches to Teaching 'Sir Gawain and the Green Knight'. Edited by MIRIAM YOUNGER MILLER and JANE CHANCE. (Approaches to Teaching Masterpieces of World Literature) New York: The Modern Language Association of America. 1986. xii + 256 pp. $27.50.

This collection of essays grew out of responses to a questionnaire about the teaching of *Sir Gawain and the Green Knight* circulated by the Modern Language Association (see pp. 43–68 for details of its content); the respondents were predominantly American, although some Canadian, Japanese, and Spanish academics were also involved. Help was requested, both in respect of 'sifting through the wealth of writing on the poem', and of teaching and examining it (p. 66). The first of these areas is explicitly addressed in Part One ('Materials' (pp. 1–39)); the second in Part Two ('Approaches' (pp. 43–212)).

Over half of the articles in this second part are grouped according to teaching-level, with two sections devoted to undergraduate courses, and a third to dual-level and graduate courses. In the first two, the romance is studied in one or other of the available translations (some idea of their merits and shortcomings was earlier provided by comparing their renderings of lines 134–37 of the original (pp. 7–18)). In the third group the poem is studied in Middle English, despite fears (happily unfounded) that this would bore the students (p. 187).In the undergraduate courses, the task of arousing and sustaining interest is sometimes acute: one thinks particularly of the class in which all the students were majoring in engineering (p. 123). At present, at least, such a situation is foreign to the experience of most British teachers of the romance, though as defined by R. Ascherl, its by-products are not always unfamiliar: a lack of real interest in literature, sketchy reading of the texts, passive acceptance of whatever the lecturer may have to say about them.

An interesting feature is the sheer diversity of texts that have been taught alongside *Gawain;* besides a wide range of medieval literature, we find nineteenth and twentieth-century novels (involving quests, rites of passage, etc.), and science fiction, and the romance has also been used as a way of throwing into relief the potentialities and limitations of various modes of literary criticism (p. 156). Of all these contexts, the most obvious proves in some ways the least comfortable; as John Ganim very properly reminds us (p. 45), *Gawain* will always tend to be a subversive and disruptive element in courses devoted to the romances. One might add, however, that it finds at least a limited counterpart in the Middle English *Havelok*, also to some extent set apart from the romances with which it is traditionally grouped, and further akin to *Gawain* in its leisurely and symmetrical narrative, and its limited and individual use of the type-scenes and conventional expressions that it might have been expected to contain.

Two of the essays in the final section of the book ('Specific Approaches') stress the importance of visual aids to the study of the romance; earlier (p. 39), M. Y. Miller had suggested that a film of *Gawain* itself might one day be made. In fact, one such was released in 1972 (directed by Stephen Weeks), but would prove more of a visual hindrance than visual aid to all but the most knowledgeable of *Gawain*-students. For here not only is Arthur grumpy, and the Green Knight no longer identified with Bertilak, but Gawain has to cope with the whole of the adventure of the spring from *Yvain* just after leaving Camelot. The film's most engaging feature is its extensive locational use of Burgess's Castell Coch (for Bertilak) and Cardiff Castle (for Arthur), with a timely cut saving Gawain and Gryngolet from being 'britned to noght' by the eastbound traffic, when they emerge from this last.

UNIVERSITY COLLEGE OF WALES, ABERYSTWYTH   MALDWYN MILLS

De Cella in Seculum: Religious and Secular Life and Devotion in Late Medieval England. Edited by MICHAEL G. SARGENT. Woodbridge, Suffolk and Wolfeboro, New Hampshire: D. S. Brewer. 1989. xiv + 244 pp. £45.00.

The papers here collected were given, with one accidental exception, at a conference held in July 1986 at Lincoln to celebrate the eighth centenary of the consecration of Hugh of Avalon as bishop of that city. The occasion (to declare at once the possible bias of the present reviewer) was one notable for the welcome that its participants received from both the secular authorities in Lincoln and from the Chancellor of the Cathedral, and also for bringing together scholars from disparate areas of expertise for three days of enlightening dialogue. The resulting volume perhaps reflects less of that dialogue than might be wished, but it certainly retains the scholarship. The contributions will be of interest primarily to those concerned with the career and early reputation of Hugh of Avalon, and to students of later medieval, mainly English, devotion. After the preface by Canon Nurser and the introduction by Michael Sargent, six contributions concern Hugh and his immediate contemporaries, six deal with major English texts or authors; between these two groups falls a single paper on a twelfth-century miracle collection, and after the second come three papers that deal in more general terms with aspects of late medieval piety.

To select individual papers for special attention here is invidious but necessary for a short review. Of the chapters devoted to Hugh of Lincoln himself, possibly the most interesting to readers of this journal will be the surveys of his career by H. E. J. Cowdrey and of his character by David Hugh Farmer. Less centrally, Richard Pfaff's discussion of the changing liturgical forms experienced by Hugh in his transition from Carthusian monk at La Grande Chartreuse to English bishop is a salutary reminder of the diversity within the experience of medieval religion. The connexion of some of the papers on later medieval English writings with Hugh is tenuous or, in some cases, non-existent. But Sr Teresa Brady's paper on the Lollard additions and modifications to some manuscripts of the *Pore Caitif* is an extremely important contribution to knowledge of this widely-disseminated collection of tracts from the person who is currently engaged in the laborious task of editing them. George Keiser has a valuable discussion of some writings that attempt 'to make the fruits of monastic piety accessible to their devout contemporaries' (p. 146), with particular reference to the assembly known as *Gratia Dei*; he makes plausible suggestions to explain why this text did not gain the circulation that comparable collections achieved. Professor Keiser notes (p. 156) the text in British Library MS Harley 2398 headed 'A short reule of lyf for euerych man in general and for prestes & lordes & laboreres in special', and comments that such a text makes the optimism of *Gratia Dei*'s author in looking for such a wide audience look more credible. Such optimism was characteristic of Lollardy: indeed, it might be worth adding that MS Harley 2398, like the other manuscripts in which the *Schort reule* is preserved, is at least on the borders of Wycliffism, and that one of those manuscripts, Westminster School 3, is amongst those included by Sr Brady with a copy of *Pore Caitif* infiltrated by Lollard views. Vincent Gillespie's enigmatic title '*Cura Pastoralis in Deserto*' masks an illuminating examination of possible answers to the question (pp. 161–62) 'Why were books of pastoral care owned and produced by an order whose way of life was minimally coenobitic and whose members were rigorously separated from the ways of the world?'

Other contributions include a re-evaluation of Giraldus Cambrensis's *Life of St Hugh* by Richard Loomis, a study of *De Quadripartito Exercitio Cellae* by James Hogg, a brief but useful survey of the audience of the medieval English mystics by Stanley Hussey, a paper by Nicholas Watson on Rolle's reputation and his *Judica Me*, an examination of *The Pomander of Prayer* by Robert A. Horsfield, and some interesting deductions from *The Myroure of oure Ladye* by Ann M. Hutchison. Martha W. Driver's paper on pictures in early printed books of devotion for lay readers is not altogether well served by the quality of the reproductions, some of which are faint and appear slightly out of focus. In all, then, this is a valuable collection of essays on a wide variety of topics.

LADY MARGARET HALL, OXFORD   ANNE HUDSON

English Poetry of the Sixteenth Century. By GARY WALLER. (Longman Literature in English Series) London and New York: Longman. 1986. xvi + 315 pp. £15.95 (paperbound £6.95).

Changing Landscapes: Anti-Pastoral Sentiment in the English Renaissance. By PETER LINDENBAUM. Athens and London: University of Georgia Press. 1986. xiv + 234 pp. $27.50.

Humanist Poetics: Thought, Rhetoric, and Fiction in Sixteenth-Century England. By ARTHUR F. KINNEY. Amherst: University of Massachusetts Press. 1986. xvi + 529 pp. £33.25.

These three books in conjunction suggest something of the present state of criticism for English Renaissance literature. One, Gary Waller's, proposes a 'revisionist view'; David Lindenbaum's adopts a conservative approach to literary history through an examination of the ideas of poets; finally, Arthur Kinney's brings the history of classical thought and rhetoric to bear on the interpretation of the ends and means of English writers of prose fiction. While Professor Waller remains a-historical, except for gestures in the direction of the new historicism, Professor Lindenbaum's historicism is limited by his subjective judgements about the state of mind of the poets he discusses. Only Professor Kinney chooses to attempt the exploration of the philosophical and rhetorical contexts within which his authors were writing.

As part of a series designed to offer 'a practical and comprehensive guide' to English literature, Gary Waller's book is described on the cover as placing the poetry of the sixteenth century 'within its own history', which apparently means that it 'argues that sixteenth-century poetry was an expression of the cultural struggle which centred on the power of the Court and which embodied many of the wider conflicts of the age'. But since the reader is also invited to let the text 'speak in the world its readers inhabit', we are advised to 'concentrate on the "dislocations" and "disruptions" in poetic texts as well as on what they "intend"'. In fact, Professor Waller largely ignores intention in the rhetorical sense; what interests him is the poets' feelings as they struggle to express themselves against 'the dominant ideology'. It is almost as if Rosemond Tuve had never written her *Elizabethan and Metaphysical Imagery* (Chicago, 1947), a work which defines the terms and sets the stage for speaking of a Renaissance poet's intentions.

Obviously the usefulness of this book cannot be gauged solely by one's sympathy for, or antipathy to, the familiar catchwords of reader-centred theory or the new historicism as they decorate the text. It is the particular judgements of poets and their poems that demonstrate how the author would apply his theories to the criticism of poetry. Speaking of *The Faerie Queene*, Professor Waller refers to 'the ideological repressiveness from which the poem was born'. Deep down inside, Spenser felt uncertainty, we are told, even about such a time-tested virtue as temperance. The writer is invariably certain about his poets' uncertainties.

In short, there is little appreciation of what cannot be described in terms of expression and repression. Even the famous affirmations of Shakespeare's Sonnet 116, on the marriage of true minds, are labelled 'acts of repression'. As for Shakespeare's *Venus and Adonis*, it has to be written off as 'regretfully (*sic.*) static, with just too much argument and insufficient flowing sensuality to make it pleasurable reading'. It is a mark either of Professor Waller's critical eclecticism or of his inconsistency that his dismissal of this poem echoes the judgement of a number of very old-fashioned critics. So much for being up to date.

David Lindenbaum sets out to examine what he calls anti-pastoralism in English Renaissance poetry. Contrasting the idealized pastoral of Sannazaro or Monte-mayor, he argues that Sidney, Shakespeare, and Milton 'are uncomfortable' with the idea of pastoral as an escape from the active life, or even as exemplifying the contemplative life. Not wishing to add complications to his argument, he has elected to exclude Spenser and Marvell from consideration, since both these poets allow more credit to contemplation as the spiritual goal of pastoral life than his thesis will permit.

Like Gary Waller, Professor Lindenbaum is much concerned with what poets feel on certain subjects; they both, for example, confidently refer to a poet's 'uneasiness', whether it is with 'the dominant ideology' or with pastoral conventions. But Professor Lindenbaum is more traditional in his approach, favouring expository clarity and giving primacy to a poet's ideas, rather than to the experience of reading the poems. He hypothesizes that the English, being both Puritanical and Humanist, were bound to find pastoral as a way of life unsatisfactory. But is this not to assume a very literal view of pastoral? Sidney does, after all, note in his *Apology for Poetry* that 'sometimes under the pretty tales of wolves and sheep' can be included 'the whole consideration of wrong-doing and patience'. To speak of 'Sidney's continued uneasiness' with the pastoral convention or of Shakespeare's 'unfairness to the pastoralist position' is to lose the element of play and masking that characterizes pastoral. The question is whether Milton really belongs in the scheme of the book. True, he confirms the idea of an 'anti-pastoral sentiment' by giving us what the author calls 'a difficult Eden', involving both work and the complications of sexual love. But Milton is dealing less with pastoral conventions in his Eden than with the myth of the Golden Age. He is concerned, as Professor Lindenbaum points out, to distinguish between 'the true mythic place' and mere fables. The link made here between Sidney and Milton as both 'ideologues' rests on shaky ground. Sidney at least has the spirit of play.

But the most central question raised by the thesis of the book is whether, as the author himself admits, anti-pastoralism should not rather be considered a part of pastoral, instead of a distinct mode. If, instead of emphasizing the personal feelings of the poets, we turn to the rhetoric they use, anti-pastoralism would take its place where it rightfully belongs, in a traditional *disputatio in utramque partem*, a form of argument that presents both sides of an issue. In fact, pastoralism and anti-pastoralism are merely two sides of the same coin. Such an interpretation would fit both Sidney and Shakespeare, not to mention Spenser and Marvell, but would leave Milton aside, in the camp of controversialists.

Rhetoric and fiction join hands in Arthur Kinney's treatment of humanist poetics. 'Being educable man might also be perfectible' — so he begins to present his thesis, that the works of fiction produced in sixteenth-century England 'hewed closely to the lessons of Tudor humanist grammar schools and university curricula'. Although he identifies the scepticism implicit in disputatiousness and wordplay, he emphasizes that only with the loss of confidence in a stable universe, around 1600, does this element come to dominate literature, and, in so doing, to disintegrate humanist fictions.

The title of this book might give us pause. To find humanist poetics limited to prose fiction flies in the face of Sidney's own definition of poetry. As fiction, he saw it transcending the distinction between prose and verse. A more accurate title might have been *Rhetoric and Truth in Humanist Fictions*.

With this quibble out of the way, we may turn to the arrangement of the selected works. The writers are grouped in three sections: 'The Poetics of Wordplay' (More and Gascoigne), 'The Poetics of Eloquence' (Lyly, Greene, and Sidney), 'The Poetics of Doubt and Despair' (Nashe and Lodge). Each writer is situated in his rhetorical and philosophical context. Only occasionally does a relationship seem a little strained, as it does when Greene's 'fiction of wonder' is linked to the Longinian sublime. For the most part, Professor Kinney's enterprise of tracing the influences, both classical and Continental, on English prose fiction of this period brings together a heterogeneous group of writers and provides convincing evidence that they were all working in accordance with contemporary educational principles.

Yet he does not shirk the fact that a rhetorical education, however officially joined to ethics, does not necessarily produce virtuous action. He quotes Cicero: 'I have often seriously debated with myself whether men and communities have received more good or evil from oratory and a consuming devotion to eloquence'. Certainly Lyly and Sidney make plain their awareness of the dangers inherent in the very art to which they subscribe. On the other side of the coin, as Professor Kinney points out, there is a constant threat to fiction when metaphor itself invites distrust. Hence it is that Sidney's defence of poetry advanced the idea of a higher truth which can *only* be served by fiction and metaphor.

It is little wonder that the author sees humanist poetics as 'a poetics that directs thought, always, toward abstractions'. But in this emphasis, justifiable though it is, he tends to neglect the other aspect of Sidney's poetics: delighting. One is led to ask whether the *Arcadia* would have been 'England's best-selling novel well into the eighteenth century' if it had not provided at least as much pleasure as instruction.

But to do justice to that aspect of humanist poetics would call for another, different book. Within the limits Professor Kinney has set himself — and they are very broad — he has performed a real service not only to all who labour in the field of sixteenth-century prose fiction but also to the writers themselves, by helping us to read them better. Not least, he has proved that it is possible to speak legitimately, and without apology, of a Renaissance writer's 'intention'.

UNIVERSITY OF ILLINOIS AT URBANA-CHAMPAIGN JUDITH DUNDAS

The Historical Renaissance: New Essays on Tudor and Stuart Literature and Culture. Edited by HEATHER DUBROW and RICHARD STRIER. Chicago and London: University of Chicago Press. 1989. x + 377 pp. £33.50 (paperbound £11.95).

The title of this volume of essays promises that a special feature will be the presence of detailed enquiry into particular historical milieux or historical movements. This indeed proves to be the case: the reader gains substantial, satisfying information from discussions of notably diverse areas of Tudor and Stuart culture, including the theological, the legal, the topographical, the political (in the sense both of evolving political theory and of particular political controversies), and the linguistic. As for the theoretical stance of the volume's contributors, the editors sensibly point out that the old and 'New' historicisms are not necessarily contrasted with each other, or even distinct; and in their selection of essays they illustrate some of the wide range of ways in which historical study of Tudor and Stuart literary culture is at present being conducted. In practice it is often mainly a matter of the preferred vocabulary of the critic which determines whether he or she should be labelled 'New Historicist' or not. Since the vocabulary undoubtedly belongs to the category which sixteenth-century Protestants called 'things indifferent', the reader, unperturbed by the chosen idiom, is free to judge the articles by the criterion of the extent to which they enhance understanding of the culture.

Janel Mueller, writing about Katherine Parr's *Lamentation of a Sinner*, not only draws attention to the significance of an original (not translated) religious treatise by a Tudor queen, but locates it securely in a tradition of early Tudor Protestant discourse which originates with Tyndale and includes Cranmer and Latimer. An aspect of sixteenth-century political theory, specifically the proper limits to the obedience owed by inferiors to their superiors, is tackled by Richard Strier in relation to the many servant-figures in *King Lear*. It is not that Shakespeare's affirmation of disobedience in certain circumstances is a particularly new idea (thoughtful undergraduates notice it for themselves); but Strier sets out the political context with exemplary clarity, drawing upon *The Courtier, Utopia*, the Marian exiles, and the Homilies, and then examines *King Lear* meticulously in this regard. Lawrence Manley provides an absorbing account of how the city of London in all its complexity and confusion was described and hence implicitly controlled through certain models and metaphors, the metaphor of the city as woman gradually giving way to the metaphor of city as monster. The language of courtly compliment employed by George Herbert in letters to patrons and in his speeches as University Orator, Michael Schoenfeldt perceptively shows, interpenetrated the language of the sacred poems, where Herbert both used and exposed the verbal techniques of submission made available by society. Brian P. Levack, in a carefully qualified essay, identifies a group of common lawyers in the late Elizabethan and early Stuart period whose political ideas were tilted in the direction of absolutism through the influence of Roman law. Dealing with the controversies surrounding the attempt to write English verse in quantitative metres, Richard Helgerson discusses the relationship between this seemingly insignificant movement and the great issues of national self-fashioning in the latter half of the Elizabethan era. This is an extremely thought-provoking piece.

Of course, dedicated analysis of an historical milieu does not in itself guarantee that the chosen thesis will win assent. In an essay which is most informative in its handling of debates concerning James I's project for the Union of England and Scotland, Leah S. Marcus offers an allegorical reading of *Cymbeline* which is so complex and elaborate that it would surely defeat most audiences, and then argues for the simultaneous presence of a critique which undermines the political symbols to a point at which, one may feel, impenetrability reigns. A quite different difficulty arises in connexion with Arthur F. Kinney's essay on 'Sidney and the Uses of History'. In this instance claims are made which are not sufficiently supported by detailed evidence: Thucydides is alleged to be a 'source' for the *Arcadia* on the basis of rather vague resemblances, and a discussion of equity versus the letter of the law in *Arcadia*, Book v is undertaken without close engagement with the fine details of the text.

Stimulating articles by Donald R. Kelley on resistance-theory, Marjorie Garber on forms of deformity in *Richard III*, Maureen Quilligan on the relationship between Sidney and the queen, Heather Dubrow on Donne's Somerset epithalamium, and Clark Hulse on two competing languages of power to be found in Spenser and Bacon, complete a most valuable collection. This is a book in which historical scholarship and sharp insight work together to illuminate many areas of Early Modern culture.

UNIVERSITY OF READING   ANTHEA HUME

The Sonnet Over Time: A Study in the Sonnets of Petrarch, Shakespeare, and Baudelaire. By SANDRA L. BERMANN. (Studies in Comparative Literature, 63) Chapel Hill and London: University of North Carolina Press. 1988. x + 174 pp. $25.00.

Petrarch and the English Sonnet Sequences. By THOMAS P. ROCHE, JR. New York: AMS Press. 1989. xviii + 604 pp. Inst: $57.50; Indiv.: $25.00.

Thomas P. Roche's *The Kindly Flame* (Princeton, 1964), a study of Books III and IV of *The Faerie Queene* as a unit, closely observed its structural patterns. A keen sense of the patterns accompanying and supplementing meaning has remained with him during the twenty-year slog eventuating in *Petrarch and the English Sonnet Sequences*, which seems to have been completed before 1983 (see p. xvii), though not published till 1989. It represents a mighty effort of will and industry rather than, strictly, of inspiration, though its insights are none the worse for being hard won. Professor Roche is always learned and attentive to detail. But whereas his earlier research was manageable and, in written form, even, the effort to render down Petrarch *and* the English sonneteers so that they make a shapely and coherent study has been too much. Here, he acknowledges, is material for two books. Even within the two musterings there is discontinuity and lumpiness, with too many enforced exclusions such as *Trionfi*, *Amoretti* and *Idea*. Nevertheless, a cover-all study like that attempted in 1929 by Janet G. Scott was rightly ruled out, and if we miss Spenser and Drayton, it is good to meet Anne Locke (1560 and, as first in the field, snatching the prize usually awarded to Watson) and her surprisingly skilled and prolific son Henry.

Professor Roche also has on hand an unwieldy number of subjects, reflecting the various aspects of his research. He holds the centre, however, so that the result is clumsy rather than chaotic. He achieves notable success in arguing and demonstrating cases which future scholars will have to take into account. That Petrarch's sequence is unified by a structuring myth or sub-text, that its structure is also numerological, that its moral is unequivocally Christian, and that the English sequences more or less follow suit — all these ideas add to understanding of the European sonnet tradition, while also extending the meaning of the word 'Petrarchan'. Later scholars, if not Professor Roche himself, will need to explain whether Petrarch's Italian, French, and Spanish successors fit in: their absence creates a historical gap within *Petrarch and the English Sonnet Sequences*.

Professor Roche's illustrations carry conviction. Thus the sub-text of *Canzoniere* is the myth of Apollo and Daphne and its 366 poems refer both to the calendar and to the Christian year, while 'il pentersi', covering the rejection of love as well as of lust, dominates the presentation of Petrarch's love for Laura. Likewise the sub-text of *Astrophil and Stella* is the Homeric myth of Penelope and her 108 suitors, that figure also dictating its numerological scheme, and Sidney too recognizes the sin pervading 'this too-much-loved earth', where men follow wrong objects of desire. And so on, with a substantial array of examples from Sidney's successors, culminating in Shakespeare.

The time-gap between Petrarch and the Elizabethans is filled with an account of early comment on *Canzoniere* and the ways in which it was read in the fourteenth, fifteenth, and sixteenth centuries. This is one of several fresh directions Professor Roche takes in the course of his book, and it lends support to his own moral interpretation of the sonnets. For even Alessandro Vellutello, for all his (reprehensible!) confidence in the 'real life' story of Petrarch and Laura, is never far from Augustinian morality. Indeed, few in those days were, a fact which prompts Professor Roche to attack, trenchantly if at too great length, Frances Yates's 'incredible' account of Giordano Bruno's *Degli eroici furori*, an account which, by representing him as a Hermetic magus, cuts him off from the common Christian and Petrarchan tradition.

That Petrarch's translators and imitators were, accordingly, more interested in his ideas than in his 'words and images' is a point well taken. At the same time, it is surely also true that he was a most influential contributor to Europe's rhetorical stock. 'Literary' criticism hardly exists before Dryden, or exists only as a branch of morals and philosophy. Neither Victorian feeling for aesthetics nor the modern armoury of critical tools were around. The Renaissance comment on the *utile* of poetry does not mean that the *dulce* was not, in practice, and is not still, a matter of importance to poets and their readers, including their academic readers. Professor Roche is almost too anxious to keep clear of the words and images which, in combination with metre and rhythm, continue to give delight over the centuries.

With the English sequences Professor Roche draws on a mass of research material relevant to his thesis, and as before strikes out constantly in new directions. With Constable, for example, he 'namierizes': the poet's contacts give a unique social and historical interest to *Diana*. With Daniel (and this as late as p. 343), he introduces a major theme of the latter part of his book, the poet's revision of his sequence and his addition to it of a related narrative poem. His study of the reworking of *Delia* in *The Complaint of Rosamond* and of *Sonnets* in *A Louers Complaint* forms a further contribution to understanding of the sonnet tradition. Furthermore, it also establishes a special link between Daniel and Shakespeare, and this is further developed when Professor Roche proposes that the numerological pattern Alastair Fowler found in Shakespeare's sequence derived from a similar Pythagorean pyramid in Daniel's.

Almost all the way Professor Roche is persuasive, but perhaps he took a holiday as the end drew nigh, a trip to the never-never land of Shakespeare's eternal triangle.

So the fair youth becomes the projection of 'Will', 'the higher reaches of himself'. But of what self? The 'I' of *Sonnets* is not Shakespeare, who is therefore now available for the part of the Rival Poet. *Sonnets*, true to the sonnet tradition, is Christian in tone, so that the triangle could be trinitarian. But for all the tendency of 'I' to play God, promising immortality, these three people are not (Heaven forbid!) Father, Son, and Holy Ghost. At this point, some mention of the eternizing topos in poetry, a legacy from the Romans, might have provided a corrective.

How strange that numbers should have gone under ground for four centuries, and that even the earliest commentators should have given them such scant attention! To what purpose did the poets, like Gosse's Creator, put these fossils in the rocks?

Sandra Bermann's scope is obviously narrower, being directed mainly to verbal and tonal analysis. She differentiates the 'poetic self' of three sonneteers, showing the metonymic, metaphoric, and ironic-allegorical styles of Petrarch, Shakespeare, and Baudelaire respectively. Each section starts usefully with a close look at a single sonnet. She is rather less successful in her glances at literary history. Her account of the sonnet between Petrarch and Shakespeare is rather potted, while the 'dramatic direction' of *Sonnets* is questionably described as 'new'. Again, what she says of Baudelaire's poems is more valuable than what she says of Romanticism and 'modernity'.

LONDON

PATRICIA THOMSON

Revisionary Play: Studies in the Spenserian Dynamics. By HARRY BERGER JR. With an Introductory Essay by LOUIS MONTROSE. Berkeley, Los Angeles, and London: University of California Press. 1988. xii + 483 pp. $48.00.

This volume offers us a reprinting of many of Harry Berger's essays on *The Faerie Queene* written and published in the sixties followed by a series of essays on *The Shepheardes Calendar* written or reworked between 1979 and 1987, and most not previously published. But this is not just a collecting together of scattered and disparate work. As I turned the last page of the lengthy and argumentative 'Afterword' I had the sense of having completed something of an intellectual, even a spiritual, autobiography to which the 'Afterword' stands as a credo, professing the current, but never, one feels, the final articles of Professor Berger's critical faith. These essays bear witness to a passionate, indeed at times a heroic commitment in his own work, over thirty years, to complexity and revision, to a refusal of what he calls the 'flatness of resolution'. In turn, what he finds and most admires in Spenser is a continually evolutionary and revisionary energy: 'no moment of union or reconciliation, of relief or triumph, is to be construed as absolute — absolute either in the sense of being final or in the sense of being totally one-sided' (p. 244).

The sequence of essays on *The Faerie Queene* is arranged to suggest a coherent uncovering of the Spenserian dynamics. We start with two essays, which expound two crucial Bergerian views of Spenser; his emphasis on complexity and difference within any, and particularly erotic, harmony ('The Spenserian Dynamics'), and his evolutionary view of the development of the individual and history ('Archaism, Immortality, and the Muse'). We then follow Professor Berger's analyses of these concepts through key episodes from Book I to the Mutabilitie Cantos. Working against this orderly arrangement is a continual revision and restatement as we move through the essays, due, in part, to their reordering for this volume to follow the sequence of the poem, not that of their publication. Thus, the 1961 essay on Book VI, 'A Secret Discipline', follows a 1971 essay on the House of Busirane and the 1968 essay on Book IV, 'Two Spenserian Retrospects'. Because each essay was originally published separately Professor Berger returns in each to his basic premises at a different stage of their evolution, producing in this collected version of the essays the impression of the critic as an embattled hero struggling endlessly with difficult and slippery material which needs constant redefinition and restatement.

It is possible to harbour doubts both about the general direction and some of the particulars of Professor Berger's analysis of *The Faerie Queene* while finding his readings often illuminating (Sylvanus as *silva vanus*, pp. 71–76; Busirane's House as dramatizing 'the male imagination's attempts at *maistrie,* p. 115; his analysis of Merlin's prophecy as describing an evolving sense of nation and national loyalty), and sometimes dazzling: the essays on the Garden of Adonis and the Mutabilitie Cantos conclude with breathtaking glimpses of complexity and subtlety: 'in the flickering and momentary resolution of a single complex image, the tableau holds a multitude of references, meanings, feelings, and suggestions together so that they continually act on each other, move and change as we look at the image' (p. 153).

Professor Berger is a champion of close reading. Acknowledging the effect on his critical practice of new theories of reading and interpretation in the seventies and eighties, he writes that he did not wish 'to leave close reading behind, since that was what I best liked doing and in the final analysis the only thing I felt I knew how to do'. The essays on *The Shepheardes Calendar* record his at times bloody encounter with new theories, particularly with 'new historicism', and his continuing allegiance to close reading. In my view, the results are not wholly successful. We are asked to view Colin as a risible figure, a puppet used to parody and thus criticize conventional pastoral, and to consider Spenser as a proto-feminist: the poem, he writes, 'implicates a pastoral of sexual politics... a cultural critique of motivational patterns inscribed in and reproduced by dominant literary genres and conventions' (p. 386). As that sentence betrays, Professor Berger, in *The Shepheardes Calendar* essays, occasionally falls foul of current critical idiom, allowing complexity to become impenetrability, and pursuing puns mercilessly (for example p. 376 or p. 379).

For all my reservations about *The Shepheardes Calendar* essays, the author's energy and openness, his willingness to encounter new critical discourses, to revise them and to revise his own, to proffer ever new, but always closely argued readings, elicit respect and admiration.

UNIVERSITY OF READING   ELIZABETH HEALE

The Human Stage: English Theatre Design, 1576–1640. By JOHN ORRELL. Cambridge, New York, New Rochelle, Melbourne, and Sydney: Cambridge University Press. 1988. xx +292 pp. £30.00.

John Orrell is a master of theoretical argument. In this book he moves from an immaculately researched study of Tudor London and its suburbs, through the surviving theatrical memorials of the Shakespearean era towards the official suppression of all dramatic activity in England following the outbreak of the Civil War. The case that he seeks to prove is that John Brayne, citizen and grocer of London, was a theatrical entrepreneur whose vision of the future embraced a radical change from *ad hoc* performance spaces, opportunistically selected, to a concept of theatrical architecture consistent with Renaissance, humanist approaches to it. It is a beguiling case, persuasively presented.

Given that premise, it is logical to take the sophisticated, Italianate Court banquet theatres of the early Tudor period as a starting point rather than the provisions made to suit local topography and convenience for performances of miracle and morality plays in churches, churchyards, market squares, and the like which continued until late in the 1570s.

Professor Orrell opens his argument with a meticulously careful study of all the surviving graphic and contractual information, fragmentary as all of it is, relating to the public playhouses of Elizabethan London. He then retreats chronologically to the 1520s to discuss the festive theatres created for Henry VIII by his Office of Tents and Toils and the Royal Works at Calais and Greenwich (which Richard Hosley and Sidney Anglo first brought forcefully to public notice) and links them to an equally detailed discussion of the Banquet House built at Westminster to entertain the Duc d'Alençon during his visit to London in 1581–82.

The central ideas presented in these discussions are: first, that although all three theatres were temporary canvas structures they were supported on heavy, but transportable, prefabricated, timber frames which could be mounted, like any Circus 'Big Top', on site and then dismantled and stored against future use; and, second, that the design and interior decoration of all three buildings was distinctively humanistic, rather than Gothic, in style, and governed by Renaissance cosmological thinking about the nature and purpose of theatrical architecture as practised in classical antiquity.

Professor Orrell then applies these ideas, without stretching the evidence he has offered to his readers beyond legitimate limits, to such aspects of London's Elizabethan public playhouses as the decoration of the heavens and the design and construction of their timber frames, thus opening up a direct route to the several chapters devoted to Inigo Jones's work as a theatre architect and designer which occupy the latter half of the book.

What has to be provided here is a chain-link with which to attach the largely speculative arguments advanced in the first half of this comprehensive survey to the virtually indisputable facts that comprise most of the second half. This link Professor Orrell finds in Simon Basil, James I's first Comptroller of his Office of Works, whose designs for the temporary transformation of the Hall at Christ Church, Oxford, into a theatre for Latin plays in 1605 were derived from his personal knowledge of the woodcuts illustrating Serlio's *Architettura* (*Il secondo libro di perspettiva*, Paris, 1545). This method of proceeding secures the additional advantage of relating these theoretical principles firmly back to those derived from classical antiquity.

Have we then finally become possessed in this book of a water-tight *schema* that unites the origins and development of all Elizabethan and Jacobean theatre design, both public and private, from John Brayne's first involvement with theatre management in 1567 forward to Inigo Jones's conversion of the old Cockpit in Whitehall Palace into a Court Theatre for Charles I in 1629–31, within a single, coherent, evolutionary process of imaginative theory advanced through practical experiment? Alas, we have not; but Professor Orrell is honest enough to admit, while yearning himself for his thesis to turn out to be true, that there are still too many gaps and contradictory elements left in the evidence he presents for any informed reader to accept his case as fully proven.

One of these is his surprising omission of any reference to Chaucer's description in his *Knight's Tale* of an auditorium for a Tournament, which he actually calls a theatre: ('Round was the shap, in maner of compas, | Ful of degrees, the heighte of sixty pas') which ante-dates John Brayne's three-storeyed timber frames by nearly two hundred years: and yet Chaucer, as Clerk of Works to Richard II, had had practical experience of building such auditoria for his royal master. Another is Professor Orrell's decision to ignore the adult actors' economic need to travel widely in the provinces where few, if any, of the idealized conditions he postulates could possibly have been supplied and where inventive adaptability remained obligatory.

In the event his honesty of approach has served him well, since he could not have anticipated, when submitting his typescript to his publishers, that the archaeologists' discoveries on the site of the Rose Playhouse would do more to confirm earlier beliefs in a wholly pragmatic and opportunistic approach among Elizabethan theatrical entrepreneurs towards design and construction than to support the case argued in this book.

In only one instance does this reader discern a wilful disregard of alternative evidence which, if included, would seriously threaten his own argument; that relates to his assumption that the Inigo Jones drawings for an unnamed theatre were those used by Christopher Beeston for the transformation of the old Cockpit in Drury Lane into the Cockpit, or Phoenix, Theatre in 1617. The case for accepting what Professor Orrell loosely describes as the 'recent identification' (p. 186) of drawings 7C and D now in Worcester College Library has always been disputed, and is only the more to be doubted in the light of Graham Barlow's researches respecting the known shape, size, and ownership of all buildings in that area throughout the seventeenth and eighteenth centuries (*Theatre Research International*, 13, no. 1 (Spring, 1989) 30–44).

Nevertheless, it would be churlish to quarrel on these grounds with what is unquestionably the best ordered and sharpest critical survey (in the best sense of those words) of all the information which an ever-swelling tide of research and discovery has uncovered during the past half-century respecting the playhouses of Elizabethan, Jacobean, and Caroline London, more especially since Professor Orrell himself provides adequate signposts to the need for continuing scepticism in most areas where the theoretical principles underpinning his argument remain open to question.

BRISTOL   GLYNNE WICKHAM

Shakespeare: Text, Language, Criticism: Essays in Honour of Marvin Spevack. Edited by BERNHARD FABIAN and KURT TETZELI VON ROSADOR. Hildesheim, Zurich, and New York: Olms-Weidemann. 1987. vi + 370 pp. DM 98.00.

The subtitle of this volume is perhaps more accurate than the title: it contains twenty 'Essays in Honour of Marvin Spevack' arranged in alphabetical order according to the names of their authors. Most, but not all of them could be said to fall under the heading 'Shakespeare: Text, Language, Criticism', but the editors have not subdivided them into these categories. There is no Introduction, no Index and, unusually for a *festschrift*, no information about the dedicatee's life and works, apart from the publisher's advertisement on the back flap of the cover. Not surprisingly, the result is rather a mixed bag, and it is difficult to offer anything other than rather a mixed review.

The largest and most coherent subdivision might have consisted of essays on 'Text'. There are five of these: G. Blakemore Evans on the Folger manuscript of *The Merry Wives of Windsor*, Harold Jenkins on the ball scene (II.1) of *Much Ado About Nothing*, Giorgio Melchiori on the additions to *Sir Thomas More*, Marion Trousdale on diachronic and synchronic principles of editing, and Stanley Wells and Gary Taylor on internal evidence for revision in *The Taming of the Shrew*.

Two out of four essays that might have been assigned to a 'Language' group reflect Marvin Spevack's interest in grammar and lexicography: Robert Burchfield examines Shakespeare's use of the bare infinitive in *The Winter's Tale*, and H. Joachim Neuhaus discusses some issues relating to structural semantics, dictionary definitions, and lexical glosses, focusing on Shakespeare's uses of the word 'bachelor'. An essay which concentrates on the minutiae of language in a different and more traditional way is Edgar Mertner's exploration of 'conceit' in relation to style and stylistic self-consciousness in *Romeo and Juliet*, while Inge Leimberg writes on Shakespeare's use of the phrase 'Give me thy hand' in a number of plays (though not, surprisingly, *Titus Andronicus*).

Most of the other essays would fall into the catch-all category of 'Criticism', though this would range from the study of sources (Michael Steppat on Shakespeare's use of the Countess of Pembroke and Daniel in *Antony and Cleopatra*) and theatrical interpretations (Marga Munkelt on productions of *Titus Andronicus* by John Barton in Stratford in 1981 and Heiner Muller in Bochum in 1985), to that of historical reception (J. W. Binns on the lectures given on Shakespeare by William Hawkins in eighteenth-century Oxford). And this category would also of course include some examples of traditional character-and-theme criticism: Jonas Barish on oath-breaking in *King John*, Richard Harrier on ceremony and politics in *Richard II*, Harry Levin on the death-scenes in *Antony and Cleopatra*, Samuel Schoenbaum on the Porter's scene in *Macbeth*, and Hans-Jürgen Weckermann on the failure of the autonomous individual in *Coriolanus*.

Finally, there are three essays which have to do with Shakespeare only indirectly: Paul Morgan on the seventeenth-century woman book-collector Frances Wolfreston, Ulrich Suerbaum on the 'myth' of the inner stage in discussions of the Elizabethan theatre, and Robert Kean Turner on the collaborations of Fletcher, Massinger, and Field in *The Queen of Corinth* and *The Knight of Malta*.

While these essays are all competent in their different ways, and some of them are distinguished, it has to be said that they are not exactly at the forefront of contemporary Shakespeare criticism. The authors make no reference whatever to developments such as feminism, new historicism or cultural materialism, and most of the purely critical pieces could have been written twenty years ago. The most innovative contributions are scholarly rather than critical, namely those which apply linguistic approaches to Shakespeare's verse and those on textual matters as well as the ones which could be described as straightforward historical research. By comparison the critical offerings seem tired and the topics overly familiar.

The collection is not helped by some evidence that it was a long time in preparation, allowing some contributions to have been overtaken by subsequent events. Marga Munkelt for example proclaims that the main question raised by her essay is still unanswered: 'whether and how *Titus* is producible', apparently writing before the much-celebrated production of the full text by Deborah Warner at the Royal Shakespeare Company's Swan theatre in 1987. Marion Trousdale discusses Stanley Wells's defence of modernization in *Re-Editing Shakespeare for the Modern Reader* (1984) without reference to his actual practice in the Oxford *Complete Works* (1986). Professor Wells and Professor Taylor present arguments about the text of *The Shrew* which have been summarized in the Oxford *Textual Companion* (1987). By the time this review appears the book will, sadly, appear even more dated.

UNIVERSITY OF LIVERPOOL   ANN THOMPSON

William Shakespeare's 'Richard II'. Edited and with an Introduction by HAROLD
   BLOOM. (Modern Critical Interpretations) New York, New Haven, and
   Philadelphia: Chelsea House. 1988. viii + 139 pp. $22.50.

The Actor in History: Studies in Shakespearean Stage Poetry. By DAVID GRENE. University
   Park and London: Penn State Press. 1988. xviii + 158 pp. $16.95.

Readers of Harold Bloom's collection may be surprised and stimulated when his insistence on Richard as a self-indulgent poet is immediately contradicted by his first critic, Ruth Nevo. Arguing that 'The Genre of *Richard II*' is tragic and that the very medium of tragedy is self-dramatization, she emphasizes the king's agonized recognition of hard facts as a consequence, not as a cause of his fall. In contrast, development of character or action does not engage the critics whose essays follow Professor Nevo's. Although described by Professor Bloom as 'a representative selection of the best modern critical interpretations', most share a preoccupation with language. Several support Professor Bloom's 'consensus' view that Richard is ineffectual, narcissistic, and self-destructive.

This collection displays a family resemblance among critics who concentrate on poetry, psychoanalysis, and deconstruction (Bloom's 'Gallic way of reading'). Their practice seems to exclude detailed theatrical and political analysis as effectively as it excludes tragedy. *Richard II* becomes a series of acutely personal encounters among a few characters whose behaviour is determined by generational conflict or ideological system. Stephen Booth's explanation of 'Syntax as Rhetoric in *Richard II*' does show brilliantly how self-delaying sentence patterns can frustrate audiences, suggestively if briefly associating our impeded comprehension with our 'moral uneasiness'. But persuaded as he is that audiences cannot detect 'syntactical likeness' among speakers, and that the play links wordiness with 'all varieties of weakness', Professor Booth does not look for subtle intrigue or tragic change. Harry Berger Jr grants that the ceremonial language shared by speakers in the opening scenes produces an 'uneasy awareness' of obscure motives, yet insists that his textual 'excavation' of conflict between Gaunt and Bolingbroke is both 'meta-theatrical' and 'antitheatrical'. Just why actors and directors alert to Oedipal tensions throughout the Henriad should *not* welcome Professor Berger's keen insights is baffling. Perhaps deconstruction loses its satiric energy unless it posits monoliths to undermine and explode. Through allegorical analogy, Professor Berger contaminates theatrical mimesis with patriarchal repression before he even begins to dig.

More genial allegories inform the readings of the other critics. Maynard Mack Jr presents the 'imaginative setting', the varying (and nostalgic) ideas of 'inheritance, time, and kingship' which provide a 'structure' for 'king killing'. James L. Calderwood's chapter uses *Richard II* to describe a metatheatrical 'fall' from 'verbal fideism' into nominalism, while that of Susan Wells situates the play amid contradictions between customary kinship society and the modern state. Presumably, her assertion that these social problems are 'mediated' through 'intersubjectivity' is meant to justify her 'hermeneutic' detachment from all specific problems and persons.

Not surprisingly, Professor Bloom concludes with a selection from *Northrop Frye on Shakespeare*. Professor Frye's university lecture surveys themes which are salient or implicit throughout this volume: Richard's 'programming himself as a loser', the play's circular, repetitive plot, and Shakespeare's 'deeply conservative' social vision. 'Shakespeare is interested in chronicle, the personal actions and interactions of the people at the top of the social order'. If Professor Frye were less exclusively interested in the 'top' himself, he might not have instructed his students that all twelve thousand Welshmen desert to Bolingbroke or have glibly confounded that sublime theory of property right, the king's two bodies, with the metaphor of the body politic. Such minor fallacies could annoy or awaken a Shakespeare class. I doubt that they qualify their author for Professor Bloom's highest praise: 'the wisdom that lies beyond method and theory of language, the wisdom critics once called imagination.'

David Grene's study, based on lectures delivered at Cornell in 1978, identifies imagination with a theory of dramatic speech. Introducing himself as a 'strayed classicist', Professor Grene writes for 'the intelligent general reader' rather than the professional Shakespearean. Apt citations from some half-dozen writers suggest his familiarity with scholarship of the last thirty years. Some professional readers may decide that he could easily have written his own study in the hey-day of New Criticism, forty or fifty years ago. Two considerations suggest, however, that his approach is more timely: his passionate delight in stage poetry and his reservations about metatheatre.

Shakespeare's words have great power for Professor Grene. His lively criticism-by-quotation can recall the romantic enthusiasm of G. Wilson Knight, the keen hearing of George Rylands. Professor Grene never pins down the momentary truths that excite him in Shakespeare's poetry. He refers to their quality as 'numinal' and 'histrionic', finding in them 'luminosity', 'enchantment', 'exultation', and, most eloquently, 'the vision of some country where the passionate truth exceeds the range of any particular character, and where the attention is riveted by images that grow or diminish with slender or indeterminate relation to their speakers'. It is as if an unabashed belief in strong presences and forces which transcend individual character ('impersonal imaginative life') comes naturally and persistently to this distinguished translator of the Greek dramatists.

Whenever Professor Grene terms a sequence 'histrionic' or 'theatrical', he generally discovers 'fusion' between a perceiving speaker and poetic language. Such fusions make speaking actors charismatic, for new truths bring forth new selves, liberating the actors from politics and plots. Professor Grene questions Anne Barton's view that in *Antony and Cleopatra* 'the play metaphor continues to express emptiness and deceit'. He celebrates the triumph of histrionic lyricism over history in this play and in *Richard II*, then sides with the 'independent theatricality' of Hotspur and Falstaff against the 'singular' main plot of the Henriad. Having taken so many speakers on and well beyond their own terms, he suddenly submits himself to the baleful facts and 'sharply prescriptive' role-playing of *Julius Caesar* and *Coriolanus*, producing sombre analyses of exploited heroes in Hobbesian power struggles, their portraits 'inspired by prodigious imaginative penetration of classical political life'. Finally, he imitates that versatility which he prizes in theatre by reforming the terms he applies to *Measure for Measure*. Its history, he decides, is richly fantastic, while its poetry insinuates a realism which lives on in our minds, disturbing them. Because Professor Grene allows the specific gravity of diverse plays to guide his responses to 'imaginative life', his performance often lives up to his description of Richard II's. As a critic of Shakespeare, this 'strayed classicist' is at many moments an 'inspired amateur'.

UNIVERSITY OF MANITOBA   JUDITH WEIL

The Merchant of Venice. By JOHN LYON. (Harvester New Critical Introductions to Shakespeare) New York, London, Toronto, Sydney, and Tokyo: Harvester Wheatsheaf. 1988. xvi + 152 pp. £7.95.

The General Editor's Preface (by Graham Bradshaw) to this new series is not exactly a model of precision. The volumes (one on each play and two on the non-dramatic verse are envisaged) are offered as 'a challenge to all students of Shakespeare'; they are not meant as an assembly of background information and standard interpretations, but set out to proceed from a discussion of stage history and critical reception to concentrate on 'those issues which seem most pressing' (p. vii). This vagueness at least has the merit of leaving each author free to pursue his own interests and methods. John Lyon is clearly more concerned with critical debate than with stage history. The couple of pages on the play in performance are too brief to be more than a grudging concession to the general concept; the bulk of the book consists in a very readable and stimulating commentary on the text and its critics. Dr Lyon rightly takes issue with all those critics who have smoothed over the play's provocative discrepancies by turning it either into a romantic comedy with a harmless stage villain or into an outraged attack on Christian hypocrisy. Instead, he insists on the 'unsettling' (his favourite term) qualities of the text, and though he is by no means the first to be aware of these, he offers a fresh and interesting reading of the play that allows us the freedom of our own response. It is, in the author's own words, only 'aggressive in its refusal to offer any single "new" interpretation of the play' (p. 131). Many of the text's traditional puzzles are nicely defined but left as puzzles and, in a few cases, as flaws in the dramatist's handling of his material. It is a pity that M. Mahood's excellent new Cambridge Edition of the play, though listed in the bibliography, appeared too late to be properly discussed because some of her general views on the play are more in agreement with Dr Lyon's approach than those of most of the critics he quarrels with, and at the same time Mahood seems more aware of the historical context of the play's perennial difficulties. What Dr Lyon describes as 'unsettling', Mahood defines as our 'complex responses', and she supplies what I find missing in Dr Lyon's account, an attempt to understand how such a play could have been written. Without such an interest in the historical ambience of this text it is difficult if not impossible to come to terms with it, unless, perhaps, in a brilliant production. It is therefore surprising that, for all his awareness of the modern reader's problems with the play, Dr Lyon has so little to say about questions of staging and about the widely differing endeavours of actors and producers to make coherent sense of this disturbing comedy.

BONN   DIETER MEHL

Hamlet's Choice: 'Hamlet' — A Reformation Allegory. By LINDA KAY HOFF. Lewiston, Queenston, and Lampeter: Edwin Mellen Press. 1988. xiv + 381 pp. $59.95.

Linda Kay Hoff's *Hamlet* is 'a "typal" allegory of the Reformation' (p. 17) to which the Book of Revelation and Fulke's *A Defence of the Sincere and True Translations of the Holy Scriptures . . .* (1583) provide most of the answers. *Hamlet* is a turn-of-the-century play whose uncertainties may well have apocalyptic overtones: it may also contain references to the Catholic/Calvinist feud which are obscured because of religious censorship, but Dr Hoff's all-inclusive allegorical reading weakens what might otherwise have been a valuable historicist approach.

The 'Hamlet's Choice' of the title is Calvinism, represented by Fortinbras who, like the second conqueror in Revelation, comes to rule with a 'rod of iron' (p. 332). Dr Hoff takes the First Quarto's claim that it was presented at the universities of Oxford and Cambridge as a declaration of the play's religious concerns since the universities, as former chantries, were 'nurseries of the Church of England' which was 'extremely Calvinist' at this time (p. 31). However, her subsequent reasoning is based on the conflated Arden text, not that of the First Quarto, and we are asked to 'assume that the players used an authentic text of *Hamlet* for these university performances, not the corrupt First Quarto in connection with which the claim appears' (p. 21). This does not convince and the detailed history of the universities seems superfluous.

The considerable detail in this study is frequently valuable, but historical documentation and textual analysis are not always successfully combined. Dr Hoff's study of Catholic and Calvinist applications of language can be fruitful in relation to *Hamlet* but the catalogue layout is unwieldy and repetition occurs between chapters.

Dr Hoff argues clearly that Denmark was a Catholic state and offers an additional insight concerning Claudius's confession, viewing this as the desperate attempt of a mortal sinner to confess and receive absolution because he considers himself to be under immediate threat of death from Hamlet. However, the narrow religious focus produces restricted vision elsewhere; for example, when she asks: 'If Denmark was Catholic under King Hamlet and remains so under King Claudius, why does Claudius' Catholic Denmark, a state in which "something is rotten", seem pervaded by an evil that was apparently absent during the reign of his equally Catholic brother, King Hamlet?' (p. 107). Here the "something rotten" has nothing to do with a hidden regicide and much to do with the allegorical explanation that Old Hamlet 'represents' the period of the apostolic fathers, 'the first "time" when "something rotten" was absent from Christianity' (p. 238), while Claudius stands for the 'Beast-*cum*-Antichrist of Revelation' (p. 116).

The religious allegorizing of characters is a limitation. Claudius is associated with the Jesuits who are 'evil, regicidal, and — most tellingly — hypocritical' (p. 114), but Machiavelli does not merit one reference. A highly suspect argument suggests that Laertes's name 'is meant to evoke *priest*' (p. 151) and through his trip to Paris he is associated with the contemporary Archpriest controversy. Polonius is seen as a Jesuit priest (p. 214) and 'Lesser Beast of Revelation' (p. 171), while we are told that, 'In Gertrude, Shakespeare emphasizes the degeneration of the Mother Church into the Whore of Babylon, the Woman of Revelation 17' (p. 207) and Ophelia represents 'the doubt that arose over the Immaculate Conception — the keystone of Mariology and Marioecclesiology — and the dissension associated with the Catholic Church's identification of the Woman of Revelation 12 as Mary' (p. 207).

It may be true that 'it is *impossible* to ignore the religious elements within *Hamlet*' (p. 4), but this book shows that much is lost if the play is seen to be about nothing else.

St Mary's College, Strawberry Hill   Marion Lomax

Shakespeare's Mercutio: his History and Drama. By Joseph A. Porter. Chapel Hill and
    London: University of North Carolina Press. 1989. xiv + 281 pp. $38.50.

Joseph A. Porter's book is full of surprises, challenges to habits of interpretation, and more or less felicitous provocations. It outlines the history of Mercutio before, during and after his appearance in Shakespeare's *Romeo and Juliet*, and it reasserts the centrality of the figure. The author calls on evidence of classical and renaissance iconography and mythography, including alchemy, to document 'the long communal thought process' (p. 9) behind the dramatic character. After a survey of this material Professor Porter moves to accounts of Mercutio's 'eloquence and liminality', his 'significance in the dialectic of Shakespeare's negotiations with the memory of Marlowe and with the notion of literary proprietorship', and what the character reveals about 'Shakespearean gender, friendship and sexuality' (p. 94). The story of Mercutio within the play and posterity's dealings with him are discussed with reference to a close reading of the dramatic text itself, a survey of critical responses to the character and an account of some stage and film interpretations. In the concluding chapter Professor Porter meditates on the significance of 'Mercutio's Shakespeare', the topic becomes (or is revealed to have been all along) the dispute of critics over Shakespeare's place in a post-structuralist world.

From his opening paragraphs, which deal with the 'ghost' of Valentine — included in Capulet's guest-list — Professor Porter makes it clear that he will find directions out by a good many indirections. He ponders the biographical significance of the play and the characters because his kind of new historicism must take on the history of men's lives, their sense of themselves, without necessarily privileging these as the source of their works of art. He claims that Mercury/Hermes/Mercutio's meanings as a watcher over boundaries, a leader of souls (a pyschopomp), and a god of eloquence are bound up with Shakespeare's feelings towards Marlowe, and that Marlowe's homosexuality and the phallicity of Mercutio are connected. Professor Porter insists on the homoerotic element of Mercutio's bawdy, and defends it from the bowdlerizing instincts of the annotators: 'The bibliographical and critical history of "open arse" [in Act Two, Scene One] is a good

yardstick for measuring Mercutio's changing phallic subversiveness and the changing containment it elicits . . .' (p. 161).

As a god of thresholds and margins, Mercury points to Mercutio's significance in
Shakespeare's emotional career and the sentimentalization of the character in
criticism and performance seems to demonstrate the desire of interpreters to claim
cultural centrality rather than marginality for the dramatist and his works. In this
respect Professor Porter's work is a major contribution to the study of the reception
of Shakespeare, as well as an unavoidable challenge to interpreters of the play and
the character. Its theoretical self-consciousness is engagingly articulate, and it is full
of statements that might be inadmissible by one canon or another of criticism, but
which could only be excluded from discourse in and around *Romeo and Juliet* by
forfeiting too much of value. It is, of course, mercurial. At times Professor Porter's
readings of events on stage or in the study seems to push too hard at one threshold or
another. He claims, for example, that one sign of Mercutio's continuing presence in
the play after his death is Capulet's decision to advance the marriage of Paris and
Juliet from Thursday to Wednesday: '*mercredi*, Mercury's day' (p. 17). Some of
Professor Porter's statements edge further towards nonsense. For example, in
explanation of Mercutio's undeniable 'decline and marginalisation' during the
nineteenth century he speculates that 'an empire the sun never sets on . . . might be
expected to have peculiarly little use for a liminal figure descended from the god of
borders' (p. 197). But even this has its uses, if it sends objectors off in search of
liminal figures in Victorian culture (Pendennis, Cardinal Newman, Oscar Wilde,
Prince Albert? Discuss). Although at times the author seems to be shifting the
goal-posts, it cannot be denied that he engages the reader in an exhilarating variety
of games. This engaging, learned work should serve to animate discussion of the
aims and issues — not least, the politics — of interpreting Shakespeare in particular
and the renaissance in general.

UNIVERSITY OF BIRMINGHAM   RUSSELL JACKSON

'This Sceptered Sway': Sovereignty in Shakespeare's Comedies. By HUGO SCHWALLER.
   (Schweizer Anglistische Arbeiten/Swiss Studies in English, 115) Bern: Francke
   Verlag. 1988. x + 251 pp. Sw.F. 56.00.

Most German, Austrian, and Swiss universities require doctoral candidates to
publish their theses in book form, whereas in England and the United States they are
charitably stacked away in library vaults and often only available on microfilm,
unless the authors decide to lick them into shape and translate them into a readable
publication. Hugo Schwaller's book seems to me a clear example of a prematurely
published piece of work that certainly testifies to the author's diligence and
familiarity with his subject, but does little to advance our knowledge or even to
present its material in an elegant and stimulating manner. The style is neither
concise nor particularly subtle, and the habit of rehearsing well-known facts,
perhaps necessary in an academic exercise, often makes for redundancy or even
triteness: for example, we are told 'Let it be remembered that to the Renaissance
mind God was the supreme authority over the entire creation' (p. 94), or 'when
reading between the lines, we are often led to believe that the playwright was well
aware of the fact that authority can be abused' (p. 94, n. 5), or 'Shakespeare was
hardly impervious to Christian thought' (p. 133). At this level, one hardly expects
new answers to old questions.

The subject is certainly interesting and may well deserve a book, although,
reading through Dr Schwaller's study, I felt that one or two exploratory essays

might be more helpful and appropriate, on the lines of Clifford Leech's characteristically stimulating and provocative article on 'Shakespeare's Comic Dukes' of 1964 (*A Review of English Literature*, edited by A. Norman Jeffares, Volume v, pp. 101–14).

Three aspects of Shakespeare's treatment of authority in the comedies are discussed in some detail. The most extensive section is devoted to the Dukes and Kings in the comedies, their dramatic function, personal qualities and political role. Little emerges that will surprise the reader, unless it be the frequent recurrence of similar constellations and themes in the majority of the comedies and the growing prominence of the ruler-figures in Shakespeare's career.

This is emphasized in the second and perhaps most useful section of the book where Shakespeare's use of his sources in relation to characters of authority is discussed. Dr Schwaller rightly points out that the dramatist repeatedly introduced Dukes or Kings in the story where there is hardly any precedent (e.g., *The Comedy of Errors*) or highlighted and complicated their function within the plot, most strikingly, of course, in *Measure for Measure*.

A brief final section considers the ruler as lover in the comedies. The King of Navarre, Orsino, Oberon and Leontes are reviewed in turn, but apart from the observation that 'love has a disconcerting effect, and throws these sovereigns out of balance' (p. 232), little is made of possible connexions or contrasts in relation to the theme of authority.

Dr Schwaller generally seems content to present his material at some length and to retrace sufficiently familiar territory, but rarely enters into a searching discussion of deeper implications and unsolved problems. Too little attention is paid to the contexts and traditions of comedy or to recent, rather more unconventional readings of the comedies. In consequence, the subject of the study, though unfolded with rather unnecessary thoroughness, is by no means exhausted.

BONN   DIETER MEHL

In One Person Many People: the Image of the King in Three RSC Productions of William Shakespeare's 'King Richard II'. By LISA HAKOLA. Suomalainen Tiedeakatemia: Helsinki. 1988. xii + 198 pp.

A conventional review of Lisa Hakola's *In One Person Many People* would begin with a long charge-sheet of critical accusations. The sub-title is that of a doctoral thesis, and the book bears many predictable weaknesses of the thesis-written-up-for-publication form. The range of the study is extremely narrow: one play, one company, three productions: *Richard II*, as produced by the Royal Shakespeare Company, and as directed respectively by John Barton (1973–74), Terry Hands (1980–81), and Barry Kyle (1986–87). The intensive focus, quite proper to a thesis, makes for empirical richness combined with theoretical blindness: while the primary materials of production history are well-researched and useful, Dr Hakola's attempt to locate them into some critical perspective is hampered by a highly uncritical reliance on secondary sources, compounded by an excessive respect for the authority of established critics — it is generally assumed that simply to quote a critical authority (which could be Peter Ure, John Dover Wilson, E. M. W. Tillyard) provides a firm basis on which to orientate a set of facts or observations, or construct an opinion or value-judgement.

Theoretically the book is an attempt to synthesize the most conventional literary criticism on Shakespeare's history plays with the analysis of drama in performance. The result is, again predictably, a brand of performance analysis that is heavily dependent on literary-critical methodologies: Dr Hakola is much more concerned with the director's or actor's 'presentation' of the text's 'literary imagery' on the stage (pp. 4–5), than with specifically theatrical resources such as lighting and sound, which are apparently 'of such an immediately perceptual nature that it is not possible to describe them accurately' (p. 6). Theatre semiotics are mentioned (p. 17), but there is no systematic attempt to employ them as techniques of performance analysis.

But a moment's investigation of the conditions under which the book has been produced should fill one with a sense of unfairness at so casual and routine a critical dismissal. The author is a Finnish journalist and translator, who completed the study as doctoral research at the University of Helsinki. She has written the book in English (how many of us could write a book in Finnish?), and in order to do so undertook 'more than forty trips to England' to view productions of the play. Surely it is 'natural' that a foreign observer interested in British culture should gravitate towards Shakespeare; equally 'natural' that her focus should be directed towards the work of our great international Shakespeare company; even more 'natural' that her critical attention should be stimulated by a theme as irreducibly English as the dramatized imagery of royalty in *Richard II*; and most 'natural' of all that so many of her pilgrimages (sixteen of her more than forty trips) should have taken her to the 'heart of England', Stratford-upon-Avon.

It seems to me therefore that our critical reservations should be focused not so much on the intrinsic character of this book, but on the ideological problematic into which it has innocently been inserted. Stanley Wells has criticized *In One Person Many People* for its narrow range, 'an exceptionally limited segment of stage history' (*Theatre Notebook*, 43 (1989), 86). This is, to say the least, ungracious, given that the book is so clearly modelled on Wells's own *Royal Shakespeare: Four Major Productions at Stratford-upon-Avon* (Manchester, 1977). In the latter collection of essays, as in so many other reviews and publications, Lisa Hakola could have found firmly established the basic parameters of her thesis. There is firstly the 'literary-critical' method of performance analysis, in which the decisive factor is the concrete presence of the sensitive observer, reading and responding to the theatrical 'text'. There is the concentration on those aspects of a production that can be readily assimilated to a literary-critical approach — the director's 'vision', the actor's 'interpretation' — with a corresponding lack of interest in specifically theatrical discourse. Above all there is that implicit assumption of the constitutive centrality of the Royal Shakespeare Company, which is clearly the most decisive factor determining the shape of Dr Hakola's study. It is that fundamentally ideological premise that encourages the foreign observer, like the dutiful tourist, to gravitate innocently towards these power-centres of British cultural imperialism: Shakespeare, the RSC, Stratford; to by-pass the real variety, heterogeneity, and contradictoriness of British theatrical culture; to experience that culture within a perceptual context provided by something akin to a *Blue Guide*, seeing only the monuments (as Roland Barthes observed) and missing the life.

When we survey the map of world drama in the later nineteenth century, what we see is predominantly a European cultural phenomenon; more particularly a *Northern* European phenomenon; and quite specifically a Russian and Scandinavian phenomenon. The drama of Ibsen and Strindberg seems by comparison to render as pettily provincial what was happening in contemporary England. Yet we read this theatrical history in a form completely assimilated to our own culture; we read the plays in English translation, and we would not dream of flying off to Oslo or Stockholm every five minutes to see the plays produced within their national languages and cultural traditions. One would be interested to know how the mythologies of British cultural imperialism have penetrated Scandinavian culture. What sort of place does 'Shakespeare' hold there, and how does that imported phenomenon relate to native dramatic and theatrical traditions? Why does a

Finnish intellectual prefer, when approaching British culture, to ape the accent of a British literary establishment, rather than to express the authentic vision of a cross-cultural experience?

ROEHAMPTON INSTITUTE   GRAHAM HOLDERNESS

Imaginary Audition: Shakespeare on Stage and Page. By HARRY BERGER JR. Berkeley, New York, Los Angeles, and London: University of California Press. 1989. xvi + 178 pp. $25.00.

With *Imaginary Audition*, Harry Berger Jr makes a formidable contribution to the contemporary debate between advocates of stage-centred interpretations of Shakespearean drama and critics who analyze this drama in terms of the literary text. A long-time partisan of the readers' camp, Professor Berger has now developed a model of the stage-text relationship and a set of interpretive strategies designed to accommodate both the textual and the theatrical. That *Imaginary Audition* still betrays a suspicion of the stage itself, with its complex performative variables, does not significantly undermine its achievements.

The first section of *Imaginary Audition* offers a series of counter-arguments to critics, such as Richard Levin and Gary Taylor, who would restrict the analysis of Shakespeare's plays to those meanings accessible during theatrical performance. Professor Berger attacks this model on a number of grounds. Against its assumption of a Shakespeare writing explicit meanings to be grasped in performance, he argues for a field of meaning often multiple and duplicitous. Against its polarization of reading and spectating, he argues that a textuality derived from reading has increasingly infused the theatrical reception of Shakespeare's plays. Finally, against its insistence upon the naïve spectator as a limiting variable with dramatic interpretation, he argues that a reading attuned to performance can posit more complex audience stances. 'Why should I read a play as if I can only take in what I could when actually watching it rather than pretending to watch a play that contains everything I see in the text?' (p. 31).

The remainder of *Imaginary Audition* presents Professor Berger's alternative to this dualistic privileging of the spectator's relationship with the play over that of the reader. 'Imaginary audition' describes a literary model of stage-centred criticism which seeks 'to recuperate standard features of armchair practice while maintaining a fairly strict focus on the drama of theatrical and interlocutionary relations' (p. 45). Drawing upon speech-act theory and theory of metadrama, Professor Berger proposes a mode of dramatic interpretation that attends to discourse as a performance simultaneously staged for the onstage audience and for the speaker's own self-audition. This approach allows him the opportunity for 'decelerated' textual reading, while disciplining this reading according to the illocutionary relationships on stage. In the extended discussion of *Richard II* that occupies the centre of the book, 'imaginary audition' focuses on the dynamics of self-address, and it attempts to describe both the psychology and the politics of this discursive operation. It produces a Richard not of lyrical weakness, but of rhetorical and political control: a character who stages his own self-effacement while positioning his adversary within the carefully delineated role of usurper, guaranteeing the paralyzing guilt that will pursue Bolingbroke throughout his subsequent reign.

Its intelligent refutation of a narrow performance criticism and its intriguing reading of *Richard II* notwithstanding, *Imaginary Audition* leaves one with a number of questions about its own assumptions and methodology. Does not the narrowing of discourse within the interlocutionary situation of dramatic characters minimize the broader discursive relationship of author-actor-audience to the point where the stage is once again effaced by a new, albeit more sophisticated, literarization? Indeed, doesn't the very focus on verbal discourse neglect the theatre's other, non-verbal components and risk yet another form of the Aristotelianism that has always sought to marginalize spectacle? The actor's body, and the semiotic and phenomenological complexities of the performance field it inhabits, are tellingly absent from Professor Berger's theatrical compromise. But if *Imaginary Audition* is not free of an antitheatrical current, it none the less offers provocative and intelligent discussions of the theatre-text relationship, the processes involved in reading drama, and the interlocutionary operations of dramatic discourse. We are deeply in need of interpretive models that will allow us to 'read the theatre' in Shakespearean (and all other) drama without denying its textuality, and while these models will eventually need to incorporate more than Professor Berger currently allows, *Imaginary Audition* is a book with which anyone interested in these questions must contend.

University of Tennessee, Knoxville   Stanton B. Garner Jr

Elegy by W.S.: A Study of Attribution. By Donald W. Foster. Newark: University of Delaware Press; London and Toronto: Associated University Presses. 1989. 320 pp. £30.00.

The Problem of 'The Reign of King Edward III': A Statistical Approach. By Eliot Slater. (New Cambridge Shakespeare Studies and Supplementary Text Series) Cambridge, New York, New Rochelle, and Sydney: Cambridge University Press. 1988. xiv + 274 pp. £35.00.

Here we have two soundly-based attempts on problems of the Shakespeare canon: the late Eliot Slater's on *Edward III*, and Donald Foster's on the 1612 poem *A Funeral Elegy* 'by W.S.' In each case the work is claimed for Shakespeare, and the arguments are statistically valid ones based on massive word-counts. Yet each study leaves its problem short of certainty. In the case of the *Elegy*, we are left waiting for a statistician's report. For *Edward III* we really need a whole new study to move from a likelihood to a certainty; for all that Dr Slater has proved is that *Edward III* is more like early Shakespeare than like Marlowe. Both books are based on doctoral dissertations, but Dr Foster's has been developed into a superbly written, produced, and exciting book, whereas the late Dr Slater's remains, unavoidably, a dissertation still.

   Dr Slater's title is a little misleading, for he covers not only *Edward III* but also the chronology of Shakespeare's plays. Results on this latter problem are not very impressive: mainly they confirm the judgements of the Arden editors, except for a few implausibilities, such as putting *Pericles* between *The Winter's Tale* and *The Tempest*. The basic trouble (and this applies also to the *Edward III* problem) is that Dr Slater's 'rare word' tests are not all that powerful. He begins his book with a very fair survey of the major triumphs of modern statistical attribution: Ellegard on *Junius*, Mosteller and Wallace on the *Federalist* papers — and then, frustratingly, announces that he is not going to follow those methods. Mosteller and Wallace found that quite common words, such as *enough*, and *while* versus *whilst*, were powerful discriminators of authorship; but Dr Slater instead extends the 1930s work of Alfred Hart on *rare* words. He certainly shows that the rare words of *Edward III* appear more often in Shakespeare than in Marlowe, but the test is not very powerful, partly because 'the two poets were using rare-word vocabularies which held many words in common' (p. 135). Yes, indeed. Rare words are often impressive, and so may be copied by one author from another, and many are nouns, and so will be affected by subject-matter. Common structural words are far better indicators of authorship.

However, I broadly agree with Dr Slater's conclusions. He shows that there is a good likelihood that all of *Edward III* is by Shakespeare. I do not accept his further contention that parts of the play are of different dates, with the more Shakespearean-sounding bits later. I do not believe his tests are powerful enough to deliver any such conclusion.

The Reign of Edward III is most probably an early play of Shakespeare alone which did not get into the First Folio for reasons unconnected with authorship. (Not a King's Men's play? Embarrassingly anti-Scottish?) If the play overall seems a bit weak for Shakespeare, that is surely because no-one could make a properly unified play out of the reign of Edward III. I am more encouraged to see Shakespeare in *Edward III* because I notice in the 1596 Quarto two instances of *whiles* (G1, G1ᵛ), and Shakespeare is rather unusual in making considerable use of *whiles* rather than *while* or *whilst*. (But that test will not work against Marlowe: he also uses *whiles*.) What is needed now is a classic attack on the *Edward III* problem: counts of fairly common words in many writers of the early 1590s, and comparison with *Edward III*. I think Shakespeare's authorship could be proved beyond reasonable doubt.

A stylistic result beyond reasonable doubt seems to be what Dr Foster has given us in the case of the 578-line *Funeral Elegy* on poor Mr Will Peter, murdered in 1612 at Exeter, aged 29. The poem was printed by George Eld and published by Thomas Thorpe, the same pair who put out Shakespeare's *Sonnets* in 1609. And indeed, as Dr Foster shows by seventeen main tests of prosody, vocabulary and usage, the style of the *Elegy* is late Shakespearean, and like no other 'W.S.' writing about 1612. Dr Foster's tests include the rare-word tests of Dr Slater, but also those tricks of more frequent usage that mark Shakespeare out from his contemporaries. My one cavil about this study is that the comparative, non-Shakespearean sample is half Spenser, and a quarter Marlowe-plus-Herbert: three-quarters, therefore, not quite contemporary in 1612. This arose from the patchy availabilities of concordances; ideally, one should sample as many authors as possible from the right period. Also, where one expects a final triumphant probability, one reads instead that 'this research has not yet been completed' (p. 154). However, I am convinced; especially as the poem (which Dr Foster helpfully reprints in his book) has nine instances of *whiles* versus two of *while*, and I know from my own work on Jacobean usage (*The Canon of Thomas Middleton's Plays* (Cambridge, 1975)) that Shakespeare was highly unusual in his use of *whiles c.* 1612. But then the real trouble begins. There are two passages in the poem where the author distinctly talks about his *youth*; and Shakespeare in 1612 was 48 years old. Dr Foster does discuss these exhaustively, suggesting that the 'youth' is metaphorical. Yet I find this hard to accept, especially in the second instance, where the author says he will

> Immure those imputations I sustain
> Learning my days of youth so to prevent
> As not to be cast down by them again (l. 558)

If this stumbling-block can be overturned, we will have an interesting new light on Shakespeare's biography. Here he is, in 1612, acknowledging a strong tie of friendship to yet another young man — another Will. It gives one to think about all those Sonnets: was the Fair Friend a composite figure, not just *one* young man, but two, or three?

University of Queensland, Brisbane   David J. Lake

Reviews 359

Shakespeare and 'Sir Thomas More': Essays on the Play and its Shakespearean Interest. Edited by T. H. HOWARD-HILL. (New Cambridge Shakespeare Studies and Supplementary Texts) Cambridge, New York, New Rochelle, Melbourne, and Sydney: Cambridge University Press. 1989. x + 210 pp. £30.00; $49.50.

This collection differs from *Shakespeare's Hand in 'The Play of Sir Thomas More'* (by A. W. Pollard and others (Cambridge, 1923)), a volume with which it challenges comparison, in so far as contributors were encouraged to go their own way, not to subscribe to a single, agreed argument. The essayists, brought together at a seminar in 1983, offer new 'facts' and ideas, some of which directly contradict each other.

The dating of the play's Additions has become a key issue. There is general agreement that the original text dates from 1592 or 1593, or at any rate from the period 1592–95. Pollard, indeed, thought that 'if *More* can be proved to be as late as 1599 I should regard the date as an obstacle to Shakespeare's authorship of the three pages so great as to be almost fatal' (*Shakespeare's Hand*, p. 31). Several essayists, like Pollard, date some or all of the Additions close to the original text. G. Melchiori has shown that two of *More's* soliloquies were transcribed by Hand C 'on the two halves of a single upended leaf, and then separated and pasted on fols. 11ᵛ and 14ʳ'. He notes that the two speeches 'must have been written practically simultaneously by different authors at a fairly late stage of the revision. If Shakespeare is responsible for the first, and he is the author as well of the earliest of the additions (that in hand D), then all the revisions of the book must have been effected within a very narrow period' (p. 89). Professor Melchiori favours an early date ('not later than 1594') for the play and the Additions. William B. Long suggests that the date at the end of *John a Kent*, a play once bound together with *More* and also a Munday autograph, was 'inscribed by Hand C', a man who 'can be seen working as company book-keeper in *John a Kent* and the plot of *2 Seven Deadly Sins* around 1590. His presence in the same capacity in *More* is a major factor in dating the play'. On the other hand Scott McMillin (whose paper grew into Chapters 3, 4, and 7 of *The Elizabethan Theatre and 'The Book of Sir Thomas More'* (Ithaca, New York, 1987)) assigns two dates to the Additions, which were written on different batches of paper. In 1603 or so 'Hands B, C, E, and perhaps A patch together some revisions which would bring the piece down to proper casting scale from its luxurious original design', whereas Hand D (usually identified as Shakespeare) intervened much earlier. 'The conclusion, which seems to me inescapable, is that Hand D wrote his three pages (or more) quite early, before Tilney censored the play and before the revisions had been performed on the apprentices and the Clown' (p. 59). Gary Taylor also wants a late date for the Additions, but — unlike Professor McMillin — thinks that Hand D, if Shakespeare, must be late as well. Professor Taylor gathers together the internal evidence of metre, linguistic preferences, parallels, and the like, whilst his colleagues rely on other forms of evidence — an interesting clash, which is left unresolved. (The contributors are aware of one another's views, but too often politely ignore each other when they differ.) It remains to be seen whether this internal evidence, drawn from a mere 147 lines of dialogue (in verse and prose) is more convincing than the internal evidence for the ninety lines of *Shall I die*.

T. H. Howard-Hill and G. Harold Metz carefully survey recent work on *More*. Charles R. Forker shows that Hand D cannot belong to Webster (as has been suggested), its Addition being 'significantly more congruent with Shakespeare's habits of vocabulary'. John W. Velz explains that when R. W. Chambers wrote on Hand D's 'expression of ideas' in 1923 he was diffident about evidence drawn from *Henry VI*, and that even in 1931 he still 'made no use of *Titus Andronicus*, a play that can be mined, as will appear, in important support of his analysis'. Our view of the Shakespeare canon has changed; Professor Velz lists rhetorical and situational parallels which suggest 'that Shakespeare knew the whole of *More* well enough to draw on it many years later', and even includes parallels from scenes in *Henry VIII* that are more often assigned to Fletcher (II. i, ii; v. iii). John Jowett argues, from internal evidence, that Chettle wrote six or seven scenes of the play — 'at a minimum, over one-third of the original text'. He believes, though, as do other contributors, that Munday 'plotted' the play, a belief that seems to be based (how securely?) on the later description of Munday as 'our best plotter'. Having read Professor Melchiori on the 'dramatic unity' of *More*, and Professor McMillin on its 'sophisticated dramaturgy', I find it hard to accept that the same man devised its subtly resonating 'plot' and the crude patchwork of *John a Kent* and of the Robin Hood plays. And would 'our best plotter' not have noticed, as Professor McMillin did, the 'clashes' in staging (McMillin, 1987, p. 109 ff.) that necessitated some rewriting? Is there any hard evidence that Munday prepared the 'plot'? If Professors Melchiori, McMillin, Velz and Jowett are correct in their general findings the time has come to ask whether the 'plot' might not have been roughed out by a greater man, by an experienced dramatist who could be brilliant and also careless. Marlowe — or even Shakespeare?

NEWCASTLE UPON TYNE   E. A. J. HONIGMANN

John Ford: Critical Re-visions. Edited by MICHAEL NEILL. Cambridge, New York, New Rochelle, Melbourne, and Sydney: Cambridge University Press. 1988. xii + 287 pp. £27.50.

John Ford remains the most elusive of the great pre-1642 English dramatists. Few now treat his work as symptomatic of a mythical decadence; yet, if critical opinion is more sympathetic to his achievements than formerly, the nature of the latter remains as critically contested as ever. One contributor after another in the present volume notes this fact before launching a fresh attempt at clarification. In the process, they allude frequently and generously to the efforts of a wide range of predecessors, while fully registering the scale of the disagreements that still persist. (Only the blinkered reductivism of Mark Stavig's interpretations is persistently recalled and damned). Yet there is unmistakably a collective mood of optimism that progress can yet be made.

Our problems with Ford are compounded by the paucity of the information we possess about the dating of some of his key plays and the details of his life. Only one essay here assists us on this front. Andrew Gurr's cautious, but cumulatively revelatory, exploration of 'Ford and Contemporary Theatrical Fashion' places his work illuminatingly in the context of rivalries between factions associated with different playhouses. Not all its claims about differences in repertoire between theatres seem to me absolutely secure. What definition of 'swordplay', for example, do we need to work from in order to conclude that *The Jew of Malta*, with its fatal duel between Mathias and Lodowick, 'has no fighting in it' (p. 84)? But his essay as a whole succeeds in situating some of Ford's output with fresh precision in a closely mapped theatrical environment.

Other contributors, with varying degrees of plausibility, seek for assistance in other directions. Michael Neill, for instance, looks to the 'Renaissance belief in the capacity of images to seize and possess the mind' (p. 153) for help with the last scene of *'Tis Pity*; Harriet Hawkins invokes Augustine on theatre to negotiate the perplexities of *The Broken Heart*; and Kathleen McLuskie argues that patterns of construction by the scene familiar from the *lazzi* of the *commedia dell'arte* also underpin Ford's practice. This last essay exemplifies a welcome aspect of the volume as a whole in its willingness to pay detailed, sympathetic attention to such neglected works as *The Fancies Chaste and Noble*, and her method yields rich dividends with the works she debates. Yet her subsequent attempt to extrapolate from her commentary on these plays conclusions about Ford's dramaturgy in general seems to me rushed and unconvincing, given that her only remarks here about any of the three masterpieces on which Ford's reputation is centrally founded are two brief paragraphs on *'Tis Pity* in which much is asserted but little documented. My instinct would be that a thorough application of her ideas to that play, *Perkin Warbeck*, and *The Broken Heart* would be more likely to reveal discontinuities than close kinship in dramatic method; but I would be very interested to see her make the experiment.

At several moments like this, the more interesting contributors seem to need more space than the essay-form permits in order to investigate the full potential of their ideas. This, however, is also a clear sign that in at least some of the chapters genuinely fresh approaches are being tabled. Three of the writers, Dr McLuskie, Brian Opie, and Martin Butler, have been drawn to another of the more neglected plays, *Love's Sacrifice*, and develop ambitious and intriguingly inter-related arguments about the intricacy of Ford's strategies in it. Though Dr McLuskie and Dr Butler acknowledge each other's contributions in notes to their own and Dr McLuskie adds a postscript to hers specifically raising questions about divergent approaches to the same phenomena, the essays themselves seem to have been largely written in ignorance of their shared interests. Their perspectives on the play overlap, but also distinctly diverge, as both also do from Dr Opie's. The editor of such a volume usually has a sufficiently difficult task in trying to ensure that all the planned contributions actually reach him at some point not too long after the original deadline. But it is a pity that in a case like this it was not possible for each essay to be designed from the start as part of a group exploration of a shared text. Each of these contributions is, as it stands, challenging and innovatory, but could only have gained extra sharpness of definition from its author's being aware of his or her collaborators' differing emphases. More co-ordination between contributors would have been an advantage at other points also. For example, Jean Howard's striking essay on 'Gender and Legitimacy in Ford's *Perkin Warbeck*', seeking to revise the received view of an astonishing play, closely investigates its handling of Katherine Gordon; whereas Roger Warren's earlier celebration of the one professional modern revival of *Perkin* — at Stratford-upon-Avon in 1975 — says nothing about how that role was interpreted. Dr Warren seems to me to over-rate a flawed and problematic staging, one of whose major demerits was the jejeune playing inflicted on that part by an inadequate actress. Given his intense admiration for the production generally, we are likely to differ about this; but it would have been illuminating to hear his views on it. So, in conclusion, a volume in which a number of interesting new approaches are aired, but one in which greater co-operation between the contributors could well have yielded yet more stimulating results.

UNIVERSITY OF YORK   MICHAEL CORDNER

Images of Love and Religion: Queen Henrietta Maria and Court Entertainments. By ERICA
     VEEVERS. Cambridge, New York, New Rochelle, Melbourne, and Sydney:
     Cambridge University Press. 1989. xii + 244 pp. £35.00; $49.50.

Though Caroline drama and court festivals are academically fashionable, court culture and its political implications are usually approached from the standpoints either of the King or his opponents. Erica Veevers, however, examines the court entertainments of the 1630s in relation to the Queen and her conflicting loyalties: to France, to her Catholic faith, and to her husband. It is Dr Veevers's thesis first, that Henrietta Maria brought with her to the English court the fashions of *préciosité* and

Platonic love; secondly, that she expressed these interests principally through theatrical spectacle; and thirdly, that these shows were vitally concerned with the political and religious developments of the 1630s.

The intellectual and religious context of Henrietta Maria's entertainments is established in a survey of the 'Queen's Fashions', showing how *préciosité* and the Devout Humanism of St François de Sales and his followers were adapted to the English court in the concept of *honnêteté*. Especially important was the systematization by Du Bosc whose *L'Honnête Femme* was translated by Walter Montague — a leading figure in the Queen's intellectual circle and the link between 'the interests she left behind in France and those she developed in England'. These fashions placed religion at the centre of court life by insisting that pleasure and piety are mutually interdependent.

A chapter on the 'Tone of Court Drama' surveys the different conventions of treating love on the stage. Here attention to context enables Dr Veevers to demonstrate the exaggeration of arguments, both in the seventeenth and twentieth centuries, that sexual immorality at court was reflected in the moral decadence of the drama. On the contrary, the representation of women tended towards the ideals of *honnêteté* — good manners, moderation, and good sense. Obviously, such ideas could be presented without political implications: but the moment they became connected with religious ideals, as was the case with Henrietta Maria, then they could advance well beyond the realm of personal relations and neoplatonic ingenuity. The Queen's marriage was seen by Catholics as a religious vocation — to convert first her husband and then the heretic English nation — and, at first, her over-zealous and inflexible approach antagonized those whom she was supposed to win over. Later she became less naïvely insistent, and the atmosphere she encouraged at court in the 1630s enabled Papal agents to enjoy much freer access not only to herself and her circle but also, informally, to the King himself; while the play on the language and ideas of religion, common in discussions of Platonic love, facilitated treatment of more serious religious issues. Certainly Puritans recognized this and it seems likely that, as Dr Veevers suggests, their fear of women tempting men to sexual impurity was heightened by their fear of women tempting men to a hostile religion. Thus accusations of immorality against the Queen's circle had a religious rather than a purely sexual basis.

Heavenly images of love and beauty were a feature of the art of the Counter-Reformation, and Dr Veevers rightly emphasizes the distinctive visual character of the Queen's entertainments and the religious tone created by Inigo Jones's imagery, while pointing out that Rubens's work in the banquet house recreated something of the atmosphere of Renaissance and Baroque churches. A careful discussion of *The Temple of Love* (1635) and *Luminalia* (1636) reveals how these masques reflected Henrietta Maria's religious convictions and thereby assumed political significance. *Luminalia, or the Festival of Light*, for instance, was conceived as a courtly answer to Laud's proclamation on the enforcement of the anti-Catholic laws. The Queen had initially responded with a Midnight Mass in her chapel followed, just over a month later, by the celebration of Candlemas — a festival of light, interpreted by Catholic theorists as a ceremony dedicated to the Virgin Mary. The connexion between all this and *Luminalia* (performed four days after Candlemas) is supported by literary evidence expertly marshalled by Dr Veevers whose conclusion, that this masque was a significant assertion of the Queen's Catholic interests, is compelling. Equally convincing is an analysis of the relationship between religious ceremony and the masque, especially in a discussion of the analogies between the staging of these entertainments and the settings for religious ceremony in Continental churches. The connexion between religious expression and scenography, so evident, for example, in the Roman *quarantore*, was made physically manifest in the Stuart masques where

Jones's architecture and staging came very close to the setting for worship in the churches of the Counter-Reformation.

Dr Veevers deals finally with 'Love and Religion', stressing the Queen's role as intermediary between rival religions; relating the preaching of peace and love in her chapel to the similar themes of her masques; and analysing *Tempe Restored* (1632), *Coelum Britannicum* (1634), and their Valois antecedents: showing how the personal happiness of the royal marriage was also presented as a pattern for religious harmony. A brief 'Puritan epilogue', citing contemporary satirical play on the word 'mask', highlights the attitude of Henrietta Maria's opponents who clearly recognized the crucial links between her theatrical interests and her religious convictions.

This book gets off to a slow and laborious start; there is, throughout, a tendency to repetition; the treatment of literary analogues (and, in particular, the French background) could, with profit, have been greatly condensed. Nevertheless, the force of Dr Veevers's argument is cumulative and ultimately impressive; and her study is a good illustration of the way in which careful attention to the inter-relationship between a variety of political, ideological, and intellectual contexts can illuminate seemingly familiar material.

BRIGHTON   SYDNEY ANGLO

The Conversation of the Sexes: Seduction and Equality in Selected Seventeenth- and Eighteenth-Century Texts. By ROY ROUSSEL. New York and Oxford: Oxford University Press. 1986. x + 178 pp. £15.00.

It is part of Roy Roussel's modishly provocative strategy to tackle Donne's 'The Flea', Cleland's *Fanny Hill*, Richardson's *Pamela*, Laclos's *Les liaisons dangereuses*, and finally Congreve's comedies in achronological order. Since the book purports to examine works about women written by men, and boldly addresses the central cognitive problem of *men*'s conception of women's sexual experiences, it is most questionable to deny from the outset any validity to the time-factor. Obviously, sexual mentalities had not remained static between Donne, the Restoration, and the eve of the French Revolution, a point now made abundantly clear by the current research in that slippery field. Why should Dr Roussel bother to mention '17th- and 18th-Century Texts' in his subtitle, if he pays no attention to chronology? Nancy K. Miller in her *The Heroine's Text: Readings in the French and English Novel, 1722–1782* (New York, 1980) had chosen to regard such works as historical documents, whereas Dr Roussel has deliberately 'taken the opposite approach'. His interests lie in 'those qualities and experiences — masculine control and unity versus feminine submissiveness and fragmentation, for example — which are usually assigned to male and female, respectively, but which in some way can be experienced by both men and women' (p. 4).

Within its self-imposed limitations, Dr Roussel's study of the emotional dialectics of distance and desire is carried out in a subtle, urbane fashion, pleasantly remote from the harpy-like stridencies of some feminist writings, especially in America. His 'sotto voce' dialogue with recent feminist criticism would have been more complete if he had taken up the same texts as Nancy K. Miller, not to mention such fascinatingly complex cases as Defoe's *Roxana* (1724), Molière's *Dom Juan* (1665) or Casanova's posthumous *Memoirs*, to remain as achronological as the author.

In a work dealing with the 'conversation of the sexes' in the seventeenth and eighteenth centuries, the chapter on Cleland's *Memoirs of a Woman of Pleasure* (1748–49), usually, if inaccurately known by the title of its abridged and expurgated version, *Fanny Hill*, may be taken as the touchstone to assay the book's metal. Surprisingly, Dr Roussel's edition of reference is totally inadequate: that edited by

P. Quennell (New York, 1963), although it may be 'the most widely circulated' (p. 166). Nowhere does he indicate that *Fanny Hill* and *The Memoirs of a Woman of Pleasure* are different versions of Cleland's notorious international bestseller in pornography. Peter Wagner's edition (Penguin, 1985), and Peter Sabor's (World's Classics, 1985), which both offer a reliable text and adequate annotation, must have come out too late. Again, the author of this study chooses to ignore completely the socio-historical circumstances, as well as the literary and philosophical backgrounds of *Fanny Hill*. He tends to pay too much attention, regrettably so, to modern considerations on pornography, not always directly relevant either to *Fanny Hill* or to his analysis of it. But his guiding notion that 'the novel moves toward a certain idea of androgyny in which the equality between masculine and feminine triumphs over the difference between the sexes and allows the man and the woman to converse freely across this difference' (p. 41) is a highly operative concept which serves to illuminate the pervasive feminization of Charles's desire for his long-lost and now experienced Fanny. Charles no longer tries to dominate Fanny, because of his and *her* range of past experiences, which he accepts on her own terms. Thus, although the reunited couple are still capable of experiencing the difference between masculine and feminine, they are no longer estranged by it, because they are now able to transcend it, and thus satisfy each other completely. Dr Roussel's final chapters on *Pamela*, *Les liaisons dangereuses* (possibly the most sophisticated analysis of ambiguous communication in the book), and Congreve's comedies, display the same qualities of provocative subtlety, marred by his questionable refusal to take into account the historical context. But, as it stands, it remains a valuable contribution to the feminist debate over seventeenth and eighteenth-century literature. Should a paperback edition be called for, the author would be well advised to give his readers an index worthy of the name, a select bibliography, and to correct our French colleague's surname on pages 171 and 178 to Versini.

PARIS III-SORBONNE NOUVELLE   PAUL-GABRIEL BOUCÉ

Eighteenth-Century Women Poets: An Oxford Anthology. Edited by ROGER LONSDALE. Oxford: Clarendon Press. 1989. xlvii + 555 pp. £20.00.

Readers of Roger Lonsdale's *New Oxford Book of Eighteenth-Century Verse* (Oxford, 1984) will expect much from the present volume, and will not be disappointed. According to his wise and informative Introduction, 'nothing has been included which did not seem to offer some degree of interest in manner or matter' (p. xlv). The only predictable element is a sense of intimately shared experience. Some magic casements open onto the foam of perilous seas: it dashes romantically against cliffs in Charlotte Smith's 'Sonnet. On being Cautioned against Walking on an Headland Overlooking the Sea, because it was Frequented by a Lunatic'; it arouses more immediate, if less picturesque, terrors in Jane Cave's 'Written the First Morning of the Author's Bathing in Teignmouth, for the Head-Ache'. Many poetic vistas start in enclosures: dairies, nurseries, sickbeds, or washtubs. Thanks to female wit, imagination, and defiance, they seldom end there.

Overlaps with *Eighteenth-Century Verse* are rendered insignificant by the influx of about eighty extra contributors. Frequent anonymity precludes greater precision: for example, 'On a Gentleman's complaining to a Lady that he could not eat Meat, owing to the Looseness of his Teeth' strongly resembles entries by Elizabeth Amherst. More generous representation of individual women affords scope for subtle readjustment. Hannah More's sole contribution to *Eighteenth-Century Verse* is the piously resigned dialogue 'The Riot; or, Half a Loaf is Better than No Bread.' This particular dose of mass opiate is not readministered among Hannah More's entries in *Women Poets*; the closest substitute is 'Patient Joe', where a miner is saved by a dog who providentially steals his dinner. Susanna Blamire's 'Wey, Ned, Man!' provides abundant compensation for the missing dialogue.

Preferring the 'less pretentious flights' of most eighteenth-century poets, Dr Lonsdale gives disproportionately limited exposure to 'the more ambitious or morally earnest genres'. Failure to recognize this 'misrepresentation' (p. xliv) may create false impressions. Terry Castle's observation that 'when women poets did turn to loftier forms, such as the ode, they usually did so mockingly' (*TLS*, 10–16 November 1989, p. 1227) describes this selection better than their total output. A conspicuous unacknowledged omission is drama. Its absence from *Eighteenth-Century Verse* makes the present shortage easier to understand: who could reject Allan Ramsay's *Gentle Shepherd* (1725) and include Hannah Cowley's *Albina* (1779)? Still, a case might have been made for Regulus's speech on glory in Hannah More's *Inflexible Captive* (1774), or Susanna Centlivre's anatomy of the adulterous Bassino in *The Perjured Husband* (1700). Compiling anthologies entails hard choices.

Noteworthy minor admissions include the sequel to Lady Anne Lindsay's 'Auld Robin Gray': Robin's deathbed confession that he forced Jenny to marry him by stealing her cow is classic feminine wish-fulfilment. Irony fades when 'Woman's Hard Fate', a lady's bitter indictment of male domination, appears without the gentleman's 'Answer' that originally followed it (*Gentleman's Magazine*, July 1733, p. 371). 'The Answer' reassures the lady that a father 'Restrains her mind, too apt to rove' (l. 7), a brother 'sure is kind' (l. 10), and that 'woman reigns supreme' (l. 18) in the 'halcyon days' (l. 17) of courtship. This exercise in sexual politics proves the lady's point: not even her poetry is allowed out alone. Among the unintentional lacunae is the first appearance of Mehetabel Wright's 'Wedlock. A Satire' (*Gentleman's Magazine*, October 1733, p. 542).

Women Poets contains a mass of well-documented biographical information. Even more details are promised in the second edition, which should find an eager market. Interest in Women's Studies has increased the demand for texts and biographies beyond the supply. This book may not change lives, but it should certainly alter courses.

UNIVERSITY OF READING   CAROLYN D. WILLIAMS

Orwell and the Politics of Despair. By ALOK RAI. Cambridge, New York, New Rochelle, Melbourne, and Sydney: Cambridge University Press. 1989. xii + 192 pp. £25.00.

What are we writing about when we write about Orwell? According to Alok Rai, 'it is "Orwell" that is the text, and Orwell is only *one* of its authors'. Putting the name 'Orwell' in quotation marks is a habit that can be traced back to Raymond Williams's *Orwell* (1971), and Williams also spoke of the need to address not only what Orwell wrote but 'what was writing Orwell'. *Orwell and the Politics of Despair* is a most subtle and penetrating study on these lines, setting its subject's often ambiguous commitments and beliefs against both the myths that surround them and their changing political and ideological contexts.

Orwell the imaginative writer (in the conventional sense) gets rather short shrift here. Dr Rai deals very summarily with the early novels apart from *Burmese Days*, dismissing *A Clergyman's Daughter* and *Keep the Aspidistra Flying* as clumsy potboilers. Orwell's formal breakthrough consisted, we are told, in the creation of his autobiographical persona, but Dr Rai is interested in this more as a political than as a literary device. His terse though never imperceptive comments on Orwell's stylistic and narrative achievements are incidental to the main argument.

Nineteen Eighty-Four, as one might expect, is Dr Rai's centrepiece. The view that the key to Orwell's last book lies in its rationalization of a state of paranoid anxiety, deriving not from an objective analysis of modern political systems but from the 'blocked, hemmed-in, impotent but undefeated' state of mind of a protagonist who is a surrogate for Orwell himself, has seldom been better argued. Dr Rai presents, in meticulous detail, the evidence that a widespread failure of nerve (affecting both democratic socialism itself, and Orwell as its trapped and 'bemused' spokesman) led to the writing of the book and to its vast success. Whatever one makes of this, Dr Rai is at one with most recent critics in seeing the portrayal of external tyranny as accessory to the experience of internalized repression, 'the love of Big Brother burned into the psyche'.

Another strength of this book is its fine and sustained examination of Orwell's anti-colonialism. Against this must be put its reduction of *Animal Farm* to a mere appendage to *Nineteen Eighty-Four*, and Dr Rai's tendency, from time to time, to pull off the Orwellian rhetorical trick of advancing a palpably unexamined assertion or point of view with an air of unchallengeable authority: unchallengeable, that is, by anything except what the author himself may happen to say next. Thus we hear a great deal of Orwell's 'aesthetic strategy' of writing pseudonymously even though the Orwellian persona, considered as a formal device, is not shown to be different in kind from the personas of other self-mythologizing modern writers who used their own names. At another level, Dr Rai concludes the book by announcing that he will leave the question of the 'real' Orwell to the 'metaphysicians and the mantle-snatchers', only to offer his own sketch of 'what is most characteristically Orwellian' a page later. Overall, this is a highly intelligent and engaging study in which even the blemishes suggest Dr Rai's understanding of Orwell's predicament and sympathy with it.

UNIVERSITY OF READING   PATRICK PARRINDER